WITHDRAWN FROM STOCK

D0274827

The Asquiths

The Asquiths

COLIN CLIFFORD

JOHN MURRAY
Albemarle Street, London

BEXLEY LIBRARY SERVICE	
	Cu
02194851	
Cypher	22.11.02
941.083 ASQUITH	£25.00

© Colin Clifford 2002

First published in 2002
by John Murray (Publishers) Ltd
50 Albemarle Street, London W1S 4BD

The moral right of the author has been asserted

All rights reserved. No part of this publication may be reproduced
in any material form (including photocopying or storing it in any
medium by electronic means and whether or not transiently or
incidentally to some other use of this publication) without the
written permission of the copyright owner, except in accordance
with the provisions of the Copyright, Designs and Patents Act 1988
or under the terms of a licence issued by the Copyright Licensing
Agency, 90 Tottenham Court Road, London W1T 4LP.
Applications for the copyright owner's written permission to
reproduce any part of this publication should be addressed to the
publisher.

A catalogue record for this book is available from the British Library

ISBN 0-7195-5457 8

Typeset in Monotype Garamond by Servis Filmsetting Ltd

Printed and bound in Great Britain by
Butler and Tanner Ltd
Frome and London

To my mother

Contents

Illustrations

The author and publishers would like to thank the following for permission to reproduce illustrations: Plates 4, 5, 10, 11, 23, and 33, Bodleian Library (Margot Asquith papers); 6 and 7, Oxford Union Society; 14, 15, 17, 21, 22, 35, Anthony Pitt Rivers; 16, Illustrated London News Picture Library; 18 and 39, David McKenna; 19, David Parsons; 26 and 32, Mrs Mary Rous; 28 and 30, Jon Stallworthy; 31, the Bonham Carter family; 36 and 37, Imperial War Museum; 38, Hertfordshire County Record Office (Desborough Papers)

Acknowledgements

THIS BOOK COULD never have been written without the help, guidance and encouragement of Priscilla Hodgson, the grand-daughter and sadly the sole surviving descendant of Margot Asquith. The core of the book has been Margot Asquith's voluminous diaries (covering, with gaps, the years 1875 to 1922) and other papers, which Mrs Hodgson generously donated to the Bodleian Library while at the same time insisting that I be given access to them. I am deeply grateful to her, not only for permission to quote but also for unstinting support.

I am grateful also to Arthur ('Oc') Asquith's daughters, Mary Rous and Susan Boothby, who allowed me to see and quote from their father's papers, as well as sharing their memories of him and of other members of their family and circle. Violet Asquith's granddaughter, Virginia Brand, gave me permission on behalf of the Bonham Carter family to quote from H.H. Asquith's letters and the diaries and correspondence of his daughter Violet, as well as letting me see and quote from the letters to Asquith of his first wife, Helen. I have been very generously helped and advised by other Asquith descendants and relations also, including Lady Bonham Carter, Raymond Bonham Carter, Jane Bonham Carter, John Jolliffe (editor of the letters of his grandfather Raymond Asquith), Michael Asquith and his late wife Hase, and Didi Holland-Martin.

The Earl and late Countess of Oxford and Asquith kindly allowed me to see H.H. Asquith's letters to the Earl's grandmother, Frances

Horner, as well as Raymond Asquith's letters to his father. I greatly appreciate their insights, as well as those of Lord Oxford's sister, the late Lady Helen Asquith. I very much regret that Lord Oxford and his son, Viscount Asquith, felt unable to agree with much of what I had written about Lord Oxford's father Raymond, particularly on the subjects of his relations with Lady Diana Manners (later Cooper) and his attitude to the Great War, and that they preferred not to let me see Katharine Asquith's letters to him or the letters of condolence she received after his death during the Battle of the Somme. In the end I thought it better to forego permission to quote Raymond's letters rather than to give up the freedom to write what I believed to be true, and I hope that they will accept that I have tried my utmost to be accurate and fair.

I am grateful for help, insight and, where necessary, also permission to quote, to Bridget Grant, daughter of Aubrey and Mary Herbert; Juliet Henley, daughter of Sylvia Henley and niece of Venetia Stanley; Anthony Pitt-Rivers, grandson of Sylvia Henley (who also kindly made copies for me of photographs from his family albums); Virginia, Marchioness of Bath, and David Tree, daughter and son of Viola Parsons and grandchildren of Maud Tree; Anna Mathias, granddaughter of Edwin and Venetia Montagu; and David McKenna, son of Reginald and Pamela McKenna. Lord Aberconway discussed with me his parents' friendships with the Asquiths and shared his reminiscences of Margot. Lord Neidpath guided me on Charteris family history and conducted an (unfortunately fruitless) search for letters from Lady Cynthia Asquith.

Christopher Collins and Charlotte Mosley (who is editing Margot Asquith's earlier diaries for publication) have both taken an interest in the book for several years, and readily shared with me material from their own researches. They both kindly read the manuscript and made many useful suggestions, as well as saving me from a number of stupid errors. The responsibility for any that remain, however, is of course my own.

The late Professor Colin Matthew patiently answered questions on Liberal politics and generously lent me his notes on the Haldane Papers when the National Library of Scotland was closed. The late John Grigg helped me understand Lloyd George's relations with the Asquiths, though I suspect he would have disagreed with some of my conclusions. Dr Martin Farr, researching a forthcoming biography of Reginald McKenna, and Jane Ridley helped me with political background and Ann Hoffman helped me with queries concerning the Churchills. Christopher Page, Arthur Asquith's military biographer, in doing the spadework for his own book did much of mine too, and generously gave me guidance besides. Patric Dickinson, Richmond Herald, helped with genealogical and other points. My brother Dr Rollo Clifford answered miscellaneous medical questions, and my cousin, another Rollo Clifford, explained the engagement at Qatya. I am obliged to Dr Clyde Binfield for any insight into the Asquith family's social and religious background, though much of what I wrote on that had to be sacrificed to help reduce the first draft's length. My thanks are due also to Dr Michael Brock, who is editing Margot Asquith's Downing Street diaries for publication.

I am very much obliged for help and information to Major and Mrs N. Stevenson, Jean Pryor, Andrea Whitaker, Stuart Gough, Lord Crathorne, Barry Darling of the City of London School, Dr R. Custance and Suzanne Foster of Winchester College, Maurice Keen and Dr Alan Tadiola of Balliol College, Oxford, and Isla Brownless of Lambrook School.

My researches at the Bodleian were made immeasurably easier by Elizabeth Turner, who put up with regular interruptions of her marathon task of cataloguing the Margot Asquith papers while drawing my attention to any that might be of particular interest. Colin Harris and his staff (particularly Nicky Kennan and Rob Wilkes) in the Western Manuscripts Room proved likewise unfailingly helpful and patient, as did the staff of most of the Record Libraries I visited, as well as those at the London Library and the Bristol University Library. I am grateful to the National Library of Wales and to the Clerk of the Records of the House of Lords Record Office (acting on behalf of the Beaverbrook Foundation) for permission to quote from the letters of David Lloyd George.

I would like to thank for their generous hospitality during my researches William and Sally Alden, Giles and Diss Bowring, Sherard and Bridget Cowper-Coles, Nic and Amanda Gray, Sarah Rutherford and Ross Dunlop, Michael and Vron Hodges, Patrick and Claire Mansel Lewis, Christopher and Maureen Page, David and Lexi Soskin, Mary Strang and Simon Walker, Mary Tingey, James and Prim Yorke, and particularly my mother Sheila Clifford. Thanks also to Peter and Marjorie Moncrieffe for watching my house while I enjoyed this hospitality. I particularly want to record my gratitude, also, to Victoria Schofield, who proved the most stalwart and supportive of all my friends.

The idea for this book was originally suggested to me eight years ago by my literary agent, Andrew Lownie, and he supported me loyally through all the difficulties of such an ambitious first project. At Murray's, Grant McIntyre spurred me on through the obstacles thrown up by the research as well as the complications in assembling the material, as well as proving the most brilliant of editors; Hazel Wood drew much to my attention that I had overlooked or not properly explained; Caro Westmore provided thoughtful and unobtrusive help in innumerable ways; Gail Pirkis capably steered the manuscript to printed form; thanks also to John Murray, Steph Allen and Jane Blackstock for their help and support and Caroline Knox for her sympahetic ear during difficult periods. I am particularly grateful to Douglas Matthews for his outstanding index.

Anthony Burton, Humphrey Burton, Humphrey Carpenter, Stephanie Hughes, Brian Kay and other presenters on BBC Radio 3 might well be surprised to know how much I have valued their company. Finally, no list of acknowledgements could be complete without my dog Finn Flynn, whose limitless and uncritical friendship has wonderfully alleviated the solitary business of authorship.

Author's note

IN THE INTERESTS of clarity, I have adopted a policy of quoting all abbreviations in letters or diaries in full, whether published or unpublished, except on a few occasions leaving an initial to represent a name where the meaning is obvious. I have also not hesitated to change punctuation in the original text to improve the sense of passages I have quoted: Margot and Violet, for instance, both resorted to little else beside the hyphen as their sole punctuation mark, as well as frequently running sentences together. So far as monetary values are concerned, I have decided not to make direct comparisons with present-day values, since it is exceedingly difficult to compare fairly. Not only was consumer expenditure very different, but the relative value of many goods and services varied greatly from today's: while property was comparatively cheaper, few people owned their homes and the poor spent a far higher proportion of their income on food, while the middle and upper classes all employed large numbers of servants. However, according to Bank of England statistics, the value of the pound in the period between 1850 and 1914 remained remarkably stable, fluctuating, as a rough guide, at between approximately 40 and 60 times its present value. It depreciated rapidly during the Great War from about 40 times today's level to around 20 times.

I

The Asquiths

To MOST BRITONS the name Asquith has an exotic ring. A mere two dozen Asquiths are listed in the London telephone directory. However, in Yorkshire Asquiths are not difficult to find. The name is probably Scandinavian in origin: in Denmark or Sweden the equivalent Askvist – meaning ash branch – is quite common.[1] It is far from fanciful to suppose that some distant Asquith forebear first rowed ashore in a Viking longship. Nowadays the only signs of the Prime Minister's family to be found in his home town of Morley (now almost smothered by nearby Leeds) are some impressive stone monuments covered in undergrowth in a forgotten graveyard along a litter-strewn track between the municipal gardens and a redundant Indian restaurant. The nearby chapel that once served the town's thriving Congregational community (of which the Asquiths were prominent members) was abandoned by its dwindling congregation in 1967, when it became a furniture store before one dark night local villains removed the whole building stone by stone.

Joseph Dixon Asquith, the father of the future Prime Minister, was born in 1825, the son of another Joseph Asquith who owned one of the town's more enterprising small cloth mills. Instead of following his father into manufacturing, Joseph junior established himself in business as a wool merchant, supplying the local mills with top-quality cloth from all over Europe, with outlets in Leeds and Huddersfield as well as Morley. Joseph's celebrated son gathered from local and family tradition that his father 'was a cultivated man, interested in literature and music, of a retiring and unadventurous disposition, and not cut out in the keen competitive atmosphere of the West Riding for a successful business career'.[2] Nonetheless, helped by family money, Joseph was able to provide a comfortable living for his family when, in 1850, he married Emily Willans, who came like himself from the close-knit group of families which formed the backbone of Yorkshire's Congregational community. The family lived above the town at Croft House, a substantial six-bedroom stone house with a coach house, various cottages and barns, and a magnificent view over the dales towards Leeds. It was in Croft House that Emily's first three children were born: a son in 1851, named after her father William Willans and always known as Willans; Herbert Henry, known to his family as Bertie, soon afterwards, on 12 September 1852; and a daughter, Evelyn (Eva). According to a family friend, Joseph was a devoted husband and father and took a keen interest in the education of his children.[3] Although Emily was a profoundly religious woman, she was not a stern parent and was remembered by her son as 'a devoted and sagacious mother' who 'made herself the companion and intimate friend of her children'.[4]

In 1857 the Asquiths moved to Mirfield, a village some seven miles to the south-west of Morley, where Emily had two more daughters, both of whom were to die within weeks of their birth.[5] Then in June 1860 Joseph died after twisting his intestine while playing cricket. Emily and her children turned to her father, a leading Huddersfield businessman, for support, and when he in turn died two years later, she was thrown on the charity of her four brothers. By now she was an invalid, suffering from chronic bronchitis and a weak heart, and for health reasons moved with her two daughters (Lilian had been born in 1860) to St Leonard's on the Sussex coast. The emotional effect of all this would have marked both boys, who were too young to deal with the loss of their parents and would have pushed the trauma into the deepest recesses of their psyche. Here, surely, lie the origins of the bouts of melancholy and panic with which Bertie was to struggle at times of crisis throughout his life. Beneath the apparent reserve, there was always a vulnerable man craving emotional support. The family's tragedies were not quite over, for Lilian died a few weeks before her fifth birthday.

The two boys were entrusted to the care of their newly married uncle, John Willans (Emily's eldest brother) and his twenty-three-year-old wife, Charlotte, at their home in Canonbury in London, from where they attended the City of London School. When their uncle John returned to Yorkshire after a couple of years to set up a carpet factory, the Asquith boys found themselves farmed out as lodgers with a succession of Congregational families in Islington and Pimlico.[6] The youthful new headmaster of the City of London School, the Reverend Edwin Abbott, was to have a huge influence on Asquith. Over the coming years, Bertie hoovered up all the school prizes for Classics and English and also dominated debates at the debating society, whereas Willans, although almost his brother's intellectual equal, was held back by poor health, never growing beyond the height of five feet one inch.

In Bertie's final year, Abbott made him school captain, praising him for 'keeping up the tone, as well as the intellectual standard, of the higher classes'. That year he also won the top Classics Scholarship to Balliol College, Oxford. At the end of a career full of glittering prizes he was to write: 'I can honestly say that, after more than fifty years of later experience, this was the proudest moment of my life.'[7]

The Michaelmas term of 1870 when the young freshman came up to Balliol was also the term that Benjamin Jowett, one of the towering figures of Victorian Oxford, moved into the Master's Lodge. Jowett saw Balliol's role as educating the future rulers of the British Empire and under his stewardship the college was to nurture not just a future Prime Minister, but three Viceroys of India as well as host of distinguished cabinet ministers, colonial administrators and academics. No one would have called 'the Jowler' an easy man. Undergraduates used to dread the periodic invitations to breakfast or dine with the Master or to accompany him on a walk. One former pupil recalled being served 'lukewarm tea out of a large metal pot, in big clumsy cups' and being made to feel 'indescribably stupid'. J. A. Spender, Asquith's official biographer and himself a Balliol man, described how 'the time passed in almost complete silence. Now and again I used to venture an embarrassed remark, but as likely as not the reply would be "You wouldn't have said that if you'd stopped to think", and after a silence more glacial still, he dismissed me with a brief "Good morning".'[8]

Although Asquith was never one of Jowett's greatest fans, once remarking that 'his talk is like one of those wines that have more bouquet than body'[9], there was never a better exponent of what Asquith himself called Balliol man's 'tranquil consciousness of effortless superiority'.[10] However, what some of his Oxford contemporaries saw as Asquith's 'superiority' was in fact a convenient disguise for shyness: 'I am hedged in and hampered in these ways by a kind of native reserve, of which I am not at all proud,' he once confessed to a close woman friend.[11] To another of his friends, he was 'a man who had a plan of life well under control' with 'a remarkable power of using every gift he possessed to full capacity'.[12] Without seeming to work particularly hard, he managed to gain outstanding Firsts in both 'Mods' and 'Greats' and win the prestigious Craven prize as well as being the runner-up for the other two great University Classics prizes, the Hertford and the Ireland.

Asquith's main interest – apart from his Classical studies – was the Oxford Union, where he rapidly established himself as the leading debater of his generation. Founded in 1823 as an undergraduate debating society, the Union had transformed itself by Asquith's time into a gentleman's club with its own premises in Frewin Court off the Cornmarket, where it remains to this day. The present imposing, if pretentious, debating chamber was not built until 1879, before which debates were still held in the more intimate surroundings of what is now the Old Library. The chamber was, as now, modelled on the House of Commons with opposing 'Government' and 'Opposition' benches and the President and other officers seated between them at the far end of the room. Here Asquith quickly made his mark. His speaking style was, according to a contemporary, 'cool and courageous, intellectually alert, well informed, sure of himself, with a voice clear and sufficiently strong and flexible, if not specially powerful, and a striking command of apt and incisive language'. He 'seemed sometimes to make too little effort to conciliate opponents, but neither friend nor foe could fail to listen to him'.[13] He moved steadily up the Union hierarchy until he eventually won the Presidency in March 1874. The high point of the term was the debate held in May 1874 advocating an Imperial Federation of England and the more important colonies. Asquith himself spoke against the motion, while the leading proponent was a young fellow-scholar from Balliol, Alfred Milner. The debate was the beginning of a close friendship between the two men, a friendship that would one day turn, on Milner's side, to the bitterest enmity.

After his outstanding results in his Finals, Asquith was elected a Fellow of Balliol. But he only remained another year in Oxford before ambition and a youthful romance drew him back to London.

Herbert and Willans Asquith spent their vacations from the City of London School and Oxford with their mother and surviving sister, Eva. Around the time of the Asquith boys' first year at Balliol, they met the two daughters of Dr Frederick Melland, a prosperous Manchester physician, who were staying with cousins in St Leonard's at the same time as Willans and Asquith were visiting their mother and sister. Asquith was immediately captivated by the fifteen-year-old Helen, the younger of the two sisters, who shared his fondness for literature and poetry (Wordsworth and Coleridge were among her favourite poets).[14] After her death, he tried to describe her personality to a woman friend:

> Her mind was clear and strong, but it was not cut in facets and did not flash lights, and no one would call her clever or 'intellectual'. What gave her rare quality was her character, which everyone who knew her agrees was the most selfless and unworldly that they have ever encountered. She was warm, impulsive, naturally quick-tempered, and generous almost to a fault'.[15]

Although they were rarely able to see each other, Asquith remained constant to Helen throughout his time at Oxford, and in his final year they became secretly engaged. He was called to the Bar at Lincoln's Inn in September 1876. With few briefs as yet, he initially survived on the income from his Balliol fellowship, supplemented by lecturing at the Law Society and writing occasional articles for the *Spectator*. Helen was an heiress in a modest way with a private income of a few hundred pounds a year, and by that summer the young couple decided that they could afford to set up home together. In September 1877, shortly after his twenty-fourth birthday, Asquith plucked up courage to approach Dr Melland to ask for his daughter's hand. The doctor – like the Asquiths a keen Congregationalist – had many acquaintances in common with his would-be son-in-law, and was soon convinced of his prospects. On 2 November, in a quaintly Victorian letter, he gave Asquith his blessing: 'I have the fullest conviction that your industry and ability will procure for you in due time that success in your profession which has attended you in your past career.'[16]

Asquith took the train to Manchester to spend weekends with his fiancée whenever he could and they wrote to each other every day. Helen was enraptured by her fiancé's letters, confessing 'it seems to me that the whole day has been spent in reading and re-reading them, except the time I was looking at your photograph, or the ring . . . while I have it on, I feel so completely encircled by your love'. She told him 'there is not an hour in the day but I long for your advice and help in something and above all your love', assuring him 'I mean to devote my life to making you happy.' It grieved her 'to think of your coming home tired and having no Helen to light your pipe and warm your slippers'. Faced with her fiancé's obvious brilliance, she worried about her own lack of erudition, constantly referring to herself as 'the heathen' and wondering 'what I have done to deserve such happiness, and sometimes I feel a little sad as the awful thought comes across my mind that perhaps he may not find me all that he expects. That he will awake from a daydream and find that the wife he is going to marry is a different person from the ideal woman of his imagination.'[17]

The wedding eventually took place on 23 August 1877 at Rusholme Congregational Church.[18] The marriage was, in Asquith's words, 'a great success, from first to last it was never troubled by any kind of sorrow or dissension'.[19] The couple set up house together in Hampstead at Eton House in John Street*, a quiet road shaded by poplars, limes, catalpas and plane trees, next to Hampstead Heath, then a wild expanse that 'faded away into films of grey and purplish mist'. The Asquiths' new home was a cream-coloured Georgian house, surrounded by a large garden full of fruit trees. Helen was particularly thrilled to hear that they had a mulberry tree, telling her fiancé how her sister Josephine 'suggests that the temptation will be too strong and we shall spend our whole lives in playing round the Mulberry bush'.[20] On 6 November 1878 the Asquiths' first child, Raymond, was born. A second son, Herbert ('Beb'), followed in 1881, to be joined by Arthur ('Oc') in 1883. After a gap of four years their only daughter, Violet, was born in 1887, followed by a fourth son, Cyril ('Cys'), in 1889.[†]

---

*Later renamed Keats Grove after the celebrated poet who had earlier lived there.
†As children, Raymond was also known as 'Ray', 'Rub' and 'the Captain', Herbert as 'Bertie' and Arthur as 'Artie'. Violet was sometimes called 'Bunting'. For purposes of the narrative I will use the names the children called themselves as adults: Raymond, Beb, Oc, Violet and Cys.

Asquith's legal career was slow to take off and it was to be five or six years before he could provide comfortably for his growing family. During these years Helen's support, both financial and emotional, was of vital importance. Beb, the couple's second son, later described how his mother 'gave the impression of having found a quiet happiness of her own'. She had 'little desire for the obvious prizes of the world, little care about her own position, no taste whatever for personal fame; her ambition was not for herself; her main desire was that her husband should fulfil his powers, and that his life should have a background of amusement and happiness remote from the dust of conflict'.[21]

The couple were devoted to their children. Asquith was later to describe Helen as 'more wrapped up in her children than any woman I have ever known',[22] while a family friend noted Asquith's own 'almost boyish pleasure' in his children's exploits.[23] Beb described his father's attitude as 'usually one of mellow and spacious indulgence', recalling that both his parents 'allowed their children a full measure of liberty; they used the snaffle rather than the curb and their control was very elastic in nature'.[24] Helen delighted in recounting the boys' games and mischief-making to their father. When the two-year-old Raymond smashed a box of Afghan warriors 'and then proceeded to break the soldiers by stamping on them', his mother treated his tantrum with amused detachment, reporting to Asquith how when she asked him: 'why he is so naughty and destructive, he answers in the most threatening voice "Don't ask silly questions – you must not ask silly questions."'[25] When Oc was about the same age, she described in a letter to her husband, dated 4 October 1886 how:

After being out yesterday morning I peeped quietly into my bedroom where Arthur [Oc] was supposed to be asleep – I wish you could have seen the scene – the little monkey sitting up in bed placidly eating a piece of butter scotch and the floor round his crib perfectly strewn with the white and silver wrappers of the butter scotch slabs. The drawer where I keep it was wide open and surrounded by more pieces of paper and the packet containing it had only two pieces left – he must have eaten 5 slabs. He looked rather guilty and began to cry the moment I spoke to him – which I did pretty severely. Several times afterwards he kissed me very lovingly and said he 'did not steal the butterscotch purposely'. Luckily he is none the worse for his feast, little rogue – but he gets none for his night spice, the remains being reserved for the other two.

In later life, Beb would fondly remember long walks with his mother on Hampstead Heath after they had dropped Raymond off at the little school run by a Miss Case. In the summertime, the boys would help Helen to pick gooseberries from the bushes at the back of the garden, or mulberries for the cook to stew in a cauldron in the kitchen to make mulberry jam, 'a rare and delightful confection, whose scent pervaded the basement and floated invitingly up the stairs into the hall'.[26]

When Asquith came home from the Temple, he would sometimes play cricket with his sons. He was, recalled Beb, 'rather a diffident bowler, delivering high-pitched lobs with a faintly sardonic expression, as though he were criticizing the limitations of his own style'. And contrary to his later reputation for never being seen to run, 'after hooking one of Raymond's round arm balls to the leg side of the wicket, he would often cover the ground at a very respectable pace'.[27] Helen would read to the children every evening before they went to bed. Beb remembered how his father 'would sometimes come in while we were listening to *David Copperfield*, *Alice in Wonderland*, or some other work, but more often at the end of the reading, when he would pace up and down near the window in rather an absent manner, asking us questions about the book', although it was clear 'that a large part of his mind was engaged elsewhere on some problem very remote from John Silver, Mr Pickwick, or the White Knight'.[28]

The children's imaginations were sometimes fired in unusual ways by the stories they read. One summer evening when Raymond was about seven or eight he was inspired by tales of the Greek gods to build a small altar from bricks and stones gathered from around the garden. A fire was kindled from a pile of twigs and the five-year-old Beb despatched to fetch a suitable libation from the decanter of claret which stood on the dining room sideboard. When Janet, the children's strict nonconformist nurse, arrived on the scene to see her employer's best wine being poured over the flames, she was solemnly informed by Raymond that it was a sacrifice to Zeus. Fortunately the boys' father – on his evening walk with his wife beneath the apple-trees – took a more lenient view of his sons' pagan activities. Beb recalled how 'he pursed his lips in great good humour, whispered something to my mother, and passed on with a tolerant smile in the direction of the sunset'.[29]

Asquith delighted in spending his limited income on indulging his children in pleasures forbidden in his own childhood by his mother's strict religious principles. Predictably top of the list was the theatre, with the children enjoying a regular diet of melodramas, pantomimes and Gilbert and Sullivan operas. On occasion he would bring home a box of fireworks – 'nominally, for his children', as Beb later wryly observed. On Guy Fawkes night and on Raymond's birthday the following evening, huge numbers of squibs and Roman candles would be let off among the fruit trees, while a nervous Helen stood watching at the window. Her misgivings about her husband's competence were often borne out: his Catherine wheels 'would frequently jam in mid-career' and on one occasion he badly burnt his hand when a squib exploded as he was he was tossing it over the bough of a pear tree.[30]

Whatever compensations a happy home life could provide, the lean years at the Bar were unbearably frustrating for the young Asquith. After Helen's death, Asquith confided to his friend, Frances Horner, how he viewed his early married life:

> I was content with my early love, and never looked outside. So we settled down in a little suburban villa, and our children were born, and every day I went by the train to the Temple, and sat and worked and dreamed in my chambers, and listened with feverish expectation for a knock at the door, hoping it might be a client with a brief. But years passed on and he hardly ever came . . . of all human troubles the most hateful is to feel you have the capacity for power and yet that you have no field to exercise it. That was for years my case, and no one who has not been through it can know the chilling, paralysing, deadening, depression of hope deferred and energy wasted and vitality run to seed.[31]

It was during these first years of struggle in the Bar that Asquith met Richard Burdon Haldane, the fellow barrister who was to become his closest male friend. Haldane, who was from a junior branch of an old Scottish landed family, had gone on from Edinburgh University to study philosophy at Göttingen and Dresden. Haldane soon became a regular visitor to Eton House, developing a close bond with Helen and her children, who loved to tease and be teased by him and were enthralled by his ghost stories. 'Throughout my life,' Violet was to recall, 'his spheroid figure, his twinkling benignity and pneumatic bulk reminded me irresistibly of those familiar and dearly loved figures the "old men" of Edward Lear.'[32]

By 1885 Asquith was finally earning a good enough income at the Chancery Bar, where he was picking an increasing amount of work from Railway companies, to splash out £300 on a diamond necklace for Helen.

In the General Election of December 1885 when Lord Salisbury's minority Conservative Government was defeated by a coalition of Gladstone's Liberals and Charles Stewart Parnell's Irish Nationalists, Haldane was elected as the Liberal MP for East Lothian, ejecting the sitting MP, Lord Elcho, the heir to the Earl of Wemyss (whose daughter, Cynthia, born two years later, was destined to marry Beb). Asquith was among the first to congratulate his friend, adding 'my wife was equally pleased and looks to you to secure her a place in the Ladies' Gallery'.[33] Helen, however, was much less pleased when, the following June, Haldane persuaded her husband to apply for the vacant Liberal candidacy in the neighbouring constituency of East Fife. Asquith could sense that his wife 'did not really wish it, but she was an angel and never murmured'.[34]

The country had been plunged into another General Election campaign following the defeat of Gladstone's proposals for Home Rule for Ireland. Asquith, a keen advocate of Home Rule for Ireland since his days as an undergraduate debater at the Oxford Union, threw himself with enthusiasm into a campaign that centred on Gladstone's recent conversion to the cause. It was a bitter contest, with his main rival – the former Liberal Member, now standing as a Liberal Unionist – backed not just by local Tories, but also the powerful Church of Scotland clergy. Helen plaintively wrote to ask Asquith whether she could 'not be any help – your mother seems to think I ought to go and try, and if I could you know how gladly I would come to you'; at the same time she confessed: 'I simply can't bear to read the horrid little griselling bits in that Tory paper'.[35]

Against the odds, Asquith scraped in with a majority of only 376.[36] He was to continue to represent the constituency for the next thirty-two years. Triumphantly returning home to Hampstead, he found his family gathered on the small lawn in front of Eton House, waiting to welcome him. Beb later recalled how they had spent hours making a huge white banner emblazoned with the words 'WELCOME M.P.' in large vermilion letters:

Raymond climbed the catalpa tree and hung this splendid creation from a bough which spread out over the front wall of the garden, where he remained aloft, ready to signal my father's approach, while behind him a number of Union Jacks fluttered from the bedroom windows. At last there was the clatter of hoofs in the narrow road, the sound of a hansom cab trotting down the hill with its jingling silvery bells: my father came through the garden gate, a slender figure, rather tired with the stress of his campaign, but full of merriment, with my mother, who was never ambitious for herself, smiling happily at his side, filled with delight and radiant at his victory.[37]

However, beneath his wife's obvious pleasure in his success, Asquith could sense a foreboding 'that this was the beginning of the end of our quiet unruffled uneventful companionship'.[38]

Asquith's early years as an MP were marked by intense hard work as he tried to juggle his political commitments with the need to support his growing family from his earnings at the Bar. Nonetheless, he quickly impressed his Party leaders as well as establishing himself as the leading figure in an influential grouping of young Liberal MPs, who included Haldane and Sir Edward Grey, a youthful Northumberland baronet.

In 1887, shortly after the birth of Violet, the Asquiths moved from John Street to 27 Maresfield Gardens, a larger, brand-new house half a mile away.[39] The children were upset to abandon their beloved mulberry tree and wild orchard for a garden with nothing but freshly laid turf, and the change was aggravated by the death of the family tortoise. However, there was now more room for their parents to entertain; Beb would later fondly recall how he and his brothers, in bed at the top of the house, would lie awake listening to 'the sounds of talk and laughter that poured intermittently out of the dining-room door, when it was opened to admit a new course'. Raymond would enthral his younger brothers with scary tales about the 'Scollion's Deep', a saga of his own invention that took place in a misty twilight land at the bottom of a vast imaginary cleft in the earth, lit by the flares of erupting volcanoes. The 'Deep' was peopled by a fantastic mix of pygmies, giants, dinosaurs, bishops and bat-like creatures with faces with an uncanny resemblance to the revered Mr Gladstone. They would keep the boys wide awake until 'long after the clopping hoofs and jingling bells of the hansoms that carried away the guests below, had faded into the night'.[40]

Although funds were necessarily tight, both Asquith parents delighted in indulging their children. While Asquith was visiting his constituency a few months after the election, Helen wrote to excuse a particularly extravagant expedition to a toyshop when her sons had inveigled her into buying them seventeen boxes of soldiers. 'It was in vain that I tried to limit the number: nothing would induce them to stop till every penny was spent. The three boys are now happy playing with the soldiers in a state of complete bliss.' The next day she reported 'the 400 soldiers have all been out this morning and all my historical powers have been put to the test to think of a battle in which French, Prussians, Turks, Zulus, Burmese, Chinese and numbers of other nations fought'.[41] Some years later the boys would be called upon to play at soldiering for real. After experiencing the carnage of Arras and Passchendaele, Beb wistfully recalled his innocent boyhood war games with his brothers when their artillery consisted of nothing more lethal then leaden pellets and pea shooters, and how after 'General Burnaby', their army's battered commander, was decapitated in a particularly fierce encounter, the boys held a military funeral: 'our little bronze guns fired a salvo, and the blue smoke of their powder floated up to the ceiling in a last salute'.[42]

In the autumn of 1889, Raymond was sent to board at Lambrook, a preparatory school near Ascot. The school was probably chosen on the recommendation of his uncle, Willans Asquith: Lambrook's headmaster, E. D. (known to his pupils as 'Teedy') Mansfield, was a former housemaster at Clifton, the Bristol public school where Willans was now a schoolmaster. Mansfield quickly built a reputation as an educational innovator. Although the Lambrook boys wore a traditional uniform of Eton collar, Norfolk jacket and knickerbockers, the school was well ahead of its time, with a heated indoor swimming pool, a well-equipped gymnasium and a carpentry workshop. There was a debating society and 'concerts' which might consist of anything from a lecture complete with 'magic lantern slides' on the destruction of Pompeii to playlets where the pupils acted out abridged Shakespeare plays or played 'nigger' music. And at a time when organized school sport was unusual, the Lambrook boys played rugger, cricket, shinty (a kind of hockey) and a full range of athletics. The older boys were even allowed to attend meetings at Ascot racecourse as a special reward for good work.[43]

Raymond settled in quickly and his father proudly forwarded to Helen – staying with her sister Josephine in Altrincham – a letter from Mansfield full of praise for their son. 'As you may imagine I have read and re-read Mr Mansfield's letter', she replied. 'Schoolmasters see too much of boys to be enthusiasts, and you may be sure he thinks very well of the Captain* to write as he does.'[44] Raymond's absence seems to have provoked some ructions in the family pecking order with Helen complaining to her husband that 'Bertie [Beb] is going through a most unhappy phase just now grumbling and scolding everybody and everything – especially Arthur [Oc]'. Helen herself unwittingly seems to have given Beb a new idea with which to torment his younger brother when she read the boys an account of the horrors of the slave trade, only for Beb, far from being shocked, to be so taken with the idea that he persuaded his younger brother – craving chocolate and short of pocket money – to sell himself for sixpence. The 'slave' was not liberated from his servitude until Raymond came home and judicially pointed out that slavery was outlawed under the British Crown.[45] Violet, as the only girl, inevitably fell under the influence of her brothers and was soon proudly boasting to her mother that she knew a few boys' words, giving as examples 'mucky' and 'slimy'. 'I regret to say,' Helen informed her husband, 'she is far from the lamblike character she was.'[46]

Asquith, as a good-looking, charming and ambitious MP, soon found himself much sought after as a dinner-party guest. Helen, who tended to prefer small, intimate dinner parties at home or with friends, would rarely accompany her husband to the larger social functions at which he thrived. One mild evening in late March 1891 he found himself seated next to Margot Tennant, the vivacious twenty-seven-year-old youngest daughter of his fellow Liberal MP Sir Charles Tennant, at a large dinner party at the House of Commons. Margot was trying hard to extricate herself from a long-standing romance with Peter Flower, the dashing, but utterly hopeless younger brother of their host, the Liberal MP Cyril Flower (soon to be ennobled as Lord Battersea). Never a man to take much care with his clothes, Asquith presented a somewhat dishevelled bohemian appearance. But what most struck Margot was her new friend's

---

*The family nickname for Raymond.

'clear Cromwellian face'. She decided 'this was the man who could help me and who would understand everything'.[47] Asquith's feelings, however, were much stronger. A couple of years later, he confessed to a mutual friend that Margot 'took possession of me . . . The passion which comes, I suppose, to everyone once in life, visited and conquered me.'[48]

2

Miss Margot Tennant

M ARGOT'S FATHER, SIR Charles Tennant – known to his family as 'the Bart' after he was made a baronet in 1885 – was one of the richest men in Victorian Britain. The family fortune had been founded by his grandfather, also Charles, a former handloom weaver who patented a formula for manufacturing 'bleaching salt'* and went on to build a factory at St Rollox in Glasgow, which eventually became the largest chemical works in Europe. Sir Charles became even wealthier thanks to his own flair for speculative investment. Sir Charles's wife and Margot's mother, Emma Winsloe, was described by their daughter 'as more unlike my father than can easily be imagined'. Although one of her great grandfathers had been an admiral and another had founded *The Times*, she herself had been brought up in genteel poverty after her father had walked out on her mother, a penurious parson's daughter. 'She [Emma] was timid as he was bold, as controlled as he was spontaneous, and as refined, courteous and unassuming as he was vibrant, sheer and adventurous.' And, far from enjoying her husband's riches, 'her preachings on economy were a constant source of amusement to my father'.[1]

In 1853 Charles paid £33,140 for Glen, a 4,000-acre estate near Innerleithen in Peebleshire, some 30 miles from Edinburgh, where

---

*Until then cloth had to be whitened by an endless rigmarole of boiling acres of fabric, laying it in the sun, soaking it in sour milk and then repeating the whole process over and over again, sometimes over a period as long as eighteen months.

he commissioned the leading Scottish architect, David Bryce, to build a huge neo-Gothic castle complete with towers, turrets and grimacing gargoyles. The mansion, with its six reception rooms and twenty-nine bedrooms, was completed in 1858. The setting was spectacular, with the house set in a valley surrounded by wooded hills and wild moorland. It was at Glen that Margot was born on 2 February 1864, her parents' eleventh child. Three of their first four children (all boys) died before the age of eight and in 1866 Janet, the eldest girl, succumbed to the tuberculosis that was to haunt the family. The Tennant boys, Edward, Francis (Frank) and John (Jack), were introverted characters, most at home fishing or shooting round the estate. It was the five girls – Pauline ('Posie'), Charlotte ('Charty'), Lucy, Laura and Margot – who dominated the scene. Their youngest brother, Jack, memorably described them as 'more like lions than sisters'.[2]

Posie married Tom Gordon Duff in 1875 after her first London season, thus leaving Glen when Margot was only eleven. Charty, tall and graceful with fine features and golden hair, was considered the best-looking of the girls. 'She had,' wrote her friend, Frances Horner, 'a gaiety of spirit and a transparent nature which made her the most delightful of companions.'[3] In 1877 Charty married Tommy Lister, who had just succeeded his father as 4th Baron Ribblesdale. Lucy, the third daughter and a talented artist, was her mother's favourite. At the age of seventeen she became engaged to Thomas Graham-Smith, an eccentric guards officer and impoverished Wiltshire landowner, whose interests started and ended with foxhunting. Margot, who was just fourteen at the time, later blamed what turned out to be a disastrous marriage on her father's 'want of judgement', her mother's 'extraordinary weakness' and Lucy's own 'great self-will and obstinacy'. Margot saw her future brother-in-law as a crazy Don Quixote-like figure and 'begged and implored her [Lucy] not to marry him'.[4] Laura was by all accounts an extraordinary young woman. Fair haired and barely five feet tall, she had an intense, spiritual nature, a quick mind and soulful grey eyes. Her fans included men as different as Gladstone, Tennyson, Burne-Jones, Balfour, Dilke and Curzon. Mary Gladstone (later Drew), daughter of the Liberal statesman, visited Glen in 1882 and described Laura as 'the sharpest little creature, like a needle, delicate and yet able to do everything beautifully, like riding, lawn tennis, playing, etc., full of life and fun and up to anything in the world, and yet some *Weltschmerzen* in her eyes'. However, it was Margot – then eighteen years old – who struck Mary Gladstone as 'perhaps the most really pretty and clever of the lot, her hair curling darkly all over her head, eyes large and deep, skin very pearly without much colour, and the most bewitching mouth. She sings, draws, plays violin and pianoforte, all with originality and charm.'[5]

The children's upbringing was entrusted to a string of nurses and governesses, whose regime included forcing them to sleep in thick flannel night gowns with their hair wrapped in white crêpe nets and with the windows tightly shut to mitigate the supposed harmful effects of 'night air'. Margot found her schooling just as constricting:

> Pianos were thumped, hard paints out of wooden boxes were used to copy flowers and fairies on week-days and illuminate texts for school-children on Sundays; English History was taught and re-taught, from Alfred the Great to the reign of Queen Elizabeth, and we recited French fables in the presence of Swiss governesses to pained but interested parents after tea in the evenings. The mildest questions put to any of our teachers were called 'impertinent'; and it was only because my father had a fine library, and we were fond of reading, that I learnt anything at all before I was sixteen.

Parental influence was minimal. Margot's cousin John Tennant observed that although his uncle Charles was 'a man of warm affections', he was 'too much occupied with his many successful business schemes to be a very helpful influence for good in the house; [he was] very fond and proud of his children, but not, I think, a serious factor among those that moulded their deeper natures'.[6] He was so often absent on business that his youngest son, Jack, is once supposed to have asked his mother: 'Is Papa really Papa, or only a kind of visitor?'[7] Margot herself, although fond of her father and always ready to acknowledge his gentleness and generosity, later described him as 'one of the most self-centred selfish men I have ever met'.[8]

Emma had been shattered by the loss of her first four children and lived in constant anxiety about the sickly Posie. Her relationship with her remaining children was, as Margot put it, 'tepid'. The girls were constantly told how plain they were: this was a good thing, according to their mother, as 'it protects one from temptation'. Many years later Margot recalled how 'I can never remember kissing my mother without her tapping me on the back and saying "Hold yourself up!" or kissing my father without his saying, "Don't frown!"'[9] The Tennant girls had little contact with other children and the sisters had to rely on each other for company. 'I can't imagine even a future husband <u>ever</u> being as much to me as my sisters,' Margot once confessed to Posie, 'they are the salt and essence of my existence.'[10] Charty was her 'ideal of everything that is beautiful and good', but her favourite sister was Lucy: 'I would rather <u>talk</u> to Lucy than anyone in the world because she understands me.'[11]

However, Margot's closest relationship was with Laura. The two youngest girls were only a year and a half apart and shared a bedroom until Laura's marriage in 1885. By the time Margot was fourteen her three other sisters were married and Laura was by far the most important person in her life. After Laura's death she managed to convince herself – and almost everyone else – that the two of them had been inseparable companions enjoying a sympathy that was 'telegraphic'.[12] However the journals that the sisters kept give a different picture of their relationship: while Laura rarely mentions Margot, her sister was obsessed with sibling rivalry: 'an inborn jealousy of each other has always spoilt our intimacy'.[13] Laura had a moody side to her character which her friends rarely glimpsed. She could be restless, impatient and sharp-tempered. Her diaries and letters show a young woman tortured by self-doubt and unfulfilled spiritual and religious longing. Laura and Margot would have frequent and furious rows and their bedroom was dubbed the 'Doo'cot', a corruption of 'Dovecote', in ironic recognition of the noisy arguments that would rage there.

Margot was much the wilder character, by her own admission 'self-willed, excessively passionate, disconcertingly truthful, bold as well as fearless and always against convention, I was no doubt, extremely difficult to bring up'. She longed to escape 'the nagging of nurses, the boredom of Sundays, and the daily routine of monotonous moral theories reiterated in our schoolroom'. When not in the schoolroom, the girls were free to roam the local countryside, and much of Margot's time was spent riding over the local moors or accompanying her brothers on shooting or fishing expeditions. 'There was,' she claimed, 'not a stone dyke, peat bog, or patch of burnt and flowering heather with which I was not familiar, and I made friends with wandering tramps, and every shepherd, farmer and fisherman on the Border.'[14]

For Margot, the most important event of her mid-teens was her introduction to foxhunting at Easton Grey, the lovely Cotswold stone village near Malmesbury where Lucy and her husband, Tom Gordon Duff, lived in the manor house on the banks of the River Avon, and in the heart of Duke of Beaufort's famous hunt. The Duke himself was so impressed by Margot's daredevil riding he at once allowed her to wear the traditional dark-blue Beaufort hunting habit. The sport quickly became one of her great passions. 'For pure unalloyed happiness those days were undoubtedly the most perfect of my life,' she wrote later. 'The beauty of the place, the wild excitement of riding over fences and the perfect certainty I had that I would ride better than anyone in the whole world gave me an insolent confidence which no earthquake can shake.'[15]

In the summer of 1878 Margot's parents decided to send her and Laura to Dresden for a couple of months of culture supervised by 'Frolly', their German governess. The idea – which was probably Frolly's – was an unusual one since Dresden was not yet the fashionable resort for young English aristocrats that it was to become for a future generation. In spite of a rough North Sea crossing and an exhausting railway journey, Margot was immediately captivated by Dresden's fairytale baroque streets and 'saw the Elbe spangled with the most brilliant lights'.[16] The girls shared a neat little room in a lodging house at 28 Luttichau Strasse run by Frau von Mach, who was half-English and had been abandoned by her soldier husband, driven insane during the Franco-Prussian war. Much of their time was spent at concerts at the new theatre on the banks of the Elbe: 'mad Hungarian music, Rhapsodies of Liszt, Wagner overtures, Beethoven symphonies, Rubinstein's ballet music, all these and 10,000 more'. On their first night the girls had their first taste of Wagner, listening 'spell bound' to *Lohengrin*. Margot felt a 'joyousness [that] seemed to swell my veins and my head reeled . . . Wagner is my musical hero! I know he is a wicked vain man but I love him!'[17]

Dresden also had a subtle effect on Margot's religious beliefs. She had never shared Laura's near-obsessive interest in Christian doctrine, but to the end of her life she retained a deep if unconventional faith. It was not something the girls owed to either their parents or the church. Margot noticed how her father would doze through the dreary sermons preached at the local Traquair kirk, while she and Laura would often be close to dissolving into giggles. Nonetheless the kirk was part of the family's life and Margot at first was shocked to find that neither Frau von Mach nor any of her German lodgers went to church. She and Laura regularly attended the 8 a.m. service at Dresden's Anglican church – probably as much as a means of keeping in touch with their homeland as for spiritual reasons – but henceforth she was more willing to question the puritanical Scottish Sunday regime, no longer 'convinced of the sin of running or drawing or even sewing on Sundays'.[18] In later life she liked to argue that 'the only thing that stands between us and true religion is the Church'.[19]

Margot's father was elected to Parliament in 1879 at a by-election for the St Rollox division of Glasgow (he switched to representing his local Peebles seat at the General Election the following year). Margot and Laura joined the local bigwigs on the platform at St Andrew's Hall in Glasgow for a huge rally to be addressed by Gladstone and his glamorous Scottish protégé, Lord Rosebery. Margot later recalled how the sisters were breathless with excitement as they 'gazed with rapture at the blue and yellow bunting, floating banners, and Liberal mottoes, that decorated every part of the hall'. When Gladstone and Rosebery stepped on to the platform 'it seemed as if the thunder of cheers would only cease when the roof had fallen in. Men and women scrambled onto their seats waving hats and handkerchiefs and Laura and I hardly dared to look at one another for fear of bursting into tears.'[20]

The evening was the beginning of a long friendship between Margot and the two men under whom her future husband would serve as Home Secretary. According to his biographer Philip Magnus, 'as Gladstone grew older, the repressions of a lifetime were insensibly lifted a little, and he found it possible to relax simply and naturally in the presence of young, pretty, and vivacious women.'[21] The venerable Parliamentarian was enchanted by the two youngest Tennant girls, whose irreverent flirtatiousness presented an appealing contrast to his usual diet of political toadyism. In January 1890, when Rosebery was staying at Hawarden, Gladstone's estate on the North Wales borders, he complained about the impossibility of having a private talk with his host because his time was 'wholly monopolised by Miss Margot Tennant'.[22]

Charles Tennant's election to Parliament was the catalyst for a sea change in the life of his family. The new MP purchased No. 40 Grosvenor Square (then No. 35) as a London base. It was decided that Laura and Margot would 'come out' in London society, and as preparation they were sent to a finishing school in Gloucester Terrace run by a Mademoiselle de Mennecy, described by Margot as 'a Frenchwoman of ill-temper and a lively mind'.[23] A combination of sticky food and being kept awake at night by the roars and whistles of the Great Western Railway drove Laura out within a week. Margot lasted a few weeks longer, her rebelliousness overlooked by the snobbish Madame who was keen to keep on board the daughter of a rich MP. However, shortly after Margot had blown a kiss to a passing engine driver, the railwayman was spotted by Mademoiselle enthusiastically responding to another pupil from a less wealthy background. The wretched girl was expelled, prompting Margot into a stormy confrontation with Mademoiselle, after which she flounced straight home to her parents.

The Tennants dared not risk introducing their two youngest daughters to London society at the same time. As one family friend put it, 'the effect on London of the two of them would be devastating'.[24] Instead, Margot returned to Dresden, where she devoted her time to a busy daily programme of music practice, literature, drawing and attending concerts and operas. She now had an almost defiant desire to educate herself, writing in her journal: 'Dresden Dresden you are a school for one's ambitions.' By the time she returned to Britain, she had seen every one of Wagner's operas except *Tristan und Isolde* and acquired a lifelong love for Germany and German culture.[25]

At first, the impact of the Tennant girls on the London social scene was limited by the obscurity of their background. Invitations were sparse and Margot spent much of her time riding in Rotten Row gazing at Lily Langtry and other beauties of the day. One day her brother, Eddy, took her to the Royal Enclosure at the Ascot races where she was spotted by the Prince of Wales who sat her next to him at lunch in the Guards Tent. This very public royal patronage – which Margot no doubt played for all it was worth – prompted many more invitations and it was not long before the sisters were welcomed everywhere as a refreshing counterblast to the stuffy atmosphere of mid-Victorian society. When their new friends were invited home to Glen or 40 Grosvenor Square they were amazed by an almost complete absence of the inhibitions and restrictions normal at the time in England. One new friend, Aldolphus 'Doll' Liddell, then a staid thirty-something, described a 'joy of eventful living that I had never thought could exist except in a book. There was no attempt at anything like chaperonage, all the old fashioned restrictions as to the manner or place of companionship between young men and maidens being entirely ignored, but with such an entire freedom from self-consciousness that after a time it seemed just as natural as it does to suspend the ordinary rules in regard to the attitude of the sexes during a *valse*.'[26]

A more ambivalent reaction came from Gladstone's prudish daughter, Mary Drew, whose approval of Margot and Laura piously praying before the altar of the local kirk was soon wiped out when she saw a self-portrait of a naked Margot lying openly in the drawing room. 'Isn't it beautiful?' said the disingenuous Laura. 'Margot did it from herself in the looking glass.' Mary has left a half-horrified, half-enthralled memoir of the atmosphere at Glen:

> There was a kind of Star and Garter freedom and recklessness of manners and talk, there was no reserve, no restraint, no holy places kept sacred. All day it was one fury of fun and games and music and discussions, at meals you tore through subject after subject with the rapidity of lightning, retort, repartee, contradictions, capping, flew across the table with a constant accompaniment of shrieks and peals of laughter. Parting at bedtime only meant leaving the oldies below and adjourning the game to the next floor. Here pranks and fun and frolic grew faster and more furious, apple-pie beds, sponge fights, pillow games, nobody minding whose room was invaded. And still with all this reckless freedom, so risky, so near the wind, there was a breezy innocence and frankness, the fun and freshness of pure animal spirits and childlike joy in living, that kept it from being the really unwholesome atmosphere one would expect from hearing the raw facts.[27]

Over the next few years, the Tennant sisters made Glen and 40 Grosvenor Square the hub of an extraordinarily eclectic social set where artists mixed with aristocrats, Conservative MPs with their Liberal opponents, and the hunting set with academics, artists and writers. There was even room for the young Oscar Wilde who dedicated a short story to Margot.* Laura and Margot became popular additions to aristocratic house parties where they could be guaranteed to liven things up: Margot once amazed fellow guests by dancing a furious can-can on the landing of one country house where she was staying.[28]

---

*The Star Child. Wilde also wrote several poems for Margot. Although Margot invited him to Glen, she was soon to find his egotism and affectation unbearable.

Outside the 'season' Margot and Laura operated within very different social sets. Laura's friends, like her interests, tended to the intellectual and artistic. Her male admirers included two of the future leading lights in the Conservative Party, George Curzon and Arthur Balfour, while her closest girlfriends were Mary Drew (*née* Gladstone) and Frances Graham, whose father was also a successful Scottish businessman and Glasgow Liberal MP as well as being an early patron of Burne-Jones and the other pre-Raphaelite painters. Frances, an art lover herself, became a close friend of Burne-Jones, but in the end opted for convention and married John (Jack) Horner, an intelligent but modest and taciturn Somerset squire sixteen years her senior. She remained, though, a link between the artistic and social worlds.

By contrast Margot's world revolved round the hunting set: athleticism and dash were what she looked for in a man. A typical suitor was Lord ('Rocky') Rocksavage, summed up by Margot as 'a good sort, faintly unrefined, very sporting, not too much intellect, good company'.[29] Her first serious crush seems to have been on Charty's husband, Lord (Tommy) Ribblesdale. She was thrilled one day when Ribblesdale carried her in his arms over some boggy ground. 'I could have crushed his life out.'[30] However, Ribblesdale was soon supplanted in her affections by Walter Long, a young Tory MP and Wiltshire landowner, with whom the sixteen-year-old Margot was immediately smitten when she met him out hunting with the Beaufort. She devoted pages and pages of her journal to eulogizing Long who was 'as brave and strong as he is sympathetic and polite and take him all round the most perfectly refined intelligent soul I ever met'. She was impressed by a man who 'talked to me as if I was worth talking to, and looked at me out of the sternest but most fascinating dark blue eyes and my heart jumped whenever he spoke to me'. The fact that he happened to be married does not seem to have bothered her – she complained about the injustice of not being able to love a married man 'even in private'.[31]

By Margot's eighteenth birthday she had decided that 'unless I find a man I love as much as Tommy [Ribblesdale] or Walter Long I shall marry for money or position or not at all'. Until then she was determined to play the field untrammelled by all the conventional restrictions on what was proper behaviour for a young unmarried girl. 'Why should I appear indignant when I am kissed or angry when fondled, it's humbug when I like it. Yes, love being cared about even if its not the way we call right! . . . Why should one only love one man and he must be what we call right, not any one else's husband not even in private . . . why such an adjective as fast or flirt? – it's sickening!'[32] In this mood, it is hardly surprising that after her first season Margot allowed herself to be bulldozed into a disastrous engagement at the age of seventeen to John Gratwicke ('Gratty') Blagrave, the twenty-six-year-old younger son of a Berkshire squire, whom, inevitably, she met out hunting. Margot's hilarious account of Gratty's courtship is one of the highlights of her early diaries.

In June 1892, Gratty persuaded Margot to accompany him on a trip to Boulogne chaperoned by her younger brother, Jack. Afterwards the three of them put up at the West Cliff hotel in Folkestone, where after Jack had gone to bed, Margot and Gratty stayed up talking. As night wore on, Gratty, wrestling to overcome his 'funk' and declare his love, became more and more agitated. Let Margot herself take up the story:

He went on tearing at his handkerchief, a huge one with a blue border. He then bit his finger and made a most hideous gash and I was frightened and seized his hand – and I said 'd'you want me to marry you?' He said 'Yes, yes', never looking at me but still tearing his hankey and I got a great gulping shock and said 'Oh Mr Blagrave, I couldn't marry you, never, as I love Walter better than you.' And then I felt his whole body and arms trembling. His face was hidden and he shook so and bit his hands . . . I saw he was crying and all his lips bleeding and he wouldn't speak to me or look at me, and I begged him not to be angry, to make it up. I never felt so miserable in my life. I'd never thought of such a thing and I cried and held his knees and prayed him to listen to me. His ugly little face looked quite ghastly.[33]

To no avail Margot told Gratty he was 'too good, too dear, too ripping a man not to have a woman's first and best love', as he set about biting his arm, declaring 'I shall go away out of the country, sell every hunter I possess, give up my racing . . . and never set foot in England or get on a horse again.'

The thought of Gratty sacrificing his horses for love appalled Margot so much that she began to tear out 'handfuls of my hair, and lay on the ground and sobbed' as she pleaded with him to be reasonable. Gratty would have none of it, pressing her in his arms, 'he kissed my eyes, my lips and pressed my little cold white face against his rough coat.' It was after six in the morning before Margot managed to get to bed, but not before Gratty had threatened suicide.

The following morning, Gratty refused breakfast and ran off towards the sea with Margot and Jack in hot pursuit. They found him eventually lying prostrate with his legs dangling over a cliff. He refused to speak to them and Margot, worried by the effect of the heat of the midday sun, covered his head with her parasol before escaping to the beach. It was then Gratty's turn to pursue her: 'crunching down the pebbles' he caught up with her and 'stretched his arms to the sea and looked like a maniac'. She then agreed to marry him! Deliriously happy, Gratty promised her £2,000 a year and hunting six days a week.

Margot's sisters treated the whole affair as a huge joke, but her father angrily ordered his footmen to bar Gratty from his house. Parental opposition added to the attractions of the affair and Margot revelled in clandestine meetings with her fiancé in Kensington Gardens on the pretext of attending a service at the nearby St George's Church. She teased Gratty – and doubtless appalled prim passers-by – when she slung her night gown on to the pavement in front or him. She was thrilled by 'the feeling of his arms round me and his clean cool hands lifting my face to his', she 'would nip back and be let in by Henry [the footman] too well bred to turn a hair' and just have time to ensconce herself in the library before 'Mama, Papa and Laura would come in and find me yawning over *Democracy* or whatever book was there'.

After a few weeks Margot came to her senses and broke off the engagement, to relief all round. Gratty promised to renew his suit the following year, but by then, as Margot smugly noted in her diary, he was 'to be married to Miss Sheriffe, a young lady with not much reputation left!'.*

The following year Margot and Laura fell passionately in love with the same man: Alfred Lyttelton, the eighth son of Mrs Gladstone's brother, the 4th Baron Lyttelton. A successful barrister and aspiring Liberal politician, Alfred could have stepped straight off the pages of a novel by John Buchan or Rider Haggard. Asquith – who also knew

---

*In fact even Miss Sheriffe appears to have had second thoughts. Blagrave eventually married Fanny Dixie, the seventh daughter of a baronet in 1898 The whole affair is chronicled in glorious detail in the entry for 6 June 1882 in Margot's journal.

Lyttelton well – described him as 'the ideal of manhood which every English father would like to see his son aspire to, and if possible attain'.[34] Tall, athletic and a superb all round sportsman, Alfred played football for Cambridge as well as captaining the cricket eleven and scoring the decisive innings when the University team trounced an Australian team that had beaten county after county. He went on to represent England in both sports as well as becoming the amateur 'real' tennis champion every year from 1889 until 1896.

Margot was soon in raptures about 'Alfred Lyttelton in the splendour of his manhood with everything at his feet . . . a man whose wholesome vitality and bounding life-spark knew nothing of illness or exhaustion, whose comprehensive intelligence and confident ambition defied defeat'. Laura quickly realized that her younger sister 'was madly in love with him. You see she is too clever and too fine a character to love a man whose one recommendation to her is his seat on a horse and his nerve and Alfred besides having brains and backbone has all the physical qualities, the out of doors talents she most admires.' When Lyttelton was invited to Glen over the New Year of 1885, Margot realized that it was Laura and not her that Alfred loved and 'felt as if I could have bitten her and that my teeth were full of poison like a mad dogs'. On 5 January Laura accepted his proposal of marriage, writing in her journal how 'I never felt so sorry for anybody as I did for little Margot that week. She behaved splendidly, generously, silently, with dignity.'[35]

Laura and Alfred were married on 21 May 1885 at St George's, Hanover Square. Afterwards Margot was nearly hysterical with grief. Although she seems to have spoken to no one about her own love for Alfred – her upset was put down entirely to the loss of Laura's companionship – she turned for comfort to Laura's friend, George Curzon, perhaps sensing he was feeling something similar. 'I can't help it, it may be selfish, but it's true, I mind Laura's going', she wrote to Curzon. Laura was 'part of myself and I shall shriek at the empty bed now and work off what I've wanted to say by biting my pillow and banging my head. No one takes that place say what you like . . . just we two in the most perfect closest intimacy you can imagine . . . and now it's all over – I mind – her letters, her kisses, her hair round my neck.'[36]

As the date of the birth of Laura's first child approached, Margot was sent to stay with Lucy at Easton Grey. Laura's tiny figure meant a difficult birth was almost inevitable and her mother did not want her youngest daughter put off marriage altogether by witnessing the suffering of a painful confinement. Laura herself was full of foreboding, telling Margot 'I am sure I shall die with my baby.'[37] On the night of Friday 16 April 1886, a baby boy was born after a terrible struggle that left Laura shattered. The same day Margot was thrown whilst hunting, concussed and her face badly cut. On the Sunday, when it became clear that Laura was indeed going to die, she was summoned to London. Somehow Laura clung on to life until the following Saturday, Easter Saturday. Margot was woken at daybreak and found Laura's room was full of people but she was conscious of no one but her dying sister. 'I put my cheek against her shoulder and felt the sharpness of her spine. For a minute we lay close to each other, while the sun, fresh from the dawn, played upon the window blinds . . . Then her breathing stopped; she gave a shiver and died.'[38] Laura was buried in the family plot in a corner of the little churchyard surrounding Traquair kirk. Margot recorded her agony in a stark entry in her journal – the last entry for over five years: 'I will never be able to speak to her again never laugh cry read pray think love or live together again. Oh God my God why hast thou forsaken me? I didn't love her enough and never loved her enough and now I can't say so to her.'[39]

Laura's little boy was adopted by Charty, but died a month after his second birthday. In December of the same year Posie succumbed to the chronic tuberculosis that had dogged her for years. By now Margot was almost too numb to feel anything but relief that her eldest sister's terrible suffering was over at last. The loss of Laura had already changed her for ever: a tendency to melancholy that had always been part of her make-up took a far stronger hold. From now on, what she called 'the black helpless moments when all the stars are hid and I do not see the sun' were never far away.[40]

If Margot had hopes that Alfred would now turn his attention to herself, she did not admit it even in her journal. Guilt mingled with grief led her to try to assume her dead sister's personality, throwing herself into self-education and social work. She and Laura had founded a crèche for the working women of Wapping, but whereas slum work gave Laura real pleasure, to Margot it was more of a penance for her privileged background. Like many young women of her class, she expected to carry out 'good works' towards those less fortunate, but although she did not mind visiting cottagers on her father's estate or teaching Bible stories to local children, she found slum dwellers much less attractive: 'I confess I find the poor just as uninfluenceable and ungrateful as the rich', was her verdict many years later.[41] Nonetheless, looking for a further outlet for her charity, Margot began to pay regular visits to a box factory in Whitechapel to talk to the female workers during their lunch hour, later taking them on outings to the country – although she was shocked when she took the girls to Caterham, only to have them spend the day ogling the soldiers at the barracks there.

Hunting remained Margot's passion. She was a frequent visitor to Easton Grey, where she would hunt with the Beaufort, but her favourite hunting county was 'High' Leicestershire, the home of the ultra-smart Quorn, Belvoir and Cottesmore hunts, where much of fashionable London would decamp for the winter months and where she would base herself at Cold Overton, Oakham, the hunting lodge of Hoppy and Con, Lord and Lady Manners, whom she met in the mid 1880s at a country-house party given for a Quorn hunt ball in Leicestershire. The couple became her most devoted friends and gave her a home from home. Con Manners, Margot later recalled, was 'a saint of goodness. Her love of flowers made every part of her home, inside and out, radiant; and her sense of humour and love of being entertained stimulated the witty and the lazy.'[42]

During the hunting season, Margot's attention was almost completely absorbed by the horses she rode, the hounds she followed and the foxes she chased. It was while hunting in Leicestershire that she met Peter Flower, younger brother of the Asquiths' politician friend, Cyril. A couple of months after Laura's wedding, Margot recorded that Peter Flower had already 'become quite part of my life and I can with difficulty imagine anyone getting to know me so intimately or vice versa'.[43] Peter was fourteen years older than Margot, a dashing and courageous horseman and a chivalrous lover, but unfortunately also an inveterate gambler and incapable of any serious occupation. In spite of all Margot's efforts, she utterly failed to harness him to a successful career and make him a marriageable prospect. Yet she could not bring herself to give him up. Their love affair was to last for nine years.

Meanwhile, outside the hunting field, Margot began to adopt Laura's more intellectual and artistic friends, becoming the central figure in a social set that soon came to be dubbed the 'Souls'. The term was a mocking one, originally coined by Admiral Lord Charles Beresford at a dinner party given by Lady Brownlow. 'You all sit and talk about each other's souls – I shall call you the "Souls".'[44] The central male figures among the Souls were George Curzon and Arthur Balfour. Margot first met Curzon in 1884, a couple of years before his election as Conservative MP for Southport. Writing of this early friendship, then uncomplicated by politics, she wistfully recalled a man who was 'sweet-tempered, affectionate and gay, he was an enchanting companion'.[45] However, although she found Balfour 'an irresistible companion', she always found the enigmatic bachelor 'as puzzling to understand and as difficult to know as he was easy for me and many others to love'.[46] She probably never appreciated the depth of his genuine affection for her, liking to say 'he had a taste for me as a collector might have in clocks or stamps'. When, in the early years of their friendship, Margot was criticized by the waspish Mary Drew, Balfour was quick to defend her:

> I think you are a <u>little</u> hard on my Margot – perhaps not making quite sufficient allowances for a nature whose faults and whose merits alike arise from an absolute and half '<u>phenomenal</u>' 'naturalness' – a naturalness which knows no rules and recognises no conventions, which therefore sometimes induces her to violate the canons of perfect taste and do and say things which had infinitely better be left unsaid and undone, but which nonetheless has in it some of the merits of sincerity and veracity – and is I think quite unalloyed with any kind of meanness.[47]

However, it was the Souls women who gave the set its unique ambience. Several were accomplished artists or lovers of art – Violet Granby (later Duchess of Rutland), Margot's sister, Lucy Graham-Smith and Frances Horner among them. Margot's closest friend among the Souls women was Ettie Desborough. Tall, willowy and combining a quiet charm with a sharp intellect, Ettie became one of the great hostesses of the era, bringing an unmatched panache to her house parties held at Taplow, her hideous neo-Gothic mansion beside the Thames. She was married to Willy Grenfell, Lord Desborough – six foot five and with a physique to match. Grenfell was an Oxford rowing blue and an Olympic fencer, but his intellect was as puny as his body was athletic. Although the marriage seems to have been a relatively happy one, Ettie was a notorious man-eater and satisfied her restless intellect in a series of passionate *amitiés amoureuses*.

Margot and Ettie were always linked with a third Souls woman, Mary Elcho – the wife of Haldane's beaten rival for the East Lothian constituency – in a half-jocular rivalry for the love of the supposedly unattainable, Arthur Balfour. Margot once chided Balfour that he would not miss them even if they were all to die. 'I would mind if you all died on the same day,' was his characteristic rejoinder.[48] Margot herself, however, was closer to Mary's mother-in-law, Lady Wemyss, whom she adopted as a mother figure.

Margot and her friends always professed to dislike the sobriquet 'Souls', preferring to call themselves 'the Gang'. There was certainly more to their activities than philosophical and intellectual discussions: they excelled at charades and word games of their own invention, and burnt off their youthful zest and high spirits in games of lawn tennis and that other Victorian sporting craze, bicycling. What annoyed the Souls was not so much the fun poked at their metaphysics, but the idea than they were cliquey or clannish. Balfour complained that the term was 'meaningless and slightly ludicrous', implying that the organization had come about spontaneously, 'born of casual friendships and unpremeditated sympathy.'[49] It was a fair point. One of the great characteristics of the Souls was their openness, not only to the new intellectual and artistic currents of the day, but to a much wider circle of friends than would ever be contemplated by most of the landed gentry. Besides most of Margot's hunting friends, this circle included the pre-Raphaelite artists William Morris and Edward Burne-Jones, the writers Henry James, Edith Wharton, H. G. Wells and Oscar Wilde, and even actors such as Mrs Patrick Campbell, Herbert Beerbohm Tree and Tree's wife Maud.

Margot's peripatetic efforts to educate herself received a boost when she met Benjamin Jowett in the late 1880s[50] at Gosford, the Scottish seat of Lord Elcho's father, Earl of Wemyss. Quickly captivated by Margot's unaffected precocity and – like Gladstone – no doubt flattered by her flirtatiousness, Jowett appointed himself her intellectual mentor. He told her that 'her cleverness almost amounts to genius. She might be a distinguished authoress if she would – but she wastes her time and her gifts in scampering about the world and going from one country home to another in a manner not pleasant to think of 20 years hence when her youth will have made itself wings and fled away.' He recommended she adopt 'a noble and simple life', exercise 'more self discipline' and 'have a natural love for everyone, especially for the poor'.[51] Margot took Jowett's strictures about her lifestyle with a large pinch of salt: 'I felt his warnings much as a duck swimming might feel the cluckings of a hen on a bank,' she later wrote.[52] Nonetheless, he left his mark and she became a regular guest at the Master's lodgings in Balliol. She in her turn invited Jowett to stay at Glen and introduced him to her own friends. The Master of Balliol's lodgings soon became a regular haunt of the Souls.

By now Margot and Asquith had many friends in common. Apart from Jowett and Cyril Flower, their principal link was ironically Margot's great unrequited love, Alfred Lyttelton, whom Asquith had first met in March 1880, since when they had become close friends – the Asquiths were among the guests at Laura's wedding.[53] Nonetheless, although Asquith and Margot met on a number of occasions, they seem to have made next to no impression on one another until that fateful dinner at the House of Commons in March 1891.

3

'You have made me a different man'

A SQUITH WAS FAR too proper ever to have admitted to Margot the strength of his passion. He was always careful to refer to her respectfully as 'Miss Margot', even behind her back. The nearest he came to admitting his feelings was to thank her 'for the brightness and vividness and inspiration to better things, which you have brought into my life'. For Margot, he was always 'Asquith' and his role in her life that of a slightly more glamorous Jowett: someone to guide her reading, flatter her and, most importantly, give her fatherly advice – particularly on what to do about Peter Flower. When Asquith met Peter he was careful to insist that 'I liked him very much', but he refused 'to sit still' and watch 'a power which might do so much either frittered away [or] dammed up in a narrow pond which will grow nothing but weeds and water flowers; picturesque, placid, purposeless'. After such a long and emotionally fraught relationship, he considered that a break now was 'better than the prospect of two broken hearts and two broken and squandered lives'.[1]

Asquith's friendship with Margot marked even more of a sea change in his life than his election to Parliament. She became the genie who opened up a social life of country house 'Saturday to Mondays' and elegant London dinner parties, peopled with women as clever as they were pretty. It was a diet on which he was to thrive. Asquith was never a Soul in the sense of enjoying their games, either intellectual or sporting. Yet contrary to the generally believed view that he was – in the words of Hilaire Belloc – 'jeered at behind his back' for his 'ridiculous middle class manner',[2] he was well liked by almost all of Margot's Soul friends. He always got on well with Balfour in spite of their fierce political antagonism, while George Curzon became a close friend and one of the few men with whom he was on Christian name terms. Even Curzon's dissolute fellow-Soul Harry Cust* came to regard him with an 'abiding and abounding depth and breadth of admiration and affection'.[3] But it was above all with the Souls' women that Asquith was to become popular. 'Never was better company than Henry Asquith in those days: keen, courteous, giving you always of his best,' Frances Horner was to recall. 'We never thought any party complete without him.'[4] Margot's sister Charty became another close confidante, as did Ettie Desborough.

Asquith was careful to conduct his correspondence with Margot from the House of Commons or his Chambers in the Temple. If Helen suspected anything, she sensibly chose not to fight Margot, probably believing that this was a passing infatuation; and had she lived, it would probably have been just that: her husband would after all subsequently succumb to the charms of many other women. There was, in any event, little threat to her marriage: Asquith, like many a spouse before and since, reassured himself that 'there are as we know "one way" and "another way" of love', and there is no doubt that his love for his wife was deep. Certainly, Helen gave no hint of jealousy and managed to convince her husband – if not herself – that 'though she knew Margot very slightly, she admired and even loved her enthusiastically'.[5] She even told him 'there is something a little noble about Margot Tennant's expression'[6] and made a point of befriending her, taking her to see her husband perform in court, accompanied by Raymond. On one particular hot and sultry day Margot made a strong impression on her future stepson by playfully throwing her handkerchief from the gallery on to the heads of the nodding lawyers beneath them.

---

*Henry ('Harry') Cust (1861–1917) was educated at Eton, where his teachers predicted that he was more likely to become Prime Minister than either Curzon or Rosebery. He went on to win a scholarship to Trinity College Cambridge and was elected a Conservative MP in 1890, by which time he was a well-established member of the Souls. Margot recalled him as the most brilliant young man she had ever known, with the exception of her stepson Raymond. But Cust chose to dissipate his talents in heavy drinking and serial womanizing: Margot's sister Lucy Graham-Smith figured among his unhappy conquests, as did her friend, Violet, the wife of the 8th Duke of Rutland, by whom he notoriously fathered Lady Diana Manners (later Cooper).

It was natural that Asquith should want his wife to share his new friends. Although Helen was never comfortable in 'high society', she did agree to accompany him for a weekend with the Desboroughs at Taplow, where she seems to have got on well with Ettie. According to Margot who was also there, 'everyone liked her'. Nonetheless, she could not resist a gentle put down, telling Margot 'she did not think she would ever care for the sort of society that I loved, and was happier in the circle of her home and friends'. When Margot told her 'she had married a man who was certain to attain the highest political distinction, she replied that that was not what she coveted for him'.[7]

In the early days of their marriage the Asquiths spent their summer holidays first in Cornwall and then west Wales, where by a strange irony they rented a cottage in Marine Terrace, Criccieth, the home town of Asquith's future colleague and political nemesis, David Lloyd George. Later on, the Lake District became their favourite summer haunt. However, for the summer of 1891, the Asquiths decided to spend the holidays on the newly fashionable Isle of Arran off the west coast of Scotland, renting Altachorin, a red sandstone house about a mile from Lamlash with a magnificent view across the bay to Holy Island. Altachorin had one fatal drawback: bad drains.* On 3 August Helen and the children travelled up by sleeper to Ardrossan where they were met by Charlie Melland, Helen's uncle. The boys were delighted with house and island and specially thrilled by the Royal Navy warships that steamed into the bay every night, searchlights ablaze, to anchor near the Naval base on Holy Island. The sole dissident was Violet, who seems to have had a foreboding of disaster. 'Poor Bunting does not like the house <u>at all</u>,' her mother reported, 'it is rather puzzling.'[8]

Asquith took the sleeper up to Scotland on 14 August, spending much of the time writing a long letter to Margot, with whom he was now corresponding every few days. There followed a happy week with his family, fishing, bathing and walking along the coast. On

---

*The house, now known as Altachorvie, presently serves as holiday home for a Christian fellowship.

Thursday 20 August, Beb became feverish and his mother moved in to his room to nurse him. On the second night Helen herself was suddenly taken ill with repeated attacks of faintness. Beb wanted to wake his father, but she refused to let him be disturbed, insisting that her illness was trivial and would soon pass. Over the next few days her condition deteriorated, but it was not until 27th that her family insisted that a doctor be called. He diagnosed typhoid. Helen's capable sister, Josephine, arrived the following day to take charge of nursing her. Helen was judged too ill to see the children, but maintained contact by sending down brief notes every day. Beb sent up to his mother little drawings of ships to help to cheer her. On 4 September Asquith reported to Margot 'there has been a decided change for the better. She no longer gives herself up, which is a good sign, and sleeps better and looks more like herself.' But six days later she took a sudden turn for the worse and the following day (11 September) Asquith wrote a brief note to Margot: 'She died at nine this morning. So end twenty years of love and fourteen of unclouded union. I was not worthy of it, and God has taken her. Pray for me.'[9]

Helen was buried four days later by the low stone wall marking the edge of the graveyard in Lamlash. Exactly a year after her death, Asquith described her to Frances Horner as 'an angel from Heaven and God took her back from this noisy world with unstained feet and an unspotted heart'.[10]

There was no shortage of sympathy for Asquith. 'Nothing could exceed the kindness of my friends, who do not allow me to spend much of my time in loneliness,'[11] he wrote to Ettie. However, it was from Margot herself that above all he sought support. 'There is something in the look of your face, in the touch of your hand, even in the sight of your handwriting, which is soothing and healing, which unseals the springs of hope, which makes me feel for the moment that I live again,' he told her. There was already more than a hint that his feelings for her were more than those of friendship: 'Are you unchangingly mine, Margot?' he asked. 'In your sense, yes – for you would never lie – but in my sense? I don't know. I don't like to think.'[12] Sensing she might be shocked at his apparent fickleness, the following day he sought to explain how his love for her in no sense undermined his love for Helen:

I love my darling Helen as truly now as when I kissed her dear cold hand, and looked for the last time at her angel face. I shall never cease to love her; you would despise me if I did. I even try to believe, as you believe, that she herself, as I knew her – the love of my youth, my companion and helper in all my struggles – still not only lives, but in some way that we cannot understand, is still the same. My love for you is not disloyalty to her. As she lay dying, with the intuition that often comes then, she divined (I am certain) that it was to be, and when she sent her sweet little message to you, she sanctioned and blessed it. But I am not going to force it upon you. It will keep. You know that it is always there, waiting if the time shall ever come when it can give rest and shelter and protection to that storm-tossed little heart.[13]

It would be easy to dismiss as wishful thinking Asquith's belief that his dead wife had given her blessing to her successor 'as she lay dying', except such a gesture would have been typical of Helen. He sent Margot a photograph of Helen ending his letter 'I am yours – and perhaps you somehow some day – but I can't finish the sentence.'[14]

It was all too much for Margot, who had decided to break with Peter and was still trying to cope with the emotional shock. Asquith was 'truly sorry, and a little ashamed' to add to her own worries but he pleaded that 'you have created it, and it is there, and there it will remain so long as you and I live'. But he asked nothing of her, still less did he dream of asking her to say that she loved him. But, he wrote, 'the very fact that I now know I love you – deeply, passionately with the whole strength of my being . . . fills me with resolve to leave you free to think and act and feel as your own heart and judgement dictate. Unless I am weaker than I think myself – and God knows I am weak enough when I see your dear face – you shall never hear from me one word of entreaty. You shall decide your own fate in your own time and in your own way.'[15]

Asquith's most immediate task was to find someone to look after the children. 'The main thing,' he wrote to Eleanor Birrell,* 'is that she should be really fond of and interested in them, and ready to give her time and ingenuity to making them happy. They have been accustomed to a mother who was always with them, and lived for them, and was their constant companion and playmate and friend.'[16] In the

---

*The wife of Liberal MP Augustine Birrell.

end he chose a Miss Weber, 'a German, but well anglicised and highly recommended . . . I hope she will be a success, tho' I confess that I hate the sight and the thought of her – not for any demerits of her own, but because she is what and where she is.' The children liked her, which was the main thing, although she grated on her employer. 'Her geniality,' so he told Margot, 'is of the hilarious and resonant kind, and not soft and diffusive and winning.' He took exception to her 'strong German accent, and my latest fear is that she will infect with it my poor little baby who is just beginning to talk. Fancy having a child who talked like a Rothschild!'[17]

The family's first Christmas without Helen was bound to be harrowing. Their mood was not helped by the weather. 'We spent the whole of Xmas week here in London in an unbroken fog, which shifted from black to yellow to black again from yellow and black, but for five days never allowed us a glimpse of sun or sky,' Asquith wrote to Ettie, herself enviably ensconced in the 'gorgeous East'.[18]

After the Christmas holidays Beb joined Raymond at Lambrook. Beb was the most sensitive of the Asquith children and for him, the loss of his mother – and such an ideal one at that – must have been made all the more harrowing by the memory of sharing with her the first night of her fatal illness, and perhaps feeling some sense of responsibility that his own illness may have had some role in making her ill. Now, a few short months after this trauma, he was to find himself at the mercy of British prep school boys at their nastiest. This is his account of his initiation at Lambrook:

> I was made to fight another small boy: I had no grievance against him, nor he against me, and we had never met before until we faced one another on the edge of the gravelled playground to make sport for the others, like a pair of cocks, transported from different parts of the country, who see one another for the first time in the cockpit. Urged on by the crowd we both took the offensive at once, and as we were not wearing gloves and neither of us had any idea of defence, our lips and noses were streaming with blood in the course of the first few minutes. We were both fairly strong for our ages and in our prolonged offensive each of us must have scored a good many points, but after three or four rounds the result was declared a draw, and another pair of pugilists, who had only recently left the nursery, were set up to take our places.[19]

Despite his ordeal, Beb seems to have settled down reasonably well. He was put into Raymond's dormitory and by the end of the year was placed top of his form. He got on well with the headmaster, 'Teedy' Mansfield, whom he described to his father as 'awfully jolly'.[20] At the end of the summer term Raymond won a scholarship to Winchester 'without an ounce of pressure and with really light hours of work', Mansfield assured his father, 'so that he is in no sense played out, but goes to Winchester as fresh as paint, and will, I have no doubt, presently walk by some of the boys who were above him'. It was a pattern of achievement without effort that was to be the blueprint for the rest of Raymond's life.

Meanwhile, Beb 'goes along merrily and ought also to do well bye and bye',[21] reported Mansfield. Oc, who replaced Raymond at Lambrook the following term, failed to measure up to his brothers' aptitude in the all-important Classics, but he did well enough in other subjects. Mansfield praised his diligence, but confessed 'his work disappoints me. He works slowly and cannot yet get through the ordinary translation lesson of the form, and I find him unsound in elementary work. Yet I think he tries.'[22]

The boys' surviving letters to their father show an easy and relaxed relationship and a confident assurance he would share their amusement at pranks that would have dismayed many parents – and indeed prompted severe rebukes from most fathers of the Victorian era. Thus, Raymond, laid up at Winchester with a 'nauseous skin disease' sweeping the school, blithely informed his father that meanwhile they did not have a bad time, making a good deal of noise, and that afternoon when the other boys were in chapel they were going to have some target practice in the Meadow with rifles borrowed from the school volunteer corps' armoury.[23] At about the same time, Beb, at Lambrook, relates how

> Today coming home from church in the morning we saw four high bi-cycles coming down the hill abreast. Someone said 'wouldn't it be decent if one of the outside ones fell over and knocked all the rest down', when Marsden (i.e. an awfully kiddy little chap who sleeps in my dorm and snores awfully) got in the way of one of them and was run into naturally; this knocked the bicycle over and the next one tripped over it.[24]

Both Raymond and Oc excelled at sport and ended up as captain of games at Lambrook. Beb was rather more nonchalant, proudly telling his father how during an eight-mile paper chase 'I and a few other chaps lost the scent ("by accident on purpose") and because we were awfully hot, ran and waded about in a stream for about 5 minutes. Then we went round instead of across the field where the scent was laid and consequently went much further. We came in ten minutes after the 1st pack (which was only made of the most swag runners).' However, he was loyally impressed when 'Rub-kin [Raymond] came in 1st in the ¼ mile, 250 yards, 100 yards, 20 yards. He did the ¼ mile in 71 seconds which was awfully good.' When Raymond arrived at Winchester he generously tried to supplement the monotony of his younger brother's diet by sending him slices of ham with his letters, which were duly welcomed and consumed despite the occasional ink stain.

However disturbed Margot might have been by Asquith's now open declarations of love, within a few weeks of Helen's death she was canvassing her friends' opinion about him, informing Ettie: 'I am full of longing to hear what Arthur [Balfour] said about me and Mr A. I must know even if it was only one sentence. I want to know so much and how he praised me and what about Peter, did he mention him and did he say he would like me to have 5 step children etc.?' At the same time she admitted 'I hate myself for clinging with tenacity to what I love and yet I am not strong enough to marry Peter.'[25] This was hardly indicative of a final rejection of her handsome lover.

Peter was for the moment out of the way in South Africa to inspect a 'gold crusher' on a mineral reef in Mashonaland in which he had bought a share. The venture – a desperate last attempt to render himself a marriageable prospect – proved predictably fruit-less.[26] Margot's mother, worried by her daughter's state of mind, thought this an excellent opportunity to get her away from the hunting set and proposed that she accompany her parents on a voyage to Egypt. In Cairo was an old Balliol friend of Asquith, Alfred Milner, now financial secretary to Sir Evelyn Baring*, the British agent and effectively the ruler of Egypt. The capable and ambitious thirty-seven-year-old Milner, one of Jowett's most brilliant protégés, was exactly the sort of man likely to meet with the Tennants' approval as a suitor for their daughter. Asquith correctly

---

*Later Lord Cromer.

predicted that 'Milner will be in clover, and will of course fall madly in love'.[27] He knew Milner and Margot well enough to know that the former was far too reticent for the tastes of the wild woman of Glen. His main concern was that after meeting her regularly since Helen's death, she would be away for such a long time: 'It is all very well to hold out alluring visions of smoke and conversation in a loose-box some time in January. Such dim and distant possibilities are very poor consolation for the certainty of two months' absence.'[28]

When the Tennants reached Cairo, Milner appointed himself Margot's guide to the sights, and after she departed for a Nile cruise in December they kept in regular touch by letter. Her return to Cairo coincided with the death of the Khedive and she was able to witness the splendour and chaos of his funeral procession sitting with her legs dangling over the roof of the British army barracks. The hysterical Cairo crowd was kept strictly in check by soldiers under the command of a British officer whom one day she was to get to know well and who would become her future husband's right-hand man in the Great War: Colonel (as he was then) Horatio Kitchener. 'A man of energy and ambition, a little complacent over his defects, he has not got an interesting mind,' was Margot's first impression. More to her taste was the poet Wilfred Scawen Blunt, whom she visited at his Bedouin desert camp, where three years later he was to seduce her friend, Mary Elcho ('One of the most beautiful men I have ever met', gushed Margot*).

Margot also saw a great deal of Milner, who, in stark contrast to the womanizing Blunt, was an intensely shy man with little experience of women, who put it about that he did not intend to marry and would concentrate his energies on his career – no doubt to duck the issue, rather than any real inclination towards celibacy. Much of Milner's awkwardness can be traced back to a peculiar and unhappy childhood. He had been born in Germany to English parents. His

---

*Margot's appreciation of Blunt's beauty lends superficial credence to the celebrated claim in his 'secret' diary to have seduced her in her bedroom at 40 Grosvenor Square, in 1893 (see also Longford, *A Pilgrimage of Passion*, p. 298). However, Blunt was a notorious sexual fantasist and a letter by Margot to Curzon (9 September 1893) gives the lie to the claim: 'No being could inspire me with less thrill and if he kissed me he would give me a headache.' Almost the only mention of Blunt in her own candid diaries concerns a dinner party on 5 July 1897, when she was 'too edgy with the poet whom I don't know enough to like, and therefore mind his small vanities, his hopeless mediocrity and utter want of critical faculty' – hardly the description of a man specially selected to deflower her.

mother was nearly twenty years older than his father, Charles, whom she had originally taken on to tutor her two other sons after being widowed. Charles Milner failed to make it as a doctor and ended up scraping a living teaching at Tübingen university. When his wife died in 1869 the fifteen-year-old Alfred was packed off to lodgings in London with a widowed cousin and his alcoholic daughter to complete his education at King's College. Under the circumstances his scholarship to Balliol was even more remarkable than Asquith's.

As Asquith had predicted, Milner fell head-over-heels in love with Margot. Asquith was kept well briefed: 'How can you have the impudence, you little witch, to ask me if I don't think you "are good for him?"' he replied to one letter, although he assured her 'it isn't your fault. You can't expect to get yourself to a nunnery . . . or cease to be the most fascinating and insidious and mischievous and loveable bit of womankind that was ever created, simply because men will be foolish enough to lose their hearts to you.'[29] However, Margot still could not drag herself away from Peter. In a letter to Balfour, who strongly disapproved, she not only defended her lover's character, but hinted that she was once again considering marrying him. Although Peter lacked 'honourable ambition' he had 'courage, temper, chivalry, humour' and, most importantly,

> He has really cared for me, and cares for me still . . . Of course, marrying him would mean many denials, but perhaps this would be good for me. I can imagine more suitable and better marriages from every point of view, but the perfect unions that might have been, do not come to pass and for the rest, if one has to marry (which I am told one should) attraction has its merits. The duty marriage of union with character of a high type and intellect and education and career, may be better – a marriage of deliberation with a man like Milner or Asquith may be the best, but it wants pluck and may be an undertaking more than one can quite manage.[30]

When Margot referred to 'the perfect unions that might have been' she was thinking of Alfred Lyttelton, the one man capable of driving Peter from her heart. The only other man to whom she was physically attracted was Evan Charteris, the sixth son of the 10th Earl of Wemyss, and one of the few Souls who also hunted. But she instinctively knew they were not suited, describing him as 'the forbidden fruit', and she was well aware that his mother, Lady Wemyss, considered her far too strong medicine for her gentle, passive son.

However, 'if Alfred had chosen me instead of <u>Laura</u> it might have been different'.[31] Any remaining hopes she may have harboured about Lyttelton were shattered shortly after her return from Egypt when Alfred himself broke the news that he had become engaged to Edith ('DD') Balfour. Margot was heartbroken and spent the rest of the day with Charty in tears. She gamely congratulated DD, but could not resist hinting at her own unhappiness ('there is a loneliness in my life which few suspect').[32] Given the impossible combination of qualities she looked for in her ideal mate, it would have been hard to expect otherwise: 'Ah! If I could mould him and make him – he should have Peter's pluck and figure and manners; Ribblesdale's artistic genius; Evan's face, complexion and charming sense of humour; Arthur Balfour's mind and distinction; Asquith's character and will; Milner's soul; Alfred's variety of tastes.'[33]

When Milner returned to London a few months later to take up his appointment as chairman of the Inland Revenue Board, Margot kept her 'dear <u>dear</u> friend' in tow, leaning on him for emotional support while weighing up the rival attractions of Peter, Evan and Asquith*. She always gave him just enough to encourage a glimmer of hope. A poem he wrote her was praised as one 'any woman would be proud of and every woman touched by'. She even 'cut off a little bit of my hair as the most intimate thing I can give you to show my love and confidence', assuring him 'that if I ever care enough for a man to marry him it will be through the approval of my head and the certainty that I shall find strength, rest, companionship and similarity of taste'.[34]

Asquith, meanwhile, was content to bide his time, assuring Margot that he had 'never been so fully happy as since I have loved you. You have made me a different man – better and stronger I believe – but certainly brighter and happier.'[35] He explained that 'my real happiness lies, not in the luxury of loving you, but in trying to surround you with an atmosphere of love, which without weighing upon you or fettering your freedom, will keep all evil things from you and make the "path before you always bright" '.[36]

---

*To be fair to Margot, she did appreciate Milner's sensitivity and shyness and tried to protect his dignity by keeping his love for her secret – something she never did for Asquith or Evan Charteris. Milner confessed his love to Ettie, who told Spencer Lyttelton. Margot begged him to keep it to himself: 'for Milner's sake I have told no one else so please don't'. (Margot Asquith Papers. Margot to Spencer Lyttelton, 23 May 1892)

Asquith and Margot did not see a great deal of each other even now. She resumed her hunting for most of the rest of the winter and then at the end of April she returned to Switzerland with Charty where her brother Frank's wife, Helen, was in the final throes of tuberculosis. This provoked a fresh bout of melancholy and intro-spection. 'There is almost too much sorrow in life and too much difficulty,' she wrote to Balfour. 'I don't feel it is so much worth living as I did. I look forward to nothing.'[37] When Helen died a fortnight later Asquith wrote sympathetically 'I know the darkness through which your poor brother is passing. It was your darling voice that broke and dispersed it for me.'[38]

Many of Asquith's letters to Margot during this period are taken up with political gossip interspersed with glimpses of his own polit-ical philosophy, but all served up in a way calculated to interest and amuse her: his approval of 'Essex man' after a successful political meeting in Halstead ('it enables one (in spite of Oscar Wilde and other depressing signs of the exhaustion of English manliness) to understand and believe in the perpetual virility of the stock'); his friendly but intense rivalry with Joseph Chamberlain ('I long to dust his jacket for him'); a dinner with Sidney and Beatrice Webb and other 'pallid socialists' ('when you get her [Beatrice] on her own sub-jects – political economy, labour movements, socialism etc – she is extremely interesting and suggestive', but 'I don't feel that she has any personal attraction and would as soon marry an automatic machine'); a speech by 'your Hyde Park friend the Kaiser, in which he speaks of God as his "ally" who will "not leave him in the lurch". On the whole the most fatuous and feather headed of his utterances. Read it.'[39]

Despite Asquith's avowals not to put Margot under any pressure to marry him, the prospect of their getting married seems to have been seriously discussed soon after she returned from Egypt. She was already possessive enough about their relationship to be jealous of his other women friends, notably her sister, Charty, of whom he was seeing a great deal and even taking to the theatre ('a delightful companion and an excellent critic', he called her). An outburst of sibling jealousy from Margot prompted him to respond: 'I don't believe there is any great danger – do you? – of my forgetting "the other little sister".'[40] However much Margot might like to deny it, jealousy was part of her nature and, as Asquith would later discover, she was acutely sensitive to any threat to her own position.

Margot's main objection to marrying Asquith was the daunting prospect of taking on five stepchildren. 'I had no reason to think I was maternal,' Margot admitted many years later. 'I realized the natural prejudice that all children since the beginning of time must have against stepmothers.' Asquith tried to convince her that 'the prospect is not quite as appalling as it appears at first sight'. With the three elder boys at boarding school 'the normal infantine population of the establishment consists of 2 small children, one of whom (Violet) could, I am certain, be an interest and a joy to anyone with a "genius" for the species . . . You shall never be a *hausfrau*.'[41]

Although Asquith rarely mentioned his children in his letters to Margot, when he did he showed intense pride in their achievements. Thus on Christmas Eve 1891 he related how 'Raymond has come back from school after a very good term: he has 2 prizes and is about 2000 marks ahead of any other boy. How delighted and proud Helen would have been. Wouldn't you like to be the mother of a really clever son?' Or, five months later, 'My two younger boys, Bertie [Beb] and Arthur [Oc], came back from their school yesterday and Raymond from Winchester to-day [where he was taking his scholarship exam]. They have all done well, being each of them either first or second in his class in the examinations. I don't think they are any of them extraordinarily clever, but they are tremendously keen and make the most of such wits as they have.'[42] Evidently Asquith had yet to discover that his eldest son was indeed 'extraordinarily clever'.

*

In the summer of 1892, the publication of *Dodo*, the first novel by E. F. (Edward) Benson, the younger son of the Archbishop of Canterbury, made Margot suddenly notorious. Benson had been introduced to Margot the previous year by his elder brother, Arthur, an Eton schoolmaster and an old friend, who had been walking with her in the Alps that summer. The younger Benson, according to his biographer, Brian Masters, was 'entranced by her, completely captivated by her wild, theatrical manner and unconscious verbal tricks'.[43] To the end of his life, Benson was to deny any connection between Margot and Dodo; however, the parallels between his fictional heroine and his brother's friend were too numerous and too singular for the resemblance to be coincidental and almost everyone else was only too eager to make the link.* Margot was a brilliant dancer and 'Dodo danced with peculiar abandon. Every inch of her moved in perfect time and harmony to the music.' Dodo, like Margot, made character sketches of people and passed them to their friends. Both smoked – then a daring vice for a young woman – and both fired off epigrams like bullets from a Gatling gun. To cap it all, Dodo's sitting room, with its collection of hunting whips, fox masks and brushes, bore an uncanny resemblance to the Doo'cot at Glen, right down to the skull that had pride of place on a little altar.

The plot of the novel is thin enough: Dodo, an amoral upper-class girl whose life is devoted entirely to pleasure-seeking, has just becoming engaged to Lord Chesterford, an immensely rich blockhead, for whom she cares not two straws, while simultaneously carrying on a love affair with her fiancé's equally stupid but much more glamorous foxhunting cousin. The amusement of the book – and its attraction – lies in the heroine's extraordinary personality. Unfortunately, Dodo's genius is marred by a complete lack of either scruples or conscience, deficiencies that could hardly have been better calculated to wound Margot, who may have been extravagant but was certainly not mercenary. Her objection to Peter was not his lack of money but his lack of any ambition. Although Dodo's view of babies is brilliantly Margotesque ('they were not nearly so nice to play with as kittens and they always howled'), Margot professed to adore children. And while she may not have enjoyed her charity work with working women in the East End of London, her motives for doing it were perfectly sincere; Dodo's remarkably similar munificence is 'cosmetic', undertaken because 'success was of such paramount importance in her eyes, that even a successful organiser of days in the country for match-girls was to be admired'. None of this would have mattered much if *Dodo* had disappeared without trace. However, to the astonishment of its young author as much as anyone else, the book became a runaway success. The sensible thing would have been to laugh the whole thing off, but Margot took herself too seriously for that and hated to see herself publicly mocked. 'Outsiders will always think after all the talk that it <u>must</u> be like me,'

---

*Margot was finally reconciled with Benson as he lay dying of lung cancer, when she wrote to congratulate him on his book on the daughters of Queen Victoria – <u>brilliantly</u> written – I read it through to 5 a.m.' (Brian Masters *E. F. Benson,* 285)

she wrote to Spencer Lyttelton.[44] She was particularly mortified when the Princess of Wales addressed her as 'Miss Dodo' at a ball. 'If young Benson did but know the harm he had done me with that book,' she lamented to another friend, 'not that I mind what he says about my character, but I am sick of hearing it, it is so stupid and vulgar.'[45]

Even worse, most of Margot's friends read *Dodo* and most were amused by it. She was incensed when Mary Drew described the novel as a 'refined and brilliant book'. To rub salt into the wound, Gladstone's waspish daughter – who seems to have gone out of her way to hurt Margot – told her to her face that 'a great man friend of Laura's and a friend of yours said to me "the only mistake in Dodo is the conversation. Margot talks nonsense well, but never brilliantly and has never said anything anyone could remember." '[46] The one person who could be relied upon to share her own reaction to *Dodo* was Asquith. He became almost as irritated as she by a novel constantly commended as an antidote to his well-known infatuation with her. Rosebery told him 'there is a great deal of truth in it'.[47] When Frances Horner left a copy in his room while he was staying with her, he angrily tossed it out of the window.

Coincidentally 1892 was also the year in which Asquith rose to fame, although the circumstances could not have been more different. When the General Election campaign opened in June, he knew that if the Liberals were victorious Gladstone would probably appoint him to the Cabinet. However, rather than feeling excited that his lifetime's ambition was already within his grasp, his mood was overwhelmingly gloomy. He knew his children would keenly resent his absence from their first summer holiday since their mother's death – aunts and uncles, no matter how solicitous, were no substitute for a much-loved father. But the overwhelming cause of his despondency was Margot, who had chosen the day before he left for his constituency to tell him that she would definitely never marry him. He begged her to reconsider. 'Upon my knees, which I bend too rarely to God, I implore you to think twice and thrice before you shut the door . . . For your love is life, and its loss black darkness and despair.'[48] In the midst of the campaign he did manage to meet her – when speaking in support of her brother, Eddy, who was standing for a Glasgow constituency – but although

she agreed to reconsider her decision, she upset him by the calcu-
lating manner she adopted:

> I don't suppose that you can in the least realise how like it is to having a
> knife driven steadily and relentlessly into one's most sensitive part to hear
> you calmly balancing, as you did to-night, the pro's and con's of a possible
> decision. You are quite right to determine your own destiny in your own
> way . . . but O! Margot − love of my life − if you had the least idea how I
> love you, and how you hold in one of your little hands all that I am or
> hope to be, you would − well at any rate you would pity me'.[49]

When the election result in Fife was declared Asquith scraped in
with a majority of just 294 votes. The following night he spent at the
Tennants' Glasgow house to await Eddy's result in Partick. He
described to Frances, how, despite Eddy being badly beaten, 'we
were drawn in triumph thro' streets by an enthusiastic mob'. They
finished the day with a midnight visit to the *Mail* offices, where a
large crowd had assembled to await the election results.

> It was an extraordinary sight − 20,000 people, the papers said − and when
> we were recognised at the windows there were loud demands for a
> speech. Ultimately to appease them we went down and from the steps I
> bellowed a paragraph of roaring platitudes about the flowing tide etc. etc.
> Eddy Tennant followed, and then there were deafening cries for 'Miss
> Tennant', who proceeded to deliver a highly successful maiden speech. It
> was an amusing experience.[50]

Despite his mood of outward cheerfulness, Asquith felt no sense
of triumph or even relief. The day after the celebrations in Glasgow
he went over to Arran to sit by Helen's grave to mourn not just the
loss of his first love, but also the apparent hopelessness of his new
one. 'I was more pleased with my boy's [Raymond's] election than my
own: on the day that I was returned he got a scholarship at
Winchester,' he confessed to Frances. 'I am not in high spirits about
the future − the country's, the party's, my own.'[51]

In the new Parliament, the Liberals, far from winning the comfortable majority for which Gladstone hoped, ended up with just 273 seats,
only four more than Lord Salisbury's Tories, making them dependent
on the support of the 81 Irish Nationalists. Asquith was offered the
post of Home Secretary in the new Government. Yet, on the threshold
of a triumphant future, he could not have felt flatter, writing to Margot:

Here I am, full from my earliest days of political ambition, still young, and just admitted to one of the best places in the Cabinet, and yet I undertake to say that there is hardly a man in London more profoundly depressed than I am to-day. You know why. What shall it profit a man to gain the whole world and lose his own soul? What use to me or through me to the world are honours, power, a career, if I am to be cut off from the hope and promise of all that is purest and highest in my life?[52]

Margot melted before this appeal and sent 'a heavenly letter – wise, tender, soothing and strengthening. It has made a different man of me.'[53] She may have had an ulterior motive – in the same letter Asquith mentions having received a letter of congratulation from Peter, who was angling for a job. He agreed to see him but doubted he could do much for him, although he did manage to find a place for Margot's youngest brother, Jack, as one of his three private secretaries.

The new Government was dominated by Gladstone's last attempt to introduce Home Rule to Ireland. The Bill was doomed from the outset and, as predicted, the House of Lords eventually sank it in September 1893 with a vote of four to one against. Five months later the 'Grand Old Man' of British politics finally bowed out at an emotional Cabinet meeting, to be succeeded as Prime Minister by Lord Rosebery.

Asquith and Margot regularly sparred over the issues of the day, particularly Home Rule and reform of the House of Lords. Margot, heavily influenced by the Unionist views of Balfour and Milner, thought self-government for Ireland 'a mad scheme' and considered Asquith's longstanding hostility towards the unelected and hereditary Second Chamber 'very silly indeed'.[54] However, he refused to see these political disagreements as a bar to marriage, insisting that 'the worst thing that could happen to me would be to have a wife who was an enthusiastic partisan on my side of politics'. What he needed was exactly the opposite: a woman with insight, imagination, keen sense of proportion and of the larger horizons which one so often fails to see, neither Tory nor Radical, and yet interested in it all and capable of moulding not only her husband, but other men.[55]

Soon after he became Home Secretary, Asquith took steps to adapt his domestic arrangements to the family's new circumstances, renting a house at Box Hill near Dorking in Surrey for the children as a country home* while taking an apartment at 27 Mount Street (close to his former bachelor quarters) as his own London base, where he was looked after by Cave, his remarkable valet who, according to Beb, 'might almost have served as a model for Jeeves'.[56] To his relief Miss Weber, the younger children's governess, chose this moment to 'retire permanently to the Fatherland and to the addresses of her Teutonic admirer',[57] to be replaced by the kindly – and impeccably English – Mrs James, who took charge of Violet and Cys at the Surrey house.

Asquith knew that he was in for a long haul if he was ever to win Margot. He confessed to Frances Horner that 'she does not love me, at least not in the way that I love her. Her passion long since went elsewhere, and whomever she marries her husband will have to win his way. I am under no illusions, but I love her, and my love for her is the best thing in my life.'[58] Margot, as was her wont, continued to give mixed messages, alternately raising his hopes and then dashing them to the ground. Desperate for solace, he poured out his anguish to Frances:

> There have been moments when we were almost more than lovers, and then a cloud sweeps down out of the blue, and she seems separated from me by the whole width of heaven. I sometimes feel that she, for whom I would shed every drop of my blood and every ambition of my life, is the appointed instrument of a relentless power. I am only just forty, and have had more than my share of the gifts of fortune: can it be that through her God means to teach me the vanity of hope and the nothingness of human will? And then, when the light turns low, you suddenly flash into my life, radiant, helpful, smiling through your tears, and you tell me that you will be with me and surround me with your love – and I am content.[59]

Since Helen's death Asquith had been seeing more and more of Frances, and after Margot herself, she and Charty became his two main female companions. During Frances's prolonged stays in London, they would often be seen at the theatre together and would even attend the occasional concert or opera, although she was scarcely more musical than he. Frances would also act as hostess at

---

*Haldane had introduced Asquith to the area when he took him to visit his friend, the writer George Meredith, who lived there.

the little dinner parties he liked to give. Soon the friendship deepened into something much more intimate as Frances became the first
of the *amitiés amoureuses* on which he was to depend for emotional
support throughout the rest of his life.

Frances was described by one of her close women friends as a
good thinker as well as a brilliant talker. She was 'well read, had a
considerable knowledge of English literature and she inherited a love
of art – as well as many fine Italian and English pictures – from her
father'.[60] Her dinner parties were famous for their eclectic mix of
politicians, painters, writers and the more amusing members of
London society. Her marriage to Sir John ('Jack') Horner was, as
marriages go, a perfectly contented one, but there was not much
romance. Back in 1884, while Frances was staying with the Tennants
at Glen, she had a long discussion with Laura on the subject of marriage in general, in the course of which she gave an illuminating
insight into her own when she described how she believed most
Victorian women came to be married: 'Well, you know, I think one
talks to him and likes him and one says to oneself "if he worried me
very much to marry him, I might – perhaps". And then he does –
one marries him. It is so rarely that perfect ideal affinities meet . . . it
is doing things for people every minute of one's life that makes one
love them.'

Frances coyly went on to confide how 'Jack's always awfully late.
He has never yet gone to bed before me. I am always asleep first –
and then he wakes me . . .!'[61] Although Jack Horner was a scholar and
had travelled widely abroad, he was less well attuned than his wife to
urban and artistic society, and was happiest leading the life of a
country squire in Mells in Somerset, where his family had lived for
centuries. Nevertheless, much of their time was spent in London
where she kept up with her artistic and literary friends.

Frances's early relationship with Asquith hovered in that Victorian
never-never land between a close friendship and a love affair in
which the Souls were so adept. She always knew her place. She
promised not to be jealous of Margot, but pointed out that jealousy
was a beautiful virtue, having its roots in affection and diffidence.

Margot never seems to have suspected how close Asquith was to
Frances, but she continued to have bouts of jealousy over his relationship with Charty, her beautiful and charming elder sister. On 1
January 1893 he tried to reassure her: 'O Margot, you ought to know
better than to write or think such things. I love Charty very much,

better far (as you know) than any woman but yourself . . . But no one knows better than she does that your place is your own – sacred, unapproachable, secure.'

Asquith himself still figured a long way behind Peter or even Evan Charteris in Margot's affections. When she did mention him in her diary or letters to friends he was always 'Asquith' or even 'Mr Asquith'. In the end, he decided he would be better off seeing much less of her rather than make himself miserable 'crying for the moon'.[62] In March, after dining with the Tennants, he told her he was ready to give up any idea of making her his wife, but she would always be 'his genius and his joy, the light of all his day, the hope of his life beyond politics'. She in turn explained how she would like to have married him and had tried to love him, but was 'not worth his little finger'. She had 'neither his morals, his brains or his courage'. But when he held her in his arms, as she confessed in her diary, 'my heart felt leaden', a response which 'touched him unaccountably'. After he had gone she cursed herself: 'I found ideals crystallised – a noble life, a brilliant man, a strongly intellectual circle, a life of public prestige and all this I give up for what? For a fancy about love, a dream of passion.'[63]

In April Margot's parents took her to Paris, a welcome distraction but no solution to the central dilemma in her life. 'I feel inside my soul the awful fight and the fearful struggle between what I <u>know</u> to be great and good and above all passionately devoted <u>to me</u> and what I am equally sure attracts me – to save the situation something has to be thrown overboard and when that something means all I <u>know</u> of happiness then it becomes terrible – I dream of Peter by reason of thinking of Asquith.'[64] When Margot returned from Paris, she started seeing Asquith again. In May he took her to see Jowett and in the train coming back she 'reopened the door'.[65] It was only the latest twist as she led him through 'mazes and zig-zags', always 'a baffling elusive little figure, sometimes tormenting, sometimes mocking, sometimes full of sweet gravity and a kind of wistful almost compassionate tenderness . . . at once the hope and despair of my life, so near and so far, revealing to me the unseen and unattained, now opening and now seeming to shut the gate of paradise'.[66]

Margot consulted several male friends – Balfour, Curzon, Wilfred Scawen Blunt, even Peter himself. They were unanimously in favour of her marrying Asquith. Curzon told her he would bring her 'devotion, strength, influence, a great position – things that last and grow'.[67] But still she refused to commit herself. At the beginning of October Asquith, perhaps sensing she was weakening, accepted an invitation to stay at Glen. It was a glorious autumn, but to Margot the brilliant gold and yellow hues seemed 'like triumphant love affairs staring me in the face'.[68] In her melodramatic way, she confided to DD – who was also at Glen – that she had asked for three months' grace to make up her mind: 'I feel every day now that my life is closing in on me – not fettered by Asquith but by the slow in-burning sense that I must put out to sea. I hope if I marry Asquith I shall die with my baby then I shall have done the right thing.'[69]

Asquith buried his personal troubles in political speeches, while Margot sought oblivion amongst horses and hounds in Leicestershire. There she met up with another old admirer, Evan Charteris, and warned him that she had made up her mind to marry Asquith, sticking to her position in spite of 'the narcotic of his close embrace'. A few weeks later – in spite of her marital plans (of which Asquith himself was still unaware) – she and Evan were thrown out of St Paul's Cathedral when a verger was shocked to discover them canoodling in a dark corner at the start of the morning service.[70]

Margot returned to London in December for a 'tragic dinner with Peter'. The wretched man was physically and emotionally crushed and was about to leave for Brindisi to recuperate. It dawned on Margot that 'his passion for me had gone. I killed the flower because I thought it was killing me, but I did not guess the scent would go so suddenly.'[71] The abrupt death of Peter's 'passion' seems to have been decisive. After spending Christmas and New Year with her family at Glen, her mind was made up. On 9 January she wrote to tell Asquith she was coming to London to see her dentist and would like to meet him – it was exactly three months after their last meeting.[72] She had decided she would marry him after all. Afterwards Asquith wrote:

> The thing has come which I have most longed for, waited for, prayed for, willed, as I never did with any other aim or object in my life. I swear you shall never repent it. Whatever happiness the will, the tenderness, and the worship of a man can bring shall encircle you. To that I pledge my soul and devote my life . . .
>
> I don't want you to alter. I like to think of your marriage not as a contracting and impoverishing, but (if that is possible) as an expanding and enriching of your life. You will have to give up much – every wife has: but the things you sacrifice shall be as few in number and as unessential

and <u>unvital</u> to your nature as I can make them. And there are some things which you will have, not to learn for the first time, but to practise in a new way. First and foremost, will you be very patient with me? I know you will find me very slow in some ways and summary in others . . . I shall quicken up in time, you will see; in these ways you will make a new creature of me. But you must be kind and encouraging and rather tender – will you? The next, and only thing I ask you <u>to-day</u> (there are others but they will keep) is that you shall feel <u>free</u>. The tie will always be there to keep us close, but I couldn't bear that it should chafe you.[73]

In spite of these eloquent assurances, Margot was still tortured by doubt. Writing in her diary, she tried hard to convince herself she was taking the right step. It does not show her in an attractive light. Behind all her protestations that 'Asquith is too good for you . . . he worships you and understands you', the tone is condescending and self-righteous. She carped about his lack of 'this power of making love' and at the same time smugly consoled herself that 'marrying as you are from the highest motives, you will be repaid . . . Depend on it with your rich and warm nature you will get to love Asquith and above all will prove yourself a woman of courage and nobility.'[74]

4

'An abyss of domesticity'

O NE DAY IN February 1894, the twelve-year-old Beb was trotting back from a football match at Lambrook when he remembered being handed a letter just before the game, which – not having time to read it – he had hurriedly stuffed into his pocket. The envelope was now caked in mud, but he was just able to make out his father's writing. Inside was a crumpled letter with the startling news that he was to be married to a Miss Margot Tennant. Beb remembered his father having mentioned Margot's name from time to time and he thought he might have once caught a glimpse of her, but that was the extent of his preparation for the arrival of a woman who was going to turn his family's little world upside down. Judging by his reply, he seems to have taken the announcement in his stride:

> Dear Pakin,
>   I am glad to hear Miss Margot Tennant is a decent person; I expect she is the same one whom Rub [Raymond] said chucked her handkerchief into the court when Piggot was being tried.* I am 2nd this week. I hope you get a decent house somewhere. It was very wet yesterday.
>   Goodbye from your loving son, H. Asquith.[1]

Apart from meeting Raymond at the law courts some three years earlier and occasionally coming across Violet in their father's apart-

---

*Beb was almost certainly mistaken: it was the Baccarat case (see Spender and Asquith, I, 98).

ment in Mount Street, the Asquith children were an unknown quantity to Margot. Her fiancé wrote a brief introduction to her new step
family:

> Your remark that you didn't know the boys' names amused me, but why
> should you? I think it is time I gave you a little elementary family informa-
> tion. The children are (1) Raymond- age 15 whom you know (2) Bertie –
> age 12 – red hair, and rather a quaint creature, but very generous (3)
> Arthur – age 10 – more of the Raymond type (4) Violet – age 6 – rather a
> little dear, and (5) Cyril (would you like to change his name?) age 4 – of the
> same type as Bertie: still wild and untutored, but I sometimes think he
> may be the genius (if there is one) of the family. Do they bewilder you?
>   At the same time (this being a business letter) I will ask you two ques-
> tions: (1) What are you going to call me? We shall have to arrange this
> before long. (2) What are the children to call you?[2]

It is extraordinary that Margot had become engaged while managing
to avoid calling her future husband by his first name, Herbert, which
she disliked. Henceforth, she was to call him by his second name,
Henry, and she was to be 'Margot' to her future stepchildren.* A few
days later she wrote to Raymond to introduce herself:

> You must not think that I could <u>imagine</u> even a possibility of filling your
> mother's (and my friend's) place. I only ask you to let me be your compan-
> ion – and if needs be your help-mate. There is room for everyone in life if
> they have the power to love. I shall count upon your help in making my
> way with Violet and your brothers . . . I should like you to let me gradually
> and without effort take my place among you, and if I cannot – as indeed I
> <u>would</u> not – take your mother's place among you, you must at least allow
> me to share with you her beautiful memory.

Raymond replied by return with reassuring friendliness that he was
sure they would all like her very much and that she would get on very
well with them.

The announcement of Asquith's engagement to Margot had
been delayed until mid-February to give her time to recover after

---

*Asquith approved of his new name: 'it is like a name of your own invention, and seems
therefore to link me with you, but you are not to write to me "dearest Henry" instead of
"dearest" alone. The one puts me on the same footing as a dozen (or perhaps a hundred!)
other people: the other I like to think belongs to me alone.' (Asquith to Margot, 1 March
1894)

breaking her collar bone out hunting a couple of days after accepting his proposal. Now her main priority was to resume hunting as soon as possible. She returned to the Manners family at Cold Overton and was back in the saddle as soon as her collar bone had mended. It was not until mid-April that she and her fiancé took the train to Redhill to meet his children. Raymond, who met them at the station, made a good first impression on Margot: 'a nice looking lissom boy with <u>lovely</u> eyes, a poor mouth and very jolly clever head and good hair'.

> I put my arms round him and kissed him which he did not mind but seemed to rather like and take naturally. We got into a fly and drove to a hideous jumped up villa quite the ugliest I ever saw and hardly what one would expect to belong to an artist . . . Mrs James, an elderly plain good tempered lady who does duty as nurse and lady superior greeted me at the door with Violet, a keen bright faced little creature (not pretty but charmingly dressed) in one hand and the baby in the other. Little Cys is 4 and has a jolly ragamuffin face topped by scarlet hair in thick curls – he flung himself against my legs like a puppy and seemed full of life and mischief, showed me his new trousers and a small wire arrangement which he had been making out of heaven knows what . . . We wandered down a slippery path into a little wood, Raymond and I in front and my man with the tinies behind. I talked of Winchester to Raymond and he pulled the brambles back for me with a nice unselfconscious manner and I felt I could get fond of him. The children picked flowers all the way and pressed them hot and faded into my hands and I romped a little with Cys and tore my petticoat. We all sat down to lunch, Mrs James opposite Henry, Violet and her Swiss governess opposite Raymond and myself and little Cys next to Mrs James. After a little talking down to the children and their frank sort of chatter to us, we all relapsed into a domestic silence relieved by the sound of knives and forks. I felt as if a sort of spell had been cast over me and I had been married 100 years. My spirits slowly but perceptibly sank but I pulled myself together – it was not noticeable to any one.[3]

The ordeal of being introduced to the Asquith children over, Margot was able to spend the rest of April in Paris with her parents buying clothes. Otherwise it was all parties and rides in the *Bois de Boulogne* with her Parisian friends Gladys Rothschild and Daisy White, whose husband was serving in the United States Embassy. 'I flung myself with passionate eagerness into the fun of the life feeling as if I were burying my bachelor days,' she noted in her diary.

Back in London Margot's mood soon soured. She found the round of dinners in the run-up to the wedding a trial. At the home of the Liberal MP, Sir Henry Campbell-Bannerman, she lost her temper when, after the women had withdrawn, she found herself being instructed on the duties of a politician's wife by her hostess, Mrs Gladstone, and the other wives present. Worse still, Margot resented the constant presence of her fiancé, irritated by what she called his 'want of grace', and could scarcely disguise 'a chilling revulsion of feeling' towards him.

On 10 May, her wedding day, Margot was helped into her satin wedding gown by her sister, Lucy and Gee, her maid. The dress had double puffed sleeves with a chiffon sash and two bows of orange blossom at each hip and a bodice open at the neck to show her pearls. She pinned on to her breast her Louis XVI diamond and sapphire brooch with a sprig of myrtle from Con Manners' home in Clovelly. Finally, as if to underline her ambivalence to the whole business, she wore a chain Evan had given her, to which she attached a little heart on black velvet containing a lock of Peter's hair. After showing off her wedding dress to the family servants, Margot emerged into a rain-soaked Grosvenor Square to loud cheers from a large crowd of onlookers, who had braved the bad weather to enjoy the spectacle of a society wedding involving a senior member of the Government. The crush of the crowds outside both her home and the church, St George's, Hanover Square, made Margot a quarter of an hour late. The best man, Haldane, writing to his mother, described the bride as looking 'very pale and nervous'.[4] At the start of the service, cheering from the crowd outside the church interrupted the opening prayers by the Bishop of Rochester. It was the Gladstones making a late arrival. 'A blasphemous interruption', spluttered Lord Rosebery to Charty afterwards. Margot, however, was thrilled by 'this old couple bringing their late blessing to us'. Afterwards Gladstone and Rosebery, past and present Prime Ministers, met in the vestry to sign the register, along with two of their future successors: Arthur Balfour and Asquith himself.[5]

After the service, a bewildered Beb and Oc emerged into Hanover Square to be submerged in the huge crowd milling around the church. Not having a clue how to get to the Tennants' house in Grosvenor Square – in fact a few minutes' walk away – the boys hailed a cab only to find themselves jammed in a long column of carriages. They were thrilled by the spectacle of majestic glossy horses impatiently champing at their bits and tossing their heads to the jangle of their silver bells, as immaculate coachmen in top hats tried to keep them calm amid the confusion. There was the added bonus of putting off the mortifying moment when the boys would have to display to the world the embarrassing lavender blue trousers which Mrs James had carefully chosen for the occasion, and which had already been greeted by Cave, their father's valet, with unspoken, Jeeves-like disdain. The brothers spent most of the wedding reception standing behind a table guzzling ice cream and trying hard to conceal their shaming trousers from public view. Having missed Margot's visit to their home in Redhill, they were encountering for the first time their new stepmother – 'a short slight figure, vital and alert, passing through a throng of friends', Beb was to recall many years later. 'When she greeted us, we were much attracted by the impulsive frankness of her manner which took shyness by storm.'[6]

Margot did not keep up her show of bonhomie for long, sheltering under the stairs, close to tears, and being comforted by Balfour and Curzon. The latter was almost as emotional as the bride: 'so you cried a little', she wrote to him a few days later. 'Well, I too could have <u>sobbed</u>, but I felt it would have been like a wine glass in the sea so deep was my emotion.' When Charty came over to kiss her goodbye on the platform at Paddington station as she waited for the train to Frome, en route for Mells (where they were to spend the first few days of their honeymoon at the Horners' house, Mells Park), she burst into tears. 'It has all been a terrible mistake,' she wrote to Curzon. 'With a wave and a gasp I sank back in the train <u>knowing</u> I was married.'[7] Managing to choke back her tears as her new husband sat down opposite her, Margot took out a cigarette and, handing him another, avoided any conversation by answering the congratulatory telegrams.

The village of Mells, set in Somerset's Mendip hills, was the nursery rhyme 'plum' which the original Jack Horner pulled out of the pie when he bought the village and surrounding farms from Henry VIII after the dissolution of nearby Glastonbury Abbey during the Reformation. When Frances first came to live at

Mells after marrying Jack Horner in 1883, she found the place almost feudal: boys were banned from playing marbles and villagers were expected to consult the Horners about their babies' names. The cottages dated from medieval times and, although picturesque, had smoking chimneys, damp walls and leaky thatched roofs. Frances found it hard to understand the affection in which her husband was held by his tenants in view of his apparent indifference to his duties as a landlord. But he was devoted to Mells, and made up for leaking roofs and smoking chimneys by charging practically no rent and performing all manner of charitable acts.

The Horners themselves lived in genteel poverty at Mells Park, the huge mansion completed in 1800 for an extravagant forebear who never had the funds to keep it up. Most of the forty bedrooms were either empty or used as storerooms, there were few curtains and carpets and every available drawer was crammed with collections, made by various family members, of everything from minerals to birds' eggs and dried fish. The only lighting was provided by oil lamps with white globes, apparently in imitation of nearby Longleat. Nonetheless, in daytime the setting could not have been more romantic: light poured through high Georgian windows opening on to a high terrace set over a large lake full of ducks, moorhens and other waterfowl, which nested among the rushes and islands. The sloping south-facing parkland on the far bank was planted with trees and shrubs and covered with wild flowers.

Dinner at Mells passed amiably enough as they reminisced about the early days of their friendship. But by the time Margot heard the clock strike eleven she felt worn out and 'at a certain risk of being thought bold' said she was going to bed. As she undressed and put on the smart night gown she had bought specially for the occasion, she thought how much she would have preferred it if it was Peter or Evan rather than her new husband who would come through the bedroom door. She said her prayers, got into bed and drank the glass of milk and munched the biscuits her maid always left her, while reading the day's biblical selection in *Daily Light** as she prepared for

---

*'A devotional text book for every day in the year in the very words of scripture.' It is no wonder that Margot spent so much time at the dentist.

the coming ordeal.* There was a knock at the door and Asquith came in swathed in an Indian dressing gown, grinning as he caught sight of his new wife sipping her milk. He knelt down and clasping Margot's hand to his forehead, said his prayers. He then walked round to the other side of the bed, but she refused to let him put out the candle. Trying to adopt a mock playful tone, she asked 'Do you propose to come into my bed?'

'Yes,' was the abrupt response. She wished he had responded with a tone of mock formality 'with your permission', but cursed herself for always finding fault as he got into bed and put his arms around her. 'I lay very tired with my head on his shoulder and felt him shudder under my most restrained embrace. We lay quite still and silent and I felt very low and tired and then I said "I think we will go to sleep."' She put out the candle. 'Then he kissed my hands and my hair very sweetly and we retired to the opposite sides of the bed.' All she felt was 'immense drowsiness mixed with gratitude to him for his fine control and understanding'. Margot was awoken the following morning by the birds singing and slipped into Asquith's arms and 'lay in a close and very tender embrace for some time – my face pressed between his hair and the pillow and with great peace'. Gee called at nine-thirty and her new husband went to dress as the maid poured the bath.

Over the next few days, apart from what Margot called 'a heavenly day at Bath' with the Ribblesdales, the honeymooners spent most of the time walking, talking and reading. Margot found herself contrast-

---

*Margot later told different people different things about the extent of her sexual experience before she married. In 1916, Beb's wife, Lady Cynthia Asquith, reported Mrs 'Florry' Bridges (married to General 'Tom' Bridges) telling her that Margot talking of Peter Flower had often said, 'I slept with him every night – every night of my life – everything except the thing itself.' However, four years later, when Evan Charteris took umbrage at an imagined suggestion in her *Autobiography* that they had been lovers, Margot herself indignantly insisted in a letter to Arthur Balfour that 'I was no man's mistress and never had a lover in my life', while at the same informing Lady (Ettie) Desborough: 'I hardly knew where infants came from when I knew Evan, and certainly knew nothing of <u>how</u> they came!' Whatever the truth, unless one believes the highly dubious claim by the poet Wilfred Blunt to have seduced her (see footnote on p. 40), Margot was almost certainly a virgin at the time of her marriage, although she had undoubtedly indulged in plenty of passionate kissing and petting with a number of lovers. (See *Lady Cynthia Asquith Diaries 1915–18*, p. 232, 5 November 1916; Balfour Papers (Edinburgh), MA to AJB, 18 August 1920; Desborough Papers, D/ERV C71 f. 66, MA to ED, 18 August 1920.)

ing their feelings for the countryside, where she felt she was a native, her husband a tourist. For Asquith, going for a walk was exercise, for Margot it was 'lolling and straying and stopping in the country. I can lean over a gate and lose myself in the landscape'. She carped at his lack of athleticism. 'He has not the limbs or balance that come from constant idle country life – he has not the deftness that springs over broken ground.'[8] Even the lovely spring weather and the profusion of wild flowers failed to lift her stubbornly downbeat mood: there was 'something sad about the Spring – a sort of abundant self-sufficiency which makes it less sympathetic than autumn'. She tried to console herself – or so she informed Curzon – that she ought to feel pride in bringing '"real good" to one who spreads everything dear and joyous that the world can give around him'.[9] But her diary reveals the extent of her harshness towards the man she had just married:

> I realized that in some ways with all his tact and delicacy, all his intellect and bigness, all his attributes, he had a common place side to him which nothing could alter . . . It is not in his nature to feel the subtlety of love making, the dazzle and fun of it, the tiny almost untouchable fellowship of it . . . He has passion, devotion, self-mastery, but not the nameless something that charms and compels and receives and combats a woman's most fastidious advances.*

A day or two later she found herself wishing 'for him to sleep in his dressing room. He felt it all and knew by my change of manners instantly what had happened but I myself am incapable of measuring the depth of my own misery. I longed to die, I only wanted to have everything stopped.'

When the Asquith boys broke up from their schools for the summer holidays they had to get used to exchanging their modest Surrey villa

---

*Margot reread this entry (15 May 1894) twenty-two years later and, on 23 April 1916, appended the following comment: 'When I wrote this I was the most spoilt, impulsive, egotistical creature – over-loved and over-tired. Never was such a bad criticism of Henry! It would be laughable if it was not pathetic! No woman ever had such passion, sympathy, tenderness and fun with her husband as I've had. But he wasn't a professional lover which Peter Flower was and Evan Charteris and others. Power to love and to love-make was given to me in a higher degree than to any woman I've ever met.'

for a grand Georgian house in one of the most fashionable West End addresses: No. 20 Cavendish Square, a wedding present from Margot's father.* They were thrilled to discover the house possessed a long subterranean tunnel connecting it to the kitchen quarters and stables in Henrietta Street, through which meals would be brought in a specially heated trolley. Above the tunnel was another delight for the children: a small conservatory containing a vine which produced numerous, but unfortunately very sour, grapes. A thirty-foot frosted glass wall separating the Asquiths' garden from that of their reclusive next-door neighbour provided an outlandish touch to the landscape.

The children's excitement about their grand new home paled before their wonderment at the extraordinary personality of their new stepmother. Violet remembered how she and her brothers were filled with a mixture of 'admiration, amazement, amusement, affection' and 'a vague sense of uneasiness as to what she might, or might not, do next'.[10] Violet's relationship with Margot got off to a bad start. After her mother's death, her father – following Helen's own practice of letting one of the children sleep with her when he had been away from home – had his daughter's bed moved into his own bedroom when she stayed at his London flat and would talk to her about politics and politicians when he came in. During these years a deep and lasting bond grew up between father and daughter. The other important adult in Violet's life was Mrs James, to whom she was very attached.

Margot was keen to take charge of mothering the younger children herself and immediately dismissed the housekeeper. It was a silly thing to do – particularly as she intended to spend most of the autumn hunting in Leicestershire. When Violet discovered that she was not only being turned out of her father's bedroom but also having to bid farewell to the woman who had been her proxy mother for the past couple of years, she became hysterical. Asquith, at a loss to know what to do, massaged her wrists with eau de cologne (a favourite Victorian remedy).[11] This had the desired effect of calming her down for the moment, but the damage was done and the foundation laid for years of rivalry between his wife and daughter.

Margot got off to a better start with the three elder boys, who were away at school most of the time and naturally of an age to be more

---

*The house only had an eighteen-year lease, so the Bart's present was not as generous as might be supposed.

independent. Beb's first significant experience of his stepmother came a few days into the summer holidays when she took him to the dentist – in those days an alarming experience for adults, let alone children. It was a fine morning and their destination was soon forgotten as they drove through Hyde Park in Margot's open carriage while she regaled him with tales of her adventures out hunting, such as how she ploughed up a whole row of turnips trying to free herself from being dragged along by a runaway horse. 'Then very suddenly, in the middle of a story,' he recalled 'we pulled up at a door with a brass plate, the horrid goal of my journey, which for the last hour, under the spell of this new interest, had faded away from my memory.'[12]

The children had been used to a very lax regime up to now and the house-proud and fastidious Margot soon put a stop to such habits as 'throwing everything on the floor or covering blotting paper with huge dirty blots from filling pens too full and having lots of open windows and big baths'.[13] She seems to have been clever at getting her way without confrontation: when Beb cluttered up the front hall with his model of the Great Northern Railway, she delighted her stepson by ordering an extra forty feet of line from Hamleys. The gift, of course, had the intended effect of making the rail system too big for the hall and ensuring its relegation to the garden.

Beneath her initially tactful exterior, however, Margot felt distinctly antipathetic towards her stepchildren. She never appreciated the traumatic effect, especially on the two younger children, of the loss of their mother; nor did she understand how intimidating her own powerful personality could be. All she could see was the contrast between the anarchic personalities of herself and her siblings and what appeared to her to be the overly serious Asquith children. Many years later she explained to a family friend, the actress Viola Tree, how

> having been brought up in an atmosphere of glowing love, criticism, discussion and compassion, I often <u>marvelled</u> at the want of temper or temperament in my adopted blood – never a quarrel! Not even a cross word, never a temptation except to say brilliant – always witty often unkind – never reverent things . . . never an adventure, or enthusiasms or beliefs, or soaring ambitions – all cool headed, cool hearted highly almost nervously intellectual elderly critical children.[14]

Margot was used to having her own way and to amusing friends and family with her long, always entertaining, and often outrageous, monologues, and felt threatened by the way her 'steps', as she used to call them, could unexpectedly derail her. 'One day when he [Raymond] was at home for his holidays and we were all having tea together, to amuse the children I began asking riddles. I told them that I had only guessed one in my life, but it taken me three days. They asked me what it was, and I said: "What is it God has never seen, that kings see seldom and that we see every day?" Raymond answered instantly "a joke". I felt that the real answer, which was "an equal", was very tepid after this.'[15]

For the summer holidays after their marriage the Asquiths went to stay at Inverewe, a grand shooting lodge on the Moray Firth along the coast from Inverness, which they shared with Margot's brothers, Eddie and Jack Tennant. She was by now pregnant and suffering constant indigestion, toothache, sleeplessness and other ailments, and as a result, irritable throughout the holiday. Her noisy stepchildren maddened her with what she called their 'want of refinement' and 'hideous accents'.* In the evening, 'luckily the boys played whist', but she was upset by the way their father noisily threw the pack of cards on to the table which he neglected to cover with a tablecloth. He smelt of smoke and was lax about correcting his children. When Asquith took his three older boys fishing, she confessed in a letter to Balfour that 'I revel in being left to myself – children are so fatiguing and <u>between ourselves</u> I marvel at the life I have selected for myself – Thank heaven our public schools aren't threatened! . . . They are nice children, all clever, but with ugly voices and ways, and the two small ones are quite uninteresting.' She reserved her harshest comment for her diary, where she described the seven-year-old Violet as 'a hard, common-place, clever, graceful, logically-minded little girl with a frightful voice'.[16]

Asquith tried hard to be understanding of his new wife, admitting to Frances Horner that 'it was a formidable trial for her to be

---

*After twenty-two years of marriage Margot claimed that one of the few things she had ever influenced in her stepchildren was their pronunciation, getting them to use 'long As instead of short'. Apart from this and a few other 'habits of <u>mild</u> exterior kind . . . I never altered a single Asquith by one hair except Cys. It was thro <u>me</u> that Cys realized cleverness is <u>nothing</u>.' (Margot to Maud Tree, 14 August 1919 (Tree Papers, ADMAN 62126)

plunged headlong into such an abyss of domesticity, and sometimes she found such a profound change from anything which she has known for a long time, difficult and depressing'.[17] The boys at least seem to have thoroughly enjoyed their holiday. Beb later recalled:

There was a deer forest at Inverewe, good trout-fishing in the lochs, and fishing in the sea, which more than once resulted in an exciting battle with a conger eel. I never saw my father cast a fly, but he was persuaded one day to stalk a red deer: he had never fired a rifle before, but after a few practice shots at the target he consented to go out on the hill. The result was entirely successful, and when evening came, he returned with an expansive smile, ruddy and weathered by the wind, followed by a pony carrying a stag, which had been killed with his first shot.

Shortly afterwards, having returned to Lambrook, the eleven-year-old Oc wrote to congratulate his father: 'I am awfully glad you shot another stag and that Eddie and Jack got so many rabbits and some partridges and wild duck.' According to Beb, 'for the rest of his life he [Asquith] abstained from stalking, remaining content with a record which it was difficult to maintain and scarcely possible to beat'. Some twenty years later, during the Great War, Asquith (as Prime Minister) was inspecting the Channel Fleet with its commander Lord Jellicoe when the Admiral started to blaze away with a rifle at what he thought was a German mine. When it failed to detonate, he invited Asquith to have a go, but the offer was refused on the grounds that he did not want to spoil his record of 'two stags with two shots' – fortunately, as it turned out, for the 'mine' was discovered to be an empty tin canister.[18]

After the start of the foxhunting season the Asquiths divided their time between London and Leicestershire, with Margot coming home to Cavendish Square for a few days in the middle of the week, while Asquith would come up by train to be with her at weekends. It must have been quite an ordeal for him, since most of her hunting friends considered it a 'terrible waste' that such a brilliant horsewoman should marry a non-sporting man. However, Asquith's stock rose measurably when, during what must have been for him an insufferably dull dinner party, he contradicted a remark one of the guests made about the pedigree of some Derby winner.

Knowing her husband's retentive memory, Margot doubled her host's wager that he must be wrong. The whole table then listened 'in awed silence' as Asquith correctly gave the name and date of every winner since the inception of the Derby. When he had finished everyone stood up and drained their glasses in a toast for the health of him and Margot, who later recalled how 'some of my friends whispered as I said good night to them, "he's a fine chap, and you're damned lucky!" '.[19]

Margot herself was beginning to appreciate her husband's qualities, won over little by little by his kindness and his understanding as, now pregnant, she suffered acutely from morning sickness. She was touched when one day, riding home wet and shivering from a day's hunting, she met Asquith out taking a walk. He immediately took off his coat and hung it round her. 'How wonderful Henry has been,' she wrote in her diary two days after Christmas, 'I have cried so much with my head in the hollow of his shoulder in bed.'[20] But hot-blooded as she was, she found it difficult to understand his reserve, complaining about how he had 'no impulse – appears to take everything for granted'. Whereas 'in public speaking or writing he has more power of expression than anyone I know', he was 'curiously slow at seeing the nuances of intimate easy talk'. But she did praise his 'infinite sympathy, tenderness and consideration for other people's feelings, common sense that amounts to genius, personal humility, detachment and breadth, unconscious nobility of character . . . truthfulness, generosity and fearlessness'.*

By now Margot knew that her mother was suffering from cancer of the liver and had not long to live. As soon as she heard she had gone straight from Leicestershire to spend Christmas at Glen with her family, leaving her husband and his children to celebrate the season's festivities in London without her. Emma's bravery and stoical refusal to cause any trouble were not much consolation as it was evident to everybody how much she was suffering, with morphia and brandy the only palliatives. 'I cannot tell you how terribly it breaks

---

*Margot Asquith's Diary, 27 December 1894. In a note added on 28 April 1916 – apparently the first time had she reread the passage since writing it – Margot wrote 'I can truly say no words of mine today can at all, describe how differently things have turned out for me!!!! My in-loveness (for 9 years) with Peter Flower – my love for Evan, my hundred and one loves and friendships are like so much waste paper!! . . . My criticisms of Henry are pathetically stupid narrow and crass. The fact is I was . . . a sort of drunkard of all social caresses up to the moment of marriage.'

into our hearts,' Margot wrote to Milner on Christmas Eve.[21] Her mother died on 20 January.

Asquith, who had joined Margot at Glen for the New Year, returned to London a few days before Emma Tennant's death. He seems to have been a model of restraint and understanding in the face of carping and bad temper from Margot, who had still not reconciled herself with settling for less than her ideal as a husband, writing in her diary: 'for ten years I looked out for a man who would be serious, sporting and intellectual. I did not find him.'[22] Back in London, Asquith wrote to excuse himself: 'I know my defects in these ways, and not sharing the pessimistic creed as to the unchangeableness of character which you sometimes profess, I don't despair of mending (if not ending!) them.' Meanwhile, he did his best to comfort her: 'what can we do but fall back upon our old trust in the infinite purposes of God? But for that faith we might well despair, when we are brought face to face with the littleness of life, the futility of our work, the hopelessness of keeping what we have loved best.' The day of her mother's death, he wrote: 'Your two little letters this morning wrung my heart: they bring before me such a scene of desolation and break-up in surroundings that have almost always been bright with the sunshine of gaiety and happiness. You are strong and brave my angel, and you need all the strength and bravery that God can give you now.'[23]

Few women could fail to be moved by these letters, all the more so as they were written in the face of such tetchiness on Margot's part. When she arrived back at 20 Cavendish Square on 31 January 1895 feeling 'cold and very tired and very low',[24] Margot found that Asquith had been called away to make a speech in Newcastle and was not home until the following day. Longing to be comforted, she found – for perhaps the first time in their marriage – that she was really missing him.

Margot's gloomy mood was not helped when five days after she returned to London she was badly shaken up after a dinner at the House of Commons: their coachman got drunk while waiting for them and then allowed the horse to bolt up Whitehall, where it reared up and impaled itself on the railings in front of the Home Office. Margot was now six months pregnant, but miraculously, neither she nor her unborn baby were harmed. Nonetheless, Asquith summarily dismissed their errant servant.

Politically the situation was looking grim for the Liberal Government. Rosebery, for all his mercurial brilliance, had neither the natural authority nor the administrative ability to be an effective Prime Minister. Margot caught the prevailing mood of pessimism within the Liberal Party in a letter to Milner written on Christmas Eve, lamenting 'how low our political fortunes seem to have fallen and what a disappointment Rosebery is'.[25]

Over the next few months Asquith was rarely at home as he carried the burden for the two main pieces of legislation in the Government's programme: his own Factories and Workshops Bill (intended to tighten up 'health and safety' rules) and the highly contentious Bill for the Disestablishment of the Welsh Church.[26] As a result, Margot 'never saw him till next morning unless he came back from the House before 1 a.m'.[27] The Welsh Church Bill was under attack not just from the Conservative Opposition, who hated the slightest interference with the privileges of the established church, but also from the Liberal Party's own radical wing. Notable among the rebels was the newly elected MP for Caernarvon, a thirty-two-year-old solicitor, David Lloyd George, who wanted the church stripped of the bulk of its wealth. An exasperated Asquith, seeking a compromise deal which would preserve the Government's dwindling majority, complained to the Chief Whip, Tom Ellis (another Welshman), that he was far too lenient in the face of Lloyd George's 'underhand and disloyal' tactics.[28]

Margot made no attempt to conceal her antipathy to the very principle of disestablishment. On one occasion she was in the Ladies' Gallery to hear her husband speak in a debate on disestablishment and got up to leave as Sir Michael Hicks Beach rose to reply for the Opposition. Balfour's sister-in-law, Frances, who was sitting next to her, quipped 'I see you don't want to hear the other side.' 'I have just heard it,' replied Margot, whose own political views on almost every issue were much closer to those of her friend, Balfour, than to Asquith's.[29]

Margot's feelings for her husband himself, however, were undergoing a sea change. During her mother's painful final illness she had been profoundly touched by his patience, sympathy and unstinting love in the face of her own ill temper; over the next few weeks, as his political duties kept him away from home, she discovered just how much she missed his comforting presence. In early March the Asquiths took advantage of some mild weather to take a short holiday with Charty and her husband in Sandwich, where Margot recorded in her journal how, while the Ribblesdales played golf:

> Henry and I sat in a sand hole and talked over our early courtship and the sorrows of the honeymoon . . . it is wonderful what a lot love can do in the way of growth and conquest and it would be a very flimsy woman who could not have been touched by Henry's love and nobility . . . we lolled in the sun listening to the larks soaring and hovering in undivided happiness between the earth and sky.[30]

Margot's baby had been expected in April, but was late. She began to go into labour on 15 May while she and Asquith were lunching at her father's house at 40 Grosvenor Square.[31] Violet Granby* accompanied the couple home to Cavendish Square and plied Margot with champagne while servants were sent to fetch her sisters, Charty and Lucy, and her doctor, the fashionable Sir John Williams (the Princess of Wales's gynaecologist). By the time Williams arrived Margot was nearly hysterical, cowering in an armchair sobbing and screaming in 'the awful panic of pain and fear which no one can realise who has not had a baby', while Asquith knelt beside her clutching her hands. Lucy was so affected by her distress that she had to be sent away. The sleeping draught Williams immediately administered had no effect and he was forced to resort to chloroform, after which Margot became delirious and passed out. The doctor, with Charty and Asquith in attendance, was up all night with Margot and it was entirely owing to his skill that she survived at all. The baby, however, had to be sacrificed to save her. She did not recover consciousness until the following day, but was too sick for the news of her baby's death to sink in. For four days she ran a high fever and was unable to keep down any food, while the nurses tried to keep her temperature down by repeatedly rinsing her mouth with cold water and sponging her forehead with iced vinegar.

The loss of the baby seems to have affected Margot less than might be imagined – initially, at least. Asquith told Catherine

---

*Later Duchess of Rutland.

Gladstone that the doctor was surprised that she had 'not suffered more from the tremendous shock. Happily she does not at present dwell much on her loss.'[32] However, her nerves were so shattered that she trembled at the slightest noise, startled even by someone unfastening the shutters or opening the door. Her legs were badly swollen and Dr Williams, diagnosing phlebitis, kept her still for six weeks and prescribed injections of morphia every night.

Before her confinement Margot left a letter for Asquith to read in the event of her death. He did not open it until he knew she was out of danger. His reply, dated 19 May 1895, touched her more than she could ever have imagined at the time of her marriage:

> Darling sweetheart and wife,
>
> I have just read for the first time your inexpressibly dear and touching love-letter written more than 3 weeks ago. I have resisted the temptation of opening it all this time: somehow I dared not, until all was over. But I am rewarded for my patience, for it is the dearest tribute that has ever been paid me by woman or man, and I shall carry it with me as a blessing and inspiration until I die.*
>
> I am not worth what you say or think of me. No one knows it better than I do. But I love to think and believe that it is true that in the great decision of your life – so painfully and so nobly worked out by you – you have not been mistaken, and that together – ever nearer and closer to one another – we may be able to do more and to live better than either of us could alone.
>
> To me from the first hour I knew you until now, you have been the best that I have known. I have loved and love you truly and loyally and with all my nature: and now we are more bound together than ever by the hopes and the fears and the loss which we have shared. God make us ever more and more to each other and help us both to do and to bear. Your own true husband and love.[33]

Little by little Margot regained her strength, while a constant stream of visitors helped to cheer her up. As well as her women friends, most of the leading politicians of the day called on her and regaled her with the latest gossip. The Tories Balfour and Brodrick, close friends from her Souls days, were regularly joined at her bedside by senior Liberals, although Rosebery and Harcourt studiously avoided one another. Margot and John Morley, whom she had got to know through Asquith, would discuss the novel they planned to write together when

---

*Like the rest of Margot's letters to him, it has disappeared.

the Liberals lost power, although he could hardly anticipate how soon that would be. 'One of the extraordinary and satisfactory things about this first year of marriage,' she wrote in her diary, 'is the way all our colleagues trust me.'[34] Despite her Tory views she was already regarding herself as an ex-officio member of the Liberal Front Bench.

On 21 June the Government was defeated out of the blue on a vote of censure on the War Minister, Campbell-Bannerman, about (of all things) the supply of cordite to the army. Harcourt only left Cavendish Square in the nick of time to vote in the crucial division, while Morley, unable to drag himself away, missed the vote altogether. The Liberals were badly beaten at the General Election in July, with the Conservatives and their Liberal Unionist allies returning to power with an overall majority of 152. Fortunately the Liberal vote held up well in Scotland and on 19 July Asquith cabled Margot: 'We have given Tories tremendous beating; 4332 Henry 3616 Gilmour. Bless you H.'

By October Margot was strong enough to accompany her husband to his home town of Morley, where he had been asked to open the town's imposing new neo-classical town hall. They were both moved by their 'Yorkshire' welcome, particularly when they were driven past Croft House, Asquith's childhood home, where strung across the gateposts was a large banner emblazoned with the words WELCOME HOME LAD. The ordeal of a vast ten-course banquet that lasted from three o'clock to nine o'clock – and they had already had lunch at the mayor's house – was less welcome. Not surprisingly, by the end of the day Margot was feeling 'quite ill and restless and hot and tired'.[35] Afterwards the Asquiths went to recuperate with Margot's sister, Lucy, in Easton Grey. Margot's health had soon recovered sufficiently for her to be back in the saddle hunting with the Beaufort* as well as managing a round at Minchinhampton golf course. When they returned to London she was able to enjoy the theatre again, praising Mrs Patrick Campbell's performance in *Romeo and Juliet*, although she noted 'her voice when excited is ugly – it closes in her throat instead of expanding'.[36] Margot was herself once more.

After the Liberals' loss of power, Asquith became the first former Cabinet minister to resume practice at the Bar and was soon earning

---

*Apparently Margot's doctor had suggested 'that I had better start hunting again to see if this would cure my sleeplessness'. *Autobiography* II, p. 27.

between £5,000 and £10,000 a year. He needed a substantial income with five children to educate and an expensive London house with a full complement of servants to maintain, plus substantial expenses. Most of the £3,000 allowance Margot received from her father was swallowed up by the cost of maintaining her horses and their grooms as well as her expensive taste in clothes, which alone absorbed at least £600 a year.[37] Anyone who imagined Asquith had married a rich wife was mistaken: Margot and the lavish entertaining that went with her cost far more than she ever brought in.

Margot had now truly come to love her husband, steadily won over by the strength of his own love for her, his kindness over her mother's death and – perhaps decisively – their shared grief over the death of their child. Over the next year she also began to appreciate her three eldest stepsons, even if still she resented her role as a mother to Violet and Cys. During the summer holidays in 1896 the Asquiths and Ribblesdales took a house close to the golf course at St Andrews, and for six weeks Asquith, Margot and the three eldest boys played golf every day. 'It is a great thing to have a joint holiday amusement,' she remarked in her diary, noting how well Charty and Ribblesdale got on with the boys 'who certainly are very nice and good – unquarrelsome, manly and happy. Raymond is the most remarkable, Bertie [Beb] the most loving and Arthur [Oc] the least elastic, but if anything the most liked. Henry is a model with them, much the same age in pursuits and intercourse and on occasions a vigorous parent.'[38]

Golf turned out to be a great bond between the whole family and a source for ribbing as well as rivalry. 'I suppose you have been playing golf lately a good deal at Innerleithen,' Oc had written to his father the previous autumn, adding archly 'I saw rather a funny cutting out of some paper or other about you and Margot golfing. It was not exactly complimentary to your golf ("They are about as bad as they make them").' A year or two later Beb threatened 'Oc and I are going to beat you, Margot and Jack next holidays!'[39]

By now Margot was pregnant again, which brought about a return of her irritability towards her two youngest stepchildren. She was irked by Cys's constant coughing and complained about 'Violet making little dull old maidish remarks with her narrow long face [which] makes me feel so old and done for – as if all the youth had gone out of my life and there was nothing left except to look forward to bringing Violet out and seeing Cys sitting in a heap in his chair, square and ungainly not uttering. I held my book before my eyes and sobbed.' And yet Violet tried her best to ingratiate herself with her grumpy stepmother, asking if she had a headache and trying to make Cys stop coughing. For a Christmas present, she gave Margot a pair of tiny socks she had made for the expected baby, which even her hyper-critical stepmother had to admit were '<u>beautifully</u> knitted'.[40]

Beb had joined Raymond at Winchester in September 1894. Raymond was already beginning to distance himself from his siblings and seems to have taken little notice of his younger brother. 'I see very little of Beb now-a-days,' he wrote in response to an enquiry from their father, 'but he seems to be getting on all right and enjoying himself pretty well.'[41] Unlike Raymond, Beb failed to win a scholarship, which must have been a disappointment as he was always near the top of his class at Lambrook. He and Oc – who, surprisingly, did slightly better in his own scholarship exam two years later* – were fortunate to have the Reverend J. T. Bramston as their housemaster. 'Trant', as he was always known to the boys, had 'a rare and delightful personality,' Beb later recalled. Trant's benevolent rule and the (no doubt connected) decency of the House prefects – whose 'powers were so supreme that it seemed highly improbable we should ever be able to exercise them again in any period of our lives' – did much to mitigate the harsh regime which the new boys had to endure as 'sweaters' (as 'fags' were known at Winchester).

Although Raymond's relationship with his stepmother was ostensibly free and easy, one senses that sometimes he deliberately set out to shock her – and particularly her religious sensibilities. Thus after a weekend visiting the Winchester mission to the poor of Portsmouth he complained about people whining around for money, and when they got it spending it on incense and candles. He was no more respectful about the recipients of the College's charity, gleefully recounting how many of them were drunk.[42]

Raymond got on well with his father, with much banter on both sides: he blithely quoted a newspaper report describing one of

---

*Raymond informed his father Oc was 'in the first 25: 14 scholarships were given', but the competition was apparently considered weaker than in Beb's year.

Asquith's speeches as 'philanthropic but foggy'. A constant theme running through his school reports is how his brilliance was blighted by his indolence. Raymond's indifference to effort even extended to sport, for which he also had natural flair. He did become second captain of the school 'Winchester football' team,* but he pitied those who had the misfortune to play cricket all day, who could have no idea of the bliss of lazing around on a summer evening in lovely woodland; although, to be fair to Raymond, he made this remark after describing a day's activity that also included 40 miles of bicycle riding (and tea at a village pub).[43] Raymond made no attempt to conceal his indolence from his father, boasting about how much he appreciated a lazy existence of playing fives and doing a little work in the daytime, while spending his nights gossiping into the small hours with some of his more intelligent friends.[44] Asquith seems to have made no attempt to reform his eldest son, probably realizing that he did more work than he let on, or perhaps believing that sheer ability would win through in the end. Raymond was well aware of a flaw in his character, in a letter to his friend Bob Ensor,[†] comparing himself to the beggar who always walked with the wind at his back, and claiming that he had no inclination to do or be anything that needed effort.[45]

Richard Rendall, Raymond's housemaster (who went on to become headmaster) seems to have adopted the same *laissez faire* policy towards Raymond as Asquith, and as a result the two of them got on well. The same could not be said for the Winchester headmaster, the Reverend W. A. Fearon, whom Raymond treated with ill-concealed contempt, informing Margot that 'the Bear' (as Fearon was always known to the boys because of his bushy black beard) as a typical product of Oxford – good manners and a good brain, which would be even better if he learnt how to use them properly. Writing to his father, he caricatured one of the headmaster's sermons as full of ingenious but contradictory arguments aiming to prove that the objective of life was to be a clergyman, and the objective of a clergyman was to grow a black beard and become headmaster of Winchester College. Although Fearon's delivery was clear enough for the first fifteen minutes, after that the wretched man's lips began to crack and he started going to pieces.[46]

---

*An energetic game peculiar to Winchester and usually played six a side.
†The future Oxford historian R. C. K. Ensor.

Raymond was, as might be expected, less forthcoming in his letters home about the homosexuality that seems to have been rampant at Winchester. He had no such scruples with his friend, Harold 'Bluetooth' Baker, who left school a year before him, regaling him with an account of how, after some boys had been caught *in flagrante delecto*, 'the Bear' had summoned all the prefects and then proceeded to lecture them for twenty minutes in a breaking voice on the drawbacks of unorthodox vice, elucidating in hushed tones the awfulness of the crime and urging them passionately to try every kind of prostitution and bestiality rather than sodomy. When Fearon confided that he and his fellow headmasters were discussing with the Government raising the penalty from two to fourteen years, a shiver ran through the assembly, at least eight-five percent of whom, by Raymond's estimate, were in peril of imprisonment for the crime. The more intrepid amongst them took comfort from the fact that the law had not yet been amended, and vowed to take advantage of the breathing space.[47] Raymond himself does not seem to have participated in any 'unorthodox vice', although a couple of younger boys wrote him 'love letters', but seem to have desisted when they received no encouragement.*

Raymond, however, had a very different side to his character to the caustic wit displayed in his letters, which were calculated to amuse or shock. One of his closest friends was a fellow scholar, Frank Lucas,[†] whose own letters home portray a very different impression from the 'devil may care' picture Raymond presents of himself. Lucas, Raymond and William Weech were 'thick as thieves', their main occupation being to 'hold long philosophical discussions'. When Lucas introduced Raymond to his parents he was specially anxious to check that Raymond had 'created a good impression', assuring his father that 'he has extraordinary merit'.[48]

Raymond, Beb and Oc all participated in the Winchester debating society, always a minority interest but where the politically interested

---

*One boy was identified by Raymond simply as 'A.P.H.' in a letter to Bob Ensor (Ensor Papers, 24 September 1897). The letters of the other, Geoffrey Smith, have survived and are charmingly innocent in a pre-Freudian way, for example, 'Your soul, my dear Raymond, would be such an adornment to my ideal land' (Jolliffe, p. 27). Here again Raymond seems to have lost contact. Smith was killed in France in 1916, shortly before Raymond himself.
†Francis Lucas, born in 1878, scholar at Trinity College, Cambridge, and later Financial Secretary to the India Office. He died of typhoid in 1920.

boys could thrash out the issues of the day. Raymond's own references to politics in his letters home are rare. Thus in February 1895
he asked his father how long the present government would last and
whether he wanted a General Election.[49] But it is a rare reference to
his father's work, and he was evidently much more concerned with
the freezing weather.

The first report in *The Wykehamist* – the Winchester boys' own
magazine – of a speech by Raymond appeared only in December
1894, by which time he was sixteen and his friends Bluetooth and
Bob Ensor were already regular speakers. Raymond proposed the
motion 'that in the opinion of this House it is high time to put a
check on the influx of destitute aliens'. According to *The Wykehamist*,
'on the whole the anti-Jew cry was too prominent. Asquith . . . made
it the staple of a sensible and at times epigrammatic speech. Had
he arranged his matter better, instead of revolving round a Jew
centre . . . he would have been quite effective.' The anti-'aliens'
motion was passed overwhelmingly by thirty-five votes to four: in
those days few people had any inhibitions about forcibly expressing
their views on mass immigration. What is more remarkable is
Raymond's own specifically anti-Jewish line, not because such views
were unusual at the time but because his opinion was so much at
odds with those of Margot and his father (who, incidentally, later
opposed the Tory Government's attempts to try to halt 'alien' immigration) and who had many Jewish friends.

Raymond seems to have spoken regularly at debates. His speeches
were praised for their fluency, wit and clever epigrams, although he
was evidently not a natural performer: 'he must learn to be louder,
more emphatic and interesting in delivery' was a criticism of *The
Wykehamist*. On most issues Raymond's views seem to have been
similar to his father's – supporting trade unions and the right to
strike, attacking Salisbury's foreign policy and condemning Dr
Jameson's abortive raid into the Transvaal.[50]

Nearly all Beb's letters have disappeared, but he seems to have
been just as cheeky to his father as his brothers. Asquith was once
amused to receive a letter begging him to organize his style better
when speaking in public, after Beb had been asked to
'Demosthenize' one of his father's speeches – a task which he apparently found 'unduly hard'.[51] Beb himself was an even more gifted
speaker than his elder brother, rapidly making his mark as a popular
and effective debater in the Winchester debating society, of which he

was elected Vice-President.* A speech in favour of 'the social liberty of America' (in which he particularly favoured the transatlantic policy of 'mixed education as emancipating both sexes from prejudice and priggishness') was described by *The Wykehamist* as 'by far the best speech' in the debate, and praised for its 'well-chosen, spirited language' and its 'complete command of the situation and his audience'. 'Another speech, in support of the House of Lords being in urgent need of reform', was thought 'worthy of Lloyd George'.[52]

Oc was less political than either of his elder brothers, but it was not long before he was roped in by Beb to speak in a debate – this time on the total abolition of the House of Lords – where he showed that he shared his brothers' flair and wit as well as his family's radical views, arguing in an 'able and vigorous speech' that 'old families were merely robber chiefs in origin, and retained their characteristics, they still hunt foxes when they cannot hunt men'.[53] One can almost feel the shivers running down the spines of Margot and her hunting friends.

---

*The President was the supervising don who, in Beb's time, happened to be Richard Rendall, Raymond's housemaster.

5

'Diverted from the sterner
mode of life'

———————————◆———————————

ROSEBERY ABRUPTLY RESIGNED the leadership of the Liberal Party
in October 1896. Although Asquith was seen by many as his
natural successor, there was no question of him being able to afford
to give up his income from the Bar with no private means except
Margot's £3,000 annual allowance from her father. Eventually a
compromise was cobbled together whereby Rosebery stayed on as
the titular Party leader, while handing over the Liberal leadership in
the House of Lords – and thus the need to deal with Harcourt, the
Commons leader, whom he hated – to Lord Kimberley.

Asquith never relished the business of Opposition. For him, argument had to have some practical purpose. Harrying the Government
for its own sake held little attraction. For the next few years his main
contribution to the Liberal cause was outside Parliament, as he criss-
crossed the country to keep up Party morale with speeches to local
Liberal associations, where he was always a popular speaker, able to
command large audiences. However, the rarity of his appearances in
Parliament soon gave rise to snide remarks about him 'preferring
society and amusement to the House of Commons'.[1] Inevitably,
Margot's influence was blamed.

On 26 February 1897 Margot successfully gave birth to a daughter, Elizabeth. Her birth pains, although not as traumatic as her first
tragic confinement, still taxed to the limit the courage that had
bravely born countless hunting injuries. The new mother was suitably soppy: 'to feel the little wee breathing, living, being close in my

arms with her lovely little hands pressed against my mouth was so marvellous that it filled my soul with quiet and my brain with prayers'. It was unfortunate that in the immediate aftermath of Elizabeth's birth, Asquith had to spend many evenings in the House of Commons as he took the leading role in opposing the new Government's Education Bill. This prompted many tears from Margot, who suffered severe post-natal depression. When she asked her doctor whether 'a baby generally takes away one's husband's love', he replied tactfully, 'Oh no, Mrs Asquith, a baby is a great bond.' When Margot repeated the remark to her husband he always referred to Elizabeth as 'little bond'.[2]

Margot had recovered sufficiently to host her first dinner party within five weeks; the guests included Balfour, Haldane, Morley, Harry Cust, Sir Alfred Lyall and Milner who – aided, so she liked to believe, by her energetic lobbying of Balfour on his behalf – had just been appointed Governor of the Cape of Good Hope. Asquith hosted a large *bon voyage* dinner for his old Balliol friend and Margot had a suitably emotional farewell *tête à tête* with the new proconsul (this was the occasion when Milner told her that she was 'the only woman he had ever wanted to marry').[3]

Margot had now become genuinely fond of her stepsons. 'My step children become dearer and dearer to me every day,' she wrote in her diary a couple of months after becoming a mother. 'If I had to choose among the children of my friends which five I would annex I should turn to Henry's: they are clever and manly, full of high spirits and innocent enjoyment. I love them very much and think they love me.' She noted how 'they have been sweet to my tiny – all amusing her in turns and watching her dear little naked body in contortions over dressing or in her bath'.[4] Margot was later to describe the turning point with Cys in her autobiography:

I told the children one day to collect some of their toys and that I would take them to the hospital, where they could give them away themselves . . . and a few days afterwards I was invited to the nursery. On arriving upstairs I saw that Cys's eyes were scarlet; and set out in a pathetic array round the room was a large family of monkeys christened by him 'the Thumblekins'. They were what he loved best in the world. I observed that they were the only unbroken toys that were brought to me; and he was eyeing his treasures with anguish in his soul. I was so touched that I could hardly speak; and when I put my arms round his neck, he burst into sobs:

'May I keep one monkey . . . only one, Margot? . . . *Please*? . . . *Please*, Margot?'

However, it seems that Margot still found it difficult to feel much affection for Violet. It would take another two years before she would grudgingly admit that her stepdaughter possessed a few good qualities: 'she is very plain, but graceful and clever . . . old as the hills, a trifle secretive and pedantic, but good and well intentioned. She is sweet with baby which pleases me.' 'Baby', of course, was 'a genius' as well as 'passionate and daring'.[5] Elizabeth, it seems, was thoroughly indulged by her siblings and father alike.

Asquith could not have been more thrilled when Raymond won the top Classical scholarship to Balliol in November 1896: 'RAYMOND CAME IN FIRST – HURRAH!', he cabled to Margot, who was in Paris. 'Darling boy, I can't tell you how proud I am of you,' Margot wrote to congratulate her stepson. 'I cannot but feel how proud your mother, had she lived, would have been and how inadequately I can refill her place either in sympathy or joy, but you must just believe in my pride and affection and gratitude for having you as a step-son and friend. God bless you and give you a worthy future.'[6]

Raymond treated his triumph with disdain. While he was at Balliol sitting the scholarship exam he facetiously dismissed most of his fellow examinees to his father as sick and repulsive. What most pleased him about his success was the irritation it caused Fearon, his despised headmaster who, he told Ensor, had not concealed his exasperation, even suggesting that the results published in *The Times* might be in alphabetical order. After Raymond squashed this theory, Fearon angrily showed him the door. However, on the threshold of Oxford, Raymond was looking back not forward, regarding his five years at Winchester as a golden age, never to be repeated. Quoting Heine, he told Ensor that the world smelt of dead violets. He expected nothing of Balliol and Oxford, which reeked of snobbery. He then gave a revealing insight into his deepest feelings, by proclaiming that the Biblical character whom he most admired was the Prodigal Son – or would have been if the Prodigal had had the courage to go on living off acorns. He would give anything to be a destitute beggar with nothing but the freedom to forge his own destiny, but unfortunately he had what were supposed to be 'advantages', which meant that he received no credit for success, but was in disgrace if he failed.[7]

Paradoxically, it was probably his father who was unwittingly responsible for Raymond's feelings. While Asquith left Margot in no doubt about his joy over his son's triumph, he himself gave Raymond a subtly different message: 'I am delighted that you have taken the first place, and I must confess that I would not have been quite satisfied had you taken any other.'[8] Success was no more than what was anticipated: Raymond had been granted prodigious talents and he was indeed expected to triumph. He was never allowed to know just how proud his father was of him, or indeed the depth of his affection. Behind Raymond's carefully contrived indifference to what 'the world' (as against his chosen friends) thought of him was an attempt to affect disdain at the expectations heaped on him by a father he loved and admired and whose affection and esteem he craved more than anything else. It was a misunderstanding that marred their relationship right up to Raymond's premature death.

Far from revelling in the lifestyle that his father's marriage to Margot had brought in its train, Raymond resented the constant round of house parties with the same ever-shifting kaleidoscope of Souls and their families.* He wrote to 'Bluetooth' Baker from Hyndford House in North Berwick, which the Asquiths had rented as their base during the summer before he went up to Oxford, complaining of the ceaseless round of smart but vacuous joviality. The only part of the holiday he seems to have appreciated was his stay at Cloan, Haldane's Perthshire seat, where he appreciated his host's sense of humour and his fine cellar and excellent table, both of which he reckoned to be the best in Scotland. After a weekend with Rosebery at Dalmeny, Raymond went to Grasmere where – he wrote to Ensor – he could commune with the mountains in solitude, armed with an Aeschylus as an antidote to the crude sentimentality of Wordsworth, whose most absurd rubbish was, in his view, inspired by the district.[9] The Lake District was, of course, for ever associated with happy family holidays while Helen was alive, and

---

*This hostility to their parents' large social circle was apparently shared by Beb and Oc. The latter responded to Asquith's suggestion that he and Beb take leave from Winchester join him and Margot for the weekend by specifying 'that there is not a large party of strangers there, in which case our coming over would be out of the question'. (Clovelly Papers, AMA to Asquith, 24 June 1900)

Wordsworth was her favourite poet – one of few things she had in
common with Margot. Perhaps this was Raymond's way of trying to
recapture his mother's spirit, while denying any 'sentimentalism'.
John Jolliffe, Raymond's grandson and the editor of his letters, is
surely right to wonder whether 'on his mother's death he formed a
self-protective mask from behind which he gave vent to merciless
and aloof observations'.[10]

Margot's hunting and her husband's frequent speaking engage-
ments round the country meant that the Asquiths were often apart,
and it was not long before she became suspicious about what
quarry her husband might be pursuing while she was chasing foxes.
The couple's first jealous spat was in 1898 over Lady Ulrika
('Mouche') Duncombe, the spirited daughter of Lord Feversham,
whom Asquith described to Margot as 'a delightful and noble creature'.[11] At first Margot had designs on marrying Mouche off to
Milner. However, the shy and studious Milner was hardly to
Mouche's taste; flirting with confident and attractive married men –
as Margot knew well – was much more fun. It was not long before
Asquith was having to reassure his wife that 'you remain and will
always be to me, not only the sweetest and dearest and most
desired, but by a long way the cleverest and most brilliant among
women, and I should never dream of putting Mouche – much as I
admire her – or anyone else, within miles of the same class.' In
August 1898, though, he could not resist recounting how he had
been invited by Mouche's compliant mother, Lady Feversham, to
spend Sunday with them, although 'of course, I refused. I long to
see you again my own darling love.'[12] Margot's suspicions were re-
ignited and a couple of months later, while she was at Glen, she
fired off a wildly jealous letter. Asquith threw up his hands in outraged innocence:

> My own darling, how could it enter your head to write such things . . . I
> burnt your letter – so as to have no trace of it. You surely know that
> nobody ever can or will take your place, or any part or inch of it, in my
> heart and life. As for Mouche, have you not always said that one ought not
> to shut out of one's life new sources of interest and confidence and affec-
> tion – so long as one is not disloyal to that which is and ought to be at the
> centre.[13]

It was going to be a regular refrain throughout the Asquiths' married life. In this case Margot had not much to worry about, since her husband's ardour soon cooled, helped by a dose of cold water from Mouche herself

As it happened, Margot's furious letter about Mouche crossed a more significant one from her husband. On the evening of 25 October 1898 Asquith had been summoned to meet his father-in-law, who had announced that he was going to marry again. The Bart (as his family called him) was nervous about how his children would take it, and eagerly grasped at Asquith's suggestion that he write to Margot, at that moment at Glen with her siblings. Asquith adopted a jocular tone in his letter to Margot, recounting how her father 'went on (this is too characteristic to be omitted) that he had always lived a "celibate" life – had never kept a mistress (!) – and was quite strong enough for the part. "I dare say people will say that it will kill me – but I shall know how to take care of myself." '[14]

Margot was not in the least amused. What really grated about her father's choice, Marguerite Miles – apart from being, at thirty, forty-five years her fiancé's junior, and indeed four years younger than Margot herself – were her 'hideosity' and her being very much of child-bearing age, evidently sharing the Bart's confidence in his continued virility.[15] Nonetheless, when the Bart appeared at Glen, his children could see his obvious happiness and tried to make the best of the situation. He was married within a month of announcing his engagement in 'a rather depressing ceremony', as Asquith acidly remarked to Raymond: 'the lady wore at the altar with complacency a cope of pearls presented by the Bart at a cost of £2,500'[16] – a sum which, it would not have escaped his son-in-law's notice, was nearly as much as his daughters' annual allowances. He was not slow off the mark in demonstrating his continued virility, and by early in the New Year Marguerite was pregnant.

Margot's main concern about her father's remarriage and the prospect of his having more children was that it was now unlikely that he would ever agree to increase his daughters' allowances. After the wedding, Asquith had what Margot described as 'a serious talk' with her about her extravagant lifestyle; explaining that 'some day he might have to lead the party, in which case he could not make what he does at the Bar', he insisted she must cut back on her expenditure. The most obvious economy was her dress bill of over £600 a year.

She solemnly promised to purchase just one Court gown during the coming year and otherwise to restrict her new clothes to a habit and 'a golfing gown or two made at home of stuff'. And to show she was serious she signed a piece of paper to this effect.[17]

Asquith could hardly have predicted just how soon a vacancy in the Liberal leadership would arise, with Harcourt resigning a couple of weeks after the Bart's wedding. After a long discussion, the Asquiths decided to ask Balfour and Haldane to lobby Margot's father to increase her allowance to enable Asquith to lead the Opposition. She dared not ask him herself. What Balfour's colleagues would have thought of his mission can be scarcely imagined: Haldane appreciated the 'humorous' predicament of the Tory leader in the House of Commons helping to pave the way for the man likely to prove his most effective opponent, although this never seems to have occurred to the Asquiths. Loyal friend that he was, Balfour swallowed his scruples and wrote, but the Bart replied 'promptly and firmly to say I was not to think of it', taking – in Margot's words – 'the man in the street's view that there was no party to lead (which is great rubbish as no regiment can work or keep together without a colonel) saying Henry's time would come etc'.[18]

In the circumstances, Asquith had no option but gracefully to support his only serious rival, Sir Henry Campbell-Bannerman, or C.B., as he was always affectionately known. C.B. had the advantage, at sixty-two, of being fifteen years Asquith's senior and, as Margot put it with characteristic candour in a letter to Curzon, 'is not young or very strong and is not likely to prove a formidable [long term] rival'. In the meantime, she resolved to make the biggest sacrifice she could to help finance her husband's political career: 'I've taken the bull by the horns and sold my horses and let my groom go and with tears in my heart said goodbye to hunting.'[19] However, she soon had second thoughts; and it was to be another seven years before she would say her final Tally Ho!

*

Raymond's prejudices about Oxford survived his arrival at Balliol in October 1897. Soon after going up he informed Margot that those parts of the day not taken up with eating, the athletic spent drinking, while the more intellectual smoked or played poker. He dismissed his fellow undergraduates as mostly Scots and niggers,* who spoke a blend of Gaelic and Hindustani, not easily understood by a Londoner.[20]

By now Jowett had been dead four years and, although his ideas still influenced strongly the College's academic ethos, the atmosphere at Balliol was more relaxed. The new Master, the philosopher Edward Caird, exuded what Beb was to call a 'gentle air of tranquil benevolence',[21] and encouraged the younger dons to fraternize socially with the undergraduates, whose education benefited as much from late-night fireside chats – lubricated by port and tobacco – as from formal tutorials. Balliol had become a much more fashionable College than it had been in Asquith's day. Although most of its undergraduates were still drawn from the 'lesser' public schools and came from what might loosely be described as the 'professional middle class', about a quarter of its intake were now old Etonians: 'Balliol seemed to me an older edition of Eton,' wrote the Eton-educated diplomat Maurice Baring, who was in Oxford at the time to study for the Foreign Office exams.

Raymond, despite his initial misgivings, soon found himself even more in his element at Oxford than he had been at Winchester. Asquith, who spent a weekend with his son towards the end of his first term, reported to Margot that he 'has got nice rooms, not badly furnished, tho' he is not well off yet for pictures. Ribblesdale's 18th century men will be a great improvement to his walls.' The Asquiths, father and son, together with Bluetooth Baker, were given dinner at the Gridiron Club – a private undergraduate dining club – by fellow Wykehamist, Arnold Ward, whose other guests were 'two young dons called Simon and Smith'†: both of whom Asquith was to get to know very well one day. Afterwards, Asquith recounted how they all repaired to Ward's rooms in Balliol: 'I sat there smoking and talking

---

*At the time the term 'nigger' encompassed any non-European and was sometimes stretched to include Spaniards and Greeks and was not thought offensive, at least by those who used it. Among the 'niggers' cavalierly dismissed by Raymond was Pasha Mohammed Mahmoud, a future Prime Minister of his country. The Scots included Lord Haddo, the eldest son and heir of the Earl of Aberdeen, whose brother Archie Gordon was to have a tragic romance with Violet, James Balfour, the son of the Lord Justice General of Scotland, and Arthur Keith, who went on to become Regius Professor of Sanskrit and Comparative Philology at Edinburgh University.
†John Simon and F. E. Smith, later Viscount Simon and Earl of Birkenhead, both future Lord Chancellors.

till late. Sunday I spent entirely with Raymond, who was in his most forthcoming mood and a very agreeable companion. I think the place has already done him good in these ways. He seems to know everybody and certainly has some very nice friends . . . Altogether I think he has made quite a good start, and he is certainly in good spirits and happy.'[22]

For both Raymond and Beb – who joined his elder brother at Balliol in 1900 – their years at Oxford proved to be a golden age, although not, as with their father, a launching pad for greater things. The Asquith boys mixed primarily with the sportsmen and College swells who made up the members of the Annandale, in theory a College debating society, but in practice a riotous dining club. The 'Anna' set, although they included a few approved Scots and even the odd colonial, was dominated by old Etonians. The Club's termly dinner was dreaded by the more serious members of College, who invariably found (at best) their sleep disturbed by the post-prandial revelry, even if they were spared having their rooms wrecked – although, to be fair, the 'Annas' would invariably pay for the damage they inflicted. 'Annas' never got drunk, they merely became 'buffy'.

The Annandale's Minute Book*, with its painful record of the debauched proceedings, is perhaps more illuminating of the club's ethos. 'Misdemeanours' were punished with fines levied in claret, port or sloe gin from the Society's cellar. The twenty or so diners (mostly from Balliol with one or two favoured outsiders such as Bluetooth, who was at New College) usually managed to drink fifty or so bottles of wine during dinner, supplemented by a few magnums of Pol Roget champagne beforehand and a generous allowance of port and brandy afterwards. After dinner the 'Annas' would considerately save the College servants the trouble of washing up by sending most of the crockery crashing down Number XIII staircase in a semi-sanctified ritual known as 'the waterfall'. Then there might be a spot of persecution for some innocent (usually Scottish) scholar as a prelude to a raid on one or both Balliol's neighbouring Colleges, St John's or Trinity. During Raymond's term as President of the Annandale he tried to raise the

---

*Appropriated by Sir Maurice 'Bongie' Bonham Carter during his time as the Club's Secretary and only recently returned to the Balliol archives by his family.

tone of the membership by introducing a pet goat to the Society's proceedings.*

Reports soon reached Margot of the debauched way her brilliant nineteen-year-old stepson was spending his time at Oxford. When she wrote him a suitably tactful letter about her concerns, she cannot have been wholly comforted by Raymond's rebuttal of what she had been told. Although he assured her that she had nothing to worry about and promised to consult her should he get into any difficulties, he was delighted to find himself accused of Byronic profligacy. However, pleading he had neither the time nor the opportunity, he informed her that gambling and women were unfashionable among saner undergraduates, and that, while the place swam in wine, few people drank too much – and many were improved by their drinking: for someone with a strong head, there was not much to fear.

Margot's scandalmonger of an informant – so Raymond maintained – had got the wrong idea about the life he led. His stepmother should realize that he was a scholar, and different standards applied to scholars than to commoners, particularly at Balliol, which was an academic hothouse. A clique of three younger dons – anaemic pedants to a man – wanted them to live like women in a Turkish seraglio, stooped over their books and cut off from any temptation to be frivolous. They were horrified when he started making speeches at the Union. Although most scholars surrendered to these unwritten rules, they were all half-witted, as well as filthy, hideous, ignorant and antisocial. Most of Raymond's own Balliol friends – so he told Margot – were athletes, who were on the whole the best company: he maintained that an intrinsically intelligent but untrained mind was

---

*One senior don complained that 'the public-school psychology' permeating Oxford at the time, had 'some affinities with the drill-spirit of Prussia'. At least one undergraduate who participated in the Annandale's drunken raids was later ashamed of his behaviour. Laurence Jones, a friend of the Asquiths, wrote: 'It was part of the ritual, before the waterfalls began, to climb the turret stairs to the high room where "Moonface" was certain to be found at his books, and to worship him . . . But no flicker of amusement relieved the solemnity of Moonface's large, white, perfectly circular countenance . . . It is probable that he felt not so much contempt as utter incomprehension. For Norman Campbell was a dedicated man; dedicated partly to scientific research, but wholly to the succour of the poor and weak . . . most of us missed our chance of getting to know a remarkable human being, probably worth more than the rest of us added together.' Campbell went on to teach science at Trinity College at Kandy in Ceylon (now Sri Lanka), where his pupils regarded him as a saint. He was killed at Arras in 1917. (Lewis R. Farnell, *An Oxonian Looks Back*, p. 131; L. E Jones, *An Edwardian Youth*)

invariably preferable to the useless overburdened contraption that passed for a brain in most scholars. As a result his way of life was much more entertaining and healthy than that of the average scholar. At first the dons were incensed by his attitude, and even had the temerity to suggest that he should see more of his fellow scholars. Now that they realized that he always beat the idiots at their own game anyway, they were much more amenable.[23]

The following term Raymond reported to his father how he had taken part in a combined assault by Balliol and Trinity on St John's. After the attackers had successfully driven the outnumbered defenders back through their College gardens and the quads towards the main gate and made ready to hunt them into St Giles, the President of John's appeared on the scene and unsportingly broke up the proceedings. Raymond was recognized as one the ringleaders and although the authorities seem to have taken the usual indulgent attitude to 'undergraduate high jinks', he found himself deputed to collect contributions from his fellow Balliol raiders towards the broken windows and other damage. The President of Trinity apparently paid his own undergraduates' share since, according to Raymond, he approved of the destruction of John's.[24]

At 'Handshaking', the end of term meeting with the Master and College tutors, Raymond found himself berated for living on his capital and urged to work harder to counter the growing threat to Balliol's intellectual supremacy from New College. It was suggested, he reported to his father, that he should discuss Plautus with redheaded Jews and liverish Paulines,* instead of wasting his time with 'exquisite' rakes. Raymond had responded as urbanely as he could and, so he believed, parted on excellent terms.[25]

It was a far cry from Asquith's own studious undergraduate days, but he seems to have refrained from criticism. Presumably he was amused and perhaps a little envious of his firstborn. Raymond's years at Oxford were not only the happiest in his life, but the period when he was closest to his father. Their correspondence shows a resumption of their easy relationship and shared sense of humour, while Raymond's letters to his friends are peppered with praise and admiration for his father, whether his intensely witty speech at a St Andrews golf club dinner or the expert way in which he evaded a journalist's questions

---

* Pupils of St Paul's School, London

about Home Rule.[26] When he was irreverent, it was affectionately so. Thus he reported to Bluetooth how, while he was dining at the House of Commons with Balfour, Curzon, Cranborne and other young Tory MPs his father came in half-way through after making some ridiculous speech, which he proceeded to recount with delightful cynicism, corroborating his view of the statesman of the day.[27]

Asquith and the headmaster of Eton, Dr Warre, were the guests of honour at a Balliol dinner in 1901, when Raymond was asked to reply to his father's speech proposing a toast to the College. With Warre's son Felix sitting beside him, Raymond proposed the health of 'the fortunate fathers of two very distinguished sons'.[28] Asquith proudly recounted to Margot how his eldest son's speech had completely outshone his own: 'I made them laugh and thought I got on pretty well', but 'R's chaff of us two as fathers was excellent and made everybody roar. It was a really witty speech, but in such perfect taste and so quietly delivered that it had a tremendous success with the critical and rather fastidious audience. Beb was there and highly delighted.'[29]

Margot had little to fear about the malign influence of her stepson's Oxford friends. Eccentric and amusing as they were, they were hardly likely to lead him seriously astray and she was soon to welcome many of them into the family circle. Bob Ensor was already a close friend from Winchester days. Hugh Godley and Maurice (always known as 'Bongie') Bonham Carter — and another Wykehamist — were both to fall in love with Violet and Bongie was ultimately to marry her. She was not to meet the most outstanding athlete among them until many years later, when F. S. 'Cleg' Kelly, the best rower of his generation as well as a brilliant musician, had become one of Oc's bravest comrades-in-arms on the battlefields of Gallipoli and northern France. Another rowing blue, Auberon 'Bron' Herbert, the nephew of the fourth Earl of Carnarvon and a cousin of Ettie Desborough, was later to become a member of Asquith's Government. Bron's cousin, Aubrey Herbert, Lord Carnarvon's fourth son, who came up the year after Raymond, was the most remarkable figure of all in that extraordinary Balliol generation.* Nearly blind since childhood, tall and gangly with gesticulating hands and clear piercing blue eyes staring out of a small, close-cropped

---

*Lord Carnarvon had died suddenly in 1890, when he was succeeded by Aubrey's half brother 'Porchy', famed for his role in the discovery of the tomb of Tutenkhamun by Howard Carter.

bullet head, and invariably scruffily dressed, Aubrey presented a picture of wild eccentricity. He was renowned for such daredevil feats as traversing the tall houses in King Edward Street, forty feet up swinging from ledge to ledge by his fingertips. His homes – at Pixton, near Dulverton in Somerset, which his widowed mother had bought from his half-brother, the fifth Lord Carnarvon, and the family's villa at Portofino on the Gulf of Genoa – became a mecca for the Asquith children and his other friends.

Outside Balliol, Raymond's circle included Bluetooth at New College, Maurice Baring – studying for the Foreign Office exams – and John Buchan at Brasenose, all of whom were regarded as honorary Balliol men. Three years older than Raymond, Buchan had come up to Oxford in 1895 after graduating from Glasgow, and had already published his first novel. At first sight, they made an unlikely pair. Buchan was the son of a Scottish Free Church minister, serious-minded, distinctly puritanical and a fervent Tory. 'No two friends were ever more unlike than he and I,' Buchan admitted later. 'He chaffed me unmercifully about my Calvinism.'[30] For Buchan, his friendship with Raymond and Aubrey (on whom he later modelled Sandy Arbuthnot in his novel *Greenmantle*) represented his final metamorphosis from son of the Manse into a man of the world, whereas for Raymond his fondness for Buchan showed that underneath his cynical devil-may-care pose there lurked a serious young man. He readily joined Buchan's Horace Club, which beside supping 'on nuts and olives and fruits' and imbibing 'what we made believe was Falernian', was a poetry society meeting in the President's garden at Magdalen to hear each other's compositions. Buchan later recalled:

> There were times when he [Raymond] was almost inhuman. He would destroy some piece of honest sentiment with a jest, and he had no respect for the sacred places of dull men. There was always a touch of scorn in him for obvious emotion, obvious creeds, and all the accumulated lumber of prosaic humanity. That was a defect of his great qualities. He kept himself for his friends and refused to bother about the world. But to such as were admitted to his friendship he would deny nothing. I have never known a friend more considerate, and tender, and painstaking, and unfalteringly loyal.[31]

Buchan has provided a striking image of Raymond at Oxford, clad in an old shooting-coat of light-grey tweed and grey flannel trousers and regarding the world with his 'deep-set grey eyes and his lips parted as if at the beginning of a smile. He had a fine straight figure, and bore himself with a kind of easy stateliness. His manner was curiously self-possessed and urbane, but there was always in it something of a pleasant aloofness of one who was happy in society but did not give to it more than a fraction of himself.' Raymond had 'seen much of distinguished people who to most of us were only awful names, so he seemed all his time at Oxford to have one foot in the greater world'.[32]

Raymond may have picked up a disdain for politics and politicians, but nonetheless both he and Beb were keen to follow their father into the House of Commons, to which the Oxford Union was seen as a natural stepping stone. The venue for debates was no longer the intimate book-lined surroundings of the Old Library, but the recently built grandiose new debating hall. The Presidents in the three years before Raymond came up included three of the Union's most outstanding speakers: F. E. Smith, Hilaire Belloc and John Simon. All of them were still around in Oxford and still spoke regularly. F. E., as he was already universally known, was now a Fellow of Merton, while an already embittered Belloc – having failed to secure election to All Souls' – held court in his little house in Holywell, while making a living coaching.[33]

Raymond's maiden speech from the floor, on the question of the Indian frontier, 'seems to have been quite a success', so his father heard during his visit to Oxford a few weeks later.[34] He was given his first 'paper' speech* the following term, dealing, according to *Isis*, with some cheap jibes about his father from the preceding speaker, Reginald Hills,† 'in a spirit of forbearance that did him infinite credit', before launching into a typical tirade against a string of British politicians. The rival *Oxford Magazine* praised his speech as 'extremely good, his language polished, and his manner clear and incisive. He made a great impression on the house, and sat down amidst cheers.'[35] The following Michaelmas term Raymond spoke in the 'Presidential'

---

*'Paper' speakers are those listed on the official order of debate as opening the cases for and against the motion, after which it is thrown open to the 'floor'. The debate was held on 17 February 1898.
†Sir Reginald Hills (1877–1967), who became Recorder of Winchester.

debate – in support of Buchan, who was one of the candidates for the Presidency – on the motion 'that this House does not believe in international morality'. The subject was tailor made for Raymond's talents of satire and epigram and he made 'the best speech of the evening', according to the *Oxford Magazine*. 'He reduced International Morality to cant and convention', said *Isis*.[36] Buchan's speech was good enough to secure him the Presidency with Raymond elected Librarian (Vice-President).

On the whole Raymond's political views mirrored those of his father. If anything he was slightly to the right of him*, though his speeches rarely displayed genuine conviction. Nonetheless, he was capable of real strength of feeling as demonstrated in a most unexpected way. One of the Librarian's tasks was to seek the House's approval for a weekly list of books recommended for purchase by the Library Committee. Usually the list went through with little comment, but on this occasion a work attacking the Oxford Movement was challenged.[†] Raymond could not have been less interested in the book itself, which he considered trash, but he was angry at what he saw as unwarranted censorship by religious zealots. Even in that post-Darwinian era Christianity could still raise enormous passions and not only was the floor of the debating chamber packed, people were standing cheek by jowl in the gangways with the gallery, according to the *Oxford Magazine*, 'full to overflowing'. A great pack of clergymen had come to Oxford specially to bay their opposition to the book. After Belloc had led the attack, Raymond defended the proposal 'in a speech of great fury and eloquence'. Buchan recalled how he spoke 'with a white face and an unwonted passion in his voice. He asked where such censorship would stop. There were books on the shelves, he said, by Roman writers which poured venom upon the greatest man that ever lived. Were these books to be expelled? 'I assure you,' he told the angry ranks of Keble and St John's, 'that the fair name of Caesar is as dear to me as that of any dead priest can be to you.' The original subject for debate was soon forgotten as heated argument over the book raged on into the night until eventually a compromise motion was passed handing the issue over to adjudication by three ex-Presidents of more than ten years' standing.[37]

---

*In a letter to 'Bluetooth' Baker, Raymond described socialism as fraudulent, contradicted by history, expediency, equity and common sense (Jolliffe, p. 33).
†Walsh *The Secret History of the Oxford Movement*.

Raymond's stance on the Oxford Movement book cost him the Presidency at the end of the Trinity term of 1899 – he had refrained from standing the previous March, probably to avoid clashing with his Mods exams. When the Boer War broke out the following term, infecting even the Oxford Union with jingoism, Raymond's chances of ever winning the Presidency must have seemed bleak, with the handicap of his Liberalism aggravated by his anti-war stance. That summer he again stood aside in favour of his friend Ensor, who despite his 'pro-Boer' views was elected. Ensor gave Raymond a speech in the traditional 'no confidence' debate on the Unionist government in which he was opposed by Algernon Cecil, the grandson of the Prime Minister, Lord Salisbury. *Isis* reported Cecil had 'several altercations with Mr Asquith in which both sides drew blood'. Raymond was able to poke fun at Balfour, Cecil's cousin, for 'opinion without knowledge and of assurance without conviction'.[38] It was a remark Balfour himself would have enjoyed and indicates what a good House of Commons performer Raymond would have made had he ever been given the chance.

It was not until March 1900 that Raymond made another bid for the Presidency. This time the Winchester mafia worked in his favour with Bluetooth agreeing to stand for a second term as Librarian rather than oppose him. No doubt he would have preferred to have avoided the contentious subject of South Africa altogether; however, just before the election he was asked to stand in for the sick proposer of a motion in favour of giving 'a fair measure of independence to the Boer Republics'. For once, Raymond found himself outshone by, of all people, the visiting President of the Cambridge Union, Edwin Montagu, a man whose destiny was to be closely entwined with that of Raymond's father. Raymond believed that Cambridge speakers were as repellent a gang as he had ever seen and that they sounded like Welsh missionaries. Montagu, however, was praised by *Isis* for his 'delightful flavour of satire'. His cynical argument that 'the Boers would ultimately like our rule, and it would be wrong to deprive them of the opportunity of enjoying it', was worthy of Beb at his best.[39]

This time, in spite of his pro-Boer stance, Raymond was elected President, successfully beating off the challenge of Algernon Cecil by 197 votes to 162. Most undergraduates can find better things to do on long summer evenings than spend them at Union debates, and Raymond's term of office was unremarkable, with most meetings lacklustre and poorly supported. The one high point of the term was the traditionally lighthearted 'Eights Week' debate* held on the motion 'that members of Somerville College and Lady Margaret Hall should be eligible for election to the Union'.† The carnival atmosphere was heightened by the news just in that the British garrison in Mafeking had been relieved after a 217-day siege and the House voted for a message of congratulations to be sent to Major General Baden-Powell for his gallant defence of the town. The presence of women students in the gallery ensured a full house and, according to *Isis*, 'an air of festivity pervaded the society's rooms', with supporters of the motion cheered on and opponents showered with a variety of missiles including crinolines and even pots of marmalade.[40]

Raymond's academic record turned out to be as good as his father's. He was not only awarded a double First in Classics, but went on to gain another in Jurisprudence (Law) in his fifth year, having already won the Ireland, one of the two great Classics prizes for which his father had only managed to be *proxime accessit* (runner-up) as well as the Derby and Eldon scholarships in Law.‡ He capped it all by the ultimate accolade of being elected a fellow of All Souls' College in 1902. When one takes into account that Raymond also played a great deal of sport – he boxed, fenced and played tennis and racquets, besides captaining the College soccer eleven and rowing in the Balliol Eight in Torpids§ – and played a prominent role in the Oxford Union, his academic achievements are truly astonishing.

All Souls', which has no undergraduates, did not require its fellows to reside at the University, so Raymond, after an expedition to Egypt (which he dismissed as a hideous country whose monuments had nothing to commend them but their antiquity),[41] began reading for the Bar at the Inner Temple in the spring of 1901.

---

*Held during the Summer College Head of the River races.

†Although women were allowed to attend lectures they were not eligible to take degrees until the 1920s, when one of the early beneficiaries was Raymond's elder daughter, Helen.

‡It was left to Cys to complete the family hat trick in the University Classic prizes by winning the Hertford.

§The Lent term 'bumping' races. Admittedly Raymond's eight was not very successful, being bumped twice.

6

'Of presidential stock'

T HE REUTERS TAPE carrying news of the relief of Mafeking
reached Winchester at 10.42 p.m. on Friday 17 May, 1900. Within
minutes a patriotic mob had assembled round the Guildhall to sing
Rule Britannia. Oc, who had just turned seventeen and shared none of
his two elder brothers' anti-jingoism, was asleep in his dormitory
when he was awoken by the sound of cheering. Writing to his father
three days later, he gave a graphic account of the celebrations by the
citizens of Winchester:

Another fellow and I affected an escape out of one of our dormitory
windows at the peril of our lives, and after climbing over several gables, at
last reached the ground by the aid of a drain pipe and a pig-tub, without
the least hope of ever being able to get back again.

We reached the Guildhall at about half past 11 and there found a
roaring reeling crowd, most of whom were all already half soused. We
tried to find out whether the news was official, but could obtain no reasonable answer. At last we thought that the least we could do was to make
a sensation in the school, so we got hold of a leader of a gang of roughs,
who were beating tin kettles and tea trays, and told him to lead his men
round to our House. We then shouted to the rest of the crowd, about 250
in number, I should think, to follow. And so we had a kind of triumphal
procession, led by my companion and myself, past all the houses, waking
them all up by the fiendish noises which our crowd emitted. They tried to
batter in the doors of one House, and would have done it if we had not

shouted to them with all our might. At last we got them round to this House, where Trant [the housemaster, the Reverend J. T. Bramston] addressed them from his bedroom windows not dreaming in the least by what agency they had been brought there. My friend and I then managed to climb in unseen.

Yesterday the whole school went up into the town with banners etc. etc. They shouted and sang patriotic songs out of tune, were addressed by the Mayor and generally made a demonstration. When passing the Guildhall again the Mayor tried to make another patriotic speech, but the first seemed to have been quite enough for everyone. He got a very bad time of it, being pelted with a diabolical kind of cracker called a 'go-bag' which goes bang on striking any hard substance. At length he beat a precipitate retreat indoors.

Yesterday night I managed to climb out again with some other men. We went up to the top of St Giles Hill, where there was a bonfire. The crowd, however, had left the bonfire and were swilling down beer, which was being given to them free, in the streets. We took up some rockets, and directed them into the town, which caused a certain amount of consternation. When we were going back through the streets, everything and everyone were in a disgusting state – terribly beery. We got back to bed at 12.45.

Like most Winchester boys, Oc was as overwhelmingly behind the war as the rest of population. Beb's anti-war stance must have strained his popularity to the utmost.

The Boer War was a disaster for the Liberals, causing a split in the Party's Parliamentary ranks every bit as bitter as the one over Ireland which had led to the defection of Joseph Chamberlain's Liberal Unionists. The anti-war faction included Harcourt, Morley and Lloyd George, while the 'patriotic' wing was led by Rosebery, with Grey, Haldane and – somewhat half-heartedly – Asquith in support. Margot was torn between her patriotism and her loyalty to Milner on the one hand, and her admiration for the Boers as sturdy yeoman farmers 'fighting for their national existence' on the other.[1] In November 1899, soon after the outbreak of hostilities, she had accompanied Charty and Ribblesdale to Birkenhead to see off their elder son Tommy Lister, about to embark with his regiment (the 10th Hussars) for South Africa. She was moved to tears as she watched Tommy in his new khaki uniform 'leading his beautiful charger and giving orders to his soldier servants in a vast shed full of horses and soldiers'. Even the usually self-controlled Ribblesdale broke down in his son's arms.*

Although the British forces found themselves outnumbered and outgunned by the irregular Boer forces, the overwhelming majority of the public remained fervently jingoistic. As the tide of the war began to turn, Lord Salisbury's Unionist Government was comfortably returned to power at the 'khaki' General Election opportunistically called in October 1900. The prospects for the divided Liberal Party looked bleak.

The following month personal woes were added to political ones for the Asquiths when Margot's third baby died after five hours of struggle in Wanborough Manor near Guildford, the country home of the Asquiths' friend Sir Algernon West. 'I showed no sort of courage but screamed with agony declaring it could not be true,' the distraught mother wrote to Ettie afterwards. 'Poor Henry, his grief was far the most remarkable thing I ever saw: my doctor and nurse were quite dumb before it and told Lucy they had never seen anything the least like it.' After showing the tiny corpse to his wife, Asquith and Lucy attended 'a touching little funeral' at Wanborough church.[2]

This episode marked a new stage in the gradually improving relations between Margot and Violet. Margot proudly forwarded to Ettie her stepdaughter's letter: 'Violet is 13 and a very susceptible age with a passion for babies and I think it's a remarkable letter, so well thought out and expressed and full of feeling.'[3] The flaw in their relationship had always been that whereas Violet wanted a mother, Margot treated her as a sister. Violet's close relationship with her father helped to compensate for Margot's lack of maternal affection, however, throughout her childhood she clearly tried her best to inspire affection in her stepmother, something Margot came to appreciate as Violet grew older. Yet it was a far from ideal relationship that was bound to be severely tested once a crisis developed in Violet's own life.

Beb had joined Raymond at Balliol for the Michaelmas term of 1900, after the three eldest Asquith boys had spent part of the summer holidays on a climbing expedition in the Swiss Alps organized by 'Trant'. The trip was not a success. Oc, writing home from the Grand Hotel in Zermatt, complained of 'the smallness of pleasure in comparison

---

*Tommy Lister survived the Boer War, only to be killed by Somali tribesmen in 1902.

to footsoreness and the enormous guide's fees', while Raymond, who was feeling thoroughly out of sorts, hardly exchanged a word with his brothers throughout the holiday.[4] He complained to Bluetooth that he was thrown perpetually into deep gloom by the reflection of his nothingness. He had done nothing worth doing, knew nothing worth knowing, felt nothing worth feeling, and was worth nothing. He described mountaineering as altogether the most tedious and painful sport he could imagine. Even the scenery did not match up to Scotland's.[5] There was, so he told Margot, an inflated and almost tin-selly prettiness about it.[6]

Raymond was clearly experiencing the depression from which all of Helen Asquith's children suffered at times of stress in their lives, almost certainly related to the trauma produced by her loss. The previous summer Raymond had learnt of the death of Bluetooth's mother just after his stay in the Lake District, an area that would always evoke happy childhood holidays with his own mother. When he wrote to console his friend, Raymond gave a few rare clues as to how much pain his mother's death had given him, and also the extent to which he had attempted to suppress his grief. The only consolation he could offer was the commonplace plea that time would soon dull the pain of his friend's sorrow. This had been Raymond's own experience when he had lost his mother at the age of twelve. She was, he admitted, the only person he had ever really loved and when she died he had felt that life was not worth living: yet within a couple of months life seemed to get back to normal. He believed that Nature herself provided consolation for the death of someone with whom one is linked by blood rather than choice. While admitting that his efforts to offer solace might appear clumsy, he pleaded that he himself was not good at either receiving or giving sympathy and that he had always preferred to suffer his sorrows in silence. Even for an emotionally inhibited young man – and Raymond was not quite twenty-one at the time – it was an extraordinary belief that one could suffer more from the loss of a close friend than from the death of an adored mother.[7]

Beb cannot have found the holiday an ideal preparation for joining his elder brother at a university where he was bound to feel in his intellectual shadow. Beb was no slouch academically. But he had no desire to be compared unfavourably with Raymond, and almost went out of his way to cultivate a reputation for indolence. Beb became as enthusiastic a member of the Annandale set as Raymond and had soon adopted many of his brother's friends, most notably Aubrey Herbert. He became secretary of the club in 1902 and his 'minutes' of the dinner held that Trinity term give an idea of the goings-on at one of the more innocuous evenings. The meeting coincided with a rival party being held by the Dean in the room below attended by 'a large bevy of ladies', which one of the Scottish members, Mr Baldwin Graham, attempted to drown out with a 'Gaelic lilt'. After dinner, the Annas 'called upon a Mr Beal', as a direct consequence of which the unfortunate Mr Beal's possessions 'fell in value by £25'. Thereafter

> the society embarked on a variety of hazy and romantic adventures under the command of Mr Bill Farrie. The only two events which we [i.e. Beb] can recall in any detail were the shampooing of Mr Tritton's head, who had for some reason been surrounded by a noisy halo at this period of the evening, with Eno's fruit salts, a combination of chemicals which resulted in an immediate explosion: and the gallant attempt of Mr Bill Farmer to secure a death mask off one of the guests [presumably at the Dean's party] with the help of a malleable tin bath. 40 bottles of wine were drunk at the dinner and 9 afterwards.[8]

On another occasion, Beb seems to have been the main mover behind a motion 'that Mr Bonham Carter should appear at every dinner given by the Society during the next year without his trousers; an amendment was also carried, in the interests of sanitation, that the said Mr Bonham Carter should be previously shaved and scented by some competent hairdresser'.

Beb had no intention of matching Raymond in debauchery alone. He knew that he could do so in at least one other field: the Oxford Union. Although his maiden speech – in favour of Home Rule in Ireland – was not a great success (*Isis* criticized 'an extraordinary lux-uriance of repetitive metaphor'[9]), he was given a 'paper' speech the following February (1902) by the new President, Algernon Cecil, who apparently harboured no ill feeling after his defeat by Raymond two terms earlier. The motion – that 'the necessity of conscription is one of the chief lessons of the [Boer] war' – foreshadowed the con-troversy which was to rage at the heart of Asquith's Government in the Great War. Beb followed the proposer, Aubrey Herbert, who, according to *Isis*, 'was lacerated and down-trodden by the massive eloquence of his successor'. Some of the colour of his language can be gleaned from quotations in *Isis* and the *Oxford Magazine*: 'indifferent soldiers were like bad eggs, they did not improve by multiplication', and 'the scum of Whitechapel, conscripted, will hardly be a desirable addition to the life of the regiment'. It was a point of view which his own experience of warfare was to turn on its head.[10]

Beb's 'eloquent defence of sane imperialism'[11] in May 1901 helped secure his election to the Union's Library Committee. His popularity seems to have grown fast and the following term he made the spectacular leap to election as Treasurer on the back of a brilliant speech against the motion that 'any interference with the liberty of the Press would be inexpedient and dangerous'. Here again was an issue that was to rear its head during his father's wartime premiership. Beb's argument that 'liberty was a most dangerous weapon in unscrupulous hands' and about 'the mental dyspepsia of the average newspaper reader' would have appealed to those who vainly tried to persuade Asquith to curb the destructive bile of the Northcliffe press that was ultimately to destroy his Government.[12]

In February 1902 Beb was back on the subject of the Boer War, opposing Aubrey on the motion that the 'opinion expressed by a section of the opposition are to blame for the difficulties of the Government in South Africa and on the Continent'. The laboured wording referred to the split in the Liberal Party in the wake of a speech by Campbell-Bannerman condemning the 'methods of barbarism' employed by the British forces to crush Afrikaner resistance (most notably the world's first civilian 'concentration camps'). Joseph Chamberlain, the Colonial Secretary, blamed the Boers' reluctance to negotiate a surrender on the supposed encouragement they were receiving from the Opposition, in effect lumping all Liberals together to exploit the unpopularity of the anti-war view. The tactic might have been specious, but it proved so successful that a near riot forced Lloyd George to flee a meeting at Birmingham Town Hall by escaping through the cellars disguised as a policeman. Beb, an opponent of the war himself, argued that 'the fact that their champion had a town hall about his ears, and had been obliged to escape through a coal-hole in the guise of a policeman, was not very likely to deceive the Boers as to the sentiments of the majority of Englishmen'. *Isis* gave 'the blue ribbon to Mr H. Asquith (Balliol) for the speech of the evening. Though he spoke for twenty-seven minutes he was never for one moment tedious. He delighted the House with an endless succession of epigrams and antitheses, which Macaulay himself could not have excelled.'[13]

In March Beb was elected Librarian, but the following term he was beaten, like his father and Raymond before him, at his first attempt for the Presidency. For once, his speech – opposing 'a tax on bachelors' – was a flop. But in November, helped by a fierce anti-Government speech more in keeping with his talents, he bounced back to victory, achieving the family treble. At the start of his term as President Beb was given the traditional profile in *Isis*: 'He comes of Presidential stock, and no one who has heard him speak doubts that his success is no greater than he deserves.' The article concluded with perhaps the finest tribute of all from the usually cynical student magazine: 'Wherever he may be, by sea or land, in town or country, his friends wish for no better companion.'[14]

The following year, after gaining a second in 'Greats', Beb followed Raymond to London to read for the Bar.

Margot recovered physically from her latest failed pregnancy remarkably quickly. The mental scars, however, took longer to heal. She remained ill and tearful for weeks afterwards, and in February 1901 it was decided to send her to Switzerland for two months. By March she was walking and skating and generally more cheerful, although she remained frail for many months to come. The family's problems were aggravated when Violet was struck down by infantile paralysis, a condition that was to cripple her for the best part of two years. That November her health suffered a further blow when she developed appendicitis. Appendectomy was then in its infancy and potentially dangerous even for an otherwise healthy patient. The doctors tried everything to avoid the operation, from hot water bottles to a belladonna plaster round her waist. But in the end they had no choice. Mercifully the operation, carried out by the distinguished Scottish surgeon William Cheyne, was a success, although Violet remained too weak even to stand for the best part of a year.

In spite of all the dangers and discomforts, Margot had still not given up the hope of having another child, although it appears that she kept this from husband, who was shocked when in the spring of 1902, while he was staying with Jack and Anne Poynder in Monte

Carlo,* she wrote to say she might be pregnant again. 'I hope the "suspicion" you mention', he replied, 'has not turned out to be well-founded as, like you, I cannot but dread the prospect of your being thrown back again in health, just when you were regaining the old ground: delightful as it would be for Elizabeth not to remain a solitary child.'[15] The 'suspicion' turned out not only to be right, but, on Margot's part, intended. Writing to Curzon that August, she admitted to being not over-hopeful about her prospects, adding that she 'would hardly have dared risk it again except for Elizabeth's sake'. She was being disingenuous, the real reason, as she confessed later, was 'I have a devouring passion for children'[16] – a sentiment unthinkable at the time of her marriage. And on 9 November 1902, three days after Raymond's twenty-fourth birthday, she successfully gave birth to a son. Anthony, as the baby was christened, was soon affectionately dubbed 'Puffin' by Violet thanks to his prominent nose.

Asquith was by now almost completely disillusioned with C.B.'s leadership, even quoting with approval to Margot a letter from Raymond describing a speech the Liberal leader made to the Oxford 'Eighty Club' as dull and feeble; CB never got to the point, Raymond thought, but just rambled round it.[17] C.B.'s 'methods of barbarism' speech against British efforts to crush the Boers, forced the stalwartly patriotic Asquith decisively off the fence and into Rosebery's 'Liberal Imperialist' pro-war camp. The Party's chances of regaining office in the foreseeable future seemed remote when Balfour succeeded his uncle, Lord Salisbury, as Prime Minister in 1902. For the first year of his premiership, as Margot put it, Balfour 'had a stronger hold on the House than Mr. G[ladstone] or Dizzy ever had – a hold not merely on his own men, but on ours – this hold came primarily from charm'.[18]

Meanwhile, the Liberals were perilously close to another split. Rosebery launched 'the Liberal League', caricatured by a cynical Raymond in a letter to Buchan, as appearing to consist of three men, Rosebery himself, Raymond's father, and Grey, backed up by a band of women who reckoned that the snobbery of the lower orders outweighed their greed;[19] but probably intended by its founder as the

---

*Sir John Poynder (1866–1936), Unionist MP for Chippenham 1892–1910. Later he was created Baron Islington and made Governor General of New Zealand. Anne Poynder was one of Margot's closest friends until they fell out when Asquith refused to appoint her husband Viceroy of India in succession to Viscount Hardinge in 1916.

embryo for a new political party. Then, on 15 May 1903, Joseph Chamberlain, the Colonial Secretary, exploded a political bombshell with a speech in Birmingham advocating a system of preferential colonial tariffs. Margot has described how the following morning her husband came into her bedroom brandishing a report of the speech in *The Times*. '"Wonderful news today," he said, "and it is only a question of time when we shall sweep the country." '[20] Chamberlain had picked the one issue guaranteed to split the Unionists and unite the Liberals in the defence of 'Free Trade'. The topic was tailor-made for Asquith and for the next few months he shadowed Chamberlain's every speech, systematically tearing his argument to shreds. The Liberals were on the march again. By the summer of 1905, with a General Election now imminent, the Party was on the crest of a wave and it was clear that the man who had put them there was not their leader, Campbell-Bannerman, but his deputy, Asquith.*

The imminent prospect of the Liberals regaining office and the likelihood that sooner or later Asquith would become Prime Minister inevitably cast the spotlight on Margot's suitability as a Prime Ministerial consort. It was a prospect viewed with trepidation in royal circles where her loose tongue and ever-ready quips had the potential to become a serious embarrassment to her studiously diplomatic husband. An incident at a reception in November 1905 held at Windsor Castle for the King of Greece, and shamelessly described by Margot in her diary, reinforces the point. The trouble started when Margot spotted Queen Alexandra chatting to Lord Halsbury, the octogenarian Tory Lord Chancellor: 'very short and bow legged and comic', as Margot put it, but nonetheless one of the all-time giants of the English legal system. Afterwards, she could not resist telling the Queen (who 'giggled like a little child') that together they looked like 'Beauty and the Beast'. Unfortunately, Halsbury's 'narrow, hard featured second wife' overheard the remark. When

---

*One person Asquith failed to convince was Margot's father, a diehard Protectionist. 'I had a long letter from the Bart (after a long silence) – quite friendly in tone, but giving me a few "facts" as to the terrible case of his own trades,' Asquith wrote to Margot on 30 November 1903. 'I have sent him a polite answer, but of course telling him that the proposed "remedies" would make everything that is bad worse and everything that is good bad . . . I hope he won't try to continue the controversy.'

later on she and Margot found themselves next to each other, 'She gazed at me with her head in the air in so marked a manner that I thought my tiara must have got on one side, so I said quite simply: "What are you looking at?" To which she replied in a glacial voice, moving her skirts slightly away from me: "I would really rather not speak to you, Mrs Asquith. I heard what you said to the Queen about my husband." '

Margot travelled back in the train to London with St John Brodrick (a former Soul who was now Minister of War) and his wife, Alfred and DD Lyttelton and Gerald Balfour (Arthur's brother) and his wife, Betty, all of whom were good friends and were 'convulsed with the story'.[21] Even so, the incident should have taught Margot a lesson. Needless to say, it did nothing of the kind.

*

When Oc left school, instead of following his father and brothers to Balliol, he opted for Winchester's sister foundation, New College, where he won an Exhibition to read Classics, going up in the Michaelmas Term of 1902. However, the attractions of Varsity life had little appeal for him: he was not interested in the Union and not much more in his degree course, nor had he his elder brothers' enthusiasm for tomfoolery, pranks and riotous drinking. In December 1903 he informed Violet that he had 'suddenly and sadly realised that I have just 3 months in which to make up for a year of idleness. And though I'm afraid I have no ambition to do well in my Exam in March (for it does not interest me), I think Father would probably be rather bored if I did disgracefully badly.'[22]

Violet at the time was attending a finishing school in Dresden with a group of girlfriends. The lovely Saxon capital, which a generation earlier Margot had found devoid of compatriots, had now become a fashionable playground for Edwardian English upper-class youth. Beb and Oc naturally leapt at the opportunity of joining their sister and her pretty companions during the Christmas vacation. Among Violet's group of friends were Mary Vesey, who was later to marry Aubrey Herbert, and her cousin, Cynthia Charteris, then seventeen years old (the same age as Violet), green-eyed and auburn-haired and destined to become one of the great beauties of her generation, painted many times by, among others, Sargent and Augustus John. Cynthia was the granddaughter of the diehard Tory peer, the Earl of

Wemyss. Her mother was Margot's fellow Soul, Balfour's confidante Lady (Mary) Elcho. Although the ancient and notoriously snobbish Charteris family would have hated being compared to the comparatively *nouveaux riches* Tennants, Cynthia's anarchic upbringing at Stanway, the family's medieval mansion in north Gloucestershire, had much in common with Margot's childhood at Glen. Stanway was – as Cynthia herself dubbed it – 'Liberty Hall to children and dogs'. The tomboyish Cynthia readily competed with her brothers at practical jokes and cricket as well as tree climbing. She also shared Margot's love of foxhunting, which she called 'sheer ecstasy'. And, like Margot, Cynthia had had little formal education (apart from a few weekly lessons at Cheltenham Ladies College); since the age of ten she had been tutored by 'Squidge' ('a dear, bird-witted Viennese')[23] who allowed her to run wild. Although Cynthia could not match Margot's musical talents, she also caught the Wagner bug, later recalling those 'eight rapturous weeks in Dresden, where life was one long intoxicating Wagnerian dream'.

Cynthia's first encounter with Beb was more a scene from a Tchaikovsky ballet than a Wagner opera. Sitting quietly beside a frozen lake, 'reclined in a carved and painted chair, constructed in the image of Lohengrin's swan, I suddenly found myself being propelled over the frozen waters by a tall young man on skates. Not a single word did he say, and it was not for me to break the silence, but I remember a sense of momentousness out of all proportion to the event.'[24] Although Beb was immediately smitten, Cynthia fell for his younger brother.[25] Oc's affections, however, were already strongly engaged elsewhere: with Molly, the eldest daughter of Hoppy and Con Manners, Margot's longstanding hunting companions.

Oc was sufficiently invigorated by his stay in Dresden to put in a last-minute spurt of study which proved enough to secure him a respectable Second in his 'Mods' exams at the end of the Hilary term 1904. However, after thus saving his father from 'boredom', he insisted on abandoning the rest of his Classics degree course. The big question now was what he was to do next. With few ideas except a vague notion of going into business, he even resorted to asking Violet to poll their friends for suggestions.

That summer Oc's great love, Molly Manners, became ill and died at the age of seventeen while on holiday in India. He was devastated: 'her companionship and friendship and the thought of her meant more than any I have ever known before or since,' he was to write in

his diary two years later.[26] Another brief reference to Molly is followed by three pages that have been ripped out. There is no doubt he
mourned Molly long and deeply.

Molly had also been close to Violet – indeed she was her first close
friend. In the circumstances, the Asquiths decided to send Oc and
his sister to Paris together in October for five months to improve
their French, which would be useful if Oc decided to go into com-
merce. In any case, the trip would give him a breathing space to get
over Molly's death before deciding on a career. For Violet, this was
her first thrilling taste of freedom – and in Paris, in the company of
her favourite brother: 'with whom Siberia would be Elysium', as she
wrote on the second page of the diary she had just begun.[27] Oc and
Violet rented a flat in the Rue Gay-Lussac off the Boulevard St
Michel in the Latin Quarter, conveniently close to the Sorbonne
where they attended lectures. 'This is far and away the most beautiful
town I've ever seen,' she recorded. 'I love the great open places (like
the Place de la Concorde) surrounded by fine buildings and monuments and flooded by light and air and sun.'[28] Her admiration for her
brother was boundless: 'I think for sane, sound judgement and level-
headedness Oc surpasses anyone I've ever met. He has the rare
faculty of cutting himself and his personal prejudices loose and of
looking on any question however near it may be to him, however
entangled with his wishes, his hopes or his fears – with as much coolness and impartiality as if he had been the man in the moon.'[29]

In March 1905 Violet and Oc spent three weeks in Italy seeing the
sights of Genoa, Pisa and Florence before returning to Paris for
Violet's eighteenth birthday on 5 April. After a disastrous family
holiday with their father, Raymond and Cys in Dinard, the pair
rounded off their trip in style staying with Margot and Elizabeth at
the Paris Ritz, the object of the exercise being to buy clothes for
Violet's first London 'season'.

Margot herself was in cracking form, having spent the winter
hunting in Leicestershire. This was perhaps the last period in her life
when she was really happy. The Manners had given up Cold Overton
and taken a much smaller house in Oakham, where there was no
room for Margot and her family. Another friend, Lady Angela
Forbes (the mistress of Cynthia's father, Lord Elcho), stepped into
the breach and agreed to share her own 'tiny' house in Manton with
Margot, her children and Elizabeth's much-loved German governess, Anne Heinsius (affectionately known as 'Frau'). 'I don't suppose

I shall ever spend a more peaceful winter than this,' Margot recorded at the beginning of a new 'Children's Diary'.[30] She took Elizabeth hunting for the first time and was delighted with the ease with which she jumped the fences and ditches. Margot herself, Lady Angela noted, 'still went very well . . . except possibly that she rode a little too fast at her fences'. It was the story of her life. Asquith came down at weekends and, according to his hostess, 'never talked his shop, but listened to our description of a day's sport, and asked endless questions on the subject . . . He didn't know one end of a horse from the other, so it must have been pure kindness on his part.'[31]

In Paris Margot thoroughly enjoyed Violet's company, remarking on how, despite suffering from severe toothache and so having every excuse to be grumpy, 'she was sweet with my *vendeuses* and shop people. She has naturally good manners coming from a warm heart and sensitive nature.'[32] Violet's presentation at Court had to be delayed until 2 June. Margot made her practise her curtseys in front of the nursery rocking horse: 'too jerky and spasmodic', she commented and then 'lowered herself slowly with a melting look'.[33] The long wait to be presented at Buckingham Palace, cooped up with nervous debutantes and their fussing mothers, might have been tedious, but not with Margot. None of the Asquiths had much respect for Court etiquette or the Royal Family: 'kindly louts' was how Asquith dubbed them, while Margot regarded them as 'stodgy fluent people who scatter my brain like a kaleidoscope'.[34] She now selected a vantage point with a good view of the King and Queen where she and Violet 'watched strings and strings of people making the <u>most</u> comic curtseys – the heavy chin-scoops and projecting backs and extreme archness of most of them made us shake with laughter – we became quite hysterical when a lady in feathers diamonds and a <u>flowing</u> beard came through'.[35]

Violet's season opened on 22 May with a ball given by Margot and the Bart for Violet herself and his granddaughter, Frances Tennant (Frank's daughter), Sir Charles generously presenting each girl with a diamond necklace for the occasion. Afterwards Violet had only the haziest recollection of her dancing partners: 'in the intervals of being whirled giddily round by a young man who was new every 5 minutes'. The one young man whom she did remember meeting was Archie Gordon, the twenty-one-year-old youngest son of the seventh Earl of Aberdeen who was now up at Balliol and who sat next to her at dinner. She considered him very attractive and easy to get on with, even though his 'knees coil round one valsing rather too much but this is a detail'.[36]

The rest of the summer passed in an exhausting whirl of dinners, dances and balls, the Eton versus Winchester cricket match, racing at Ascot and Violet's first dinner at the House of Commons, hosted by Haldane. Violet rapidly found herself at the centre of a circle of young men, mostly friends of her brothers or the sons of her parents' friends. These included several Balliol contemporaries of Beb and Raymond, including Arnold Ward, Hugh Godley, Bongie Bonham Carter, Aubrey Herbert and his younger brother, Mervyn. Then there was Bluetooth Baker, now very much a friend of the whole family and, of course, Archie Gordon and later other younger men: Edward Horner (brother of Katharine), Cynthia Charteris's brothers, Ego and Guy, Ettie Desborough's two wild sons, Billy and Julian Grenfell, the Ribblesdales' surviving son, Charles Lister and the Manners' son, John. Here was the male core of the social set who would soon become known as the 'corrupt coterie'. Few would survive the Great War.

Margot was fascinated and slightly baffled by Violet's social success, and at the same time disapproved of a life devoid of any serious purpose, writing in her journal:

> Violet is not pretty but every-one is in love with her. I never saw a more conspicuous instance of how little beauty matters than in Violet. She is not even very soignee or prettily arranged. She has very dirty, untidy ribbons and waistbelts half below her sash, her shirts crooked, her cuffs and collars never really nice (like I had at her age – I was always most particular and neat), very little natural taste; but somehow her wits and vitality, her wonderful manners, keenness and sweetness of nature all triumph over torn and dirty clothes, not a very good complexion and not pretty teeth, just as if they were unnoticeable trifles. She has lovely hair and a pretty figure and looks very much prettier in the country.
>
> What Violet has really got is brains and kindness – the right things appeal to her but she has an insatiable love of pure amusement. I never saw a clever, highly intelligent girl so unable to spend an evening in London – however tired she was or crushingly hot – but it was without some form of entertainment.[37]

Violet loved being at the centre of so much male attention: 'every dance I longed to be with 3 different people', she wrote after one ball. 'I can see no horizon to my powers of loving – and the more friends I have the more I am capable of giving to each.'[38] It was all very Margotesque. The problem, as her stepmother had discovered during her own youth, was that some of the men with whom Violet so enjoyed flirting had much stronger feelings about her: Arnold Ward, a fellow barrister and contemporary of Raymond (and later Tory MP for West Hertfordshire), was clearly besotted and would regularly get moody and jealous when Violet's attentions were engaged elsewhere. When Archie Gordon asked her for eight dances at the New College Commem Ball and then took her off for a long talk by the College chapel until sunrise, it dawned on her that he was not just 'an unselfish and energetic youth discharging a duty towards his "party"'.[39]

Violet gleefully recorded how after one ball Beb and Oc grabbed Arnold and 'slung him up kicking and struggling in their arms and carried him down the street', as the other guests looked on cheering. Afterwards the three of them walked home with Violet and Archie, but calm did not last long and Violet recalled 'the last sight I saw was Archie up a lamp-post at the corner of Cavendish Square and Arnold tie-less at the bottom reproving him. The boys were in such high spirits that Beb snatched the electric light globes off the nursery landing and sent them crashing down the stairs! Silly boy!'[40]

In December 1905 Violet and Beb were invited to stay at Haddo, the Aberdeens' Scottish seat. They knew they had to be on their best behaviour with Archie's good-natured but formidable mother, though Archie himself was on tenterhooks about what Beb, the eternal joker, would get up to. 'If either Beb or I had flinched at holy water we should have had a very bad time, for prayers went on intermittently during most of the day,' Violet wrote to Hugh Godley. 'Archie seemed a good deal relieved at Beb and I behaving so orthodoxly and well.' Nonetheless, Beb could not resist – to his sister's mortification – pinching Archie's calves at dinner, prompting Lady Aberdeen to lean forward and ask: 'What are you giggling about Archie?' By the time hymns were sung after dinner, Violet admitted: 'I dared not look at Beb for fear of losing my composure.'[41]

Raymond was by now an aloof figure to all his younger siblings. Cys was later to recall how it was not 'easy to forget the expression of nausea with which, having risen courteously in an ill-lit room to welcome what he [Raymond] supposed to be a stranger, he discovered

that he had been unwittingly polite to his brother Arthur [Oc]'.* The
age gap with Violet – eight and a half years – was that much bigger and
Raymond seems to have made little effort to get to know her. On one
of the rare occasions when neither Beb nor Oc was on hand to see
Violet home from a party, Margot rashly entrusted her stepdaughter
to Raymond, only for him to push off early without even telling her he
was leaving. Although Violet was able to cadge a lift with Frances
Horner, she had no latch key and broke her nails trying to wrest a
piece of stone from the pavement to hurl at one of her brothers'
windows. In the end she had to ring the doorbell and rouse a sleepy
and dishevelled footman from his hard-earned sleep.

The truth was that Raymond never much liked London society.
He confessed to Aubrey that there were half a dozen women and
perhaps a dozen men whose company he enjoyed, but he found
intolerable the myriad of insincere conventions and pompous
restrictions with which one had to contend, to say nothing of twittering women and vacuous men. He was no more enamoured of the
Bar. Writing from his dingy chambers whose windows were
encrusted with pigeon droppings, he described his fellow lawyers as
hundreds of tedious men, as like real men as a pianola was to a piano,
reading dust-covered books reeking of decay, which were as like real
books as a beetle was to a butterfly.[42]

Raymond had by now fallen passionately in love with a young
woman very different from the 'twittering' debutantes: Katharine
Horner, the younger daughter of his parents' friends, Sir John and
Lady (Frances) Horner. He had first met her at Mells in the summer
of 1900, when she was fifteen years old. But at the time he had been
more struck by the beauty of her elder sister, Cicely; however, the
following year, when he saw the sisters again at Clovelly, the home of
Con Manners' sister, Christine Hamlyn, it was Katharine who
attracted him the more. He described her to Bluetooth as having a
broad low brow, a charming voice and lively eyes. He thought her
very clever and was impressed both by her knowledge and instinctively sharp mind. Katharine's gentleness and her quiet and thought-

---

*To be fair, Cys went on: 'Notwithstanding their cool and casual contacts, the family as
a whole were united by a powerful freemasonry, and its members would even on occasion furtively fight each other's battles: but a horror of emotional nudism led them to
clothe their mutual appreciation with a semblance of judicial indifference, and to deny it
all ordinary expression.' (Spender and Asquith, II, pp. 222–3)

ful intelligence may well have reminded Raymond of his dead mother, to whom she bore a striking physical resemblance.

Raymond's admiration for Katharine grew steadily into love and by the summer of 1904 she can have had no doubt about the strength of his feelings when he told her how he would give her not just the whole world if it were his, but the sun, the moon and the stars. He told Con Manners that Katharine had eyes capable of pulling a limpet off a rock or deadening the conscience of an archangel.[43] Raymond's correspondence with Aubrey Herbert suggests that he was almost as inexperienced with women as Katharine was with men – she was his first and, as it turned out, his only real love. He was perpetually belittling himself to her: thus his clumsy behaviour towards her at some ball left him moody and angry. He thought she must be almost ashamed to be loved by such a feckless, clumsy oaf, his sole defence being that never before had he much inclination to have a solitary talk with a woman, so he had never learnt any tricks.[44] And in spite of all his achievements, intellectual and social, Raymond was extraordinarily sensitive about his perceived social inferiority to the aristocratic Horners, calling himself a middle-class charlatan full of fraudulent pride.[45]

On 4 December 1905 Balfour caught the political world by surprise when, instead of calling the expected General Election, he abruptly resigned, thus forcing C.B. to attempt to form a minority caretaker Government. It was a clever ploy which the Unionist Prime Minister hoped would expose the divisions in the Liberals' own ranks, where it was well known that many senior figures were profoundly dissatisfied with their leader. The move caught Asquith, Haldane and Grey on the wrong foot. The previous September the three men had met at Relugas, a fishing lodge on the River Findhorn in Scotland's Grampian region, and had agreed that they would all refuse to serve in a C.B. Government unless he consented to go to the House of Lords and allow Asquith to lead the Government in the House of Commons as well as giving him the Exchequer, while Haldane would become Lord Chancellor and Grey Foreign Secretary.

However, Balfour's ruse meant that instead of being in a position to dictate terms to a Liberal Prime Minister with a large Liberal majority behind him, the three men risked splitting the Party and jeopardizing its election prospects. When C.B. called their bluff and refused to become a Lord, what had seemed such an excellent idea in the autumn glow of a remote Scottish fishing lodge, began to look like a shabby plot to put pressure on an old man at the moment of his greatest triumph. Asquith, always the Party loyalist, was ready to give way rather than wreck the Party's chances of winning the coming election, particularly as C.B had always intended to make him Chancellor of the Exchequer; however, it took all his powers of persuasion – and enormous pressure from other senior figures in the Party – before his two friends agreed to serve In the end, although Grey did go to the Foreign Office, Haldane had to accept the Ministry of War and not the Woolsack.

Balfour's gamble had backfired and the Liberals were able to march into the coming election strong and united, routing the disunited Unionists, who lost over 200 seats and were reduced to a rump of 157 MPs. Asquith's own campaign in Fife saw the political blooding of Violet: 'her excellent manners, and her almost Ettie-like faculty of persuading people that they interest her intensely, are very useful', her proud father reported back to Margot.[46]

The sacrifice of Asquith's lucrative legal practice for the more modest salary of a Cabinet Minister finally made Margot decide to give up hunting after a last season with the Manners in Leicestershire. She compared the rupture to the abrupt end of a love affair, but was equally upset about sacrificing what she called her 'peaceful cottage life' with Hoppy and Con at Manton, which had been so much part of her winter routine for two decades. When Margot returned to London on the evening of 31 March after her final outing in pursuit of a fox, Asquith met her with the news that her father was seriously ill. He died nine weeks later. The trauma of the occasion was aggravated by the Bart's will, when his children were astonished to discover just how rich he had been. Margot and her sisters already knew they would be getting nothing further, but were still shocked to learn that their brothers Jack and Eddy had each been bequeathed sufficient capital to give them an income of £40,000 a year, with Eddy, the elder son, inheriting the Glen estate and an income of £80,000 per annum. Margot wrote in her diary: 'I confess without bitterness of any sort that I think papa made a mistake,' commenting 'my brothers have not the size or scope or ease to spend such fortunes – £5,000 a year less to each would have been <u>quite</u> unfelt by any of them and just made the difference to the 3 girls.'[47]

Margot's horses were sold at Tattersalls just two days before the will was read. Her brothers, although generous with their hospitality and presents, refused even to pay for the upkeep of a horse. Their stinginess was to become a lasting source of resentment as her own financial situation deteriorated, particularly as Eddy was to be given Cabinet office and a peerage by her husband. The first Lord Glenconner's very moderate abilities would never have earned him a senior ministerial post under any other Prime Minister, and his barony would have proved very costly indeed if he had had to wait to purchase it from Lloyd George.

What made the perversity of the her father's will especially galling was that, at the age of forty-two, Margot was pregnant again and wondering how they were going to cope with the expense of an eighth child.

7

'How dare you become Prime Minister when I'm away'

———————◆———————

IN 1905, AFTER MUCH dithering about what career to pursue, Oc applied for a post in the newly established colonial service in the Sudan and returned to Oxford to study Arabic, a requirement for the entrance exam. In August his father wrote to tell Margot, 'Oc was one of 12 selected from about 130 candidates, at least 100 of whom were well up to the mark.'[1] There followed a year's special course at the University in book-keeping, surveying and first-aid, as well as more Arabic.

An Anglo-Egyptian Condominium in the Sudan had been established in the wake of General Kitchener's defeat of the Dervish forces of the Mahdi in 1898. A couple of years later Lord Cromer, the British agent in Egypt, laid the foundations for a civilian administration of the territory, setting out to recruit 'active young men endowed with good health, high character and fair abilities' to run it.[2] The first six recruits arrived from England in 1901 and by 1905 there were fifteen civilian inspectors, who formed the nucleus of what was to become the 'Sudan Political Service', one of the elite administrations of the British Empire. The intake comprised mainly Oxford and Cambridge graduates with a strong bias towards the sporting types best suited to survive the rigours of the tropics and most likely to appreciate the limited range of amusements available, which consisted mainly of riding, shooting and polo. The racially diverse Sudan was soon dubbed 'the land of Blacks, Browns and Blues'.

Oc divided his final summer holidays in 1906 between Clovelly, the north Devon village owned by Christine Hamlyn, sister of Con Manners, 'where life tastes of fresh milk and smells of hay', and 'days of energy and air at Rothes' on the River Spey in Scotland's Grampian region, where the Asquiths had taken a house for the summer. There he spent 'long hours in the butts with drowsy spells of sunshine lying over the sweeps of the far flung moor and the far seen sea, in one's ears the soft rumble of carts carrying peat and in one's nostrils the fragrance of the warm heather'.[3]

It would be eighteen months before he would be entitled to any home leave and, his departure was bound be emotional, even if, in true Asquithian fashion, most feelings were left unspoken. 'I simply daren't think of Oc's going away on the 26 August,' Violet wrote to Hugh Godley a fortnight before her brother was due to leave. 'He feels to me at this moment quite, quite indispensable.' When the time came to say goodbye she called it 'one of the acutest physical wrenches I've ever had'.[4] Oc himself later described in his diary the three worst moments of his departure from Rothes:

> First when Violet gave me a hug in her bedroom on Friday evening and broke down entirely: then shaking hands with Father in the hall after lunch – we had had a little talk in the billiard room before, neither of us venturing beyond money matters and banalities: he had to go off and play golf with Algy West, so he said he could not come to see me off and he was nearly crying. Finally, Margot, Violet and Elizabeth hugged me passionately and tearfully, and I should have choked before I saw their backs huddling away in the sunshine if Violet had not been very brave and cold and stiff.[5]

Margot recorded how her stepson 'felt his going very much and had tears in his eyes'. She loved his 'rare and very lovely nature. He is sound and manly, very kind and straight and most capable. I think more capable than any of the family. He has not such fine brains, but a much better head. He never forgets and has rare powers of organisation.'[6]

Oc bade a final goodbye to Violet and Margot at Elgin railway station. Margot gave him a diamond 'M' to remind him of Molly Manners, his father a government despatch case, Violet a rug, Elizabeth a writing case and a blue sponge bag, and Puffin (or rather, Margot on his behalf) a photograph of himself and a lock of his hair in a little mulberry morocco case. Beb, generous and impractical as ever, presented his brother with an ornate silver inkpot: 'a fit wedding-gift for the inhabitant of a Louis XV boudoir', Oc wryly observed, 'but utterly unsuited to the vagrant life of an Empire-building cadet!'.[7]

After a quick visit to Cavendish Square, Oc travelled to say goodbye to the Manners family and Cynthia Charteris, who was staying with them at Avon Tyrrell, their house near Christchurch on the Hampshire coast. In its way, this leave-taking was as emotionally charged for Oc as his farewell to his own family. Con had come to know the Asquith children through Margot and, for Oc in particular, had become as important a maternal figure in his life as she had been for his stepmother. The relationship had been cemented by shared grief over the death of Con's daughter, Molly who, everyone had assumed, would one day become Oc's wife. 'Con has been my mother for six years, as well as being Moll's,' he wrote in his diary. He was annoyed to be 'tactfully left with Cynthia for a starlight walk when I was panting for an intimate talk with Con, or an educational discourse with Bet' (one of Molly's younger twin sisters). Con was aware of Cynthia's fondness for Oc and wrongly assumed that, after Molly's death, her feelings were reciprocated, whereas, although he found Cynthia 'intelligent, kindhearted, <u>very</u> pretty', he was 'not <u>really</u> very fond of her and she is in quite a different category of my friends to that of the Manners family. She is prose and they are poetry.'[8]

The following evening it was Katharine Horner's turn for a final sunset walk with Oc. This time he was happy to be left *à deux* as it gave him the chance to reminisce about Molly. He had 'always been faintly jealous of her [Katharine] as the intimate confidante of all her [Molly's] secrets, whereas for me she was then and is now mainly "*la vague elle de tous les volumes de vers*" as Flaubert says'. He pictured Molly 'in a sunbonnet running up the steps that lead into the hall at Clovelly to welcome me when I arrived and again at Mouth Mill in a sponge bag bathing cap, swimming out to sea with me – turning her head with a smile full of joie-de-vivre as a sunlit sea, and stretching out her hand to shake mine'.[9]

When Oc returned to Cavendish Square he found letters from his father and Margot waiting for him. Asquith's letter, posted from Rothes and dated 11 September, neatly encapsulates his austere yet close relationship with the son who, he privately admitted, was his favourite:

My dear Oc,

Just a line to tell you how much we are all missing you, and wishing you every kind of luck and happiness in your work and life.

I have always had and have the most perfect confidence in you.

Ever your loving Father.[10]

Margot's letter, posted from Rothes the same day as her husband's, was much more emotional, but in the end she was most concerned with the effect of Oc's departure on herself and her children:

My darling boy,

It was with a very sad heart I left you at the station for what seems such a long time. Partings when one is very young are less severe – human nature is recuperative and a life together in the country can always make things gay, but I am never [gay] and have suffered a great deal in my life. Posie, Laura and my mother died with my arms round them and Jack's first wife, Helen had a most tragic death in St. Moritz with me. I rather feel with George Eliot that in every parting there is a shadow of death. Little Elizabeth's eyelashes have clotted with tears tho' she was sound asleep when I got to bed – she feels things <u>very</u> deeply.

. . . If anything happens to me at the end of December or early January, I trust to you more than to any one after your father to look after the children. I think you would see that Elizabeth's many love affairs which she is sure to have shall be guarded and watched – she is reasonable and with tact and sympathy would give up a silly thing. She has not got Violet's cool head and steady heart and is more likely to get into trouble I think. Puffin only wants his nerves guarded. He doesn't want noise.[11]

Margot's choice of 'December or early January' was, as it turned out, eerily prophetic. The baby was not due until the end of February. There was another reason why her thoughts turned so easily to death: her sister Charty had recently been diagnosed as having tuberculosis.

It was a very sad Oc who caught the P & O Express that left Victoria Station at 11 a.m. on 13 September 1906 for the first stage of his journey to a remote outpost of the Empire. He was only twenty-three years old, but far from looking forward to the future, his thoughts were overwhelmingly in the past. Margot's parting quotation from George Eliot kept coming back into his mind as he thought of her 'with her unborn child and the certainty of change. Marriages and the dissolution of our home circle are at any rate inevitable.' His mind went back to his last Channel crossing, nearly two years earlier, with Violet on their way to Paris soon after Molly's death, as his thoughts turned towards Molly's younger sister: 'I thought I saw for the first time a glimmering of emotion in Betty's lovely passionless eyes as we shook hands for the last time and the train moved away.'[12]

Oc's mood perked up when he reached Marseilles on 14 September and boarded the SS *Arabia* bound for Egypt. There was a telegram from Violet awaiting him and now he had the companionship of his seven fellow recruits to the Sudan civil service, one of whom, Thomas Leach, was a fellow Wykehamist.* 'They are good fellows all of them,' he noted in his diary, but he was disappointed to see 'nothing subtle, speculative or very *sympathique* about them'. The exception was Colin Scott-Moncrieff, who became his main companion during the voyage across the Mediterranean, which they whiled away in long discussions on such abstruse subjects as whether they would be prepared to be martyred if forced to become a 'Mohommedan at the point of a sword'. Scott-Moncrieff hoped he would be brave enough to choose martyrdom rather than apostasy,[†] while Oc said, 'I don't think I should be a martyr except before a gallery of women!'[13]

After being 'beset by villains crying "cigars, cigarettes, smutty photographs"' at Port Said, Oc found Cairo more to his taste, recording: 'what I liked best was Old Cairo, and the bazaars; but it is a bore having to pocket one's nose when seeing the best sights'. He and his new colleagues were put up at the celebrated Shepheard's Hotel, from where he tracked down Fanous, a Coptic friend from New College. Fanous took Oc, Scott-Moncrieff and Leach to see the Pyramids, now spectacularly silhouetted in the seasonal floods. The youthful visitors were far from overawed: 'We all went shrieking and howling and racing and roaring with laughter into the chamber of the Princess – with a mob of Arabs accompanying us as pleased as small children by our indecorous hilarity.'[14] In Khartoum, Oc and Leach

---

*Leach remained in the Sudan Political Service and in 1925 was appointed Governor of Halfa province.
†Scott-Moncrieff was not to be given the choice: in 1908, when he was Inspector of the Gezira region, he and his Egyptian assistant were murdered by a disgruntled ex-Mahdist.

were billeted in the government bungalow of the Civil Secretary, Major Phipps, where they 'had the bath of a lifetime and slept in the cool air of the verandah on stationary beds'.[15] There was an affectionate letter from Betty Manners:

> My dearest Arthur,
>
> I have been miserable ever since you left thinking <u>how</u> I wasted those few precious minutes that I had with you by talking about silly Archie Gordon, when there are such <u>thousands</u> of things that I longed to say and do long [sic] – I knew that both of us were on the verge of breaking down and somehow it has become so part of our daily life to dread tears that we all of us waste <u>precious</u> opportunities that may never come again by such futility. I am weeping as I write when I think of all the love and tenderness and fun that has gone out of our <u>daily</u> life with you.
>
> Love your <u>loving</u> Betty

Oc carefully copied her words out into his journal, commenting: 'I don't know whether to pity myself at being such as to receive such words of endearment from a girl who is not in love with me – till I remember what a <u>child</u> dear Bet is in some worldly ways: and that the words she uses to express her affection mean no more than the same words would mean from a child of ten.'[16] The following pages in his journal have been cut out. On his long journey from Cairo to Khartoum, he confessed to longing for Betty to be 'sharing the sensations'. This apparently innocent admission is followed by a reference to 'my folly and infidelity' after which two more pages have been ripped out.[17] He was already torn between his love for the dead Molly and the stirring of feelings for her younger sister.

The following morning a pair of servants appeared, one wearing a tarboush and the other a turban. The two young Englishmen made them toss a coin for masters and the tarboush won Oc who, a few days later, was pleased to note that 'he has turned out very well so far – though his first acts showed a tendency towards extravagance'.[18] Extravagance was one thing he wanted avoid. He was determined to live on his salary of £420 a year (rising by £60 after two years) and asked his father to pay three-quarters of his allowance into his bank in London. He boasted to Violet that he was 'a rich man now – a prospective horse owner', while reminding her that her tuppeny ha'penny stamp was a needless extravagance as the imperial postal rate was only a penny.[19]

The day started at seven o'clock for the new 'deputy inspectors', as they were now grandly known, with an hour's drill as part of their training for police work and to teach them the native words of command. Afterwards Oc and Leach were assigned to the secretariat of the Governor of Khartoum province. There should have been plenty to do in the Governor's office: 'everything of interest passes thro' it, boundary disputes, explorers' reports, and scandals of all sorts', Oc told Violet. However, when their boss, Major Phipps was away they would 'sit and yawn from 9 – 2.45 every morning'. Phipps' absences were frequent, since he had to make tours of inspection in the interior, so they spent a lot of time suffering what Oc called 'the contagion of mental flatness and lethargy'. The unpleasant summer climate of 'thunderstorms, damp oppressive heat and "huboobs" i.e. sandstorms' and the constant threat of fever or dysentery all conspired to aggravate his 'grumbling mood'.[20]

The 'suckling deputy inspectors', as Oc called himself and his colleagues, were 'regarded individually with tolerance, but collectively with disapproval'.[21] Oc disliked 'the rough-tongued, heavy handed martinet military types' who dominated the administration, and was bored by Phipps, whose house he shared and whose lengthy monologues at dinner he compared to 'the Khartoum golf-course, long and flat and sandy: and one is often inclined to break one's clubs across one's knee in the bunkers of his self-complacency'.[22] Khartoum, he complained to his father, was 'hideously European, crammed with Government officials and Greeks' and 'a preserve for the middle-aged and married'. He was scornful about a levee held by the 'Sirdar' (Governor General), Sir Reginald Wingate, to mark the Moslem feast of Bairam:

> to see officials dressed in black frock coat and red tarboush riding in state on donkeys to the Palace gates was very ludicrous. In the afternoon we went over to Omdurman to see the Sirdar distribute money to the wives of Sudanese soldiers, and grain to the poorest women of the town. These last crouched in circles and kept up a twittering chorus of animal gratification – spurred on by sedulous officials whenever they showed signs of flagging: the squat Sirdar and his staff strolled from group to group, majestic as gods.

Oc was equally cynical about colonial social life, describing a dance as: 'ten English women, and about thirty English officers looking absurdly like the male chorus that comes rollicking onto the musical comedy stage in white Eton jackets'.[23]

Fortunately there were more agreeable diversions: Oc acquired 'a most promising little native bred pony' for £11 and spent 'a good deal of time trying to educate and fatten it'.* He and three companions made use of a couple of days' holiday at Bairam to go on an expedition to shoot gazelle. Their journey took them past the battlefield where Kitchener had defeated the Mahdi eight years earlier and, as he told his father, 'we passed the graves of the 21st Lancers, and rode through the "Khor" which was such a trap to them'.[†24]

In December Oc and Leach escaped Khartoum for the cooler climate of Omdurman on the opposite bank of the Nile. 'Six miles of straggling mud-huts, only three European houses, gum, donkey and camel markets, bazaars of the various crafts and nothing but natives.'[25] Although only a few minutes' journey by steam-ferry separated them, the two cities were divided by 'centuries of time', according to a fellow deputy inspector:

> Omdurman was as African as Khartoum was European. The steep riverbank of Khartoum, crowned with bungalows and luxuriant gardens, was replaced in Omdurman by a sloping, stony foreshore on which were heaps of gum, dura and hides, and all the busy commerce of a thriving population. The greenery of Khartoum contrasted vividly with the treeless, sandy streets and the arid compounds of Omdurman. The carefully planned alignment of the broad Khartoum streets presented a very different spectacle from the maze of little alleys and by-ways which seemed to start from nowhere and lead nowhere. In Omdurman, instead of the spacious shops of the European merchants, were the booths and mud stores of an African market, lit by oil lamps or candles.[26]

---

*Oc became very fond of this tough little beast, devoting seven sides of a letter to his father (7 July 1907) to an account of how he rescued the pony after he fell down a well shaft in his eagerness to reach some fresh grass. Oc had eight policemen heaving on pulleys, and after several setbacks they managed to pull the animal up 'more dead than alive', but he made a full recovery.

†This was the foolhardy cavalry charge during the battle of Omdurman in 1898 in which the young Winston Churchill took part. More than half of the forty-eight British soldiers killed in the battle were Lancers.

Much to their delight, the two Wykehamists were lodged in the Mahdi's House and the day after their arrival, Oc could not resist writing to Violet with his grand new address firmly underlined, although the 'palace' was hardly majestic: 'one story high, built of mud-bricks'.[27]

The ostensible purpose of assigning the trainee Deputy Inspectors to Omdurman was to give them some judicial experience by allowing them to try petty cases before being posted to their permanent posts. More immediately, they were needed to do the legwork in assessing the town's houses for a new land tax. Oc described his work to Violet:

> Each of us is President of a Board of which there are two other members — the Sheikh of the Quarter in which we work and a Notable of the Quarter — remarkable, fat men who roll up on colossal donkeys and try to get their friends' houses assessed low and their enemies' houses high: and dissolve in perspiration as one bustles them from house to house. By house you must understand one story of mud kneaded with hands into a habitable shape, roofed — usually with matting, and surrounded by a compound inhabited by donkeys, goats and camels. The interiors are more primitive than any Bible illustration. I worked from 6.30 a.m. – 1 o'clock, with an hour for breakfast, and only got thro' about fifty of my seven thousand. After that I tried two women who were fighting over the body of a slave girl and did not get back to lunch till a quarter to three. So you can see one has lots to do.[28]

Oc got on well with his new boss, Captain Young, although he complained about him being 'secretive' and having 'no idea of devolving responsibility'. Most mornings were taken up with the Land Commission and although, as he admitted to his father, there was a good deal of sameness about the task, it brought him into contact with such exotic people as 'Dervish Emirs, sons of the Mahdi, and men who were besieged with Gordon'.[29] He was characteristically dismissive about his judicial duties: 'I despatch a large number of civil and criminal cases every day with a minimum of knowledge of procedure and the codes, which I cannot find time to learn.'[30] However, he had a brief moment of glory when a fire broke out in a timber yard and spread to the nearby British Girls' School. He sent home a cutting about the incident from a local newspaper, which a suitably impressed Elizabeth stuck in her scrapbook:

A brisk wind was blowing at the time, and the fire threatened to become very serious. But the heroic efforts of Mr Asquith and Ahmed Effendi Darwish, Mahmoud Effendi El-Ezmirli and Aziz Effendi Fehmi, who hurried to the scene with a number of policemen and soldiers, checked the progress of the fire and finally totally extinguished it. Great admiration and praise were expressed for the courage and energy exhibited by Mr Asquith in fighting out [sic] the fire. He imperilled his life several times and once was seen to jump from the roof of the school to the ground, a height of some 20 ft. The officers who assisted him showed similar courage. Mr Asquith and Ahmed Effendi Darwish came out of the affair with their clothes completely torn.

An interesting sidelight of the affair is that Oc made sure that his Sudanese colleagues received due credit, as, later in his life, he was to do with those under his command in the Great War. But as he told his father, he himself 'got no thanks for it from my superiors here whose one wish was to be rid – without compensation – of the scrubby shops and market huts near which the fire occurred'.[31]

Oc's letters home give the impression that he was enjoying the colonial life. Apart from the interest of his work and the entertaining personalities he came across, his spare time seems to have been agreeably occupied. He went on regular hunting expeditions and by mid-1907 he had two ponies and was on the point of buying a third for polo. And there was golf', in which he proved his prowess by winning the Sirdar's medal: 'the blue ribbon of Sudan golf', as he teasingly described it to his father.'[32] But, six months after his arrival in the Sudan, Oc poured out his true feelings in an entry in his journal:

Health and a clean conscience and open air alone are not enough for my happiness and peace of mind. The transition from theory to practice is painful. Romance at first hand is often prosaic, sometimes squalid. My work is that of a land-agent: my interests and inclinations are at an opposite pole. In my heart of hearts I cannot help feeling that training of character which involves cramping natural aptitudes to extinction in such narrow boots must be a mistake. I have been trying hard to pretend that I am enjoying my profession. I have tired myself out physically day after day in unacknowledged fear of letting myself think. I have written reams of cheerful correspondence to blind others and myself. Is it merely the mill through which I should have to go in any profession? Is it the homesick weakness against which I believed myself fully armed?

If I had the courage, after such a fuss had been made of me at my departure, to go back, to say I had chosen the wrong profession, and try another, should I be able in any other to do as much good to my fellow creatures, keep the flesh under control, and be happier? Or should I always look back wistfully from a miasma of mammon upon my time here and wonder how I could have been discontented with sun and moon, brave free winds, and first hand dealings with the little cares and tragedies of men?

Shall I have the desire and courage to give it up a year hence? And if so shall I spend all my life falling in love with people far too good for me: and philandering thro' vanity with others, but not letting myself go whole-heartedly with these, because they do not satisfy my ideal – an ideal which will always plague me without giving me the energy to make myself worthy of those who do satisfy it? *Dieu disposera*.[33]

Absence from home and loneliness (Oc's closest friends in the Sudan, Leach and Scott-Moncrieff, were now far away in Halfa and Gezira) no doubt contributed to Oc's melancholy. He was also increasingly restless to see Betty again. Betty had suggested that they should both read George Eliot's *Middlemarch* and share their thoughts on the novel by letter. The idea of corresponding in the first place was Oc's: 'I thought it was the best chance of keeping in touch with her as she is so splendidly keen about educating herself, and is so utterly indifferent to my "solicitous amiability". I am not in love with her as I was and am with Molly. But her fresh clean sensible simplicity and joy and her coldness and beauty fascinate me.'[34]

When Betty's mother mentioned in one of her letters that she had heard that Cynthia was in love with him, Oc showed a characteristic (albeit touchingly naïve) concern for his flirtatious friend's feelings, wondering whether

I must have been unconsciously guilty of philandering and cowardly court-liness . . . I must now resign myself to the strange and uncongenial role of the womanhunted, and to the difficult task of making the terms of our friendship perfectly clear to her . . . It sounds like an insult to say you are not in love with a beautiful young woman friend: and worse than an insult to admit that it has occurred to you that the faintest dose of sentiment has entered into her friendly feelings towards you . . . There is a passage that struck me in *Middlemarch* in which George Eliot speaks of the quality of soul that makes a man's passion for one woman differ from his passion for another 'as joy in the morning light over valley and white mountain top differs from joy among Chinese lanterns and glass panels'. My friendship for Cynthia was, I am afraid, a friendship of Chinese lanterns and glass panels, – in crowds on the ice and at the opera in Dresden, and as my most agreeable partner at routs, balls and water parties last July; and in a desultory, joking, dispassionate correspondence since I have been out here.

. . . I think it probably a waste of ink to tell you that your Bet attracts me more than any living being.[35]

*

Oc's friends and family kept him well abreast of the latest news among their social circle. He was pleased to hear that 'fiery Felix'*, Beb's bullying pupil-master, had taken silk and he hoped his brother 'will get back some of his self-confidence now that the shadow of the whip-hand no longer falls across the sunlight of his day'.[36] Meanwhile, 'that rattle Bluetooth' fed him with the latest gossip, notably the latest developments in Archie Gordon's much-vaunted love affair with Ettie Desborough, seventeen years his senior, who, Oc reported to Margot, he heard was 'trailing her passion before an unsympathetic world'.[37]

Margot's baby, a boy, was born on Christmas Eve, and although he was two months premature, he seemed healthy and the doctors were hopeful; he was wrapped in cotton wool to keep him warm – it was snowing hard outside – and put to sleep in his father's dressing room (the warmest spot in the house) with a nurse in attendance. But he died suddenly at six o'clock on Christmas morning. Margot became hysterical when Dr Williams broke the news to her three hours later:

I screamed and I hid my face with my arms and fell back in an anguish on the pillow. I felt as if my eyeballs had been plucked out of my head with red hot needles – stab after stab went through my tired body. I threw back the bedclothes and Henry came and put his arms round me, moved to the depths and the doctor left the room. Henry knelt down more and more tender and heartbroken at my passionate grief . . . I had never thought of this – why had I felt so certain that once it was born alive all would be well? I never even asked after the little creature . . . I had never even seen it, my Christmas angel visitor.

___

*The Right Honourable Sir Felix Cassel, Bart (1869–1953).

Ironically, the baby's premature birth probably saved Margot's own life, for at forty-two she might not have survived another difficult delivery. She tried to make Christmas as normal as possible, even putting the children and their nurses through the ordeal of singing Christmas carols to her; however, Violet was deeply affected by her stepmother's plight: 'I've never felt such helplessness – such blind misery and agonizing ignorance,' she wrote shortly afterwards to her friend Venetia Stanley. Margot's 'courage all through has been marvellous. Poor, <u>poor</u> darling how inexplicably cruel it seems that all her hopes and pain and looking forward should end in death.'

Asquith held a short service of prayers in the drawing room to thank the servants for their kindness to the family. Con Manners was the only outsider there. On 28 December he and Violet drove down to Wanborough through countryside 'all white and silent with snow' and, after a brief funeral service with their chauffeur and the parson the only other people present, the baby was buried in the churchyard beside his little sister.[38]

Margot's health never fully recovered from this ordeal. She now had to accept that she could never risk another child, although she had originally hoped for five or six. The trauma turned her hair grey and she suffered from pain, nausea and mental anguish for many months afterwards. An agonizing operation in March – ten veins in her bowel were burnt and one cut by her surgeon, William Cheyne – only added to her misery. When she came round from the anaesthetic she 'shrieked and bit and screamed for nearly an hour', while two nurses and her maid tried in vain to hold her still before a strong dose of morphia eventually took effect. She then spent 'three weeks of misery and anguish . . . drugged in every way' before being sent to a convalescent home in Folkestone. She only returned to London to hear her husband's budget speech on 18 April 1907, sitting with Violet and Elizabeth's governess, 'Frau', in the Speaker's Gallery.

After the speech, while Asquith dined with his Permanent Secretary, Sir Edward Hamilton, Margot, Violet and Beb were entertained by his new Parliamentary Private Secretary, Edwin Montagu, and 'Loulou' Harcourt, the new Commissioner of Works and the son of the former Liberal leader Sir William Harcourt. This seems to have been Margot's first meeting with Montagu, the visiting President of the Cambridge Union who had spoken so effectively against Raymond seven years earlier, and who was destined to play an important role in the lives of the Asquiths. Margot seems to have shown little interest in him at this stage, but the dinner ensured that she again felt part of the political world, and as such acted as the best possible tonic for her spirits.

Asquith's brief term as Chancellor of the Exchequer was to have a huge impact on the country's finances, foreshadowing big changes in the tax system as well as paving the way for the introduction of old age pensions and the genesis of the Welfare State. However, the Asquith family life went on much as before. They rejected the option of moving into the Chancellor's official residence, 11 Downing Street, as not large enough, allowing the new Home Secretary, Herbert Gladstone, and his wife Dolly to live there instead. Beb later described an encounter with his father during his time as Chancellor that 'is typical not only of his concentration but also of a certain reticence in his nature'. Beb had brought some friends home one evening after the theatre and they were chatting in the small library at Cavendish Square which his father used as his study, when 'he [Asquith] came into the room, sat down at his writing-table, picked up a pen and asked us several questions about the play and those who had acted in it. He continued writing and talking at the same time, and it was only by accident that we discovered that he was preparing the speech which he was to deliver on introducing his Budget the next afternoon.'[39]

In late April Margot received a visit from the recently ennobled Lord Milner, who had resigned as Governor General of South Africa when the Liberals returned to power. In his maiden speech in the House of Lords, Milner had bitterly attacked the new Government's moves to give Home Rule to the two breakaway Boer republics (a policy in which Asquith was playing a leading role) as a betrayal of everything for which the war had been fought. He was still smarting from attacks by Campbell-Bannerman and Lloyd George on his policy of allowing South African mine-owners to import indentured Chinese labourers, which they compared to legalising slavery. In one of those extraordinary twists that so often were to entwine the personal with the political in Margot's life, it was an issue that linked Milner, her most ardent unrequited lover, with the Colonial Secretary, Alfred Lyttelton*, the man for whose love she herself had once so hopelessly yearned. She now felt the full force of her old admirer's pent-up bitterness as Milner lectured her on how 'your people have got the mine-

---

*In 1895 Lyttelton defected to Chamberlain's Liberal Unionists (who later merged with their Tory allies).

owners on the brain'. Although he tried to reassure her that 'these political differences make no difference whatever to my personal feelings towards you or Henry', she sensed his deep-seated anger and 'wondered what it was that had produced the violence of his mind',[40] putting it down to his upbringing in Germany. (She remarked in her journal that he was 'not quite an Englishman'.) She failed to appreciate that there was now yet another reason for Milner to hate her husband, the man who had married the one great love of his life. It would take another eight years, a World War and even more bitter divisions over Ireland and conscription before all this accumulated poison burst forth.

These political distractions proved only a temporary break in Margot's tribulations. Cheyne recommended another operation to cure 'acute inflammation' in her ears, apparently without anaesthetic. 'I screamed till I broke down,' she wrote afterwards. 'I didn't know any one could live thro' <u>such</u> pain. No baby pains or indeed physical anguish of any sort can be compared to my suffering . . . It has done for my nerves.'[41] She went to recuperate at Easton Grey with Lucy and her amiably eccentric husband, 'Grambo' Graham-Smith. Frau took time off from her tutoring duties to help to nurse her and Violet came down as often as she could. Margot was touchingly grateful about 'how much I owed to Violet. She has a most charming and beloved nature and the temper of an <u>angel</u>. I am perfectly <u>devoted</u> to her and long for her when she is away.'[42] All the family were concerned for Margot's health. Asquith, in the midst of piloting his historic Budget through the House of Commons, came down to see her as often as possible, advising her strongly against consulting a nerve doctor. ('They are mostly quacks, and those who are not live upon guess work.'). The sixteen-year-old Cys also did his best to boost Margot's morale in a touching letter, assuring her she had been very brave. Anyone might be excused for breaking down with all she had been through.

> But I'm sure your depression is only physical and will lift as soon as your nerves are restored. Depression always does leave one sometime, although while it is on one is sure it never will. That is the same with tooth-ache and ear-ache and almost any trouble of that kind. Please don't be gloomy, Margot, you will soon be well again, and the world will be all the happier in contrast with the pain you have been through. Goodbye and God bless you, Margot. Write to me sometimes. I shall never meet any one so wise and kind self-sacrificing as you.[43]

At first, with a combination of good nursing and doses of bromide, sal volatile and veronal, Margot seemed to get better and put on weight. Then in June she had a bad relapse with a return of insomnia, breathing difficulties, nausea and stomach ache. 'I have never felt so low or desperately unhappy in my life,' she wrote to Ettie.[44] When, in just eleven days she lost four pounds of the weight she had worked so hard to put on, she feared she had cancer and convinced herself she was going to die (this time Elizabeth was entrusted to Violet, rather than the absent Oc, 'to defend her from rich rotters'). When Violet went down to Easton Grey, she found her stepmother 'in a state of utter breakdown here, sleeping badly, losing weight, constant deadly sickness and no progress of any kind in spite of a fortnight's peace and air'.[45]

Fowler, a local retired doctor whom Margot trusted, was at least able to reassure her that there was no sign of any cancer, diagnosing 'acute irritation to the pneumo-gastric nerve' and prescribing ether and bismuth with powder of bromide of soda to be taken with milk at night time. This seems to have at least cured the nausea and stemmed the weight loss. 'At last thank God, I've taken a real turn and feel like a prisoner reprieved, not to penal servitude but a free pardon,' she wrote in her diary at the end of June. Thankfully she was well enough to attend Raymond's wedding on 25 July.[46]

By the beginning of 1906, Katharine had decided that Raymond was definitely the man she wanted to marry, much to the chagrin of Bluetooth who was also desperately in love with her. However, she was only nineteen and her parents were understandably reluctant to allow her to marry before she had the chance, in the words of her grandson, John Jolliffe, 'to see a little more of the world, and a few more potential husbands, before making up her mind'.[47] For all his long-term prospects, Raymond had yet to make his mark at the Bar and was still partially dependent on his allowance from his father. But the Horners did nothing to discourage the love affair, even including Raymond in their family holidays to Venice in September 1904 and Ireland the following summer. Raymond's parents, for their part, thoroughly approved of his choice: 'a dream of beauty' was his father's view of Katharine, while Margot admired her 'marvellous sweetness of temper' and, far from considering marriage premature, thought the couple 'the most perfect combination of in-loveness and friendship, marrying at the right age after the right knowledge of each other that

I have ever seen'.[48] Asquith offered to increase Raymond's allowance, no doubt remembering the support Helen's father had given himself as a penniless suitor, and this seems to have tipped the balance in convincing the Horners into letting marriage go ahead.* The couple became officially engaged in February 1907. Raymond confessed to his future mother-in-law his relief that it was all fixed at last. Although he hated asking favours, particularly of his family, he thought in this case it was alright to accept, particularly as the help came unsolicited and both Margot and his father seemed to think that they could provide the subsidy without pinching themselves too much.[49]

Although Raymond and Katharine wanted to keep the betrothal 'as secret as possible for as long as possible',[50] as Con Manners wrote to tell Oc, by the beginning of April the news had leaked out:

> Much to Katharine's <u>dismay</u> and fury she had several letters of congratulation. We think Raymond is still under the impression that no one knows and here [at Avon Tyrrell] they hardly spoke to each other, they were both so self conscious and shy! Neither Ettie nor Evan nor <u>any</u> of them dared mention it to Raymond! Frances [Horner] is very impatient of their 'nonsense' and tried to persuade Mary Crawshaw who came over here for the day to congratulate them openly, as she so longed to see Raymond's face! But I would not allow it, as I would not have them teased in this house. Since I began this I heard from Raymond, <u>furious</u> at having received a letter of congratulation from Eddy Marsh,[†] he says their secret is out owing to the garrulity of their parents and he wanted to save Katharine as long as possible from the 'coarse felicitations of maiden aunts when they speak of the great happiness that is in store for her'.[51]

Con was amused when she came across Beb, who was staying with her at Avon Tyrrell, 'struggling with a letter of congratulations to

---

*Although Margot professed that 'as far as I am concerned Raymond has always been most dear', she believed (with reason) 'his family appear to have bored him a great deal'. She could not help noticing that he – alone among her step-children – showed no interest in her own children. In her diary she recounts how once when he came into the room in Cavendish Square where Puffin was, 'baby [Puffin] looked up at him not having seen him for months: "Are you new"? Raymond does not care for children. He can be very fascinating to them if he takes trouble [for example] to Monica or Betty Manners, but he hates grind of any sort – he is quite generous but he is selfish.'(Margot Asquith's Children's Diary, Ms.Eng. d. 3205, pp. 34–5, 26 July 1905, pp. 162–3, 1 August 1907)
†Sir Edward Marsh (1872–1953), Cambridge Classical scholar and 'man about town'. He was Private Secretary to Winston Churchill from 1905.

Katharine and [he] said to me what he dreaded more was writing to Raymond. So I said: "But as you will see him so soon it is not necessary to write", and he said "but you don't think I shall speak to him of it, do you!!" Oh! what an odd family you are.'[52] Oc did write to congratulate his eldest brother. Raymond replied misanthropically that he had expected that being engaged would be unbearable, but it was really almost no worse than not being engaged, save that it released floods of 'Heygatism'* which seemed to exist, at times unsuspected, in most men and apparently all women, who, at the least excuse of this kind, let forth a sticky flood of fifth-rate sentiment and saucy humour over pages and pages of writing paper.[53] Asquith, even though he was 'frightfully busy' with seeing his Budget Bill through the last phase of its Committee stage, managed to find time to help Katharine with her house hunting and reported to Margot that he approved her eventual choice of 49 Bedford Square as 'bright and clean'.[54]

The wedding was held at St Margaret's, Westminster, on 25 July 1907, with Elizabeth and Puffin among the bridesmaids and pages. It was an emotional occasion: the bride's sister, Cicely, was cruelly reported by one guest to be 'shaking with sobs like an elephant (they are all very tall). Mrs Horner was weeping copiously and steadily and "Old Jack" was striding up and down gulping down his sobs'. The reception was held at 11 Downing Street, lent by the Gladstones for the occasion, and there was a dance afterwards at Cavendish Square. The bridegroom's father drank far too much and had to be helped upstairs by Ettie, who cattily reported finding Margot in her bedroom, 'arrayed in a kimono and having a little invalid supper (just like the powders you give dogs)'.[55]

Raymond and Katharine spent the first part of their honeymoon partly with the Manners at Avon Tyrrell in Hampshire, before going on to Mells. A few years earlier the Horners had abandoned the huge Mells Park and gone to live in the more manageable and comfortable gabled Elizabethan manor house, built of the same local grey stone as the nearby early Tudor parish church. The walls of the manor were crammed with paintings by Burne-Jones and other Pre-Raphaelite artists that Frances had inherited from her father. Raymond seems to have enjoyed his honeymoon at Mells, except for one dreadful day

---

*Heygate was a notoriously dull Eton schoolmaster whose name became 'coterie' parlance for anyone considered tedious.

when, as he later reported to Violet with his usual hyperbole, some thousand of the Horners' faithful retainers assembled in the Park to celebrate the nuptials with rustic sports, accompanied by fireworks and music-hall songs played on a gramophone by Katharine's fifteen-year-old brother Mark. The nearest Raymond came to acknowledging married bliss was to inform his sister that if she pressed him for his first impression of married life, it was incomparably preferable to being single.[56] Katharine struck a more ominous note when she wrote to Ettie that she was happier than anyone had a right to be; her only apprehension was exciting the jealousy of God.[57]

The Asquiths spent the rest of the summer and autumn of 1907 at Highfield, Muir of Ord, in Ross, according to Margot, the most expensive and ugliest house they had ever rented, redeemed by being in the 'finest country in Scotland'. Initially the youthful company of her stepchildren's friends helped to cheer up Margot (she was particularly fond of Archie Gordon and Hugh Godley), but she became irritated by all the gossip, complaining that 'the rottenest of my lovers never talked of his women admirers or showed letters: kissing and telling was like cheating at cards, it is not so now'.[58]

Asquith and Beb returned to London at the beginning of October. Cys was already back at Winchester, while Margot, her children and Violet decamped to Archerfield House in East Lothian, lent to them by Margot's brother, Frank Tennant. This house, with its own nine-hole golf course, was to be the Asquiths' Scottish base for the next five years. Here, little by little, Margot began to regain her strength. In December came the tremendous news that Cys had emulated his father and Raymond by winning the top Classical scholarship to Balliol: 'We were all over the moon with joy,' gushed Margot in her journal. 'It is too splendid and he <u>does</u> deserve it richly. He is brilliant and really kind and dear, I love him deeply – he is more like Henry than any of the children.' Asquith could not resist a little *Schadenfreude*, confiding to Margot: 'I can't help a feeling of satisfaction that his old opponent Billy Grenfell [Ettie's second son] was fourth, while he was first.'[59]

When Margot returned to London in the New Year she felt, in her own words, 'a different creature'. The same could not be said of Violet, whose delicate health was now aggravated by a persistent cough. Margot lamented her stepdaughter's obstinacy in not taking her advice: 'poor darling in these things it is so hard on her not to have a mother, as they can insist – <u>I cannot</u>'.[60] In the end everyone was relieved when Violet's friend, Venetia Stanley, persuaded her to go to Switzerland at the beginning of February with Elizabeth and Frau. Venetia, the youngest daughter of the deeply eccentric Liberal peer, Lord Sheffield, and now Violet's closest and most trusted friend, joined them later.

One thing that especially irked Margot in her prolonged period of illness was missing out on the political world during the Liberals' first year back in power. And there must have been more than a twinge of jealousy when she heard how well Violet was performing in her place at official functions. 'I long to be of some use and of no anxiety to Henry again,' she wrote from Archerfield in October to the newly retired Sir Edward Hamilton. 'How I hope and pray he may make a real success of his political future, he has waited a long time for his chances hasn't he?'[61] He would not have to wait much longer.

It was already clear that Campbell-Bannerman's health was breaking down under the strain of being Prime Minister. During the course of 1907 he suffered four heart attacks. In February 1908 the King, who was about to depart for Biarritz, called in Asquith to make it clear at he would be sending for him in the event of C.B.'s resignation. Margot, who was staying with friends, was thrilled when her husband telephoned over a crackling line to tell her what the King had said. 'This is a great day in my life,' she wrote at the time. 'I should love to have been with him on the great day, after such a long wait to jump at last into the position of all the others that I would most wish him to have.'[62]

Violet, far away from it all in Switzerland, could hardly contain her frustration at missing all the excitement, confiding to Edwin Montagu, who had been keeping her abreast of all the latest gossip, that 'the thought he might die when I was away kept me awake at night! And I'm sure I kept him alive by sheer prayer. Poor old boy.'[63]

C.B.'s condition continued to deteriorate, with Asquith acting as *de facto* Prime Minister and in the meantime, as Asquith put it to Violet, 'the whole world is given up to every kind of idle and mischievous gossip'.[64] On 27 March C.B. summoned the man he knew would succeed him for a final, emotional farewell. When Asquith got home to Cavendish Square later that evening he was close to tears as he told Margot how his Chief, after speaking about the words he wanted on his gravestone, went on to thank him for being 'such a wonderful colleague, so loyal, so disinterested and so able'. At this, no doubt recalling his part in the shabby Relugas plot (when he, Haldane and Grey had unsuccessfully conspired to force C.B. to go to the House of Lords), he broke down. Margot put her arms round her husband's neck and they both cried.

For all her excitement at the prospects ahead for themselves, Margot now saw the real tragedy of C.B.'s position. Here, for all his defects, was probably the most decent man ever to hold the office of Prime Minister. Childless and a widower since the death of his beloved wife the year before, he was now facing death bravely, with no family to comfort him. The following morning, as a final gesture, Margot took round to 10 Downing Street a huge bunch of pink roses and white lilacs.[65]

Meanwhile, Edward VII – who with characteristic selfishness was reluctant to break his holiday – was urging C.B. to stay on until he was ready to come home. On 1 April, the dying C.B. painfully dictated a letter to the King seeking his permission to give up office. C.B. was finally released by telegraph two days later, while the following day a royal messenger was despatched to summon Asquith, the new Prime Minister, to Biarritz to 'kiss hands'. By now Press speculation about a change of Prime Minister had reached fever pitch and 26 Cavendish Square was besieged by reporters.

The King's messenger finally turned up at 6 p.m. on Monday 6th, and after an early supper with Margot and Mrs Mahaffy, an old Irish friend of hers, Asquith caught the boat train to Paris, finally reaching Biarritz at 10.15 the following night, where a telegram from Violet – now in Bellagio – was awaiting him: 'How dare you become Prime Minister when I'm away.' After putting on his frock coat and 'kissing hands' the next morning, Asquith breakfasted with the King. Afterwards he wrote to Violet: 'The only thing that makes me sad is that you should have been away in these trying and exciting times.'[66] He then wired Margot: 'BACK FRIDAY ASK GREY DINNER & ONE OR 2 NICE WOMEN – BLESS YOU – ALL MY LOVE. H.'[67]* The following morning, Thursday 9 April, the new Prime Minister was on his way home.

---

*Margot characteristically omitted the reference to the women in the version of the telegram she reproduced in her Memoirs – as she omitted them from her invitations to the dinner. (See *The Autobiography of Margot Asquith*, II, p. 98.)

8

'The governess of all the world'

―――――――●―――――――

O N THE DAY Asquith received his seals of office from the King, Margot drove to Richmond with the thirty-three-year-old Winston Churchill, to 'take the air'. After abandoning the Unionists for the Liberals in 1904, Winston, as everyone called him, was appointed Under Secretary at the Colonial Office by C.B. Asquith had always got on well with Winston's father, Lord Randolph Churchill, admiring 'his vitality and a certain freshness in his mental atmosphere',[1] and it was the same qualities that attracted him to the young Winston. As Violet remarked, 'no one knew better how to how to perform the public service known as "putting the cat among the pigeons"'.[2] In old age, Violet famously recalled her own first meeting with Winston at a dinner party given by Lady Wemyss, when she was nineteen and he thirty-one. 'We are all worms,' he told her. 'But I do believe that I am a glow-worm.'[3] Although the words have taken their place in the Churchill legend, Violet makes no mention of the encounter in the diary she kept at the time. Whether or not her memory was playing tricks with her – she was writing nearly sixty years later – the remark is pure Winston. Violet came to like him very much. 'He's got the uncertain sense of humour of the last gener-ation – which (for me) invests conversation with a new excitement.'[4]

Margot always had a soft spot for Winston, but she never trusted him: he was, she thought, 'as sincere as a rather unscrupulous person can be'. Nonetheless, she rated him 'a much better fellow' than his father, 'less malignant and disloyal and abler altogether', and included among his qualities generosity, good temper, candour, a willingness to accept criticism and 'a jolly sense of humour'. He was also – surprisingly for a self-confessed 'school dunce' – the only young man whom she thought cleverer than Raymond.[5]*

On the way to Richmond, Winston and Margot discussed the morning's edition of the *Daily Chronicle* containing an accurate prediction of all the most important Cabinet changes, including his own promotion to the Cabinet as President of the Board of Trade in succession to Lloyd George (who was to take over from Asquith as Chancellor of the Exchequer). Margot narrowed down the source of the leak to 'Winston himself, whom I was sure it was not, or Lloyd George whom I was sure it was'. Churchill vigorously defended his friend and colleague, giving Margot 'some admirable advice about taking any part against colleagues, saying he feared I had been prejudiced by McKenna who certainly does not like Lloyd George'.[6]

However much Margot might agree in theory that she should not interfere in Government, she had not the slightest intention of heeding the advice. As soon as she got home she set about collecting evidence to prove that Lloyd George was indeed the source. She instinctively distrusted him, disliked his noisy radicalism and firmly believed – as she forcefully pointed out to Winston – he had been 'boomed beyond his merits'.[7] Her first port of call was Reginald McKenna, who had become a good friend since becoming Financial Secretary at the Treasury under her husband, and who had been tipped to succeed him as Chancellor. McKenna, in appearance and ability the archetypal technocrat, was a consummate political gossip. He detested Lloyd George, eagerly telling Margot how Robert Donald, the editor of the *Daily Chronicle*, had dined with Lloyd George and heard all the information he wanted to hear. Even more damning was the intelligence provided by the Prime Minister's senior Private Secretary, Vaughan Nash (who had no axe to grind), that the 'unworldly' Donald had asked if he could 'add anything to what Lloyd George had already told him'.

Armed with this apparently conclusive evidence, Margot wrote to inform Asquith of Lloyd George's perfidy, hoping to catch him in

*Raymond himself was not yet a great Winston fan, complaining after they were both guests at a house party in 1905 that he made a political speech that went on for eight days. He was the autocrat, not only at breakfast, but at lunch, tea, dinner, bridge and billiards. (*Raymond Asquith: Life and Letters*, p. 123)

Paris and fully expecting there would be 'an awful row'.[8] What exactly she thought her husband ought to do at this stage is difficult to judge – he could hardly send a telegram *en route* informing the miscreant that his offer of the Exchequer was now off. Margot was further stirred at breakfast the following morning when a furious Haldane called to insist that a firm line must be taken with the culprit: he 'of course knew it was Lloyd George'.* One can imagine the scene, with Margot munching her toast and marmalade while Haldane 'walked up and down and we found ourselves in violent agreement'.[9]

On Friday afternoon, 10 April, Margot picked up Raymond and Katharine on her way to meet Asquith at Charing Cross Station. By the time his train pulled in just before six o'clock – three-quarters of an hour late – the station concourse and platform were crowded with friends, politicians, journalists and onlookers. As her husband emerged from the train, Margot was nearly knocked over in the rush to get a glimpse of the new Prime Minister, who was protected by only two police constables. The station master beckoned furiously to her and, well schooled on the hunting field on how to get ahead, she pushed her way through the throng and managed to grab hold of Asquith's elbow. They walked triumphantly arm in arm through the cheering multitude to their motor car, where Horwood, their chauffeur, greeted them with a broad grin. As the driver skilfully manoeuvred through the onlookers, the Asquiths were showered with flowers thrown by supporters standing on top of the red Royal Mail carts drawn up outside the station.

Asquith called briefly at 10 Downing Street to ask after C.B. before returning to Cavendish Square, where he found the First Sea Lord, Admiral Sir 'Jacky' Fisher, waiting for him. As the two men discussed the threat from the rapidly expanding German navy, Margot, 'the Governess of all the World',[10] as Charty aptly dubbed her sister, sat down to write to Churchill, who was dining with Lloyd George that evening: 'I <u>wish</u> you <u>would</u> speak to him and tell him quite plainly that the staff of the Daily Chronicle have given him away to three independent people.' She had no scruples about revealing

---

*In spite of his political differences with Lloyd George, Haldane was not one of those to belittle his merits. Three years earlier Margot recorded him saying: 'there were only three men who were essential to the new ministry: Asquith, Grey and Lloyd George'. (Margot Asquith's Diary, d. 3204, p.20)

two of her sources, although she suggested he had 'better perhaps to keep McKenna's name out'. Neither of the other two – Nash, who would have to deal with the new Chancellor of the Exchequer on a regular basis, and Walter Runciman, who was about to succeed McKenna at Education and would be looking for extra Treasury funding – would thank her for her indiscretion. She then proffered this advice: 'Lloyd George's best chance, if he is a good fellow, <u>which</u> I take <u>your</u> word for, is not to lie about it when Henry speaks heavily to him, but to give up the whole Press campaign. He will be done as a dog if he goes on – I think <u>you</u> might save him and the Cabinet if you do this courageously.'

In case Winston might imagine she was not acting with her husband's support, she ended: 'I've just driven Henry from the station and he said to me he "hoped to God" Winston will give it to him. He is perfectly furious.'[11] Furious or not, Asquith had no business in allowing his wife to involve herself in running the Government within days – one could almost say minutes – of his becoming Prime Minister.* Nonetheless, with a great deal more tact, he himself had already asked Churchill to quiz Lloyd George about the allegations.

Margot, as suggested, asked Grey to dinner, but naturally enough she 'never thought of obeying Henry's wire to get a few nice women – it would have ruined our dinner. I know very few really clever discreet women.'[12] Instead, she invited Haldane, Morley, McKenna and Lord Crewe, the new Colonial Secretary and husband of Rosebery's daughter, Peggy. All might have been – and probably were – hand-picked for their hostility towards the new Chancellor of the Exchequer. As soon as she was able, Margot steered the conversation on to the subject of Lloyd George. Encouraged by the reactions of Grey and Morley, who 'were <u>most</u> violently down on him', she excitedly warned the latter that the new Chancellor 'would be a danger to our Cabinet and begged him to keep Henry up to the mark', a remark which her husband, who had enough problems already, apparently overheard. He immediately motioned to her to leave the room, an instruction which, for once, she meekly obeyed.[13]

After dinner Churchill called to report on his meeting with Lloyd George, who predictably had indignantly denied the accusations.

---

*Even if Margot herself did not admit to her husband what she was up to, Nash would have almost certainly warned him.

Asquith, having got Churchill to ask Lloyd George to put his denial in writing, sensibly decided not to press matters further, informing his errant colleague that although he was annoyed by the leak, he accepted his disclaimer without reserve.

Margot had lost this particular battle, but the war was only just beginning. And she had some powerful allies: McKenna, for one, may have lost out on the Exchequer, but his 'consolation prize' – becoming First Lord of the Admiralty – ensured he was one of the most powerful men in the Cabinet. He now made himself useful by soothing the battered ego of Margot's brother, Jack, after Asquith had refused point blank to give him a job, calling him 'foolish and disloyal' for reacting like spoilt child after his earlier exclusion from C.B.'s Government. 'My brothers are uninfluenceable,' lamented Margot.[14]

As 20 Cavendish Square filled up with 'secretaries, messengers' and 'anxious ex-Cabinet ministers waiting to hear their fate', Margot, still weak after suffering nausea and weight loss, retired to bed, exhausted by all her politicking.[15] However, she typically rose to the occasion when a few days later, 15 April, 'Grambo' Graham Smith, her sister Lucy's husband, was horribly burnt after he knocked over an·oil lamp in his bedroom. Lucy was in Rapallo, nursing Charty, whose tuberculosis had taken a turn for the worse, so Margot hurried to Easton Grey to do what she could to comfort her dying brother in-in-law. Lucy arrived just before he died five days later – the day after Easter. His funeral on the Wednesday coincided with the death of C.B, and Margot could not help contrasting the simple village ceremony with C.B.'s magnificent state funeral in Westminster Abbey the following week.[16]

Violet arrived home just in time to attend C.B.'s funeral, having been diverted to Venice, where Beb and Cys had joined her for an emotional reunion with Oc, who landed on Good Friday on leave from the Sudan. Violet reported to Venetia that her brother was 'very thin and I think not looking well, but over the moon with joy and exactly like himself. I don't think I've ever been so excited by anything as the thought of seeing him.' After a few days in Switzerland, Oc soon put on weight and the four siblings arrived back in London 'looking splendid', according to Margot.[17]

Margot had known 10 Downing Street under four Prime Ministers (Gladstone, Rosebery, Balfour and Campbell-Bannerman), but she had little affection for the house, which she regarded as 'liver-coloured and squalid', claiming that before she moved there it was so little known that she had to give directions to taxi drivers if she did not want to end up in Down Street, Piccadilly.[18] Violet's return added further to her woes. Relations had been strained by Margot's refusal to let her return to England earlier, fearing that the bad weather in London might set her health back. Apart from missing all the excitement of her father's elevation, Violet had to celebrate her twenty-first birthday away from home. 'I can't tell you what the torture was of sitting still near that damned lake [Como] at Bellagio – with what I'd dreamt about and prayed for all my life happening at home,' she wrote to Bongie. 'I cried over every paper for days and wired at last begging Margot to let me come home as I felt quite ill with wanting to. But she wouldn't – she is sometimes unimaginative as she would have realized that no journey could have tired me so much as staying still.'[19]

Violet's 1908 season proved to be every bit as exhausting as her two previous ones, and by the time of the family's summer holidays she was as much in need of a break as Margot and her father, who was tired out after combining the jobs of Chancellor of the Exchequer and acting Prime Minister for most of the year.* The Asquiths took Slains Castle (belonging to the Earl of Erroll) on the rugged Aberdeenshire coast for the late summer and early autumn that year. Margot travelled up on 31 July with Elizabeth and Puffin, with the rest of the family and the usual bevy of guests arriving at various intervals later on. Margot believed herself to be 'at the very end of my tether and looked and felt a perfect "scarecrow"'; she desperately missed the companionship of Frau, who had gone home to Munich for the summer holidays. But 'it was heavenly sitting on the rocks with nothing but the sea between us and the North Pole'.

The arrival of Asquith and Violet soon threatened the atmosphere of peace and harmony. Violet was missing Oc, whom she had recently seen off back to the Sudan, and was suffering from an unspecified but unpleasant skin ailment about which, according to Margot, she 'became almost hysterical'.[20] Margot, with her worries over her own and Charty's health, was in no mood to be compassionate.

Violet's skin problem eventually cleared up in the sun and fresh air of the Aberdeenshire coast. But any relief from stress was short-

---

*After Asquith became Prime Minister, he himself, and not his Chancellor Lloyd George, introduced the year's Budget with its provisions for the introduction of old age pensions – for which Lloyd George, typically, claimed the credit.

lived. The trouble began when Violet, out for a solitary walk along the cliffs on the evening of Saturday 19 September, apparently slipped on the wet grass and fell on to the rocks below, knocking herself out. The Asquith parents were in the middle of dinner with their older friends when Venetia burst in with the news that Violet was missing. The younger members of the party – who included Beb, Aubrey Herbert, Arnold Ward, Jasper Ridley, Viola Tree (the actress daughter of the celebrated actor-manager Sir Beerbohm Tree) and Venetia herself, together with the household servants – immediately set out to scour the surrounding countryside with lanterns and car headlights. The coastguard was alerted and soon the search party was joined by local lifeboatmen and fishermen.

As midnight approached and there was still no sign of Violet, her father became, in Margot's description, shattered with worry, as 'we stood in the dark, little Elizabeth, he and I and watched feats of heroism on every side – men and women risking their lives in a still warm, heavy, dewy night with an angry sea obliterating every sound and a blank sky with a few stars painted on it. Emotion, terror, hope, despair filled every heart.' One of their guests put a comforting arm round Margot and they knelt down and prayed on the wet road. As they got up from their knees they heard the sound of cheering. Violet had been found. Margot fainted.

Violet later explained how, after recovering consciousness, she saw lights above her and heard her name being called. She managed to climb back on to the coast path and then struggled to a stile beside the road where she collapsed before being found by some fishermen. When Margot came round from her own swoon, she saw her step-daughter being carried half-conscious into the castle by Archie Gordon. Apart from the shock, Violet was unharmed. Margot helped her to undress and put her to bed, apparently accepting her explanation of what had occurred. Nonetheless, it is odd that she could have been unconscious for so long and yet apparently suffered no ill effects apart from 'nerves'. Archie expressed surprise at this aspect of Violet's 'accident' when he wrote an account of the incident to Ettie, 'especially as she had apparently <u>fallen</u> on the back of her head among the rocks'.[21] It is tempting to speculate that her 'disappearance' was an attention-seeking device that got out of hand. Even so, the suggestion that this was a botched suicide attempt following the news that Winston Churchill had become engaged to Clementine Hozier is wide of the mark: far from being in love with

Winston, as is often supposed, she never regarded him as anything other than an amusing friend. Indeed, she greeted the news of his engagement with the comment to Venetia that 'his wife could never be more to him than an ornamental sideboard . . . and she [Clemmie] is unexacting enough not to mind not being more. Whether he will ultimately mind her being as stupid as an <u>owl</u> I don't know.'[22]

There is another explanation for why Violet may have faked her accident: the clue is in the fact that it was Archie Gordon who carried her up to her room. Archie had been one of Violet's most ardent suitors; but while she recognized his qualities ('undefeated hopefulness and the greatest capacity for joy I have ever seen'), his famed charm never worked on her. In any case, Violet had no desire to be dragooned into an imperfect match. When her friend Pamela Jekyll (the niece of Gertrude, the celebrated gardener) had become engaged a few months earlier to the First Lord of Admiralty, Reginald McKenna, nineteen years her senior, she had written to Ettie: 'Most marriages seem to me to present the awful alternative of cramping one: either emotionally (by marrying a well-to-do Funny who gives one practical scope) or intellectually – by living with a nice pauper (whom one likes) among the dankest of the dank.' Like many strong women, Violet tended to attract men with weaker personalities than her own, whereas she was always looking for the impossible partner who would match the qualities she saw in her adored father. Until now she had spurned Archie's love while praying 'I may not hamper or injure him.'[23] But Archie's charm was matched by his good looks and, as Margot believed, she may well have 'succumbed to what is called "the physical side" '.[24] Now that, far from pining for her, Archie was enjoying his much-talked-about affair with Ettie, Violet might have felt spurred into re-asserting her own hold over him.

Whether Violet's accident was genuine or otherwise she could scarcely have anticipated the field day the national newspapers would make of her disappearance. Any sympathy Margot may have had for her stepdaughter's ordeal soon drained away as she watched her revel in the attention, commenting in her journal:

I was considered very unsympathetic. I didn't think this unfortunate, foolish and most <u>dangerous</u> escapade should be made too much of: constant talk of all that was said and that happened, charts of her temperature copied out and distributed, newspaper cuttings, letters and telegrams . . .

put into her hands at all hours, could not be good for any one of Violet's temperament. I wanted her just to thank the fishermen and poor people who had found her and say nothing more about it; poor Violet! Nothing was further from her ideas and she felt hurt, I could see, by my attitude.[25]

Margot made matters worse by criticizing Violet's enjoyment of the publicity to her stepdaughter's own friends: Violet soon got to hear about what was being said and was hurt, which made Margot, in her turn, feel guilty. She vented her frustration in a talk with Ettie who, in the near-incestuous world in which they lived, played the same sort of maternal role with Violet as Con Manners had with Oc. Afterwards Margot wrote to Ettie:

> I felt so horribly <u>disloyal</u> to Visy yesterday, but the fact is <u>I</u> have been very stupid in taking her men friends into my confidence about <u>her</u> health and <u>my</u> irritation. I think they <u>all</u> gave me away and she made no allowances for my desperately <u>miserable</u> condition and was stunned at my criticism – dear child she has never had any! I have always found her so good and dear, but this summer it seemed as if she changed suddenly and I felt as if there was not enough love to go round somehow.

Margot hoped Ettie would mend matters by writing to Violet that 'I said sweet things of her – I <u>meant</u> to because she has been very kind to me.' The nub of the problem was, of course, Margot's own depression. As she admitted, 'I ought to make allowances for <u>her</u> [Violet] – but alas! I am too <u>miserable</u> about myself.' She had now lost so much weight that her doctor 'can feel my spine thro' my stomach, I'm such a skeleton'. She ended her letter with an appeal: '<u>Do pray for me</u>. I'm <u>so</u> depressed and ache all over.'[26]

Violet not only rapidly recovered from her ordeal, but, in her stepmother's view, 'looked better than she did before her accident'.[27]

By the time Margot returned to London from Scotland in early November, the family had a new member. In October Katharine gave birth to a daughter who was christened Helen after Raymond's mother. Her delighted grandfather wrote to Margot: 'it is a very healthy little creature weighing 9lbs, wreathed in fat, and with a good complexion considering its age. K. seems to be doing well.' Bongie informed Violet that Raymond 'accepts his daughter as if she were a Varsity scholarship. I do not mean he is not pleased, as he obviously is, but I do not think that he would dream of mentioning it to anyone as a possible piece of news of interest.'[28]

Curiously, Margot made no mention of the new baby in her journal, possibly feeling a twinge of jealousy so soon after the loss of her own last child. She was, however, thrilled when the new First Lord of the Admiralty, her friend McKenna, asked her to launch the Royal Navy's latest 'dreadnought', HMS *Collingwood**, and at the time the biggest battleship the world had ever known. 'I am the first Prime Minister's wife who has ever launched a man of war,' she proudly recorded in her journal, calling it 'the most remarkable ceremony I ever performed at and far the most moving'.[29]

On 7 November the Asquiths arrived at Devonport dockyard just after 3 p.m. on 'a brilliant day, the sea dancing and crowded with hundreds of little boats bobbing about between the evil-looking, silent, steely men of war'. Margot was dressed in her best garden party kit: a clinging, biscuit-coloured skirt with a string blouse and a chic new fawn hat with vast wings. As she climbed the red cloaked steps to the special platform erected beside the battleship, it was clear the hat was a mistake. There was a strong wind and with a boisterous all-male crowd of 20,000 dockers and sailors watching below, it was a struggle enough to keep her skirt from billowing up, without having to hold down a hat that might have doubled as a kite. Fortunately, standing beside her on the dais was the twenty-nine-year-old Nancy Astor, whose husband was the Conservative Parliamentary candidate for Plymouth. As everyone lustily bellowed out the mariners' hymn *Eternal Father strong to save those in peril on the sea*, Nancy, with admirable presence of mind, snatched away the winged hat and 'bunched down a heavy fur toque on my scattered curls, ramming my new, beautiful hat with 100 Yankee pins onto her neat little head'.[†]

As soon as the ship had been blessed, the flustered constructor bustled up to Margot and urged her to be quick as the ship was straining at her mooring ropes. She immediately smashed the bottle against the side and said in a loud voice:

---

*Named after the admiral who took over from the dying Nelson at the Battle of Trafalgar.

†By the time Margot came to write about the launch of HMS *Collingwood* in her *Autobiography* (Vol. II, pp. 117–18), Nancy Astor had become her sworn enemy – thanks to her ill-informed attacks on Asquith's wartime record – and her contribution to Margot's naval triumph was omitted from her account.

'I name you *Collingwood*! Blessings and luck to the *Collingwood* and all who sail in you!' I raised my arm and blessed her and seized the chisel and smashed it down against my own hand and the constructor's – luckily not very hard. But in one moment I aimed a mighty blow, very straight and strong, which cut clean through the three ropes and off she went at 20 knots, silently, splashlessly into the sea and the entire company above on our platform and below in the dock sang *Rule Britannia* to the military band. There was not a dry eye as I held onto the rail praying for the beautiful, powerful, terrible ship and wondering where she would go and on what mission.'[30]*

A few days after the launch of HMS *Collingwood*, Margot found herself the object of much less welcome attention when she was spat at by one of the other women guests at the Lord Mayor's Banquet.[†] Asquith was an unrepentant opponent of votes for women and became the target for demonstrations by suffragettes as soon as he entered Downing Street, being heckled on almost every occasion when he spoke in public.[‡] Margot's own vociferous opposition to female suffrage resulted in her being regarded as a traitor to the cause by many suffragettes who subjected her to a stream of hate mail, some of it containing threats against her children as well as herself. When she was awoken one night by the sound of shattering glass as suffragettes threw stones into the room just below the one where Puffin was sleeping, the effect on her already fragile nerves was devastating. In a furious response to a complaint by Frances Balfour (herself a leading advocate of votes for women) about the harsh treatment meted out by the police to her suffragette kinswoman, Lady Connie Lytton, Margot accused the suffragettes of making her life 'a hell' and, referring to the attack on Downing Street, described how 'I nearly vomited with terror that he [Puffin] should wake and scream.

---

*HMS *Collingwood*, with the future King George VI on board as a young sub-lieutenant, was to be one of the British battleships to meet the brunt of the broadsides of the German Grand Fleet at the Battle of Jutland in 1916.

[†]When the offender was confronted by the Lord Mayor she 'burst into tears and was full of apologies'. He allowed her and her husband to remain on condition that they give their word of honour not to disrupt the speeches. (Margot Asquith's Diary, d. 3206, p. 140, 9 November 1908)

[‡]Asquith's opposition to votes for women was something of a mystery to friends such as Lady Frances Balfour, an ardent campaigner for female suffrage. The truth is that, like other politicians of the era, he was suspicious of univeral suffrage in general, and believed that ordinary women were even more likely to be swayed by the popular press (which he loathed) than men.

Why should my life be burdened by these wombless, vicious, cruel women? They say men would not be so seriously dealt with. What lies they tell! Men would be horse whipped at every street corner.'

After the incident, security in Downing Street was increased and threats against Elizabeth and Puffin (which included kidnap) were taken seriously enough for the children to be given their own police bodyguards. 'Do you think it amusing for me to lie awake and hear the detectives coughing in the rain at 4 a.m. and see my children shadowed wherever they go?' she taunted Frances, pointing out that 'Henry has many faults perhaps, but he is not a physical coward and threatening his wife's life will not really convert him to give way.'[31]

Margot's own opposition to women's suffrage might seem surprising, not only because she herself was so overtly political and relished every mite of influence she possessed, but also because so many of her friends were strong supporters of the suffrage movement. But Margot had little respect for her own sex: 'I have not one woman friend who knows or cares about politics – they love the personal aspect, the prestige, the Cabinet-making,' she had written in her journal a couple of years earlier. Women as a whole were 'd-d stupid really, and only have <u>instinct</u>, which after all animals have. They have no size or reason – very little humour, hardly any sense of honour or truth, no sort or sense of proportion, merely blind powers of personal devotion and all the animal qualities of the more heroic sort.'[32]

While the cause of votes for women divided politicians right across Party lines, surprisingly few of them considered the subject of major importance. The issue that most threatened the unity of the Cabinet – and had McKenna at daggers drawn with Lloyd George – was the Royal Navy's insistent demand for more money to be spent on countering the growing threat from Germany.

*

In late January 1909 Margot took herself off for a month to Beatenberg, above Lake Thun in Switzerland. She was accompanied by her children and Frau, as well as Violet and Cys, who was between Winchester and Balliol. The combination of mountain air, sunshine, rest and plenty of exercise skiing, skating and tobogganing not only restored both Margot and Violet to the bloom of health, but also – for the time being at least – healed the breach in their relationship. Violet 'has been most sweet out here and I pray daily that she may get strong and marry happily' wrote Margot in her journal. She was even more enthusiastic about Cys, whom she found 'independent, high-minded, quite original and really sympathetic'[33] – qualities she considered a model for Elizabeth's future husband.

By the time Margot left Switzerland on 22 February to spend a week in Paris while the rest of the family stayed in Beatenberg, she was in high spirits. She loved the French for 'their variety and cleverness' and was looking forward to a serious session of clothes buying, excusing her extravagance with the comforting thought that 'one may not be P.M.'s wife for long, who knows! I am all for enjoying the <u>Present</u>!'.[34] Margot took the opportunity to look up the French Prime Minister, Georges Clemenceau, whom she had known and admired since her teens. She had an appointment to see him at his office at 6.15 p.m., but as she had arranged a dinner engagement with her American friend, Daisy White, and her diplomat husband, she turned up early. She was preceded up the staircase by a tall, distinguished gentleman, addressed as 'Prince' by the official on guard outside the Prime Minister's office. 'This is a swell who wants to see the Prime Minister first. I can't allow this. I must impress myself somehow,' she thought. Determined that 'the Prince' should know that she was the wife of the British Prime Minister, she wrote 'Mrs Asquith' in large handwriting on the slip the official handed her, archly remarking: 'I hope, sir, you are not here on important business. If you are, of course, you must see Monsieur Clemenceau first.'

'Not at all, Mrs Asquith . . . nothing will make me go into that room first,' replied the Prince, with a deep, deferential bow, all the while looking quizzically at her and wondering, or so she fancied, whether her visit marked some new development in the *entente cordiale*. The Prime Minister's door opened and 'the old gorilla with his charming smile came out with both arms outstretched'. After greeting Margot, Clemenceau turned to introduce her to Prince Radziwill, the German ambassador – '*fin comme un renard*',* as he told her later.

'I'm afraid I shall keep you some time,' said Margot with her sweetest smile, as she shook the ambassador's hand. Clemenceau begged him not to believe her: '*Elle ne me dira que quelques injures, Prince, je vous assure!*'† And with that they closed the door on the

---

*'As sly as a fox'.
†'I can assure you, Prince, that she is just going to insult me a bit.'

Prince and hugged each other. Prince Radziwill was kept waiting about twenty minutes while she and Clemenceau discussed personal matters. Margot found herself (probably for the last time) defending Churchill, whom the French Prime Minister loathed, damning him for being 'tactless, indiscreet, untrustworthy, disloyal etc'. The conversation ended with Margot telling Clemenceau that it was 'rot' that he was tired and finished with politics. She could never have guessed that his ministerial career would outrun Asquith's.

Margot's international politicking was not quite over, for at the Whites she met Charles Cruppi, the French Trade Minister, who was 'very excited over a rumour that Lloyd George was going to raise our duties on French wine'.[35] The Minister later came to see her at her hotel and spent an hour discussing the issue with her, before leaving a document on Anglo-French tariffs for her to show to Asquith. As Margot suspected all along, the rumour turned out to be false, but the fact that a senior member of the French Government believed it worthwhile to lobby her on trade policy shows how rapidly she was establishing a reputation as a power behind the throne.

When Margot's train arrived at Charing Cross on 5 March she was met by her husband, who plunged straight into a denunciation of Churchill for blatantly leaking to the Press arguments in Cabinet over McKenna's proposed increase in spending on the Royal Navy, which Winston was opposing even more vociferously than Lloyd George. 'I am afraid to say Winston has proved himself a thoroughly untrustworthy fellow,' Asquith informed his wife. 'My heart sank,' she wrote in her journal, as she predicted that 'unless some great and new force comes to Winston's help and gives him some sort of character or conviction' he would become 'a source of danger and irritation to Henry's administration'. She too now regarded with profound suspicion the man whom a few days earlier she had been vigorously defending:

> I can't look at Winston with his bluff, swagger and leakiness without disgust. I am glad to say he has not spoken to me and I show him pretty plainly that whoever else forgives him and approves his perorations and phrases, I resent them and his personal character. He is not a gentleman and never will be. I prefer an honest outsider, even tho' provincial and limited like McKenna, to a little, treacherous, gutter genius like Winston.[36]

McKenna's decision to ask Margot to launch HMS *Collingwood* was probably one of the smarter moves in his generally clumsy campaign to persuade the Cabinet to finance six new dreadnoughts. Her own instincts matched Churchill's belief that Germany had no bellicose intentions against Britain, and she did not hesitate to cross swords even with the profoundly anti-German Queen Alexandra on the issue, forcefully telling her that 'all this foolish scare talk' about Germany was 'contemptible'.[37] Nonetheless, Margot had been thrilled to launch a battleship – a privilege usually reserved for Royalty – and had loved being cheered by massed ranks of blue jackets; there was now no firmer advocate of an expanded Royal Navy. The argument was resolved mainly thanks to Asquith's diplomatic skill in winning over the waverers in Cabinet and then persuading Lloyd George to accept a compromise deal whereby four new dreadnoughts would be laid down immediately and the money provided for four more, if justified by the rate of construction of new German battleships.

The hike in naval spending on top of the cost of old age pensions made tax increases inevitable. Lloyd George proposed not only to raise the rate of income tax (then paid by only a small proportion of the population), but also to impose a new 'super tax' on high earners and a swingeing tax on liquor licences. Ominously for landowners, the Government proposed to value all landholdings in the most far reaching survey since the Domesday Book, raising the prospect of a major new tax on land values, which caused a storm among the 'peerage' even fiercer than the licensing tax caused among the powerful 'beerage'. Lloyd George admitted he would never have got his proposals through the Cabinet without the support of the Prime Minister who 'has backed me up through thick and thin with splendid loyalty'.[38]

The Chancellor's momentous Budget speech on 29 April, 1909, signalled the start of one of the most bitter periods in British Party politics. There was growing speculation that Balfour was prepared to do the unthinkable and block the Budget bill in the House of Lords in defiance of the long-established convention that the Upper House did not interfere with money bills. Asquith's tactic was to offer the peers the minimum of provocation and hope to finesse them into giving way. Lloyd George, however, believed that the peers must be bludgeoned into submission. On 30 July he threw down the gauntlet in a speech at Limehouse in the East End of London, pouring scorn on the selfishness of rich men unwilling 'to provide for the sick and the widows and orphans', or even to pay their share of the costs of the new battleships for which many of them were clamouring. He concluded with the threat that if the peers resisted, they would be brushed aside 'like chaff before us'.

This was revolutionary stuff in Edwardian England, smacking of socialism and calculated to infuriate the Establishment. Asquith found himself under intense pressure from King Edward VII, whose support was vital if the House of Lords was to be outmanoeuvred, to rebuke his Chancellor. In the event, he delivered only the mildest schoolmasterly reproof, explaining to Lloyd George that it was important 'to avoid alienating his [the King's] goodwill . . . what is needed is reasoned appeal to moderate and reasonable men' and not to 'rouse the suspicions and fears of the middle class'.[39]

Margot was surprisingly ready to give the Budget her qualified support, summing it up as 'ingenious, highly complicated, not unsound but with a touch of "nouveau art" which may or may not come off'. She reflected the view of most observers (neutral or otherwise) when she described its provisions as 'generally popular, but by a vast minority it is loathed'. Although most of her own friends were to be found among the 'vast minority', she gave short shrift to arguments which she saw as motivated purely by self-interest, singling out for special scorn Lord Anglesey's threat to reduce his subscription to the London Hospital from £5 to £3, while at the same time buying a new yacht 'which I hear costs him £1500 a month to sail'. As for her husband's 'old step-friend and colleague', Lord Rosebery, his opposition was brutally dismissed as 'the scream of a rich man who takes himself very seriously'.[40]

On 8 October, two days after the budget completed its hard fought 'Committee' stage in the House of Commons, Lloyd George addressed a huge audience at the Palace Theatre in Newcastle and unrepentantly returned to the attack, informing some 5,000 rapturous Geordies that 'a fully-equipped duke costs as much to keep as two Dreadnoughts – and they are just as great a terror', and asking them 'whether five hundred men, ordinary men chosen accidentally from among the unemployed, should override the judgement – the deliberate judgement – of millions of people who are engaged in the industry which makes the wealth of the country'.[41]

This was a red rag to a bull and the bulls in question charged full tilt: on 30 November the peers defiantly rejected the Finance Bill by

350 votes to 75.* Asquith had no option but to call a General Election, only too aware of the delicate balance that had to be held between losing ground to the Labour Party and not alienating moderate middle-class opinion. However, a crisis within his own family was to force him drastically to curtail his own role in the election campaign.

Archie Gordon's love affair with Ettie Desborough provided the opportunity for Hugh Godley, Violet's most faithful and persistent admirer, to pursue his own suit. Or so he must have thought. Hugh's big handicap was his politics – he was a firm Tory – and he frequently found himself involved in acrimonious arguments with Violet that ended with her lecturing him about the error of his ways. In a letter to her dated 12 May, 1909, he complained that she was 'colossally arrogant about [her] views to the point of despising and rejecting people who differ from them', plaintively suggesting that his arguing with her was 'a helpless struggle for independence; as you pointed out to me not long ago'.[42]

Violet was beginning to feel the pressure on all young women of her class and generation to marry: as she admitted to her father being 'wife or mother' was 'a woman's career'. Hugh was charming, good-looking, intelligent and came from a similar background, and he was beginning to wear down her resistance. However, when she floated the idea of marrying Hugh to Asquith, he wrote begging 'don't do, or think of doing, this thing, until you and I have talked it over many times. It would break my heart if you didn't make the best of your life.'[43] Yet in spite of parental opposition, in July she raised the subject with Oc just before he returned to the Sudan after his annual leave. As she must have known, her brother's views matched their father's, as he made clear in a long letter, dated 18 July, written on the voyage back to Egypt:

Dearest Violet,
     It was sad leaving you just when I thought I might have been of some use to you. I ought to have invited your confidence before; but I was

*The Opposition cunningly managed to by-pass the Lords' inability to block 'money' bills by the ingenious device of passing a resolution refusing its consent pending the result of a referendum.

blind: the possibility of your regarding Hugh in a new light had not occurred to me . . .

I understood from you that you thought of him as a possible husband because he had been in love with you for four years; and he was the best companion you knew; and because you had not yet met anyone who stirred you to any deeper feeling than this. You were sorry for him . . . If it were not for overfatigue and Hugh's and Archie's constant badgerings, I am convinced that nothing could have brought you to contemplate as possible what you recognize would be only a second-best sort of marriage when you are only twenty two. If you were thirty, and still love had not come into your life, it would be different.

But surely you have the same sort of ideals of marriage as me. In it surely you would like to find a background of quiet and simplicity against which the real values of things would shine clear: and in a husband surely you would like to find a rock to build your house on: someone who would never allow the line of least resistance in important things: a man of broad humanity, not glib but understanding; one in whose courage and character and sense of honour and of proportion you could have implicit reliance; one who could guide your energies into the right channels . . . think of Hugh, Father and Beb put through every sort of test: don't you feel by instinct that Father's and Beb's metal would always ring true: but that possibly in Hugh's there might be a flaw? . . . Don't think I'm unsympathetic towards Hugh: I have every reason to feel for him.* For Heaven's sake tell him you cannot care for him in the way he cares for you: and that if he cannot go on being just a great friend, he had better avoid you. I would not give interfering advice of this sort, if I did not feel sure I was right: I feel all the surer because I know Father agrees with me.[44]

Oc must have known that he was hitting home when he asked Violet to compare Hugh to their father, whom she idealized. Yet still she dithered until a rival came on to the scene with whom no mortal can compete: a ghost.

On Sunday 28 November Archie Gordon was severely injured in a car smash at a crossroads near Winchester, when his brand new Daimler 'Silent Knight' collided with another car (whose driver was unhurt). He was taken by horse ambulance to the Royal County Hospital in Winchester, where the doctors diagnosed several fractured ribs, a badly broken pelvic bone, a dislocated shoulder and – most ominously – a seriously ruptured bladder.[45]

---

*Oc was, of course, obliquely referring to his own unrequited love for Betty Manners.

Violet travelled down to Winchester on 1 December, putting up at a local inn. However Archie was considered too seriously injured to be seen by anyone except his parents, and it was not until a fortnight later, by which time the doctors had given up all hope of saving his life, that she was allowed to see him. In the meantime, as she waited helplessly while her young admirer struggled for life, her feelings for him deepened. This was the first time she had faced the loss of someone close to her since the death of her mother, and long-buried childhood traumas must have come to the surface as she contemplated what she was about to lose.

Margot, in the meantime, had gone to Archerfield with Elizabeth, Puffin and Cys. She had never known Archie well, but had always liked him, considering him 'a most brave pure splendid being – far more manly than any of Violet's friends'. Now, as she heard that he might die, she convinced herself that 'had it not been for fear of getting in his and Violet's way we would have had many, many talks'. Conveniently overlooking his affair with Ettie, she believed he had always adored Violet and behaved 'quite steadily' when her stepdaughter was considering marriage to Hugh. Although far away in Scotland, she became caught up in the drama of the situation and cried daily Archie, convinced that 'if he dies part of the sunshine of our lives goes too'. So far as her grieving stepdaughter was concerned, Margot was torn between sympathy for Violet, now 'walking in the valley of the Shadow of Death', and a belief that her grief was due to remorse at having 'treated him like a dog,* a pawn and a lover in turns. She loved making him uncomfortable and held him up to ridicule before any and all of us. She was never in love with him but she liked his love for her.'[46]

Whatever the reasons for Violet's sorrow – and she was bound to be feeling all sorts of mixed emotions – she regretted more and more that she had not agreed to marry Archie. Asquith became so concerned about her distress that, in the midst of preparations for the coming General Election, he and Beb took the train to Winchester on Saturday 11 December to comfort her. Then he wrote to Margot, clearly annoyed about her lack of sympathy for Violet's feelings and irritated by her renewed harping on about their having spoilt her as a child:

---

*As a dog lover, Margot almost certainly meant that Violet exploited Archie's dog-like devotion, rather than implying that she had been cruel to him.

It is a grief to me that the two women I care for most should be on terms of almost chronic misunderstanding. Violet is no doubt often self-centred and inconsiderate, and it may be that a little more coercion would have been good for her. But she is at present suffering acutely – more than she has ever suffered in her life – and showing on the whole admirable self-control (as Lady Aberdeen [Archie's mother] assured me) though she is constantly on the verge of breaking down. No one could have seen her yesterday – when almost the last gleam of hope was vanishing – without being deeply moved.

Asquith reported how Godwin, the surgeon who had operated on Archie, had told him that he had never known anyone with such extensive injuries survive for so long. He went on:

A very serious item (so far as we are concerned) is that there is quite a possibility – Godwin, I think inclines to put it higher – that he [Archie] may never be able to be a father. Poor Aberdeen is more distressed about this than anything: he thinks Archie would not care to live in a maimed condition, and how could he marry? This is, of course, an unexpected and horrible complication, of which poor Violet knows nothing. Aberdeen talked to me for some time in great emotion about it, but I said that while Archie was hovering between life and death we need not think of such things.

I think Lady Aberdeen has abandoned hope: she telegraphed for the other children to come. She is a marvel of courage and composure. She promised me that, if the worst became certain, she would let Violet see him while he was still conscious and himself. Archie himself does not realise that he is as bad as he is . . . Violet asked me what I thought, and I told her the truth: that I was afraid he must die but that we must still put faith and hope in his wonderful resisting power.[47]

Violet received the summons to see Archie on the evening of 14 December. Venetia and Frau, who were staying with her at the inn, accompanied her to the hospital at ten o'clock in a howling wind. Leaving the others on the visitors' bench in the entrance hall, Violet rushed upstairs to Archie's room outside which she met Godwin, the surgeon, who told her that 'heart failure had set in and that the outlook was very grave'. She asked if there was any hope, but 'saw in his eyes that there was none'. She then went downstairs to ask Frau and Venetia to let her father and Beb know what was happening before settling down to wait.[48]

Archie had been asking for Violet, but he was so drugged with heroin by now that it was not until 4 a.m. that he was in any fit state to see her. After waiting patiently six hours, she 'felt the greatest joy I have ever known'. Tidying herself up, she put on her jade necklace and her hat and coat to maintain the fiction that she was 'passing through' Winchester – a rather feeble ruse suggested by the doctors so that Archie would not realize that she was only there because he was dying. He was sitting up in bed propped up on a large pile of pillows, breathing heavily in short gasps, but he managed to hold out his arms to her and say: 'Now I know what Tristan felt.'* Violet bent over and kissed him, telling him 'in the words Heaven sent me for such a moment that I loved him – that everything I had to give was his. It would be sacrilege to write of what followed – an ecstasy too holy for expression either then or now.'

Violet called in Godwin and Archie told him their news. 'Tho' perhaps at first sight I don't look it, doctor, I am at this moment in the most enviable position of any man alive. And she's *cured* me, doctor. I could walk now. I can't *feel* the beastly pelvis or the rib, no pain, no breathlessness. I'm treading on air.' Violet told him how proud she was of him, that he was like a knight of old and had covered her with his glory. He glowed with pleasure at this association with the 'Age of Chivalry' which he so loved. Then, as she recalled, 'I told him how all the things I used to expect of life and things I prized had dwindled and disappeared – how now platform oratory, verbal memory, "interest" (one of his worst bogeys!) and all my other nominal essentials were so many melted mists. All I cared about, all I longed for was just to be his wife. This seemed to me the greatest thing that could happen to any woman.'

Archie and Violet played out a charade together that all was going to be well. Archie asked her if she was up to having seven sons, and she replied: '*Quite* up to it.' He joked about her being 'my chattel before the world', while she administered sips of iced brandy and water or meat juice, interspersed with puffs of oxygen. After a while, Godwin came in to administer another injection and, as Archie slowly drifted into unconsciousness, he seemed to recall the moment of his accident, murmuring phrases like 'I can't get in the clutch'.

---

*The reference is to the hero of Wagner's *Tristan und Isolde*, who dies in the arms of his beloved. Violet and Archie, like Margot, Cynthia and many of their friends, were keen Wagnerians.

When Archie regained consciousness he expressed his sympathy for Hugh as his beaten rival. After the doctor came in again Violet stayed snuggled close to her fiancé, much to his surprise: 'Darling, you *have* changed! You used to hardly speak to me when there was anyone there – and now!'

After Archie had slept a little more, his two elder brothers, George (Lord Haddo) and Dudley, came in 'ostensibly to congratulate him', as Violet put it. The fiction was still being maintained that he would recover. Violet mentioned that Beb was also outside. As Beb poked his head round the door Archie greeted him: 'Here comes the burlesque element. Well, Beb, this is fun isn't it. This is splendid.' The sensitive Beb could see quite clearly what the others refused to recognize, that – as he later told Margot – Archie knew perfectly well that he was dying.

Venetia was the next up and Archie could not resist a little good-natured aside to Violet about the young woman who was by now very definitely 'the special girlfriend'. 'Venetia will have to nearly live with us, won't she?' Violet said something about Bongie and this seemed to make him uncomfortable. 'This does make one so sorry for all the poor fellows in the world who aren't going to marry you.'

'Not half so many want to as you seem to think. It isn't everyone's idea of fun.'

Asquith turned up at 3 p.m and was close to tears when he saw them. Violet reminded him to congratulate them and he quickly remembered himself. 'I've always wished it Archie – I've always wished it.'

'I know you're giving me the most precious thing you've got, Mr Asquith.'

'It's my very best – the best thing I've got to give.'

'I will try to make her happy.' Archie played along with the charade, talking about putting things on a business footing, before asking his 'future father in law' to kiss him and bless him. As Asquith left he said 'divine man', and then to the nurse, 'there goes the finest man alive!'.

For the next couple of hours Archie only spoke to ask for iced water or to have his forehead bathed, as Violet sat by his bedside holding his oxygen tube. Then he began to choke and Violet and Lady Aberdeen and the nurse tried in vain to adjust his pillows to help him spit. Violet could hardly bear his agony as he clutched at her. 'I'm dead, I'm done!' She tried to appear confident and serene, promising it would be all right. All the while he was asking for his father, who had been called away. Finally Lord Aberdeen came, kissed them both and Archie grew calmer.

Then Ettie arrived. Her young lover's deathbed betrothal to her much younger friend could have made this an awkward occasion, but, presumably well aware that Archie was doomed, she was characteristically magnanimous: 'Darling, this is what I've always longed for – to see you two together.' After another period of unconsciousness Archie revived, pulled Violet towards him and suggested 'I want to be married *now* – I feel such a strange impatience.' These were his last words before he lapsed into a coma.

Soon after Archie became unconscious Margot and Cys arrived. Margot had received a telegram at Archerfield that morning that Archie was dying. On her own admission she scarcely knew Archie. But by now completely absorbed in the drama unfolding in Winchester, she burst into tears and fell into Cys's arms. Cys himself, as it happened, was already thoroughly unhappy – lovesick, as he had recently confided to Margot, for her niece, Kakoo (the daughter of Frank Tennant) – but he did his best to comfort his stepmother. The two of them travelled together down to London and then on to Winchester. By the time they arrived at the hospital Archie's room was packed. Margot made a careful note in her journal of the positions of the principal actors as she came in: Violet was sitting leaning over the dying man and clasping his hand, while his mother 'was standing brave and erect the other side of the bed holding his other hand'.[49] Asquith was seated discreetly in a little chair close to a screen behind Violet, while Lord Aberdeen was slumped with his head in his hands. Ettie was sitting in another chair. Asquith got up and kissed Margot as Lady Aberdeen signalled to her to come and take her place. They all then continued to watch over him until he died at 6.40 a.m.

Margot took Violet back to her hotel and put her to bed, while Asquith, who was looking 'dead with fatigue', also went to bed for the rest of the morning. Margot then returned to the hospital with Frau, buying some flowers on the way to put on Archie's body. She found his body already surrounded by flowers. 'I have never seen anyone dead look as beautiful and arresting as Archie,' she recorded. 'I sobbed and strained over his still warm forehead in a passion of kissing and cut off his hair two curls – one I gave to Frau and one to Ettie.'

Even by Margot's standards, her behaviour was well over the top, perhaps explained by the memories Archie's death doubtless evoked of Laura's early death twenty-three years earlier. Yet in the midst of her sympathy for Violet – and there is no reason to doubt that it was perfectly genuine – she was curious to know how her stepdaughter would react: 'Violet behaved quite splendidly at Winchester showing the greatest possible self-control and tenderness,' she wrote in her journal at the time, going on: 'Poor darling, this is a most terrific crash. Her first sorrow and a crushing tragedy to those even less concerned. I shall be interested to see what the lasting effects will be upon her. Love which awakens late immediately followed by Death are the greatest emotions except Birth which can come to any human being.'[50]

9

A family crisis and a political setback

———————◆———————

THE DAY AFTER Archie died an announcement appeared in the newspapers of his deathbed engagement to Violet. Margot felt this was a bad mistake, contributing to her stepdaughter's sense of widowhood, but for the Gordon family it was a recognition of the comfort she provided in his final hours. A few hours after Archie's death, his brother Dudley wrote:

> Dearest Violet,
>
> Our hearts were too full for us to say all we felt to each other this morning: but may I be allowed to thank you for giving dear Archie such a gloriously happy ending to his life. I feel proud of the fact that you are his, and I can't put it higher when I say I feel you are indeed worthy of him. It was your wonderful courage and love which made his end so contented and peaceful, and all my life I shall remember how wonderful you were, and be made a better man for the memory
>
> Archie told me more of his feelings for you than he did to anyone else, and I can appreciate all you have meant to him.
>
> God bless you,
> Yours affectionately, Dudley[1]

A memorial service was held in London at the Temple Church on Monday 20 December. Violet sat behind the coffin between her father and Lady Aberdeen, with Margot and Cys in the next row. As the organist played music from Brahms's Requiem, Margot was overcome with misery at 'the loss of that fine, gay, pure influence in such a circle that needed every inch of it'. For Margot Archie had become the only one of Violet's friends who 'would have listened or understood me'. She had already lost all sympathy for Violet herself, prescribing 'Silence and Work' as her 'only chance'.[2] Meanwhile her sleeplessness returned and she felt weepy most mornings. The nub of the problem was that now more than ever Violet was the centre of the family's attention – particularly her father's.

Margot defied all Violet's entreaties to stay away from Archie's funeral, held three days later at Haddo. Her behaviour there must have exceeded her stepdaughter's worst fears: she burst into tears in the middle of dinner and had to be comforted by, of all people, Archie's mother. With Ettie sobbing on the other side of the table, Lady Aberdeen more than lived up to Margot's description of her as 'an angel'.

People from miles around came to watch the funeral procession from Haddo House to the Aberdeen's private chapel and its little churchyard. Violet walked behind the coffin between Archie's parents and her own father was one of the pall-bearers. Afterwards Margot and Asquith returned to Archerfield leaving Violet to spend another night with the Gordons. When she appeared the next day, Christmas Eve, she seemed, according to Margot, 'quite herself, good, bright, rather tired', but thereafter her mental state deteriorated rapidly.

The only hint in Margot's journal of what happened is an entry dated 11 January 1910 in which she admits that 'things have gone very badly for me' and 'I have not been as unhappy morally since I married.' In her last entry for 1909, written on New Year's Eve, she wrote that Asquith was 'low and anxious about Violet, who has given way completely and goes about in a wretched condition'. Her New Year prayer that Violet 'may deepen and broaden' is the only indication of her disapproval.[3] However, among Margot's papers is a note written on Archerfield headed writing paper containing a garbled account of her stepdaughter's behaviour over that New Year holiday. Although much of what Margot wrote is confused and even contradictory, it is possible to piece together roughly what occurred.

On Boxing Day, two days after Violet returned from Haddo, she became 'ill – stunned senseless and devoured by self pity and egotism'; then she started sleepwalking. Margot later reproached herself with not having guessed what was the matter: Violet was overdosing on veronal, a barbiturate she had been taking to help her sleep at Winchester. Having obtained extra supplies after Archie's funeral – Margot strongly suspected Venetia was behind this ('thinking it harmless') – she started taking large doses every night, which probably caused the sleepwalking. She was then moved to a downstairs room, which she was made to share with Venetia, much to her annoyance.

When the sleepwalking did not prove 'a success' (Margot's word), Violet resorted to the 'bold stroke' of taking veronal in the daytime, producing a state of stupor which lasted four days until she finally collapsed during dinner. Her father and Beb, in an 'agony' of worry, called a doctor, who having taken her pulse and temperature (both normal), pronounced her 'hysterical'. When she seemed to recover, she begged Margot let her sleep in her own room rather than the 'beastly little boudoir', and eventually she got her way. After Violet had gone up to her bedroom, her maid, Morrison, who had known all along that she was hoarding veronal under her bed but had been frightened to tell anyone, heard the sound of pills being rattled and rushed in, grabbed her mistress by the wrists and, as she later told Margot, '<u>implored</u> her not to touch the stuff'. As Morrison struggled to prise open her fingers, Venetia ran in with a glass of water to help Violet to swallow the pills. At this point, Margot arrived with, of all things, a sleeping draught, prescribed by the doctor.

Venetia, meanwhile, had run to fetch Bongie, telling him that 'Margot has spoilt all the effect of the veronal'. By now Margot was livid. Even before this incident she had seen Venetia, whom she called Violet's 'squaw', as an unhealthy influence; she imagined Violet and Venetia made fun of her behind her back, repeating her 'clumsily expressed sentences' which 'would return in brilliant shards, having gone round the West End of London'; now she angrily lectured Venetia and Bongie on 'how they had combined to make out of a good, brilliant, self-indulgent girl, a rag of a woman: self-absorbed and hysterical, a mere bit of sucked asparagus, unfit to have children and worse even than a physical invalid, a moral one'.

When Margot told Asquith and Beb what had been going on they refused to believe her, apparently accepting Violet's preposterous explanation that she had been taking the veronal under the influence of sleepwalking. To Margot 'this was so obviously absurd that one can hardly imagine some people believe it'. She excused 'poor Henry, who adores Violet and could never understand a character as unsimple and morbidly vain'. She later found him in his room at 2 a.m. 'almost weeping'. Margot was supported by Frau and Bongie, as well as Katharine, who was staying at the time. The atmosphere at Archerfield must have been appalling.

Margot was almost certainly correct in her belief that the root of Violet's behaviour lay in 'her longing for sympathy and attention and a certain desire to convince every-one that her great love for Archie had shattered her health'. Archie's death had indeed caused a major psychological crisis. Margot, of all people, should have realized that her stepdaughter was having some kind of mental breakdown, and that she needed sympathy. However, the drama over Archie's death had brought on a renewed bout of depression in Margot, who was too emotionally needy to provide any support for Violet; instead she felt an irrational rivalry for Asquith's attention. The result was an acrimonious row, the first real quarrel in the Asquiths' married life. She recorded bitterly how 'Henry spoke to me for the first time in his life cruelly and harshly'. Her response was to tell him 'that there was no kindness in never telling the truth to Violet or standing up to her'. Margot's fury burns through her Archerfield scribblings: 'then came in to my soul the iron that hurts and which will always bruise and burn me. Violet came between me and Henry. I don't trust her accuracy and she does not know the meaning of the word loyalty.' Her own future 'as regards Henry and Violet' was 'as black as thunder . . . that a spoilt, rubbishy, little creature should have the power and above all the <u>will</u> to make her father (and <u>such</u> a man) suffer'. She convinced herself that her husband no longer loved her, and in the following weeks lost a stone in weight.

Fortunately, Beb provided a shoulder to cry on: 'Beb has been wonderful,' she wrote. 'I shall never forget his calm and goodness and absolute understanding.'[4] By 6 January, Asquith, by now in the West Country in the midst of the General Election campaign, was able to write to Margot:

> I am delighted at the better reports and that you and Violet have had a really good talk. I never said or thought that you were hard. No one knows so well as I do the warmth and tenderness of your heart. It was simply a question of how to deal most gently and wisely with a particular phase in Violet's condition. I long for each to understand the other, and I believe you will.[5]

The last statement was wishful thinking. After Lucy left on 8 January, Margot felt 'forlorn and longed to go right away anywhere! But Henry has had such an anxious time with Violet and been so perfectly miserable that for his sake I pulled myself together.' Edward Grey, with whom she had become friendly over the past couple of years, broke off his own electioneering in Northumberland to have lunch with her at the George Hotel in Dunbar the following week. He persuaded her to join the closing stages of the campaign in Fife, where she had a 'peaceful time alone with Henry at Raith'.[6] Marital harmony seems to have been restored, although Violet, with whom Margot travelled to Cupar on 25 January to hear the result of the election in Fife, still remained 'in the same temper of gritless self-pity as she had been at Archerfield'.

Asquith's own majority in Fife rose in spite of a disappointing national trend. But much to Margot's disgust, he was prevented from delivering his acceptance speech by suffragettes who 'climbed up the lamp posts and shouted in their artificial stage voices which I know so well, "Votes for Women"'. Afterwards, there was the chance for the Prime Minister to thank a room full of his supporters in a more relaxed atmosphere over champagne and cakes. Margot's 'heart throbbed when he spoke of me as his faithful companion'. For her, her husband was 'the pluckiest, simplest, most patient, wise, kind, easily-amused man I have known'.[7] All was well with the Asquiths' marriage again.

All was most certainly not well with the Parliamentary Liberal Party, as Margot soon found out when their sleeper arrived back in London the following morning, 27 January 1910.

The election campaign had been exceptionally bitter. With Asquith largely absent dealing with his daughter's emotional problems, the spotlight fell on Lloyd George, which helped Balfour's astute strategy of portraying the main issue in the election campaign not as 'peers versus people' – which would have suited the Liberals – but a prelude to a more general attack on the property-owning classes. In the event, the Liberals lost heavily, ending up with only 275 seats, two more than the Conservative Opposition. Henceforth they would be dependent on the eighty-two Irish Nationalists for their majority. What Margot called Lloyd George's 'monotonously personal and violent speeches' during the campaign, were blamed by many of the losing Liberal candidates – and most of the Cabinet – for the Liberal Party's poor showing in the General Election.*

Violet and her father, whom Margot had never seen looking so exhausted, went straight to bed, while she had breakfast on her own. When Lloyd George sent round a messenger to ask if he could see the Prime Minister, she sent him packing: 'not till this afternoon'.[8] As it was, Asquith was up in time to see the Chancellor before lunch, recounting afterwards his colleague's fantastic theory that the Liberals' losses were due to 'the Anglo Saxon races' going against them, whercas 'we had won wherever there was Celtic blood'. Asquith had pointed out that Liberal support had held up well in Yorkshire and Lancashire, and did not think he made 'much of a case'.[9] It was in Lancashire that the other Cabinet *enfant terrible*, Winston Churchill, had conducted a barnstorming campaign while sticking to the Cabinet's agreed line not to bait the peers. When Grey came to discuss the results, Asquith could not have been more lavish in his praise of Churchill, comparing his crusade in Lancashire to Gladstone's celebrated Midlothian campaign: 'the close reasoning of his speeches was that of a real statesman', he told Grey.[10]

The following day Asquith left for a well earned break in Cannes. It is not clear why Margot did not accompany him, but his absence left the 'Prime Ministress',[11] as she now called herself, free to conduct some politicking of her own. Her first action was to summon Churchill, now back in her good books, for a pat on the back for his new 'moderation'. Having told Winston how pleased Asquith, Grey and others had been with his election speeches, she recalled in her diary:

I had never had him in my own room or talked to him *à deux* since he had talked to the Press about the naval estimates (he never even attempted to deny this – as he had completely denied it all to Violet. I was surprised, but I could see at once that he knew I knew and I was glad he didn't lie again). I reminded him of how I had sent for him to tell him what I thought to his face, but he had not come.

---

*The Liberals lost 104 seats (depriving them of their Parliamentary majority – and making them dependent on the Irish Unionists for their continuation in office). Although the effect of Lloyd George's speeches on the overall election result is difficult to gauge, his peer-baiting may have bolstered support for the Conservatives from middle-class voters frightened by his radicalism.

Margot: 'I don't want to balk at you, Winston, now. It's pretty obvious that now you see character pays more than anything in English politics. You've got a lovely wife and nice little child, why alienate <u>every</u> one – why not turn over a completely new leaf and make everyone love you and respect you? You think it's dull, but it's much duller to talk to journalists and to be always bracketed with Lloyd George. Why not walk with Edward Grey for a change? Didn't you mind Lloyd George's violent speeches? Do you realize, whether truly or not, at least 30 seats are attributed by our defeated men to Lloyd George?'

Winston: 'Well, I'm not sure he didn't win as many as he lost, but he certainly said a good many cheap things.' Putting tea in his sugar, 'I at any rate was not going to compete in the same line of business.' Before we parted he shook me warmly by the hand and held one of my hands in his and said I was the truest of women and that he would never forget what I had said.[12]

On the same day, Asquith wrote to Churchill from Cannes offering him the Irish Office. He was not to be flattered into accepting that particular poisoned chalice, however, and suggested the much safer option of the Home Office, vacated by Herbert Gladstone, who became Governor General of South Africa.

Margot delayed joining her children and Frau, who had been in the Swiss resort of Wengen since mid-January, until early March so as to be with her husband; she was particularly anxious to take advantage of the absence of Violet, who was travelling on the Continent with Venetia and her mother, Lady Sheffield. This was one of the low points of Asquith's pre-war premiership, as he appeared to procrastinate over what to do next about the peers. 'Your father is behaving with courage which masquerades as cowardice, and is the victim of Cabinet carelessness in the past,' was Montagu's charitable interpretation of his Chief's policy – or lack of it – when he wrote to Violet.[13]

Montagu, recently promoted to Under-Secretary at the India Office after four years as Asquith's Parliamentary Private Secretary, was now very much part of the family's 'inner circle' and could be expected to be among the more sympathetic of Liberal observers. The Prime Minister's supposed 'cowardice' was probably a reference to dissatisfaction on the Liberal benches that he had taken office without securing, as he had promised during the election campaign, a guarantee that the King would, if necessary, create enough new Liberal peers to force the Budget and constitutional reform through the House of Lords. What Montagu saw as Asquith's 'courage' may have been his refusal to bow to pressure from Cabinet colleagues to seek an immediate confrontation with the House of Lords, not just by threatening its power to veto legislation, but by proposing to make it a directly elected second chamber. It was a typical Asquithian case of 'Wait and See' – or rather 'don't strike before the hour', as he preferred to interpret it.* The Government, now dependent on the Irish Nationalists for its Commons majority, had a radical programme of social reform which he felt should be given priority over constitutional reform. But for the moment Asquith looked weak and indecisive.

On 21 February Margot and Churchill accompanied Asquith as he was driven to the Opening of Parliament, cheered along the way by a large crowd gathered in Whitehall. When the Prime Minister rose to speak in the debate that followed, even Margot 'could see that his speech was very coldly received and our men, one and all, were thoroughly dissatisfied'. Balfour, by contrast, was on top form 'in his best light, but poignant manner'. Nelly, the Marchioness of Londonderry, who was sitting near Margot in the Speaker's Gallery, rubbed salt into the wound by laughing loudly as the Tory leader taunted the beleaguered Prime Minister. 'I thought a less obtrusive loyalty would have been better taste and felt a little jarred,' noted Margot. 'Not a very amusing situation,' she remarked to her husband's tormentor when later on she ran into him in the corridor. Balfour smiled consolingly. 'My dear, you will be in a long time yet, I can assure you.'[14]

Asquith himself left his wife in no doubt how much he appreciated her support in his hour of need, despite their political disagreements: 'I was touched by what you said in your little farewell letter,' he wrote to Margot after seeing her off to rejoin her children in Switzerland, from where they toured northern Italy and the French Riviera. 'You have been very good to me all through these trying times – loyal, considerate, and <u>believing</u>.'[15]

Margot's departure for the Continent was the cue for Violet's return, now, according to her father, 'very decidedly better'. She was willing to see a few selected friends again: Olive [Mcleod], Cynthia, Bongie and Hugh. Her appetite and sleeping had improved, she had attended a dinner party at the Birrells with her father and had even accompanied him to a political meeting at Oxford.[16] None of this cut

---

*See p. 330–1.

much ice with Margot, who while staying with the industrialist Charles McLaren (later Lord Aberconway) and his wife Christabel at their villa in Antibes was still castigating Violet for over-reacting to Archie's death: 'Her strong will has been set on getting ill, which seems to me such a cruel selfish shallow view of Death,' she complained to Ettie. She hated 'the crepe and powder and self pity and Self Self Self that crush me. It gets on my nerves to see Puffin run up to her with his little divine, considerate nature, brimming over with sympathy and ask if he should shut the door and see her stare stonily at him and not answer – I could hit her with my fists.'[17]

By the time Margot returned to England at the end of March, Asquith had persuaded his colleagues to stick to C.B.'s original plan to restrict the peers' power to hold up Bills to two years only. Margot recorded how her husband came into her bedroom and 'for the first time in his life he praised himself', telling her: 'I don't think any-one else could have kept the party and this Cabinet together, but I think now it looks as if I have.' She kissed him and told him 'he had shown courage and patience'.[18]

On 28 April the Budget finally passed through the House of Lords without a division. Afterwards, Asquith scribbled a quick thank you to Margot: 'all through these trying weeks you have been more than anyone sympathetic, understanding, loyal and loving. I have felt it much.' He then took Lloyd George off for a celebratory dinner at the Savoy.[19] As soon as they had finished the meal, he was picked up by Reggie and Pamela McKenna and driven to Portsmouth to board the Admiralty yacht *Enchantress* for a recuperative voyage to the Mediterranean. The irredeemably seasick-prone Margot declined to accompany them.

*

Asquith was on board the *Enchantress* bound for Gibraltar when King Edward VII unexpectedly died on 6 May. Margot, who had already telegraphed news of the King's illness to her husband advising him to return at once, was awoken at midnight to be told that the King had died fifteen minutes earlier. Lucy came in and the two sisters had a good cry together before going to break the news to Beb. The next day, Margot, never one to be caught off guard where clothes were concerned, ordered a smart new black dress for the funeral. 'This is bad news, madam, the King's death will spoil the season,' remarked the shop assistant. 'I felt the smallness of human outlook,' was Margot's acid comment in her journal. Violet, who rushed back from Dublin to be in on the action, informed Venetia that her stepmother was 'in tip top form, she absolutely revels in the excitement of the sudden death of a King'.

Although Margot had heartily disapproved of Edward VII while he had been alive – only a couple of year's earlier she had described him as 'common and vulgar' and dismissed his opinions as 'commonplace'* – she threw herself into the business of public mourning with her customary enthusiasm, rising at 6.30 a.m. to make sure she was among the first to send off letters of condolence to the Queen, Sir Francis Knollys (the dead King's Private Secretary), Alice Keppel – his mistress – and his close friend, Sir Ernest Cassel. 'Poor Cassel' came round later that day 'much moved' to tell Margot about the King's final moments.[20]

The *Enchantress* berthed at Plymouth on the evening of 9 May and Margot met Asquith at Paddington Station just after midnight. When the late King's body was taken from Buckingham Palace to Westminster Hall for three days' lying in state, Margot stood beside Alice Keppel in an unseasonably bitter wind as the cortège moved off, noting that there were only two wreaths on the coffin, the Queen's and the Kaiser's, the latter 'very large and feathery, all orchids'. She went twice to see the lying in state, once with her husband and Elizabeth, and then again with Lucy and the family servants. The Asquiths' treatment of the spectacle at Westminster Hall did not go unnoticed, one member of the royal household disapprovingly noting how 'the Prime Minister was there with Miss Asquith leaning against one of the lamp standards and watching the people pass. I thought his attitude and general demeanour rather offensive, I fear he had dined well and he seemed to regard the occasion as a mere show.'[21]†

The weather had changed completely by the day of the funeral, which was held in warm sunshine. As the funeral party waited for the

---

*Examples of King Edward VII's 'commonplace' opinions included: 'all clever young men were "prigs" . . . keen Liberals "socialists", the uninteresting "charming" or "pleasant", the interesting "intriguers", the dreamers "mad", clever women "rather too advanced for me" '. (Margot Asquith's Diary, d. 3206 pp. 110–111 (June 1908))

†Winston Churchill behaved even less deferentially, taking a large party to see the King's coffin after Westminster Hall had closed for the night and then aggressively haranguing the doorman when they were not allowed in.

nine reigning monarchs to join them, Margot made friends with the dead King's little terrier, although his horse bared his teeth at her – a reflection, perhaps of his late master's feelings towards Margot. She and Lady (Peggy) Crewe, the wife of the Lord Privy Seal, both wearing 'long crepe veils and chiffon veils behind', walked in front of the soldiers, the only women in the procession.

The death of Edward VII presented Asquith with an unexpected opportunity to seek a way out of the looming constitutional crisis. The late king had refused to agree to create new peers without a second General Election; now the succession of his son, George V (in Asquith's own words 'still rather raw and rough'[22]), gave the perfect excuse to delay bringing matters to a head, while Asquith tried to find a solution to the problem posed by the House of Lords. In the circumstances, he was relieved to resume his cruise on the *Enchantress* as he pondered how to deal with the new King.

The struggle over the fate of the House of Lords, following on as it did from the controversy over Lloyd George's budget, heralded one of the nastiest periods in British politics. Most of the bile of the threatened upper classes was directed at the Chancellor of the Exchequer, but the Asquiths were far from immune. The member of the family most directly affected was Beb, who suddenly found politics interfering with his love life. He had continued to woo Cynthia Charteris since their dramatic meeting on the frozen lake in Dresden in January 1904, and once Cynthia realized that she was going to get nowhere with Oc, she gradually succumbed to his brother's combination of charm, persistence and love poems.

Beb faced the resolute opposition of the fiercely Tory Charteris family, who were determined to prevent a daughter of the house falling into the clutches of a son of the 'Robber Chief', as Cynthia's cantankerous grandfather, the Earl of Wemyss, called the Prime Minister.[23] Her father, Lord (Hugo) Elcho, had been fretting about his children's friendliness with the Asquith family for some time, with her mother confiding to Balfour that she hoped 'the result of our dinners etc. will not be a double marriage, Violet – Ego [the Elchos' eldest son and heir], Cynthia – Beb, that Cynthia spends all her nights with Beb at balls, and that V. and B. both look very second rate and that he's going to tell Cynthia and Ego so – this is the really worrying thing'.[24] When it became clear that Cynthia was serious about Beb, Elcho barred him from his homes. Leaving aside the Asquiths' politics, Beb was in any case a risky prospect. He shared

Raymond's boredom with the Law; and although he was making a reasonable living at the Chancery Bar, he dreamt of becoming a writer and a poet before following his father into politics. Every day he impatiently awaited 'the blessed hour of six o'clock' when 'the warm pulses of life began again to beat in his veins' and he was free to carouse with his friends.[25]

For Cynthia, brought up in a world where writers and artists mingled with the hunting set and the political world, the prospect of being the wife of a writer-politician seemed an attractive enough prospect. Beb might be lazy, but so was her mother's great friend, Arthur Balfour, and this had not prevented him becoming Prime Minister.* Her pet name for Beb was 'Bushtail', while he called her 'Rag': 'Go on loving your Rag,' she wrote. 'You don't have much chance of wearing it out.' She loved the poems he wrote for her: '"The winged vanguard of the free" and the preceding lines are excellent and I like the verse ending with the "heartbeat of eternity" very much, I am delighted with it all . . . Thank you for it darling, you should write some more, I should like to "discover" a poet and I will send a laurel wreath.'

Although Cynthia did not dare defy her parents openly, she circumvented her father's ban on her taking Beb home by meeting him at Raymond and Katharine's house in Bedford Square on the pretext of going to see their baby, Helen. Katharine would leave the key to the Square garden on the hall table which allowed them to be alone together there. One dewy evening she brought a blanket and the couple indulged in some heavy petting on the damp grass. 'Will you come every night to Bedford Square with the blanket,' wrote Beb afterwards. Such activities would have been risky enough in pre-First World War England even if they had been officially engaged, so Beb suggested they meet in Cavendish Square, which was then vacant. Perhaps oversensitive to his fiancée's scruples, he assured her 'if you want to stop doing that, my darling, you must tell me and

---

*Balfour himself did not have a high opinion of Beb, who like his brothers was not a great dinner party conversationalist, leaving the floor to more skilled exponents like Margot and Balfour himself. On 29 August 1910 he wrote to Ettie: 'Your accounts of Cynthia and Beb are delightful. I am now looking forward to a pleasure which, so far, I have never enjoyed – that of hearing Beb speak. Certainly in his case no one will assert that Love has shown himself blind: – so very odd that Love should have made up for it by showing himself dumb.' (*The Letters of Arthur Balfour and Lady Elcho*, ed. Jane Ridley and Clayre Percy, p. 261)

don't think it could make any difficulty between us. You must be quite open about everything like that.'[26]

In the end Cynthia managed to overcome her mother's opposition to the match, but she was so fearful of her father's hostility that she took off her engagement ring when he was about. Beb decided to beard Lord Elcho himself and formally ask for his daughter's hand in true Victorian fashion. Cynthia later recounted what happened:

> The alarming interview was opened by Papa handing Beb a huge cigar, at which he puffed appreciatively. 'You like doing yourself well?' remarked his host, interrogatively. Beb, suspecting a snare, but not knowing what to say for the best, sheepishly supposed he did. 'Well you won't be able to do yourself well if you marry Cynthia!' triumphantly declared Papa . . .
>
> Meanwhile my mother and I cowered upstairs. At long last we heard the front door bang behind the departing suitor. We listened to the tingling silence . . . Suddenly it was broken by a loud Ha! Ha! and stumping up the stairs, Papa shouted, 'What *do* you think that fellow's gone and done now, Mary? He has taken my new hat and left me one I wouldn't be seen dead in!' . . . The crisis was over.[27]

The couple's financial situation still had to be sorted out. Asquith who was already subsidising Raymond and Katharine, generously agreed to help as much as he could; however, Lord Elcho had lost most of his own capital gambling on foolish investments, which meant that Cynthia had to look to her grandfather for any subsidy; and the nonagenarian Earl of Wemyss proved immovable, as Mary Elcho, by now nearly won over to Beb's charms, wrote to Balfour:

> . . . Beb has spoken to me, has told me he earned 800 this last year and that his father would give him 600. He owns that is <u>most</u> moderate but says he wanted to know if he could be considered <u>just</u> possible and excuse his otherwise inexcusable conduct. He was very nice . . . I do think that if poor old Squith [Asquith] can allow 600 it's awfully shabby if the Earl cannot give another 600. But his bitter politics will make him mad.[28]

When Beb went to see Elcho to discuss the situation it soon became apparent that it was he himself who posed the main obstacle to a more generous financial settlement. He bluntly told his prospective son-in-law that he would oppose his father (Lord Wemyss) settling more than £200 a year on Cynthia. Beb tried to get Mary Elcho to change her husband's mind, arguing:

> Cincie ought to have at least £1500 a year in order to be decently pro-
> vided for, and I do not understand Lord Elcho's view that he ought to
> oppose his father making a small settlement upon his daughter. I think
> my father might be ready to guarantee £1,100 a year [to make up any
> shortfall in Beb's income from the Bar] if Cincie's family provide £400 a
> year.

Lady Elcho had an unpleasant row with her husband over the issue, but she could not budge him. Beb also had to contend with the resentment of other aristocratic parents about him carrying off one of the major Society 'catches' from under the noses of their own more eligible sons: the Duchess of Rutland, whose son Lord (John) Granby was one of Cynthia's unsuccessful suitors, had no scruples about trying to exploit the Elchos' worries about Beb's comparative impecuniousness in a last-minute attempt to advance her son's cause, begging Mary 'to stem the Beb tide'.[29]* There was also some residual hostility to the match closer to home, notably from Raymond's wife, Katharine, who had never been able to appreciate the qualities that lay behind Beb's notorious social shyness. Cynthia confessed to Katharine

> I am more frightened of you than any of my family. Opposition based on
> the Heygate objections† – money and so on – though inconvenient is not
> embarrassing because – though I am far from underestimating these
> drawbacks – it is quite easy to argue about that side of the question. It
> would be quite easy to justify myself to you if you were in sympathy with
> the more vital and intrinsic thing, but I know you do not like Beb and that
> the whole situation surprises you . . . But I know you are understanding
> enough to be able to guess how extraordinarily different people can be in
> different relationships and I think this applies to Beb more than to anyone
> else – I simply cannot recognise him when he is with other people, and I
> quite understand what you feel about him.[30]

---

*Ultimately, another Asquith was to be the main loser in this particular family feud when in 1916 Lord Granby married Kakoo Tennant (the daughter of Margot's brother Frank), with whom Cys was desperately in love.
†See note on p. 131.

Cynthia married Beb on 28 July 1910 at Holy Trinity, Sloane Street, where some of the guests had to be seated according to their political (rather than family) allegiance as a precaution against unchristian rows breaking out in church. Fortunately, Beb himself was a much more easy-going creature, and indeed he needed to be with a family as eccentric as the Charterises: when sitting next to his mother-in-law at Stanway, he was liable to be required to forego mint sauce with his roast lamb as his hostess liked to feed Pina, her favourite Chow, with tasty morsels from the plates of her guests and the dog apparently preferred its meat unseasoned.[31]

The couple spent their honeymoon at Avon Tyrrell, although some wag (probably Aubrey Herbert) who knew about the bride's earlier fondness for Oc, managed to fool *The Times* into reporting that the couple 'will go to Egypt, where Mr Asquith holds an appointment and will make their home in that country'.[32]

When Margot returned from her trip to the Continent that spring she found Violet 'a little better, but still very seedy and self-absorbed'; however, her attitude soon mellowed and three weeks later Violet recorded having 'rather a <u>nice</u> talk' with Margot when they dined alone together.[33] Her own subsequent stay with the Aberdeens at the Viceregal Lodge in Dublin, where Lord Aberdeen had been Lord Lieutenant since 1905, was a success in spite of (or perhaps because of) the constant reminders of Archie, and she returned home in a much more positive frame of mind. Yet rather than facing up to her loss, she was trying to deal with it by pretending that she could still talk to Archie. For three years after his death her diary entries consisted of letters to him.

Violet was determined to find a suitable memorial for Archie and canvassed opinion among his friends before deciding to set up a fund for a club for 'destitute' boys. Her idea was that it was to be 'for the purposes of <u>pure enjoyment</u> (no insidious undercurrent of improvement)!'.[34] There was, of course, a parallel between Violet's plans for a club for boys from poor families and the excursions Margot used to organize for the factory girls in Whitechapel after Laura's death. Here at last was something constructive to come out of Archie's death of which Margot approved: 'her club has been wonderfully done and she has a rare genius for making her boys – and I may say <u>all</u> young people happy', she wrote in her diary.[35] But whereas for Margot slum work was a penance, Violet genuinely enjoyed her time with her boys who, as well as broadening her horizons, gave her a purpose in life. When she and Cys went to interview 'candidates' at a school in Hoxton in October, she wrote in her diary (addressed as though to Archie himself):

> you can't think how pathetic it all was: the brave drudgery and cheerfulness of the poor little undermasters, grinding away their lives in these dismal class-rooms, the pale plants trying hard to grow in pots on the window ledge, one or two small fishes caught in the canal and kept in a small tank of opaque water in which floated one slimy strand of weed. The wild spirits of the boys in the midst of all the squalor was very wonderful – they were all let out into the stone playground at 3.30 for 10 minutes – you never saw such riotous joy.[36]

The 'Archie Gordon Club' brought Violet closer together with Bongie Bonham Carter, who had recently been appointed to be one of her father's Private Secretaries* and who was roped in to help because of his experience with the Balliol Boys' Club in Hammersmith. Together they raised over £1,000 from Archie's friends for the Club in Hackney, in the East End of London, where it looked after around a dozen boys aged between eleven and fourteen from poor local families. The editor of Violet's letters, Mark Pottle, has described how

> the emphasis of Club activities was on educational entertainment, and in spite of Violet's playful avowal to the contrary, there was an 'improving' aspect to the proceedings. She wanted the boys to have 'pure fun', but she also wanted them to have prospects, and this meant self-improvement. They were encouraged to attend night-school, to read and to debate. She enthused at the thought of their enjoying translations of the Classics, and perhaps unconsciously modelled them on her brothers. When the boys reached working age efforts were made to find them apprenticeships: to this end Violet and Bongie enlisted the help of their wealthier friends. The philanthropic aspects of the Club, though, were overshadowed by the recreational: there were annual summer camps, sightseeing trips and a weekly 'Club night'.[37]

---

*Bongie was to succeed Vaughan Nash as Asquith's principal Private Secretary two years later.

Meanwhile, in spite of his early misgivings, Oc was making the best of his life as a colonial administrator, earning the respect of his fellow civil servants and the Sudanese population alike. However, he craved wider horizons for his talents and was increasingly desperate to renew his old friendships back in England – and to woo Betty Manners. Nonetheless, he loved the country and was keen to show it off to his siblings before he left.* He had hoped that both Beb and Violet would visit him. But with his brother newly married, in the end it was only his sister and her maid, Morrison, who boarded P & O's SS *Delhi* in December 1910. They were seen off from Dover by Margot and two of Asquith's Private Secretaries, 'Micky' (Meiklejohn) and Bongie, whose 'poor faithful doe-eyes looked sad as the water widened between us', noted Violet.

Violet enjoyed the voyage across the Mediterranean, but the shock of Port Said – her first glimpse of the Orient – appalled her even more than it had Oc: 'Unlit sandy streets – where dust whirls and women and children huddle in heaps – men, with pigs, of every colour and nationality howling strange tongues at each other, diseased dogs lapping out of filthy puddles, desolate mud-stretches, horrible hovels – everywhere an atmosphere of filth, brawl and squalor.'[38]

The two women reached Omdurman on Christmas Day. Oc's bungalow, at the top of a steep path leading down to the Nile, consisted of a 'straight row of rooms with a verandah opening on a little "garden" – all beautifully cleanly and whitely and newly painted with bright green doors and shutters'. Violet was given a large cool white bedroom with a shiny stone tiled floor on which lovely carpets are strewn, a very odd, very broad bed, made of strong rushes, a little white table, a looking glass and next door a large bathroom with a stone bath'. After tea on the verandah and 'a brown bath in Nile water', Oc took his sister for an introductory drive through the city.[39] Little by little, her brother's company helped her to recover from the trauma of Archie's death. In a letter to a friend, written two and a half weeks into her stay, she described how

Oc and I are at present living the most strange and delicious life in a mud house on the banks of the Nile – gold eyed lizards dart about outside, and

---

*Oc retained an affection for the Sudan and his Sudanese friends that was to last for the rest of his life, and after the Great War he was to return to the country several times on business trips.

a stud of pitch-black servants minister to our wants: they address me as
'Your Blessedness' and 'Your Felicity', which thrilled me at first as I
thought it was a title especially inspired by myself, but I have since learned
that it is the conventional form of address of every English <u>Colonel</u> and
as such thought appropriate to me!! . . . Oc has devised a new punishment
for criminals here, which is to fill my large stone bath out of the Nile every
evening![40]

Over the next few weeks Oc and all-too-willing male colleagues
starved of European female company took Violet for moonlit camel
rides in the desert and trips by steam launch on the Nile. She even
accompanied her brother on his tours to inspect the rebuilding of
Khartoum, recording:

A Sheik accompanies us on a donkey with a sheaf of hieroglyphics in his
hand which he shows Oc – one by one – as we reach the houses they
apply to. Here the plaintiffs come out and petition to Oc in querulous
tones and Oc either (usually) refuses what they ask or refers them to
someone else – (the Survey Commission or something). I saw hardly any
boons granted. The requests were usually for things like a yard and a half
more land or to be allowed to put a wall round a well. Oc looks very judicial in a khaki coat and a sun helmet and speaks in low authoritative tones.
His verdict is accepted as final.[41]

Violet met General Kitchener's naval officer nephew, Henry
Kitchener, whom she liked very much, although she irreverently
described his famous uncle as 'the best made up <u>stage</u> conqueror
I have ever seen – iron jaw, glazed eye, well padded chest,
vile manners'. She was shown over the battlefield of Omdurman –
of special interest as she had just read Churchill's account of the
battle* – and attended a spectacular military parade headed by
Kitchener 'on a white charger looking very firm and victorious' with
'Oc's horse whinnying wildly'. She 'could have shouted with excitement. I didn't know such love of life was left in me as I have felt
today. It is the first feeling of living again.'[42]
    Violet's most faithful companion in Omdurman was Bongie's
brother, Edgar Bonham Carter, the legal secretary to the Sudan
Government, who had become friendly with Oc. 'I simply love

---

*The River War: An historical account of the reconquest of the Sudan (1899).

him – he is divinely reserved and aloof and unsusceptible and contained,' was her first impression of the forty-year-old bachelor. When
she accompanied Edgar, Oc and James Currie, the principal of
Gordon College in Khartoum, on a desert expedition, she attributed
the former's fussy solicitousness to his lack of experience of women,
noting how he 'always thinks I'm going to tumble down a well or be
kicked or bitten by a horse or do something foolish or unlikely'. But
it mattered little beside the thrill of riding a camel by moonlight and
camping under the desert stars. She was taken aback when, just
before she was due to leave, Edgar abruptly proposed to her: 'I
couldn't have been more surprised if he had shot me where I sat. My
breath literally left me,' she wrote in her journal. After trying to insist
he couldn't be serious, saying 'all the silly conventional things about
it being an honour and my being proud' and telling him how broken
she was by her experience over Archie, she promised to consider his
proposal and write to him.[43] In the end she kept the poor man on
tenterhooks until finally posting her refusal from Marseilles.

A week after Violet's departure Oc embarked on his Sudan swan-
song: a two-week hunting trip with his friend, Robin Buxton. He
ends his account of the expedition with an eerily prophetic poem:

> Time Flies and will not return.
> The Wings of Man's Life are
> plumed with the feathers
> of Death.

Oc was not to keep a diary again until the autumn of 1914, when his
quarry would be human.

10

'What a fine fellow he is to serve under'

———————— ◆ ————————

THE DEMISE OF Edward VII gave a breathing space in the constitutional crisis facing the Asquith Government. However, after an all-party constitutional conference on reform of the House of Lords broke down in early November 1910, the Prime Minister had no option but to call a fresh General Election, having first wrung from a most reluctant George V an undertaking that, if the Liberals were re-elected, he would create enough new Liberal peers to guarantee the passage of the proposed House of Lords reform.

Lloyd George defiantly opened his election campaign on 21 November with a renewed attack on the recalcitrant peers in a speech at the Paragon Theatre in Mile End in the East End of London. He compared the aristocracy to cheese: 'the older it is the higher it becomes' – or as a heckler more crudely put it: 'the more it stinks'.[1] This was good knockabout stuff, but it sent nervous shivers down the spines of more moderate Liberals. According to Margot, 'every sort of M.P. came to see me on our side with bitter complaints'. Convinced that 'no one would do anything and that we should lose seats like last time', and without consulting her husband, she decided that she herself must rein in the hot-headed Chancellor of the Exchequer, writing to him on 29 November as follows:

Dear Mr Lloyd George,
I am sure you are as generous as you are impulsive. I am going to make a political appeal to you. I say political as against personal for, if you do not

respond to my appeal, I shall be very unhappy, but <u>not affronted</u>. Don't when you speak on platforms arouse what is low and sordid and violent in your audience: it hurts those members of it that are fighting these elections with the noblest desire to see fair play; men animated by no desire to punch anyone's head; men of disinterested emotion able to pity and heal their fellow man whether a lord or a sweep. I expect the cool-blooded class hatred shown for some years in the corporate counsels of the House of Lords has driven you into saying that lords are high like cheese etc. etc. etc.

If your speeches only hurt and alienated lords it would not perhaps so much matter – but they hurt and offend not only the King and men of high estate, but quite poor men, Liberals of all sorts – <u>they lose us votes</u>. If a wave of caution and irritation bursts over England we shall have a <u>tre-mendous</u> beating in the next three weeks – don't let anyone say your speeches set this wave in motion. You are a great artist: with a little more political prevision and less self indulgence you could draw to yourself in public as you do in private, not merely the feverish curiosity, the gloomy fervour of a clammering [sic] crowd, but the growing confidence and enduring interest of the best kind of Liberalism.

Yours in affectionate sincerity
Margot Asquith[2]

Margot's letter was, even by her own standards, an amazingly foolish intervention in a matter that was none of her business. It was bound to cause offence, and it duly did. Lloyd George, tired after a hard bout of campaigning and suffering from a heavy cold, received the letter as he was leaving for a few days rest at his home in Wales. Exasperated, he dashed off a sarcastic reply:

Dear Mrs Asquith,
Thanks for your letter. I have undertaken in spite of a racking cold to address a dozen meetings before the election is over. If you would only convey to the Whips your emphatic belief that my speeches are doing harm to the cause you will render the party a service and incidentally confer on me a great favour.

Were it generally known that this service was due to your intervention it would add enormously to your popularity with the rank and file of the party and strengthen the opinion which is generally entertained of the beneficence of your influence.

There is only one other favour I would ask at your hands. I hear on all sides that you are fond of attributing the fall in the Liberal majority at the last election to me. All I ask is that before you repeat that statement in future you will be good enough to look at the result of the bye-elections before my Budget was introduced and compare them with the results after. If you do so, you will probably come to the same conclusion as the Tory managers have already arrived at, that but for the tactics you deplore you and I would have been out of Downing Street months ago.

Believe me

Yours sincerely,

D. Lloyd George[3]

When Margot received the letter the following day, she understood, probably for the first time, that Lloyd George knew what she had been saying about him behind his back. Realizing the folly of what she had done, her main concern was that her husband would get to hear about the affair, – 'he hates my missionary tendencies!', she admitted in her journal. Fortunately for her, Asquith was at an election meeting in Reading with Violet, so Margot had time to cover her tracks. She wrote Lloyd George what she called 'a most human, humble, charming letter', which she then showed to the Chief Whip, Alexander Murray (who rejoiced in the Scottish title of 'Master of Elibank'), who lived two doors away at 12 Downing Street. Murray had already received an angry letter from the Chancellor threatening to take the matter up with the Prime Minister: 'I begged him to make it up for me as I was in a blue funk lest he should tell Henry to whom the whole thing would have been a great worry.'[4]

Luckily for Margot, Murray, like the best Chief Whips, was a master at healing rifts in the political snake pit. He assured Margot that she was 'the most generous splendid woman I've ever seen. No gentleman could have written Lloyd George's letter!'[5] He then telephoned Lloyd George and did his best to smooth him down, following it up with a suitably emollient letter:

I am so distressed at this absolutely unnecessary difference of opinion between you and Mrs A. – as if we had not all enough to do! I have seen her and she sends enclosed letter which believe me is really genuine – and I'll tell you more when we meet.

The PM knows nothing about it; – nor does any one else and I do hope you will banish it all from your mind.[6]

Margot's letter, although not containing a full retraction, was about as contrite as Lloyd George could have expected:

I am sorry I have hurt and vexed you. You are too good a fellow to be really angry with what I write to you! As you know my motives were of the highest and best. I daresay it is some want in me, but I never think 'les gros mots' on either side do any good. I have never in my life publicly or privately said one word against you or your Budget: on the contrary, with my stupid rich friends I have had a very bad time from telling them with perfect truth that the Budget has brought in the maximum of money and minimum of friction – I think so far from your Budget diminishing our majority, I think it won it for us, so you need not believe that gossip. It is quite true that when you asked if I liked your Limehouse and Newcastle and Mile End speeches I have said no . . . Dear Mr Lloyd George don't be vexed with me. I can see in every line of your letter that I have wounded you – I can't bear this: may I run in and see you (only for 5 seconds) so that you may know by my face and my handshake that I am genuinely sorry?[7]

The next day Margot, who was attending a big Liberal rally in Wolverhampton with her husband, received a telegram from Murray instructing her to ask Lloyd George and himself to lunch the following day. Her guests arrived while she was tidying her hair and when she entered the drawing-room they were standing in front of the fire chatting to Violet and Lucy. Lloyd George blushed as Margot walked straight up to him and clasped his hand between both of hers. 'Is that all right?' she asked, noting how 'he looked at me with his beautiful eyes and interesting little face and squeezed my hand. I owe a lot to the Master who got me out of this. We all sat down to a friendly lunch – Lucy was much interested as she hadn't met him [Lloyd George] before. He was in excellent form.'[8]

She indeed owe a lot to the Master. Asquith would have been furious had he found out what she had done. As it was, the exchange of letters and subsequent reconciliation turned into a cathartic experience for both Margot and Lloyd George: it marked a dramatic turning-point in their relations and for the next few years they remained good friends.

The election left the balance of power in the House of Commons unchanged, but having assured the support of the Irish Nationalists with the promise of a Home Rule Bill, Asquith could just about claim a mandate for constitutional reform.

In early April 1911 Charty, now in the final stages of tuberculosis, came home to die. Margot met her emaciated sister off the boat train at Dover and then passed an agonizing few weeks watching her 'devoured alive' until on 2 May she finally expired in a nursing home in Wimbledon.[9] Lucy was now the only one left of the four sisters with whom Margot had grown up. Lucy, a widow, childless and periodically crippled by severe rheumatism, felt Charty's loss bitterly, weeping continuously and placing added strain on her sister.

Margot, as always when she was depressed, craved love and attention: her self-confidence was so low that even a visit to the oculist to get reading glasses reduced her to tears, signalling that, at forty-seven, she was 'getting old'.[10] Although she feared her husband was 'far too busy for me to worry him',[11] Asquith, in the midst of the constitutional crisis, did his best to comfort her: 'Don't give way to imaginings – especially as to middle age, isolation etc. Everybody regards you as a central figure and force, and no one will ever think of you as an onlooker – and you know that to me, there is no one else.'[12] At the time, October 1911, he was still being truthful when he said there was 'no one else' in his life. But this was soon to change.

Asquith's friends had long recognized what he himself admitted as his 'slight weakness for the companionship of clever and attractive women'.[13] Margot, after her fit of jealousy about Mouche Duncombe in the early years of their marriage, came to accept her husband's need for other female company – indeed, enjoying as she did so many close friendships with other men, she could hardly have done otherwise. She always denied harbouring any jealousy of what she jokingly called her husband's 'little harem', later claiming that 'on the contrary, I welcomed them, as they fitted the theory which I have always held about wives . . . No woman should expect to be the only woman in her husband's life . . . I not only encouraged his female friends I posted his letters to them if I found them in our front hall.'[14] It helped that, with one notable exception, the women in question were her own friends as well as her husband's.

Asquith, now in his sixtieth year, came into regular contact with a great many attractive young women in his children's social circle, known as the 'Coterie'. Violet was still living at home, while after his return from the Sudan Oc had been taken on by Franklin and Herrera, an Anglo-South American trading firm, and was based at 10 Downing Street when not travelling on business in Latin America. Raymond and Beb and their wives frequently called round. As a result, there was a constant stream of youthful visitors to the family's lunch table, where there was an undiscriminating policy of 'open house'. Young guests enjoyed rubbing shoulders with Ministers emerging from Cabinet meetings, while the latter found the high spirits and banter of the 'bright young things' an effective antidote to the atmosphere of siege that was so much part of the politics of the day.

Asquith was fond of both his daughters in law, especially Cynthia who was a natural flirt. Another of his close young female friends was Pamela Jekyll, who had married Reginald McKenna in 1908. In January of that same year Pamela drew Asquith a diagram of his heart divided between several young women: Viola Tree, twenty-three-year-old actress daughter of Herbert Beerbohm Tree and his wife Maud (both old friends of the Asquiths); Dorothy Beresford, eldest daughter of the Rector of Easton Grey; Margot's niece, Lilian Tennant; Venetia Stanley; and Pamela herself.[15] It was to Viola Tree that Asquith turned for support as he tried to cope with the strains of the political crises in 1911. Margot herself regarded Viola as 'unspoilable', once telling her husband – admittedly well after Viola was safely married – that 'after myself I would rather you had married her. She is the least hysterical of women . . . she loves you with the best kind of love.'[16] Viola was vivacious, attractive, highly intelligent, sympathetic and popular. She would provide what the beleaguered Prime Minister called 'the most perfect companionship' during regular Friday afternoon drives out of London into the still easily accessible countryside.

Meanwhile, the bitter struggle over the Parliament Bill limiting the veto of the House of Lords reached its climax on 24 July 1911, when the Prime Minister was obliged to reveal his trump card: that the King was willing if necessary to create sufficient new Liberal peers to force the legislation through. When Asquith rose to speak in the House of Commons there was what he described to Viola as 'a truly fiendish row – the worst I think I have ever seen. The base young Tories tried to howl me down, and very nearly succeeded. Our men were with difficulty restrained from throttling Hugh Cecil, F. E. Smith and other bad offenders.'[17]

It was a baking summer's day and Margot, sitting in the Speaker's Gallery with Violet, Elizabeth, Katharine and Ettie, was bathed in perspiration. 'I felt quite iced when I saw what was going to happen – they were not going to let him speak,' she wrote afterwards in her diary. She suffered every moment of 'a degrading and humiliating spectacle', all the time conscious that those around her were stealing quick glances to see how she was reacting. Ettie tried to comfort her with 'a very sympathetic little squeeze'.[18] Eventually she could stand it no longer and left the gallery to seek relief in the Prime Minister's room, where she scribbled a note to Grey: 'You are our one chance. You will be listened to – for God's sake defend him from these cats and cads!' When she resumed her seat, she saw Grey, unable to find a place on the crowded Front Bench, squeezed on to the bench to the left of the Prime Minister. She could see him toying with her note, although he never read it. After Asquith finally gave up and sat down, Balfour rose and was listened to in stony silence; then Grey, whose patrician background and bearing belied his own radical views, was allowed to deliver what one Parliamentary reporter called 'a dignified rebuke to the Unionists'.[19] However, when F. E. Smith, one of the ringleaders of the disturbance, tried to follow, it was the Liberals' turn to cause uproar, and after five minutes of further chaos the Speaker had no option but to suspend the sitting.

By the time Margot reached Asquith's room, already crowded with family and supporters, she was thoroughly distraught. She resented the fact that neither Violet nor Katharine seemed to share her rancour: 'they were watching a wonderful and most dramatic mise-en-scène, but they were not exactly feeling it.' As soon as Grey appeared, Margot hustled him outside into the corridor, ostensibly to thank him for his intervention, and dissolved in tears:

I took his hand and put it against my burning cheek and kissed it. He said nothing but he took both my hands in his hands and pressed them to him and his eyes were full of tears: 'I never read your letter till afterwards – don't, don't be so hurt. It was a horrid sight, but you mustn't feel things so deeply: it is all part of political strife. He has scored all round. Don't, don't cry, all this isn't as personal as you think.'

'Yes it was – their faces were like wild beasts! How dared they shout him down . . . You are a noble and most beloved friend. Henry loves you quite as much as I do.' He looked in both my eyes with his beautiful expression of aloofness and sympathy, his eyes quite full of tears, and put both my hands in his two and pressed them and we left each other. I joined the others in H's room. I saw at a glance Henry had been deeply moved, hurt and surprised.

In fact, Asquith realized that the Opposition had overplayed their hand and, he insisted to Viola, 'I wasn't "upset" not really: tho' I confess I minded, for it was a squalid, degrading, humiliating scene.' He even wished his confidante had been there as 'it would have amused you'. Like Oc, en route for the Sudan contemplating martyr-dom 'before a gallery of women',* the actor in Asquith appreciated fighting his political battles before an audience of pretty young women: 'I know you feel strongly and deeply, and I rely on you,' he insisted to his actress friend, assuring her 'you cannot imagine how much rest and pleasure and joy you have given me during these last 48 hours'.[20]

Given Margot's state of mind there was no 'rest and pleasure' to be had in her company. She, for one, was most definitely not amused, but she refused to blame Balfour, whose feeble attempts to call his troops to order had proved woefully ineffective. 'I felt sorry for Arthur, the most courteous of men,' she wrote to Ettie shortly after-wards. 'And to think that he should have to lead such a rabble – a eunuch like Linky [Lord Hugh Cecil] and cads like F. E. Smith . . . I felt deeply for Henry, who has never said a rude word in his life to a living soul and I was filled with wonder at the hold he has over his men in absolutely forbidding any word of retaliation from them even when they were listening to their P. M. being insulted as if he were a low adventurer.'[21]

The remark about Lord Hugh being a 'eunuch' soon made the rounds of the Asquiths' friends: 'Margot has, it seems, been wilder than ever,' a delighted Balfour wrote to Mary Elcho a few days later from Taplow Court, the Desboroughs' Buckinghamshire mansion, as he regaled her with the verbal castration of his 'shrill-voiced' Cecil cousin. In the event, it was Balfour himself who was the real loser from the rumpus: three months later he quit the leadership in disgust at his inability to control his Party's wilder spirits. The man who emerged as his surprising successor was Andrew Bonar Law, a dour Scot of Ulster descent, summed up by Margot as 'a particularly nice fellow, but he seems to live intellectually from hour to hour like a servant, and has no politics whatever'.[22]

Three days after Asquith turned fifty-nine he wrote to Viola Tree: 'I have just gone through another birthday, but I feel no older: on the contrary, younger distinctly than I did this time last year.'[23] However,

*See p. 118.

his jowly and corpulent appearance belied his youthful pretensions. Few, if any, Prime Ministers have had to face so many problems at once: fierce Parliamentary struggles over Lloyd George's Budget, the reform of the House of Lords, proposals for Irish Home Rule and disestablishment of the Church of Wales, and opposition from within his own Party to increased spending on the Navy. On top of this, there was the unrelenting campaign by the suffragette movement and serious strikes by miners and railwaymen. And, in the background there were the constant emotional demands of Margot's volatile moods, terrible bouts of depression and irrational hostility towards Violet, as well as Violet's own fragile health and emotional instability. Constance Battersea, the widow of the Asquiths' old friend Cyril Flower,* who lunched with the Asquiths at Archerfield in October 1911, gave her sister a more detached view of the Prime Minister's health and demeanour:

> The PM kind, extremely cordial – but how he is changed! Red and bloated – quite different from what he used to be. He gave me a shock. They all talk of his overeating and drinking too much. I am afraid there is no doubt about it . . . Margot is a wreck to look at, the young ones growing up, all clever – Cys, a marvel, the little Anthony, a musical genius – Elizabeth aged 14, talking like a woman of 25 – Violet very clever talks talks – I have never seen such a family![24]

Yet, whatever Asquith's physical decline, his political position had never been stronger with the passage of the Parliament Act curbing the veto power of the House of Lords. In an inspired case of appointing the chief poacher as head gamekeeper, the Prime Minister made Churchill and McKenna swap posts, giving the former charge of reorganizing the Royal Navy whose wings he had, up to now, been so keen to clip; while the latter's calmer and more liberal approach was to prove better suited to the work of the Home Office. Winston was staying with the Asquiths as a house guest at Archerfield when the Prime Minister offered him this 'plum', as Margot called the Admiralty, and 'was in the 7th Heaven of joy'.[25] McKenna, however, was distraught.

The main issue that threatened to derail the Government was the fractious state of industrial relations. Cynthia was not alone in

---

*Created Lord Battersea in 1892, he died in 1907.

fearing it was 'the beginning of a French Revolution' and could 'already hear the tumbrels' during a damaging railway strike in the summer of 1911.[26] When the dispute was eventually solved by the skilful intervention of Lloyd George, Asquith – never one to be jealous of a successful colleague – was unstinting in his thanks. Relations between Prime Minister and Chancellor could not have been better, helped considerably by Margot's almost Pauline conversion to the cause of her Downing Street neighbour. Even Elizabeth added her own precocious pennyworth of praise, writing Lloyd George 'just a line of congratulation on the magnificent way which you put an end to the strike. I do hope you won't think me horribly impertinent . . . Father's account of the way you dealt with the men and masters made the temptation of writing quite irresistable.'[27] After all the hostility the Chancellor had endured from Elizabeth's mother, he could not have been more delighted:

> Dear Miss Elizabeth,
> It is so charming of you to have written to me.
>   The Prime Minister has also written me a letter which I shall treasure to the end of my days. I cannot tell you how proud I am of it. What a fine fellow he is to serve under, generous and chivalrous and so far above the pettiness which spoils most of us public men . . .
>   Many thanks to you.
>   Ever sincerely,
>   D. Lloyd George.[28]

The bond between the Asquiths and their Downing Street neighbours was further cemented by a burgeoning friendship between Puffin and Megan, the Lloyd Georges' youngest child. The two children were almost the same age and treated their adjoining homes as a single playground, enjoying noisy games of hide and seek among Downing Street's interlinking warren of corridors and rooms, oblivious to the important visitors they might bump into.

Margot got on surprisingly well with Megan's mother, Lloyd George's first wife Margaret, although the two women could not have been more different in personality and background. Mrs Lloyd George, the daughter of a Welsh tenant farmer, hated 'society', and only felt truly at home in her beloved Criccieth. Margot described her neighbour as 'a very homely, intelligent, little servant of a woman with a heart of gold and no ambition or rise in her'; nonetheless, she was fiercely protective of her. On one occasion when they were sitting together in the Speaker's Gallery listening to a speech by Lloyd George, the Marchioness of Londonderry audibly called out 'cad', and 'liar'. For Margot 'this kind of thing is intolerable and makes my blood boil' and afterwards she confronted the aristocratic heckler ('a rich, vulgar, has-been beautiful woman') and 'told her she was a snob'.[29]

The Asquith family's academic triumphs were capped that Christmas 1911 when Cys, having already gained a First in Mods and won the Ireland Classics prize earlier in the year, was awarded the coveted Hertford Prize, the one Classics trophy that had eluded both his father and Raymond. 'Cys has really done splendidly,'[30] Asquith wrote to Margot at Archerfield, trumpeting the fact that his fourth son's achievement was 'a record'.[31]

In January 1912 Asquith departed on a sightseeing holiday in Sicily with Edwin Montagu, his thirty-three-year-old former Parliamentary Private Secretary, recently promoted Under-Secretary to the India Office. It was arranged that they would be joined by Violet, who was enjoying winter sports in Murren, and her close friend Venetia Stanley.

*

Edwin Montagu's father, Samuel Montagu (created Baron Swaythling in 1907), the founder of the eponymous merchant bank, died a few months before his son's trip to Sicily in 1912. A severe and unforgiving parent, he was little mourned by his six children on whom he had tried, without much success, to enforce his own strict brand of Judaism. Edwin found in Asquith an ideal father figure: easy going, appreciative and quick to praise, and Margot soon scooped him up into their extended family. The affection was mutual: writing to Margot from the boat to Sicily, Asquith described Montagu as 'an excellent travelling companion – clever, sympathetic, never boring and capable of well chosen silences'.[32]

Violet was delayed in Murren for a few days by tonsillitis, before picking up Venetia in Lucerne on the way to Sicily. They were met at Palermo by Montagu and Danostrio, their courier, who took them along the coast to their hotel, Villa Igeia. Violet was delighted by 'our marble balcony covered with purple bougainvillaea' and pleased to find her father 'looking very well and bird-happy'.[33] Asquith himself extolled the benefits of 'cool clean air and for the most part bright sun: above all the sense of being away from both the small and large worries of life'. Although in his letter to Margot he included the obligatory 'I wish you were here', she was probably one of the worries he was relieved to escape.[34] She had turned down the chance to join the party, preferring to be with her children in Murren, but she wept after seeing her husband off. She was already feeling the first stirrings of jealousy of Venetia, and her husband had to reassure her: 'Why should you think anything you have written has "alien-ated" me? It could not, even for a moment, and even tho' I thought some things you said (or suggested) a little less than just. I love you always wherever I am, and you know well that no one ever does or ever could take your place.'[35]

Three years later, in a letter to Venetia herself, Asquith recalled this holiday in Sicily as the 'first stage in our intimacy (in which there was not a touch of romance, and hardly of sentiment) . . . we had together one of the most interesting and delightful fortnights in all our lives'.[36] But Viola, or 'cara amica'[37] as he called her in a flirtatious letter written in Italian from Palermo, was still very much in his thoughts.

For a careworn Prime Minister, the holiday was a light-hearted interlude after the stress of the past few years: seeing the classical sights, playing chess and Piquet, teasing and being teased. Violet's description – as always addressed to the ever-present spectre of Archie Gordon – of one strenuous bout of sightseeing near Syracuse gives a flavour of the party's high spirits:

> You would laugh if you saw us rumbling off in our grotesque landau – Father, Venice [Venetia], Montagu and I, every tooth in our heads rat-tling – over the most mountainous and flinty roads, the old Downing Street fur rug spread over our 4 knees, 3 Baedeckers in our hands, La Notre [Danostrio, the courier] on the box occasionally calling our atten-tion to some simple wayside object: 'Mr Asquith, excuse if I bring to your notice the prickly pear' – etc. A church is reached, built on the founda-tions of an old temple, I struggle up the stylobate [the base of the columns] in a hobble skirt . . . La Notre proceeds, we go down to the crypt then on through some catacombs, Montagu pales at the skulls, shivers at the cold, Venetia and I rally him. We re-emerge covered with cobwebs and dripping in the warm sunlight of the friars' garden – full of the smell of Cherry Pie – the friar gives me a little bunch.[38]

Montagu delighted in playing games with the two young women, a willing butt of their good-natured 'ragging'.[39] Violet recorded how 'we played hiding in the garden and jumping out after dark. Montagu is the best person in the world to play it with. He is so frightened – and so frightening.'[40] Her father told Margot how they had nicknamed him 'Tante', after 'we discovered one morning that he had all sorts of hidden affinities to that moody and tempestuous genius'[41] – the hero of the new eponymous novel by Anne Douglas Sedgwick, which seems to have been part of everyone's holiday reading.

Montagu was by now besotted with Venetia, writing to her regularly and taking her out whenever he could. Although she was 'forbidden fruit' under a clause in Lord Swaythling's will that stipulated that his children would lose their inheritances if they married Gentiles, it had probably already occurred to Edwin that his father's executors might be satisfied if the irreligious Venetia were to go through a nominal conversion to Judaism. In any case, during the August following their Sicilian holiday, he proposed to her. Although Venetia, physically repelled by his huge head and coarse pock-marked face, refused him, she lapped up the waspish political gossip at which he excelled, and they continued to see a great deal of one another, with Montagu a regular house guest at the Stanley family homes at Alderley and Penrhos.

Venetia, now twenty-four, was not over-burdened by rival suitors. Most men of her age were mystified and even intimidated by this austere, highly intelligent young woman, so lacking in vanity that she was, in Cynthia's words, 'brutally careless of her person!'.[42] Her friend, Sir Laurence Jones, has left this impression of her in her youth:

> Venetia had dark-eyed, aquiline good looks and a masculine intellect. I delighted in her and we were close friends; but she permitted herself, in the morning of her youth, no recourse to her own femininity. She carried the Anthologies in her head, but rode like an Amazon, and walked the high garden walls of Alderley [her family's home in Cheshire] with the casual stride of a boy. She was a splendid, virginal, comradely creature, reserving herself for we knew not what use of her fine brain and hidden heart.[43]

Violet caught a glimpse of another, flirtatious, side to Venetia when they were staying together with the Aberdeens in Dublin after Archie's death, recounting to Bongie how her friend 'was a transformed <u>being</u> here! Very painstaking, feminine, bright and *avenante** – her gruff baritone changed to a siren soprano – shooting glittering glances hither and thither – wearing a new 'fish' every night and spending tête à tête days at the zoo with her A.D.C.'s!'[44] For Asquith, Venetia, as a 'lady of leisure' and Violet's best friend, had distinct advantages over Viola Tree, who was often away on theatre tours and had plenty of much younger admirers: he was not fooled when the actress tried to assuage his jealousy with a 'scientifically mapped out' account her days on tour, finding 'plenty of loopholes here, as I could point out if you were in the confessional box'.[45]

Asquith himself needed a confessor, or more precisely a comforter, as he was buffeted by seemingly endless storms of political controversy. But, Venetia was as yet not ready to fulfil the role. The holiday mood was dissipated as soon as the Prime Minister and his party reached Charing Cross, where they were confronted by an aggressive party of suffragettes. The demonstrators, he later told Margot, 'were kept well in hand by our bodyguard, Nash, Bongie etc, and Violet had the satisfaction of crunching the fingers of one of the hussies'.[46] It was not the only time women of the Prime Minister's family had to come to his aid: on other occasions Margot boxed the ears of one assailant, and Violet, who, perhaps surprisingly, shared her father's opposition to female suffrage, used a golf club to fend off women attempting to rip off his clothes at Lossiemouth golf course.[47]

The suffragettes, persistent as they were, posed no threat to the Government. More serious was a renewed bout of industrial unrest among coalminers and dockers, either group of which had the power to cripple the country. In the background the dangerous naval arms race with Germany was gathering pace, with Haldane visiting Berlin in what turned out to be a forlorn mission to secure an agreement with the Kaiser. By early March Asquith, writing to Viola, was comparing himself to St Paul at Ephesus 'fighting with beasts – Gorgons and Hydras and Chimearas dire – as Milton says somewhere'.[48]

When Margot had returned from Switzerland in mid-February she had 'rushed into the Cabinet room and found Henry in splendid form: thinner and better to look at'. However, he was soon having to deal with the first national coal strike, and it was not long before his health was damaged once again by the renewed stress, made worse by over-work, lack of exercise and too much food and drink. On the

---

*'Comely'

morning of 2 April he came into her bedroom, sat down on her bed and said 'I don't feel well.' Coming from him, as Margot noted in her diary, this was like her saying she thought she was dying: 'I looked up and saw his tired eyes looking quietly at me and an expression of exhaustion written like a railway map over his whole powerful face.' He said he had been feeling giddy for the last three weeks and she noticed how 'the strike and working day and night had aged him'. She touched his forehead and it was hot. She felt sure 'he was on the very edge of a great collapse'. He had to chair a Cabinet meeting in an hour's time, and, with Lloyd George due to introduce his latest Budget that afternoon, it was not one he could miss. Margot made him lie down for half an hour and then helped him downstairs. She then telephoned her doctor, Parkinson, and arranged for him to call that evening, making sure her husband cried off a 'Budget' dinner hosted by Montagu.

Margot herself was still far from well, suffering from persistent colitis. Now, worries about her husband's health – for which she blamed her own inability to give him the support he needed – reduced her to tears. She pulled herself together to watch Lloyd George's Budget speech that afternoon, and in the evening she attended a performance of Bach's *St Matthew Passion* at St Paul's Cathedral, during which, unnoticed in the dark, she was relieved 'to cry my heart out at the glorious music. I prayed for Henry, I <u>suffered</u> for him and begged God to forgive me and make me strong in health and faith.'[49] When Margot got home Asquith was not there. She rang Dr Parkinson, who gave her his diagnosis: 'blood pressure on an exhausted brain while eating and drinking the same amount as if he had not been using his brain to the very utmost'. Later her husband appeared. He had been in the Cabinet room all along, writing to Venetia.

This near physical collapse wrought a marked change in the Prime Minister. His strong physical constitution had enabled him to abuse his body for years, and it was a profound shock to find his health was now breaking down. Asquith's former political opponent, Joseph Chamberlain, had been crippled by a stroke and his first question to Dr Parkinson was whether he risked the same fate. Having seen how the strain of office had killed Campbell-Bannerman, he was anxious to avoid wrecking his own health. The doctor warned him to cut back drastically on his drinking. Asquith was never an alcoholic – his alcohol consumption was far less than Churchill's was when he was

Prime Minister – and excessive drinking was as a result of too much wine and brandy at the dinner table to alleviate the strain of having to cope with one crisis after another.

Parkinson's advice, strongly backed by exhortations from Margot, who even threatened to leave him unless he cut down on his alcohol intake,[50] had a dramatic effect A week later, after an Easter break at Ewelme, the home of Frank Lawson near Oxford, Asquith was able to deliver a powerful two-hour speech introducing the Bill to give Home Rule to Ireland. Margot recorded how 'my heart beat with joy' as she listened to him, 'I never heard his voice so good and he got better and better as he went on.' The following day the doctor told her that her husband's 'blood pressure had largely decreased' and that he 'had the arteries of a young man'.[51]

It seems that this health crisis and the warnings of his doctor and Margot combined to reform Asquith. Henceforward, although never a teetotaller, he seems to have taken a firm hold on his alcohol consumption. But reputation once tainted is rarely regained. Ettie's bone-headed Tory husband, Lord Desborough, was not alone among Asquith's enemies in continuing to refer to him as 'a drunken time-server, with no moral qualities and prostituted abilities'.[52] And even among his friends, the convenient sobriquet 'Squiff' was one that stuck.*

Towards the end of 1911 Margot managed to procure the 'country cottage' for which she had so long been pining. 'The Wharf' in Sutton Courtney, near Oxford, consisted of two small cottages set about eighty feet behind a redundant coal barn and wharf on the River Thames. The property belonged to Maud Tree, who had hoped to convert it into a retreat for Viola, but, as she told Margot, was now having second thoughts. Margot was immediately keen to buy. Maud wanted £1,300 for it and the architect, Walter Cave, a friend of the Asquiths, suggested that for £3,000 'he could make it all perfect'.[53]

The Asquiths were already living well beyond their means, but Margot was 'bent on buying the Barn Wharf, I've thought it all over

---

*Although stories about Asquith's supposed heavy drinking continued to circulate, most can be dismissed as hearsay. One indicator of his sobriety is provided by his letters to Venetia Stanley and other female confidantes, to at least one of whom he wrote most nights before going to bed. All these letters are perfectly lucid and legible.

most carefully',[54] as she wrote to Maud. Never one to have any scruples about accepting or soliciting gifts, she brazenly asked her richest friend, the American banker, John Pierpont Morgan, to help. The notoriously ugly Morgan, who had had a serious crush on Margot since first meeting her twenty-five years earlier, was 'delighted' to advance £3,000 towards the cost of the scheme. It never occurred to her – or indeed Asquith or Grey, who was the only person outside her family who knew about the gift – that accepting such a large sum of money from a man who had significant financial dealings with the British Government was, to say the least, open to question.

Once work on the Wharf was complete, Margot arranged a little house-warming tea party for Sunday 21 April. Asquith, Elizabeth, Puffin, Violet, Beb and Cynthia made up the party, with Hugh Godley – who had recently renewed his wooing of Violet – the only non-family member. A pall was cast over the celebration by the shocking news earlier in the week of the sinking of the SS *Titanic*. Beb arrived on the Friday evening with a pile of newspapers full of the latest heartrending details of the tragedy and, as he read out the reports of the liner's last moments, Margot noticed 'Henry was deeply moved', while she herself could not suppress her tears.

Margot was anyway in a thoroughly emotional state. A couple of months earlier she had been distraught at the prospect of Puffin, now aged nine, attending school for the first time (Mr Gibbs' famous pre-preparatory school in Sloane Street). She was more than ever jealous of Violet's close relationship with Asquith and wanted her twenty-five-year-old stepdaughter off her hands, fearing she 'would never marry and hash her life like so many women do from self indulgence'.[55] She revealed the real cause of her distress in a letter to Alfred Lyttelton's wife, DD:

> I ought to have my own husband and my own children in a home of my own – I have only been alone with Henry and my children 3 weeks in 19 years. This has got on my nerves. It is really physical and the more I control the longing or the showing of it, the iller I feel. We are always à trois – in shops, in the hills, on official occasions, round the fire and at the altar. I long to take the communion service with Henry alone. I long to talk to him – to be with him. It would be so easy if she would marry.[56]

Violet must have felt the pressure, which was probably the main reason why she was again considering the ever-faithful Hugh

Godley as a possible mate. Even Margot praised her for being 'wonderfully intimate and frank' about her feelings for Hugh, but believed she expected the impossible in a husband, noting that 'Vs deathly analysis of herself and her admirers and habit of giving silver for gold, makes it all fearfully dangerous and difficult. I shall do all I can to guide and support her but I foresee great rocks ahead from her temperament.'[57] Violet herself, in typically Wagnerian mode, explained her inaccessibility to Bongie by comparing her own longing for 'infallibility' to Brünnhilde's declaration that 'if I <u>must</u> surrender to someone, then let it be a hero'.[58] She was unlikely to find a Siegfried among what Margot dubbed 'her little court'.[59]

In early April 1912, in the northern French seaside resort of Le Touquet Violet joined Raymond, Katharine and Hugh for an Easter break (coincidentally at the same time as her father was having his health crisis), and confided in her eldest brother about her problems with their stepmother. For once, Raymond took on the mantle of protective elder brother, and wrote to Margot, who responded by going back over all the old ground: Violet 'has always been more in love with herself than with any-one else'. When Raymond vigorously defended his sister, Margot, who now had all the additional worry of her husband's health, felt guilt: 'My dearest, I feel in every word of your letter a reproach which I've no doubt I've <u>fully</u> earned. I know you are never touchy and always tolerant and good to me and about me. I am sorry I wrote as I did, especially as I feel guilty as Violet has been quite perfect to me all this year.'

After a long talk with Asquith about Violet and Hugh Margot now accepted 'the fundamental difference in temperament and outlook so clearly that I fear it would not be "a safe marriage" . . . All I meant to convey to her was when one does marry one must swallow the man whole and that I didn't think anyone met the intellectuality of her father and the physical attraction and vitality of Archie in one man: the Almighty is too good a handicapper for that.' In her final letter to Raymond on the matter, Margot quotes Violet as saying she was 'afraid of marrying a man "whom I am neither in love with, nor dominated by either the character or the brain of, whose career doesn't open a channel for me to pour my energies through to keep me riveted, interested, occupied" '. Margot saw this as another example of one of her persistent criticisms of her stepfamily, encapsulated here in one of her best epigrams: 'The whole Asquith family over-value brains. I'm a little tired of brains: they are apt to go to the head.'[60]

While Raymond was having this spat with Margot over Violet's love life, his father forwarded to him a note from the Liberal Party Central Office about a vacancy for the seat of North-West Norfolk. Murray, the Chief Whip, was keen for him to stand, but Asquith, while leaving his son to make up his own mind, pointed out that it was a 'scattered village constituency, with no towns and therefore laborious both to win and to run'.[61] Raymond agreed, and having turned down the Norfolk seat, was adopted the following year for the much more suitable seat of Derby.

Raymond was now beginning to make a success at the Bar: he might regard the Law as 'a lean casuistical business', but he was keen to succeed in his chosen profession. His breakthrough had come in 1910 when he was appointed to the legal team representing the United Kingdom at an arbitration in the Hague of a dispute over fishery rights in Newfoundland between Canada and the United States. His letters home are full of scorn for the verbosity of American lawyers and, following his father's practice in the House of Commons, he had no scruples about writing letters during their more tedious speeches. Yet there is an element of (admittedly amusing) contempt in Raymond that goes beyond anything Asquith would have said. But he did not let it affect his work: after the arbitration, his leading counsel, William Robson K.C., wrote to his father about 'how well Raymond has done at The Hague and how much he has helped me'. Robson believed him to be 'capable of great things at the Bar and, I believe, of still greater things on the Bench when he gets there'.[62] This was the opinion of a man who had the chance to observe Raymond's skill as a barrister at close hand.

Yet Raymond's friends and family were deceived by his banter. Even his ever indulgent father reproached his firstborn with pursuing 'a pleasure-hunt' and lacking a 'spark or goad'.[63] Laurence Jones, younger than Raymond but part of the same Balliol set, believed him to be 'without ambition . . . what he prized was leisure – leisure to read and re-read the classic authors, and to cultivate friendships, and to pierce with wit and irony the shams and hypocrisies of our civilisation'.[64] John Buchan, who knew Raymond much better, was beguiled into thinking it 'doubtful if he would have made one of the resounding successes of advocacy. He was too careless of the worldly wisdom which makes smooth the steps in a career, and he had no gift of deference towards eminent solicitors or of reverence towards heavy-witted judges.'[65]

Raymond learnt from his father how to compartmentalize his life. He once told Cynthia that there was a part of one's life between 8pm and midnight which was set apart for pleasure, sometimes one filled it oneself, at other times one handed over these sacred hours to another.[66] She showed the letter to Beb, who on this matter at least was in hearty agreement with his elder brother. Raymond might emphasize the sacred hours of pleasure-seeking to his friends, but the unwritten implication was that the rest of the day was set aside for work. He was now a committed family man, with two daughters to support. Helen's sister, Perdita, was born while he was at The Hague, and despite his blasé attitude (he remarked that girls were cheaper than boys until they reached the ball-gown stage), he doted on both children.

How successful Raymond would have been as a Member of Parliament is difficult to judge. A political career is a lottery since so much is dependent on luck and the actions and prejudices of others. Beb later recalled how his elder brother 'used to talk of the "bleak futility"of ordinary politics, but he was a brilliant speaker, and if he had entered the House, there is little doubt that he would have made his presence felt'.[68] Buchan thought Raymond's talents ideally suited to politics:

> He had every advantage in the business – voice, language, manner, orderly thought, perfect nerve and coolness. The very fact that he sat rather loose to party creeds would have strengthened his hands at a time when creeds were in transition. For, though he might scoff at most dogmas, he had a great reverence for the problems behind them, and to these problems he brought a fresh mind and a sincere goodwill.[69]

Perhaps, though, beneath the disdain for men and their motives, there was an idealist struggling to escape, and Beb was right in believing that, had he lived, his elder brother 'might well have found a cause which would have called forth the highest powers of his nature'.[70]

Few of Raymond's friends were allowed to catch a glimpse of the seriousness that lay beneath the sarcasm. He deliberately sought out the company of younger men who would appreciate his wit but were unlikely to penetrate its veneer. He and his circle had made Balliol

'fashionable' as well as 'respectable' and the College became the pre-
ferred destination for clever Etonians, many of them children of the
Souls. Among this select band were Ettie's two elder boys, Julian and
Billy Grenfell, Frances Horner's elder son, Edward, Charty's surviv-
ing son, Charles Lister, and Aubrey Herbert's younger brother,
Mervyn. The 'non-Souls' among 'the Corrupt Coterie' – as
Raymond's circle now called themselves – included Alan Parsons and
Patrick Shaw-Stewart. It is probably no coincidence that the latter
two were the only ones to achieve outstanding academic success.
The others, like Raymond, all suffered from high parental expectations, but did not have his talent to succeed while at the same time
adopting his devil-may-care attitude to their studies. Julian Grenfell
suffered severe depression at Oxford, Charles Lister rebelled by
joining the Labour Party and Edward Horner, six foot four and with
the shoulders – but not the brain – to match, severely disappointed
his mother by ending up with a Third. Raymond's consoling assertion that academic distinctions were all rot did not cut much ice.[71]
Margot, who admired Edward for his spirit, blamed 'Eton and
Balliol',[72] but her stepson no doubt played his part in smothering his
less gifted friend's ambition.

Raymond was the Coterie's guiding light. 'He was the King,'
recalled Lady Diana Cooper (formerly Manners) many years later:
'He was the one we liked best and he liked us better than his own
people. He was wonderful.' Diana herself, in the words of her biographer, 'read books to please him, echoed his opinions, feared his
criticism. She loved him with a fervour that only first love can
inspire.' Although 'the beautiful, daring, delightfully wicked Lady
Diana Manners' was fourteen years Raymond's junior, she, as much
as he, epitomized the spirit of the Coterie.[73] 'Our pride,' according to
Diana 'was to be unafraid of words, unshocked by drink, and
unashamed of "decadence" and gambling.'[74] Ettie banned her from
her homes and Margot disapproved of vices that included: 'love of
notoriety and stainless vanity – her boredom with the country, her
blasphemy . . . her entire want of sensitiveness . . . no imagination
and no compassion'.[75]

The older generation was surprisingly tolerant of the Coterie's
drugtaking – chloroform ('chlorers') and a variety of other narcotics
were readily obtainable from chemist shops. Asquith was amused
when Nellie Hozier (Clementine Churchill's sister) told him how she
had 'put opium into Raymond's pipes'.[76] The sex usually would not

have amounted to much more than Margot's own cavortings with Peter Flower. What really dismayed their parents was an attitude of flagrant irreverence, profanity and callousness. Margot 'was never more shocked in my life' than by Violet's account of 'Breaking the News', a game she had learnt at Stanway which involved acting out the effect of the death of a child on his or her mother. The black humour (as with many Coterie games) was a parody of the intellectual charades of their Souls parents, but for Margot 'a more <u>terrible</u> game I never could imagine: Heartless and Brutal'.[77] She was equally appalled by Raymond's teasing impiety, perhaps best epitomized by his flippant critique of Christianity to Diana that if Christ had been clean-shaven, the Virgin worn rouge and the Ghost been an eagle or a Bower Bird instead of a dove, how appreciative they all should have been. But no. God had played his cards badly from beginning to end.[78]

The iconoclastic spirit of the Coterie offended not just their parents but also many of their own friends. Cynthia, who like Viola managed to be part of the Coterie's circle while spurning its ethos, believed 'there is an insidiously corruptive poison in their minds – brilliantly distilled by their inspiration, Raymond. I don't care a damn about their morals and manners, but I do think what – for want of a better word – I call their anti-cant is really suicidal to happiness.'[79]

11

'No one was left with a shred of reputation'

———————————◆———————————

IN MAY 1912, three months after Asquith's trip to Sicily, Margot was parted from her husband again when he and Violet travelled to Genoa to join the new First Lord of the Admiralty, Winston Churchill, on the *Enchantress* bound for Syracuse and Malta. Although Asquith begged his wife to come with them, she refused, partly because of her longstanding aversion to sea voyages, but also pleading that his absence would provide an opportunity for her to sort out The Wharf. In the event, she never went near her cottage and almost immediately regretted her decision, particularly as she believed Churchill to be 'the worst sort of friend' for Violet ('his counsel is bad and his attention is vain-making') as well as a bad influence on her husband politically.* Most of the Cabinet would have agreed that one could not 'keep pace at all with his extraordinary changes of conviction'.[1]

At the end of September Margot did manage to get away with her husband and Elizabeth for what she called the 'most delicious holiday possible' in Venice, staying with Lady (Maud) Cunard† and a

———————————

*Although Margot mistrusted Churchill, she could not help liking him: 'Winston is a child and will never grow up . . . It is the side of him I am really fond of, but of course it makes me distrust his judgement very much tho' I see his real genius.' (Diary, 2 September 1913, d.3210, p. 35)

†The wife of the eccentric shipowner, Sir Bache Cunard, and a leading society hostess of the day. Violet was making a pilgrimage to the Aberdeens at Haddo to remember Archie on what would have been his birthday.

large party of her daughter Nancy's friends: 'I richly deserved my little honeymoon – the first since I married.' Without Venetia or Violet to compete with her, she was soon caught up in the youthful high jinks of what was to be one of the last flowerings of a doomed generation. Lord (George) Vernon, another rich Coterie host, had taken a palazzo near the Cunards, where his party included Raymond and Katharine, Beb and Cynthia, Charty's son Charles Lister (a diplomat in the Rome Embassy), Ettie's son Billy Grenfell, Edward Horner (Katharine's brother), Duff Cooper (another young diplomat) and Denis Anson, the eldest son of a sporting baronet. 'There was,' recalled another guest of the Cunards, Lady Diana Manners (later Cooper), 'dancing and extravagance and lashings of wine, and charades and moonlit balconies and kisses.' Margot did not begrudge the attention lavished on her husband by Diana, Nancy and Elizabeth and reported how much he enjoyed taking them sightseeing. Diana remembered how:

> On his arm I would climb the stairs of the Miracoli Church and plan to be married there. (From its slippery steps Elizabeth fell into the narrowest and slimiest of canals.) Hand in hand we would gaze up at Colleoni, read from *The Stones of Venice*, peer at Carpaccios in S. Giorgio de' Schiavoni, then quite invisible from darkness, and buy presents for Margot or white Longhi masks for the evening's masquerade.

Margot had never seen her husband 'in such splendid spirits in my life – he was very sweet to me and the young ones and we spent a lot of loose sunny time in laughing'. The Coterie fêted the Prime Minister in style, laying on a lavish late sixtieth birthday party for him when, according to Diana, they 'dressed him up as a Doge and hung the *sala* with Mantegna swags of fruit and green leaves and loaded him with presents, tenderness and admiration. I think he was ecstatically happy that day.'[2]

The Asquiths' 'honeymoon' continued with a trip to Verona and then Munich, where Frau showed them the sights of her native city and they gorged on cakes and chocolate and loaded themselves with pictures, china and other presents to take home to England. When the time came to leave, Margot felt flat. Elizabeth was staying behind in Bavaria with Frau for a few months' immersion in German culture. Margot recorded that 'My youth seemed to be left behind with Elizabeth. I fell into Henry's arms and cried myself sick, poured out that I was going back to a house I was not wanted in and a lot of wicked things – that Elizabeth needed me and Violet didn't know if I was living or dead.'[3]

Relations with Violet were now more strained than ever, with Margot complaining that her stepdaughter 'can't bear a breath of criticism from any one. I get on her nerves – it is quite natural, we were born with natures utterly opposed to each other.' Margot had recently learnt from Frau about the diary which was still addressed to Archie. But she refused to accept that her own behaviour had played a role in her stepdaughter's grief, insisting that she and Violet get on better than most mothers and daughters. Margot's carping mood was aggravated by a choppy Channel crossing and the homecoming Prime Minister being 'accosted by 'a d-d woman' (a suffragette): 'Luckily I was not near or would have certainly killed her,' observed an enraged Margot. 'Grief makes me wild and wildness gives me a sort of steel strength. Poor Henry I did feel for him.'[4]

Back in England, her colitis and nausea soon reasserted themselves. A rare island of happiness was an impromptu dinner party in November when Asquith called in his main Cabinet confidantes to discuss the political situation. Margot revelled in being the only woman surrounded by five key members of the Government. The detail with which she recorded the evening's conversation is testimony to how frustrated and bored she must have felt much of the rest of the time: 'I've never been at a more exciting and amusing dinner,' she wrote in her diary afterwards, 'only 6 of us and Henry in tearing form. I never heard him better in my life.' She was delighted at the way her husband drew out the initially nervous Lloyd George: 'He and Henry romped over the others – so much freer of self and demarcations – so much humour and rapidity, wit and insight – Winston always hampered in his very best talk by a kind of devouring self . . . his genius cannot be pooled.'

After dinner, while the other four settled down to bridge, Margot had 'a grand talk' with Lloyd George, who was worried about Liberal divisions over House of Lords reform. Winston joined them when he was dummy and chafed his colleague about being 'easily downhearted', calling him 'everything but a funk', only to be floored by Lloyd George's retort. 'What do you know about the situation! You've spent the last two months down a submarine!'[5]

Most of the time, though, Margot not only felt ill and isolated, but also disapproved of many of the Government's policies and disliked what she saw as the shallowness of her stepchildren's friends. Comparing them with her own generation, she saw 'more cocoa than blood in the veins of the men and maidens in our milieu'.[6] In September 1912 McKenna's wife, Pamela, described to a friend how 'she criticizes everything incessantly . . . and always in the unkindest way . . . but I know she never means to be wounding and 1 do feel sorry for her, as she makes herself terribly unhappy'.[7]

Yet Margot could still be witty and amusing in the right company. Lady Minto, the wife of the last Viceroy of India, who had a long talk with her while they were both guests of the Royal Family at Windsor Castle in November 1912, was fascinated by her winning mixture of outrageous indiscretion and complete lack of deference towards their royal hosts. She lit a cigarette as she left the drawing room to go to bed and had to be told to put it out before saying goodnight to the Queen. Lady Minto noted in her diary how, although Margot looked unwell:

> There is always something attractive about her. I like her unguarded, out-spoken remarks, but they are terribly dangerous: she suddenly tells you that her best friend has had all her children by different fathers, and before one has time to recover, she is telling one what a singularly good woman the lady in question is . . . We discussed the political situation, her friends etc and no one was left with a shred of reputation!

The Asquiths' stay at Windsor took place against a rising tide of tension in Ulster over the Government's Bill to establish a Parliament in Dublin. The Unionists were pressing for the exclusion of Ulster and George V, a strong Unionist, was under pressure from Bonar Law to insist on a General Election before granting the Royal Assent to the Home Rule Bill. Although George V got on well with the Prime Minister, he was overawed by his formidable intellect. Not daring to put his views on Ireland to Asquith directly, the King fool-ishly vented his frustration on Margot when, as he later told Lady Minto, she 'buttonholed him' after dinner. According to Lady Minto's account, the monarch 'told her plainly that her Party had no patriotism and were simply clinging on to office without a thought for the good of the country. He told her many home truths.'[8]

Lady Minto's account matches that in Margot's own diary, where she records how she and the King sat in a bay window discussing the Irish situation for more than an hour. Comparing his views to those of 'a most ignorant Club Tory', she wrote that 'he amazed me by his violence and foolish remarks'. Margot was fond of him, but having known him since he was a child, did not mince her own words in lecturing the monarch on how the Unionists had 'made asses of themselves at Blenheim' (at a big rally at the Duke of Marlborough's palace in Woodstock), and telling him he should have reprimanded Bonar Law and F. E. Smith at the Privy Council 'for inciting Ulster to Rebellion'.

Margot and Asquith later laughed a good deal over her conversation with the King. Mcanwhile, George V's Private Secretary, Lord Stamfordham, told Lady Minto that he wished the King 'would say the same thing straight to Asquith' since Margot would 'never repeat it correctly'.[9] There matters would have rested had Margot not taken it upon herself to write to Rosebery (the 'Lord High Steward' and as such an unofficial royal adviser on matters of State) about her conversation with George V, lecturing him on his obligation to ensure that the King understood the Government's point of view. Knowing Margot as he did, Rosebery immediately buttonholed the King and gave him a candid lecture on the impropriety of talking politics to the Prime Minister's wife – especially this one. George V took Rosebery's strictures in good part and admitted to his other Private Secretary, Lord Knollys, that he had been 'foolish' and 'imprudent'. When Margot heard how the King had been scolded for confiding in her, she 'cursed Rosebery in my heart for taking such a conventional point of view' and told him to his face that he would 'spoil our intimacy'. In the end, no great harm seems to have been done: the King apologized to Margot for his outspokenness and (as Knollys reported to Rosebery) asked her to 'keep entirely to herself the conversation which had taken place between them. This she promised "on her word of honour" to do,' while apologizing for repeating their conversation to Rosebery in the first place.[10]

In December 1912 Violet accompanied Lady Aberdeen on a trip to the United States and Canada to raise funds for the relief of tuberculosis victims in Ireland. From the moment they disembarked in New York, Violet found herself an object of fascination for the American newspapers. Her adoption of her father's usual policy of disdain towards reporters naturally wetted their interest: 'Snap me if you can,' she quipped to one photographer as she refused to pose for him. The *Washington Post* put her reticence down to 'the characteristic modesty usually attributed to the English girl'.[11] No one could believe she shared her father's opposition to votes for women and, as an amused Violet wrote home, the American newspapers reported that she was 'a passionate Suffragist restrained from action by your domestic tyranny and bigoted opposition'.

Beneath her demure façade, Violet loved being 'treated like a mixture between an Envoy Plenipotentiary and a Music-Hall star of the first water' and was transfixed by the <u>marvellous</u> vitality energy and horse-power' of New York, where she spent 'a hectic 4 days rushing over gigantic buildings – teeming with human beings – sitting through longish lunches and dinners – getting in and out of taxis, telephone rooms and lifts'. One day she was seated at both lunch and dinner next to ex-President Theodore Roosevelt, who charmed her with his '*élan vital*' and his 'continuous bubble and splutter and flow'. In Washington, she was less impressed by President Taft, whom she dismissed as a 'a distinctly unmagnetic personality', although she found the White House itself 'a jolly place – a little small for present conditions, but simple and dignified'.[12] She was, however, under no illusions about the reason for all the adulation, and she made sure that Asquith knew how much she missed him: 'beloved father – <u>all</u> my fun here comes from being your belonging – and lovingest possession'. She was certainly thinking not of him but of her stepmother when she remarked, only half jokingly, 'I look forward with a shudder to the chilly obscurity which will close round me again on my return home!'[13]

While Violet was having what Asquith described as 'the time of her life' in the United States, the onset of the British winter saw Margot back in the doldrums. Her husband, she complained, was '<u>far too busy</u> this autumn session and undertaken a Goliath amount of work' and so had little time to spare for her problems.[14] Matters were not helped by a sense that she was being steadily sidelined by Venetia.

In a 'Chapter of Autobiography' which Asquith sent to Venetia in 1915, he recalled a weekend in February 1912, just after their Sicilian holiday, when they stayed at Hurstly near Lymington in Hampshire (the house was lent by the Prime Minister's cousin Eustace Firth), together with Violet, Beb and Cynthia (Margot was in Switzerland):

I was sitting with her [Venetia] in the dining room on Sunday morning – the others being out in the garden or walking – and we were talking and laughing just on our old accustomed terms. Suddenly, in a single instant, without premonition on my part or any challenge on hers, the scales dropped from my eyes; the familiar features and smile and gestures and words assumed an absolutely new perspective; what had been completely hidden from me was in a flash half-revealed, and I dimly felt, hardly knowing, not at all understanding it, that I had come to a turning point in my life.[15]

Yet, any romance was slow to develop. Even when Viola put herself out of the frame by marrying Alan Parsons, a fellow member of the Coterie, in July 1912, Asquith made no attempt to deepen his relationship with Venetia, not writing to her more than about once a week until late 1913. As far as Margot was concerned, it was probably Venetia's closeness to Violet that made her less acceptable than other members of her husband's 'harem'. Together they threatened her own position in a way that Viola never could – or wanted to.

Venetia herself gives an interesting insight into her relationship with Asquith at this time, in a letter to Montagu written in November 1912, describing her first visit to the The Wharf:

It was delicious seeing him [Asquith] again. I hadn't any kind of talk with him since the end of the summer. He was in very good spirits I thought in spite of the crisis [over Ulster]. He didn't, as you can imagine, talk much about it and our conversation ran in very well worn lines, the sort that he enjoys on these occasions and which irritate Margot so much by their great dreariness. I love every well known word of them – with and for me familiarity is a large part of the charm.[16]

Whether or not Margot's irritation was really due to the 'dreariness' of her husband's conversation, she evidently succeeded in disguising her antipathy to her young rival. Her pride would not let her admit this antipathy even in her diary, any more than many years earlier she had been willing to confess to her unrequited love for her sister's fiancé, Alfred Lyttelton. Yet, although Venetia herself described Asquith as one of her 'favourite people', she was still far from confident about her own hold over him. Shortly afterwards, after spending most of the week at Downing Street with Violet, she confessed to Montagu that she even wondered whether Asquith sometimes found her company tedious: 'I saw not very much of the P.M. Do you remember saying how much he varied in his liking for me, and that sometimes he quite liked me and at others not at all? Well, this was one of the not at all times. He was horribly bored by my constant presence at breakfast, lunch and dinner.'[17]

Writing to her three years later, Asquith claimed that she had already become his 'pole-star' at this time, rescuing him 'from sterility, impotence, despair'; his love for her enabled him 'in the daily stress of almost intolerable burdens and anxieties, to see visions and dream dreams'.[18]

It is unlikely that Venetia was ever Asquith's mistress. After the publication of his letters to her in 1982, Lady Diana Cooper confirmed that Venetia had told her she was a virgin until her 'brutal defloration' on her wedding night in 1915.[19] The morals of the time made such a relationship almost unthinkable for a young, unmarried woman from the upper or middle classes. In any case, the opportunities for illicit sex would have been few and far between: continual entertaining and ever-present servants would have ensured that the couple were rarely alone. But Asquith, like many politicians, was an inveterate 'groper', and avoiding his attentions became something of a game among the members of his 'harem'. Diana herself, in a letter to her future husband Duff Cooper, complained of 'defending my face from his fumbly hands and mouth', and she always believed that Asquith's relationship with Venetia 'must have included some sexual contact'.[20] Among his family, the subject of his lecherous 'hanky-panky' was almost taboo: Cynthia, according to her biographer Nicola Beauman, 'violently inked over all references in her diary'. Lytton Strachey, who met Asquith a few years later, had fewer inhibitions, revealing in an essay written in 1918 (although not published until 1972) how Ottoline Morrell (an intermittent member of the 'harem') had told him how Asquith 'would take a lady's hand, as she sat beside him on the sofa, and make her feel his erected instrument under his trousers'.[21] The notoriously scandal-mongering Strachey is not the most reliable source but in this case his account rings true.

Whatever the exact nature of Asquith's relations with Venetia, by the end of 1912 an acutely depressed Margot sent her husband an anguished pencil note from Downing Street as he was attending the opening of Parliament on 30 December:

My darling,
    do write just one line, quite short. You've made me so unhappy – I'm also miserable at having been sulky to you tonight. Forgive me.
    Your loving

He returned the note after scribbling: 'Darling – why should you be unhappy? I love you and only you. Your H.'

Asquith undoubtedly found consolation in his relationship with Venetia, yet there is no doubt that he still loved Margot, was worried about her constant bouts of depression and was genuinely anxious to see her health and spirits restored. When Churchill proposed another Mediterranean cruise in May, he was insistent that this time she must join him and Violet on the *Enchantress*. Although the voyage did little to improve her health, she appreciated the cheerful company and change of atmosphere. The Churchills, Clemmie especially, did their best to make her at home on board the Admiralty yacht, although this did not stop her berating her hostess for lack of 'maternal feeling, a great deal of flimsiness, self-indulgence and considerable temper'. She was fascinated – and perhaps a little envious – by the tight hold Clemmie had over her husband, observing how 'the moment he gets back from some futile fishing shooting or inspecting expedition his first question is always "where is Clemmie?"'. What Margot hated was all the sight-seeing – 'all day every day: temples, museums, churches, palaces in boiling sunshine – hundreds of steps going up, hundreds of steps going down. I stood on my legs till I felt numbed.' She also complained about the food: 'the chef on board was an absolute fool and all felt ill in turn (except Clemmie, Violet and Henry who can eat anything).' Violet was not sympathetic, describing her stepmother in a letter to Hugh Godley as 'dwelling morbidly on digestive problems, crabbing the food, the noise, the heat, the dust, in fact most of the fun of travelling', whereas 'the rest of us are divinely happy day in day out'.

The effort of climbing the steps of the Acropolis to visit the Parthenon left Margot feeling 'like a corpse', yet when it was proposed to return the same evening to see the temple by moonlight, she insisted on joining the party. The Churchills considerately hung back from the main group to help her up the steps, but the couple had a tiff when Clemmie tried to adjust Winston's hat and he roughly pushed her hand away. Margot was left alone as Clemmie huffily walked ahead with Winston in hot pursuit. As she watched the couple hug each other in reconciliation on the steps above her, she 'felt almost ashamed of being a spectator to their embrace – I meandered away quickly feeling very ill and lonely', slinking 'under the shadow of the great columns, too numb to cry and too sick to pray'. The contrast between Winston and Clemmie's obvious physical affection for each other and her own feelings of inadequacy as a wife was all too painful.

The Marconi scandal, which had been building up for nearly a year, reached its climax soon after the Asquiths resumed to England. The origins of the affair lay in dealings in Marconi shares the previous year by Lloyd George, Rufus Isaacs (the Attorney General) and the former Chief Whip, now Lord Murray. Negotiations between the Government and the British Marconi company about setting up a chain of wireless stations across the Empire were close to a deal by spring 1912, sparking fevered speculation in Marconi shares on the London Stock Exchange.[22] In the meantime, shares in Marconi's United States affiliate had been in the doldrums after a series of financial scandals. With no prospect of tapping disillusioned American investors, the Chairman of British Marconi, Godfrey Isaacs (brother of Rufus), sought to raise funds for the American company by a share issue in London, where the Marconi name would have a much better reception. Keen for his brothers to share in the expected bonanza, he persuaded Rufus to take a large quantity of shares, and the Attorney General in turn brought his friends Lloyd George and Murray in on the deal. After the American Marconi shares were introduced on to the London Stock Exchange in April, the price quickly doubled, but instead of cashing in their profit, the three politicians greedily bought more shares at the inflated level and ended up losing money when the price fell back.

It was not long before there was City gossip about Government ministers speculating in Marconi shares – in precisely which Marconi company was unimportant at this stage. As Margot later put it in her diary: 'No one cared a fig if they had been Manchurian or Madagascuers [sic], it was the word "Marconi" over which the Government were forming a contract which mattered.'[23] The Isaacs brothers and Samuel, the Postmaster General who had been nego-tiating with Marconi, were all Jews, and dark hints of an alleged 'Jewish conspiracy' to defraud British taxpayers soon began to spice the rumours. When the terms of the contract were debated in the House of Commons in October 1912, the Attorney General – stung by stories about him dealing in the shares of British Marconi – cat-egorically denied buying the company's stock. Strictly speaking he was telling the truth, in that he had only dealt in the shares of the

American company. But he was clearly being economical with his facts.

As the political pressure increased over the coming months, Isaacs and Lloyd George both offered their resignations, but the Prime Minister, believing them to have been merely foolish in not admitting to their transactions, refused to accept them. Little by little the truth began to emerge and eventually both Ministers were forced to admit to their dealings in shares in American Marconi. Having refused to accept the two men's resignations, Asquith had little option but to give them his backing.

For Margot, feeling cut off from politics, the affair was a heaven sent opportunity to play a full part in dishing out advice, solicited or otherwise. She was more inclined to blame Isaacs than Lloyd George, who was still her blue-eyed boy and whom she rightly described as 'a green horn' as far as the stock market was concerned.[24] However, in the days leading up to the House of Commons debate on Marconi on 18 June 1913, her main concern was to protect her husband's interests. After 'hearing quite vaguely that neither of them in spite of their anguish had the least intention of apologizing to the House for their conduct, I was determined at any rate to see Rufus and for Henry's sake find out what he intended to say – I was not going to allow Henry's generosity to be taken advantage of'.[25]

Margot's first step was to consult Sir Robert Chalmers, the Permanent Secretary to the Treasury, who advised her that the two men's only chance was 'a complete white sheet'. He warned her that Lloyd George was a treacherous man who had never understood the dignity or responsibility of his position, and interestingly likened his character to that of Napoleon. Although Margot faithfully recorded the warning in her journal, it did little to shake her faith in her new friend: 'I am fond of him and think he has great affection when you are with him. He has a genuine conviction that he can help the poor.'[26] A couple of days later, Isaacs sounded Margot out on what he should do, presumably as a means of gauging how far her husband was likely to go in backing him. When she repeated Chalmers' advice that he must make a full apology, Rufus put his head in his hands and, close to tears, 'said "You don't really mean what you say – you <u>cannot</u> ask me to do this."'

Margot, adopting her best schoolmistressy tone, replied: 'But my dear Rufus what did you mean to say – surely not to justify yourself and expect my man to back you? You and Lloyd George must be mad if you think such a thing possible. He will stand by you both on this condition and this <u>only</u>. I have no sort of authority from him, but I <u>know</u> these to be his views . . . You have no alternative – neither you or Lloyd George will have a chance if you try to brave it out.' She promised to see her husband straightaway to confirm and report back on his views. Asquith told her 'you can go straight to him and tell him you have in no way exaggerated what I feel', adding as she went to the door, 'tell him, I'm going to stand by both of them'. Margot then went to the Attorney General's office:

I confess I felt very very sorry for Rufus. I found him white as a sheet sitting on a green sort of sofa and sat beside him. He turned his back and literally cried. I pulled him down and put my arm round his shoulder and begged him to buck up. It seemed incredible to me that he should not see the situation clearly. It has permanently altered my views of his judgement and alas! of his courage.[27]

She backed up her advice with a letter:

My dear Rufus,
Our conversation is burnt into me as a living coal. The agony of your face and depth of your soul and of every emotion – generosity love despair amazement – laid bare, touched me profoundly . . . A man is tested as to his character in adversity only. Great simplicity touches every-one. Cleverness and brains must be the servants, never the Masters of your soul. Later on you will not be remembered only by great achievements, but by a great apology.
    Your devoted friend, Margot Asquith.[28]

Next Margot turned her attention to steeling Lloyd George's resolve, writing to him:

To my mind they seriously overrate what will happen – <u>we</u> shall score and why? Because of the low vile charges they made without a shadow of evidence and after all is said and done the Committee have proved nothing but great indiscretion. This debate must show that nothing of the kind can <u>ever</u> happen again – and though when you realized the folly, you apologized (that part of your speech should be broad and simple in <u>no</u> way rhetorical it will have much more effect) and did your best. Henry is <u>fine</u>, the right mood and much stirred up by the caddish behaviour of Bonar Law, Lord Bob Cecil etc. <u>Do</u> see him to-day you and Rufus will be in high spirits.[29]

Asquith sent both Lloyd George and Isaacs a draft of what he felt they should say in the debate. Margot backed up her husband's advice in two letters to Lloyd George urging 'no "Hell giving" tomorrow . . . later on you will speak in the country and tell the voters how vilely you and Rufus have been treated'. She angrily dismissed the allegations: 'God's truth, it makes my blood boil – indiscreet you may all have been, but to have this fuss made by our rotten opponents is too ridiculous', and sagely advised him, 'nervous and high strung as you are, I would drink a little *sal volatile**, finally exhorting him to 'take <u>everything</u> in your stride like a race horse'.[30]

Lloyd George could not resist a little 'Hell giving' with some well-aimed abuse of his tormentors in the Press, but on the whole he followed the Prime Minister's advice and was suitably contrite. Margot was pleased with his speech although she found him 'a little impatient over his own apology'. She was less impressed by Isaacs, who made what Asquith aptly described as a 'long, diffuse, rambling, stupid speech'[31] in which he made great legalistic play with the exact meaning of the word 'intentional' to describe the way he had misled his fellow MPs.

The Prime Minister, true to his word, defended his ministers with typical vigour. In the end, both men were let off the hook thanks to the restraint of the Unionist leaders, embarrassed by the blatant anti-Semitism behind the attacks. It was unfortunate that four months after the debate Lord Alverstone, the Lord Chief Justice, retired. He was seriously ill and had put off the moment as long as he could. By convention, the Attorney General always had the 'first refusal' to be Lord Chief Justice when the post became vacant and it was well known that Isaacs had long coveted the position. After his exoneration by the House of Commons, Asquith told Margot that 'logically he had no choice' but to nominate Rufus, although Lloyd George was so worried that his friend would be passed over that as early as July he was lobbying Margot to use her influence with her husband. 'I <u>wish</u> I could do what you wish! But Mr. Lloyd George, Henry is sure to give it to Rufus, but <u>I</u> shan't influence him', she replied. The remark did not suggest any disapproval of the appointment on Margot's part, but was a measure of her own waning influence over her husband, who 'can do pretty well what he likes. He is on the top of the wave!'

---

*The traditional Victorian remedy for swooning women.

Isaacs' refusal to apologize for conduct that had put the whole Government at risk left a bitter taste in Margot's mouth: 'I have come to the painful conclusion that no Jew has courage – not that <u>last little bit</u> – they cannot help it, they are born "soft".'[32] It was, of course, unfair to reproach a whole people for one man's frailty, though she never allowed their friendship to be affected by her disapproval of his behaviour over Marconi, nor indeed by her hurt three years later when Lord Reading, as Isaacs now became, was the only leading Liberal to back Lloyd George against her husband for the Premiership.*

---

*It would be wrong to accuse Margot, who had many Jewish friends throughout her life, of anti-Semitism, although she did have some firm prejudices: a few months after the Marconi scandal she confessed that 'the Nationality I hate most is the American – after that the Welsh and my third hate is the Irish'. (Margot Asquith's Diary, d. 3210, p. 158)

12

'There's a germ of violence in the air'

———————————◆———————————

MARGOT SUFFERED WHAT she called 'a sort of nerve break-down' once the excitement of the Marconi scandal had subsided: 'I looked and felt ugly. I was irritable, over-wrought and useless.' Worst of all, she found herself, as a side-effect of the 'break-down', losing her power of speech. The trigger seems to have been the sudden death of Alfred Lyttelton in July 1913, which brought flooding back painful memories of Laura and her own early unrequited love. Asquith made the mistake of trying to spare her an extra ordeal by not giving her advance notice of the generous tribute he paid to Lyttelton in the House of Commons, and she bitterly resented not having been allowed to hear his 'glorious perfect speech'.[1]

The family's summer holiday in Scotland – this year at Hopeman Lodge on the Moray Firth, lent to them by Posie's former husband, Tom Gordon-Duff – brought some relief to Margot. The house was almost new and hideous: Violet described it as 'painfully square and bare . . . no garden, no blade of grass, no leaf of shade', but it was comfortable and set in glorious scenery: 'the sea at one's feet – glorious sunsets over it – and a lovely range of hills'. It was close to Lossiemouth golf course, where the Asquiths found a new playmate in the Labour MP and future Prime Minister, Ramsay MacDonald. He bewitched Violet with his 'beauty, fluency and vanity'.[2] At the end of September the Asquiths went to stay at Brodick Castle on the Isle of Arran and Margot was touched when one day Asquith took her to see Helen's grave at Lamlash for the first time: 'I never saw Henry

more touchingly simple,' she recorded. 'He told me of her death and
dear Beb's little drawings of ships to please his dying mother.' She
'picked a few little leaves and pressed them in my Bible for me and
Violet', reflecting 'how different Violet would have been had her
mother lived!'.[3]

However, Margot's melancholy flooded back when her latest
ailment – severe problems with her gums – forced her to return to
London in October for dental treatment. Venetia arrived at
Hopeman just before she left and almost immediately sparked
another spat with Violet by repeating some criticism Margot had
made. Curiously, Venetia seems to have been oblivious to how much
her own relationship with Asquith was contributing to her hostess's
woes: she tried hard to make it up in a contrite letter to 'Darling
Margot', in which she admitted: 'I think I've at last realized the
mistake of repetitions, they are very edged tools! Dearest Margot I
do hope you'll take great care this winter and really get strong and
well.'[4]

Margot was not the only member of the family to be seriously
depressed. Cys, after gaining a First in his 'Greats' Finals, was almost
suicidal over his unrequited love for Kakoo. In response, Margot
readily agreed to send her stepson on a prolonged holiday to Egypt
and the Sudan with Violet for company. Having her stepdaughter
out of the way would have been an added bonus. Margot was eventually persuaded to go for a rest cure in Antibes with Puffin in
January. After she left, Asquith wrote her 'one line to tell you how
much I miss you and how I long that this exile of yours will make you
really strong and well and happy for years to come. That is my one
wish.' Unfortunately, he felt he had to mention 'that there is a rather
heavy overdraft at the Bank, which will have to be provided for. But
don't say anything to Eddy [Glenconner].'[5] He was reluctant to add
to his wife's load with money worries, but they were living well
beyond their means. A letter from her bank manager informed her
that they were £950 in debt. Ignoring her husband's strictures, she
wrote to all three of her brothers to seek their assistance. However,
although Eddy gave her £200 for Christmas, they all refused to help
with her family expenses. No doubt they felt they would be merely
encouraging their sister's fecklessness and saw no reason to subsidize
her stepchildren. That said, it would surely have been reasonable for
Eddy Glenconner in particular – who after all was one of the richest
men in the country and owed his whole political career (not to

mention his peerage) to his brother-in-law – to have at least offered to pay off their overdraft.

To add to their worries, the day after Margot left for Antibes, Violet cabled from Khartoum that Cys had contracted dysentery and the doctors feared he had typhoid – the disease that had killed their mother. Violet followed up her telegram with a worried letter to Bongie, confessing she felt 'so far away – Pray for him [Cys]'. Frantic cables passed between London, Antibes and Khartoum, before the crisis passed and Cys was out of danger.

For Asquith, this new anxiety about Cys, together with their indebtedness and all Margot's problems, physical and mental, added personal worries to the seemingly endless political crises. Throughout the autumn and winter months, he had held secret meetings with Bonar Law and Carson to try to hammer out a way to give Home Rule to Ireland that would satisfy the concerns of Ulster's Unionist majority without losing the support – essential to the Liberals' Parliamentary majority – of Redmond's Nationalists.

The other big political problem was a Cabinet split over Churchill's latest proposed hike in Naval spending, which was strongly opposed by Lloyd George. Asquith was quietly trying to steer his colleagues in the First Lord's direction, and he would not have been pleased to discover that Margot, on the eve of her departure for Antibes, had been working in precisely the opposite direction, urging the Chancellor 'don't let Winston have too much money it will hurt our party in every way – Labour and even Liberals. If one can't be a little economical when all foreign countries are peaceful then I don't know when one can.'[6] Fortunately, by the time she returned in early February, Churchill had won the argument, having, so Asquith told her, 'conducted his campaign with extraordinary ability and quite won over Lloyd George'.[7]

Margot returned in altogether much better fettle, even having managed to put on eleven pounds in weight. She recorded how 'Henry and I, delighted to be alone together, rushed at every subject. I felt gloriously well. It was like a honeymoon'; he was 'so wonderfully quick, responsive, kind as well as brilliant'.[8] Her happy mood did not last long. It was soon apparent that her husband's bond with Venetia was growing stronger: he was seeing her several times a week as well as writing to her almost every day, and she had now graduated from being his 'dearest love' to his 'darling'. As the crisis over Ulster worsened, with recruits flooding in to join Carson's Ulster

Volunteers, Asquith admitted to Venetia on 22 March that 'I have never wanted you more'.[9]

Margot, meanwhile, was at the Wharf, usually confined to bed with severe headaches and once again suffering difficulties in speaking. In her isolation she became obsessive about Venetia's hold on her husband and in desperation turned to her closest confidant at the time, Edwin Montagu, apparently oblivious of his own continued interest in Venetia. Interestingly, the intensely ambitious Montagu did not regard Asquith's relationship with Venetia as an obstacle to his own efforts to woo her; indeed, he seems to have welcomed it as reinforcing his own ties with the Prime Minister. Montagu was worried that Margot, far from supporting her husband at a time of intense political strain, was merely adding to his burdens. He knew how much Asquith had come to rely on Venetia for support as much as a necessary distraction from his work, but at the same time he wanted to reassure Margot that the relationship was no threat to her:

> If he [Asquith] wins [i.e. secures agreement over Ulster] you first will share his triumph, if he loses you alone can make it tolerable . . . Don't you know what you are to him? How amused you can afford to be at his relaxation. Those who know you both would laugh at a comparison between your relations with him and those of any other woman in the world.
>
> So show him you acknowledge his right to any amusement he chooses in order that he may give every ounce of himself for the struggle. Show him how confident you are of him and yourself and you will prove to be once again the big minded great loving Margot, who has no more loyal admirer and friend than
> Yours very affectionately,
> Edwin S. Montagu.[10]

Margot not so easily reassured. A fortnight later, in a letter to Edwin dated 21 March, she confessed how she 'suffered tortures' during her husband's afternoon drives with the 'deceitful little brute'.

> If Venetia had an ounce of truth and candour like Viola [Parsons, née Tree], Mouche [Duncombe], Dorothy [Beresford] (a girl you never heard of) – and two other women whose names I shan't tell you – have got and have always shown me, I should smile, but she is even teaching Henry to avoid telling me things. My step-family think all this very good fun and that I would be a fool to mind. I'm far too fond of Henry to show him how ill and miserable it makes me, it would only worry him at a time he

should be free. Good God! To think you proposed to her! A woman
without refinement or any imagination whatever . . .

Oh! If only Venetia would marry – how I loathe girls who can't love but
claim and collect like a cuckoo for their own vanity – Venetia's head is
completely turned.[11]

At least Margot's temporary distraction from politics should have
allowed her husband to deal with the crisis over Ireland free from
family interference, if Beb had not now blundered in to fill the
vacuum left by his stepmother.

Beb disliked his work at the Bar even more than Raymond. However,
unlike his elder brother, the responsibility of being a husband and,
with the birth to Cynthia in May 1911 of their son John, a father, had
little effect on his happy-go-lucky attitude. A few months earlier he
and Cynthia had moved into the then slightly unfashionable 8 Sussex
Place, a few minutes' walk from Baker Street station. Beb nicknamed
the house 'the Pepinage' after Pepinetta, his pet name for his wife.
Although they were much less well off than most of their friends,
Beb's earnings, his parents' generous subsidy and Cynthia's small
allowance were enough to maintain the basics of gentility. The baby,
as was usual in those days, was mostly under the care of his nanny,
Miss Faulkner, and frequently parked with Cynthia's mother, while
Beb and Cynthia pursued an active social life. There were plenty of
invitations to weekend house parties at the grand country houses of
their friends and on the surface life must have seemed agreeable
enough. Yet both of them were frustrated. Cynthia, like so many
intelligent upper-class women of the day, felt unfulfilled by a life of
frivolity. She longed for Beb to become an MP, but their relative
poverty made that impossible for the moment. Beb was equally keen
to enter the political arena and throw off the chains that bound him
to the dull life of a Chancery barrister. Cynthia was concerned
enough about her husband's apparent indifference to earning his
living to ask Katharine whether 'Raymond had much work? Beb pre-
serves an ominous silence as to his profession.'[12]

In March 1913, after a prolonged, unexplained bout of ill health,
Cynthia feared she had tuberculosis and sought treatment in a sana-
torium in Scotland, leaving John with her mother. Whatever was
wrong, after a couple of months Beb became convinced that it was

not tuberculosis, and he commissioned her mother, Mary Elcho, 'to go and heckle the doctors and bail her'.[13] It may well be that Cynthia's malady was psychosomatic, brought on by depression – an affliction to which she was certainly prone later in her life. Beb installed her and John in Marylands, a cottage in the village of Kingsgate on the eastern tip of the Kent coast, where she could benefit from sea air, while they were close enough to London for him to take up what briefs still did come his way. A mile or so along the coast at Broadstairs were the novelist D. H. Lawrence and his aristocratic German mistress, Frieda Weekley (*née* von Richthofen), who was in the process of obtaining a divorce. When Eddie Marsh, Churchill's private secretary, came to stay with Beb and Cynthia in July, he asked Lawrence and Frieda over to Marylands for tea. Lawrence was already well known as a poet and had just published his third novel, *Sons and Lovers*, to good reviews and disappointing sales. But, as Cynthia later recalled, 'except the mere facts that he wrote poetry, was the son of a coal-miner, and had a tendency to consumption, we at that time knew nothing whatever of Lawrence; but the moment a slender, lithe figure stepped lightly into the room, we both realised almost with the shock of collision that something new and startling had come into our lives.'[14]

The attraction was mutual and the two couples immediately became close friends, regularly dining together and going for walks along the shore below the nearby chalk cliffs. Lawrence was a notorious snob and social climber, and the combination of the Prime Minister's son and granddaughter of an Earl was irresistible. It helped that the Asquiths were apparently unfazed by his 'living in sin' with Frieda.* The novelist was fascinated by Cynthia's pre-Raphaelite looks and her matching ethereal personality, and he was to use her as a model for a number of female characters in his fiction, most notoriously – as his ultimate fantasy – casting her as Lady Chatterley, although he always denied it. At the same time, Lawrence recognized in Beb a fellow poet struggling to cast off his legal yoke. 'You tell Mr Asquith that man does not live by Briefs alone,' he once wrote to Cynthia. 'But he won't believe you. It's no use us poets waving our idealistic banners, like frantic suffragettes.'[15]

---

*In Beb's novel *Roon* (1929), set in pre-Great War England, the eponymous heroine, after leaving her politician husband, likewise lives with her lover in a cottage on the South coast.

This was music to Beb's ears. He was only too keen to believe that he could become a writer and poet. The poverty-stricken Lawrence was hardly an advertisement for the literary life, but Beb knew from his family's friendship with John Morley and Augustine Birrell that it was possible to construct an agreeable lifestyle from a combination of journalism, literature and politics. During long walks together, Lawrence would lecture his new friend on 'his theory of art', which, as Beb later recalled, 'was strongly opposed to the "would-be" of self-conscious effort; his impressions were urgent and immediate; his theory was one of inspiration.' It was seductive philosophy for a naturally lazy and bored young barrister and Beb was soon transfixed by 'a poet living on a plane far removed from the dust of politics, but more deeply in revolt against the values of the age than any political leader'.[16]

Lawrence's encouragement made Beb for the first time think of himself as a 'real' poet, rather than an amateur dabbler in occasional poetry. He had recently written *The Volunteer*, a poem about a frustrated city clerk who dreams of glory and eventually, in death, fulfils his fantasy as he 'goes to join the men of Agincourt'. The poem voiced a long-suppressed quest for adventure in Beb, which Lawrence (ironically, a committed pacifist) now reinforced. When the poem was published two years later, it was, perhaps more than any other Great War poem, to encapsulate the ethos of a generation of bored public schoolboys, who were only too willing to march cheerfully into the 'valley of the shadow of death':

THE VOLUNTEER

Here lies a clerk who half his life had spent
Toiling at ledgers in a city grey,
Thinking that so his days would drift away
With no lance broken in life's tournament:
Yet ever 'twixt the books and his bright eyes
The gleaming eagles of the legions came,
And horsemen, charging under phantom skies,
Went thundering past beneath the oriflamme.

And now those waiting dreams are satisfied;
From twilight to the halls of dawn he went;
His lance is broken; but he lies content
With that high hour, in which he lived and died.

And falling thus, he wants no recompense,
Who found his battle in the last resort;
Nor needs he any hearse to bear him hence,
Who goes to join the men of Agincourt.
                                   (Herbert Asquith, *Poems 1912–1933*)

Beb would soon get his own chance of death or glory but in the early months of 1914 the location of the next war seemed likely to be closer to William of Orange's Battle of the Boyne in Ireland, than to Henry V's field of Agincourt; Beb, a committed Home Ruler, was the last man to seek glory with the Ulster Volunteers, many of whom, enthusiastically egged on by Lord Northcliffe and his newspapers (*The Times* and *Daily Mail*), seemed willing to fight rather than agree to be ruled from Dublin. In March, Asquith only narrowly averted a mutiny by most of the officers of the Cavalry Brigade stationed in the Curragh, but in the process lost Colonel Seely, his War Minister. He decided temporarily to take over the War Office himself, much to the delight of Margot, to whom the additional salary was specially welcome.

Milner, now more embittered than ever, re-entered the political arena to lend his vociferous support to those who opposed coercing Ulster into a united Ireland. Events seemed to be spiralling out of control when on 25 April two steamers berthed in the harbour at Larne and landed a large consignment of arms for the Ulster Volunteers. Beb looked on with horror as his father appeared to lose his grip on the situation. Many years later Tamlyn, a character in his novel *Young Orland*, voiced his views at the time:

There's a germ of violence in the air, a mania: some of the men on both sides are like mad dogs, and many of the women are worse. They all have a snap at poor Barfield [a fictional politician clearly based on Asquith]. Barfield is ruled by reason, and he can't understand that the average man is ruled by prejudice: his intellect keeps him out of touch with his followers.[17]

Beb was seeing a great deal at this time of his old Balliol friend, Aubrey Herbert, who three years earlier, in 1911, had been elected as the Conservative MP for his home constituency of Yeovil. He now decided to enlist Aubrey's help in his own peace initiative.

Until his election to Parliament, Aubrey had been better known for his hair-raising adventures in the Balkans than his political ambitions and few people were convinced by his metamorphosis into a respectable MP. Margot, who like the rest of the family, loved Aubrey dearly, went to see him take his seat in the House of Commons, and afterwards cynically remarked that he 'still fancies himself as a brigand on the Bosphorus'.[18] The Conservative Party hierarchy regarded this outlandish figure in their midst with profound suspicion, aggravated by Aubrey's well-known friendship with the Asquiths. So when a few days after the gun-running incident at Larne, Beb came to see his Tory friend – apparently with the blessing of his father – and said that to avert disaster it was essential to resume talks with Unionists, Aubrey saw it as an opportunity to demonstrate that his good relations with the Asquith family could be politically useful. He telephoned the Conservative Chief Whip, Lord Edward Talbot, to tell him what Beb had said. Carson and the Prime Minister were both due to speak in the House of Commons on Ireland that evening, so Talbot's first question was whether the talks needed to take place before the debate. Beb said no.

Aubrey then returned to the Commons, where Carson's relatively conciliatory speech found no echo in Asquith's defiant reply. Uneasy about how much Carson might have held back as a result of his message from Beb, Aubrey began to feel anxious that he had let the party down. He tried to seek reassurance from some of his fellow Tory MPs, telling them it was 'quite impossible I should have been deceived. Beb would never have come to me to get his party out of a hole at my expense, but why ask for conciliation if you are going to smack the extended palm with a cane.' His colleagues were not impressed, and one of them 'kept repeating that in every nursery in England there should be texts round the walls, "Asquith is the blackest hearted man in England" '. Aubrey recorded how Beb himself then turned up:

> He seemed in a state of great excitement. I said it was a pity that the P.M. had not been sympathetic after Carson's sacrifices and Bonar Law's, especially after Beb's message had been given and there was every chance of renewed conversations. Beb said that he came to me on his initiative and that his Father knew nothing about it. I jumped up as if a hornet had stung me. I said 'the P. M. did not send you, but he must have known of your coming'.
>
> 'No,' he said, 'I came on my own. I thought it would be a good thing.'
>
> I said 'do you mean that you came and asked me to go to my whip and

tell him the situation was so serious renewed conversations were necessary?'

'My position is this,' said Beb, 'I wanted to make peace for the sake of the country.'

I was furious. I said 'you persuaded me, under false pretences, to go and pledge on my honour to my party leaders, that your father wanted pacific steps taken. And now you say your father did not know' . . . He began 'my position . . .' but I interrupted and said his only position was that he was the son of his father; that he had under false pretences induced me, his oldest friend, to lead my people into a trap.[19]

It later transpired that Beb had mentioned to his father what he was going to do, but had specifically asked him not to comment. Coincidentally, the day after the Commons debate, 30 April, Aubrey and his wife, Mary, were due to dine at 10 Downing Street with the Prime Minister, Margot and Violet. The only other outsider was Montagu. Afterwards Aubrey wrote:

Never had a more curious dinner; Margot whispering on one side of me, Violet on the other. Nerves visible everywhere except with P.M., who looked tired and worn. People's hands spilled their wine, at least mine did. Violet began by asking if there had been a plot. I said of course there had, this led off merrily. We got through dinner somehow, Margot, Mary and Violet left, Violet returning like an ADC to give her father some papers. He then settled down to catechize me. I readily gave him my impressions of the danger of the situation . . . I told him of the Japanese spirit on our side: that people were worked up to such a pitch, that the sacrifice of their lives at a price was beginning to appear glorious. That a number of our backbenchers wanted to settle, and that if the Government failed to meet Carson's moderation in the same spirit, we should be driven into the ranks of the extremists.[20]

Five days later, having heard nothing further from Asquith, Aubrey went to see Beb at his chambers and told him that all negotiations were off, warning him that the Government must make a move soon as the situation was growing dangerous.[21] The following day Beb telephoned and told him that talks were proceeding.

The Prime Minister had hoped for some months to overcome Unionist opposition by offering to exclude part of Ulster from the jurisdiction of the proposed Parliament in Dublin. He had been conducting secret talks with, on the one hand, Carson and Bonar Law –

representing the Unionists – and, on the other, Redmond and the Nationalists. But he had always come up against the difficulty of securing agreement on the fate of the counties of Tyrone and Fermanagh, with their mixed Roman Catholic and Protestant populations. It was this issue on which Asquith and the Unionists now resumed their negotiations.

At the end of May, Asquith took a week's holiday at Penrhos on Anglesey, the second home of Venetia's parents, Lord and Lady Sheffield. The party included Montagu, Bongie and Violet as well as Hugh Godley, who was on leave from the Sudan where he was now based, and of course, Venetia herself. The holiday gave the Prime Minister the chance to catch up with War Office papers, while discussing Ireland in a calmer atmosphere with Birrell, the Irish Secretary, another house guest. Unfortunately, Asquith's absence from Downing Street and proximity to Venetia provoked a, to him, unaccountable recurrence of Margot's speech difficulties. The only comfort he could offer his wife was 'to try to keep a true perspective, and to believe that the best will work itself out'.[22]

Politics, as so often, came to Margot's rescue. With her voice now recovered, she, like Beb before her, could not resist putting in her own bid for a role as mediator. She regarded the Nationalist leader, Redmond, as a bore but, overcoming her antipathy both to him and the idea of Home Rule in general,* she asked him to meet her on 10 July at Frank Lawson's house at 104 Park Street. The Irishman turned up in a 'hideous pale grey hat and clothes', but soon won her over with some extravagant praise of her husband, whom he described as 'more trustworthy than anyone' before clasping her hands and saying: 'Mrs Asquith, there is no one on God's earth like him and I'd do anything for him.' Margot pleaded with him to avoid civil war by giving way over Tyrone. He explained that if he did his life would not be safe, and assured her there might be riots but there

---

*Margot wrote in her diary at the time: 'I've always hated Home Rule: it has been the curse of the Liberal Party since I was a little girl and I don't think the Nationalists are the least ready for it, but will they ever be any readier? And can the country [i.e. the United Kingdom as a whole] thrive at all while the question is unsettled. Everyone who goes to Ireland, however unbelieving or even Tory, comes back a Home Ruler! – so I have a veneer of conviction, but no sort of "bliss" "no rapture".' (Margot Asquith's Diary, d. 3210, p. 93)

would be no war, and that once 'the [Home Rule] Bill is on the Statute Book, we – Carson and I – will agree to some settlement'.[23]

Redmond and Carson did meet in late July at a conference between all the Parties held at Buckingham Palace, and got, so Asquith told Margot, 'within an inch of settlement', but in the end failed to reach an agreement on the area of Ulster to be excluded from Home Rule. He said they were both in tears as they shook hands as the conference broke up, laughingly commenting: 'they are an impossible lot for any one to <u>govern</u> – they <u>must</u> govern themselves: you'll see tomorrow, after sobbing round each others necks, they'll call each other liars, cowards cheats etc.!'[24]

The unfolding drama over Ireland kept the political attention of almost everybody in Britain through that long hot summer of 1914. Few people took much notice when on 28 June the Archduke Franz Ferdinand was assassinated by a Serb nationalist in Sarajevo. When four weeks later Austria delivered its ultimatum to Serbia to hand over the suspected conspirators, although Asquith admitted to Venetia that 'we are within measurable, or imaginable distance of a real Armageddon', he still believed that Germany would restrain its ally before rushing headlong to disaster.

As far as 'London Society' was concerned, the main talking point that summer was neither Ireland nor the Balkans but a tragic river-boat accident on the Thames at Battersea. Edward Horner and Constantine Benckendorff, the son of the Russian ambassador, had hired a steamer for a party on the Thames on a balmy July night, serenaded by a band made up of members of Thomas Beecham's Covent Garden orchestra. After several hours' drinking, dancing and carousing the steamer was opposite Battersea Park on its return journey, when Raymond is supposed to have offered Diana Manners £10 if she could persuade their friend Denis Anson to jump into the river. Anson, who was by now much the worse for drink, handed his watch to Diana and leapt straight over the side. Almost immediately he was in trouble in the notoriously strong Thames current and cried out for help. Benckendorff and Mitchell, one of the musicians, jumped in to help him. The Russian, a powerful swimmer, quickly realized the hopelessness of the situation and managed to struggle back to the boat where he was hauled back on board, but Anson and Mitchell both drowned.*

---

*To be fair to Raymond, it should be said that he was a poor swimmer.

At the inquest which followed the tragedy an array of the finest advocates of the day – including F. E. Smith taking time off from whipping up Ulster – persuaded the coroner to record a verdict of 'Death by Misadventure'. The newspaper-reading public were not so easily convinced, while the members of the Covent Garden orchestra were furious at what they saw as their colleague's needless sacrifice in a futile attempt to save one of 'the Idle Rich' from his own folly. Raymond, in what looked like a typical 'Establishment cover-up', was excused appearing as a witness on the feeble pretext that he was appearing in court elsewhere. Diana also managed to avoid being called.

What most shocked people, including many Coterie parents, was the apparent callousness of Anson's supposed friends who carried on partying in the days that followed the calamity as if nothing had happened. Margot noted in her diary that 'no one individual nor even the Pleasure Party was to blame for the tragedy', but she joined in the general condemnation of the way the 'young people afterwards showed no real feeling; they ran about bickering, ballrooming – to parties, operas and felt martyrdom because they were criticized'.[25] The worst stories were told about Diana: that she had mimicked Anson drowning at the Bath Club swimming pool, that she had attended an opera at Covent Garden the following evening, causing the orchestra to threaten a walk-out unless she left. None of this was true, but the tragedy and subsequent criticism haunted Diana for the rest of her life. A couple of years later, while her friends were dying like flies on the Western Front, she imagined – probably under the influence of drugs – Anson's ghost, describing the apparition to Raymond as 'not dripping slime or festering in a shroud, but he always looked at best like a "shrieking mandrake from out the earth" so it was as bad as if he had worn the symbols of my murder'.[26]

Raymond himself seems to have had little conscience about his own role in the incident. However, by the time he received Diana's letter he had seen sights far worse than any 'shrieking mandrake' and lost many better friends than the dissolute Anson.

13

The Asquiths go to war

———————————◆———————————

ON THE EVENING of Wednesday 29 July 1914, Asquith came into Margot's room, as usual to chat with her while she dressed for dinner. He stood quite still as he told her he had just arranged for the 'precautionary telegram' to go out to the Empire. It was the first stage in preparing the nation for War.

'How <u>thrilling</u>! Oh! tell me aren't you excited, darling!' was Margot's instant reaction.

Her husband, she recorded, did not smile but 'quite gravely kissed me and said "it will be very interesting"'.[1] The understatement was deliberate and typical. The Prime Minister, as ever, was coolly composed as the gravest crisis of his premiership unfolded. He still hoped for peace, but Austria's insistence that Serbia hand over those responsible for the assassination was making conflict ever more likely. Asquith had been expecting to leave on Saturday for a couple of days with Venetia and her family at Penrhos, and still hoped he would be able to get away. However, he had asked Colonel Hankey, the highly efficient Secretary to the Committee of Imperial Defence and as such the lynchpin for the nation's war effort, 'to keep within reach'. Hankey had already warned his wife that he was unlikely to join her that weekend.

As the European crisis developed the Cabinet was meeting every day, with ministers running the gauntlet of cheering crowds gathered in Downing Street and Whitehall. The mood inside was grim, with the majority of ministers opposed to Britain becoming involved in a

European war. Although at first Asquith hoped that Britain would be able to stay out of the conflict, by Friday 31 July he regarded war as inevitable. At 11 a.m. he looked into Margot's bedroom, where she usually spent the morning writing letters and supervising the household arrangements, to tell her there was no hope of peace.

However, it was not to Margot that Asquith looked for support in the coming ordeal, but to Venetia. Warning his young confidante that 'things look almost as bad as can be', he cancelled his planned trip to her family home, confessing

> I can honestly say that I have never had a more bitter disappointment. All these days . . . full of incident and for the most part anxious and worrying – I have been sustained by the thought that when to-day came I should once more see your darling face, and be with you, and share everything and get from you what I value most, and what is to me the best of all things in the world – your counsel and your understanding and your sympathy and your love. All that has been shattered by a truly devastating succession of the blows of fortune. I should be desolate, if it were not for your sweetest of all letters this morning . . . which gives me a new fund of courage and hope. My darling – can I ever thank you enough? Without you, I tremble to think what would have happened to me.[2]

By Saturday evening Germany and Russia were at war. The following day Margot and Elizabeth attended communion at St Paul's with Frau and her new husband, Rolf Meyer, who expected to be called up to the Kaiser's army at any moment. Afterwards Margot went to call on Prince Lichnowsky, the German ambassador, whose lesbian wife Mechthilde had taken a great shine to her. The ambassador had just returned from Downing Street, where he had made a tearful appeal for Britain to stay out of the coming war, only for the Prime Minister to insist 'it rested largely with Germany to make intervention impossible'.[3]

Margot found Lichnowsky 'in a state of white despair' pacing up and down beside his wife, who 'was lying on a green sofa with her little Dachshund, who yapped drearily at me . . . Her eyes were starved from crying.' The corpulent Mechthilde hugged her 'while we both cried: "to think that <u>we</u> should bring such sorrows to an innocent happy people! I have always hated and loathed our Kaiser. Have I not said so 1000 times, dear little Margot, he and his friends are <u>brutes</u>!"'.[4]

Two days later, 3 August, when Germany demanded free passage for its army through Belgium, the majority of the waverers in the Cabinet – most crucially Lloyd George – swung behind the Prime Minister's and Foreign Secretary's position that Britain could not stand on the sidelines. Only three ministers (Morley, Burns and Trevelyan) resigned when the following day Grey issued his own ultimatum to Germany to lift its threat to Belgian neutrality by midnight or find itself at war with the British Empire.

Tuesday 4 August was a cloudless summer's day, and as the Prime Minister left the House of Commons he was mobbed by an excited crowd of 'holidaymakers and loafers' gathered in Parliament Square. Unusually for a politician, he hated adulation, reminding Venetia of Sir Robert Walpole's remark: "'Now they are ringing their bells; in a few weeks they'll be wringing their hands." How one loathes such levity.'[5] The crowds continued to swell as the day wore on, singing *Rule Britannia*, *God Save the King* and even the *Marseillaise* as they moved between Parliament Square and Buckingham Palace. With the approach of the critical hour – midnight in Berlin was 11 p.m. in London – the focus of attention switched to Downing Street, and Whitehall became packed with people. Half an hour before the expiry of the ultimatum, Asquith sent a message round to Lloyd George next door to come over and join him in the Cabinet room. The Chancellor, who found Grey and McKenna already there, afterwards described to Margot how the 'very serious, very anxious' mood inside 10 Downing Street contrasted with the cheering, singing crowd they could hear outside. Grey said 'it's not all over yet', but a few minutes later a message came in that the British ambassador in Berlin had sent for his passport.

'It's all over then,' said Lloyd George. He later recalled how, as the crowds outside went quiet, and as 'Big Ben struck eleven, very slowly came the Boom – Boom – Boom – we sat in complete silence, I should say for 10 minutes after the last Boom', until their reverie was rudely interrupted: 'Winston dashed into the room radiant, his face bright, his manner keen and he told us – one word pouring out on the other – how he was going to send telegrams to the Mediterranean, the North Sea and God knows where! You could see he was a really happy man. I wondered if this was the state of mind to be in at the opening of such a fearful war as this.'[6]

The following afternoon the Prime Minister made the official announcement of the declaration of War to the House of Commons and asked for an immediate vote of credit of £100 million. *The Times* Parliamentary correspondent, Michael MacDonagh (not normally a sympathetic observer), writing in his personal diary, described Asquith's speech as 'magnificent . . . It will rank among the historic parliamentary orations.'[7] The Lichnowskys left for Germany shortly after daybreak the following day, taking with them – at the Asquiths' request – Frau's husband. Margot delayed her departure for their annual holiday in Scotland to wish 'God's speed' to General Sir John French before he left to take command of the British Expeditionary Force in France. She gave him a medallion with a saint's head on it, which he promised to wear throughout the War.

Margot was determined to resist the anti-German hatred being whipped up in the press, most notably by *The Times* and the *Daily Mail*. After discussing the issue with the Queen Mother, the Danish-born Queen Alexandra, three months later, Margot recorded that 'to her the war is the Kaiser and so it is to me. I disassociate all the Germans I've known and loved.'[8]

Frau had by now been with the Asquiths so long that she seemed one of the family. It never occurred to them that her continued presence in Downing Street could be a source of political embarrassment, even though there were already rumblings in the newspapers about pro-German elements in the Government – above all Haldane, Lord Chancellor since 1912, whose love of Goethe and Schiller was accounted incompatible with being a patriotic Briton. A couple of days after Margot left for Hopeman Lodge on the Moray Firth, Asquith wrote to tell her

> Edward Grey came to see me this this morning and spoke very seriously about Frau. He is clear that she ought not to remain in this house: everybody says that she sees and hears all that we are doing and talking about, and as a patriotic German she is bound to report it to her own people. Miss Way [Margot's secretary] has spoken to her, and she will probably go for a time to Folkestone to the Miss Neumans. Eliz's German maid we think might go to you at Hopeman: exception is also taken to her. It is a great bore but it can't be helped.[9]

The fact that the Asquiths thought that moving Elizabeth's German maid from Downing Street to Scotland would be enough to counter any accusations that they were 'harbouring enemy spies' shows how little he anticipated the anti-German feeling that was rapidly sweeping the country. When, a fortnight later, Frau did eventually embark for Munich, Margot insisted on going to Victoria Station with Lucy and Elizabeth to see her off.

The Prime Minister's most urgent priority after the declaration of war was to find a replacement for himself at the War Ministry, of which he had remained in personal charge since the Curragh mutiny. Asquith eventually offered the post to Kitchener who, after an initial show of reluctance, eagerly took up the cudgels.* He had been impressed by the hero of Omdurman when he and Churchill had met him on Malta two years earlier, and now he and Haldane believed him to be 'teachable'. Margot did not agree and wondered how long her husband would think so well of him.

Kitchener immediately set about recruiting a new volunteer army. Cynthia's father, who had recently become Earl of Wemyss after the death of his own father, patriotically responded to the call to arms by threatening to sack any of his younger male employees who refused to enlist. A horrified Mary Wemyss lamented to Arthur Balfour that 'I shall have no chauffeur, no stableman, no odd man to carry the coals', but in the end she persuaded her husband to revoke his ultimatum on condition that she do her best to get as many of the men as possible to volunteer. Cynthia, who had given birth to her second son (Michael) ten days before the declaration of War, was staying at Stanway with Beb, who was roped in as recruiting officer, deploying his best Oxford Union skills on the bemused gamekeepers, farm workers and servants gathered in a barn. Violet related to Bongie how 'Beb quoted "England expects every man to do his duty" in firm and ringing tones', adding laconically that unless her brothers themselves soon volunteered 'Father will be asked why he doesn't begin his recruiting at home'.[10]

Oc was the first Asquith to enlist, explaining to his employers, Franklin and Herrera: 'I have two older brothers, both married, and one younger brother with an ailing colon [an after-effect of Cys's bout of dysentery in Egypt] ... It is obviously fitting that one of my father's four sons ought to be prepared to fight.'[11] Violet later recalled how Oc 'never – even when he joined up – romanticized the

---

*Margot was rightly cynical when her husband told her about Kitchener's apparent reluctance to become War Minister and when the next day Ettie – with whom the Field Marshal was friendly – said to her 'Isn't it splendid of K to have offered his services at once to the Government!', she saw it as 'a sidelight on K's methods' and remarked 'I knew after that that he would accept!' (Margot Asquith's Diary, d. 3210, p. 261)

War . . . he just considered the whole thing "a <u>beastly</u> duty".[12] Beb, who volunteered shortly afterwards, shared the general mood of excited anticipation, eloquently captured in a tribute to Ares, the Greek God of War, written a few months earlier:

> Steel-hearted Ares, shaker of the Throne;
> Young God of battle, restless lover, hail!
>
> For once a man has seen thine eyes aflame,
> And mounted on the horses of the gale,
> Death is nothing, life an empty name:
> Arise and lead us 'ere our blood be tame,
> Lord of Thunder, Ares of the Crimson Mail![13]

And so it was, a few weeks after the outbreak of the War, that Beb, Oc and Cys (who despite of an 'ailing colon' and his recent bout of typhoid was accepted for military service) found themselves at Tidworth on Salisbury Plain, taking part in an infantry training course for former members of public school cadet corps. When Beb and Oc came home for the day on 9 September, their father nonchalantly reported to Venetia that both were 'much bronzed with sun and wind. They are liking it very well, and say Cys is wonderfully better for it.'[14]

Meanwhile, their eldest brother had no wish to be bamboozled into a war that he considered a thorough bore. Raymond warned Diana to beware of saying in public 'God save the Kaiser', cursing King George or professing to love war because one gets raped.

If the 'King of Chaos', as Raymond irreverently dubbed Kitchener, was right in his forecast that the War would last three years, he ruefully predicted that sooner or later they would all be under the turf. He informed Diana Manners that after wondering whether he should best do his duty by pretending to be a vet or a St Bernard dog, he had put his name down for 'the London Volunteer Force', organized by Ettie's husband Lord Desborough and Lord Lovat. This force had a number of advantages, including that the War Office might prevent it ever coming into existence, that Raymond's friend, Patrick Shaw-Stewart belonged to it, and that it could not be expected to do anything before the Goodwood races were held the following August (1915). Raymond had also called at the offices of the grandly named 'National Service League', where he found a large crowd of well-meaning and inept patriots, beavering away for fourteen hours a day classifying and then rejecting the applications of an even larger crowd of even more well-meaning and inept patriots who were applying for jobs which they were patently incompetent to fill: deaf mutes applying to be interpreters, Baptist ministers offering to run canteens, and so on.[15]

In the meantime, Raymond was determined to make hay while he could and enjoy the rest of his summer holidays at Hopeman Lodge on the Moray Firth, which he found crawling with mine dredgers and lit up by searchlights each night to guard them from Attila.[16]

The British Expeditionary Force bore the brunt of the attack as the Kaiser's forces tried to outflank and encircle the French Army massed on the German border. Several of the Asquiths' friends were among the early casualties in the retreat from Mons. John Manners, the brother of Molly and Betty, was killed when his platoon of Grenadier Guards was surrounded and fought to the last man. Aubrey Herbert was among those reported missing. Even Raymond found it 'terribly easy to be soppy' about the popular and charming John, but – as he later told Aubrey himself – 'I would put my last shilling on your luck.'[17] Sure enough, Aubrey soon turned up back in London, wounded but decidedly unchastened. Beb, whose training had now been transferred to the Crystal Palace, was among the first to see his old friend, who told him a tale that could have come straight out of a John Buchan novel.

Although Aubrey's poor eyesight disqualified him from military service, undeterred he had procured the uniform of an officer in the Irish Guards and, abetted by his wife's cousin, Tom Vesey, who was serving in the regiment, fell into their ranks as they marched along the Vauxhall Bridge Road. Once the Guards' ship was safely under-way for Le Havre, Tom introduced the impostor to his bemused Colonel who, having no better idea what to do with a half-blind Tory MP, appointed him the regimental interpreter. Ten days later Aubrey was charging across a turnip field beneath a covey of partridges put up by the German artillery. Shortly afterwards he was wounded during a desperate rearguard action in the Forest of Compiègne and taken prisoner. On the whole his captors were 'extraordinarily kind and polite', plied him with wine, water and cigarettes and assured him '*Wir sind Kamaraden*'. His wound was operated on in a local château and a few days later, sitting up quietly in bed reading, he heard rifle fire and looked out to see a squadron of French cavalry-men emerge into the garden through driving rain 'in fine style, like conquerors; one man first, riding, his hand on his hip. The German sentries who had been posted to protect us wounded, walked down and surrendered their bayonets.'[18] This was all splendid 'Boys' Own' stuff and whetted Beb's appetite for the great adventure. He speedily arranged a commission for himself in the Royal Marine Artillery. However, it was Oc who was the first Asquith to see action. A couple of days after Aubrey was freed, Asquith wrote to inform Margot that 'Winston has persuaded Oc to take a commission as lieutenant in his Naval army. He evidently means to run a war of his own.'[19]

Churchill's 'Naval army' was the recently formed Royal Naval Division, a motley collection of naval reservists and middle-aged 'stokers', as naval ratings were called, who were surplus to present naval requirements, but whom the First Lord was determined to keep out of the clutches of the War Office and under his own wing. This force of some 7,000 was beefed up by miners from the Northumberland and Durham coalfields, who had been diverted from a queue of volunteers for their local county regiments to the comparative comfort of the nearby naval recruiting hall.

When Oc arrived on 29 September to join the 2nd Naval Brigade at the makeshift training camp at Betteshanger in east Kent, the confusion that greeted him was a long way from Churchill's lofty ambitions for his 'private army': there was no unified command structure with the 1st Brigade five miles away at Walmer, and the majority of the officers – being naval, not army reservists – had no infantry training, while those who did were mostly ex-Guards officers of questionable quality. One of the most incompetent of the new officers was the pompous and overbearing George Cornwallis West, a retired Scots Guards Captain who, on the strength of being Churchill's stepfather,* was given command of the 'Anson', the battalion to which Oc was assigned. However, Oc was favourably impressed by the brigade commander, Commodore Backhouse, and was relieved that his own platoon of forty-five men was not made up of the notoriously ill-disciplined stokers,† but solid Ulstermen, whom he judged

---

*West had married Lady Randolph Churchill, twenty years his senior, in 1900.
†In a note made after the War and found among Oc's papers at Clovelly, he explained that the stokers 'felt all along that service afloat was their "métier" and their contract and that in using them as soldiers the Admiralty was trying to make a sow's ear out of a silk purse. They allowed little to escape their dry and rather cynical sense of humour.' (Note beside copy of F. S. Kelly's diary entry for 26 July 1915)

'good material' if 'rather ungainly'.[20] He was also pleased to find among his fellow officer recruits the poet Rupert Brooke, who had become friendly with the Asquiths after being introduced to Beb, Cynthia and Violet by Eddie Marsh in March 1913. Violet in particular had been captivated by the charming and good-looking poet, inviting him to her twenty-sixth birthday dinner a few weeks later.

Training began with marching and drilling before the recruits were judged ready to tackle the basics of musketry. When Oc and his comrades were awoken by the battalion band shortly after 5 a.m. on 4 October and ordered to prepare to embark for Dunkirk, everybody assumed they were being sent to France to continue their training. Oc was groggy from the combined effects of an anti-typhoid injection and a good dinner at The Black Horse Tavern in Deal in the company of Rupert and his friend (and now fellow member of the 'Anson' Battalion), the musician Denis Browne, and from then being kept awake by the 'snarlingly stertorous' snoring of Foster, the brigade chaplain, with whom he shared his tent.[21] When the brigade marched into Dover at about midday, the officers had their work cut out to prevent their men imbibing too much of the beer pressed on them by enthusiastic bystanders. They eventually embarked at 9 p.m.; and the following morning the troopships were held up for eight hours in choppy seas off Dunkirk before being allowed to land to the accompaniment of the band playing *La Marseillaise* and the cheering of townsfolk gathered on the dockside. It was only now that they were issued with such basic equipment as overcoats, haversacks and water bottles and 120 rounds of ammunition, and then informed, to general consternation, that this was no training exercise: they were being sent immediately into action to relieve the beleaguered Belgian Army in Antwerp. When Oc learnt that the battalion's medical officer had not even been issued with basic field dressings, he scrounged some 350 bandages as well as lint and gauze from the local French military hospital.

The scheme to defend Antwerp was Churchill's own. When he heard that the port was about to fall to the Germans, he paid a flying visit to the headquarters of King Albert of the Belgians and promised to send the Royal Marines and the Royal Naval Division to shore up the exhausted Belgian forces defending the city. Churchill, who had a lifelong obsession with emulating the military achievements of his great ancestor, the Duke of Marlborough, then telegraphed the Prime Minister offering to resign the Admiralty and take command of the force himself. Asquith politely declined the offer from the former cavalry subaltern, but could not resist reading his telegram to his Cabinet colleagues, who greeted it with derisive laughter.

The Allied counter-attack never came, and by the time the Naval Division arrived at Edeghen railway station, four miles south of Antwerp, the Germans had breached the outer defences and the city was all but lost, despite the valiant efforts of the Royal Marines, who had been fighting alongside the Belgians for the past couple of days. Rupert Brooke later recalled how as they marched towards Antwerp, Belgian civilians, imagining they were the vanguard of a major British force, 'cheered and flung themselves on us and gave us apples and chocolate and flags and kisses, and cried "*Vivent Les Anglais*"'.[22] Any feelings of elation soon evaporated as they passed streams of refugees and bedraggled and wounded Belgian soldiers struggling in the opposite direction, and then glimpsed the smoking ruins of the city itself.

The Anson Battalion rested for a few hours in the garden of a château in the suburb of Vieux Dieu, the bitter cold and the constant shellfire preventing anyone getting much sleep. They were roused at 3.30 a.m. and ordered to take over a thousand yards of trenches between two Belgian artillery redoubts. In front, they were protected by about fifty yards of barbed wire entanglements through which they could see a herd of piebald cows grazing, oblivious of their perilous position. But Colonel Cornwallis West refused Oc's offer to drive the cattle away in order to secure a better view of any enemy advance.

Shelling continued throughout that day and the next, but the Naval brigades escaped relatively unscathed as the German artillery concentrated on reducing the remaining forts to rubble. At about 6 p.m. on 8 October Oc caught a glimpse of his first enemy soldiers some 500 yards away. Soon afterwards the battalion was ordered to pull out as their position became hopeless, with more and more exhausted Belgian troops abandoning their trenches in the face of overwhelming German superiority. It transpired that Cornwallis West had lost the battalion's only map of the city. By now the huge petrol tanks between the Naval troops and the pontoon bridge over the Scheldt river which they had to cross were ablaze, and if the wind changed direction they would be completely cut off. The situation became farcical as the Anson's increasingly desperate commanding officer, without a clue where they were, stopped everyone he saw and asked '*Avez vous un plan d'Anvers?*' In the end, he managed to dragoon a Belgian civilian on a bicycle into acting as a guide, only for it to transpire that the man had a gammy leg and had constantly to be helped back on to his bike.[23] Brooke later compared their confused, fire-lit trek to the Scheldt River to a scene from Dante's *Inferno*, while Oc recorded in his diary their apprehension that the burning petrol tanks would explode as they marched past:

> Happily what slight breeze there was came from our left. Two Yankee flags fluttered absurdly on buildings near the tanks. Beyond the tanks was a field with grass, trees and many ditches. On this, a sort of forest fire was blazing and roaring: flames running along the surface of the ditches, so I suppose they were full of oil. Crowds of huddling refugees, and a railway blocked with three toppled locomotives, farm carts and debris of ruined houses – all in the glare of the conflagration – formed a weird and wonderful spectacle never-to-be-forgotten.[24]

The Anson Battalion reached the pontoon bridge just in time to prevent an enemy saboteur from blowing it up. The man was summarily shot. They were met on the other side by Major General Paris, the newly appointed divisional commanding officer, who was furious when he heard that West had lost one of the four companies under his command. Fortunately the unit managed to catch up a few hours later. The First Naval Brigade, meanwhile, thanks to a staff muddle, received no orders to retreat until it was too late to escape the advancing Germans. They had to flee across the border into neutral Holland, where they were interned for the rest of the War.

Oc and his comrades, who had barely slept since they had left England, struggled for some thirty miles through the night along cobbled roads, now clogged with a confused mass of Belgian soldiers and refugees, cattle, horses and mules. Many soldiers discarded their ammunition and even their rifles en route, but somehow they kept together and by morning most of them reached the railway station at St Gilles-Waes, where they caught a train for Bruges. The following night they reached Ostend, and in the early hours of 11 October they collapsed exhausted on to beds of hay on the vessel taking them home to England. Four days later the Germans occupied the port.

Oc invited Rupert to stay at 10 Downing Street, where his father was keen to quiz them on their experiences. By now most of the British

Press was in full cry blaming Churchill for the fiasco.* After talking to his son and his friend late into the night, Asquith wrote to Venetia:

> I can't tell you what I feel of the wicked folly of it all. The Marines of course are splendid troops and can go anywhere and do anything: but nothing excuses Winston (who knew all the facts) from sending in the two other Naval Brigades. I was assured that all the recruits were being left behind, and that the main body at any rate consisted of seasoned Naval Reserve men. As a matter of fact only about a quarter were Reservists, and the rest were a callow crowd of the rawest tiros, most of whom had never fired off a rifle, while none of them had ever handled an entrenching tool.[25]

While the First Lord of the Admiralty's reputation took a battering from the Antwerp expedition, Oc's calm conduct during the battle and the subsequent retreat profoundly impressed the men under his command. Private Thomas, a regular Royal Marine sent to 'stiffen' the raw Naval Brigade recruits, described his experiences to his father, who forwarded his son's letter to the *Evening News*:

> Young Mr Asquith, the Prime Minister's son, was as daring as anybody. He moved about giving us a cheery word from time to time, and nothing ever seemed to tire him. He had one or two narrow shaves, but, bless you, he never troubled about that.
>
> 'Wait and See' was his motto when the shells began to fly around, and he looked as if he wasn't going to worry until one hit him. Officers like him make a lot of difference to men, and there isn't one of us that would not go through fire and water for him.[26]

It was a view echoed many times during Oc's short military career.

*

Beb crossed the Channel five days after Oc returned, not with his artillery brigade, which was still waiting for its guns, but as a member

---

*Churchill vigorously defended himself, arguing that without his intervention Antwerp would have fallen before the Allies had managed to secure the Channel ports to the south. There was some truth in the claim, but he was being wise after the event since the original object of the exercise had not been defensive but to facilitate a counter-attack. Curiously, Margot's opinion of Churchill went up after Antwerp. She apparently accepted his explanation and was impressed by how unaffected he was by all the criticism.

of a 'fact-finding tour' organized by Violet to discover how the Royal Army Medical Corps and the Red Cross were coping with the wounded. The expedition, which left for Boulogne on 18 October, was joined by Cynthia and James Dunn, a rich Canadian banker friend, roped in for his 'huge comfortable Limoges', which the Asquiths were amused to discover 'had been made for and used by the Kaiser on his last visit to England'.[27] Beb, even more the dreamer than usual, failed to provide much masculine authority to smooth their way through the inevitable bureaucratic obstacles, which included being held up by a French official who, spotting the car's AA badge, ignored their 'cracking theatrical passports' and 'open Sesame letters' from Kitchener and Cambon, and demanded proof of their membership of the Automobile Association. 'Beb more absolutely useless and befogged and shy than anything you can imagine', Violet complained to their father, 'I wish Oc could have come.'[28]

Both Violet and Cynthia drooled over the good looks of the British professional soldiers compared to their conscripted French counterparts, who were (according to Violet) 'just like toys in their red trousers – ours in khaki about two feet taller'.[29] The more openly erotic Cynthia thought the glamour of the British garrison at St Omer 'beggars all description. Either War is an even more powerful incubator [aphrodisiac] than one thinks or else the *Daily Mail* correspondent was right and the Expeditionary Force is entirely composed of super-men with throats like towers and teeth like almonds.' She found some wounded German prisoners she met in a military hospital equally attractive: 'fine good-looking men – "blond-beasts" with large *schwärmerisch* [passionate] eyes'. Dunn, 'who enjoys a healthy collective hatred of the enemy', disapproved when she and Violet gave them cigarettes and chatted to them in German.

Cynthia and Violet were 'cruelly persecuted by cocks' crowing outside the room they shared in St Omer, prompting the former to complain that 'it did seem hard to have one's night wrecked by anything as banal as poultry when there was quite a good sporting chance of a bomb'. The reality of War, however, struck home when Cynthia met some wounded soldiers at the military hospital in Mons:

I have never been able to cross the threshold of an ordinary tidy London Hospital without feeling literally faint – but somehow this rough and ready one, though infinitely saddening, was not in the least sickening.

There were ghastly sights, but one simply had to steel oneself and not shrink because, poor darlings, they do love exhibiting their wounds. They have got the most beautiful manners – considerable gift of expression and a wonderful macabre sense of humour . . .

Their patient unpuzzled acquiescence in pain is so extraordinary that much of its horror seems diminished, but the pang which never grows blunted is the common sight of an empty sleeve and a very young face. They love talking about their families and frankly pine to get back. The most haunting sight was a man – not badly wounded – but with completely shattered nerves. I shall never forget his hunted eyes with tears pouring down his face and he was so apologetic. 'I know it's very foolish – I'm not as bad as these other poor fellows – but its me nerves.' The doctor told me he had been crying all night.

It would not be long before Cynthia was to experience the effects of 'shell shock' much closer to home. Curiously, although she was shocked by the wounded in the field hospitals being left 'in their filthy blood-stained Khaki with their heavy boots', both she and Violet regarded the Red Cross as 'unpractical sentimentalists' for demanding clean shirts and bed linen, the supply of which risked holding up munitions going to the front line troops.*

Margot hoped Violet's mission would spur her to take up nursing as many of her friends were doing, but although she did do a stint at Winchester Hospital for a while – presumably, selected because of its association with Archie – she regarded her most useful contribution to the war effort as supporting her father. Although Margot herself made a point of regularly visiting the war wounded, she took no part in organizing any war work, something for which she was later criticized. She did, reluctantly, agree to serve on Queen Mary's Committee for needlework to provide clothing for the wounded, but she burst into tears during a meeting and was scolded by Peggy Crewe for 'showing so little self control when others more directly concerned are showing such Pluck!'.

What Margot most longed to do was to involve herself in government. When her husband complained about Lloyd George being 'ill-mannered and insolent' to Kitchener in Cabinet, she promptly wrote to the Chancellor that she was 'delighted you stood up to K!'

---

*Eventually it was pressure from the fighting troops themselves – appalled by the conditions faced by wounded comrades – which forced a change of policy.

1. H.H. Asquith, aged about 24, already with 'a plan of life well under control'

2. Helen Asquith, 'an angel from heaven', in about 1888

3. Arthur ('Oc'), Herbert ('Beb'), Violet and Raymond Asquith in about 1890. Their father took 'almost boyish pleasure' in their exploits

4. Margot Tennant, aged 27, with her father Sir Charles Tennant at the Temple of Karnak in Upper Egypt, 1891

5. Margot *(left)* chatting to Mrs Blair at a foxhunt meet in Leicestershire. Margot apparently 'rode a little too fast at her fences'

6. Raymond Asquith (*right*) at the Oxford Union in 1901 beside Aubrey Herbert, probably injured after one of his notorious climbing escapades

7. Beb Asquith at the Oxford Union in 1902. *Isis* praised his 'massive eloquence'

8. Dresden, 1903: Mary Vesey (later Herbert), Cynthia Charteris (later Asquith), and Violet Asquith

9. The Asquiths at Glen in 1904. *From left*: Elizabeth, Asquith, Olive Macleod (standing), Margot (seated), Katharine Horner gazing at her future husband, Raymond (far right), Violet, Cys (seated, front), Oc (beside Violet), H. T. ('Bluetooth') Baker (standing, back) and Edward Horner

10. Elizabeth Asquith as a bridesmaid at Raymond's wedding in 1907

11. Puffin Asquith at Margate in 1908 with his German governess Anne Heinsius ('Frau')

12. Archie Gordon, later engaged to Violet after being mortally injured in a car crash in 1909

13. The Asquiths' great friend, Lady (Ettie) Desborough, who lost two sons in the First World War

14. Harold 'Bluetooth' Baker, Mr Underhill, Venetia Stanley (holding her monkey, Pluto), Cynthia Charteris (later Asquith), 'Ego' Charteris, Beb Asquith and Lord Sheffield (Venetia's father) at Penrhos in Anglesey, 1907

15. Violet Asquith and Venetia Stanley at Penrhos in 1907. Margot believed the pair made fun of her behind her back

16. Margot Asquith, having swapped hats with Nancy Astor because of the strong wind, launches the Dreadnought HMS *Collingwood* in 1908

17. On the Anglesey coast in 1909. *From left*: Sylvia Henley and her sister Venetia Stanley, Violet, Asquith, Edwin Montagu and 'Bongie' Bonham Carter

18. On board the Admiralty yacht *Enchantress* after the funeral of Edward VII in 1910: Asquith, Pamela McKenna, her sister Barbara Jekyll and Reginald McKenna (the First Lord of the Admiralty)

19. Viola Parsons (in the 1920s), the actress daughter of Sir Herbert Beerbohm Tree, and Margot's favourite among her husband's 'harem'

20. 'The beautiful, daring, delightfully wicked' Lady Diana Manners (later Cooper) in about 1914

21. Asquith with Venetia Stanley in 1910, before the start of their love affair

22. Winston and Clemmie Churchill at Penrhos before the Great War. Margot disliked Winston's 'bluff and swagger' but appreciated his 'jolly sense of humour'

23. Margot and Violet in Downing Street in 1914. 'It is a grief to me that the two women I care for most should be on terms of almost chronic misunderstanding,' wrote Asquith

24. Raymond Asquith, killed on the Somme in September 1916

25. Beb Asquith suffered shell shock, but later fought at Passchandaele

26. Oc Asquith as a Brigadier-General. A 'born soldier', he was awarded three DSOs

27. Cys Asquith was spared the trenches because of his poor health

28. The 'Argonauts' in March 1915, bound for the Dardanelles:
(*from left*) Bernard Freyberg (partially hidden), Rupert Brooke, 'Cleg' Kelly
(grinning, seated on lower gangway steps), Denis Browne (to right of Kelly), Oc Asquith
(cross legged in front of Browne), Johnny Dodge (far right)

29. Giza, spring 1915. *From left*: Oc Asquith, unknown, Rupert Brooke, Mary and Aubrey Herbert, and Patrick Shaw-Stewart

30. A sick Rupert Brooke at Port Said three weeks before his death in April 1915

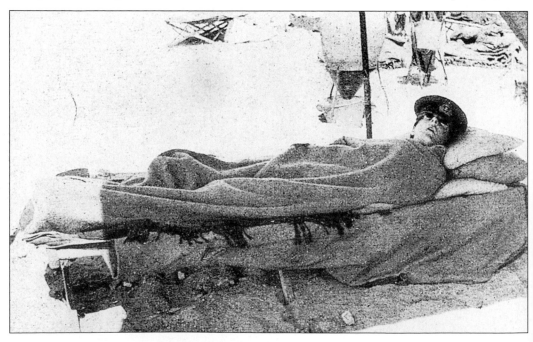

31. Violet Asquith taking tea in Alexandria in June 1915 with Oc (*left*) and Bernard Freyberg, both convalescing from wounds sustained at Gallipoli

32. Oc Asquith (hand outstretched) in the trenches at Cape Helles, Gallipoli, autumn 1915. He was sceptical about the campaign from the start

33. Margot Asquith beside a ruined Flanders church during her visit to the headquarters of King Albert of the Belgians in December 1914

34. Asquith and Lloyd George at the Wharf, probably in May 1915, when they were still on good terms

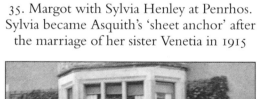

35. Margot with Sylvia Henley at Penrhos. Sylvia became Asquith's 'sheet anchor' after the marriage of her sister Venetia in 1915

36. September 1916: Field Marshal Haig,
watched by Joffre, lectures the 'shifty
and unreliable' Lloyd George

37. Colonel Maurice Hankey (*left*), the
irreplaceable Secretary to the War
Cabinet, with Lloyd George

38. Oc and Betty Asquith emerge from Avon Tyrrell Church under the swords of New Zealand soldiers after their wedding in April 1918

39. Asquith and Lloyd George with the former's granddaughter Priscilla Bibesco in the mid–1920's

Kitchener refused to take up her suggestion of a military band beside the recruiting station in Horse Guards' Parade to help wives and girlfriends appreciate that their menfolk were 'heroes', so she appealed – apparently successfully – to the King to use his influence on the recalcitrant War Minister. Grey's warning her against going around criticizing Kitchener only served to make her carp at the 'gossips' who had given her away and wish the Foreign Secretary had 'a little red blood in his veins'.[30] She was particularly irritated when Grey and Bongie tried to dissuade her from accepting an invitation from King Albert of the Belgians to visit him at his headquarters. However, she was supported by Drummond, the Prime Minister's other Private Secretary, who called the Foreign Secretary 'a governess'. She was, in any case, determined to go, even though it would mean enduring a rough and cold Channel crossing in December, made all the longer by having to zig-zag to avoid enemy mines and submarines.[31]

Margot, wearing leather breeches and waistcoat, a silk jersey and a thick blue serge skirt to cocoon her against the cold, and sporting a patriotic 'black Belgian soldier hat', was escorted by Major Gordon, a middle-aged Scottish staff officer. After a brief detour to visit the Duchess of Sutherland's hospital at Dunkirk, where she approvingly noted her niece Dinah Tennant working hard, they were driven at a 'shattering pace' over icy roads in a large Benz motor car to King Albert's headquarters in time for a 'disgusting lunch' with her friend, Colonel Tom Bridges, the British liaison officer. Margot was given a bedroom with no curtains or shutters in a small seaside villa where she had to help 'a stupid Belgian housemaid' to make her bed. There was no heating and she wore her fur coat for dinner, which was not until 9.15 p.m. However, when the King appeared at lunch the following day, she was impressed by his no-nonsense informality compared to the stuffy British Royal Family, finding him 'delightful – so wise, uncomplaining and <u>absolutely</u> real, no sort of swagger: keen, interested and asking every sort of question'.[32]

After lunch, Margot and Gordon were driven to Nieuport. Like Cynthia and Violet, she was thrilled by the sound of gunfire, but the excitement gave way to horror when she saw the result:

The houses are all smashed – avalanches of bricks and window frames standing up in the walls like dolls houses – no inhabitants, but soldiers smoking or cooking in the open doorways of less ruined houses. Every church – and some beautiful – littered with bits of bombs and debris of broken stained glass with twisted lead ribbons – tops of tombs, heads of stone saints, all pell mell on the grass of the cemeteries.

Margot's self-confidence seems to have been as low as ever: when French refused her request to visit his headquarters, pleading – not unnaturally – that he was too busy, she took it personally, reflecting that 'perhaps, Sir John thinks I am old. Henry likes very young females. It's sad to get old and feel young!'[33] Instead, she and Gordon drove to Ypres to distribute brandy, biscuits, cigarettes and other goodies they had brought for the troops. She was moved by 'the tragic ruin of what must have been a <u>beautiful</u> little town – the Cathedral and Town Hall with its saints and prophets all in fragments in the streets', and haunted by the cemetery with the British names scrawled in pencil on wooden crosses. They found the grave of the son of the former Tory Foreign Secretary, Lord Lansdowne, who had given them a 'crude ugly cross' which Margot held while Gordon hammered it into the ground.

The Major then took her to some high ground to show her the German lines. 'I felt so excited I was stunned,' Margot recorded as she gazed at the smoke of battle while shells crashed into the ground below them. When some French and Belgian soldiers suggested she should take shelter under the wall of the hospital, she tartly told them she was no more frightened than they were, which was greeted with some Gallic shoulder shrugging. One of the Frenchmen took off his dirty blue stomach belt and presented it to her as a souvenir and a Belgian soldier gave her his white one. She carefully packed both away in a cigarette box.

Gordon refused to let her accompany him to put a cross over the grave of the Duke of Richmond's son, which was much closer to the front line, so she settled down to write up her diary beside the hospital with its windows 'rattling like wine glasses' from the vibration of the shellfire. She was relieved when the Major returned – 'very pale, his face bathed in perspiration' – having accomplished his mission despite shrapnel bursting all round him.[34]

At Bailleul, Margot met up with a childhood friend, 'Artie' Wolfe Murray, now a Major in the Highland Light Infantry, noting 'the same rather pathetic look of strain in the eyes which they've <u>all</u> got'. She also managed to track down her nephew Edward Tennant, who was serving with the Royal Flying Corps, clad in his flying cap, leather coat, breeches and gaiters, 'so gay so sweet and young . . . I shuddered at the thought of the Ypres cemetery'. They then proceeded to General Sir Henry Rawlinson's headquarters at Merville, 'shaken like a jelly on the d-d pavé roads' and having to be hoisted out of the mud by some helpful Tommies after Margot made their chauffeur leave the road to let an army convoy pass. On the way they called at the billet of Gordon's brother-in-law. When four enemy mortar shells exploded some thirty yards from the door as they were having tea, their host apologized profusely. Margot herself considered the danger to be less than that of the average fox hunt and noted complacently that the shells were muffled by landing in water.[35]

Rawlinson was in fact an old foxhunting companion of Margot. His headquarters in a 'magnificent hideous' villa were far superior to King Albert's, and Margot was able to have a hot bath. Although she thought Rawlinson the 'kindest fellow possible', she had 'never found him anything but stupid'. Another hunting soldier friend, General Sir Ian Hamilton, had assured her, though, that he had 'a marvellous instinct for country'. She was aware of the tension between Rawlinson and French and could sense that he was keen to discuss his difficulties, but any chance of a confidential chat was ruined by the presence of another spectre from her girlhood in the shape of the French liaison officer, Prince Poniatowski – an 'awful rotter' who had been seen off by her mother. After a huge English breakfast with Rawlinson and his staff the following morning, Margot returned to England via Boulogne, to be greeted by newspaper hoardings announcing that Scarborough had been shelled. She felt suitably indignant about the attack on 'a perfectly innocent unfortified town and killing women and children . . . but I could not help thinking of Winston's foolish remark about digging the German ships out of their holes like rats'.[36]

By the end of 1914 the German advance into France and Belgium had ground to a halt as the Western Front settled into a stalemate. Asquith's Government, meanwhile, was resisting growing pressure in Parliament and the Press to conscript all able-bodied men. For the time being, the Liberal Party's ideological objections to the concept of forcing men to fight coincided with the British Army's traditional preference for volunteers, and Kitchener was able to recruit more than enough men for the army to train. The main problem for the Government was not the supply of men, but gearing up British industry to produce the vast quantity of munitions needed to fight war on a larger scale than anything the world had known. What Asquith and most of his colleagues failed to appreciate was the growing resentment among the Army rank and file, as casualties mounted, to the fact that so many of their fellow citizens were actually benefiting financially from the war, whether as bosses or as workers earning generous overtime payments.

Beb joined his family for Christmas and New Year at Walmer Castle on the Kent coast, the official residence for the Lord Warden of the Cinque Ports, which had been lent to the Prime Minister as a wartime weekend retreat. The castle's proximity both to London and the Channel Ports made it an ideal location for meetings between the men directing the War from England and the generals fighting on the Continent. Originally constructed by Henry VIII to forestall a French invasion, Walmer had subsequently been greatly extended and converted to residential use. The castle was steeped in history; and it was there that the Duke of Wellington had died in 1851. But its exposed position made it bitterly cold in winter and Margot duly complained about the draughts and inadequate heating, noting that Raymond, Beb, Oc, Cys and Elizabeth, as well as herself, all suffered from 'flu and sore throats. To add to their woes, Margot and Elizabeth, in particular, were missing Frau, who had shared their Christmas celebrations for the past fourteen years.

Beb, waiting impatiently for his artillery unit to be supplied with guns, was particularly irritable. Fourteen years earlier, at the Oxford Union, he had cavalierly dismissed 'the scum of Whitechapel conscripted' as 'hardly a desirable addition to the life of the regiment'*; but he was now as committed an advocate of conscription as anyone. After the War, and with the benefit of hindsight, he was to describe the year 1915, which was just beginning, as 'the complex and difficult period of transition during which England changed her ways, brought to birth a continental army composed of volunteers and mobilized her industries for War'. By then he fully appreciated the difficulties his father had had to overcome to gear up the country for war and pave the way for eventual victory:

---

*See p. 100.

During this vital period of transition my father's task was greatly complicated by strong differences of opinion between civilians and soldiers,
between Trades Unionists and conscriptionists, and between such prominent leaders as Kitchener and French on the one hand, and Kitchener
and Lloyd George on the other. Rarely had a statesman been called upon
to face so many difficulties at home and abroad at the same moment . . .

My father's Sundays at Walmer, though a change from London, were
far from being a rest: a soldier in billets or a sailor in harbour may have a
few days of ease, a respite from duties; but for a Prime Minister in the
long crisis of a great war there is no rest, no ease, no respite, no time of
leave to which he can look forward, no release day or night from the
weight and urgency of his responsibilities.[37]

However, at the time Beb was much less understanding of the
'load of Atlas' being born by his father, as he blamed the
Government for the delay in putting the country on to a full war
footing, and providing the guns which would allow him to join the
fighting. It was a mood that inevitably led to acrimonious altera-
tions. Asquith should have taken more notice of his son's views,
which reflected growing and widespread impatience in Parliament
and the Press. If nothing else, the Prime Minister needed to explain
the difficulties better and prepare the country for a long and bloody
conflict. But although the strained relations with Beb are evident in
a letter he wrote to Venetia in early January, it is clear that he paid no
more heed to his son than to his other critics:

Another rather curious figure in our party was Beb, clad in khaki and
growing an orange coloured moustache, against which all but Cynthia
protested (I heard Puffin who had been among the adverse critics, say to
her in a low and sympathetic tone 'I hope I didn't hurt your feelings,
Cynthia'). He is more slow in speech and undecided in action than I ever
remember him, and the girls say that when I asked him at breakfast if he
was going to golf, he looked musingly out of the window (it was a lovely
morning) and after a long interval replied: 'My plans have not yet crystallised'. He is full of rather argumentative fads about spies, conscription
etc, and, as Cys says, his 'bonnet is a regular bee-hive'.[38]

After the Antwerp operation, the Royal Naval Division was sent for
further training at Blandford Camp in Dorset. Oc, Rupert Brooke
and Denis Browne moved from the Anson to the Hood Battalion,

which was commanded by the thoroughly professional Colonel Arnold Quilter, an ex-Grenadier Guard and Boer War veteran who was both liked and admired by his men, and altogether different to his incompetent fellow old Etonian, Cornwallis West.*

The other Hood subalterns included Raymond's friend and Coterie disciple, Patrick Shaw-Stewart, who had succeeded Archie Gordon as Ettie's 'toy-boy'. Ettie's influence had secured him a job at Barings Bank, where he was already recognized as one of the City of London's rising stars. Another ex-Balliol man was the irrepressible Australian-born, Eton educated, F. S. 'Cleg' Kelly, a contemporary of Raymond and Beb at Oxford who, after establishing himself as the outstanding oarsman of his generation,† went on to study musical composition in Germany before embarking on a career as a concert pianist and composer. Then there was Lionel 'Cardy' Montagu, the younger brother of Edwin, but a much more flamboyant character, whose main interest – to the disgust of their father – was horseracing.‡ Another remarkable Hood officer, destined to become one of Oc's closest friends, was the twenty-five-year-old New Zealander Bernard Freyberg, a bull of a man who a few months earlier had been serving as a mercenary in Mexico – a profession in which many of his German forebears had distinguished themselves since the Middle Ages. When war broke out in Europe, Freyberg made his way to London where he bearded Churchill and badgered him into arranging a commission in the Royal Naval Division. The other non-Briton was Johnny Dodge, a high-spirited twenty-year-old American with a taste for adventure.

Rupert Brooke and Violet had begun to correspond regularly after they met again when Oc brought him to stay at 10 Downing Street after the Antwerp operation, and, if she had not already done so, soon fell for the poet. Although the sexually experienced – indeed rapacious – Brooke was far from reciprocating her infatuation, he was evidently

---

*West was summarily relieved of his command of the Anson in the wake of the Antwerp fiasco.
†Kelly won the Diamond Skills at Henley a record three times before rowing in the British Gold medal-winning eight at the 1908 Olympics.
‡When Cardy's father broached the subject of joining the family bank, his son is said to have asked what he would be paid, and on being told he would be entitled to 5 per cent of the profits, replied: 'In that case might I have 2½% and leave at lunchtime.' Cardy went off to work for his uncle's rival firm of A. Keyser and Co before enlisting in the Royal Naval Division.

amused by her, and her friendship suited his social ambitions. In November Violet visited Oc and Rupert at Blandford when they were both struck down with 'flu and arranged for them to convalesce at Lady Wimborne's house in nearby Canford. Rupert eagerly accepted Violet's invitation to stay at Walmer in early January and seems to have charmed her father and stepmother almost as much as herself.

In the mood of general frustration over the impasse in the West, Maurice Hankey put forward a bold proposal to strike at Germany's ally, Turkey, by capturing the Dardanelles straits commanding the entrance to the Bosphorus, and then marching on Constantinople. The plan was eagerly seized upon by Churchill, who soon managed to win over the Prime Minister and most of the Cabinet. At the start of 1915 the Dardanelles were poorly defended and could have been seized by a relatively small military force. The most obvious uncommitted formation was the 9,000-strong Royal Naval Division, now fully trained and a very different body of men from the raw recruits sent to Antwerp. The Prime Minister was furious when Churchill, confident that the Royal Navy alone could force the Dardanelles with no military back-up, offered his Naval troops to French without even notifying Kitchener. 'Winston just now is absolutely maddening – how I wish Oc had not joined his beastly Naval Brigade!' Asquith commented to Margot. Any element of surprise was ruined when Churchill, with Asquith's backing, ordered the Royal Navy to begin the bombardment of the forts protecting the Dardanelles on 19 February. As a result the Turks immediately hurried to reinforce the whole Gallipoli peninsula.

On 20 February, the day after the Royal Navy began to bombard the Dardanelles' forts, Quilter briefed the Hood officers on their role as part of the task force being sent to capture the straits. Their mission did not remain secret for long: Violet heard the news a couple of days later from Lady Essex, who had had it from Shaw-Stewart. Churchill himself confirmed the story to Violet the same evening at a dinner at the Admiralty. The First Lord, despite suffering from mild 'flu, was apparently on cracking form, delighted his 'private army' would at last have the chance to prove themselves to their detractors. Violet recorded how 'he discussed every aspect of the strategy, military and naval, with zest and suddenly breaking off said quite seriously "I think a curse should rest on me – because I <u>love</u> this war. I know it's smashing and shattering the lives of thousands every moment – and yet – I can't help it – I enjoy every second of it.'"[39]

Margot was for once lagging behind her stepdaughter on the gossip stakes. Asquith gave Margot no advance notice that Oc was to be part of the Dardanelles expedition, presumably fearing her loose tongue. She only heard about her stepson's imminent departure for the Dardanelles when he came to London a couple of days later to purchase supplies for the expedition, including, optimistically, a Baedeker guide to Constantinople, ironically only available in German. She was even angrier about being kept in the dark when she discovered that Violet had arranged to join Winston and Clemmie for the official farewell party at the Naval Division's base at Blandford in Dorset: 'I wept bitter tears over all this pettiness and was angry with myself for minding so much when such very big things are going on,' she recorded. 'I often wish I didn't love Oc so much and yet it is a feeble wish to want any form of Love lessened.'[40]

Violet, Clemmie and Goonie Churchill (the wife of Winston's elder brother, John) commandeered the Prime Minister's official car to take them down to Dorset, but Margot pre-empted them by taking the train to Salisbury where she was met by the chauffeur of Lady Wimborne, who drove her straight to Blandford. It was already dark when Margot arrived at the camp, which was scattered all over the heath, so she collared a senior marine officer to escort her to the hut that Oc shared with Rupert and half a dozen other officers, whisking the two sub-lieutenants* off to the Wimbornes', where they met up with Violet, Clemmie and Goonie.

'Dinner', according Margot, was 'wonderfully dull, long and cold. Like all very rich people Lady Wimborne has no idea of comfort. The fires were not even lit and we all ran and put on fur coats – the bath water was cold which disappointed the boys – I would have given anything for them to have had boiling baths.'[41]

The King was to inspect the Division the following morning, 25 February, a bitterly cold but glorious winter day with the frost-covered Downs glinting in the sunshine. Margot, who watched the parade on foot with Goonie, noted that neither Clemmie nor Violet,

---

*The Royal Naval Division retained Naval ranks for new Naval reservists and new recruits while regular officers from the Army – like Colonel Quilter – retained their Army ranks. It was an arrangement that infuriated tidy-minded martinets among the military hierarchy.

who were mounted, 'looked quite horsemen to my professional eye'. She was particularly critical of her stepdaughter's 'bad flat wide brimmed hat and her pretty hair very untidy and unbusiness-like and elbows tight to her sides'.[42] Churchill walked round the Division before the King arrived for the official inspection, while Violet and Clemmie cantered up and down the lines. 'Rupert looked heroic,'[43] noted the starstruck Violet. Margot for her part recorded:

> I felt quite a thrill when I saw Oc and Rupert with walking sticks standing in front of their men looking quite wonderful! Rupert is a beautiful young man and we get on well, he has so much intellectual temperament and nature about him. He told Oc he was quite <u>certain</u> he would never come back but would be killed – it didn't depress him at all but he was just <u>convinced</u> – I shall be curious to see if this turns out to be a true instinct.[44]

There was a two-hour delay before the King arrived. As the Division marched past, Violet felt 'a great thrill when the Hood came on preceded by its silver band – and Quilter roared like a lion "<u>Eyes Rrright</u>" and all their faces turning. I hadn't realized before what a different colour men of the same race can be: Patrick [Shaw-Stewart] was arsenic green, Oc primrose, Kelly slate-grey, Rupert carnation-pink, Denis Browne the most lovely Giorgione reddish-brown. The King looked rather *mesquin** in a Khaki coat with a fur-collar, but was more forthcoming and agreeable than I have ever known him – making quite gratuitous and good conversation.'[45]

After the parade Margot and Violet dined in the Hood officers' mess. Although Shaw-Stewart had procured 'every form of delicacy such as grapefruit, marrons glacés, foie gras and champagne', everyone felt flat after having been up since 6 a.m. preparing for the parade. Shaw-Stewart, who was suffering from a throat infection, 'looked like death', according to Margot, 'and even Oc and Rupert were very white'. Margot herself felt depressed and tired, while Rupert irritably complained to Violet 'that <u>Kelly</u> had got hold of his sonnets and was spreading them among his mess-mates'.[46]

Margot paid a final visit to Blandford camp the following day, stopping at the bank in Poole on the way to obtain £50 in gold sovereigns, giving ten to Rupert and forty to Oc: 'they were most grateful and sweet. Rupert kissed me and I wondered if I would ever see him

---

*Shabby.

again.' She and Oc sat on a wooden crate outside his hut and chatted for half an hour, but avoided the subject of the dangers that lay ahead, instead concentrating on the perennial problem of Violet. Oc said he hoped that his sister would marry Bongie and told his stepmother 'to be patient and that he understood my domestic difficulties . . . He took my hand and patted it and put his arm round me like a lover.'[47] They hugged each other and Oc shook hands with Horwood, the Asquiths' chauffeur, before he drove Margot off in floods of tears.

Violet, meanwhile, was thinking as much of Rupert as her brother. Early on Sunday morning, 28 February, before setting off to bid them a final farewell, she wrote the poet a diffident letter for him 'to read on the high seas', making clear her feelings for him while at the same time absolving him from any expectation that he could reciprocate them:

> When I have asked myself in (rare) moments of introspection in the last 2 months – <u>why</u> I loved being with you so – one of the reasons I disentangled from a skein of unanalysable and indefinable ones was that I have never spent a moment with you anywhere – not at a pounce table* or a music hall or a Downing Street lunch! – that wasn't permeated by and shot through with colour and a sense of adventure . . .
>
> I know you'll do glorious things – and want them for you – and I suppose it's no good saying don't get killed. There are so many excellent reasons why you shouldn't – much better ones than my minding. But I should mind.[48]

Violet was picked up by Dunn's chauffeur just before eight o'clock and driven through the quiet Sunday morning Bristol streets and out along the River Severn to Avonmouth docks, where the Hoods were on board the *Grantully Castle*, a converted Union Castle liner. Amidst 'a confusion of soldiers, trucks, mules, packing-cases, gangways, sound and movement', she spotted Denis Browne, who fetched Oc and Rupert. She took them to lunch at a hotel in Bristol where 'Rupert's main idea as usual was to get as warm as possible – he is a real lizard – and we coiled ourselves nearly in the fire-place – till it was time to go out and have a prescription made up for Patrick's throat'. Violet accompanied them back on board and went to see the ailing Shaw-Stewart.

---

*'Pounce' is a card game for two or more players, similar to Racing Demon.

I dawdled about with them – with a terrible pre-operation feeling – the suspended knife seemed just above us all – then the dull muffled siren booms and hoots began, charged with finality, and I knew it was falling. Rupert walked with me along the narrow crowded decks, down the little plank stairs, then I said goodbye to him. I knew by his eyes that he felt sure we should never see each other again.[49]

When Rupert disappeared below deck, Oc accompanied his sister down the gangway. There was a final 'imperious hoot' from the ship's siren and as her brother turned to go back on board he said firmly 'I shall come back. I may be wounded, but I shall come back.'[50]

The Hood's trumpeters sounded a final salute as the ship slid slowly out of the harbour. Violet stood and watched the decks 'densely crowded with splendid Khaki figures with happy confident faces', her eyes firmly fixed on her brother until he became a distant blur. She was reminded not of the ultimately victorious Greek war against Troy which was in most people's minds, but of the disastrous Athenian expedition against Syracuse during the Peloponnesian war, when the attacking army was annihilated.

14

'To make a poet's grave'

I N THE 1920s Beb visited Skyros, the island in the Aegean where
Achilles rested during the Trojan War and where, 3,000 years later,
Rupert Brooke was buried. Afterwards Beb wrote a poem, *Skyros at
Sunset*, the first stanza of which perfectly captures the spirit in which
his fellow poet and his companions set out to match the exploits of
the legendary heroes of the Ancient World who had inspired so
many of their boyhood dreams:

> Here passed of old the fleet of Persia,
>   Wine-red sails and flashing oars,
> Splintered by charging triremes of Hellas
>   And broken on her sacred shores.
> Here came Youth and the ships of England
>   Eastward across the wave;
> Here came Valour, and Hope, and Sorrow,
>   To make a poet's grave.[1]

No convicted felon ever mounted the scaffold more certain of his
fate than Rupert Brooke as the *Grantully Castle* steamed along the
Bristol Channel with her two destroyer escorts, bound for Gallipoli:
'Come and die. It'll be great fun,' the poet exhorted a friend shortly
before he left.[2] When he first learnt that the Royal Naval Division
was bound for the Dardanelles, he told Violet 'it's too wonderful for
belief. I had not imagined Fate could be so benign.' In Malta he

posted his answer to her shy declaration of love: 'Do not care much what happens to me or what I do. When I give thought to it at all, I hate people – people I like – to care for me.' Her enigmatic reply shows she was resigned to her feelings being unrequited:

> You tell me not to care what happens to you. If it is for my sake – I have made my hedonistic calculus and am ready to take the risk of your bad luck and its possible reflex action on me. But if it is for yours – if I don't fill any hole in your life and if you are bothered by the responsibility – for it is a responsibility always – of people who care for you – then I can do as you say.[3]

The mood on board the *Grantully Castle* itself was almost that of a pleasure cruise. In Malta they were joined by Charles Lister, Charty's surviving son, who had been serving at the British Embassy in Constantinople when the War began. 'Weather quite perfect,' Oc reported to his father from Valetta harbour as if writing a holiday postcard. 'So far the voyage has been very like an ordinary voyage on a rather second rate P & O steamer . . . Please thank Winston very much for arranging for us to take part in this most interesting of expeditions,'[4] he wrote to Margot a couple of weeks later from Mudros Bay in Lemnos Island, where the liner lay anchored with the rest of the invasion fleet as they impatiently waited to invade Gallipoli.

'Cleg' Kelly and Denis Browne, the two musicians on board, helped to maintain the holiday spirit by entertaining the stokers with sea shanties and popular music hall ballads hammered out on the ship's saloon room piano, while Shaw-Stewart regaled his fellow officers with tales from *The Odyssey* and *The Iliad*: 'his actors come onto the stage with the modernest dress and language',[5] Oc informed his father. Their mess was sarcastically dubbed 'the Latin table' by their less erudite companions, while they themselves preferred to be known as 'the Argonauts', after Jason's companions in his mythical quest for the Golden Fleece. Although Oc could banter with the best of them, rather than adopt the 'do or die' attitude of most of his comrades, he was already beginning to question the whole basis of the Gallipoli operation: 'The more one studies the undertaking with maps, the more it looks as if the operations may be prolonged and difficult,' he wrote to his father on 11 March, the day the *Grantully Castle* dropped anchor in Mudros Bay.

General Sir Ian Hamilton had recently arrived from England to take command of the multi-national military force being assembled at Lemnos. As well as the Royal Naval Division, Hamilton had at his disposal a French division (with a large contingent of colonial African troops), two divisions from Australia and New Zealand and the 29th British Division. Lieutenant General Sir William Birdwood, commanding the Anzac forces, was all for pressing ahead, but Hamilton, with inadequate transports, little artillery support and major deficiencies in the way of stores, decided to err on the side of caution and ordered the whole force to withdraw to Port Said to give him a chance to re-organize and refine his plan of attack.

At Port Said, Oc groused to his father that it was 'tiresome kicking our heels and not being able even to stretch our legs'. When someone had joked about the words 'On Active Service' on their letters Denis Browne had suggested substituting 'In' for 'On'. Conditions for the men crammed below deck were much worse. Fresh water was rationed and 'the result is vermin are increasingly numerous'. When one of the Ansons died, typhoid was suspected. Oc was particularly irritated by his ignorance of the operational plan, complaining to his father that 'I probably know less about the Dardanelles problem than do readers of the English press. The impression one got from the flotsam of naval gossip at Lemnos was that Gallipoli is strongly held and admirably trenched and entangled: and that the Fleet has no chance of getting through until snipers and howitzers have been turned out from both shores.' He was dubious about whether troops could be successfully landed at all and, even 'supposing this could be done, would it be possible to supply by boats upon beaches exposed to violent winds, an army of the necessary proportions?'[6]

One snippet of news that did reach Port Said was the campaign being waged by Lloyd George against drunkenness among factory workers, which was being blamed for delays in gearing up the production of munitions. When Oc heard that the King had responded to the campaign by banning alcohol in the Royal household for the rest of the war, he cabled his father:

REPORTED SPREAD OF TEMPERANCE ALARMS AND AMAZES US. STAND FAST.[7]

There was not much danger of the Prime Minister ever succumbing to a temperance campaign, but, as Oc heard from Margot, he was greatly cheered by the telegram:

My darling Oc,

   . . . Father enchanted with your drinks wire! The King's letter to my mind (and a few more) is idiotic – he never showed it to father – Lloyd George and he did it together.* The only person who needs a little stimulant is the workman. He has been cruelly maligned (even Lord Kitchener said this to me!) – fearfully over-worked – often carried out of the great heat fainting and off the ships fainting – over-time every Sunday since early war days. Lloyd George, McKenna and Kitchener have knocked off all wine and alcohol – I wish Beb and Raymond would: they are of the kind that can stand any poison. Fearful rows going on as Winston and Lloyd George (not the latter now) want total prohibition and of course that vile Times has whipped up the agitation till it has grown grotesquely.[8]

Morale began to improve when the troops were allowed ashore to a tented camp at Port Said. The officers were granted forty-eight hours' leave in batches of three, and Oc, Rupert and Patrick took the train to Cairo, putting up at Shepheard's Hotel, where Oc had stayed ten years earlier en route for Khartoum. Oc, who spoke fluent Arabic and knew the Egyptian capital well, showed his friends the Pyramids and the other tourist sights and they luxuriated in having 'one's every want forestalled by soft spoken dusky myrmidons'. They met up with the ubiquitous Aubrey Herbert, who was in Cairo with his wife, Mary, having wangled a post on Birdwood's staff. He bragged about having got a message through to friends in Constantinople, while the three Hood officers pretended they had been practising their only sentence in Turkish. 'Do not kill me. I am a friend of Herbert Effendi.'[9]

   Rupert and Patrick suffered a bad dose of diarrhoea and were exhausted by a hard route march through the desert, so Charles Lister took them to the Casino Hotel in Port Said to convalesce. Rupert insisted on being carried back to camp for Hamilton's inspection of

---

*In fact, as the King himself later explained to Margot, he had 'never intended to give up drink unless the Government passed drastic legislation on the subject – that had this been done he wanted to say he was ready to share the sacrifice of the poorest of his subjects'. However, he had been bulldozed into doing so when the newspapers – in full cry for Prohibition – misinterpreted his carefully worded letter to Lloyd George. Apparently, when the keeper of the Royal cellars locked up his domain, he had 'arranged large wreath of dead bottles outside and put a crêpe bow on them with a placard "Dead"'. (Margot Asquith's Diary, d. 3211, p. 234)

the Royal Naval Division on 2 April, lying, as he wrote to Violet, 'racked by headache and diarrhoea, under the awning on the sand while the stokers trudged past'. She heard from her brother how 'we are delighted with the choice of G.O.C. . . . Quilter was pleased as a child, so I think he must have been praised.' After the parade Hamilton came to see the young poet: 'a notable meeting, it was generally felt,' Brooke boasted to Violet afterwards, 'our greatest poet-soldier and our greatest soldier-poet.* We talked blank verse. He looked very worn and white haired. I thought him a little fearful – not <u>fearful</u>, but less than cock-sure – about the job.'[10]

Hamilton had every reason to be apprehensive about the preparations being made by his opponent, Liman von Sanders, the astute German general commanding the Turkish forces in Gallipoli, to make his much advertised visitors unwelcome. Meanwhile, in England the twelve-year-old Puffin caught the public mood of optimism when he wrote to 'Dearest Oc, I was so excited to hear that you had been sent to the Dardanelles. Are you having fun? Have you got to the Dardanelles yet? . . . Have you had any fighting yet? We have had ripping weather here.'[11]

On board the *Grantully Castle* the atmosphere, as described by Oc to Violet, had reverted to one of frivolity:

> We get through the days with Swedish exercises, signalling and machine gun classes and inspection of rifles, boots and ammunition . . . Johnny Dodge has a pot of luminous paint with which he made a nightmare of the cabin he shared with Rupert on the way out. He proposed to paint his back with it so that in night-work he might be visible to his men . . . I think we are improving Cleg [Kelly] – whose bursts of nervous laughter become less frequent and hyena-like. We have occasional Greek lessons from an interpreter whom I picked up in the island . . . Charles [Lister] is excellent company.[12]

The *Grantully Castle* reached Lemnos on 14 April to find Mudros Bay already clogged with Allied shipping, so she was redirected some seventy miles to the south to Trebuki Bay at the southern end of Skyros. Oc was almost lyrical when he described the island to Violet

---

*Hamilton discovered his talent for poetry while serving as ADC to General Sir Frederick Roberts VC in Madras, India, in the 1880s, where he befriended the young Rudyard Kipling. Several of Hamilton's poems were published.

as 'like a great rock garden of white and pinkish white marble, with small red poppies and every sort of wild flower . . . everywhere the smell of wild thyme or is it sage? Or wild mint? I enclose a sprig. Our men kill adders and have fun with big tortoises. Charles, Freyberg and I have been for a couple of swims in the bay. The water near the shore, where the bottom is white marble, is more beautifully green and blue than I have ever seen it anywhere.'[13]

To pass the time, Quilter organized a fancy dress competition, and while the men cavorted on stage in an astonishing array of improvised costumes, Kelly and Browne took it in turns to provide background music. The prize was a huge iron cross. Joseph Murray, an able seaman in Oc's platoon, described a training exercise in which the men were divided into sections and made to race each other back to the beach. When Oc discovered that some members of his platoon had mutilated a giant tortoise by cracking its shell he ordered the offenders to go back and put the animal out of its misery, an act of humanity that apparently made a profound impression, according to Murray, who recalled: 'My section lost the race, but it had a new respect for its officer, a gentleman who, even on the eve of battle, had a soft heart and a detestation of suffering.'[14]

On 21 April Oc informed Violet that 'Rupert has fallen ill again today – a swollen lip, temperature 101 and pains in the back and head'.[15] The infection was put down to a mosquito bite and no one was particularly alarmed. The following day Kelly 'looked into his cabin before breakfast, when I found him very dazed, but I had no idea he was dangerously ill'. But that afternoon Brooke was diagnosed as suffering from acute blood poisoning, which before antibiotics – particularly in his already weak state – was likely to be fatal. McCracken, the battalion doctor, decided to move him to the nearby French hospital ship, the *Duguay-Trouin*, where he would at least be more comfortable. Kelly – already full of 'foreboding that he is one of those, like Keats, Shelley and Schubert who are not suffered to deliver their full message'[16] – watched as the invalid, with Oc and Denis Browne in attendance, was gently lowered into a steam pinnace to be taken over to the French ship.

Oc and Browne stayed with Rupert for the rest of the day, only leaving at six o'clock to go across to HMS *Franconia*, the headquarters of the divisional commander, Major General Paris, to arrange for cables to Hamilton and Churchill to warn them of the poet's imminent demise. Oc sat with Rupert all the following morning, 23 April,

St George's Day and the anniversary of the birth and death of Shakespeare. The poet himself could not have written a better script. Oc later told Violet how, although Rupert was unconscious most of the time, 'at least twice when I spoke to him, he seemed to make an effort in his throat to speak: but no words came'. At 2 p.m. Oc was relieved by Browne and went to make arrangements for the funeral, which, with the flotilla due to leave for the Dardanelles at dawn the following day, would have to be carried out immediately. Rupert died at 4.46 p.m. – Browne made a precise note of the time – and after a short discussion they decided to bury him in a picturesque olive grove on Skyros, where they had all rested for lunch during the divisional manoeuvres three days earlier. Browne went ahead to prepare the grave with Lister, Freyberg and a team of stokers, while Oc procured a solid oak coffin from the hospital ship's store and, borrowing a cauterizing iron from the operating theatre, burnt Rupert's name and the date of his death on the lid.

At 8.15 p.m. a pinnace with Paris and several of his staff officers on board picked up Quilter, Kelly and some dozen other Hood officers from the *Grantully Castle*. Oc was waiting on the deck of the *Duguay-Trouin* beside the coffin which he had covered with a Union Flag on which he placed sixteen palm fronds together with the dead poet's pith helmet and his revolver in its holster. The French Guard of Honour presented arms, Oc stepped back and saluted, and the coffin was lowered into the boat to be taken ashore, where Patrick Shaw-Stewart was waiting with a group of burly petty officers to carry it to its final resting place nearly a mile away. With the moon shrouded in cloud, the bearers struggled slowly with their burden over the stony ground lit only by a flickering lantern, followed by about thirty British and French officers.

It was not until 10.45 p.m. that the little procession reached the grave site. The chaplain of First Naval Brigade read the burial service while the escort stood to attention holding flaming torches. A firing party under the command of Shaw-Stewart fired a final salute and the Hood's trumpeters sounded 'The Last Post'. Kelly noted how 'the small olive grove in the narrow valley and the scent of wild sage gave a strong classical tone which was so in harmony with the poet we were burying that to some of us the Christian ceremony seemed out of keeping'. While the others hurried back to the boats to complete their preparations for departure a few hours later, Oc, Kelly, Freyberg, Lister and Browne stayed behind and scrabbled about in the dim moonlight for pebbles and chips of pink and white marble to lay on the grave, before placing a simple wooden cross with Rupert's name and date of death at the head of the tomb and another smaller cross at its foot. The five men then stood in silence and took a last look at the olive grove. Afterwards, Kelly wrote in his journal that 'the sense of tragedy gave place to a sense of passionless beauty, engendered both by the poet and the place'.[17]

Back in London, the death of Rupert Brooke dominated the newspaper headlines. Asquith, although he had only known the poet for a short time, was as moved as anyone, writing to Venetia at midnight on the day he died:

> My darling, I can't tell you what I feel about Rupert Brooke's death. It has given me more pain than any loss in the war. We have seen a great deal of him all this autumn and winter, he and Oc being fellow officers, and the closest companions and friends. And Violet and he had a real friendship – perhaps the germ at any rate (as I once said to you) of something more. He was clean-cut and beautiful to look at, and had a streak of something more than talent: his last Sonnets struck a fine note. Altogether, by far the most attractive and winning of the younger men whom I have got to know once the war began . . .
>
>   Why should people like myself be allowed to linger on the stage, when so much vividness and promise is cut prematurely off?
>
>   And in the stress of such an event – so unforeseeable, so apparently irrational and wasteful – one gets a dazed, dim, premonitory feeling, that the next blow may come even nearer home. My much beloved Oc – or Beb, who went off to-night to the front in France. Who could have thought it possible or even conceivable a year ago?[18]

By a cruel stroke of irony, Violet was staying with the Aberdeens (Archie Gordon's parents) at the Viceregal Lodge in Dublin when she heard the news and, according to a fellow guest, 'sobbed for hours'. Writing to Aubrey five months later, when many more of her friends were dead, she claimed that Rupert's death was 'the greatest sorrow of the war – and one of the greatest of my life'. She told Virginia Woolf that she had loved him 'as she had never loved any man'.[19]

Rupert's close friend, Eddie Marsh, who had originally introduced Rupert to the Asquiths, wrote to Oc: 'It is everything to me to know that he had two such friends as you and Denis to look after him . . . I know he would have wished to die fighting, but I know how much more hideous that might have been.'[20]

By the time the five Allied divisions finally embarked for Gallipoli, the Turks had six divisions dug in on the Peninsula with further reinforcements to the north if necessary. Liman von Sanders identified three possible landing sights: Cape Helles, commanding the entrance to the Dardanelles, Gaba Tepe, a wide beach area some fifteen miles to the north, and Bulair near the neck of the Peninsula, which he thought the most likely and where the general concentrated his main force of two divisions and based his own headquarters.

Hamilton correctly guessed where his opponent expected him to land and concentrated his attack in the south of Gallipoli, sending the Anzacs ashore at Gaba Tepe, while the British 29th Division and two battalions from the Naval Division, with the French in support, landed at Cape Helles. Meanwhile, the rest of the Royal Naval Division was ordered to mount a diversion at Bulair to convince the Turks that this was indeed the Allies' main objective.

As soon as the RND's flotilla reached their objective shortly after daybreak on 25 April, the cruisers HMS *Dartmouth* and HMS *Doris* set about bombarding the Turkish positions, while the battleship HMS *Canopus* with General Paris on board, moved close inshore while troops ostentatiously boarded boats as if preparing to land. After nightfall it was planned that a platoon from the Hood would land and light flares and fire off machine guns to try to mimic an invasion. With two entire Turkish divisions waiting to receive them, the scheme was tantamount to suicide for the men involved, so Freyberg hatched up an alternative plan, which was for Oc and himself to swim ashore and light flares all along the beach. Both men were strong swimmers – Freyberg had swum for his country – and Oc enthusiastically endorsed the idea. Colonel Quilter was equally keen, but was adamant that although he was quite ready to let the New Zealander risk his life, he was not going to be held responsible for drowning the son of the Prime Minister. He also turned down offers by Kelly and Lister to go instead. Oc later informed Margot that although Freyberg 'hated going alone, Quilter insisted that he could not risk another officer'.[21] So it was on his own that the New Zealander swam ashore towing a raft carrying an oilskin containing flares, his body blacked up to make him less visible and smeared with grease to protect him against the cold. While the warships bombarded the Turkish positions, he accomplished his mission despite having to dodge back and forth into the sea as the beach was raked by machine gunfire. Afterwards, he miraculously managed to swim back to the now darkened ships although it took him two hours to locate them, by which time he was half dead from cold and exhaustion. He was awarded the DSO for his efforts.

Freyberg's ruse worked spectacularly well, deceiving von Sanders into keeping all his forces at Bulair in position for another forty-eight hours in spite of the landings taking place to the south. If the commanders of the invading forces had shown a fraction of the New Zealander's initiative, a remarkable victory could still have been achieved. As it was, the Anzac forces at Gaba Tepe were landed at the wrong place, became muddled up and having gained the heights overlooking the beach, began to drift back in search of their officers, when the local Turkish commander, Mustapha Kemal (the future leader of his country, known as 'Ataturk'), launched a series of devastating counter-attacks. Aubrey Herbert, who had landed on the beach in the expectation of interrogating prisoners, looked on in horror as, instead of Turkish captives, he saw hundreds of wounded Anzacs struggling or being carried back to the boats.

At Cape Helles, although successful landings were achieved against relatively light opposition at two beaches, there were bloodbaths on the other two – in particular at 'V' Beach where the *River Clyde*, an ancient collier, was beached to be met by a hail of Turkish gunfire. Johnny Dodge, whose platoon was helping to crew the collier, was severely wounded as he led his men to support the assault.* Meanwhile, the commanders at the other beaches dithered instead of making their way inland and harrying the Turks from the rear.

On the night of 29–30 April, the Hood battalion, after a frustrating three days steaming up and down the coast while being held in reserve, was landed at 'W' beach. It was a cold, clear night and, as they waded ashore across the barbed wire crushed by the barges, the Hoods were confronted by a scene of chaos: abandoned weapons and equipment everywhere, heaps of bodies piled up awaiting burial and the cries of wounded men pleading for help. As the sun rose,

---

*Dodge was evacuated to England.

Kelly had a good view of the beach where the French had landed and noted ruefully that 'they seem to have got things into a more orderly state than obtains on our beaches'.[22]

The next couple of days were spent digging in while the Turkish batteries and the naval guns exchanged what Kelly described as 'a colossal game of tennis over our heads'. The enemy, under von Sanders's masterful command, was concealed in innumerable well-camouflaged slit trenches and gullies running along the Achi Baba hill, with machine gunners hiding in the ruins of stone cottages. All Kelly could see was the surrounding countryside, which he thought 'quite delightful – open with a certain number of small trees, some orchards and a profusion of wild flowers'.[23]

The Turks attacked on the night of 1–2 May, but were driven off with heavy losses. The following day the Hood, supported by the Hampshire regiment, mounted a counter-attack. But having captured a ridge overlooking the beach, they were forced to withdraw as they came under fire not only from the enemy artillery but also snipers who, they were shocked to find, were positioned both in front of them and to their rear. Oc later recounted to Margot how 'the Turkish snipers paint their faces green, and dress their heads with leaves and sit in holes in the ground with a week's food and ammunition. Our troops walk over and past them without seeing them.'[24] Lister became the first Argonaut casualty when he was wounded as his platoon covered the retreat.

There was not much sleep to be had over the next three nights as an artillery duel between ships and shore batteries continued without abatement. On 6 May a big Allied offensive was mounted against the Turkish positions on Achi Baba hill and the nearby village of Krithia. The Hood and Anson battalions were positioned between the French and a makeshift brigade of British and Anzac troops, with orders to advance 2,000 yards and then to hold their position while the other units enveloped the Turks. The Hoods soon found themselves ahead of the troops on their flanks, who were held up by Turkish artillery. After about a mile Oc's platoon came under fire from the hitherto invisible enemy trenches a few hundred yards in front and Oc himself was shot in the knee. He later recounted to Margot how 'after I was hit, I rolled for three or four hundred yards through the daisies towards the nearest depression in the ground. I was sniped at all the way, and very lucky not to be hit again.'[25]

The Hood battalion as a whole suffered heavily in the attack, losing half its officers, including Quilter, who was killed by a shell: 'he was very human and lovable – the best type of regimental soldier,' Oc told his stepmother, 'he is a great loss to all of us.' Freyberg's company fared the worst, with the New Zealander himself sustaining a bad stomach wound and Kelly, Browne and Shaw-Stewart the only officers unscathed – the last was saved when a bullet was deflected by his Asprey steel mirror: 'almost as good an advertisement for that firm as Oc's wound for the Government', he quipped in a letter to his father.[26]

A few weeks later Asquith informed Venetia's sister, Sylvia Henley, that he had received a letter from 'one Bowen, an unknown auctioneer in the City, who out of sheer kindness, encloses an extract from a letter just received from his son at the Dardanelles, who seems to be a Lieutenant in the Marines: "Mr Asquith's son was wounded in the knee, and I overheard him in a heated argument with his stretcher-bearers. He wanted them to put him down, and carry a poor Tommy who was trying to struggle down in the arms of two pals. A good man". Isn't that rather touching? so like our dear Oc.'[27]

*

John Churchill, Winston's brother, who was attached to Hamilton's headquarters staff during the invasion of Gallipoli, happened to be visiting the field hospital when Oc was brought in. He noted in his diary that he was 'looking bad from loss of blood'. He cabled the Admiralty as soon as he had spoken to the surgeon:

FIRST LORD SECRET AND PERSONAL
ASQUITH SHOT NEAR LEFT KNEE. HAS BEEN SEEN BY DOCTOR. WOUND SERIOUS BUT NOT DANGEROUS, BULLET PASSING THROUGH. JACK.

Hamilton himself called to see the casualty late that evening and sent a wire to Asquith at 7.30 the following morning:

HAVE SEEN OC – VERY CHEERY. NO DANGER OF LOSS OF LIFE OR LIMB. IAN HAMILTON.[28]

Margot was brushing her hair and (as she wrote to Oc himself later that day) assumed the worst when Asquith came into her bedroom at nine o'clock clutching the two telegrams with 'his eyes full of tears'. She exclaimed:

'He's dead!' and put my arms over my head, but he said 'No, he's not' and we both cried while we read them. I had been waiting and watching and sleepless with longing and apprehension and here it is – we know the worst, please God you are safe and I pray no pain and clean surroundings. I had been reading this wonderful account of the whole thing, which I enclose for you, and was moved to the core. How <u>thrilling</u> and glorious and pathetic it must have been. <u>What an experience</u> for you my dear darling. Puff, Elizabeth and I have prayed for you all the time always. I could not think God would take you from us. 'Nothing in the History of War has ever been more wonderful' your father said when he came up from the Cabinet.'[29]

Rather than bringing the family together, Oc's wound was the cause of more tension between his stepmother and his sister. Violet described in her diary how she was in the bath when 'Margot rushed in with a telegram in her hand making loud sobbing noises and saying "He's <u>not</u> dead! He's <u>not</u> dead! He's not dead." I of course concluded that Oc tho' not killed was in an all but hopeless condition and was infinitely relieved to find a rather satisfactory telegram from Ian Hamilton.'[30]

Margot was put out when Violet said 'Goodness I thought by your face and manner he was dead! You gave me an awful fright!', noting in her own journal how she 'was surprised more than moved – surprised that I could feel emotion over a mere escape and almost put out that I had frightened her, tho' she too adores Oc'.[31]

Oc informed his stepmother that 'I have had the most wonderful luck, the bullet – a clean, small one – went into my left knee just to the right of the knee cap and came out just below the hock – missing every bone and the artery – no permanent injury has been done. One inch either way would have meant a stiff leg or the loss of it.'[32] The surgeons suggested he would be fit to return to Gallipoli after 'a fortnight of massage and fortnight of convalescence'. As Violet prepared to travel out to Egypt to be with her brother, Margot wrote that it was 'a <u>terrible</u> disappointment to me hearing you are to be kept out there', but what really bothered her was feeling 'very envious' of 'lucky little idle Violet . . . being able to go out and be with you – I would give anything to have gone and of course would, if V. and I had been partners, but alas! as you know we are not.'[33]

For some months Margot had been suffering renewed bouts of self-pity and lack of confidence, the root cause of which was her continuing resentment of Venetia. Unable to bring herself to confront her husband directly, she tried to persuade her rival's mother, Lady Sheffield, to call off her daughter. After one particularly 'upsetting episode', Blanche, Venetia's married eldest sister, wrote to their mother:

> It is difficult to know how to take such violent outbursts which I fear <u>are</u> caused by jealousy of the P.M. and also by wounded vanity and humiliation at not being able to retain the position and influence she once had. She will never know any peace of mind, I am sure, until . . . perhaps, our V. is married . . . it would no doubt be very difficult now to break off what is, after all, a very delightful friendship . . . I always feel V. is very safe, which is the main thing, as it is her cleverness and intellectual side that is involved much more than her affections, though no doubt she is very fond of P.M. – But you don't think there are any signs of her being too fond of him, do you?[34]

Whatever Venetia's family hoped about the innocence of her friendship with Asquith, by early 1915 their relationship was the subject of gossip, exacerbated by the fact that the Prime Minister would sometimes make use of tedious exchanges in Cabinet to write to Venetia. All Margot would admit in her journal was to being 'out of spirits – it is sad getting old! I should not feel it so much – or indeed at all – if I was <u>quite</u> sure I would keep my place in the hearts of those I love best, but I am not vain enough to feel <u>sure</u> of this!' A few days after her fifty-first birthday, she pathetically tried to seek reassurance about her own place in her husband's affections: 'I went to Henry's dressing room and hugged him – I said "You have got <u>everything</u> – Fame, Power, Success, Love, Friends, Health, children – <u>everything</u> but a young wife!" He said with that wonderful emotion which I miss so much in his children – "I have got the youngest wife in the world!"'[35]

Asquith may well have been referring to this conversation – which was no doubt a great deal more charged than his wife let on – when he wrote to Venetia: 'I believe I am endowed with rather more than an average stock of patience, but sometimes (this morning for instance) it is tried almost to bursting point, and like the Psalmist, I have to put a guard on my lips that I "sin not with my tongue".'[36] He was more candid with Violet when three months later he came to her bedroom and stayed until 3 a.m., telling her how 'I have sometimes walked up and down that room till I felt as tho' I were going mad. When one needed rest, to have a thing like the *Morning Post* leader flung at one – the obvious reasons for and against things more controversially put even than by one's colleagues.'[37] Venetia gave him respite from all this.

In truth, however much Asquith might try to disguise the intensity of his feelings for Venetia from Margot, he was by now besotted with his young confidante, writing to her at least once every day and sometimes as often as three times. 'I love you more than ever – more than life!' he told her on 12 February, assuring her six days later that 'I can honestly say that not an hour passes without thought of you'.[38] He was not only emotionally dependent on her, but sought her advice on how to deal with his fractious colleagues, and even on questions of wartime strategy. 'You are the only woman I have known who can think in the real sense,' he told her, and 'there are only 2 or 3 men to my mind in the same class' so far as her judgement was concerned.[39] He believed that their relationship was

> the most ideal comradeship that a man, 'immersed' as they say in affairs, ever had with a woman since the foundation of things. And from being first a luxury, then a recurring pleasure, it has become to me not far off from being a necessity. I cannot imagine a day passing in which I would not tell you my doings and my thoughts and my hopes and fears; with the certainty of sympathy and understanding and response, the wisest counsel, the most tender and unselfish help.[40]

It is hardly surprising that as the Prime Minister became more emotionally demanding, Venetia tried to back off. When in early 1915 she began training as a nurse at the London Hospital, it became a convenient excuse for not being always at his beck and call, but when in February she suggested going to the Balkans to nurse, she hastily backed down after he protested that she risked exposing herself to typhus – 'let alone my own selfish reluctance even to dream of you so long so far away. Darling, it would afflict me night and day more than I can tell.'[41]

Although Asquith rarely even hinted at the possibility of Venetia marrying, it was always in the back of his mind, and he was increasingly worried by his dependence on her and his fear of losing her. He confessed that 'sometimes a horrible imagination seizes me that you may be taken from me – in one way or another; with you would vanish all the colour and "point" of my life'. On 23 February, he admitted to 'a suicidal mood' and beginning 'to think that the happiest thing would be to become the sudden prey of one of Fate's lurking submarines. One would at any rate carry down with one to the bottom a golden freight of memories, and escape the living hell of frustrated hopes and unattainable desires.'[42] Venetia did her best to re-assure him, and on 5 March, he wrote:

> My own darling – I had a very healing hour and a half with you and feel far happier than 24 hours ago I thought would ever be possible. I didn't really exaggerate in what I said to you: the *coup foudroyant* (in the literal sense) would have been welcome all yesterday afternoon and night. It may not be wise to be so dependent: to have put everything that one hopes for into one investment: to stand or fall entirely by one person: but it is too late now to make these calculations, and to attempt to draw up a balance sheet. *J'y suis – j'y reste.* I can never make out tho' I often speculate, exactly how much it means to you: naturally not nearly so much as it does to me: but still I have (except in bad moments) an unshaken faith that it is a real and vital part of your life, and that if anything were to crush or annihilate it, you would feel a certain mutilation, or, if that is too strong a word, a sense of permanent loss, and that is something – a great deal – indeed everything to me.[43]

Asquith was, of course, not the only man in love with Venetia. Edwin Montagu was also very much on the scene. In February the Prime Minister himself helped to enhance his rival's attractions when he appointed him Chancellor of the Duchy of Lancaster two days short of his thirty-sixth birthday, making him the youngest member of the Cabinet. The post was a nominal one – a Minister without portfolio – but it represented a real promotion: 'I am sure he has gone back to his tent – for once in his life – a genuinely happy man,' Asquith told Venetia.[44] She for her part was keen to assure Montagu that 'you won't stick in the Duchy for long and I am very ambitious for you (!) I welcome this step greatly.'[45] Now Asquith was not the only Minister writing to Venetia during Cabinet meetings.

Asquith was well aware how much Venetia was seeing of Montagu, but he thought his colleague's physical unattractiveness a bar to his becoming her husband – to say nothing of the seemingly insuperable provision in Lord Swaythling's will. Nonetheless, there were occasional flickers of jealousy as Asquith envied 'the Assyrian'* the innumerable little opportunities he seems to find or make for seeing you', while Montagu complained to Venetia: 'Can you possibly expect me to go on being allowed to see you only when he [Asquith] is not free and refused either interview or speech or message except when he is busy or away?'[46]

Margot unwittingly completed this star-crossed circle by continuing to confide in Montagu about what she euphemistically referred to in her journal as 'a trifling domestic discouragement which has baffled and bothered me for a long long time'. All her pent-up unhappiness boiled over while the Asquiths were staying with the King at Windsor in mid-April. When Asquith had to go to London to attend a Cabinet meeting, she gave a letter to his valet, George Wicks, to put in his car: 'I told him how much I loved him and how well I knew I was getting older – that I was irritable – that there were other females in the world etc, that I had no common jealousy that would deprive him of unshared leisure or pleasure . . . my love was constantly re-equipping him for Happiness, but that in moments of discouragement I also wanted re-equipment and a little stimulus.'[47]

As soon as Asquith reached Downing Street he sat down in the Cabinet room and wrote a reply which he immediately dispatched to Windsor by special messenger. His letter clearly shows the pressure he was under, and why he craved the succour provided by his relationship with Venetia:

My own darling,
    Your letter made me sad, and I hasten to tell you that you have no cause for the doubts and fears which it expresses, or suggests.
    You have and always will have (as no one knows so well as I) far too large a nature – the largest I have known – to harbour anything in the nature of petty jealousies. But you would have just reason for complaint, and more, if it were true that I was transferring my confidence from you

_____
*One of Asquith's affectionate nicknames for his Jewish friend, and a reference to his Middle Eastern ancestry.

to anyone else. My fondness for Venetia has never interfered and never could with our relationship.

She has *au fond* a fine character as well as great intelligence, and often does less than justice to herself (as over this Hospital business) by her minimising way of talking. She is even now trying to arrange for a fresh spell of what is to her not at all congenial work.

I wish, with you, that Violet had rather more of the same sense of the futility of much of the life they have been leading.

But to come back to the main point, I <u>never</u> <u>consciously</u> keep things back from you and tell them to others. These last 3 years I have lived under a perpetual strain, the like of which has I suppose been experienced by very few men living or dead. It is no exaggeration to say that I have on hand more often half-a-dozen problems than a single one – personal, political, Parliamentary etc – most days of the week. I am reputed to be of a serene 'imperturbable' temperament, and I do my best in the way of self-control. But I admit that I am often irritated and impatient, and then I become curt and perhaps taciturn. I fear you have suffered from this more than anyone, and I am deeply sorry, but believe me darling it has not been due to want of confidence and love. Those remain and will always be unchanged.

Ever your own <u>husband</u>[48]

There is no doubt that Asquith genuinely loved his wife, and the tenderness of his letter demonstrates clearly why their marriage survived all the strains. Nonetheless, Margot was not slow to infer an unspoken message that her husband needed Venetia because she herself – with her moodiness and insecurities – could not give him the emotional sustenance he needed. Desperate for reassurance, Margot turned to Montagu, seemingly the only person in whom she confided about her husband's relationship with Venetia. In a long letter she enclosed Asquith's letter to her. She tried to belittle her worries about Venetia, wondering if her rival 'hadn't ousted me faintly – not very much – but enough to wound and humiliate me', and assuring him that her husband 'shows me <u>all</u> his letters and all Venetia's and tells me every secret'. She ends with the astonishing injunction that '<u>your</u> part to play is to persuade Violet and Venetia that if they don't marry they will be formidable egoists and amateurs'.[49] It is just possible that Margot was seeking to spur on Montagu to renew his own suit with Venetia, although until now she had shown no knowledge of his continued interest.

After cold-shouldering Montagu's own advances for so long, Venetia was now seriously contemplating marriage to him. One does not have to look far for the reason for her seemingly strange *volte-face*: she was now twenty-eight, and almost every day brought news of the death of another potential suitor. She tried to prepare Asquith for the blow by hinting about the possibility of marriage in a letter, but without suggesting any names. She was delighted when he seemed to grasp her point, replying 'I can understand every word of it, and (what is more important) I can read between the lines.'[50] Comforted by this reassurance and after a good deal more pressure from Montagu, Venetia eventually gave way and on 28 April agreed to marry him. As part of an extraordinary deal between the two of them, he conceded any right to insist on sex – his fiancée would still not allow him even to kiss her – while at the same time giving her a free rein to have extramarital love affairs. She for her part consented to go through a nominal conversion to Judaism to please his mother and (most importantly) satisfy the terms of his father's will.

The one remaining problem for the couple to resolve was when and how to break the news of their engagement to Asquith. The Prime Minister travelled up to Alderley with Venetia that weekend apparently oblivious of her plans, since although she dropped more hints that she might marry, she gave him no indication that the idea was more than hypothetical. Afterwards he wrote that 'we will leave the future, till it comes; and when it comes I will try to face it with courage'.[51] On 10 May, after a walk with Montagu, Asquith told her that 'I don't honestly believe that, at this moment, there are 2 persons in the world (of opposite sexes) from whom I could more confidently count, whatever troubles or trials I had to encounter, for whole-hearted love and devotion than you and he.'[52] After this, Venetia could hardly procrastinate any longer and the following day she finally broke the news in a letter to Asquith.

'This breaks my heart,' he replied, 'I couldn't bear to come and see you. I can only pray God to bless you – and help me.'[53]

In desperation, Asquith turned for comfort to Venetia's thirty-three-year-old married elder sister, Sylvia Henley, who was conveniently staying at their parents' house in Mansfield Street. On the day that Venetia dealt her devastating blow, Sylvia managed to equal her sister's record of receiving three letters from the Prime Minister in a single day. The second letter shows both his state of despair and his determination to maintain – as far as the outside world was concerned – his usual 'serene imperturbable temperament':

Dearest Sylvia,

Since I wrote to you this morning I have gone through a Cabinet, a lunch-eon with Prince Paul of Serbia and Sir R. McBride of British Columbia and a rather searching question time at the House and I hope I got through them all without any sign of disquietude or impotence. All the same, I don't suppose there is in the kingdom at this moment a much more unhappy man.

I had never any illusions, and often told Venetia: and she also was always most frank about her someday getting married.

But this. We have always treated it as a kind of freakish, but unimagin-able venture. I don't believe there are two living people who, each in their separate ways, are more devoted to me than she and Montagu: and it is the way of fortune that they two should combine to deal a death-blow to me . . . I am really fond of him, recognise his intellectual merits, find him excellent company and have always been able to reckon on his loyalty and devotion. Anything but this!

It is not merely the prohibitive physical side (bad as that is) – I won't say anything about race and religion tho' they are not quite negligible factors. But he is not a man: a shamble of words and nerves and symptoms, intensely self absorbed, and – but I won't go on with the dismal cata-logue . . .

She says at the end of a sadly meagre letter: 'I can't help feeling, after all the joy you've given me, that mine is a very treacherous return'.

Poor darling: I wouldn't have put it like that. But in essence it is true: and it leaves me sore and humiliated.

Dearest Sylvia, I am almost ashamed to write to you like this, and I know you won't say a word to her of what I have written.

But whom have I but you to turn to? in this searching trial, which comes upon me, when I am almost overwhelmed with every kind and degree of care and responsibility. Don't think that I am blaming her: I shall love her with all my heart to my dying day; she has given me untold happiness. I shall always bless her. But – I know you will understand. Send me a line of help and sympathy.

Always, dearest, your loving and devoted, HHA.

Sylvia, whose cavalry officer husband was serving on French's staff, was only too willing to pick up the baton abruptly cast aside by her sister and provide a shoulder for the Prime Minister to cry on, writing a 'sweet and understanding' reply, prompting Asquith's third letter that day: 'I must see you: I cannot say a word to anyone else, and you are wise and loving and know everything.'[54]

Margot did not hear the news until the following morning, when her husband came into her bedroom to tell her that 'a very sad thing has happened'. Her first thought was that Beb had been killed. 'Oh not as bad as that,' he replied (it should be mentioned that, up until this moment, Beb's predicament in the front line in Flanders had featured in neither his father's letters nor Margot's diary), 'but Venetia has engaged herself to Montagu and good and devoted fellow as he is, this will spell disaster and sorrow to both of them.'

Asquith was right. Venetia could never give Montagu the affection he craved. But it was disingenuous of him to expect his wife to believe his disinterested concern for his friends' interests. Needless to say, Margot herself was delighted to see her rival depart the scene, though her joy was tempered by worry about the effect on her husband's ability to cope with his awesome responsibilities, 'harassed as he is by everything just now'.[55]

15

'A terrible gamble'

———◆———

ON THE MORNING that Margot heard the news of Venetia's engagement, 13 May, she later ran into Lord ('Jacky') Fisher, the First Sea Lord, in Bongie's office as he waited to see the Prime Minister. Fisher was in the midst of an acrimonious quarrel with Churchill over sending naval reinforcements to the Dardanelles, which the Admiral was resisting. His temper was not improved when Margot told him that he was being blamed for leaking the quarrel to the newspapers. She herself could not have been feeling happier after hearing about Montagu's marriage plans, and to cheer Fisher up, she suggested they waltz, whereupon the Admiral seized her round the waist and they waltzed together round the room in one of the more bizarre scenes that 10 Downing Street has witnessed.[1] The respite in Fisher's mood was only temporary. The following day, a renewed demand from Churchill for more warships and aeroplanes for the Dardanelles provoked him into sending in his resignation to the Prime Minister after which he promptly disappeared. When he was eventually tracked down to the Charing Cross Hotel and brought round to 10 Downing Street in the afternoon, it was clear that, after innumerable previous resignations, this time he really had had enough of working with Churchill.

Things would have been bad enough if another huge bombshell had not exploded under the Government the same morning in the shape of an obviously well-sourced report in *The Times* by the paper's military correspondent, Colonel Repington, blaming the large number of casualties in French's most recent offensive on the British artillery's lack of shells. The report directly contradicted a recent speech by the Prime Minister in which he had unequivocally denied any shortages of munitions. His assertion was based on an assurance French had given Kitchener that he had adequate supplies of ammunition for his immediate needs. Asquith knew he could not defend himself properly without dragging his two senior generals into the controversy. What he did not know – although Kitchener strongly suspected it – was that French himself was behind *The Times* story as he sought to deflect criticism of his own shortcomings as a commander.

There was no respite for Asquith that weekend at the Wharf with much of his time taken up discussing the political situation with the Home Secretary, Reginald McKenna, who was staying with his wife, Pamela. No sooner had the McKennas departed on Sunday afternoon than the Churchills invited themselves to dinner. 'It seemed hard on Henry that on such a glorious day he should be kept jawing to colleagues whom he is obliged to see every day of the week,' noted Margot in her journal. She was even more irritated when, after Churchill had finished with her husband, she saw him walking up and down with Violet and Clemmie:

> the 2 females hanging on to his words like maid servants on the arms of soldiers in the Park – I wondered if Winston had had 2 more remarkable female friends who had, instead of flattering him, really stood up to him, it would have made any difference to him and I came to the conclusion it would not. I always think he and Violet would have been good for each other – had they married. Her cleverness would have delighted him and their mutual egotism would have been an interesting combat.[2]

In fact, on this occasion, Churchill – as Violet recorded in her own diary – 'was very low', having never realized until now that 'he was on the edge of a volcano in his relations with Fisher'.[3]

Churchill knew that the Tory Opposition would be only too keen to exploit his differences with Fisher over the Dardanelles. Although the Gallipoli campaign had yet to be seriously questioned, Churchill's premature bombardment of the Dardanelles' forts was widely blamed for jeopardizing the chances of a speedy victory. His overall conduct of the War, from the Antwerp fiasco to the ease with which the German Navy had bombarded British ports, made him a target for attack from his former Unionist colleagues, who had never for-given him for his defection to the Liberals and continued to regard him as an untrustworthy adventurer.

As far as Asquith was concerned, the dispute between Churchill and Fisher, serious as it was, posed less of a problem than the growing acrimony in relations between Kitchener and Lloyd George. The War Minister despised politicians in general (the Prime Minister being an exception) and distrusted Lloyd George in particular, while the latter (egged on, as we have seen, by Margot) resented the Field Marshal's autocratic and secretive approach to his Cabinet col-leagues. Over the past few months the supply of munitions had become a major issue as it became clear that despite Kitchener's efforts – which had increased the production of shells twentyfold – the supply of arms and ammunition was still far less than required by the hugely expanded Army. Lloyd George blamed Kitchener, while the War Minister regarded with contempt what he saw as the Chancellor's uninformed interference. A further problem was posed by McKenna who, if anything, disliked Lloyd George even more than Kitchener did, and was convinced that the Chancellor was plot-ting with Press baron Lord Northcliffe, the Tory owner of both *The Times* and the mass circulation *Daily Mail*, to supplant Asquith as Prime Minister.

The evening after Churchill's visit to the Wharf on 17 May, Margot was 'swamped in the biggest big bath in London', when her husband came in and abruptly told her:

> 'I've had to take very drastic measures. I wrote to all my colleagues to resign. I shall form a Coalition Government. I've just seen Bonar Law – he was pleased and happy, of course, they long to be in it.'
> This announcement flabbergasted me. I flung the towel round me and said with horrified eyes 'Oh Darling – so its come to that!! How terrible – our wonderful Government and wonderful Cabinet' – I could not trust myself to say another word for tears.[4]

The Prime Minister's uncharacteristically sudden decision had been the result of a flurry of discussions between himself, the Tory leaders and Lloyd George (an advocate of a coalition government for some time), which convinced him that this was the only way to avoid a damaging Party conflict on the conduct of the war. Asquith gave no clues as to what was going on when he wrote to Sylvia Henley that evening. But he did admit how much he was missing Venetia's soothing presence:

> I am in the stress of the most arduous and exacting things that you can imagine, and I miss (more than I can say) what has helped and guided me so often during these last 3 years. I can't describe to you the depth of the unbridged gulf. It has been, all that time, so natural and necessary to me. It is not easy to reconcile one's self to such a breach. I feel almost like one half of a pair of scissors.[5]

It was clear from the outset that the Unionists would never tolerate the continued presence of Churchill at the Admiralty. Bonar Law was also seeking the dismissal of Kitchener, who was blamed for continued problems in the supply of munitions, and there was pressure from Fleet Street for Lloyd George to replace him as War Minister. Margot was worried that the post would end up as a trap for her Welsh friend: 'I know what soldiers are, he will get nothing but kicks,' as she put it in her journal.[6] She was also concerned that the Lloyd Georges, who had no London home of their own, would be turned out of 11 Downing Street, the Chancellor's official residence. This would also mean Puffin losing the companionship of his friend Megan. For some while she had been urging Asquith 'to create a separate Department for Munitions alone and give it to Lloyd George, [and] put Bonar at War Office',[7] believing the Welshman could remain as Chancellor (and thus hang on to his house) if Montagu became his deputy and did most of the work. On the Tuesday morning she ran next door to propose her plan to Margaret Lloyd George, who enthusiastically endorsed the idea.

Margaret telephoned the Treasury and sent for her husband, who arrived a few minutes later 'quite white', having assumed something had happened to Megan. He was relieved, and no doubt astonished, to hear the reason for his summons, and quickly agreed with Margot's proposal before excusing himself. Margot does not seem to have been aware that her idea of a Munitions Ministry was already being widely discussed, but when the Prime Minister did adopt the plan, Lloyd George was happy to give her the credit, telling Asquith how 'she ran across to my wife suggesting this and we both thought it <u>excellent</u>'. Margot, understandably nervous about how her husband would react to this latest bit of unsolicited interference, was delighted when he too congratulated her: 'I confess I clapped my hands like a child and jumped up and kissed him!', she noted in her diary.[8] And although Lloyd George had to hand the Exchequer over to McKenna, he was allowed to keep 11 Downing Street.

The main casualty of the reshuffle was Haldane, who from the beginning of the War had been subjected to regular scurrilous attacks by the Press for being 'pro-German', receiving sacks of hate mail from gullible readers. Rather than publicly defend his friend, Asquith adopted his usual attitude of contempt towards journalists, failing to realize how much Haldane had been hurt by the slanders. Margot had tried to persuade Kitchener to speak up for the embattled Lord Chancellor, only to find that the Field Marshal's loathing of journalists fully matched her husband's. Another soldier, the Quartermaster General Sir John Cowans, although he had a high regard for Haldane's achievement as a War Minister, was equally unhelpful, responding that the Lord Chancellor 'can well afford to despise and over-look his attackers'.[9]

The Prime Minister had to face the consequences of his failure to take on the Press barons when Bonar Law insisted that Haldane must be dropped. Margot, who had been long frustrated by her husband's failure to impose 'a proper press censorship', lamented in her journal that 'I can never understand why our Government is so amazingly weak about the Press. It gets on H's nerves my asking him questions, but till I die I shall think this one of the stupidest blunders we've made in the whole war. I must get someone to explain why we allow Northcliffe to write any and every lie that he thinks copy.'[10]

Margot did her best to whip up support for Haldane, telling Crewe 'if you want to please Henry, make a stand for Haldane's inclusion'. It was to no avail, and Haldane, with characteristic loyalty, departed without a murmur. A myth has grown up, based on nothing more than constant repetition by historians, that Asquith neither fought very hard for his oldest friend nor properly thanked him for his years of service. Both allegations are nonsense. On the evening of 22 May, Asquith joined Margot at the Wharf, and she recorded in her diary that he told her how he had pleaded with Bonar Law and Balfour to be allowed to retain Haldane in the Government, telling them that he was his oldest friend, who had been 'subjected to a Press campaign led by the *Morning Post* etc of the foulest, lowest, most mendacious character fostered by the anti-German mania'. Although the

Unionist leaders were moved by his appeal, they remained adamant that feelings against Haldane among their own MPs were 'so strong that it would be quite impossible for them to enter into a coalition at all if he were kept'. Although Margot reacted with indignation to what she saw as 'blackmail', her husband assured her that he had no choice. The following day Haldane himself wrote to her: 'The one important thing is to secure a Cabinet which thoroughly commands the confidence of the whole nation – and I could not fulfil this condition – I knew it and told Asquith so from the first. He has been affection itself to me and I shall never forget the way he took it and the tenderness he showed.'[11]

Asquith replaced Churchill with Balfour at the Admiralty, giving Bonar Law the nominally more important Colonial Office. He did manage to retain Churchill in the Cabinet as Chancellor of the Duchy of Lancaster, which Montagu generously agreed to give up, returning to the Treasury as Financial Secretary under McKenna. The Prime Minister immediately received a wild letter from Clemmie Churchill angrily accusing him of caving in to the Press, arguing that 'if you throw Winston overboard you will be committing an act of weakness . . . he has the supreme quality which I venture to say very few of your present or future Cabinet possess – the power, the imagination, the deadliness to fight Germany'.[12] Margot was outraged by Clemmie's letter, which she told her husband 'shows the soul of a servant – that touch of blackmail and insolence'. Although he agreed with his wife's suspicion that Churchill himself was behind the letter, Asquith was more tolerant, calling it 'the letter of a wife', to which Margot made the predictable response: 'a fishwife!'.[13]

Margot later heard that Clemmie was 'behaving like a lunatic and crying daily over Winston being turned out of the Admiralty', and tried to appease her by asking her and Winston to dinner a couple of weeks later, suggesting that she come early and they had tea together. The gesture seemed to have worked when Clemmie 'answered pleasantly on the telephone and arrived looking cool and handsome in a muslin dress'. However, when Margot put her arms round her and gave her 'a little squeeze . . . she pushed me resolutely back and put up her veil. I saw I was in for it and scanned a very hard insolent young woman with little or no sense of humour (a great sense of truth), not really unkind, but quite unoccupied (and unimaginative over the war) frivolous, bad tempered, ungrateful and common au fond.'

Margot responded to the rebuff with the typically tactless jibe that although she 'detested Coalition' and regarded it as 'a source of weakness and a terrible gamble', Winston had 'always wanted one'. Clemmie refused to rise to the bait and steered the conversation into a denunciation of Lord Northcliffe, whom they could both agree was 'a vile man', but she could not resist a quip that 'Lloyd George thinks he is a hero!'. When Margot told her she was talking rubbish, she repeated Winston's belief that the Welshman – whom she herself regarded as 'the direct descendant of Judas Iscariot' – had 'black-mailed' Asquith into a coalition by threatening to resign. Margot called the story 'pure fabrication' and could not resist a dig that 'Winston wasn't loyal to McKenna over the naval estimates', while appealing to his wife to 'think of poor Henry and all he has gone through'. This was a red rag to a bull for Clemmie:

> 'That's good!! Why he has thrown his dearest friend and his most remark-able colleagues, Haldane and Winston, to the wolves!' She got up held on to the tea table and harangued me in fish-wife style on Henry's defects till I got up and sat at my writing table calmly while she screamed on a long rodomontade till I stopped her and said 'Go Clemmie – leave the room – you are off your head – I had hoped to have a very different kind of talk.'

As Clemmie got up to go, Margot launched into a denunciation of her letter to Asquith and lectured her on how she was 'a hard little thing and very very foolish as you will do Winston harm in his career'.[15]

Incredibly, after this vicious row, both women managed to get through the dinner party – Margot, who sat next to Kitchener, actu-ally called it 'probably the most interesting in my life'. After dinner Asquith, alerted to his wife's row with Clemmie, managed to inveigle the latter into the Cabinet room and, as he later reported to Sylvia, 'we parted on good and even affectionate terms: and I trust I have dispelled her rather hysterical mutiny against the Coalition and all its works'.[16] A little later, when Lloyd George got up to leave, Margot accompanied him downstairs to quiz him about Clemmie's allega-tions about him blackmailing Asquith, which had begun to prey on her mind. They sat down on two chairs beside the grandfather clock outside the Cabinet room and he dismissed the Churchills' story as rubbish, pointing out that McKenna, just back from the Wharf, had been with him when Bonar Law had called to see him on the Sunday evening. However, when Margot asked whether he had really told

Winston that he 'thought Northcliffe a hero', she was less happy, as she recorded in her diary:

> 'No,' he replied, 'but I said I thought he had done the right thing over the shells.'
>
> 'Then you said a very wrong and foolish thing. Winston will go all over London saying this and mark my words, I've said this before and I'll say it again as a warning, Lord Northcliffe will run you against Henry. He has already tried and he will go on and I shall back <u>Henry</u> to score if this happens.'
>
> Lloyd George smiled: 'My dear friend, wicked I may be, but I'm not a damned fool. As I said to Winston, 'do you <u>really</u> think I don't know what Northcliffe is?! Why he'll turn on me and stab me in the back at any moment.'

As they were talking, Margot, to her horror, spotted Churchill coming downstairs. Feeling 'like a conspirator', she fobbed him off by praising his recent speech at Dundee while he put on his coat. After he had left, Lloyd George remarked 'I'm afraid he'll never forgive me.' However, Margot's thoughts were elsewhere. She had recently told Oc how Northcliffe had been 'fool enough' to say in front of her solicitor friend, Charles Russell, 'I will do for Asquith and get rid of him – he must go. Lloyd George must be P.M.'[17] But until now she had never questioned Lloyd George's own loyalty. Now Clemmie had revived all her old suspicions about him. Her parting words were pregnant with mistrust: 'I warn you, never <u>see</u> Northcliffe and don't let him run you against Henry as I know quite well what will be the consequences. It will hurt and damage <u>you</u>.'[18]

Margot got her chance to get her own back on the Press a few weeks later when the *London Mail*, a small-circulation scandal rag, repeated a rumour that she had been playing tennis with German officers imprisoned at Donnington Hall in Oxfordshire. Although Simon (the Attorney General), Nash (Asquith's still influential former Private Secretary) and other 'old women' advised her it would be 'most undignified of me to take any notice of such a low paper',* she instructed her solicitor, Charles Russell† to threaten legal

---

*After Margot's action had proved successful Bongie wrote to Violet (in Egypt) 'I think it was right to take this up.' (*Champion Redoubtable*, p. 68. Letter dated 10 June 1915)
†Son of Asquith's friend and former colleague at the Bar, Sir Charles Russell QC, later Lord Russell of Killowen.

action. He extracted a grovelling apology from the journal and a contribution of a hundred guineas to the British Red Cross.[19]

A couple of weeks after forming his coalition Government, Asquith was already wondering whether his judgement during those few fateful days had been warped by his emotional turmoil over Venetia's engagement. Writing to her sister, Sylvia, he confessed that: 'I am not at all happy about this coalition and its prospects. I rarely go back on my original judgement. This time I feel an unusual uncertainty. Venetia, who as so often and now for so long my best counsellor, was gone . . . you were not yet by my side.'[20]

As is apparent from the letter, Sylvia herself had already replaced her sister in the Prime Minister's affections. Margot was only too pleased to encourage the relationship, and made a point of asking Sylvia to lunch at 10 Downing Street as a prelude to her taking Venetia's place on her husband's regular Friday afternoon drive. She had always liked Sylvia, who had the supreme advantage of being happily married, and she underlined her approval, not only by inviting the 'very dear creature and friend of Henry's' to spend a weekend the Wharf, but asking her to come again the following weekend when Asquith himself was away visiting the Army in France.[21]

Venetia herself had had few illusions about the uniqueness of her relationship with Asquith. Only three weeks before telling him of her engagement, she perceptively observed to Montagu that 'I know quite well that if it hadn't been me it would have been someone else or a series of others who would have made him just as happy'.[22] What Asquith saw in her was an idealized woman, and he was perfectly capable of creating another. Within a fortnight of declaring that Venetia had broken his heart, Sylvia had 'become my sheet anchor, and I <u>love</u> you', and by early June he was assuring her that 'whatever storms blow, or tidal waves menace, I can always feel that I am safe and sure'. She possessed 'qualities which <u>you alone</u> can contribute to one's life. Personality – humanity – intuition – judgement – wisdom: and above and around them all, a delicious and untranslatable atmosphere of warmth and love which no other woman can create or maintain in the same degree.'[23]

Sylvia was to remain Asquith's main confidante for the next year or so, by which time her role had been gradually diluted by several other 'leading ladies'. Nonetheless, whether or not Venetia granted the Prime Minister sexual favours, Sylvia was standing no nonsense and firmly slapped him down when he tried to go too far. He threw up his hands in outraged innocence 'that you could <u>ever</u> have suspected that I should be tempted to convert our wonderful relations of love and confidence into – what shall I call it? – an erotic adventure? . . . Perfect love, as the scripture says, casteth out fear, and still more distrust.'[24] But the fact that the rebuke hardly seems to have affected the relationship shows that what he was after was not extramarital sex, but 'mothering' – something that was not in Margot's nature. Sylvia's beneficent influence rapidly worked wonders. Cynthia, who lunched at Downing Street on 8 June, noted in her diary 'P.M. looking quite restored and serene again'.[25] Indeed, had they been closer in age, Sylvia, with her combination of kindness, composure, firmness, intelligence and good sense, might have made an ideal spouse for him. Whereas Venetia's vanity had been flattered by the idea of the Prime Minister writing to her in the middle of ministerial meetings, her more sagacious elder sister sternly rebuked him for his folly: he was suitably penitent, thanking her for 'a great deal of good advice' and coyly promising that 'I shall <u>never</u> write to you again from a Cabinet or War Council!'[26]

As Asquith's sense of personal loss diminished, what seemed most shocking to him was Venetia's willingness to convert to Judaism. 'Even to a person who had no dogmatic beliefs,' he wrote to Sylvia 'to turn your back (for that is what it means) on the main force which has created the West, and, with countless follies and absurdities and crimes, has remoulded and transformed the world, and made us what we are, and . . . adopt in its place the narrow sterile creed, which has no doubt kept alive and separate the Israelite sept.'[27]

Reactions to Venetia's conversion amongst the rest of the Asquith family were, as Bongie reported to Oc, 'sharply divided . . . I need not tell you I think in which camp each individual is found.'[28] Oc himself took a typically pragmatic view of the match, writing to Violet that 'I hate the whole business; but my social self-indulgence or natural immorality is such that the crimes of my friends rarely make me wish to forego their society.'[29] Violet was torn between uncharitable squeamishness about Montagu's 'physical repulsiveness . . . the thought of <u>any</u> erotic amenities with him is enough to freeze one's blood', and being shocked by Venetia's willingness to 'renounce England and Christianity'.[30] She confided to Oc that 'the whole thing simply <u>revolts</u> me both in its physical and spiritual aspect – and I think it <u>vile</u> of Montagu to drag Venetia thro' the mud of this bogus conversion – the first of its kind since the Crucifixion I verily believe! – to save his income'.[31]

Margot was much more sympathetic to Montagu, realizing that his insistence on Venetia's conversion to Judaism was hardly an imposition, pointing out (in a letter to Oc) that Venetia 'recants nothing – as none of the Stanleys believe in God. I would rather marry into the Jewish faith than the Roman Catholic . . . I think Venetia is marrying a <u>very</u> good fellow.'[32] As for Raymond, he found a number of typically irreverent reasons for approving the match, among which were: because any marriage was preferable to perpetual virginity for a woman; because Venetia – having had ample other opportunities during the past dozen years – was probably incapable of feeling passion for anyone at all; because it <u>was</u> a marriage of convenience: in that if a man possessed both a private income and private parts (especially if both were substantial) he was certainly a convenience to a woman; because it annoyed Venetia's parents, the Sheffields; and because it shocked the whole Christian Community.[33]

Violet had been due to leave to visit Oc in hospital in Egypt when the triple crises over Fisher's resignation, the munitions controversy and Venetia's engagement burst upon her father. Asquith pleaded with his daughter to delay her departure, leaving a note on her pillow: 'don't go away from me now – I need you'. Touched by his vulnerability Violet wrote in her diary: 'it is so wonderful to feel he really needs me'.[34] Those few extra days were to be critical for her future, as before she left she took the seemingly sudden decision to marry Bongie. Only a fortnight earlier Margot had been lamenting to Oc what she called the 'triple attente'* of Hugh Godley, Bongie and Violet, regretting Asquith's refusal to do '<u>his</u> duty' and 'tell Violet to marry Bongie'. Violet's own shock at Venetia's engagement and feeling of loss of her best friend (relations between the two of them never regained their former intimacy) probably had a role in her sudden decision. And no doubt, she too shared the feeling of so many women at the time that soon few of their male friends would be left alive: Bongie at least seemed safe from becoming cannon fodder.

---

*'This is what Italy, Rumania and Greece have been wittily called!' (Margot to Oc, 13 May 1915)

The match was kept secret for the moment, ostensibly because of Violet's imminent absence from England, but no doubt also to allow her to have second thoughts: 'you know me well enough to know that I am already wondering how long it will persist – but there it is for the moment – and perhaps for life', she admitted to her new fiancé on the eve of her departure for Egypt. When the engagement was officially announced on 5 July, many of her friends were disappointed at what they saw as the timidity of her choice. Although Cynthia was 'glad really' and considered her sister-in-law's choice of mate, 'wise', after discussing the match with Katharine, she concluded 'it seems almost incestuous to marry someone you know quite so well'.[35] Even Aubrey Herbert, who had known and liked Bongie since their days at Balliol together, wrote to his wife, Mary: 'How can one congratulate on something that is tepid?' When he wrote to Violet, she sensed his reservations and explained that Bongie 'has known, understood and endured everything that has ever happened to me – and is big enough to hold it all and a lot more! – without cavilling or grudging. To him I need never bowdlerize, or explain or translate. I feel him a foundation of rock on which to build my life.'[36]

Cynthia noted that Margot was 'over the moon' at the news.[37] In her journal, Margot called the day she heard of Violet's engagement 'the most fateful day of my life excepting May 10, 1894 my Wedding Day'. Although she had her reservations about Bongie's abilities as a Private Secretary compared to his predecessor, the supremely able Vaughan Nash, she believed that 'no girl will ever marry a better fellow. I prefer him to all V's admirers and think she will find he has a much stronger character than she knows.'[38] Her one concern, she confessed to Oc, was that 'she won't bully him – he deserves the best wife in the world and if Violet can surrender her own will and completely forget herself and her own "ego" she will make the best of wives, of this I feel sure'.[39]

Violet reached Port Said as the end of May. On the train to Alexandria she was handed a cable from Oc to say he would meet her at Sidi Gaber station, where 'sure enough when I put my head out of the window, there he was hopping down the platform in the white glare like a lame jackdaw'. She found that the wound in his knee was 'quite healed and the mark tiny' though he was 'still very lame but extremely agile'. He was receiving daily massages to restore his movement and expected to return to his battalion in about a fortnight. She was soon introduced to Freyberg, whose stomach wound was now nearly healed, recording in her journal how:

> I liked his simplicity, singleheartedness, eagerness, ambition, and a quality of firsthandness which impregnated all he said and thought. Also a sort of intuition very sensitively tho' directly conveyed – without questions or answers or apologies or explanations – of how things stood between me and Rupert. He really loved Rupert – and felt him to the bone.
>
> We bathed together at Stanley Bay several times – a crowded, confined little inlet of sea containing alas! all Alexandria, but also the biggest waves I have almost ever seen – terrifying to my water-cowardice which is as great as ever. Freyberg used to take me in – right in – and then as they came towering darkly <u>feet</u> above us, he would give a great leap lifting me right off my feet and over it and we would be borne in together in a swirl of foaming surf! My terror never failed nor the succeeding thrill of relief – he is the only person who has ever given me water confidence. It really was his element – he went bounding and shooting through the very centre of the waves like a porpoise when unhampered by me.[40]

On 7 June, the eve of Freyberg's departure for Gallipoli, Violet and Oc took him to the Savoy restaurant in Alexandria for a farewell dinner. The meal was interrupted by the arrival of Schlesinger, the Howe battalion surgeon, with the terrible news of the latest fighting in Gallipoli three days earlier: the Royal Naval Division had been badly cut up spearheading a futile frontal assault on heavily fortified Turkish trenches. Its Second Brigade had been all but annihilated when French Senegalese troops on its flank left it exposed by scuttling back to their trenches and refusing to emerge in spite of the valiant efforts of Shaw-Stewart who 'was seen running along waving his cane and shouting, "*Avancez, Avancez*!"'[41] The brigade lost over two-thirds of its strength in the ensuing débâcle, with Shaw-Stewart one of only nine officers out of seventy to survive the battle unhurt. After listening to the surgeon's inevitably sketchy account of the fighting, Freyberg insisted he didn't want to know anything more about it as he wanted to enjoy his last evening. Violet could see he was upset: his elder brother, Oscar, had just arrived with one of the new battalions, the Collingwood, and she sensed he felt his brother was dead.

The following morning the New Zealander asked her to go for a drive with him round the Nassa garden as he told her his life story and how 'he had been wandering since he was fifteen'. Afterwards, he dropped her off at her bank while he went sailing. He returned later in a distressed state, saying 'I need you very badly – my brother's killed.' She recorded that 'I went out with him – poor, poor thing. He was so inarticulate – and so wretched.' They later met up with Oc at the Regine restaurant for lunch, where a tearful Freyberg admitted: 'I've never had any friends – and now I do for the first time in my life – and they're all being killed.'[42] Among those missing was Rupert's musician friend, Denis Browne, who had been shot in the stomach after bayonetting two Turks. He scribbled a brief farewell message to Eddie Marsh in his pocket book and gave it to his Petty Officer, ordering him to escape before they were overrun by the Turks who, so Oc reported to Margot (no doubt with Denis in mind), had 'committed every horror of torture on our wounded – burning, flaying and pricking with bayonets'.[43]

Cleg Kelly, who had been shot in the heel, was among the more lightly wounded casualties to arrive at Alexandria. He remained as droll as ever, describing his injury to a friend as 'an obliging little wound that will give him a short holiday in Egypt'.[44] Oc and Violet were also reunited with Charles Lister, who had been convalescing in Malta, and came ashore for a night on his way back to Gallipoli. Violet stayed on until the second half of June when her brother was finally passed as fit to return to the front. 'Oc said to me quite seriously: it is simply a choice between being killed and being disabled for life,' she reported to Bongie, 'which ices my blood rather.'[45]

By the time Violet arrived back in England at the end of June several more of the Asquiths' friends had been killed, among them Ettie Desborough's eldest son, Julian Grenfell, who after four weeks' struggle had succumbed to wounds. His cousin, Francis Grenfell, who had won one of the first VCs of the War (shortly after the death in action of his twin brother), had also been killed: 'Margot was devoted to him,' Asquith told Sylvia, calling Francis 'as fine an example of clean and unselfish manhood as was to be found in the country'.[46] Two months later, the Desboroughs' second son, Billy, disappeared under the mud during an attack near Hooge.*

'I can't and won't believe either of these grand boys have come to the end of their powers,' an anguished Margot wrote in her journal, pleading: 'Oh! God how I long to have one glimpse of thy purpose –

---

*The Desboroughs' surviving third son, Ivo, was killed in a motor accident in 1926.

<u>one</u> gleam of hope as to our sure immortality.'[47] She shared the sense of national anguish and bewilderment as people struggled to come to terms with the human cost of the conflict, writing to Ettie: '<u>Oh!</u> what a Horrible War! and on and on it will go till we are all left staring at God and <u>longing</u> to know why it all happened and what it is all for.' By now Margot's own family had also suffered their first deaths: her cousins Charlie and Willy Tennant had recently been killed in action, together with a cousin of Bongie's, Guy Bonham Carter – a Winchester contemporary of Oc. When Edward Horner, serving with the North Somerset Yeomanry, suffered a severe stomach wound, Margot arranged for Sir Arbuthnot Lane, a top London surgeon, to travel out with Frances and Katharine to the hospital at Bailleul where Edward was being treated.

Amidst all the carnage, Beb seemed to have got off comparatively lightly when he returned on leave on 14 June with a gashed cheek, badly swollen lip and a couple of teeth shattered by a shrapnel splinter.

16

'Feeling as if he would crack up'

———◆———

BEB SPENT THE last period of his gunnery training at a barracks in Portsmouth, while Cynthia flitted between her parents' home, Stanway, where she had left their two boys, and a hotel in Southsea. Their house in Sussex Place was let to Belgian refugees as an economy measure. As the date of Beb's departure for the Front drew closer, Cynthia developed a nervous rash which she feared was measles, but once her doctor had reassured her it was not, she joined her husband on Thursday 22 April for a final night together at his billet at the Mermaid Tavern in Rye ('the most perfect specimen of "Ye Olde Inn" I have ever seen'). When Cynthia arrived Beb was away dealing with last-minute preparations for the guns, so she was looked after by his battery commander, Captain Ammon – 'good-looking and very young' – and another officer, 'a huge burly, jolly man called Arkwright' who turned out to be a former captain of the England soccer eleven. When Beb finally turned up at 8.15 p.m. he was so covered in dust that 'one could have written with one's finger on his face'. His fellow officers tactfully left him to dine with his wife at a little table by themselves. Cynthia recorded that 'I could not realise the reality of the situation and grasp that I had really come to see Beb off to the Front, the setting of that lovely old inn full of soldiers and everything was so extraordinarily theatrical.'

The couple were woken at 5.30 a.m. to accompany the guns to Dover, Cynthia travelling with Captain Ammon, while Beb ('looking very official with maps and paraphernalia') brought up the rear of the convoy. She spent the rest of the day sitting 'stupifiedly in the lounge' of the Lord Warden Hotel, while the guns and their lorries were being loaded on to the *Princess Victoria* – coincidentally, the same vessel on which Margot had crossed the Channel four months earlier. At about 4 p.m. Beb's driver, who Cynthia characteristically remarked was 'almost the best looking man I have ever seen', drove her to the pier where her husband, 'very well disguised as a soldier, gave orders to brilliantly efficient-looking N.C.O.s'. There was then just time for tea together at the hotel, before Beb embarked at 6 p.m.. After saying goodbye, she waited in the cold by the quayside, until they left:

> I felt strangely and mercifully numb, curiously narcotised and unimagina-
> tive. Luckily there was no band, nothing to dramatise the situation. They
> just slunk stealthily, surreptitiously, away with their grim iron freight. No
> cheers, no waving, and but few jokes – just one or two 'Are we down-
> hearted? No's'. I was the only woman seer-off, and I could not convince
> myself of the reality and momentousness of the occasion. I couldn't
> believe it was really Beb who was going, or myself who was watching him
> go.[1]

Raymond also was now in uniform, having become a part-time soldier in January, when he had joined Cys in the Queen's Westminster Rifles. As the months went by with no sign of the regi-ment being sent abroad, Raymond and 'the more dashing officers' became increasingly frustrated with such futile tasks as stopping sus-picious vehicles approaching London from the North-West. In the spring he briefly toyed with the idea of following Oc into the Royal Naval Division, but the prospect of being subordinate to his younger brother probably put paid to this.

Katharine, who dreaded her husband's growing inclination to seek a transfer to a Guards regiment as a means of seeing action, tried to interest him in his prospective constituency in the forlorn hope that he might be satisfied with serving his country in Parliament. Raymond was having none of it, retorting that people in Derby could not expect him to be a soldier boy and go on the stump at the same time. When Bongie asked him to deputize for his father at the annual meeting of the Fife Liberals, he reluctantly agreed to what he saw as a repellent proposition, involving two expensive and uncomfortable night journeys and doing nobody – so he believed – any earthly good.[2] Clearly, he was losing his appetite for politics.

Even London life had fewer attractions for Raymond. Most male members of the Coterie were on active service, while Katharine spent much of the time at Mells with her parents and children. Sitting alone one evening at Brooks's club, Raymond wrote to Diana Manners describing his comatose fellow members as shapeless men on whom and in whom toads had laid eggs since the dawn of time, whose sex could only be determined after exhaustive laboratory experiments.[3] This was no longer a world to which he belonged.

For a while, an increasingly ardent flirtation with Diana provided a welcome antidote to Raymond's lassitude. But even this started to pall as more of her time was taken up with nursing duties at Guy's Hospital, while she liked to escape London altogether when she was off duty. When she was absent all the world was a morgue and all the men and women mere mummies, he once parodied Shakespeare in a telegram to her. He had done his best to discourage her from becoming a nurse in the first place, pointing out that the hours were long, the drudgery unendurable and the uniform hideous, while a hospital had all the material discomforts of a convent without the spiritual glamour of chastity. On one occasion when she was free, Raymond was called away to take part in nocturnal manoeuvres, and bitterly complained about having to crawl around on his stomach in a dark swamp when he might have been worshipping at the high altar of her beauty.[4]

Although Katharine can hardly have approved of her husband's letters to Diana (or rather Dottie or Dilly, as he usually called her), she had little to fear in the way of competition from her closest woman friend. She was right to be secure in Raymond's love for herself, knowing Diana well enough to realize that she relished having a clutch of men in her thrall. The arch exponent of the 'tease', Diana knew that she possessed more power over her admirers as a *femme fatale* than as the brazen harpie many believed her to be. Raymond was tantalized when she wrote to him from her bath, regarding any words written by her naked as more precious and consecrated then the sonnets of Shakespeare, and as for her bad spelling, he could stomach even the Apostles' creed if it were misspelled so seductively.[5]

While Diana was probably at least half in love with Raymond, he had few illusions that he was ever going to get very far with her: in a letter written to her at 2 a.m. on 26 April 1915 as he packed for a military camp after a particularly frustrating evening with her he lamented the brazen purity and haughty perfection of her breasts, telling her that he worshipped everything about her with the religious idealism of a nun and the passion of a goat. She was everything to him even if he were nothing to her.[6]

Six weeks later he ruefully sympathized with her having to juggle in order to humour three or four lovers, while striving to keep them all airborne at the same time.[7] With fellow Coterie members George Vernon, Patrick Shaw-Stewart, Edward Horner and Duff Cooper, as well as Raymond himself and even to an extent the Prime Minister, all in Diana's thrall, he was, if anything, underestimating the number of his rivals.

When Beb reached Belgium, he found that his Royal Marine Artillery Brigade and its much-needed guns had been distributed all along the British line. He was posted to a battery in Nieuport, where the western flank of the trenches met the coast, commanded by Captain Barr – 'a charming and genial spirit'. The Belgian town presented a bizarre contrast between seaside resort and military strongpoint. Beb was struck by the incongruous sight of 'a rank of bathing machines . . . torn by shells and riddled with bullets', still standing amidst the barbed wire and iron stakes which decorated the beach. The unit's guns, which had the dual role of anti-aircraft defence and harassment of enemy communication trenches, were positioned behind a railway embankment close to the front line. The morning after their arrival, Beb and Knight, a fellow subaltern, were sent to locate suitable 'forward observation posts'. The two inexperienced subalterns clambered up the broken staircase of a ruined church tower to get a better view. On either side was the Yser canal, smothered in oil and clogged with the wreckage of barges, and nearby 'a train which may often have carried the family parties of Flanders to their summer holidays, lay on its side, like a broken toy, twisted and bent'. The sand between them and the German lines was, as Beb later recalled, a scene of macabre horror:

> The ground was scattered with large numbers of the dead, French and German, lying on that powdered and shell-pitted soil, on their faces or their backs, tangled on the barbs of the rusted wire, or tossed over the

brink of a shell-hole, and here and there a rigid arm stretched upwards
aimlessly to the sky. But in the long line of the German fire-trench and the
torn streets and shattered houses of the village behind it, there was no
living German to be seen, no sign of the mysterious enemy who had disturbed our night with his machine guns and trench mortars, though at
that moment there must have been many hundreds in the cellars of the
village and many thousands hidden behind the parapet of the trench.[8]

The officers' first reaction 'this curious and sinister view' of anonymous dead bodies was one of excitement rather than shock. They
did not have long to take it in before a shell burst among the tomb-
stones below them rapidly followed by others exploding either side
of the tower, as they realized that their precarious eyrie was a handy
ranging-point for the invisible German guns, and hastily abandoned
the tower.

After the initial excitement, Beb settled into an almost routine
existence of artillery duels, intensified twice each day in two bombardments known as 'morning and evening hate'. The Germans had
used gas for the first time a couple of days before Beb's arrival and,
with as yet no protection against this new and dire form of warfare,
much of their time in the forward observation posts was spent
'sniffing at the sea-mist that drifted across No Man's Land in search
for the scent of chemicals'. Beb later recalled how

> We heard that people at home were working feverishly at the manufacture
> of gas-masks. The first form of protection which was sent up to our part
> of the line was a pad treated with chemicals, and so designed that it could
> be strapped over our noses and mouths, but it afforded no cover for our
> eyes. This was soon followed by the first gas-mask, a grey flannel bag with
> eye-holes of talc. This mask was fairly comfortable to wear, unless it was
> raining, when the chemicals with which it was soaked were apt to run into
> the eyes of the wearer.[9]

In spite of the discomfort and constant danger – the guns regularly had to be moved as the German counterparts discovered their
location – Beb almost relished his first experience of War. At the end
of May, after receiving three letters from her husband, Cynthia
recorded in her diary that 'he sounds really extraordinarily happy and
says it is a great holiday from the Bar. It makes the whole difference
to know he is enjoying it, so that one has no vicarious suffering
added to anxiety.' Asquith, who saw his son soon afterwards during

a tour of the British positions, told Cynthia that 'he had never seen him look so well and that he was in very good form'.[10]

Asquith's visit to French's headquarters in St Omer provided Beb with a short break from his front-line duties when he was ordered to escort his father. The High Command were probably not motivated by simple altruism, but believed it would be useful for the Prime Minister to hear about the shortage of shells from his own son. Beb himself found it difficult to adjust to the sudden comfort after weeks of living in a dugout scraped out of the railway embankment. He accompanied his father on a tour of commanding officers, as well as going to see a factory converted to a bath house for the troops, and also Bailleul hospital, where Edward Horner had been treated. Asquith described to Sylvia 'one poor officer whose face I shall never forget, breathing shortly and heavily for the 5th day from asphyxiating gas, and plainly doomed'. He then made a short speech to the men of the 16th Brigade, who were about to go on leave, and their commanding officer 'called for three cheers which were wonderfully and touchingly given'.[11]

Beb later recalled his father's 'great sympathy for soldiers in these difficult days; he liked meeting them and talking over their difficulties in an atmosphere removed from Whitehall'. When they lunched with the commander of the First Army, General Sir Douglas Haig, he noticed how much his father 'was enjoying himself and deeply interested in his talk'.[12] It was to be a critical meeting for both men, for although the Prime Minister found Haig 'curiously inarticulate', he was impressed both by his knowledge of the science and practice of war and by the clear superiority of his 'carefully thought out and constructed'[13] trench system to that of the Second Army under Plumer. When six months later he decided to replace French as Commander-in-Chief, Haig was his choice to succeed him.

It was early June, shortly after his father's visit, that Beb was hit in the face by shrapnel when a shell-burst near him as he was running up to take over one of the guns. Several of his teeth were broken by a splinter which penetrated his cheek and, as he was shortly due for some leave, Captain Barr suggested that he had his injuries treated in London. He wired Cynthia, who met him at 10 Downing Street the following morning, pleased to see that Margot was 'very affectionate' to her wounded stepson. When Beb had left for the Front she had been hurt that he 'went off without one line or wire of farewell of any kind'[14] – a neglect prompted, perhaps, by tensions with his father about the time taken for his Brigade's guns to arrive.

After lunch Cynthia whisked her husband off to see the eminent dentist, Sir Francis Farmer, who said he could kill the nerves and keep the stumps to be crowned. She insisted on watching the operation and very nearly fainted. Beb himself, apart from his face wound and some signs of strain, looked well and obviously enjoyed showing his family an impressive array of souvenirs from the battlefield. Cynthia was impressed by how her husband, usually so taciturn in the presence of his loquacious stepmother, spoke 'extraordinarily well about his experiences'. Everyone was amused when the *Daily Mail* captioned his photograph with a report that he had been wounded in the Dardanelles.

Beb was soon absorbed in his pre-war London life of dinner parties and other social occasions. There was the added excitement of the official announcement of Violet's engagement to Bongie, with even the usually hostile Tory newspapers celebrating 'the Downing Street romance', and Margot, as Cynthia noted, 'triumphantly tearing Violet round from dressmaker to dressmaker, ordering a sumptuous trousseau'. There were visits to see their two boys, whom Cynthia had parked with their nanny, Miss Faulkner, in lodgings at Littlehampton on the Sussex coast while she – with no home of her own since renting out their London house – continued her peripatetic existence 'cuckooing' at the homes of her friends. Beb was delighted with his eleven-month-old son, Michael, but less impressed with their fellow guests at the hotel. When Cynthia told him 'they represented England and were what he was fighting for', he nearly resigned his commission.

On one of these visits to Littlehampton Cynthia invited D. H. Lawrence and Frieda, who were living nearby in Greatham, over to tea. Afterwards the two couples went for a walk along the shore. Cynthia 'wanted Beb and Lawrence to have a talk, so lingered behind with the Hun', as she now affectionately referred to Frieda. Lawrence, a passionate pacifist, accused Beb of 'subconscious blood-lust' and lectured him on his belief that 'destruction is the end, and not the means to an end, in the minds of soldiers'.[15] Beb later recalled their argument, which was perfectly amicable throughout:

> I did not agree with his contention, and argued that a delight in the mere act of destruction, such as that of a child in shattering a toy, though it

might often be seen in grown-up iconoclasts, was not at all typical of soldiers. When I began to throw stones at a bottle that was bobbing about in
the ripples, Lawrence regarded me for a moment with a humorous but
baleful glance; he continued his mystic refrain about 'will to destroy', and
it was in vain that I protested that I had no passion for the destruction
even of a medicine bottle.

The real difficulty, as it seemed to me, was not that the motives of individual soldiers were bad, but that they were admirable; for each of them,
on whatever side he was fighting – English, French, Russian, German, or
Italian – believed that he was defending his home and that God was on
the same side as his own country.[16]

Cynthia was struck by how her normally equable husband was
'bitter on the subject of generals and ammunition shortage', while
her cousin, Mary Herbert, reported to Aubrey, who was still in the
Dardanelles:

Beb lisps [through his broken teeth] all day long his hatred of politicians.
I suppose they must go on, but you must abolish this mouldy generation
and their shibboleths of parliamentarism, even [Lloyd] George and his
steel shavings are better than this dry rot. Beb wants to bring back an
army at the end of the war and string up his father and Bonar and all old
men to lamp-posts and then have a great and glorious army rule England
and let everyone be democrats and soldiers together.[17]

For Beb, who loved and admired his father, to speak of lynching
him – even in jest – shows the strength of his feelings. Unlike Oc,
who spent a great deal of time during his home leaves in the
company of comrades who had become friends, Beb must have felt
isolated among uncomprehending civilians. All the time he was on
leave his thoughts were with the comrades he had left behind. He
tried to use his time in England to exert any influence he had to help
them. A dinner party at 62 Cadogan Square, the Wemyss's London
base, was an opportunity to lobby Balfour – who as the new First
Lord of the Admiralty was responsible for the Royal Marines – for
more anti-aircraft guns. Beb was impressed by the former Prime
Minister's 'quick pointful questions' and 'high degree of technical
knowledge'. He, in turn, must have made his point effectively for he
was promised eight more guns for his unit.[18]

Given Beb's truculent mood, sparks were bound to fly with his
father. Having created the new Ministry of Munitions and overridden

Kitchener's objections to putting Lloyd George in charge, Asquith's strategy at this point was to conduct a 'holding operation' on the Western Front while concentrating on achieving a decisive victory in the Dardanelles. He was having to argue through his view both with fractious Cabinet colleagues and his French allies; he was also facing an increasingly hostile Press at home, and was in no mood to continue the debate at home with one of his sons. Margot, who naturally took her husband's side, complained in a letter to Oc that

> Beb talked wonderful rot. He even made your father angry by his Northcliffe views and his new and to me bewildering pomposity. Poor Beb, he drinks too much and has not the head for it. He is quite addled at times and yet there is <u>great</u> sweetness of temper and soundness and unselfishness about him. Most people – Violet and others – thought him a little mad!![19]

Beb may indeed have drunk too much while on leave – Margot had already complained to Oc about both his elder brothers' excessive consumption of alcohol – but that did not make his views any less valid. However, what was new was the vehemence – or 'pomposity' as his stepmother called it – with which he argued his case. He had disagreed about politics with his father before now, most notably during the Boer War, but had never fallen out with him. The uncharacteristic emotion that Margot put down to too much drink was probably an early symptom of shell shock. But Beb refused the offer of a 'soft' job teaching recruits at Eastney and insisted on returning to the Front when his face wounds had healed in mid-July. His growing disillusion with the War – which went hand in hand with his admiration for the fighting men – was reinforced when he arrived back at Nieuport:

> I heard that our guns had again been bombarded and that my friend Knight had been hit, and had died of his wounds. He was one of many thousands who had already fallen, scarcely more than a boy in years, but bearing the fullest burden of a man. I had seen little of him at home, and our friendship had been formed, and suddenly ended, in the queer, unearthly conditions of that strangely twisted world, the line in Flanders; within it he stood forth as a splendid example of boyhood tempered beyond its years by stark experience, now and then impetuous, but a first rate officer, full of care for his men, gay, gallant, and loved by all.[20]

A short while later Beb himself had a narrow escape approaching an observation post near the railway when a shell burst close by, knocking him to the ground and covering him with debris, but otherwise leaving him no more than badly shaken. Over the next weeks the gunners had to be constantly on the alert as each side mounted raids to probe each other's defences, 'resulting in sudden concentrations of fire and long lines of flares and rockets'.[21]

At the end of August, Cynthia was staying at Gosford, her family's house in East Lothian, when she heard Beb was coming home on 'short leave'. He first called on Violet, who was convalescing in Sandwich in Kent after contracting typhoid in Egypt. She reported to Oc that their brother looked 'very strained and tired'.[22] The following day, 31 August, Cynthia and the now four-year-old John met Beb off the overnight sleeper at Drem station. He told her that 'he was feeling as if he would crack up' and explained that they had 'been having a very bad time – dysentery, poisoned water, and ceaseless tension. One of his officer friends has gone off his head from sheer strain – horrible. Beb still rather angrily pro National Service' (i.e. conscription). Cynthia took Beb to see Dr Ewart, a local doctor, who, unaware that his patient was displaying clear symptoms of shell shock (a condition still barely recognized even by Army medics), prescribed him a fortnight's leave.

The ambience of Gosford was hardly conducive to relieving nerves strained from weeks of unremitting shellfire. Cynthia herself had never felt comfortable in her family's Scottish seat, a huge eighteenth-century Palladian pile originally designed by Robert Adam and then extended in the 1880s. She compared it to 'a handsome person without charm. The rooms were airless and except with the aid of a long hooked pole, it was impossible to open and shut any of the heavy windows.'[23] The arid atmosphere was not helped by frequent rows between Cynthia's father, Lord Wemyss, and his mistress, Lady Angela Forbes, who openly lived with him. When Cynthia's mother appeared, there were more tears over the Earl's attempts to shut down her beloved Cotswold home Stanway as an economy measure. Cynthia's sister, Mary, and Letty, the wife of their eldest brother, Ego (now Lord Elcho), were distraught at the imminent prospect of Ego and Mary's fiancé, Tom Strickland, being sent to Gallipoli. Then, shortly after Beb's arrival, the doom-laden mood was intensified by the news that the much-loved Charles Lister had died.

Beb's strained nerves were scarcely helped by Cynthia's lack of understanding of what he had been through. While he was at the front, she had gaily informed a friend that he was having 'great fun potting Zeppelins'.[24] D. H. Lawrence wrote after meeting Beb that 'the war is the only reality to him. All this here is unreal, this England, only the trenches are life to him. Cynthia is very unhappy – he is not even aware of her existence. He is spell bound by the fighting line.'[25] Beb himself said that, like his elder brother, he 'preferred to eat his sorrows in silence'; even Raymond once complained to Viola Tree about how 'secretive' Beb was.[26] However, although Beb is unlikely to have confided to anyone his feelings about Cynthia, some idea of what he was thinking is apparent in a clearly autobiographical passage in his novel *Roon* (1929), where he describes the eponymous heroine's feelings on meeting her wounded lover, Dick Napier (significantly, also in 1915):

> She felt that a large part of him was still away from her in the other plane, where he had left and lost so many of his friends; it was as though a veil lay between her and him, through which she could still see the light of his welcome, and she longed to draw it aside. Besides her joy at seeing him she felt faintly envious of those who had shared his dangers, and could move with him on that other plane which few women reach in modern war, however anxious they might be to do so.[27]

There may well be some element of wishful thinking here, in that there is little evidence in Cynthia's diaries that she wanted to face what was happening over the Channel. None of her immediate family had yet been killed, and by her own admission, 'I begin to feel a horrid numbness creeping over me. The Tragedy is so spendthrift. Either Billy's [Grenfell's] or Charlie's [Lister's] death a year ago would have absorbed one's thoughts for ages.' The War even had a certain fascination: she was acutely disappointed at missing the excitement of a Zeppelin air raid on London of which she heard 'thrilling accounts', and she was even fascinated by the novelty of cutting pads for gas masks, remarking in her diary that: 'it is such fun feeling a factory girl and it gave me some idea of how exciting it must be to do piece-work for money' – although she did at least admit: 'I must say I was very glad I hadn't got to do a twelve-hour day – it is quite tiring.'[28]

At Gosford, the Charteris family and their friends tried to forget the conflict, immersing themselves in Coterie word games, tennis matches or gossip. The conflict did impinge a little when in the week after Beb's arrival they saw off Cynthia's nineteen-year-old youngest brother, Yvo, who was off to join the Grenadier Guards on the Western Front. Cynthia had to comfort her grief-stricken little sister, 'Bibs' (Irene).

Faced with all this forced jollity, Beb became increasingly withdrawn, shutting himself up in his room to write poetry that relived his recent experiences in Nieuport and brought him closer to the comrades who were always in his thoughts. It was almost certainly with Knight in mind when he wrote *The Fallen Subaltern*,

> Who looked at danger with eyes of laughter,
>   And on the charge his days ended well.
>
> One last salute; the bayonets clash and glisten;
>   With arms reversed we go without a sound:
> One more has joined the men who lie and listen
>   To us, who march upon their burial ground.

Margot, Elizabeth and Puffin spent the summer and autumn of 1915 at a villa in North Berwick, her first summer holiday without her husband, her stepchildren and their usual gaggle of young and high spirited friends. Asquith decided that the state of the War meant he must remain in London throughout the summer, and he only travelled up to Scotland for the occasional weekend with Margot and her children. Without the usual bustle of family and friends to cheer her up, Margot was in a grim mood. In Downing Street she had been frustrated by the continued presence of Violet, whose typhoid had caused the postponement of her marriage to Bongie. The death of Charty's son Charles Lister, of whom she was particularly fond, had hit Margot hard, and now there was the additional worry of Raymond, who in July had successfully applied for a commission in the Grenadier Guards, in spite of opposition from Katharine. 'If Raymond and Cys go into the fighting lines as well as Oc and Beb . . . the strain will be terrible for all of us,'[29] Margot wrote in her diary. She was also increasingly worried by the strength of the campaign for conscription, which she suspected was being exploited as a means of ousting her husband. The issue was far from the simple matter of recruiting the maximum number of fighting men.

Kitchener, who like most of the High Command preferred a volunteer Army, was still able to recruit enough men, and there were real concerns that a general call-up would deprive industry of the skilled men vital to the campaign to increase the supply of munitions. Besides, with the Trade Unions still opposing any compulsory call-up of their members, there was a danger of unleashing a wave of industrial unrest, if the issue were not carefully handled. However, this did not prevent Lloyd George from intriguing with Churchill, Curzon and other Tory members of the Cabinet, backed by a vociferous newspaper campaign, trying to railroad the Government into introducing immediate conscription.

For the time being Margot's fury was directed against the Press lord whose newspapers were spearheading the campaign for conscription, and campaigning stridently for Lloyd George to become Prime Minister. 'Northcliffe ought to be shot' was her own preferred solution to the problem (in a letter to Oc), although 'it's too good a death'. But she was in no doubt as to the Welshman's complicity: he had, as she informed her stepson, 'allowed Northcliffe and his swine to run him in every way against your father'.[30] In frustration at her husband's apparent refusal to take any action either to muzzle the Press or rein in the Cabinet dissidents, Margot turned to her friend Arthur Balfour, to whom, in a letter marked '<u>Very Secret</u>', she wrote on 18 August 1915:

> Are we – the Government – really powerless to deal with Northcliffe?? You don't perhaps see the *Daily Mail* (<u>I</u> don't – but it is sent to me in batches of letters from strangers <u>cursing</u> Henry and the Cabinet for what I agree appears weakness not dealing with Northcliffe). I don't know enough about war laws or ordinary laws, but the chief use of a coalition government appears to me to be if it could deal with the Press. If we have not the powers under the Defence of the Realm [Act] could you not suggest at the Cabinet that we should take powers? You are too busy to know what is going on just now in that strange Welsh world next door and it is too private to write about, but I warn you that Northcliffe has backed himself to break this Cabinet and he will do it. Henry never takes any interest in the papers that attack him, but <u>our allies</u> do: they are very brittle.[31]

Margot even resorted to exploiting Kitchener's '<u>loathing and distrust of Curzon</u>' since their days in India together to lobby for his support against 'the wreckers', as she called those ministers conspiring to force conscription on the Government.[32] Ironically, just as Margot was beginning to appreciate Kitchener's qualities, her husband was becoming disillusioned with his management of the war effort, and was seeking a means to replace him as War Minister.

Margot's hatred of Northcliffe was further fuelled by the way articles in his newspapers were exploited by the enemy. Disabled former British prisoners of war at the King George Hospital, who had been repatriated from Germany, told her of their disgust with the way in which quotations from *The Times* and *Daily Mail* were being used as propaganda by the German press. On holiday in Scotland, Margot vented her frustration over the War and her lack of influence over events. Cynthia described a visit by her stepmother-in-law to Gosford as leaving 'a wake of weeping, injured people. Both nurses mortally offended. She said [her son] John had no roof to his mouth and [his brother] Michael looked like a Red Indian.' Cynthia went to North Berwick 'meaning to tell her what pain she gives and try to stand up to her, but as usual all my resolution evaporated . . . She is disarming, I always resent her so much more in theory than in practice.'[33]

Beb's mental condition, far from than improving, was becoming ever more fragile as he shut himself away for hours on end to write poetry. The local doctor gave him another fortnight's leave, but in his quiet Scottish practice he was ill-equipped to realize with what he was dealing. Beb began to suffer fits of dizziness, and on 17 September he insisted on working on one of his poems after dinner rather than join the others at poker. Later on he appeared in Cynthia's room while she sat chatting to her sister, Mary, and her brother Ego's wife, Letty. He complained that he felt 'queer' and confessed that he had just smashed a vase because it 'wasn't pretty'. Cynthia noted her reaction in her diary:

> I remembered Lawrence's statement that Beb's destructive spirit had been aroused, and that he couldn't bear 'to see a house with its roof on' and I felt alarmed. I believe the desire to smash is a recognised symptom of nervous strain from Artillery work, and I do so understand it, only one must drastically discourage it, for there is nothing that it mightn't lead to, and his arguments when scolded were rather unhinged. 'Gallant and wonderful soldiers

were being killed, so why should ugly things survive?' Such logic might lead to the smashing of Lady Horner's face.

Of course, Cynthia did not understand – how could she? A different doctor was summoned but all he could suggest was that Beb stay in bed. A couple of days later Cynthia thought he seemed better, but he insisted on eating dinner in the sitting room rather than listen to the boisterous Charteris family's word games. As autumn set in, Beb tagged along with Cynthia's life of 'cuckooing', as she called her nomadic wartime existence. It was now her turn to be irritated by her husband's unwanted presence. She had been seeing a great deal of Bluetooth Baker, who had long been in love with her. Although she had never reciprocated his feelings, Cynthia was flattered by his attentions and revelled in his political indiscretions; as she wrote in her diary, she now found it 'awkward à trois while Beb was there'.[34] Bluetooth got his revenge by tastelessly making fun of him to Raymond, informing him that Beb was not really wounded but had run a fork through his cheek in a frenzy of gluttony'.[35]

More of a threat to Beb's marriage was a much more recent friend of Cynthia's, Lord Basil Blackwood, the son of the Marquess of Dufferin and a Balliol contemporary of Hilaire Belloc and John Buchan. Blackwood, who is now best known as the illustrator of Belloc's *Bad Child's Book of Beasts*, was one of those charming, multi-talented people who are never quite able to find their niche, or indeed in his case the right woman to marry. He had joined up at the beginning of the War at the age of forty-four but after being wounded had returned to his previous job as Private Secretary to Lord Wimborne, Viceroy of Ireland. Cynthia and Mary had been to stay with him in Dublin and he met her in England as often as he could. For Cynthia, having Beb around when she was with Basil was very definitely 'dentist wrecking'.* In October she noted how her husband 'complained very bitterly at the prospect of an à trois dinner, but it went off very well',[36] apparently oblivious to the fact that Beb was on the brink of a breakdown.

---

*The Coterie word 'dentist' was later defined by Cynthia as 'a pre-arranged tête-à-tête' with, as the editor of her diaries puts it, 'flirtatious overtones, so that the intervention of an unwanted third party playing gooseberry was known as "dentist-wrecking"'.

17

'To know more dead than living people'

IN OCTOBER 1915, after a short training course at the Guards'
depot at Bovingdon, Raymond was posted to the 3rd Battalion of
the Grenadier Guards in France. 'In the Guards he was extraordinarily happy, and seemed to have found again the light-hearted companionship which had been the charm of Oxford,'[1] recalled his friend
John Buchan. 'Raymond has gone to France, poor love, so unfit and
so pathetically keen,'[2] a rueful Diana wrote to their Coterie friend
George Vernon, who had recently been evacuated from Gallipoli to
Malta with severe dysentery. Meanwhile Violet, who was staying with
the Horners at Mells when Raymond left, wrote to Oc:

> He and Katharine came down here to say goodbye to Frances and the
> children. He rather happy and excited – poor K. of course quite
> wretched. Cys was to have gone last week but was again rejected as med-
> ically unfit [his health never recovered properly from his bout of typhoid]
> ... I am continuing my very slow convalescence at Mells – which is lovely
> and lulling as ever – the garden flaming with hollyhocks, red hot pokers,
> Michaelmas daisies, dahlias and that delicious half rotten autumn smell in
> the air – the lichen peacefully creeping on over the old stone churches
> and walls. It is all so calm and normal and undisturbed, it is almost
> impossible to imagine the horror that is shaking the world – and you
> poor darling far away hanging on to the edge of your grim and bloody
> Peninsula amongst flies and half buried Turks. How I long to get you
> back again.[3]

The Guards' depot did not lack comforts for the officers. Raymond shared a hut with a fellow subaltern complete with, so he reported to Diana, hot baths, champagne, roast partridge and bridge – all the trappings of civilization save intelligent conversation and sex. However, they had little time to enjoy the facilities before they were on the move towards the front line and had to survive on condensed milk and hard boiled eggs, with the only women in sight being the gelded Hebes serving in the Y.M.C.A canteens. Progress was infuriatingly slow. Raymond complained bitterly about them being treated like cattle, only on the move at night (and thus getting little sleep) and waiting five hours at every station. When they reached Rouen, the men – to Raymond's mortification – were locked up in a dingy shed with some Indian troops, while he and his company commander, Captain Vaughan, were able to procure a hot bath and a shave at the Grand Hôtel de la Poste before indulging in a drunken lunch of lobsters and brandy with, as he disclosed to Diana, but not to Katharine, four or five admirably spirited and pretty harlots for company.[4]

Raymond was fortunate to join his battalion just as it finished a stint in the trenches. He was welcomed by the adjutant, Oliver Lyttelton (Alfred and DD's son), and his brigadier, John Ponsonby, entertained him to dinner. He was comfortably billeted in a farmhouse some ten miles behind the lines, where there were liberal supplies of fine wines and hampers of goodies from Fortnum and Mason. He was able to reassure Katharine that they were living a life of comparative ease, with a moderate drill in the mornings, an afternoon stroll with Lyttelton or somebody else, dinner washed down with a bottle of wine, and a feather bed at night. On 6 November he celebrated his thirty-seventh birthday with a large dinner party where his guests feasted on pâté de foie gras, preserved ginger, champagne and vintage brandy.[5]

The only annoying interruption was a parade of the entire Guards Division for one of the Kaiser's relations (George V), which was cancelled after a six-mile march through drenching rain. Raymond's only chore, so he informed Katharine, was reading and censoring the soldiers' letters, which he complained were very long and very dull, excusing himself for the criticism with the unlikely observation that probably his own letters were not much better. Writing to Diana (who often brought the worst out in him), he attempted a laboured parody of a guardsman's letter home, addressed – as he implied all such letters were – to 'Bella and Will'. Raymond's con-descending mixture of slang and semi-literate expressions do him no more credit than his weak joke that his invariable policy as a censor was to cross out anything he had seen in any previous letter – which usually meant crossing out everything after the words 'Bella and Will'.[6]

On 19 October, barely a week after Raymond left for the Front, the reality of the War suddenly struck home to Cynthia when she heard that her little brother, 'darling, darling little Yvo – the perfect child and youth', had been killed:

> How can one believe it, that it should be the <u>object</u> to kill Yvo? That such a joy-dispenser should have been put out of the world on purpose. For the first time I felt the full mad horror of the war . . . How immune my life has been! The extraordinary difference between people – even Billy [Grenfell] whom one thought one was so fond of – and one's own little brother. Somehow with the others who have been killed, I have acutely felt the loss of them but have so swallowed the rather high-faluting platitude that it was all right for them – that they were not to be pitied, but were safe, unassailable, young, and glamorous for ever. With Yvo – I can't bear it for him. The sheer pity and horror of it is overwhelming.

The whole Charteris family was devastated. Cynthia described her father as 'heartbroken and just like a child – tears pouring down his cheeks and so naively <u>astonished</u>.' Her thirteen-year-old sister Bibs' sobs 'poured and poured ceaseless rain all day'.[7]

For Beb, still suffering from strain which had not yet been diag-nosed as shell shock, there was some temporary comfort with a visit to Aubrey and Mary Herbert at Pixton, their Somerset home, although he could not bring himself to accompany his friend on a shoot. Aubrey had been ordered home from Gallipoli after contract-ing dysentery and, like Beb, was suffering from nervous strain after witnessing, week after week, dead Anzac and Turk soldiers lying unburied and the wounded crying for water between the trenches, while Hamilton refused to allow him to arrange a truce.[8] He too was blaming incompetent generals and stubborn politicians for the suffering of both sides. 'He is badly physically haunted by his experi-ence,' Cynthia later remarked in her journal, noticing 'exactly the same expression on his face as Beb had that night at Gosford when he smashed the vase'. Nonetheless, she could not help wryly observing that 'I think Lawrence would rejoice and say Beb and Aubrey were looking "chastened".'[9]

Beb and Cynthia returned to London, where they were now stayed at the Herberts' house, 28 Bruton Street, to be greeted by the news that their friend George Vernon had died of dysentery in Malta. She asked in her journal: 'Oh why was I born at this time? Before one is thirty to know more dead than living people?'[10] A memorial service was arranged for Vernon at Stanway church on Sunday 14 November. The day before Cynthia received a wire from Beb saying he had a chill and would not be able to attend, followed by a vaguely ominous cable from Margot: 'Think you had better come up tomorrow evening see Parkinson about poor Beb.' She complained irritably that it was 'too tiresome – just as I had got back here. If only Beb had come down with me on Friday . . . I loathe going to Downing Street. Damn!' However, at Beb's suggestion she stayed for the service and travelled to London that evening, arriving just before 10.30. She found her husband in bed and looking very pale. He merely admitted to a 'a fainting fit at luncheon on Saturday', but she got the full story from Violet:

> He had been looking ill all the time, turned a ghastly colour, shook all over, and fainted. Mary Herbert was there and supported him. He had a rigor and was unconscious for quite a long time, and his heart very bad. They sent for Parkinson. He says he is on the verge of spinal neuritis.* There is a quantity of cases of this kind affecting people in various ways resulting from strain at the front. He says he must be quiet in bed for a fortnight, but that he may be moved down to the country. He is not to smoke or drink at all, poor darling.

Beb had a good night's sleep but remained very weak and drowsy and Cynthia had 'to feed him like a baby'. She was frustrated at not being able to coax the fire into burning properly in his cold, draughty room. Mary Herbert called at about eleven, followed by Margot, who ushered Cynthia into her bedroom and, with a 'glance of melodramatic commiseration', confided: 'This is a fearful blow, isn't it?'

---

*A contemporary medical description of symptoms of the condition better known as shell shock.

Cynthia replied that at least that they now knew what the problem was; then, as she recounts in her diary, 'the most amazing scene ensued':

> Margot: 'Ah, but do you think he <u>will</u> be able to pull himself together? I don't. Oh my poor Cynthia, you've got years of anguish before you! I know it so well with poor Lucy.'
>
> I gasped, wondering what she meant, as I knew Beb was not suffering from arthritis. Gradually I realised her meaning – that poor Beb was suffering, not really from his experiences at the Front, but from a protracted course of drunkenness. She fabricated corroborating words for Parkinson . . .
>
> She has an obsession about drink: her grandfather and Lucy's husband both died of it*, and she has had anonymous letters about the P.M. Beb often what I call 'takes off the receiver' and is very *distrait*, especially when bored – as he is by her – and on these occasions has an odd almost dazed manner. This she attributed to drink . . .
>
> What I am <u>positive</u> about is that I have never seen Beb 'drunk': in my opinion his misfortune is that he has too strong a head, and is able to drink more than is healthy. She couldn't believe that I didn't realize that Beb was a regular drunkard, and was astonished to hear Parkinson had not told me . . . She poured out a lot of novelette twaddle about my being the only person who could save him, and so on. It was altogether a horrible scene. I cried and was furious, but very inarticulate.

The following morning Cynthia and Violet interviewed the doctor themselves and found, as they had suspected, that 'the words put into his mouth were pure fabrication'.

It would soon become apparent that even if Beb had been drinking too much, this was more a symptom of his condition that the cause of it. He was clearly suffering from shell shock, a condition which, with military psychiatry in its infancy, was only just becoming recognized. The British Army, in particular, was slow to recognize the cumulative effect on front line troops of having to withstand continual bombardment by high explosive shells while confined to trenches. The problem was significantly mitigated once the High Command adopted a policy of rotating front line troops every few days, with units doing 'fatigues' behind the lines and everyone receiving regular

---

*This is palpably untrue in the latter case, although drink may have been an indirect cause of 'Grambo' Graham Smith's setting fire to himself.

rest breaks well out of range of enemy gunners. Later in the War, when he was mentally better prepared, Beb was to withstand battle conditions far worse than anything he experienced in 1915. But for the moment his febrile mental state was aggravated by the incomprehension of those around him. By contrast, when Oc came home on leave from Gallipoli (where, in any case, the artillery on both sides was inferior to that on the Western Front), he had the company of several comrades in arms.

Cynthia was at least quick to realize that the last place Beb needed to be was 10 Downing Street, under the 'care' of Margot. The following afternoon she took him 'with glorious paraphernalia of bath-chair, hot-water bottle, and thermos flask' by the 4.45 train to Stanway, where they consulted the Charteris' family doctor, Halliwell, who advised them: 'it will be a long business'.[11]

The one person from whom Beb received no sympathy was Raymond, who on hearing about his brother's illness (no doubt caricatured by Bluetooth's poisonous pen) could only bring himself to feel sorry for Cynthia, apparently going along with Margot's diagnosis that Beb's main problem was a surfeit of alcohol. There was no end to his brother's eccentricities, Raymond remarked in a letter to Katharine, wondering if spinal neuritis was a new illness and whether anybody else had contracted it after being shelled – or getting drunk. To be fair to Raymond, when he wrote this he had just had his own first taste of life in the trenches and was in a bad mood after having swapped his comfortable billet for a Spartan farmhouse.[12] He was still determined to treat the War with scorn and tried hard not to be downcast even when friends were killed. When he heard from Diana about George Vernon's death from dysentery, what most upset him – or so he maintained – was that she was distressed. All he would admit on his own part was to feeling a bit sentimental over the memory of their glittering junketings in Venice three years earlier, eclipsed by the rapid progression of Denis Anson, Billy Grenfell and now George Vernon from the Lido to the Styx. Meanwhile, as he awaited his own turn to be ferried across to Hades, he consoled himself with the thought that he had not missed out on any of the fun.[13]

The Grenadier Guards had been in the thick of the fighting since the beginning of the War and were severely under strength by the time Raymond joined them at the front. When the regiment returned to the trenches, it was posted to one of the comparatively quiet sections of the front line, where shelling was sporadic. He was more concerned by the discomfort than the danger, complaining about being up to his neck in dense, sticky blue clay; at the same time he was puzzled that while the sound of rifle fire seemed no more far off than the next gun in a partridge drive, nothing seemed to happen.[14]

The Grenadiers' 3rd Battalion, in particular, was chronically short of officers. Raymond was typically dismissive of the casualties, ascribing most of those among his fellow officers to fright. Nonetheless, he may have had Beb in mind when he admitted – as one who had never been shelled – to being surprised by how many men with seemingly average nerves became hysterical when subjected to shellfire, although he added that once he himself had experienced it, he would probably be surprised that there were not more.[15] He does not seem to have appreciated that he was one of the beneficiaries of the new policy of only deploying forward units in front-line trenches for forty-eight hours.

As a result of the officer shortage Raymond found himself second in command of his company. The only other officer besides Vaughan, the company commander, was Second Lieutenant Alfred Yorke, the genial forty-four-year-old younger brother of the Earl of Hardwicke. Raymond described his fellow subaltern to Diana as a complete philistine and obstinate anti-radical. Yorke was the kind of reactionary buffer he would have avoided in normal peacetime circumstances; however, in the alien conditions of the trenches, he appreciated a companion with whom he had many friends in common; and they consoled themselves in the dark, dank trenches by gossiping about wine and women. Diana herself featured in their banter, with Raymond stoutly defending her against accusations of abominable wickedness, while Yorke chaffed him about his passion for her.[16]

Even Raymond's fatalistic cynicism could not prevent him feeling frustrated with the deficiencies of generals and staff alike. He complained to Katharine about the lack of dry trenches and the idiocy of the authorities in making no adequate preparations for winter. Although everyone ought to have trench boots in their division, half the men had to do without them, and other divisions were probably even worse off. Yet he stubbornly maintained his cheerful façade, even remarking on the daring of the huge number of well-fed rats, which after having had their fill of the corpses would hurtle over their faces. It was fortunate, he added, that he had always been an animal lover. When they did come under fire, he maintained that the shells and bullets created a diversion rather than panic. He really didn't know where they would be without them. Nonetheless, he did not disguise his apprehension about taking part in one of the attacks which, in his view, everyone but the staff not only dreaded, but regarded as pointless.[17]

Raymond's fears about another push before Christmas proved ill founded. At the end of November, he was put in charge of a redoubt consisting of three small forts behind the lines, part of the second line of defence should the Germans break through the front-line trenches – an eventuality he viewed as remote since, as far as he could judge, they had broken the spirit of the Hun in their part of the line. He did, however, get his first taste of being directly targeted by German artillery, although he tried to reassure Katharine that as long as they were well dug in, shrapnel was not frightening. After being bombarded by a hundred shells, only one of his men was injured, and not seriously.[18]

A few weeks later, after experiencing a great deal more bombardment, Raymond gave a graphic account to Diana of what it was like to be shelled, describing yellow and red flames, great pillars of dust and smoke and sand-bags flying up all around, as they were showered with clods of earth, while shells whizzed over their heads making a noise like a thousand defective harmoniums played in unison by a lunatic. The most respected soldiers would appear absurdly solemn, while the most ignominious would bellow with laughter while emitting a torrent of obscene jokes. At first it seemed as if everyone else in the trench must be dead; but once the shellfire had subsided it was discovered that the only casualties were two men with slight wounds. Every so often soldiers would gingerly peer over the parapet to find out whether their artillery was doing much harm to the Boches, and see a row of sensational volcanoes erupting along every five yards of the German line. But if a soldier put his head above the parapet for thirty seconds a hundred bullets would whistle past.[19] Raymond had a narrow escape when a bullet penetrated the wall of his dug-out three inches above his head while he was having dinner, an incident which he characteristically pretended was almost too mundane to mention to Diana, who every evening had to suffer the drama of escaping from corked champagne, bores and dozens of things far more disagreeable than nickel-coated bullets.[20]

Few of the men under Raymond's command were as nonchalant about being under fire. Most of them had endured many months of bombardment far more severe than anything he had yet encountered, as well as participating in – or helping to repel – the murderous attacks which he so dreaded; in the process they had seen many of their comrades killed, maimed or driven out of their minds. Yet Raymond seems to have felt a curious lack of responsibility for calming his men's frayed nerves, and (however he acted in reality) was happy to give the impression to Diana that his main concern was to maintain his own dignity and *sang froid*. After experiencing, just before Christmas, his worst bombardment yet, he bragged to her how he was relieved to discover that on each occasion he could remain standing and watch the spectacle for an hour at a time, while calming himself by intoning 'Bugger'. He was openly contemptuous of more battle-scarred fellow soldiers who he told her seemed scarcely human as they lay in the yellow mud, scraping dementedly with their hands at the trench wall.[21]

If Raymond seems hard on his Grenadier comrades, he was much harsher about a detachment of Welsh fusiliers from the new volunteer regiments, who were temporarily attached to his platoon for instruction. He dubbed these midgets in black spectacles without discipline, experience or stomach, and with a superabundance of nerves and words – the sort of fellows who he supposed gave animated lectures on medicine to first-year students at some lesser Welsh university. They groaned, coughed, snivelled and vomited throughout the night in a manner that was most upsetting; they took so little notice of their duties that if they had been grenadiers, he would have had half of them shot. If these men were a fair sample of Kitchener's volunteer army, it was easy, he claimed, to understand why so many offensives had failed.[22]

Yet, it would be wrong to see Raymond as lacking in any humanity. His letters were written to amuse and should not be judged by the impression of printed words on a cold page. It is clear from the letters received by his family after his death, not just from fellow officers but also from ordinary soldiers (those that survived him, if only for a while), that he amused his comrades as much as his friends, and that he was regarded with as much affection as respect. Like his brothers, he disliked delegating a task he could perform himself, often crawling out at night to check the wire, when he could just as well have sent one of his men.* He would occasionally let down his

---

*The author was not granted access to these letters and must trust the account of them by Raymond's family.

carefully contrived emotional guard even to Diana. He once described to her how, on returning in torrential rain from a night patrol during his final stint in the trenches, before going home on leave, he found the sentries singing, the duty officer splashing around in three feet of water, and the off-duty guardsmen asleep in attitudes of exhaustion and so thickly plastered in mud that he could scarcely make out their equipment: it was, he said, a scene impossible to depict, and one which would pierce the coldest heart.[23]

What Raymond admired was panache. For him, the man who emerged from the war better than anybody was Winston Churchill, who had recently resigned from his father's Government and was now attached to the headquarters of the 2nd Battalion of the Grenadier Guards. The former First Lord of the Admiralty rode over to Raymond on 23 November, reporting to Clemmie that 'we had a pleasant talk and some tea. He is quite a soldier now, and much improved by the experience.'[24] The fact that Churchill's relations with his father were strained would not have worried Raymond, who, as he wrote to Katharine three days later, was fuming over the fact that he had not received a single letter from any member of his family since he had left for the Front. Although he pretended that there was no reason why they should write, it is clear that in fact he was deeply hurt by his family's apparent indifference, telling Katharine that at least it was something to throw back at them if anyone started to lecture her about his supposed heartlessness.[25] It did not prevent him sending Violet his good wishes for her wedding to Bongie on 30 November. But there was a touch of malice in the way he disloyally regaled Diana with unpleasant rumours which had reached him from the Italian Riviera (where his sister and Bongie were honeymooning) that she retained her virginity several weeks after her marriage.[26]

Raymond can hardly have been surprised by the lack of communication from his brothers or sisters. He had displayed little interest in his siblings since their childhood, and while Violet was constantly in the company of Beb and Oc – and later on, Cys – she was, if anything, closer to Katharine than Raymond. Although Raymond seems to have charmed Elizabeth once she reached her teens, Puffin later told Margot that he could not 'remember his ever speaking to me'. Margot may well have been right when, at the time of Raymond's marriage, she wrote in her diary that 'his family appear to have bored him a great deal'.[27] Yet after his death she wrote: 'I loved him much . . . when I first married he was my favourite step-child, he appeared to have the most distinction and to the end was more punctual and less self-indulgent than the rest . . . We were such friends till he went to the Bar.'

There is little evidence, however, to show that Margot was particularly fond of Raymond while he was still alive. At the time of her marriage she had little affection for any of her stepchildren, so being her 'favourite' meant little. Certainly she was worried about Raymond's behaviour at Oxford, and after the death of her third baby in 1900 she sent his letter of commiseration to Ettie, commenting: 'it is just like him, showing the finest taste and dearest most loving understanding and so clever and perfect in literary style without a trace of self consciousness'. Yet when she was stressed or depressed, she never turned to him as, at different times, she turned to his three brothers. In a rare but telling diary reference to her eldest stepson in her 1909 diary, Margot noted that 'as I grow older I long for two things! One is Imagination and the other Heart. Raymond tho' understanding <u>everything</u> you say to him and really not crabbing considering his rather glacial intellectual standard, is deficient in both these qualities.'[28]

Raymond had much greater justification for feeling aggrieved with his father for not writing. Whatever the defects in their relationship, there was real pride and affection on both sides, and Asquith's failure to write to him – or indeed to Oc or Beb when they were at the Front – is very hard to understand. If he could find time to play bridge and write to at least one member of his 'harem' most evenings, he surely could find time for the occasional letter to his sons as they faced the daily danger of death.

Beb, who curiously was less affected by his father's 'neglect' than Raymond, once explained Asquith's apparent indifference to Cynthia as 'an excessive belief in the powers of the unspoken word'.[29] Perhaps the truth was that the Prime Minister, with his well-known tendency to ignore unpleasant facts, simply did not want to face up to the possibility that at any moment one of his sons might be killed. A letter to one of his women friends allowed him to unburden himself or seek a momentary distraction from the crushing responsibilities of the War, while writing to his sons at the Front brought him face to face with the personal consequences of the decisions he had to face every day. His first duty was to his country, and the longer he could keep his fears for his sons at bay the better.

Raymond seems to have expressed no resentment to his family about the lack of letters. When he lunched at 10 Downing Street on 29 December, Margot recorded that he looked 'very well and handsome' and 'told us a lot about the trenches and effect on one of the first fire etc. He told it well, I wish he would write a verbatim account of his experiences.'[30] It may well be that his ill-feeling evaporated when he saw how pleased his family were to see him, or it may be that he now appreciated the gravity of the political crisis confronting his father, whose closest Liberal colleagues were up in arms and threatening to resign when he seemed to bow to the pressure to introduce conscription. There was also a serious Cabinet split over Gallipoli. After the defeat of the last Allied offensive in August, argument had raged over whether to evacuate or reinforce the peninsula. Bonar Law and Lloyd George were pressing hard to withdraw, while Curzon and Kitchener, the only two ministers who knew the region, were for once united in opposing an admission of defeat, which they believed would have a disastrous effect on British prestige in Asia. In November, after visiting the Dardanelles himself, Kitchener finally recommended evacuation. But although the bulk of Allied troops were successfully pulled off the peninsula by mid-December, it had not yet been decided whether to keep the one remaining Allied bridgehead at Cape Helles, where withdrawal in the face of armed opposition from an alert Turkish army risked a military catastrophe. The decision, as Raymond would have realized, could not have been more poignant: for among the sick, cold and ill-fed British forces grimly hanging on to the tip of Gallipoli was his brother, Oc.

On Christmas Eve Asquith informed Sylvia that he had just received 'a rather depressing letter this morning from Oc – who never grumbles – giving a very gloomy account of winter conditions at Helles'.[31] The letter had taken four weeks to reach Downing Street. In the meantime, as the Prime Minister and his colleagues argued about the pros and cons of abandoning Gallipoli altogether, the Turks were preparing to drive his favourite son and his comrades into the sea.

*

Oc was full of confidence when he and Charles Lister rejoined the Hood battalion at their rest camp on Imbros island, just off the Gallipoli peninsula, on 28 June. 'The general tone is optimistic,' he complacently told Violet. 'I may soon be back with rugs from Stamboul for you.' Fresh, rested, well fed, happily reunited with his friends Lister, Freyberg and Shaw-Stewart, with his wounded knee now fully healed, it was easy to feel cheerful, and even to enjoy the spectacle of Royal Navy warships and newly arrived French field guns hammering the Turkish positions: 'last night it was a wonderful sight, with flares and guns and a background of thundercloud and forked lightening'.[32]

Oc's sunny mood did not last long. The state of the Royal Naval Division was dire. A few days later, in a letter to Margot, he admitted that most of them 'suffer from acute diarrhoea with which the doctors cannot cope'. After a spell in the front line, he welcomed some respite from the deafening bombardment. Censorship of letters home was a convenient pretext to spare his family the worst details of what they were having to endure: 'Excuse a dull letter,' he wrote to Margot, 'anything interesting one is not allowed to say.' Yet, as Violet pointed out, if he had written directly to his father his letters would not have been opened and he could have said what he liked. His family could glean few clues about conditions from references to thunderstorms being 'disagreeable for dug-out dwellers', or that 'the rapidity of fire' of 'Asiatic Annie' (the most formidable of Herr Krupp's guns ranged against them) 'comes as great a shock of surprise to all as do my rare victories at "Pounce"'.* The only bombardment he described was a shell 'landing among our camp kettles and tearing to ribbons with the splinters a tunic of Patrick's [Shaw-Stewart] which was hanging on a tree'.[33]

Conditions for the Allied troops on the Gallipoli peninsula were appalling. Those soldiers not suffering from dysentery were likely to have jaundice, and many were afflicted by both. The air was thick with the stench of thousands of rotting corpses lying unburied in No Man's Land, the latrines were disgusting and the food little better. They lived on cans of heavily salted bully beef which the heat turned into repulsive greasy soup. Any fresh meat that did appear, if it was not instantly covered by swarms of flies bloated on the flesh of the dead, was infested with maggots within twenty-four hours. The troops derived most of their nutrition from condensed milk, pilfering extra supplies by 'accidentally' breaking the crates as they were being unloaded. The only fruits available were fly-ridden, overripe

---

*See note on p. 250.

figs sold at exorbitant prices by the Greek merchants who set up stalls on the beaches: no one was sorry when one stall holder was summarily shot after being caught signalling to the Turks.

The Royal Naval Division, devastated by casualties and sickness alike, was officially sidelined from front line duties to give it time to regroup. Five fresh divisions were on their way to reinforce Gallipoli and it was planned to invade Suvla (to the north of the existing bridgeheads) and advance across the peninsula to the 'Narrows' at the neck of the Dardanelles, with the aim of cutting off the Turks defending the south of the peninsula. Meanwhile, Major General Aylmer Hunter-Weston, in charge of the Helles area, was under orders from Hamilton to maintain an aggressive stance to convince the Turks that the main threat was from the south. The consequent pressure on front line troops resulted in the RND being held in reserve rather than allowed to re-train: Oc spent the week after his return sleeping in his boots, expecting any moment 'to be sent up to the firing line'.[34]

The haemorrhage of Hood officers was such that Freyberg, as the senior survivor, was catapulted into command of the battalion – their fourth commanding officer in three months. Oc replaced him as commander of D company, jumping two ranks from sub-lieutenant to lieutenant commander (the naval equivalent of major), a title, he explained to Violet with typical Asquithian disdain, 'of rather unattractive associations, with none of the romance or knight-liness that hangs about "Captain". My progress reminds me of a series of books which Beb and I read as boys called "The Three Midshipmen"; "The Three Lieutenants": "The Three Captains"; "The Three Admirals."' Violet was thrilled by her brother's 'rocket like career', telling him 'I long for you to be a Commodore', while Cynthia, the wife of a mere subaltern, was 'swollen with pride on your account and boasting of my relationship with you as I hear from all quarters that you are such a wonderful soldier and I observe you striding up the military ladder'.[35]

Oc's flippancy belied daunting new responsibilities. His company was not only seriously depleted by casualties but in dreadful physical condition and suffering from plummeting morale. The Hood's *esprit de corps* was not helped by an influx of men from two fresh battalions recently arrived from England, which were broken up and dispersed amongst the existing formations. The new arrivals understandably resented being separated from comrades with whom they had trained, while the veterans were suspicious of fresh-faced novices drafted in to replace battle-hardened officers now transferred to other companies. Oc complained to Violet that 'our delightful mess – Charles [Lister], William [Egerton], Cleg [Kelly], [Edward] Nelson and I – is broken up now by this influx of new officers . . . who give us our "Sir" to excess', spoiling the informal atmosphere in which all the officers had hitherto been on Christian name terms, regardless of rank. Oc was relieved to retain Patrick Shaw-Stewart as his second-in-command, but his other officer, 'a little frightened boy from one of the new battalions', was 'worse than useless'.[36] He soon lost both of them: Shaw-Stewart, once he had seen action, began 'to wonder whether this is any place for a civilized man',[37] and had no hang-ups about accepting a post as liaison officer at the French head-quarters, where he would be comfortable and well fed. Fortunately, both Patrick and the 'frightened boy' were replaced by four keen young sub-lieutenants.

On 12 July Hunter-Weston launched an ill-judged offensive which resulted in the virtual destruction of the 52nd Division, made up of Scottish territorial regiments. The following day two Marine and three Naval battalions, until now considered unfit for front-line duties, were thrown into the battle to recapture the trenches abandoned by the Scotsmen. The Royal Naval Division's historian Douglas Jerrold described how after almost forty-eight hours of continuous fighting amidst 'some of the worst scenes ever experienced on the battlefields of France or Mesopotamia . . . many hundreds of men lay dead or dying, where a burning sun had turned the bodies of the slain to a premature corruption, where there was no resting-place free from physical contamination, where the air, the surface of the ground, and the soil beneath the surface were alike poisonous, fetid, corrupt'.[38]

The Hood and the other Naval battalions held in reserve were sent to relieve the shattered remnants of the 52nd Division. Before they could begin to rebuild the defences, they had the appalling task of burying the dead. Oc characteristically spared his family a description of their experience, merely admitting in a letter to Violet to having 'fallen into indescribable lassitude' after 'five tiring but exciting nights in the most advanced trenches'.[39] However, in a note written after the War on his typewritten copy of Kelly's diary, he recalled that 'the Turks who had been killed on July 12 lay everywhere, unburied and half-buried, in these newly captured trenches.

The weather was sweltering, the stench overwhelming, and many of our officers and men were sick again and again. Reluctance to face this nauseating experience was so strong that during the afternoon there were three cases of self-inflicted wounds . . . the only cases I can remember in the Battalion.'[40]

Charles Lister wrote to his father that 'Oc has been extraordinarily dogged, and is practically responsible for all this corner, which will be known as Asquith triangle. He hadn't a wink of sleep all the four days.'[41] A few days later, when Lister and Freyberg were wounded by French shrapnel while trying to deal with a Turkish sniper, Oc described the prevailing chaos in a letter to Violet:

> When I came up, Freyberg was collapsed on the ground, calm and conscious but helpless, and thinking he must be done for: while Charles was careering about in the open in front of our trench, covered with blood . . . The congestion at the debouching point of the trench became a perfect nightmare: sandbags, bandoliers and water bottles being passed up to the barricades; Freyberg collapsed in the gangway, with a dead man beside him. Water and ammunition parties arriving from the supports: and then a man to extend the telephone – all at the junction of three trenches 3 ft wide.
>
> Then the officer who had brought up water from the supports was shot in the head, and died soon after in the gangway. By this time Freyberg had been moved in a blanket, and Charles had been persuaded to go to the rear for treatment. I was senior officer left in the firing-line – and second senior in the Battalion. We were warned to be prepared for a Turk counter-attack. Happily they did not come: it was most difficult to keep the men awake for this – their fifth – arduous night running. Next morning we were very glad to be relieved and to get back here to our Rest camp.[42]

The Royal Naval Division was now a pale shadow of the proud body of men inspected by the King six months earlier, barely able to muster 5,000 men compared to its initial strength of over 16,000. According to Jerrold, 'at the beginning of August, not 10 per cent would have been considered fit in France for duty in the quietest part of the line. In Gallipoli at this time all officers and men who could actually walk to the trenches were reckoned as fit.'[43]

There was also a real risk that the Division would be broken up: the Army had always resented its separate command structure, its confusing mix of army and naval ranks and its men being allowed beards; now the Royal Navy had no scruples about removing 300 stokers from its depleted ranks for service with the Fleet. Hamilton, who for all his deficiencies as a commander was a humane and compassionate man, gave his impression of the Naval troops in a letter to the Prime Minister dated 2 September:

> I went over ten days ago and saw some of the Naval Division who were out of the trenches, and had a long talk with old Paris who commands them. They are stout fellows and are sticking it out well, but they are very tired – whereas they used to invalid out 8 to 10 men a day, their sick rate now runs sometimes as high as 60 men a day. Simply the poor fellows are worn out and some of them are as weak as cats. I do hope Mr. Balfour is going to keep them fed up to strength, for there is a devilish fine spirit about this particular Division, and it would be ten million pities if they were allowed to peter out.
>
> Paris was horrified at the youth of some of the boys who had been sent out to him, and wanted to send them home. He found one of them crying in the trenches because he was so frightened. He was only 16 years of age and no doubt these Turks, great hefty fellows, are alarming neighbours when you are only separated from them by about 15 feet of mud. But I told him not to send them home but to keep them for light duties in camp, and doing messages, cooking etc. etc. I assured him they would grow up and have time to fill out into fine men before the war came to an end.[44]

The Hood was particularly badly affected by the removal of the stokers, losing 140 of its most seasoned veterans; nonetheless, Freyberg, who quickly recovered from his latest wounds, was determined to turn the battalion into an elite fighting force. Not everyone appreciated the young New Zealander's brash approach to his duties: Lieutenant Colonel Crauford-Stuart, who briefly commanded the battalion after the death of Quilter before being badly wounded himself, met the Asquiths in Scotland that summer and told Margot that Freyberg was 'pushing and egotistical' and 'not the least like a gentleman', having bragged about Violet having a crush on him.[45] Oc vigorously put his stepmother right about his friend:

> He is a 'gentleman', in every sense that has any importance to me, so far as I can judge, and I have seen a great deal more of him than Stuart has. I do not believe that he suggested to anyone that V. was in love with him: nor do I believe that he has ever fancied himself in love with her . . . He is

very young – 26 – and commands this Battalion with several officers – critical men, too – five to ten years older than himself. I have never heard one of them suggest they would prefer any other commanding officer. He has had no education: his love of adventure is his strongest trait: he has great energy, is very affectionate, knew every man in his company by name and knew a good deal more about most of them.[46]

Oc and Kelly (also now recovered from his wound) played a critical role in helping Freyberg to lay the foundations for giving the Hood what Jerrold described as 'a brilliant standard of efficiency'. In the process, they earned not just the respect of their men, but also their affection. In his notes to Kelly's diary, Oc noted how at Blandford Cleg paid for his entire platoon to visit a dentist and then bought them all sunglasses on Malta. When Oc took command of 'D' company he made sure he had the addresses of the next of kin of each member of his company, as well as conducting painstaking enquiries about the fate of those reported missing in the recent fighting, appreciating how important it was for their families to know. According to Oc's military biographer, Christopher Page, he 'was able to discover what had happened to thirty-nine men'.[47]

The other side of the coin was Oc's insistence that his platoon commanders keep their men up to the highest standard of tidiness, conducting regular checks of the state of their gear and haircuts. At the same time he did his best to ensure that they had fresh fish to eat – even if this was by the unecological means of exploding grenades underwater. He did not hesitate to appeal to Freyberg when the regimental quartermaster questioned his demands for rations: 'I do not care a fig for what Petty Officer Roberts says or for the QM's knowledge of the working classes, all I ask is that they should be supplied with what they actually do want in so far as their wants do not exceed the ration allowed.'[48]

Throughout these trying months the Hood officers relied on one another to keep up their spirits. Charles Lister's 'sense of humour is a great stand-by', Oc told Margot, and he delighted in recounting to Violet how 'Patrick has just received from the Horners an amusing hamper which includes a magnum of <u>complexion restorer</u>: he says he wishes it had been champagne instead as his complexion is half mottled amber and half hidden by his burnished beard'.[49] Cleg Kelly was a particular source of amusement. The huge, muscular and now bearded veteran oarsman presented so outlandish an appearance that on one occasion, as he waded ashore after a swim with Oc and Egerton, an alert sentry from the King's Own Scottish Borderers detained him on suspicion of being a German spy. His companions then mysteriously disappeared, leaving the naked former Olympic gold medallist volubly protesting his loyalty to King and country until one of the sentry's own regimental officers arrived and ordered the prisoner's release.

Oc and Cleg developed a close bond, frequently swimming together and enjoying their brief respites from the battle-scarred Gallipoli landscape on the island of Imbros, where they shared their love of nature and wildlife. 'I have grown fond of Cleg – laugh and all,' Oc wrote to Violet on 22 August.

> He is very vital and his readiness to challenge any and every statement leads to good fun arguments. <u>Freyberg</u> (with rather colonially over-enthusiastic sentiment): 'By God, T. died a very game death.' <u>Cleg</u> (immediately and furiously): 'Why?' Charles and I in fits of laughter. Cleg explains that T. was leading his platoon and doing no more than his duty when he was shot: so why go into superlatives about it. Also T. was insufferable when alive.[50]

Oc delighted in showing his friends the entertaining letters he received from his family (though not his father) in England. Freyberg recalled 'being enthralled and delighted by Asquith's constant flow of intimate letters from his devoted stepmother and brilliant sister Violet, all of which he shared with his friends and I often think with gratitude of their help. They did us more good than all the material comforts supplied by Her Majesty's Government.'[51]

Hankey, who saw Oc while on a fact-finding tour, wrote to the Prime Minister on 5 August that his son 'looked well, tremendously sunburnt and in good spirits'.[52] The following night British troops made their long-awaited landing at Suvla Bay, but instead of encountering light opposition as predicted, they were met with fierce rifle fire. Lieutenant General Stopford, the distinguished military historian in charge of the invasion, lost his nerve and failed to press inland, with the result that the operation was a dismal failure. Oc, who was already showing greater military insight than many of the generals cluttering up the higher echelons of the British Army, communicated his scepticism about the whole strategy to his father:

The Suvla fiasco was naturally a great disappointment; not that many of us were very optimistic about its chances. We – by which I mean the Hood Company commanders mess, with Charles as Turkish expert – have the dismal satisfaction of having always said that this campaign was being treated by England as one of Divisions when it should have been treated as one of Corps or Armies. I remember Charles' outburst of indignation when someone came in rubbing his hands with news from Lemnos that five divisions had arrived. It would be interesting to see Stopford's orders: but if we had got across, could we possibly have held the line both ways with the numbers at our disposal?'*[53]

As the heat of summer gave way to autumn, Oc described the climate to Violet 'as perfect now', telling her how he, Freyberg and Kelly enjoyed bathing at sunset off an old stone jetty at Sidi el Bahr against a background of 'pink mists along the coast of Asia, a lazy interchange of shells between the coasts and two destroyers and a trawler fussing up and down at the mouth of the straits'.[54] However, with the first chills of September came worries about how they would cope with winter on the peninsula, a prospect that, ill-equipped and weakened by sickness as they were, filled them with dread, as Oc made clear to his father:

Where we here are worse off than those in France is in never getting away to a house or even a tent because everywhere we may be shelled. Also we have no wood or corrugated iron to roof, wall, or floor our dug-outs with. We get on as best we can with waterproof sheets. Happily we have had little rain yet, and the Turks must have been badly off for guns and ammunition. With guns and ammunition on the German scale I think it would have been utterly impossible for us to have remained on the Peninsula. As it is dysentery is the chief trouble. Our men have been going sick at an alarming rate, and new drafts cannot keep pace with it. The whole corpus of a Battalion changes kaleidoscopically from month to month: but it is always wasting away, and one feels some unreality on talk of preparations for the winter months, snows in January etc, when a simple mathematical calculation seems to show that in a month or two one's Battalion will be wasted to nothing by sickness.

---

*Oc is referring to the plan to advance across the Dardanelles from Suvla and thus divide the Turkish forces defending the Gallipoli peninsula.

Oc had by now resigned himself to spending winter on Gallipoli and asked his father for 'porridge, chutney and pickles and tinned *café au lait* – Milk Maid brand it is called – and a light Etna with solid fuel such as Margot uses in her bedroom so that one could make a hot drink at night without the light of a fire'.[55] However, his criticisms of his Commander-in-Chief hit home, and Asquith forwarded this part of his son's letter on to Lloyd George: 'You will think I am a grouser, but this Ian Hamilton is the limit, and it is so obvious to all out here what a terrible mess and massacre he has made of the expedition from the start. I don't believe he has ever been in any of the front trenches, and I can honestly say that I have never seen any of his staff officers there.'[56]

The letter seems to have sealed Hamilton's fate. Even Margot was impressed by her stepson's damning indictment of her old friend, citing 'our boy' in a letter to Hankey in which she railed that 'the demoralisation out there is complete and Hamilton useless. For God's sake get someone to show a little action soon.'[57] In fact, the Prime Minister had already secured the backing of the Cabinet's Dardanelles Committee to recall Hamilton. That Asquith no longer confided in Margot about strategic decisions may be a result of the influence of Kitchener, who blamed much of the 'leakiness' of the Cabinet on ministers gossiping to their wives and other women friends. However, Margot's attempt to sway Government policy through Hankey is surely a reflection of just how much she felt her influence with her husband had slipped.

Even though Asquith considered Oc's opinions worth citing to Cabinet colleagues, he never replied to his letter. Unlike Raymond though, Oc does not seem to have resented his father not writing. However, he was upset when heard nothing from Margot. When she did finally write, his reply, dated 13 October and starkly addressed 'In trenches, Dardanelles', sardonically informed her that 'after four leaden months of silence it is a delight to hear again your silver accents'. He was being a bit unfair as she had written two months earlier, but nonetheless he clearly felt neglected as well as homesick:

I had almost decided that, if I survived the war, I would shake the dust of England and of all friends and relations, forgetful and inconstant, from my feet, and that I would spend a sunny, contemplative middle and old age among the orange groves of Paraguay where women are constant and devoted and industrious and men are few. Your delightful letter came just in time to save me from taking an immutable decision. Please write again often and wean me from the desire to forswear kith and kin. Your mention of Archerfield and of your delicious holiday in North Berwick already shakes me. It must be lovely there now in October, clean, frosty days with beech leaves turning: and it must be lovely at the Wharf too.

For once, Oc did not mince his words about the conditions, describing how there was

no shelter either in the trenches or rest camp except such as we can rig with waterproof sheets in our dug-outs – which become uninhabitable after rain which so far has been rare, thank goodness. We had two thunderstorms this week, and were draggled and miserable till after an hour or two of sunshine. Such – very few – of our men as have not been wounded or sick – have now been living in the open air and have not been under a roof or so much as a tent, or drunk a drop of beer or seen a town, or a woman, for six months. It is getting very cold, and if you hear of mufflers, mittens or jerseys being on offer by rich Americans we could find homes for them.[58]

By now the campaign had settled into stalemate. The main weapon available to British infantrymen to harass the Turks was a primitive elasticated catapult, which often proved more lethal to the thrower than the quarry: on one occasion Oc recommended Able Seaman George Ramsay for a medal after he saved his comrades from one of their own rebounding bombs by tearing out the fuse before it exploded. 'Turkish morale probably suffers more from our vocalists' parodies of Turkish melodies,' he dryly observed in a note to headquarters.[59] The main problem posed by the Turks themselves were 'some redoubtable snipers'. Oc described a duel with a particularly skilful sharpshooter, of whom they would catch an 'occasional glimpse through our periscopes of his tall forehead and dark moustache . . . and then a bullet would destroy the periscope'. Eventually they managed to shoot him by means of 'some very cunning loopholes'.[60] Oc's own efforts to deal with a suspected sniper caused him much ribbing from his comrades. During a night reconnaissance close to the Turkish lines he spotted a soldier apparently dozing in a slit trench, but not considering it gentlemanly to shoot a sleeping man, he stealthily crept up on him with the intention of taking him prisoner, finally grabbing him by the throat and putting a pistol to his head, only to discover that he was already dead.

It was around this time that Kelly was shocked to note his 'complete absence of feeling' after visiting one of his men who had been shot.[61] However, when it was a particular friend who was killed, the strong bonds that had grown up between them meant the loss affected them all the more. The popular Charles Lister's lingering death on a hospital ship after his third wound 'plunged all of us into the deepest grief', as Freyberg confessed in a letter to Violet. 'We have got extraordinarily fond of all the Old Hood's and as each one goes it hurts like nothing else.'[62]

Hamilton's replacement, Lieutenant General Sir Charles Munro, was from the start convinced that Gallipoli should be abandoned. But the commander of the Australian contingent, Lieutenant General Sir William Birdwood, the Royal Navy and a powerful clique in the Cabinet continued to oppose evacuation, and in early November Asquith sent Kitchener out to give his assessment of the situation. Afterwards, on 28 November, Oc made his own contribution to the debate, sending his father 'a cold unexaggerated account of the state of affairs here in so far as they have come under my eyes as a mere Company Commander'. He described British forces at Helles as utterly unprepared for winter, outlining a damning catalogue of deficiencies in their equipment, which included 'a solid pier at which it would be possible to disembark stores and men in all weathers', noting sarcastically that 'the British, who are I suppose the greatest pier-builders in the world' were obliged to land their supplies 'by courtesy of the French at their pier'. They lacked not only 'deep level wells to replace the shallow pits of liquid sewage which have been giving our men dysentery all through the summer', but even 'winter clothing for the troops', with only sixteen pairs of rubber boots 'per battalion' to cope with the trenches now knee deep in mud. There was a lack of corrugated iron for roofing, and tarpaulins had to be begged, borrowed or stolen to cover even the officers' mess, while the men had to make do with rigging shelters out of groundsheets. 'Drying arrangements. There are none. Washing arrangements. Our Battalion has a stove which boils less water than could be contained by two ordinary washing basins.'

Oc reported how when he visited Shaw-Stewart at the headquarters of the French contingent, 'the contrast was painful', their soldiers having well constructed shelters, 'stacks and stacks of firewood . . . excellent washing places: carpenters shops with steam-saws: all arranged with perfect orderliness and precision', and – the most bitter pill of all – their equipment was 'largely bought in England'. He concluded: 'If we do not have terrible wastage from rheums, pneumonias etc it will not be the fault of our generals.'[63]

It was this letter that reached 10 Downing Street on Christmas Eve, a disgraceful four weeks after it had been written. On 7 December the Cabinet had finally decided to pull out of Suvla and Anzac Bay, leaving Helles – as a sop to the Royal Navy – the sole bridgehead on the peninsula. The very same day Kelly, with almost uncanny prescience, noted in his diary rumours that Gallipoli was to be evacuated, with Freyberg hoping the Hood would conduct a 'glorious rearguard'. A few days later Oc, in a letter to Bongie, revealed he had heard 'under seal of secrecy' from Shaw-Stewart 'some interesting news – you will guess what'. At the same time he angrily lambasted as 'utterly irresponsible' a speech by Ribblesdale in the House of Lords in which he had said that it was an 'open secret' that Munro had recommended evacuation. He pointed out that 'secrecy and speed would be our only chance of avoiding heavy losses. R. and his fellow makers of sterile "chin music" (you will remember Franklin's phrase) could not do better if they were in the pay of the Boches.'[64]

Yet the following week Allied troops were pulled off Suvla and Anzac with a skill hitherto unmatched throughout the Gallipoli campaign. This left the Royal Naval Division and the rest of the garrison on Helles in a precarious position, buffeted by winter storms and not knowing whether they were to stay or not. As morale began to deteriorate, there were even recriminations between the Hood officers, with Kelly complaining on 20 December about 'one of our officers making an unnecessary display of alleged rheumatism – we have had several similar cases and the temper of the battalion is against letting another one slip through its fingers'.

On Christmas Eve the Turks mounted a heavy artillery bombardment and everyone expected a big attack the following day. When it did not materialize Freyberg and Kelly amused themselves by sniping at the unexploded shells littering No Man's Land. Cleg noted that Oc 'adopted a croaking attitude as to the silliness of it etc'. Having had no response from his father to his damning indictment of incompetence and neglect, he had lost even his sense of humour. However, it was that very day that Asquith received his letter. It seems to have been decisive, contradicting as it did much of what the military authorities were telling the Prime Minister. Five days later, when Freyberg received orders to instruct his men that they were going to be relieved, he suspected a cover for evacuation. As they prepared to leave, the ever-cheerful Kelly recorded 'a thrilling feeling of both armies being on the watch like cats for indications of the other's movements'.[65]

Oc, as he later made clear to his father, believed that leaving evacuation so late was 'a wicked gamble on the weather'.[66] The order for withdrawal did not come until 8 January, with the Hood, as Freyberg had hoped, acting as the rearguard. When the Battalion's turn came to make its way to the sunken ship from which they were to be picked up by a destroyer, it was Oc's company which covered their retreat; then, as the rest of D company filed off, Oc stayed behind with a handful of men whom he made run up and down the trench to deceive the Turks into believing it was fully manned, before they themselves made good their escape, the last British soldiers to leave the ill-fated peninsula. At the beginning of the Gallipoli campaign, Quilter had refused to let Oc join Freyberg on his celebrated swim. At its conclusion, no one questioned the Prime Minister's son risking his life.

The Royal Naval Division was now handed back to the Royal Navy, which assigned them to garrisoning the islands, sending the Hood to Lemnos. It was announced that fifteen percent of officers were to be granted home leave in England, but no mention was made of the other ranks. The Hood officers reacted with indignation to what they saw as the snub to those who had shared the dangers and endured even greater discomforts, refusing any leave themselves unless it was granted to their men on the same terms. No one was more angry than Oc, whose admiration for those under his command was unbounded: 'Our men in the Hood have been wonderfully cheerful and brave – wet through sometimes for 3 days on end and no fires or hot food: mud, and daily casualties from shells,' he had written to Margot in his last letter from Gallipoli, recounting how 'one of my men bandaged three others before he fainted: he had not mentioned that he had been badly wounded in the thigh'.[67] Now, as Freyberg organized a meeting of battalion commanders to back the Hood officers' demand, Oc angrily appealed to his father, informing him that his men had not seen families since the previous Christmas and that Paris had failed to fight for his Division, and expressing 'contempt for our divisional staff'.[68]

Asquith asked Margot to send his son's letter on to Balfour. She did not hesitate to make her own appeal personal: 'Henry adores this boy and is <u>longing</u> like a mother to see him . . . He is the joy of our hearts. General Paris, his commander is not a clever or wise man.'[69] Once again, Oc's influence seems to have been decisive, for soon afterwards the military authorities caved in and allowed the men leave on the same basis as their officers.

On 21 February Oc, Freyberg and Kelly, all of whom were among those who had spent the most time on Gallipoli, heard they had been selected for home leave. Five days later, along with Shaw-Stewart, they boarded HMT *Olympic* (the sister ship of the *Titanic*), which had just disembarked 10,000 typically belated reinforcements for the Royal Naval Division. On board, Kelly took delivery of three dozen bottles of champagne he had originally ordered for Christmas, and the four friends celebrated in style as they set sail for Marseilles.

18

'The awful anxieties of Downing Street'

━━━━━━━◆━━━━━━━

IN FEBRUARY 1916 Frances Stevenson, Lloyd George's secretary and mistress, wrote in her diary 'Mrs A[squith] herself has been heard to declare that "Nothing but God Almighty will drive Herbert out of Downing Street".'[1] The comment was not actually made by Margot, who of course never called her husband 'Herbert', but was based on a remark made to her by George Moore (a friend of Sir John French), who, just after the political crisis that led to the formation of the coalition Government in May 1915, had assured her that Northcliffe would never succeed in toppling her husband.[2] Margot rashly repeated the prophecy to all and sundry, with the result that it was soon thought to be her own. Her enemies eagerly seized on it as yet another example of the Asquiths' hubris.

Margot's relations with Lloyd George had been steadily going downhill again since she had warned him not to allow Northcliffe to 'run' him against her husband. Far from heeding her advice, he had been seeing a great deal of the hated Press lord, and she believed, with some justification, that the two men were now working hand in glove. The Minister of Munitions was well aware of what Margot was saying about him behind his back. Although most senior Liberals shared her distrust of Lloyd George, they, like Asquith himself, appreciated his contribution to the war effort, and they blamed her for widening the chasm opening up between the Prime Minister and his most powerful lieutenant. In August 1915 Lord

Reading (formerly Sir Rufus Isaacs) and Walter Runciman* persuaded her to invite Lloyd George to lunch, insisting that 'he felt
deeply aggrieved that I should have thought him capable of intrigue
against his Prime Minister'. Judging by Margot's account the gesture
did little good:

> As I had written before and he [Lloyd George] had taken no notice, I
> added to my invitation that I should not discuss the past with him. He
> arrived and hung on to Puffin's shoulders: he seemed hearty and in good
> form but never really looked at me or spoke except to the company at
> lunch – I was much amused. Directly after lunch Violet made him go to
> see her which relieved him and incidentally was a relief to me – I didn't
> want to make him lose his temper and I didn't want him to think he had
> convinced me. He hates a breath of criticism, like all vain people.[3]

By now even Bonar Law was warning the Prime Minister about
secret conclaves between Lloyd George and the Tory leader's own
two chief troublemakers, Curzon and Carson. Asquith, however,
remained confident that he could handle his awkward but useful colleague, rather as a skilful circus ringmaster persuades a truculent
tiger to jump through a hoop: 'I've got him tight now – he'll do anything I like for the time,' he said to Margot after an emotional
meeting between the two men in September 1915.[4] Margot was less
sanguine about the strength of her husband's position: 'It is only a
question of time now – the Government will break,'[5] she wrote in
her journal in October.

Any fair assessment of Asquith as a war leader must conclude that,
for all the mistakes that are a feature of any wartime administration, it
was his Government which laid the foundations for the eventual
victory, whether in terms of army manpower, munitions production
or the selection of the most effective Commander-in-Chief and
Quartermaster General – Haig and Cowans. The Lloyd George
Government which followed, while taking the credit for winning the
war, probably prolonged the conflict by at least a year, and as we shall
see, very nearly lost it altogether. The main accusation that can be lev-
elled against Asquith was his slowness to act. However, what his
enemies caricatured as an attitude of 'Wait and See' was to Asquith
himself – as he once explained to Sylvia – a matter of 'don't strike

---

*Respectively Lord Chief Justice and President of the Board of Trade.

before the hour'.[6] He was a supremely practical, tactical politician who always liked to examine all the options, as well as ensure the maximum of agreement, before embarking on any course of action. The way he tackled conscription was typical of this approach: although he disliked the idea of compelling men to fight, he was ready to give way on the issue if the army proved unable to recruit sufficient volunteers. His Achilles heel – and ultimately the reason for his downfall – was his failure fully to explain the difficulties that must be overcome, to prepare the public for a long war and rally them behind himself, and, above all, to appreciate the damage done by a hostile Press both to his own reputation and to public morale.

Margot was as powerless as the Prime Minister's colleagues to take a firmer lead with public opinion. This did not stop other people trying to influence him through her. Stamfordham, George V's Private Secretary, sent for her in October 1915: 'He opened by saying how devoted to Henry the King was and how miserable to think his Cabinet might be wrecked by foolish wild men and went on by saying Henry had only to lift his little finger and tell the country how things were going, and it would stifle all restlessness, that he wasn't prominent enough and people wanted to hear what he had got to say.'[7]

Yet, to Margot's frustration, Asquith stubbornly continued to insist there was 'no danger in any press campaign',[8] and saw no reason to alter his usual practice of treating most newspapers and journalists with contempt. Cys later quoted Boswell's *Life of Johnson* to illustrate his father's attitude towards what he euphemistically called 'his noisier critics': 'I never wrestle with a chimney sweep.'[9] Margot was also increasingly worried about any weakening of support for her husband from his Tory colleagues. Curzon, as one of the principal supporters of conscription, had always been difficult, but she had doubts too about some of the others (even when they were personal friends), wondering 'if Arthur Balfour and Lansdowne and Walter [Long] will really be dragged at the heels of two such curs as Lloyd George and Winston – they will be <u>mad</u> if they are.'[10] Although she had been close to Balfour since her teens, she regarded him as untrustworthy, and now she believed him to be 'jealous politically of Henry'. As early as March 1915 she warned Lloyd George (then still in her good books) that 'Arthur is really au fond <u>hostile</u> – <u>very</u> hostile. You and Winston don't know AJB as well as I do: that cool grace, easy mind and intellectual courtesy takes the eye off like the three card trick – he is a bitter party opponent.'[11]

By the autumn of 1915, with Lloyd George now rivalling Northcliffe as Margot's arch-villain, she felt Balfour's support for her husband to be crucial. Hesitating to make a direct appeal to her old friend, she sought the aid of Hankey, one of the few men trusted and respected by all, entreating him to use his influence to persuade the former Tory leader to support Asquith on the conscription issue. 'Does Arthur Balfour realise what is happening? It is clear as day that Lloyd George, Curzon and Winston are going to try and wreck the Government.'[12]

On this occasion, Margot underestimated the strength of the Prime Minister's political position: Churchill's resignation in November caused scarcely a ripple and whatever Asquith's problems with the Press, he still retained the support of most of the Cabinet. The most immediate threat was not his colleagues or the newspapers, but his own health: the strain of having to co-ordinate the nation's military and industrial resources had taken its toll. On 18 October, three days after Margot's letter to Hankey, he collapsed in the middle of a Cabinet meeting. Margot was called and found her husband lying on his bed under the counterpane with the blinds down and windows shut, suffering from a high temperature and severe headache. After sleeping most of the rest of the day, he came into her room at 1 a.m. and told her 'I feel very ill and have come to the reluctant conclusion that I must give up.' She felt 'the sky had fallen'. Fearing the worst, she blamed the Northcliffe Press, telephoning the Lord Chancellor, Lord Buckmaster, and telling him to lobby Simon, the Home Secretary, to 'make a case for suspending The Times and Daily Mail – I said they were all going to kill Henry'.[13] Of course, the Prime Minister himself was the main obstacle to drastic curbs on the Press, for which several ministers and indeed the King were pressing. Fortunately, the admirable Dr Parkinson assured Margot that her husband was simply suffering from over-exhaustion and prescribed starvation and sleep. After a few days' rest he was able to resume his duties.

It was just as well: in November, when Kitchener was despatched to report on the Dardanelles, Asquith once again took over the War Office on a temporary basis and was shocked to discover the administrative chaos he had to clear up: 'no man was ever so unlike his reputation – muddle-headed, secretive, even irresolute', he told Margot.[14]

The first big test of Cabinet unity came in December 1915, not from Lloyd George or the Tories, but from a quartet of Asquith loyalists –

Grey, McKenna, Runciman and Simon – who continued to hold out against any form of conscription, even after the Prime Minister himself had backed a compromise deal (suggested by Hankey) to conscript unmarried men. Ultimately, with a shrewd mixture of cajolery and appeals to their loyalty, Asquith managed to keep all but Simon on board. Whatever her criticisms of his political tactics, Margot marvelled at the way her husband was able to maintain his composure and good humour throughout the crisis: 'Nothing rattles Henry,' she wrote admiringly in her journal. 'Nothing changes the sweetness and perfection of his nature. He never hardens up or scratches or even retaliates in an ugly way.'[15]

Margot played her own part in the drama, shamelessly exploiting Asquith's renewed dalliance with Pamela McKenna who, having rather faded into the background since her 'bachelor days' as Pamela Jekyll, was now running Sylvia a close second as a correspondent and favoured member of the Prime Ministerial 'harem'. Cynthia heard how 'Margot had written to Pamela, asking her to use her influence with Reggie [McKenna] as the P.M.'s friend'.[16] When the crisis was over, Margot ordered three green cigarette cases to give to Reading, Hankey and Montagu to thank them for their part in its resolution, inscribing each to 'a real friend from Margot Asquith in memory of the last week of 1915'.[17] The gesture helps to explain the affection she inspired despite her frequent lack of tact and sensitivity.

Violet's marriage to Bongie, which eventually took place on 30 November 1915, should have heralded better relations with her volatile stepmother. But on the day of the wedding Margot wrote to the bride, confessing:

> I have often been clumsy and tactless and un-understanding, but darling you will forgive all this now and remember and believe that I have never failed you nor will I ever fail you (should you want me) in times of stress, but I daresay (poor darling!) – and I also hope – you will want no one but only Bongie. If I ever see an unimaginative female daring to cast even a shadow between you and Bongie, I will kill her with my own hand. You shan't have a moment's depression or neglect if I can prevent it.

It is a bizarre letter, even by Margot's standards. A wedding day is hardly the moment to raise the possibility of infidelity, and in any case Bongie was not likely to stray: given Violet's own tortured pre-marital love life, any 'shadows' were likely to be cast by her. Of course, Margot's main concern was that Bongie would not prove a sufficiently powerful magnet to draw Violet away from Asquith. And as Margot feared, far from marriage weakening the bonds between father and daughter, it was the occasion for renewing their vows to one another. Asquith wrote to Violet: 'we have never failed one another: thank God!' and went on: 'You have always understood me, and I believe I have always understood you. It has been a perfect relationship . . . Do not ever let us break or even suspend the chain which has always bound us together. Let us maintain the close intim-acy – as it always was and always ought to be.'

Violet's answer was in its way as extraordinary as Margot's letter to her. She assured her father 'you have always meant <u>everything</u> to me – since I can remember – and are still the <u>closest</u>, the most passion-ately loved of all human beings to me'.[18] It was a degree of filial affec-tion that her stepmother continued to resent bitterly: 'I'm a fool to mind and wicked too,' she wrote in her journal in January 1916, 'but she gets on my nerves to <u>such</u> a pitch that when she is away on her holidays I feel a different being!'[19]

Asquith stayed in London over New Year, to work on the details of the new conscription measures, while Margot – exhausted by 'the awful anxieties of Downing Street' – took her children and Violet and Cys to spend Christmas with Lucy at Easton Grey. In the New Year it was announced that Margot's niece, Kakoo, was engaged to the Marquess of Granby, the eldest son and heir of the Duke of Rutland and the brother of Diana Manners. Margot was too immersed in her own problems to appreciate the effect of the news on Cys, whose unrequited love for Kakoo had so blighted his early manhood. She suspected nothing when he spent much of the New Year period at Easton Grey rectory, and was flabbergasted when a few days later Cys wrote to inform her that he was engaged to the rector's youngest daughter, Mary Beresford.*

Margot considered Mary 'a rubbishy little animal quite without vice – full of vanity and gossip, without occupation or interest of any kind', and believed her to be dominated by her blind father, who made her read to him and act as his guide on his rounds of the parish.

---

*Mary's eldest sister, Dorothy – 'now an iron clad old maid', according to Margot – had been a semi-approved member of Asquith's 'harem' some years earlier.

Cys's letter, wrote Margot in her journal, 'shattered me with grief', but her reaction had more to do with her own overwrought state of mind than any rational concern for his welfare. Cys 'was my own little boy' and her lack of influence over him sparked another bout of regrets and confused feelings about her role as a stepmother. She had always had a stormy relationship with Violet and had never been close to either Raymond or Beb, but she longed for Helen's other two sons to return her intense love for them, confessing: 'How I wish Oc and Cys had been my own children – how different my life would have been with these props.'[20]

This was hardly the ideal frame of mind in which to offer Cys sensible guidance, especially if, as Margot believed, he had agreed to marry Mary because he was sorry for her. Instead she wrote him a hysterical letter full of grouses about the cold-bloodedness of the Asquith family, berating him for being 'bored' by her. Though Cys was deeply hurt by this tirade, he did not rise to the bait but assured her that he loved her 'intensely' and (rather futilely) tried to rebut her criticisms of his family:

> It's rather unfair to lump all 'Asquiths' together and condemn them as frigid, heartless and unimpulsive – were any two people more different than Oc and Raymond? Beb is an oddity who falls within no class – Violet and Father are not very alike. What is true of all of them to my mind, is a certain reserve about emotion, which is not at all the same thing as lack of heart – they are as ashamed of naked emotions as of their naked bodies. That's ultimately a question of temperament.

Cys ended by assuring Margot that whether or not he had expressed it, he was completely devoted to her. Margot admitted his letter 'touched me to the quick', yet she continued to bludgeon him into breaking off the engagement, even refusing to allow him to bring Mary home to 10 Downing Street, thus forcing him to meet her at Violet's house.[21] This sparked yet another spat with Violet who, although she too disapproved of the proposed match, was appalled at her stepmother's tactless handling of her younger brother. Asquith sensibly suggested a long engagement while encouraging Cys to see as much of his fiancée as possible, in the belief that 'he was pretty sure to chuck her'. In the end, his low-key approach worked and eventually Cys was coaxed into admitting that he had been emotionally blackmailed by Mary's father, who had accused him of 'compromising' his daughter and insisted he either marry her or say 'goodbye'. Once it became clear that Cys was motivated by compassion and a misguided sense of honour, he was persuaded to break off the engagement. Violet and Bongie then accompanied him to Easton Grey where he explained his decision to Mary, while his sister, like some avenging guardian angel, bearded the errant rector.

Mary, who was genuinely in love with Cys, apparently accepted the situation with amazingly good grace. According to Margot, Violet 'cried without ceasing most of the day at Mary's wonderful goodness and self-less behaviour'. Bongie cast his stepmother-in-law as 'the villain of the piece', writing her a letter of 'the greatest severity – it might almost have been written by Violet'. Margot was '<u>furious</u>', considering that 'it was practically through me minding so much that Cys's engagement was broken off. Everyone was alright except me.'

Asquith, meanwhile, had quite enough on his plate without having to mediate in yet another squabble between his wife and children. In Margot's words, he was by now '<u>tired</u> and <u>bored</u> by the whole thing'.[22]

*

At 9 a.m. on 9 January 1916, the day after Raymond returned to his battalion, his brigadier, John Ponsonby, burst into his room to press him to act as 'Prisoner's Friend' – or defence counsel – to Captain Sir Iain Colquhoun of Luss of the Scots Guards, who was being court-martialled with a fellow officer for 'allowing their men to fraternise with the Germans on Christmas Day'. After the celebrated truce in 1914 when men from the British and German armies spontaneously emerged from their trenches to sing carols and even play football together in No Man's Land, the Army High Command had resolved to make an example of any officer permitting even a semblance of camaraderie with the hated Hun. However, in picking on Colquhoun, a courageous, popular and well-connected Scottish baronet who had recently married Margot's niece, Dinah Tennant, his accusers risked antagonizing the powerful Guards' Division: it was up to Raymond to prevent one of their own being punished for allowing a tiny element of old-fashioned chivalry in a thoroughly unchivalrous war.

Raymond was summoned to meet Major General Fielding, the Guards' new commanding officer, ostensibly to discuss the Colquhoun case, but really to be shown a letter from GHQ, suggesting that he could be usefully employed on intelligence work. Raymond suspected that Katharine was behind the move, since she had made him promise to accept a staff job if one were offered. It seems that the Prime Minister, under intense pressure from his daughter-in-law (who was now expecting her third child), had tipped the wink to Haig to find a place for his son on the staff.[23]

As a result of Raymond's role in the Colquhoun case, his pleading to return to his battalion for its remaining forty-eight hours in the trenches was ignored and he was ordered to report to GHQ immediately. This laid him open, as he admitted to Diana, to the cynical jibes of his fellow Guards officers, since they were unlikely to believe that he had no advance knowledge of, still less had opposed, being given a staff post. Instead, they would imagine that he had spent his leave seeking some means to evade the spring offensive. As a result, he would have to attempt to rejoin his regiment in time for the next battle. If he were killed, he remarked sardonically, it would solve a number of pressing worries. He was beginning to wonder whether his only purpose was to finish up as a corpse. At least being wrapped in a shroud would give him public recognition.

In the meantime, Raymond threw himself into a ferocious battle with the Court Martial on behalf of Colquhoun, who soon won his admiration for the vigour and nerve with which he faced his accusers. Raymond told Diana that he gave his client full marks for his performance, delighting in his insolence, aplomb, courage and elegant virility.[24] The Court Martial apparently failed to share Raymond's appreciation for the haughty disdain of the young Scottish nobleman in the dock (and perhaps noticed the same qualities in his counsel), and Colquhoun was convicted. Thanks to Raymond's efforts, though, he escaped with a reprimand, went on to win the Military Cross for valour and was one of a handful of Guards' officers to survive the Great War from beginning to end.

After the drama of the Court Martial, Raymond resigned himself to being part-civilian, part-soldier at Haig's headquarters in St Omer, as he fumbled with a mass of paperwork, indexed out-of-date documents and became totally befuddled by the boredom endemic to office life. Fortunately, his new boss, Brigadier Charteris, was very friendly, as was his mentor, Lord Onslow, whom – he told Katharine

– he remembered dimly from Oxford days. Another Balliol man, Philip Sassoon, was well ensconced and already offering his friends battalions and brigades with Oriental generosity, while Maurice Baring was nearby at the headquarters of the Flying Corps, and there was even the chance of a reasonable game of bridge at the junior officers' mess.[25]

Raymond agreed to give the job three months, but he was soon complaining to Katharine that the moss was starting to grow on his mind and body, which would soon be encrusted with barnacles. He compared his pencil moving over the paper to a cab horse climbing a steep hill. Marooned in what he saw as a backwater, he could be forgiven a twinge of jealousy for his shell-shocked younger brother when he recognized him as the author of an anonymous poem about a ruined Flemish church published in the *Spectator*, and quipped that Beb must be making a fortune during his rest cure.[26]

The publication by Sidgwick & Jackson in December 1915 of a slim volume entitled *The Volunteer and Other Poems* by Herbert Asquith proved a runaway success. Beb himself, still convalescent at Stanway, was unable to enjoy his literary triumph, but Cynthia thoroughly relished basking in her husband's reflected glory, doing her best to boost sales by ordering copies at bookshops all over the West End. On New Year's Eve she proudly recorded buying the last copy at Hatchards in Piccadilly, where the shop assistant told her 'they had sold two lots of them yesterday – each lot would be about two dozen – so that's good for one bookshop. At Sotherans they were sold out and at Bains, to my glee, I saw them "titty up" in the window.'[27] Some of the book's success was due to many people assuming that the author was the Prime Minister himself. But the poems struck a genuine chord with a public hungry to find some element of redemption in the carnage. The book attracted enthusiastic reviews and fervent praise from Beb's friends and family: Asquith told Cynthia that he thought '*The Volunteer* was incomparably the best war poem', while Balfour confessed 'I like them all, but the first [*The Volunteer*] most';[28] even the supposedly indifferent Raymond was spotted in a bookshop surreptitiously purchasing the last volume in stock.

Margot received her copy of Beb's poems at Easton Grey, and soon convinced herself that she alone among the family had always appreciated her stepson's talents as a poet, noting in her journal: 'I think <u>very</u> highly of them. The first lines I ever saw of his in Violet's album I admired tremendously: none of the rest of the family admired them tho' Violet liked them – Elizabeth was a baby and I don't know if Henry ever saw them.'[29] Margot's obvious pleasure in the book's success helped to heal the rift with Cynthia after the row over Beb's supposed drunkenness. When Cynthia heard that the *Spectator* editor, John St Loe Strachey, thought 'Beb better than Rupert Brooke', she persuaded Margot to invite the celebrated journalist to lunch at 10 Downing Street, where 'I sat next to him feeling like a sort of Mrs. H. G. Wells – very much Beb's wife. <u>He raved about the poems</u>.'[30]

A more critical note was struck by D. H. Lawrence in a letter to Cynthia:

> At any rate he [Beb] is not a deader, like Rupert Brooke: one can smell death in Rupert . . . I think Herbert Asquith is a poet – which is after all the most valuable thing on earth. But he is not writing <u>himself</u> at all here – not his own realities. Most of this is *vieux jeux*. Still it is the writing of a poet, thank God – only let him burst through the dead old self that is on him like a snake, come out his fresh real self: and he is a poet and a leader. But it needs the death of the old world in him, and the inception of the new – not Ares, not Aphrodite – these two are old hat, and not <u>real</u> in us (neither him nor you nor me). No gods but truth – that's the motto. I hope we shall be friends, one day – he and I – fighting together another kind of fight: the fight of that which is to come, not the fight of that which is passing away.
>
> When are we going to have a shot at preparing this nation for peace?[31]

Beb, like most of his countrymen, was not yet ready for peace: he still had something to prove. Lawrence's criticism that he was 'not writing <u>himself</u>' misses the point: Beb was regretting the passing of a pastoral idyll bleeding to death on the killing fields of Western Europe. The last two verses of *The Broken Spire*, the poem spotted by Raymond in the *Spectator*, encapsulate his feelings of anguish:

> On pavements by the kneeling herdsmen worn
> The drifting fleeces of the shells are rolled:
> Above the Saints a village Christ forlorn,
> Wounded again, looks down upon his fold.

> And silence follows fast: no evening peace,
> But leaden stillness, when the thunder wanes,
> Haunting the slender branches of the trees,
> And settling low upon the listless plains.[32]

The acclaim which greeted the poems was profoundly therapeutic to Beb, acting as a catalyst for a marked improvement in his mental and physical well-being. After his collapse at Downing Street, he had been kept quiet at Stanway, away from any possible stress. Although he still could not face joining the Charteris family for their Christmas dinner, his mother-in-law, Mary Wemyss, reported to Balfour that 'Beb seems better and goes out for little walks and he and Hugo [Wemyss] play chess'.[33] He continued to write poetry and Cynthia was delighted when the *Sunday Pictorial* commissioned a new poem for its New Year edition for £50. On 5 January he took up Dr Halliwell's suggestion that he 'practise his "town" head in Cheltenham with a view to going to London, so I motored him there and made him walk up the promenade'.[34] A fortnight later the couple took the train up to London together, staying with Aubrey and Mary Herbert in Bruton Street, where Violet (in the throes of moving into her new marital home in Dorset Street) came to see her brother.

Beb did not feel up to accompanying Cynthia to Dublin, where she had been invited by Basil Blackwood to spend ten days at Viceregal Lodge. 'I decided to harden my heart, leave him in Mary's charge and go over for the jaunt myself. Rather flippant conduct I fear,' was her half-guilty, half-relieved diary comment. When Basil was in London a couple of months earlier, with Beb safely tucked up at Stanway, she had been free to indulge in 'an orgy of dentistry',* admitting in her diary, 'I get fonder and fonder of him [Blackwood], and <u>love</u> being with him.'[35] The Viceroy's house party in Dublin included Augustine Birrell, the Irish Secretary (a great favourite with Cynthia), as well as the Montagus and Goonie Churchill. The latter teased Cynthia about Basil 'being madly in love' with her. Cynthia herself, if not really 'in love', thrived on the attention, believing with characteristic vanity that 'the mere vicinity of Basil is more effective than all the cosmetics in the world'. There was, however, little prospect of an affair, at least yet: whatever his feelings, Basil was decidedly proper and Cynthia, recently discussing 'lovers' with a woman

---

*Coterie speak for flirtation.

friend and 'whether it was the fact, or the reputation' they liked, had confessed: 'it was testimonials I wanted'.[36]

Meanwhile Beb had by now recovered enough to take up an invitation to dinner on 18 February from Sir Ian Hamilton and his wife who, apparently bearing no ill will to the Asquiths over his removal from the Gallipoli command, were both enthusiastic admirers of Beb's poems. A fellow guest, Mrs Flora Guest (the American mother of Oc's former comrade-in-arms Johnny Dodge), even 'offered to come and rub Beb's spine with olive oil' – presumably to treat his 'spinal neuritis'.[37] Cynthia does not record whether the offer was taken up.

It was not until 1 March that Margot heard that Oc was coming home on leave. Three days later she was at Walmer Castle with Elizabeth when she received a message that her stepson was expected for lunch at Downing Street and that Asquith would bring him to see them that evening. Her mood of despondency lifted instantly as she enthused about the returning soldier's qualities: 'Oc is so wonderful – the greatest and best friend I have in the world, so much the best regulated of Henry's children and with far the Finest character . . . I can't imagine a greater joy than for me to have his protecting love just now.' He and his father arrived at 7.30 p.m.: 'I heard his jolly voice shout "Margot!" as he tore his coat off in the Walmer passage and we were in each other arms. He took me on his knee in Elizabeth's bedroom as if I were a little girl and put his arms round me and thoroughly coozled me. Henry and I could not speak for joy – I spent 2 hours in his bedroom on Sunday 5th and told him all my sorrows and all the news and he was thrilled.'[38]

Suddenly Margot had distractions aplenty. When the Asquiths returned to London she was introduced to Kelly and Freyberg, making instant friends of both and holding a large dinner party at 10 Downing Street in honour of them and Oc. For Kelly, it was his first chance to perform in England a piano transcription of his *Elegy to Rupert Brooke* for harp and strings, composed the previous summer in Egypt while he was convalescing from his wound. The theme had come to him quite suddenly while witnessing the poet's torchlit obsequies on Skyros, and he was justifiably proud of what was to become his most frequently performed composition. After dinner, while Asquith and the less musical guests retired for bridge, Kelly entertained the others on the piano, later describing in his journal how

> The Prime Minister, whose two sole hatreds – so Oc told me afterwards – are music and dogs, paid a few amused visits to our neighbouring room during dummy hands, and I heard stage whispers to Violet Bonham Carter, such as 'Is this really good?' On his last visit I was in the middle of my *Elegy* and I had just an impression of a slight rebuff administered by Mrs Bonham Carter, who, as a great friend of Rupert, was keenly inter-ested – at all events whispers ceased and there was complete silence for the remainder of the piece.'[39]

The following Friday, Violet arranged a small concert party at her home, Dorset House in Portman Square, for a quartet made up of the Hungarian string players, the sisters Jelly and Adila d'Arányi (great-nieces of the legendary violinist Joachim), and a pair of tal-ented amateurs: Adila's Greco-American husband, Alexandre Fachiri, and Hugh Godley, who had been a contemporary of Kelly's at Balliol. Kelly knew the d'Arányis well and had performed with Jelly at concerts before the War, and the evening was an ideal oppor-tunity for Jelly to premiere the violin sonata he had composed for her at Gallipoli after completing his *Elegy*. Bongie and Oc, he noted sardonically, rounded off the entertainment with a rendition of *Green Grow the Rushes, Oh!*.[40]

Over the next few weeks Kelly was much in demand in London society as he was asked to perform his *Elegy* almost nightly. He still managed to see a great deal of the Asquiths, and spent part of the fateful Easter weekend at the Wharf, where, in blissful ignorance of the Nationalist revolt taking place in Dublin, he accompanied Viola Parsons in songs that included some of his own.

Meanwhile, the fate of the Royal Naval Division hung in the balance as argument raged between the Admiralty and the War Office as to whether it should be disbanded. Oc and his comrades made full use of their leave to lobby hard for its retention, and while they were in England it was decided to keep the RND, but to place it under direct Army command and send it to France. A fortnight later Kelly heard from Freyberg that a second Hood battalion was to be formed, which Oc, with the temporary rank of Commander, was to lead, with Cleg as his number two. They were instructed to leave for Marseilles on 5 May to rejoin their comrades in the

Eastern Mediterranean before accompanying the men to the Western Front.

The three RND officers spent their final evening in London at a *soirée* given by the leading society beauty, Irene Lawley.* Cynthia, who dropped in on the party after the theatre, noted caustically that 'led by Kelly, several of them were making an infernal noise joke-singing round the piano'.[41] The following morning Margot accompanied Oc and his two comrades to Charing Cross station, giving each man a large bottle of *eau de cologne*. A genuinely touched Kelly wrote in his diary: 'I felt she was a dear hearted soul when she embraced all three of us just as the train was leaving.'[42] He remembered that he had left his tennis racquet at the Wharf and asked her to look after it for him. He was never to reclaim it.

Ironically, while Margot was entertaining Oc and his fellow Gallipoli veterans an article appeared in the *Globe* alleging that she had been providing 'dainties and comestibles' to German officers imprisoned at Donnington Hall – a variation on the tennis party story that had appeared the previous year in the *London Mail*. One version even claimed that she had concealed military secrets inside her food parcels. For Margot it provided an opportunity to hit back at her tormentors in the Press and nail the 'insolent lies spread and generally believed by the sort of asses this war has turned up like sands in the sea!'. Vowing that '<u>no-one</u> shall ever lie about me', she once again instructed Sir Charles Russell to sue for libel.[43] This time she had to make an appearance in the witness box; but it proved worthwhile, for she secured £1,000 in damages.

Margot's legal victory for the time being frightened off the Press from publishing blatant falsehoods, but it did nothing to halt the 'violent and hideous letters of abuse' that she received daily.[44] Amid what Asquith dubbed 'loathsome agitation about the aliens' in the Press[45] and riots in the East End of London directed against people of East European origin, branded as potential spies or saboteurs, Margot, with her well-known admiration for German culture and her many German friends, was specially vulnerable to accusations of being 'pro-German'. She blamed the War on the Kaiser and his generals and pointedly refused to join in the blanket condemnation of the German nation as a whole. Recalling her days in Dresden, she remembered them as 'more like the Scotch than any other people – a kindly, comfy,

---

*Only child of the 3rd Baron Wenlock.

over-eaten, material race with great intellectual temperament for
books and music – hardly any spirituality and very honest'.[46] With fantastic rumours circulating about enemy sympathizers at the heart of
Government, this was not a popular view among newspaper readers
encouraged to believe they were fighting a race of baby-eating savages.

The Asquiths were particularly disgusted when their own friends
were targeted. In March 1915, when a young Tory MP had publicly
questioned the loyalty of the Lancashire-born industrialist, Sir Alfred
Mond,* Margot indignantly complained to Balfour: 'I never thought
I should live to hear anything so vulgar and <u>terrible</u> as young Ormsby
Gore's speech yesterday! To hear an ugly unpopular man like Mond
called a Jew and German by an Englishman of breeding made me
shiver. He apologized, of course, but alas! no apology screens the
nature that can say that kind of thing of a kindly man like Mond.'[47]
Three months later Asquith recounted to Sylvia the travails of
another friend of German extraction: 'poor thing, she and her
husband are assailed by venomous, anonymous letters, and threatened with death should a Zeppelin reach London. The War brings
out the worst, as well as the best, qualities of our race.'[48]

Public criticism of Margot was not, however, confined to her supposed pro-German sympathies. She was reproached by even her
friends and family for her supposed failure to provide an example for
the nation's women. This meant not just her lack of 'war work' but also
the way she continued to entertain lavishly at Downing Street while
everyone else was being urged to tighten their belt. Cynthia, for
instance, complained in March 1916 about having to sit down with
over twenty people at dinner when 'with few exceptions their only
status was as bridge players. If you must have bridge, why not have one
or two tables? Why shock London by feeding twenty bores in order
that you may have your bridge?'[49] Cynthia criticized both her parents-
in-law a few months later for frivolity in wartime, when they entertained guests with what she called 'the greatest breach of taste I have
ever witnessed'. They had discovered that Yeo, their temporary butler,
was a superb mimic and summoned their guests to watch him perform:

They made him do very good imitations of various prominent guests at
Downing Street, their voices and walks – McKenna, Haldane, Lord

---

*Created Baron Melchett in 1928, Mond was the founder of Imperial Chemical
Industries.

Morley and so on. It was a very pungent scene. The P.M. lolling in glee, chuckling away at his butler ridiculing his colleagues; Margot, as though she were producing Patti, rating anybody who made a noise; and all the guests rather embarrassed and giggly. The funniest thing was the way Yeo – in his most professional, deprecating butler voice – gave out the name (just as if he were announcing him) of his victim: 'Lord Morley' and so on. I had the rare luxury of being <u>shocked to the core</u>. None of the family – except Beb, who was horrified – saw anything odd in it, but I canvassed a good many of the other guests and they agreed with me.[50]

Fifteen years after the end of the Great War, Margot's friend, Edith ('DD') Lyttelton revived the issue in a review of her *More Memories* for the *Spectator*:

Her [Margot's] desire to shine was too strong for her to be content to serve; a disability as she truly says, that her husband never suffered from. This is the explanation of why, with all her talents and her unique opportunities during the War, she gave no lead, no inspiring call of encouragement to the women working themselves to the bone in the background. I have often heard her scoff at Committees; the undeniable fact that many women are stupid was enough excuse for her to stand aside. I do not think she ever realized the disappointment, culminating in resentment, which women felt about her in the War, or the big opportunity which her astigmatic ambitions caused her to miss.[51]

It was an accusation Margot bitterly resented, as is clear from the angry justification of her wartime record she made to DD after reading her article:

I <u>detest</u> and despise committees, as they are a waste of time and an opportunity for personal vanity. I went to the hospitals every day of my life, and saw soldiers, sailors, and poor people, of whom you never could have heard. I never changed my clothes the first weeks of the war and lost a stone in weight from over-work and private anxiety. Do not believe in the *Daily Mail*, as to be an 'Asquith' was quite enough to make us <u>loathed</u> by the Press; and we <u>were</u> loathed (Thank God). Rumour is seldom right, my dearest DD, and I can see that you – like most of the London world – have no idea of what took place in 10 Downing Street during the War . . . what I <u>do</u> mind is that <u>you</u> should have been taken in by the 'Pro German' *Daily Mail* rot written of me in the War . . . What do you mean by 'leadership'? – listening to foolish females at committees? – or doing <u>real</u> work.[52]

Margot not only regularly visited wounded soldiers, she also took blinded servicemen at St Dunstan's* for drives in her car. But any idea of publicizing her charitable activities for propaganda purposes was anathema to her. What most upset her was criticism of her husband for his supposed 'Wait and See' attitude towards the War and the way his life was caricatured in the Press as a long round of country weekends and bridge parties. In March 1916, while Asquith was in bed with a severe chill, she was incensed when he was accused of pleading illness as an excuse for avoiding a statement on recruitment: '*The Times* would be pathetic if it were not <u>contemptible</u>: when he [Asquith] is ill he is shamming, when he is Kodaked smiling he is taking things lightly when he is serious he is overstrained, when he is silent he is asleep, when he speaks he is oratorical – "We do not want oratory we want deeds".'[53]

The Prime Minister's enemies, both within the Government and outside, were intent on driving him from Downing Street. Asquith had no foe more remorseless than his old Balliol friend and former rival for Margot's love, Alfred Milner. Since January 1916 a secretive group, the so-called 'Monday Night Cabal', with Milner as its driving force, met weekly with the clear objective of overthrowing the Asquith Government. The Cabal attracted powerful supporters: Geoffrey Robinson[†] (the editor of *The Times*), Waldorf Astor (husband of Nancy and owner of the *Observer*) and Carson, who had resigned from the Cabinet in October 1915 and rapidly became the focus of discontent with the Government on the Unionist benches. More dangerously for the Prime Minister, the Director of Military Operations at the War Office, General Sir Henry Wilson, a devious and embittered Ulsterman, was drawn in to the conspiracy, as was a member of Asquith's own Cabinet: Lloyd George.

In April 1916, the Cabal, acting in concert with Northcliffe and his newspapers, and abetted by Lloyd George within the Government, engineered a Cabinet crisis over conscription. Although Asquith by now accepted that universal military service was inevitable, he believed it essential to convince the doubters within his own Party, as well as the still hostile Trades Unions and the Labour Party. While Margot was 'assuring Henry that this is the worst crisis in all his political life',[54] he was determined not be rushed by hysteria in the

---

*Founded in 1915, originally for soldiers blinded by mustard gas.
†Later Dawson.

Press, and against all the odds secured all-round support for a Bill which authorized the Government to call up any man between the ages of eighteen and forty-one.

Margot saw the result as proof that her husband's political instincts were as good as ever, writing in her diary: 'Henry's patience and skill in keeping Labour in this amazing change in England has stunned everyone – the betting was 100 to 1 against these Islands <u>ever</u> adopting Conscription.'[55] However, the Prime Minister's enemies were only too keen to damn him for procrastination over the introduction of National Service, oblivious both to the practical difficulties and to the strength of opposition he first had to over-come. The Cabal knew that before long they would get another opportunity to oust him. Lloyd George's close friend and golfing partner, Sir George Riddell, the owner of the *News of the World*, wrote in his diary on 21 May: 'There is no doubt that Lloyd George and Northcliffe are acting in concert . . . Lloyd George is growing to believe more and more every day that he (LG) is the only man to win the War. His attitude to the PM is changing rapidly. He is becoming more and more critical and antagonistic. It looks as if Lloyd George and Northcliffe are working to dethrone Mr A.'[56]

19

The brink of doom

———————◆———————

RAYMOND WAS STILL serving at Haig's headquarters (recently moved from St Omer to Montreuil) when he heard about Margot's successful libel action. He had had his own arguments with her about the treatment of German prisoners-of-war when he backed Churchill's policy of treating captured enemy sub-mariners as war criminals and putting them in solitary confinement*, but on the issue of the 'bosh' printed in the newspapers, Raymond was as indignant as anyone, telling Katharine that he had reached the stage when he would rather defeat Northcliffe than defeat the Germans. The Press lord seemed to him just as belligerently crass and crassly belligerent as the enemy were, but far less courageous and capable. Raymond had hoped that Margot would receive more damages, although he quipped that she was not likely to waste her winnings on charities. As for the troublesome Minister of Munitions, he would be mortified if Lloyd George became Prime Minister for the final six months of the War and took the credit for winning it, which he most certainly did not deserve.[1]

Raymond returned to England at the beginning of May for what was to be his final home leave. On 22 April Katharine had given birth to their third child, a son, whom they called Julian, but nicknamed

———————

*The policy, as Margot predicted, backfired and had to be abandoned when Germany took retaliatory action against the captured sons of prominent Britons.

'Trimalchio', soon abbreviated to 'Trim'.* Raymond informed
Patrick Shaw-Stewart – after congratulating him on his congenial
and tranquil sinecure with the French headquarters staff in Salon-
ica – that Katharine was not yet out of bed, but was well and in good
spirits. On the first and last evenings of his leave he, Diana and Duff
Cooper dined with her in her room, feasting on lobsters and champagne.[2] The rest of Raymond's leave, so he informed Shaw-Stewart,
was as lascivious as the Song of Solomon. He had seen as much as he
could of Diana, whom he teasingly informed Shaw-Stewart – a keen
aficionado of her charms – was looking radiantly beautiful.

Katharine's pregnancy had not prevented her indulging in bouts of
drug-taking with Diana. The previous December, Diana described a
rare moment of happiness to Raymond when she had injected herself
and Katharine with morphia and they had lain in 'ecstatic stillness
through too short a night'. She found it 'strange to feel so utterly self-
sufficient – more like a Chinaman, or God before he made the world
or his son and was content with, or callous to, the chaos'. Duff
Cooper, who was to marry Diana in 1919, strongly disapproved of
the Coterie's drug-taking, as did Aubrey Herbert, who once forcefully
dragged his wife, Mary, away from one of their parties. Duff worried
about Katharine becoming 'a *morphineuse*', which, he told Diana,
'would spoil her looks', but Raymond himself does not appear to
have minded. He himself seems to have done nothing more licentious
than gambling at the Montagus, where, after the women had left, he
lost his nightly ten pounds or so before daybreak.[3] As for Diana, his
main object was probably to tease Shaw-Stewart: she was, as he told
her herself, for ever Tantalus to him.[4]

On 16 May, after his agreed term at GHQ had expired, Raymond
rejoined his regiment in the Ypres salient, where he found his
middle-aged fellow subaltern, Alfred Yorke, in cheerful spirits, if a
bit shaken by his recent spell at the Front. Raymond noticed how
since his own last stint in the trenches his fellow officers seemed
more war-weary and more afraid of shells, and talked more about the
chances of peace. He himself remained blasé about the horrors that
surrounded him, informing Shaw-Stewart that he found the Ypres
salient more agreeable than he had been led to believe, although with

---

*Trimalchio was the host of the obscene dinner party described in the surviving frag-
ment of Petronius's *Satyricon*: a bizarre, if (for Raymond) characteristic nickname to
choose for one's son and not one, as it happened, 'Trim' was to grow up to deserve.

the onset of warmer weather it stank abominably of dead Scots, Patrick's Bible-bashing compatriots having taken too literally Christ's injunction to let the dead bury the dead.* The Grenadiers suffered a few casualties from shell fire, and one night the Boche had launched an attack on their lines some 200 yards to the left of Raymond's platoon, but were driven back, leaving behind some large corpses.

Raymond was as dismissive as he had always been about 'shell shock', which he attributed to boredom, telling Shaw-Stewart that it was ludicrous to claim, as some did, that war involved continual nervous strain. Although he conceded that shelling did produce increasing stress, even around Ypres there was barely more than a day each month when it was serious enough to induce real anxiety.

After Raymond had been only five days in the front line, the Guards were withdrawn to a so-called 'rest camp', which, Raymond informed Shaw-Stewart, belied its name since they were buggered around from dawn to dusk.[5] The one bit of light relief was when the regimental padre pronounced the battalion mess room, which was festooned with pictures of nude women, an unsuitable venue for a religious service. The relief was only temporary, for a few days later Raymond was complaining about having to listen to the padre's drivel in a field where even the buttercups drooped their petals.[6]

Shortly afterwards the Grenadiers marched off to a training camp to practise attacking enemy trenches. Raymond was pleased how well he stood up to a twenty-mile march in the heat and the dust with nothing to eat or drink between 6 a.m. and 3 p.m. He boasted to Katharine that despite having had little exercise during the past three months he was hardly at all footsore or tired. But he did admit that he would have fared less well if he had had to carry a pack like his men. No sooner had they settled into new quarters in an agreeable little town than the military authorities discovered that the whole area was under crops with nowhere to train. They duly endured a further tediously slow march to another location. Yet for all his frustration, Raymond enjoyed the sensation of being part of a well-drilled formation, appreciating the majesty of a full brigade on the march with its drummers beating time. His own company marched at the front of the brigade, whose four battalions stretched back along the road behind them for some one-and-a-half miles. He was

---

*St Matthew 8, v. 22.

particularly proud of the smart way they marched past the commander of the 2nd Army in the square of a small town on the way.[7]

In the end, the Guards had no time for training, but were rushed up to the front line at Hooge to relieve the broken remnants of a Canadian division. Raymond realized that the Dominion troops were not at their best after weeks of heavy fighting, but he was still shocked to see the Canadian soldiers reel past them swigging rum, having abandoned all their equipment, including their rifles and ammunition. Fortunately for the Grenadiers, by the time they reached the trenches, the enemy gunners were concentrating their attentions elsewhere, and Raymond was able to enjoy the impressive spectacle of the British and German artillery engaging in a colossal duel over their heads, watched over by a yellow full moon above a line of poplars, while the whole horizon was lit up by a ring of flames, as the muzzles of the guns flashed and shells burst around them.[8]

In the clear light of day, even Raymond was horrified by the sight and, more particularly, the stench of the carnage in which the Canadians had been involved. He spared neither Katharine nor Diana in his description of the nearby Sanctuary Wood as the foulest, most desolate and utterly loathsome place he had ever seen. Every single tree had been felled by shellfire in the preceding week, leaving nothing but obscene, blackened stumps surrounded by craters awash with blood, filth and putrid corpses, amongst which a legion of well-fed rats scurried about. The hedges were littered with the remains of human limbs and entrails, while the sole dug-out was swimming in sewage, rotting eye-balls and other indescribable detritus. And everywhere was a stench of death and decay so abominable that the scent of every flower in the world could not have masked it.[9]

On Tuesday 6 June – the day 'Trim' was to be christened – Margot recorded how 'at 10.30 a.m. Henry came into my bedroom with a look of tragedy on a new and worn face. I thought Raymond or Oc had been killed.'[10] In fact, it was Kitchener who was dead, drowned when the cruiser HMS *Hampshire*, taking him to Russia to advise the Tsar, was sunk by a German mine off the Orkneys. Whatever Asquith's reservations about Kitchener as an administrator, he always appreciated his value as a strategist and had become genuinely fond of him; he was in tears as he gave the news of his death to Margot, who, never one to be upstaged in a show of emotion, started crying herself. By the time she reached St Paul's Cathedral for the christening, Violet had already broken the news to her friends. When Raymond (who was not given leave to attend) heard from an irritated Katharine about the commotion caused by his sister and stepmother as they discussed the tragedy throughout the service, he acidly remarked on how characteristic it was of Margot and Violet to make such a fuss about Kitchener: as if the death of old men mattered.[11]

Kitchener's death bought a new spurt of hate-mail for Margot, voicing the preposterous but widely circulated rumour that she had tipped the Germans off about the position of the *Hampshire*. Margot's own most immediate concern was who was going to take over the War Office. Her favoured candidates were Crewe or McKenna. When she tackled her husband about the issue the following evening, she was appalled when he said 'he thought *au fond* Lloyd George had the best claim', recording how 'like a perfect fool I was violent which spoilt all our talk – I said to have a sly dishonourable brilliant man in the War Office and a Northcliffe [supporter] was unthinkable!! – the whole army would rebel and War Office resign etc, that I would rather leave Downing Street forever than see such a hideous blunder.'[12]

Margot spent a sleepless night at the prospect of what she considered 'the greatest political blunder of Henry's life time'.[13] When she heard from Reading, Montagu and Bongie the next day that Lloyd George had threatened to resign and 'stump the country with the backing of the Northcliffe Press against his own P.M.', if he were not made War Minister, she was convinced that her husband had given way to blackmail and set out to sabotage the appointment, lobbying General Sir William Robertson, the Chief of the Imperial General Staff, to 'warn Henry he would not stand a Pressman in the War Office'. She was delighted to discover that not only was Robertson sympathetic, but that other senior generals, led by French (now commanding Home defence), were openly voicing their opposition to Lloyd George, so she was mortified to discover that Montagu – hitherto 'our wisest counsellor, our truest friend, the most loyal and in many ways the cleverest of all Henry's colleagues' – backed the appointment.[14] However, after arguing about the issue with Montagu, she finally admitted defeat, noting ruefully in her journal:

> I need hardly say the Press made a huge ring led by Northcliffe in favour of Lloyd George's appointment – he was boomed day in, day out, hailed

as Jehovah. The effrontery with which Lloyd George rigged the Press disgusted me – !

It is too late now and I played my cards badly with Henry: I said I would rather see him dead before he should make such an appointment, that I would go to Scotland and cease to take the faintest interest in the Cabinet or politics and was far too vehement and out of proportion. I have cried bitter tears over it and foresee great trouble.[15]

Margot considered her husband was in a no-win situation: either Lloyd George's tenure of the War Office would turn out to be a great failure (as she believed would happen), in which case the Prime Minister would take the blame, or else 'if it is a great success he will take good care to cut Henry out'.[16] The die was cast: Lloyd George took office as Kitchener's successor on 7 July. Six days earlier, Haig had launched his offensive on the Somme. Asquith's survival as Prime Minister now depended on the outcome of the battle.

Cynthia, meanwhile, was becoming increasingly concerned about Beb's 'absolute content without occupation'. The Army was by now inundated with cases of shell shock far more serious than Beb's. And with no agreement on how to treat the casualties – only the lucky ones ended up, like his fellow poets, Siegfried Sassoon and Wilfred Owen, being treated by William Rivers at Craiglockhart Hospital near Edinburgh – it seems likely that Beb, along with many others known to have suffered battle fatigue, was simply 'forgotten' in the hope he would seek his own treatment and report back for service one day.

Beb was still a long way from being fit to return to the Front, but his health was steadily improving. However, to Cynthia's consternation he showed little inclination to find employment other than writing poetry, which was certainly not going to pay the bills. She was appalled when he told her that 'even if the War stopped now, he would never return to the Bar but intended to become a novelist!'.[17] With the awful example of the Lawrences' poverty as a stark warning of the perils of the literary life, she considered it essential that he had a steady source of income. There was the additional problem that, despite her earlier indignation over Margot's accusations of drunkenness, she now accepted that Beb was drinking too much. He had even been warned to cut down by his doctor. She was furious when she heard from her parents that he 'had had claret, brandy and port

for lunch', recording how 'I went and abused him and I'm ashamed
to say lost my temper and when irritated by a hopelessly <u>irrelevant</u>
argument actually boxed his ears.'[18]

As a favour to Cynthia, F. E. Smith, Attorney General in the coalition Government, gave Beb the sinecure of Junior Counsel to Her
Majesty's Customs and Excise, but the position turned out to be
worth only some £150 to £200 a year, rather than the £2,000 which
Beb himself had fondly imagined. Cynthia asked Asquith if he could
find a job for his son, and after he 'proved characteristically inert'
and 'distressingly lacking in nepotism', she lobbied Hankey, Balfour
and French, all of whom fobbed her off. In desperation she turned to
Ettie to use her influence with the doomed Kitchener to secure a
post at GHQ. This did the trick, although not in the way that Cynthia
might have wished. Beb's embarrassment at discovering that Ettie
was touting for a Staff appointment for him – ironically just as
Raymond was returning to the trenches – spurred him into applying
to the War Office to be allowed to return to active service. He eventually managed to secure a commission with the Royal Field Artillery,
and in June he was sent for further training to a camp near Brighton,
much to the relief of Cynthia, who had feared him being marooned
on Salisbury Plain.

The rigours of military life completed Beb's rehabilitation.
Cynthia remarked that he was 'looking wonderfully better – quite
different'.[19] However, as Beb recovered another serious shadow
loomed over the lives of himself and Cynthia: the mental health of
their elder son, John. As early as May 1915, when John was four,
Cynthia had noted in her diary that he was 'very silent and unrespon-
sive these days'. But he was obviously talented – Puffin was particularly impressed by his musicality – and although over the next few
months his behaviour became increasingly volatile, with unexplained
ferocious temper tantrums alternating with being 'demonstratively
affectionate', her son's problems were pushed to one side as she
coped with the death of her brother, Yvo, and Beb's shell shock. She
even tried to make light of it being 'funny having a mad husband and
a mad child'. However, as John seemed to get worse, even at times
physically attacking his younger brother, Michael, Cynthia was at a
loss to know what to do. John was in fact displaying classic symptoms of autism, a condition that is ill understood even now, but was
then not recognized at all. Cynthia, in a 'cold terror about John', consulted friends, family members, even two 'specialists', all of whom

suggested different diagnoses and different solutions, often provoking arguments between herself and Beb. In the summer of 1916 she decided to take on a governess, Miss Quinn, to look after John separately from Michael, who was by now thoroughly frightened of his brother. From then on John passed a sad and painful life with a series of 'keepers', being moved between the homes of his grandparents, his parents and various rented flats, until he was sent to a special school in 1920. He was then confined to a series of institutions until he eventually died in 1937. Cynthia certainly felt guilt, grief and helplessness, but at the same time comforted herself with what D.H. Lawrence had told her: that she herself was 'quite wrong' for him, being 'not positive enough, and that John would see lack of conviction'.[20]

In the meantime, for the summer of 1916 she installed Michael, two that July, with his nanny in lodgings in Brighton, and herself spent as much time as she could with Beb, even watching him practising gunnery on the South Downs. When he was on leave there was a perpetual tussle over where they stayed, with the epicurean Beb wanting to stay at the comfortable – and expensive – Royal York Hotel, while the more economical Cynthia preferred a cheaper boarding house. However, despite tiffs over money and Beb's resentment at often having to spend his free time *à trois* with Basil Blackwell, these were almost carefree days for the young couple. The many limbless ex-servicemen from the nearby military hospital to be seen around town served as a constant reminder of the dangers that lay ahead, but like many people in wartime, Cynthia and Beb tried to live for the moment.

Cynthia had by now become numbly resigned to the prospect of more of her close friends and family being killed. Her state of mind was not even broken when her eldest brother, Ego, now Lord Elcho, was reported missing in Palestine. His squadron of Gloucestershire Hussars was ambushed by a whole Turkish brigade on Easter Day, 23 April, while guarding some sappers drilling for oil at Qatia in Sinai. Although hopelessly outnumbered, the Hussars held out for over seven hours before being overwhelmed.

The details of the battle were soon known, yet Cynthia, like most of the rest of her family, seems to have shown an astonishing lack of concern. Perhaps unable to face the likelihood that another of her brothers had been killed, she simply assumed, against all the odds, that Ego had been taken prisoner. Even when, several weeks later, they heard via the Red Crescent that Tom Strickland (the husband of Cynthia's sister Mary) was one of only two Yeomanry officers to be taken prisoner, the Charteris family still clung to the hope that Ego had been wounded and was being held apart from his comrades, and so had been overlooked. It was not until 1 July that they received definite confirmation that he had been killed at Qatia and reality broke in on an anguished Cynthia. 'Oh God – Oh God, my beautiful brother that I have loved so since I was a baby,' she wrote in her journal: 'Can it be true that he'll never come back?'[21]

Coincidentally, 1 July was also the first day of the Battle of the Somme. Raymond did not hear about Ego's death until ten days later. Amidst the slaughter of tens of thousands, even Raymond's self-protective armour of cynicism was pierced by the death of this gentle, good-natured and widely loved friend. He complained to Diana that a blind God stumps around the globe with a pair of sensitively malevolent antennae seeking what deserves to live and using iron hooves to grind it to dust. It was extraordinary that the skeletal fingers of Spite and Fate should penetrate what appeared to be the least dangerous theatre in the War, and pluck the most exquisite flower there. Forecasting what he saw at his own inevitable fate, he reflected that they were all living so completely on the brink of doom, liable at any instant to join the main cortège, that the order of their leaving hardly mattered.[22]

As soon as Oc, Freyberg and Kelly reached Malta, they were ordered to return to northern France ahead of their units to seek out suitable billets. No one complained about what they regarded as an extension to their holiday, as they enjoyed a leisurely tour of the picturesque villages around Abbeville, close to the mouth of the Somme. They eventually settled on Citernes, where the local Mayor (described by Kelly as 'a big honest bourgeois') not only offered to put up the three officers in the *mairie*, but insisted they dine *en famille* with his wife and 'two pretty daughters'.[23]

The next most urgent task was to divide up the Hood into two battalions. Kelly described in his journal how Freyberg and Oc, the two battalion commanders, sat down with their respective seconds-in-command (Kelly himself and Egerton) after dinner to settle how it would be done:

The procedure adopted was the alternate choice of officers (with whom went their platoons), the first choice resting on the toss of a coin. Oc won the toss, and by this we were able to avoid having one of the obvious undesirables. It was an amusing little symposium – in which either side was much concerned to keep its counsel secret. Oc and I were at an advantage here, as we relapsed into French, which the others did not understand.[24]

A couple of days later the Second Hood received a visit from their new Brigade Commander, Brigadier General Lewis Philips. Philips had begun the War as a forty-four-year-old major and owed his promotion – over-promotion as it turned out – to the shortage of senior officers brought about by the vast expansion in the British Army. Kelly's first impression was favourable, but Oc detected signs that the brigadier 'might be impulsive': an instinct that was to foreshadow a stormy relationship between the two men.

Oc now enthusiastically threw himself into knocking his battalion into shape, although he was hampered by the unit constantly being assigned to fatigue duties, as well as by officers and men being called away at short notice for various courses in tactical warfare and weaponry. Kelly, who was sent for instruction in trench warfare, did his bit to reinforce Army prejudices about the obstreperousness of the Naval soldiers by refusing to shave off his beard, and insisting, as a member of 'the Senior Service', on taking precedence on parade over his Army counterparts. A top priority for Oc, as always, was the welfare of his men and he soon became aware of 'a spirit of discontent and lack of keenness' among them because of 'the small amount of leave they have received in comparison with other troops in France'.[25] When he raised the issue with Philips, he did not disguise his irritation at the brigadier's curt refusal to countenance any extra.

At the end of June, the Royal Naval Division underwent yet another reorganization: henceforth it was to be known as the 63rd (Royal Naval) Division and, as a further step to absorbing it into the Army, was assigned a third brigade made up of four Army battalions. The 2nd Hood was abolished and its men reabsorbed into Freyberg's battalion; Oc reverted to being a company commander, losing his temporary rank of commander; and Kelly was given command of another company.

During the first two months of the Battle of the Somme both the Guards and the Royal Naval Divisions were deployed in essentially defensive duties to the north of the offensive. Trench warfare, even in the 'quieter' parts of the line, was not without its dangers. On 7 July Raymond wrote to Katharine that almost every night there were raids on the German lines accompanied by the usual ridiculous artillery barrage. He considered the whole business to be a charade, usually causing far more British than German casualties.[26]

After the temporary disturbance of Hooge, he soon recovered his usual *sang froid* and his letters reverted to their habitual bantering tone, even when recording brushes with death, such as when, during a night reconnaissance into No Man's Land to check the barbed wire, they suddenly found themselves lit up by German rockets. Some beggar chucked a grenade at them as they tried to take cover, and they were only saved by his orderly having the biggest buttocks on the Western Front: they counted ten holes in them after helping him back to their own lines.[27]

Behind Raymond's jesting tone was a contempt for the whole business of warfare. He agreed with Katharine about the complete absurdity of war, but contended that the idea only bothered him about once a week. Apart from enlarging the number of one's acquaintances, he could think of nothing to recommend it. Theft, murder or sewing mailbags would serve just as well. One can almost hear the yawn as he informed Diana that, except for the tedious boom and flash of the artillery, they could be attending an old-fashioned ball in Arthur Grenfell's Roehampton garden – the same monotonous hum of an electricity generator too close by, the same scrawny oak trees, the same scrabble for sandwiches, the same people. The enemy's efforts to make life uncomfortable were treated with equal disdain. In a letter to Katharine the same day (21 July) he nonchalantly complained that the Huns had started mounting idiotic little air raids in their section of the line at 7 o'clock every morning and 5 o'clock every evening. They generally took cover and drank tea while they were going on. Even the death of a university chum (a civilized and most congenial fellow, always ready to laugh louder than anyone at his coarsest jokes) was greeted with the insouciance of a world-weary octogenarian perusing the obituary column of *The Times* over the breakfast table.[28] However, Raymond by now did not disguise his genuine respect for the men under his command, whom (in a rare letter to Margot) he described as an excellent bunch to have on one's side: mostly game-keepers, miners, policemen and farmers, whom he found far more reassuring at sticky moments than the bureaucrats and charlatans in Kitchener's new volunteer regiments.[29]

Amid the discomforts of army life, the luxuries sent out from home assumed a disproportionate importance, especially for Raymond who always appreciated the good things of life. When Haldane, keenly aware of the Asquiths' lack of funds, generously gave Katharine a large cheque for cigars and brandy for her husband, Raymond was full of suggestions on what the money could be spent after ruling out cigars and pointing out that he had ample supplies of good brandy. Instead he suggested Gentleman's Relish, honey, tinned chicken (plain or curried), and – after evidently giving the question much thought – anchovy paste (but not too much), tinned grapes, and – if practicable – smoked haddock and kippers (ideally from Stornoway), as he was particularly missing fish in his diet. Yet, even seemingly innocent food parcels could take on a sinister signifi-cance, as when he blithely thanked Katharine for sending morphia, alongside marmalade, cold chicken and a magnificent ham supplied by Mrs Gould, the Mells' cook. Even the innocuous-sounding request for scent was to counter the all-pervasive stench of decay and death.[30]

All the while the Guards were being deployed ever closer to the holocaust taking place to the south. On 30 July Raymond reported marching for three hours under a burning sun through gently sloping chalk downs full of corn and poppies interspersed with beautiful woodland. It sounds almost idyllic but for the fact that, loaded down with steel helmets, gas masks and all the other trap-pings of modern warfare, many of the men collapsed. Raymond himself, fortunate to be able to march light, was not fatigued at all.

At least the Guards Division commissariat was superior to that of the Royal Naval Division. Raymond praised the tremendous punctu-ality and exceptional quality of the men's meals: tea, raspberry jam and bacon laid out in the shadiest corn field en route, and an Irish stew, good enough to satisfy a shooting party on a grouse moor, faultlessly served up in the yard of the farmhouse where they were billeted, with the sun shining, the drums playing and guns booming safely in the background – the whole affair was altogether most agreeable. But fine weather was, of course, the key to everything.[31]

After Raymond's unit was ordered to repair a trench in one of the hotter sections of the front line, he reported to Katharine a nasty encounter with what he regarded as the most frightful weapon of

war, the notorious *Minnenwerfer*, or trench mortar, which he
described as approximately the shape and size of a large rum jar, with
a range of about 400 yards, travelling very slowly, very high up. At
night they would spot them nudging their way through the stars
leaving a trail of sparks. Usually there were too many men in the
trench for you to get as far away as you might wish before the
Minnenwerfer landed; it would fizz around on the ground before
exploding with the most deafening roar imaginable.

On one occasion Raymond was supervising trench repairs when
all of a sudden he was surrounded by a throng of gibbering men
from the battalion holding that part of the line (the Grenadiers were
only working on it). The terrified soldiers cowered in the bottom of
the trench, holding their hands over their eyes and behaving, as
Raymond saw it, as if the world was about to come to an end. It was
most disquieting. Apparently the men had spotted one of those con-
founded rum jars and he had not. Sure enough, the device exploded
some five seconds later, fortunately just on the far side of their
parapet. The sky was shrouded with smoke and dirt, and soldiers
kept bumping into him in the gloom, yelling out more from terror
than any physical harm.

Raymond told Katharine that the explosion was about as agonizing as a noise could be, cracking your eardrums and seeming to crush
your skull. Just before the device went off, he made up his mind that
he was about to die, but when he realized that he had survived, he
decided that this must be shell shock and he would be sent home at
last. But it was not, and he was not a great deal worse off than before.
Although he had felt a splinter from the bomb strike his leg, unhap-
pily it only caused a tiny blood blister. He had plucked another fragment from his jacket shoulder (it had penetrated his uniform but not
his shirt), and there was a respectable dent in his steel helmet. A most
discouraging outcome.[32]

It was not until mid July that the re-organized Royal Naval Division
was deemed ready for front line duties and assigned to the relatively
quiet 'Souchez' sector (named after the local river) between Vimy
and Lens. Kelly found the trenches 'much inferior to those in the
Gallipoli Peninsula,' complaining that the deep dug-outs were
'death-traps' and sections of the front line so shallow that 'if the
Germans had felt disposed to snipe we made excellent targets', while

'the wire was in very poor condition, as was also the parapet – sand-bags being just heaped up with no apparent consideration as to whether they afforded cover from fire'.[33] Their efforts to improve the defences were constantly interrupted by bombardments of mortars, rifle grenades and – when the wind was favourable – gas canisters. To add to their problems, a particularly wet summer had not only left most trenches at least ankle deep in water, the hot, damp weather brought a plague of mosquitoes. They proved an even greater menace to health and comfort than the ubiquitous rats which, as Kelly wryly observed, at least 'serve a very useful purpose as scav-engers'.[34]

It was not long before Oc was complaining to Freyberg about his men's rations, which 'reach us in the most abominable state. Tea, sugar, cheese, bacon, bread, and tins of beef are put without any attempt at separation or covering into one sandbag together, and a mixture of tea, sugar, cheese and blue paint is imbedded in the bacon.'[35] His field notebooks also bear witness to his repeated – and usually unsuccessful – efforts to obtain leave for the men who most needed it. He always replied personally to enquiries from their anxious families: 'Your son is fit and working well, as he has done throughout', he re-assured one anxious father, while commiserating with him about the authorities' refusal to allow his son home.[36] He raised with his own father the question of soldiers' identity discs, which were stamped with ink liable to rub off, meaning that an unnecessary number of those killed were never identified and thus deprived of individual graves. As a result, the Prime Minister inter-vened personally with the War Office to ensure that servicemen were issued with stamped metal identity discs.[37]

Oc always attached great importance to intelligence about the enemy and, never one to delegate dangerous assignments, would regularly lead nighttime sorties into No Man's Land. On 1 August Kelly recorded accompanying him on a reconnaissance to inspect a German listening post: 'a very arduous and somewhat painful crawl along the edge of the river through longish grass and a great many nettles and frequent encounters with barbed wire', before they were eventually forced to beat a hurried retreat when lit up by enemy lights.

Kelly himself remained keen and amazingly cheerful, a constant source of inspiration and amusement to his men and fellow officers alike. He was a great animal lover and always had at least four stray

cats in his care, which his men carried in sandbags between positions. He not only took charge of the Hood Battalion band but also
set up a choir which he aptly named the 'Minnie-singers' (after
Minnenwerfer),* commenting in a letter to Jelly d'Arányi: 'they can't
sing and the noises they make would make one wince in normal
existence'.[38] But his greatest musical achievement, which he had to
badger the authorities to allow, was to conduct the Hood Battalion
band in a performance of Tchaikovsky's *1812 Overture* to the accompaniment of a real artillery barrage.

Oc did his best to put as cheerful a gloss as possible on life on the
Western Front. After one 'wet' stint in the front line, he reassured
Violet that there was 'more noise than casualties'. His description of
a training session in a beech wood as 'a panorama of men playing like
puppies in a sunny field, rolling one another into odd contortions
with sheathed bayonets', sounds more like a holiday game than practice for one of the most brutal forms of hand to hand combat, while
a barrage aimed at the German lines in late August 1916, which he
witnessed after dining with Freyberg and Cardy Montagu,† sounds
like a firework display: 'We could not see the gas-attack – the Huns
light fires all along their parapets to counter gas – but a night bombardment is always a remarkable sight, sky quivering with gun-
flashes and balls of red flame when the shells explode.'

At the beginning of September Oc was granted five days' 'local
leave'. After spending the first couple of days at the Hôtel de
Normandie in the coastal town of Deauville, which, apart from a
sprinkling of soldiers, was 'full of American children and "Chic
Parisiens"', he caught a train to Paris, where he stayed at the Ritz and
took the opportunity to see 'an excellent Yankee dentist' who
'stopped seven of my teeth in one hour and a half on Saturday afternoon'. It was pouring with rain which inevitably brought thoughts
that 'the trenches will be very disagreeable', but he assured Violet
that 'everyone here is full of optimism'. The Hood had 'not yet what
they call "been over the bags"', but, of course, we expect to do so
before summer is over, and I personally rather look forward to it as
a change from the monotony of trenches'.[39]

---

*As a fellow musician, Jelly d'Arányi would have been aware that there was a double pun,
with the name of Kelly's choir also being a play on the *Minnesang* performed by German
medieval troubadours.
†Edwin's younger brother.

20

Nemesis on the Somme

A S THE SUMMER of 1916 wore on, Raymond's letters home gradually dropped their veil of cynicism and gave occasional
glimpses of the homesickness and frustration that lay beneath. When
Diana wrote of the beauty of the English countryside that August, he
confessed to envying her, longing to share with her the sunbeams
dappling the ground beneath the oak trees. He had always felt a bit
sentimental about nature, and agreed with her that the world had
never seemed more wonderful than it was that summer. If only, he
added, he could be wounded and sent home.[1] It was a state of mind
which made Raymond specially sensitive to the continuing lack of
letters from his family. When he heard from Katharine how her
mother, Frances, had vigorously defended him against Margot's
latest attack on the coldness of 'the Asquiths', he was touched, telling
his wife how glad he was that Frances had tackled his stepmother for
calling him 'heartless'. The result was a letter from Margot, the
second he had received from Downing Street since the start of the
War. He made a point of replying straightaway and at considerable
length, but he did not delude himself that anybody but his stepmother's maid would read it.[2]

In fact, Margot copied every word of 'the delightful letter from
our boy Raymond' into her journal.[3] Such are the misconceptions
and unspoken emotions that bedevil relationships in most families.
Raymond was much more upset by the lack of communication
from his father. His hurt is apparent in a letter to Katharine dated

22 August, in which he complains about having to write to 'the Prime Minister' to ask him to pull his finger out over his (Raymond's) candidature for the Derby Parliamentary seat. He was not sure that his letter would encourage good relations between them. He had also reminded his father that his last quarter's allowance was almost two months in arrears, so he hoped soon to be able to send his wife another cheque. Meanwhile he told Katharine that if she heard any more rubbish from Margot about the callousness of her stepchildren, she could point out to her that during his ten months in France he had not received a single letter from the Prime Minister. Raymond then added, perhaps to try to disguise his real hurt, that of course there was no reason why he should write. He was extremely busy, as was Raymond himself.[4]

Whatever the explanation for the lack of correspondence, Asquith eagerly seized the chance to see both Raymond and Oc when, on 7 September 1916, he crossed the Channel to confer with Haig about the progress of the offensive. Raymond had recently returned to his battalion after another Court Martial, this time defending an officer accused of homosexuality. He told Katharine that the case was hopeless from the start: most witnesses were awful liars and he had some fun cross-examining them as they all shared the defendant's sexual tastes. One compensation was that the case earned Raymond twenty-four hours' local leave in Amiens with Soper, his company commander. The Prince of Wales lent them his car and they were able to luxuriate in hot baths, soft beds, delicious meals and some reasonable champagne, as well as amusing themselves by paying a visit to the ladies of the town although he assured her, he at least remained celibate.[5]

At any moment, the Grenadiers expected to take part in the next 'push'. On the morning that Raymond was summoned to meet his father, he had been up since five o'clock participating in an exercise designed to simulate an attack on enemy trenches behind a 'creeping barrage', the recently devised tactic of laying down a steadily moving curtain of shell fire some fifty yards in front of the infantry as they advanced. In the exercise the barrage was simulated by drummers, allowing him to give full rein to his sense of the ridiculous. To him the sight of four battalions walking in lines at a funeral pace across cornfields preceded by a row of drummers was more like some ridiculous religious ritual ceremony performed by a Maori tribe, than a brigade of Guards training for battle. When he was ordered to report to his brigadier, he imagined at first that he must have committed some dreadful military blunder, so was relieved when he was commanded to rendezvous with the Prime Minister at 10.45 a.m. at crossroads K.6d. He leapt on to his horse and trotted off to Fricourt, arriving punctually.[6]

After ten days of rain, the sun was shining brightly when, an hour late, the Prime Minister and his entourage (which included Bongie) drew up in two staff cars to inspect a captured German strongpoint close to where Raymond was waiting. Asquith described what was to be their last meeting in a letter to Margot:

> He was very well and in good spirits. Our guns were firing all round and just as we were walking to the top of the little hill to visit the wonderful dug-out, a German shell came whizzing over our heads and fell a little way beyond . . . We went in all haste to the dug-out – 3 storeys underground with ventilating pipes electric light and all sorts of conveniences, made by the Germans. Here we found Generals Horne and Walls (who have done the lion's share of all the fighting): also Bongie's brother who is on Walls's staff. They were rather disturbed about the shell, as the Germans rarely pay them such attention, and told us to stay with them underground for a time. One or two more shells came, but no harm was done. The two generals are splendid fellows and we had a very interesting time with them.[7]

Raymond was impressed by his father's coolness under fire, reporting to Katharine that whereas the GHQ driver holding his horse threw the reins into the air and himself flat on his tummy in the mud, the Prime Minister was not in the least put out.[8] All was well once again between father and son.

Three days later (11 September 1916), as he waited to go into action, Raymond reported to Diana that the Court Martial had just convicted his homosexual client: the wretched officer had not only been cashiered, but also sentenced to a year in prison. The military police had arrived the previous evening and had cut off his buttons before marching him off to Rouen in custody. Could she imagine anything so barbaric? Raymond wished he could tell Diana where he was and what they were about to do. But he assured her it would be fun, and that they were going to be centre stage, adding that she would love it. He then bade what he now knew was likely to be a final 'Goodbye' to his 'darling darling' friend.[9]

The Guards Division, in the words of their Commanding Officer, General Lord Cavan, had been assigned 'a superhumanly difficult task' in the coming attack, one of the biggest since the start of the Somme offensive,[10] and the occasion when the British Army first used its new secret weapon, the tank. Raymond optimistically informed Katharine that the Boches were expected to shorten their line by withdrawing some fifteen to twenty miles to a new line approximately between Lille and Cambrai. If the enemy could be effectively harried during their retreat, it might make life difficult for them. Now facing death, he wanted to survive, assuring his wife that it would nice to return to England for the winter and take some post at the War Office. He was becoming awfully fed up with being away from home, and not seeing his beloved Fawnia (his pet name for Katharine).[11]

The Guards' objective was the village of Lesboeufs. On the right flank of their line of advance was one of the most heavily fortified fortresses on the whole German line, the notorious 'Quadrilateral'. The chances that this strongpoint would be captured that day were close to nil, which meant that the Guards were almost certain to be subjected to devastating fire on their flank as well as their front. On 14 September, the eve of the attack, Raymond wrote a final moving farewell to Katharine and scribbled a few typically facetious words to Diana, thanking her for some Morny soap she had sent him, while hoping he would survive long enough to use the remaining two tablets. He was preparing to leave the detestable place where he now was for one infinitely worse. He feared it would be a matter of a peerage or Westminster Abbey – the grimmest of all those grim dilemmas with which he and Diana were so often confronted.[12]

Twelve years later, in an obituary tribute to Asquith, Winston Churchill (who despite all their differences remained a good friend to the end) recalled the final moments of the Prime Minister's eldest son:

> It seemed quite easy for Raymond Asquith, when the time came, to face death and to die. When I saw him at the Front he seemed to move through the cold, squalor and peril of the winter trenches as if he were above and immune from the common ills of the flesh, a being clad in polished armour, entirely undisturbed, presumably invulnerable. The War which found the measure of so many, never got to the bottom of him, and when the Grenadiers strode into the crash and thunder of the Somme, he went to his fate cool, poised, resolute, matter of fact, debonair. And well we know that his father, then bearing the supreme burden of the State, would proudly have marched at his side.[13]

The end for Raymond came more quickly than for most of his comrades: as he clambered out of his trench and led his company forward into the hail of shell and machine gun fire, he was hit by a bullet in the chest. 'Such coolness under shell fire as Mr Asquith displayed would be difficult to equal,' Needham, his soldier servant, wrote to Katharine afterwards.[14] Raymond knew straightaway that his wound was fatal, but in order to reassure his men, he casually lit a cigarette as he was carried on a stretcher to the dressing station. He gave his flask to the medical orderly who attended him, asking him to send it on to his father. The man thoughtfully wrote to the Prime Minister to assure him that it had not even been necessary to give his son morphia 'as he was quite free from pain and just dying'.* Asquith placed the flask on his bedside table.[15]

Only five of the twenty-two officers in Raymond's battalion survived the battle unscathed. It took another three days' heavy fighting to capture the Quadrilateral, and Les Boeufs did not fall for a further week. The tanks, many of which broke down, caused more shock to the German soldiers than damage to their defences; the hoped for 'breakthrough' proved as elusive as ever.

News of Raymond's death did not reach his family until two days later. Margot had organized her usual large weekend party at The Wharf, which included Elizabeth and Puffin, Margot's half-sister Nan Tennant, the dashing Colonel Tom Bridges and his wife Florry, General Sir John Cowans (the Quartermaster General) and Maud Tree. Asquith was in good form, having, according to Margot, returned from France looking 'well and happy. He was delighted with his visit to the Front, and all he saw (our tanks and troops and grand organisation). Our offensive was going amazingly well, munitions satisfactory, the French fighting magnificently.' He also 'talked a lot about Raymond'.[16]

It was 9.45 p.m. when Margot was called away to the telephone. The men were still lingering over port and brandy in the dining room, while Puffin, about to start his first 'quarter' (term) at Winchester, as a special treat had been allowed to come down in his pyjamas to play bridge, partnering his mother against Maud Tree and

---

*This contradicts an account given to Katharine by another witness, who said Raymond was given morphia. (See Jolliffe, p. 296).

Florry Bridges. Margot asked Elizabeth, who was gossiping with Nan in the hallway, to take over her hand while she answered the call. As soon as she picked up the receiver and heard the voice of 'Da' (David Davies, a close Wykehamist friend of Cys's, recently appointed the Prime Minister's Second Secretary), she guessed why he had called.

'Terrible terrible news, Margot,' said Davies. 'Raymond was shot dead on the 15th. Haig writes – no details – he writes full of sympathy. Where is Katharine? Shall I tell her?' Margot told him to ring Frances Horner, who was with Katharine at Mells, to break the news to her daughter. Choking back her tears, she sat down and tried to pull herself together. Across the hall she could hear Elizabeth teasing Puffin, while the whiff of cigar smoke and the hum of the men's voices emerged from the dining room down the passage. Crossing back into the bridge room, she told Puffin and the women what had happened. Nan burst into tears and Elizabeth, who had been particularly fond of her eldest half brother, 'sobbed convulsively'. Mrs Bridges, whose only son had been killed the previous year, implored Margot 'not to tell Henry yet'. However, Cowans was due to be picked up by his chauffeur at 10.30 p.m. to be driven back to London and it was already 10.10, so she felt he must be told at once. She asked Clouder, the butler, to call him out.

As soon as Asquith saw his wife's face at the other end of the passage he guessed what she was about to tell him. He covered his face with his hands and, his voice already breaking, asked how and where it had happened. She filled him in with the sketchy details she had had from Davies. By now they could hear Cowans putting on his coat in the hall, and Asquith, struggling to control himself, went across to say goodbye. 'Our boy Raymond was killed on Friday.' The general gently clasped the Prime Minister's hands in his own and promised to find out everything he could, before disappearing into the darkness.

It was the moment when everything against which Asquith had steeled himself came flooding in; worries he had tried to push to the darkest recesses of his mind as he strove to concentrate all his energies on steering his country through the bloodiest war in history. He silently followed Margot into the now empty 'bridge' room where he slumped into a red Chinese arm chair, 'put his head on his arms on the table and sobbed passionately'. Margot flung her arms round him and sat on his knee, for once speechless, as she listened to her husband's lament for his lost son: 'Oh! The awful waste of a man like Raymond – the best brain of his age in our time – any career he liked lying in front of him. I always felt it would happen – Oc may get off, but not Raymond.' It was a phrase he was to repeat many times over the next few days. Again and again he asked his wife what Davies had said, what Haig had written. At a loss to know what to do 'to stop his emotion', Margot asked Elizabeth and Puffin to come in and to try to comfort their father. Elizabeth sat on his knee, while Puffin, overwhelmed by his father's grief, rubbed his head against his sleeve. After a while, the boy silently took himself to bed. Later Elizabeth too left him alone with his thoughts.

Margot found him well after midnight sitting in the same chair 'his poor face set with tears but quite simple and natural – a wonderful exhibition of emotion, self-mastery, and unselfconsciousness', she wrote later in her diary. 'I was never more struck by the size and depth of his nature, the absence of bitterness and largeness of his heart and purpose than that night.'[17] She took him up to his bedroom and he talked to her of Raymond long into the night, of his son's childhood, the rebelliousness that was already beginning to worry Helen shortly before her death, his prodigious gifts and his hopes that one day he would fulfil them. 'I can honestly say,' Asquith wrote to Sylvia two days later, 'that in my own life he was the thing of which I was truly proud, and in him and his future I had invested all my stock of hope.'[18]

Over the next few days and weeks, the Asquiths were overwhelmed with telegrams and letters. Margot alone, a 'mere' stepmother, had over 200. The messages came from all over the world and from all kinds and conditions of people: family, friends, political colleagues and opponents, officers and men who had served with Raymond and complete strangers touched that their Prime Minister now shared their grief. Asquith, according to Margot, 'answered nearly all of them himself'.[19] 'I don't believe that any man was ever more loved than he, or loved by so many whose love was worth having,' he wrote to Viola. 'And he has died gloriously, still young and without a stain or scar on his memory . . . Counsellors tell me that I ought not to be sorrowful. But I am: like a man out of whose sky the twin stars of Pride and Hope have both vanished into lasting darkness.' Viola and Sylvia both rallied round splendidly to 'minister to sore and shattered hearts'.[26] Margot appreciated their support for her stricken husband more than ever, describing Sylvia in her diary at this time as 'a great joy to Henry. She is perfectly true and straight and a fine creature.'[21]

On Tuesday 19 September, after Margot had returned to London to get Puffin ready for Winchester, Asquith drove the eighty or so miles to Mells to see Katharine and her children. 'I have never seen anyone so stunned and shattered,' he wrote to Sylvia afterwards. 'All she wants is to die. I spent an hour with her and I hope I did some little good.'[22]

Margot, torn apart by guilt and regrets over her relationship with Raymond, had to contend with yet more grief as two more of her nephews were consumed in the maelstrom on the Somme. Her brother Frank's son, Mark Tennant, was blown apart by a German shell while returning to his trench after going over to congratulate Iain Colquhoun on them both surviving the attack in which Raymond was killed. Shortly afterwards, Margot's eldest brother Eddie (Lord Glenconner) lost his nineteen-year-old youngest son, 'Bim'. The three memorial services at the Guards' Chapel, for Mark, Bim and Raymond, were held in the same week. Raymond's, held on Saturday 13 October, was the last; the dead Grenadier's father and stepmother wept openly throughout the ceremony.

It was the first time Margot had seen Katharine since Raymond's death. After the service she accompanied Katharine, Frances and 'little Helen' down to the Wharf, later noting: 'I shall never forget her [Katharine's] sorrow – her beauty, and the pain of seeing her will remain with me forever. She was wonderfully generous too as she knew I had often criticized him, but she said she knew he had always loved me and she felt <u>sure</u> of my love for them both – Katharine is a fine creature.'[23]

Katharine's generosity and forgiveness helped Margot to deal with her own grief and guilt. She tried to purge her feelings of remorse about her relationship with Raymond by devoting pages and pages in her journal to analysis of his character, which had baffled so many others besides herself. 'Why,' she asked 'with his amazing brain, wit, industry, sense of duty . . . charm, beauty and health he did not make the world <u>ring</u> with his success?' She recalled his supposed corrupting role as a mentor to a younger Oxford generation, what she called his 'unfortunate' influence on 'Edward Horner, Ettie's boys, Patrick [Shaw-Stewart] and others'. This view of the malign power, wielded by 'the King' of the Coterie (as Diana called Raymond) was apparently shared by Ettie herself, as well as Rendall (the headmaster of Winchester and Raymond's former housemaster). Cys, though, had told her that he thought his eldest brother's acolytes (who were his own contemporaries) were as bad for him as he was for them, and that 'it was Raymond's disciples copying him that did him harm'. But above all Margot reverted to her own tortured feelings about her role as stepmother:

> A wonderful mother would have made all the difference . . . If I had been his mother – If!! We were such friends till he went to the Bar. After that I used to sit in my Cavendish Square boudoir with my door open to hear him come in, and watch him walk upstairs past my open door nearly every night – (not to go and see Violet who was ill, or Elizabeth, who was the baby – but to smoke alone). If I had been his mother I would have brought him in to smoke his pipe with me . . . I could have easily got Raymond away from shyness by chaffing and fagging him and making him put himself in the pool, if I had been his mother.[24]

While Margot agonized over her flawed relationship with Raymond, Asquith tried to lose himself in his work, as he had a quarter of a century earlier after the death of Helen. After nearly nine years at 10 Downing Street, the last two trying to mobilize the country's War effort in the face of immense political and administrative obstacles, the strain on the sixty-four-year-old Prime Minister was now almost unbearable. Five weeks after Raymond's death, he confessed to Ettie: 'I am a broken man – but I try to go on day by day.'[25]

By now, the fate of the Asquith Government was inextricably bound up with the success or failure of the Allied offensive on the Somme. Had Haig achieved a decisive victory, Asquith's position would have been unassailable. However, as the British troops ground to a halt in the mud of that exceptionally wet autumn of 1916, the Prime Minister's enemies in the 'Monday Night Cabal' scented blood and prepared to move in for the kill.

*

On 18 September, three days after Raymond's death, the men of the Royal Naval Division were ordered to hand over their trenches in the Souchez sector and to proceed south for training in trench assault: Kelly noted fatalistically in his diary that it looked as if their turn had come to 'follow the way of all flesh to the Somme'.[26]

Moves were soon afoot to make sure that the life of another of the Prime Minister's sons was not going to be put at risk. It seems that Margot got a message through to Haig begging him to remove Oc from front line duties, warning of the dire effect on the Prime Minister if he too were to be killed. Haig needed little prompting: although he was the least 'political' of generals, he dreaded any further weakening in Asquith's position since that would lead to his replacement by Lloyd George, whom he regarded as 'shifty and unreliable'.[27] On 20 September General Haking, commander of the XIth Corps, wrote to Oc offering him a position on his staff.* The same day, Major General Paris, commanding the RND, sent a letter of condolence on his 'gallant brother's death', making it clear that he would place no obstacles in his way if Oc wished to accept the staff job: 'You have served with us for almost 2 years – and if you must go elsewhere I can well understand the advisability of such a course. I would like to tell you how I have always appreciated your good work. The whole Division will keenly feel your departure and you will take with you the good wishes and sympathy of all ranks.'

Oc himself had not the slightest intention of ducking out of danger. Never one to be over-deferential to those in authority, he replied curtly to Haking that 'unless or until the time comes when the shortage of Staff Officers compels Generals to order Officers to go to be trained for Staff duties, I do not think it my duty to leave my present work, which I understand to some extent and enjoy'.[28] He then accompanied the rest of the Royal Naval Division to their training area near Ranchicourt, where they were put through their paces being made to launch repeated simulated assaults on a trench system laid out to replicate the German fortifications on Vimy Ridge.

On 13 October the Hood relieved the 11th Royal Sussex in front line trenches opposite the German-held village of Beaumont Hamel. They now knew that they were to take part in what was to be the last big attack of the Somme offensive, with the aim of driving the Germans out of a strongly fortified salient around the River Ancre, the one section of their original front line in the Somme area to have successfully withstood every effort to capture it. The next day Paris

---

*Margot later told Cynthia that Haig had ordered Oc on to the staff 'because he thought the P.M. must be shielded from further blows' – which seems to imply some connivance between the two of them. (*Lady Cynthia Asquith Diaries*, p. 239: entry for 24 November 1916)

was severely wounded by a German shell during a trench inspection, and lost a leg. The Army High Command, who continued to resent the free and easy atmosphere of the Naval battalions, seized the opportunity to replace him as divisional commander with one of their own, Major General Sir Cameron Shute, who was determined to shake up a bunch of men suffering from what he called 'lamentable discipline'.[29] He immediately put up the backs of his new command by rubbishing their effectiveness, ridiculing their insistence on retaining naval ranks, trying to enforce army rather than naval salutes (with palms down) and, most tellingly, banning beards.*

Shute ordered up two shifts of 500 men from reserve units to dig fresh assembly trenches to be used as jumping off points in the planned assault on the enemy lines; and hoping to surprise the Germans and minimize casualties, he instructed that this must be done in a single night (20–21 October). Freyberg, charged with providing cover for the working parties and fearing that the operation would end in chaos, put Oc in charge of making sure that the working parties found their correct positions. When the Germans started to bombard them with *Minnenwerfer*, Oc and five other members of his team were buried and badly concussed. Although Oc's eardrums were ruptured, he ignored the excruciating pain, shook himself down and tried to rally the diggers to continue with their work, to no avail as they panicked and bolted back to the relative safety of Hamel. In the end, the task was accomplished by miners serving with the Royal Naval Division itself. So much for Shute's opinion of the Division's 'lamentable discipline'.

Oc knew there was something seriously wrong with his ears, but he was determined not to miss the forthcoming action and tried to ignore his deafness and acute earache. However, a couple of days later he received a written command to report to Corps headquarters: Haking had accepted at face value his insolent challenge to order him to join his staff. There was now no point in avoiding medical advice and the doctors immediately diagnosed perforated eardrums and invalided him home for treatment at the King Edward VII Hospital for Officers in London. Oc's first concern was the

---

*This last action led to A.P. Herbert – then serving with the Hawke Battalion – writing the celebrated *Ballad of Codson's Beard* (eventually published anonymously in *Punch* in January 1918), in honour of Sub-Lieutenant Codner, who invoked King's regulations and refused to shave.

effect on his father when he saw his son's name on the casualty lists, so he wrote to Violet to ask her to reassure him: 'I doubt whether anyone, except Fritz [Freyberg] or Cleg [Kelly] can realize what a very bitter disappointment it is for me not to be with them just now. In case I may appear as a Casualty under the heading "Shell Shock", will you please tell Father how things really stand – that I am perfectly well except for my ears, and that I do not mind Shells any less or any more than I did before.'[30]

Asquith did not disguise his relief that Oc was, for the moment, out of danger, writing to Sylvia: 'the great news here is the return of Oc', who was '<u>ordered</u> (not offered) to take a place on the staff of 5th Corps Command'.[31]

The Royal Naval Division had to wait until 13 November for their long-planned assault. The Germans defended their positions doggedly and successfully held off almost all of the attacking units: not, however, the Hood. Freyberg, displaying amazing personal bravery as well as extraordinary leadership, turned the whole course of the battle in a brilliant flanking attack, capturing the key fortified village of Beaucourt. The New Zealander, who was severely wounded in the course of the action, was awarded the Victoria Cross and instantly became a national hero in Britain. The battle cost the attackers dear: the Royal Naval Division alone sustained 3,000 casualties. Even Shute could not now deny their bravery and commitment.

As soon as Oc read the first reports of the battle in the evening paper, he wrote to Freyberg, 'very anxious to see the casualty lists. I do hope we got off reasonably lightly in killed at any rate . . . I can't tell you how flat I feel at not having been in it. It's too bloody. I hope no serious harm has come to any of the old guard, officers or men.' His first eyewitness account was a letter from McCracken, the Hood battalion surgeon:

> Words fail me when I try to describe our men . . . They stuck to the barrage like heroes . . . [Cardy] Montagu [commanding Oc's old company] was splendid and all his men swear he should have had a VC too. Really he was grand. He was slightly wounded in the back and had a lump of stuff through his helmet. He smoked his pipe and cigars all the time and carried a walking stick – a most dignified and imposing fellow . . .

Your little Castle [Oc's nineteen-year-old soldier servant] was killed, or rather died of wounds. I found him lying in a shell-hole playing the hero with an H.A.C. [Honourable Artillery Company] fellow who was kicking up Hell with a bullet through his leg. I felt like crying, and then next I found Cleg shot through the back of the head opposite a dug-out in the German 3rd line.

A few days later Cardy Montagu wrote with more details of Kelly's death: 'Poor Cleg was killed right at the beginning. He was so enthusiastic about the whole thing and told me the night before he was really glad to be in it . . . He went on to lead an attack on a bombing post . . . and they showed fight.'[32]

Thanks to Kelly's inspiring leadership, his men went on to overrun the enemy strongpoint, which had been holding up the whole battalion. The death of the man who, along with Freyberg, had come to be his closest friend was what Oc had most dreaded. It left him, as he confessed to Freyberg (who was recovering in hospital from his wounds), 'very bitter. Cleg had such a wonderful enjoyment of life and communicated his electricity to those he was with.'[33] The simultaneous death of Castle ('the most devoted brave little fellow') added to his distress. Kelly's sister, Mary, asked Oc to contribute an obituary tribute in his old school newspaper, the *Eton College Chronicle*. It shows the qualities which Oc himself had so admired in his friend:

He [Cleg] was not, and I think never would have made, an enthusiastic soldier. He spent most of his leisure time composing music and reading books . . . But he had a true artist's desire to perfect his Company. He was an uncompromising disciplinarian, spared neither others nor himself, and rarely turned a blind eye. Highly strung, and as brave as a lion, aware and utterly contemptuous of all risks, he commanded the confidence and respect of all under his command . . . He was contentious, always happiest in argument: interested in the psychology of his friends, highly critical of them, and warm-heartedly loyal to them; and violently intolerant of anything that bore the faintest tinge of cheapness, insincerity, pretentiousness and bad manners.[34]

After Raymond's death, Oc had written to Violet: '"After the War" becomes daily a more parched and flowerless prospect for most of our generation: and the killing of Boches less unpalatable . . . There is little of the old world of fun left to us.'[35] Now Cleg too had been killed, he was more determined than ever to return to the Front. With Freyberg out of action for some time, he was the obvious replacement to command the Hood. Violet, for all her concern for her brother's safety, understood how he felt. When she wrote to Freyberg to commiserate over Kelly's death and his own wounds, she seems to have known nothing about Margot's supposed efforts to lobby Haig to put Oc on the Staff:

> Oc arrived here very deaf and looking strained and shattered I thought – tho' he hasn't had a trace of shell shock – and now hears almost perfectly again. He is of course moving Heaven and Earth to get out again and back to the battalion, and has I think wired to the Brigadier to apply for him. Whether there will be any Staff hanky-panky about it I don't know. It is hard on Oc I do think, and was not <u>in any way</u> prompted or inspired from home, tho' of course it would be a relief to us to know him safe.[36]

For the time being, the most useful thing Oc could do was to write to the families of his men who had been killed: among them Petty Officer George Ramsay, a twenty-year-old Scot, who had won the Distinguished Service Medal in Gallipoli on Oc's own recommendation after he saved several lives by throwing back a Turkish grenade. Ramsay's father, a miner from Bannockburn, replied: 'We were looking for a letter from you, for George spoke so highly of you in his letters, he told us you were the bravest of the brave, he said he would follow you anywhere.'[37]

Oc was not alone in his stubborn wish to join the growing legion of the dead. News had just come in that Aubrey Herbert's cousin, Lord ('Bron') Lucas, who had resigned from the Cabinet to join the Royal Flying Corps, had been shot down and killed. Beb had recently received his inoculations prior to being posted back to the Front and Cynthia's diary entries at this time veer wildly between her 'terror about Beb going out' and feeling 'absurdly secure' about him. She was much more frightened for her now 'indispensable' admirer, Basil Blackwood, who had seized the opportunity of Lord Wimborne's resignation as Viceroy in Dublin in the wake of the Easter rising, to return, at the age of forty-eight, to his regiment, the Grenadier Guards, as a subaltern.[38]

Cynthia went to see Basil off to France on 7 October with a draft of new recruits – 'nearly three hundred magnificent men almost all over six feet, marching along with women hanging on to them' – on their way to replace those slaughtered alongside Raymond in the struggle for Lesboeufs. Since then, she had written to her admirer every day since his departure for the Front. In spite of her habitual *frisson* of sexual excitement at the sight of uniformed men marching to War, she had little sympathy for the kamikaze tendencies of so many of their middle-aged friends and family. She raised the issue with her father-in-law a couple of weeks after Raymond had been killed and noted his reaction:

> Poor P.M. looks very, very sad. He deplored Basil being in the Guards and said it ought to have been absolutely forbidden instead of only made difficult. Certainly it oughtn't to be left to their own choice whether people with brains like Raymond should go on a Staff. Appalling as the waste is, no individual can put it even to himself that he is too potentially useful elsewhere to throw away his life as a Subaltern in a function which anyone else could fill equally well. But, if the Staff needs an individual's brains, it ought to come as a direct command. As it is, no one sensitive will go on a Staff now, so invidious has it become, and all our intellect is being chucked away in the trenches.[39]

It was not a sentiment that Beb, as he now prepared to return to the Front, appreciated any more than his brothers. Nonetheless, Cynthia detected a tinge of bitterness once when he returned 'jarred' from a 'big Downing Street bridge dinner – and the contemplation of the men who will survive the war, Jimmy Rothschild, McKenna etc'.[40]

Cynthia and Beb invited Oc to spend his last weekend in England with them in Brighton. Cynthia's cousin, Mary Herbert, completed the party (Aubrey was with the Anglo-French forces in Salonika). For a brief moment, the four friends were able to forget the War as they passed 'a very happy, amusing evening together'. Cynthia put up Oc and Mary 'unchaperoned' in the Royal York Hotel and was delighted when she heard that 'the maid who showed Mary her room, archly informed her that "the gentleman was next door"'. The hotel staff's presumption of an illicit affair provided 'an excellent standing joke for our Sunday party'. Cynthia had 'never seen Beb in such good form. Very "loose" too, chaffing Mary about her "turgid passions".' No mercy was shown to Oc, with Mary ribbing him about Cynthia's confession that she had been 'very much in love' with him in Dresden: 'Dear Oc,' noted his sister in law, 'he was so embarrassed – even at so posthumous a declaration – that he nearly twisted one of the tails off Mary's sables. However, he was able to murmur: "Not more than I with her".[41]

On the Monday morning, 4 December, Cynthia, Mary and Oc caught the eleven o'clock train to London. At the station news stand Cynthia spotted a headline in the *Daily Mail*: 'An Asquith Flag Day', and naïvely hoped it was 'a suggestion for an Asquith benefit collection', only to discover that the newspaper was urging 'everyone against Asquith should buy and wear a red flag, thus painting England red'.[42] Her father-in-law was fighting for his political life.

21

'An aerial tornado, from which I cannot escape'

B Y THE BEGINNING of December 1916, the political world was awash with rumours of plots against the Prime Minister. Cynthia had been kept well abreast of the latest gossip by Bluetooth, who warned her in mid November that Lloyd George was 'hand in glove with Carson and Winston', who were 'doing their best to unseat the P.M.', having '"got at" Bonar Law'.[1]

Until the Battle of the Somme, Asquith's popularity remained remarkably impervious to the best efforts of Northcliffe and others to undermine it, his calm unruffled manner presenting a soothing antidote to the panic mongers. The sense of national shock over a military campaign which resulted in more than 400,000 British casualties for little territorial gain was tremendous. Margot, writing to Freyberg about the loss of 'dear Kelly', expressed the widespread sense of bewilderment: 'I know I know nothing, but it does strike me that the soldiers must be very wanting in cunning and cover and care. We always fling ourselves at death – we don't creep and crawl and we always go too far . . . Can it be right to lose nine to ten thousand in casualties every two or three days? Is there no way of surprising the foe? I feel terribly unhappy over it all.'[2]

While the attention of Margot and most of the country was focused on the black hole that continued to suck in the nation's menfolk, the plotters in the Monday Night Cabal sensed in the public's horrified bewilderment at the carnage on the Somme a perhaps never-to-be-repeated opportunity to overthrow the despised

'Squiff'. Thanks partly to Margot's own loose tongue, they knew Asquith had been badly affected by his son's death: in late November Sir George Riddell, the proprietor of the *News of the World*, heard from Robert Donald, the editor of the Liberal *Daily Chronicle*, how Margot had told him over tea at Downing Street that 'never a day passes but that he weeps about him in his bedroom'. Riddell commented in his diary: 'it seems as if he is breaking, poor man, under the strain'.[3] Few others in the Northcliffe camp were remotely sympathetic as they readied to topple the Prime Minister.

Margot, whose nose was usually so adept at sniffing out the latest threat to her husband, was for once completely off the scent. Still 'heart broken with the Folly of the appointment' of Lloyd George as War Minister back in June, she had refused to discuss politics with Asquith ever since.[4] When in November he was considering the formation of a small committee of ministers to run the War, he did not confide in his wife even though the idea was one she had long supported. As a result, Margot was thunderstruck when, on the morning of Saturday 2 December, she read in the newspapers of a fresh – and very public – political row involving Lloyd George, who was reported to be demanding the setting up of a three-man War Council, consisting of Carson, Bonar Law and himself, as Chairman. It was clear to everyone in the know that Lloyd George had, in the understated words of Hankey's diary, 'obviously inspired' the reports.[5]

When Margot made enquiries about what was going on she learnt that Asquith had reached a deadlock with Lloyd George over his insistence that he, as Prime Minister, must chair the proposed War Council, whereas the War Minister wanted to exclude him from the body altogether. The Asquiths were about to depart for the weekend to Walmer Castle where they were hosting a house party, and Margot was horrified that her husband could contemplate leaving London with his Government 'tottering and on the eve of collapse'. She begged him to remain in Downing Street; however, exhausted by the events of the last few weeks, he stubbornly refused to change his plans, insisting he needed 'sea air and rest from the awful strain of colleagues etc'.

Margot collared Hankey and begged him to see Bonar Law and find out what the Tory leader intended to do; then, 'exhausted and anxious and miserable', she joined her husband and their guests on the train, shutting herself away in a compartment all by herself on the pretext that she wanted to sleep. 'I felt it was <u>all up</u>,' she recorded in her journal: '<u>that I was living among the blind</u>, that Henry was going to be betrayed.'[6] Margot's political instincts were now spot on. Lloyd George's threat of resignation was, for once, serious. The ultimatum was the culmination of weeks of plotting and planning with his allies in the Monday Night Cabal, who had by now sucked into their intrigue a potent coalition of politicians and newspapermen. Few men in this nest of vipers trusted any of the others, and no one trusted either Lloyd George or Northcliffe. However, all of the conspirators by now accepted, in some cases with extreme reluctance, that Lloyd George was the only credible alternative to Asquith as Prime Minister, and that their cause was nought without the powerful backing of Northcliffe and his newspapers.

Whatever his wife might imagine, Asquith himself was well aware of the seriousness of the crisis confronting him: 'Alas! the whirlwinds are blowing, and the windmills are whirling: in short, I am in the centre of an aerial tornado, from which I cannot escape,' he had written to Pamela McKenna a few days earlier, sounding like some Homeric hero preparing to meet his doom.[7] Meanwhile, activity among the Cabal was frenetic. 'The rumpus here is simply awful,' Milner wrote that weekend to his future wife, Lady Edward Cecil (formerly Violet Maxse). 'My telephone suddenly went mad and it has not completely recovered sanity yet. L. G. is really making a Gigantic Effort to get rid of Asquith.' Nonetheless, Milner still did not trust 'the Goat' as, until recently, he had scornfully dubbed Lloyd George, confiding: 'My fear is there will be another compromise and a patch up.'[8]

On the Sunday morning, with the newspapers full of Lloyd George's threat to resign if he did not get his way, Hankey despatched Bongie in a War Office car to bring the Prime Minister back to London, where he, Reading* and Montagu had been making frantic last ditch efforts to stitch up a compromise with the wayward War Minister. Margot, brushing aside the pleas of her guest, Lady (Beatrice) Granard, to stay at Walmer, insisted on accompanying her husband back to London, although she did at least allow him to travel with Bongie in the Asquiths' own car, while she took the War Office vehicle. The two cars reached Downing Street at 2.30 p.m. in time for a late lunch with Montagu, Cys and Davies, after which Margot took

---

*The Lord Chief Justice, formerly Sir Rufus Isaacs.

herself off to the Prime Minister's study overlooking Horse Guards
Parade to write letters. Looking at 'Disraeli's hideous chairs', she
wondered if she would 'look out of the windows or observe the ugly
furniture for many more days in 10 Downing Street'. She vented her
frustration on poor Reading, who was genuinely striving to broker a
deal, writing to castigate him for his continuing familiarity with Lloyd
George: 'No one can serve two Masters. He that is not for me is
against me.' She later recorded how a deeply hurt 'Rufus brought this
letter of mine back to me and burnt it in my drawing room fire in 10
Downing Street. I never turned a hair <u>or took back a word of my
letter</u>. I only said and <u>felt</u> sorry that I had hurt him.'[9]

Asquith was closeted with Lloyd George most of the afternoon.
They were later joined by Bonar Law. It appeared that the three men
had hammered out an agreement on the basis that the Prime
Minister would not sit on the War Council, but would reserve the
right to veto any of its decisions and would retain 'supreme and
effective control of War policy'. On the surface, it seemed to be just
the 'patch up' that Milner had feared; in fact, as would soon become
apparent, Asquith had fallen into a trap.

Margot quizzed her husband about the outcome of the meeting
when, as usual, he joined her at 7.45 to dress for dinner, which that
evening was with the Montagus in Queen Anne's Gate. Asquith said
he thought 'the crisis looked like being over', although he remained
uneasy and 'was not <u>very</u> confident'. Apparently Lloyd George had
used all his wiles in order to reassure the Prime Minister that he was
not after his job, 'protesting his perpetual <u>devotion</u> and <u>loyalty</u>', so
Asquith told his wife. 'He almost put his arm round my neck and
begged me not to believe all the stories that McKenna was spreading
about that he (Lloyd George) wanted to take my place, and was disloyal etc.' Margot, at least, was not deceived. When Asquith confessed that he had allowed the War Minister to 'oust' him from the
chairmanship of the proposed War Council, she set about berating
him: 'No one will ever forgive you or him [L.G.] or believe in you
ever again if you sit in the next room while the War is conducted
without you – they are all <u>mad</u> to have advised this.' After days of
wrangling with colleagues, Asquith was in no mood to be hectored
by his wife, who later recorded:

I felt sure that Henry had not made it clear to Lloyd George that as
President of the War Council he – <u>Henry</u> – <u>was</u> controlling the war and

that <u>nothing</u> would induce him to abandon this position tho' he was quite willing, if the Council had merely to register decisions of transport and unimportant things, to let Lloyd George take the chair in his absence. Henry swore to me that he had made it clear enough and that I was <u>quite</u> wrong – Lloyd George did <u>not</u> want to oust him. (Once someone <u>sets</u> themselves to think <u>all</u> you say is prejudice! and all they think is correct! you are helpless!) Henry practically agreed with me and said he had not the '<u>faintest</u> intention of giving up the direction of the war to Lloyd George or anyone else!!'.

It was clearly a frustrating exchange for both of them. Margot was not prepared to let the matter drop when they arrived home from their dinner party, continuing to pester her husband on the issue until 'far into the morning'. This time she tried to be more conciliatory, sitting on his knee before cloyingly asking him whether he had made it 'quite clear to Lloyd George about his (Henry's) never giving up the direction of the War, he was quite surprised and almost irritable: he asked me if I took him for a fool – I said "No, but I took Lloyd George for a knave".'[10]

What neither of the Asquiths knew was that their host that evening, still hoping for an agreement, had met Lloyd George before joining them for dinner. As Montagu left the War Ministry he spotted Northcliffe waiting in the wings, but kept what he had seen to himself: to have told Asquith would have scuppered any last chance of a reconciliation with Lloyd George, and he was naïve enough to hope the meeting had an innocent purpose. However, at the best of times Northcliffe and Lloyd George were hardly bosom buddies, and recently they had fallen out over the Press lord's new enthusiasm for Haig. But both men needed each other. Lloyd George, without a strong base of Parliamentary support, drew his political strength from the support of Northcliffe's powerful newspapers, while Northcliffe knew that Lloyd George was the only realistic alternative to the despised 'Squiff', who had so far resisted all his efforts to oust him from power. There could be only one reason for their meeting that evening: for the War Minister to brief the newspaper magnate on his meeting with Asquith and Bonar Law, and to plot their next move.

The result of the duo's parley was to be seen in the following day's edition of *The Times*, where there was a clearly first hand report of the agreement to set up a War Council, deliberately angled to appear as humiliating as possible to Asquith by implying that he had been forced to concede control of the War and effectively reduced to a puppet Prime Minister. The trap had been sprung.* All the warnings of Margot, McKenna and others about Lloyd George's duplicity now came home to mock Asquith. He was cornered: either he could ignore *The Times* article, which, as he himself put it to Sylvia, 'must have been inspired' by Lloyd George, and go ahead with the deal, in which case he would seem a mere figurehead; or else he could denounce the agreement and give Lloyd George just the pretext he needed to resign and stump the country attacking the Government.

There was, of course, only one course of action open to the Prime Minister: he must finally face down his vexatious colleague. He wrote to Lloyd George insisting that after all he himself must chair the new War Council. 'I confess,' he told Sylvia, 'to feeling a certain sense of relief. Nothing can be conceived more hellish than the experiences I have gone through during the last month. Almost for the first time I have felt I was growing old.'[11]

The following day, Tuesday 5 December, Lloyd George resigned. Asquith summoned a meeting of the other Liberal ministers in the Cabinet room to secure their backing for the reconstruction of his Government without Lloyd George. He had little difficulty. Most of them believed the exclusion of their troublesome colleague was long overdue. The one dissenter was Montagu who persisted in believing Lloyd George's insistent denials of complicity with Northcliffe. The Tories, however, were a different story. Bluetooth had been near the mark when he told Cynthia that Bonar Law had been 'got at'. The Tory leader, as Margot graphically put it, had 'always been terrified as a bird with a snake' of Carson, and now he found himself in essence being blackmailed by the Irishman and his allies: either he back Lloyd George against Asquith or else face a direct challenge to his own leadership of the Unionist Party. With Tory backbenchers, stirred up by Carson and his acolytes, increasingly restive over the lack of progress in the War and the Prime Minister's public invisibility, there

---

*Most historians have been as credulous as Montagu, accepting Lloyd George's version of these events, viz. that Geoffrey Robinson (later Dawson), *The Times* editor, wrote the article without reference to Northcliffe and on information supplied by Carson. Yet apart from the fact that Carson's own source must have been Lloyd George, the idea that the editor of a national newspaper would write a leading article during the gravest political crisis of the era without consulting his proprietor – particularly one as power-crazed as Northcliffe – is preposterous.

was the real prospect of a rebellion within Bonar Law's own ranks. When Asquith refused to reinstate the agreement that Lloyd George and not himself would chair the War Council, Bonar Law, in Margot's inimitable phraseology, 'with the intrepidity of a rabbit and the slyness of a fox, determined to break the coalition . . . rather than let them [Carson and Lloyd George] <u>break him</u>'.[12] When Asquith met 'the three C's' – Curzon, Lord Robert Cecil and Austen Chamberlain – later that afternoon, they made it clear that if their leader would not serve, neither would they. Yet Asquith was still not ready to give in. That evening he sent in his resignation to the King, believing that, when it came down to the wire, most of his Tory colleagues would prefer him to Lloyd George.

Cynthia had been due to go to the theatre with Oc, as a farewell before he returned to the Front where, having apparently outwitted all the efforts to save him, he was about to take command of the Hood. At the last minute he asked her to join him for dinner at Downing Street instead. 'The atmosphere was most electric,' she noted afterwards. The only person present who did not seem in the least perturbed was Asquith himself:

> I sat next to the P.M. – he was too darling – rubicund, serene, puffing a guinea cigar (a gift from Maud Cunard), and talking of going to Honolulu [for a holiday if he was ousted]. His conversation was as irrelevant to his life as ever . . . I had a great *accés* of tenderness for the P.M. He was so serene and dignified. Poor Margot on the other hand looked ghastly ill – distraught . . . and was imprecating in hoarse whispers, blackguarding Lloyd George and Northcliffe.

Afterwards Oc walked her to the Underground station 'very sad to say goodbye and he had a tear in his eye'. The following morning, 'Beb came up in great excitement, having secured two days' crisis leave' to support his father.[13] He lunched in Downing Street and, much to Cynthia's irritation, stayed there all afternoon, while Asquith attended a conference at Buckingham Palace called by the King to try to resolve the crisis. When the Prime Minister returned, having spurned all efforts to persuade him to serve under either Bonar Law or Lloyd George, he called another meeting of his Liberal colleagues. When he entered the Cabinet room, according to the account Margot later gave Frances Balfour, 'they got on the chairs and cheered . . . He put it to them should he join a Lloyd

George ministry and they replied "they would rather see him dead".[14]

The game was up. Twelve years later Churchill, who was to join the new Government in July 1917 as Minister of Munitions, summed up the national mood at the time: 'The impossible was demanded. Speedy victory was demanded, and the statesman was judged by the merciless test of results. The vehement, contriving, resourceful, nimble-leaping Lloyd George seemed to offer a brighter hope, or at any rate a more passionate effort. Asquith fell with dignity. He bore adversity with composure. In or out of power, disinterested patriotism and inflexible integrity were his only guides.'[15]

As the irreplaceable Hankey prepared with a heavy heart to serve a new Prime Minister lacking in any of these qualities, he wrote of the Asquiths in his diary: 'I felt very much affected at parting with both officially, seeing the desperate times we have lived through together. In many respects he was the greatest man I have ever met, or ever hope to meet, and Mrs Asquith's kindness and hospitality to me, treating me in every respect as one of her own family, are such that I can never forget or repay.'[16]

Hankey, who as Secretary to the Committee of Imperial Defence and then to the War Cabinet, had worked alongside Asquith almost every day since the beginning of the War, knew better than anyone the Herculean efforts he had made and the obstacles he had had to overcome to put the country on a war footing, and ultimately pave the way for victory. He wrote to the outgoing Prime Minister:

> What I most esteem is the privilege of having witnessed . . . your masterly and courageous handling of one desperately difficult situation after another from the moment when war became imminent until to-day. I confess that I have often wondered how any man could find it physically possible to carry on simultaneously so many heavy burdens. The country at present has only a slight conception of what it owes to your courage, nerve, tact, unswerving straightness, incredible patience, and indomitable perseverance. History, however, will record it.[17]

*

The most pressing problem facing the Asquiths after their abrupt ejection from 10 Downing Street was where to live. 20 Cavendish Square was let to Maud Cunard, and although she generously agreed to move out as soon as possible, she had to find somewhere herself and, in any case, Margot found the house in a 'filthy condition' and badly in need of redecoration. Fortunately, Lady Granard invited Asquith and Margot to stay with her at Forbes House in Halkin Street, while Cys was farmed out on the Crewes and Elizabeth went to friends in Richmond Terrace.[18]

The timing could hardly have been worse for Bongie and Violet, who was now five months pregnant. With her husband now jobless, they were obliged to let Dorset House and move in with his parents. 'I shall never be able to perch and cuckoo with Cynthia's aplomb and addresse!' she wrote to Mary Herbert. Her 'great dread' was that her baby 'will be born looking exactly like Lloyd George! whose face and personality have been branded deeper on my soul during the last weeks than any other human being's!'. In case Mary misunderstood her jocular tone, she confessed:

> I am so afraid of being hysterical and bitter and violent and all the things one should avoid like the plague. What I _feel_ about it is beyond expression ... How I long for the whole story to be told in all its sordidness ... But Father's magnanimity and bigness about it all is a heavy trial in some ways! He will hit always _three feet_ above the belt at least. The best humour of the situation so far has been Lloyd George sending for Bongie and begging him quite seriously to continue to run Downing Street for him.[19]

Lloyd George's offer to Bongie was probably a clumsy peace gesture to the Asquiths; in the event, it backfired. After being rejected as unfit by the Army, Bongie eventually accepted a post in the new Ministry of Reconstruction. His father-in-law acknowledged his work as his Private Secretary by recommending him for a knighthood in his Resignation Honours list. Violet informed Hugh Godley that 'we were both _very_ averse to having it ... But on consultation with Edgar [Lord d'Abernon] and one or two men of low City cunning I was told that it _would_ materially enhance his chances of making money in the City.'[20]

Asquith, Violet and Bongie spent the first week out of power at Walmer Castle, while Cys, who was suffering from flu, preferred the less charged atmosphere of Brighton, where he joined Beb and Cynthia. The sudden release of pressure after months of relentless strain triggered a complete physical collapse in Asquith himself, who was confined to bed for four days. He informed Sylvia:

I think I was really tired, as for a couple of days I was completely indifferent to the outside world, and not only didn't read a newspaper I was quite
incurious as to what it might contain. Violet has been with me all week.
Margot hurried here on Monday with Parkie [the family doctor], but the
sense of being 'out of it' was too much for her, and by cock crow on
Wednesday she rushed back to London where she has been ever since,
apparently in a maelstrom of gossip and quidnunckery – what do you say
to that for a word, invented for you on the spur of the moment?[21]

Predictably Margot was the member of the family worst affected
by the disaster, bitterly blaming herself and everyone but her
husband for not forestalling the crisis. She desperately missed the
stabilizing support of Oc, whom, she lamented, was 'with his Naval
Hood Battalion in France (waiting for Death)'.[22] At the same time,
Bongie, so often a prop in recent years, was temporarily in her bad
books for his *sang froid* throughout the drama:

> I can truthfully say I never saw Bongie shocked, distressed, indignant or
> in the smallest degree surprised. He was kind, sympathetic, understand-
> ing and, as always, most unselfish in little and big ways, but as imperturb-
> able over the whole catastrophe as if it had been a daily occurrence. He
> saw Henry wounded and stabbed to the heart – me an absolute wreck!
> morally disgusted and shocked – the Government smashed to atoms in
> the greatest war and at the most dangerous moment in the life of this
> country, and men put in its place of the lowest possible type (a Press
> Government – Lloyd George, Northcliffe, Rothermere, Aitken,* Carson
> etc), but not one sign of indignation of any sort did I or anyone else
> see.[23]

Margot's greatest ire, however, was reserved for her childhood
friend, Arthur Balfour, who threw in his lot with the 'scoundrels'
and, having studiously avoided becoming involved in the dispute
between Asquith and Lloyd George, accepted the Foreign Office in
the new Government: a change of allegiance that Churchill memor-

---

*Lloyd George raised Northcliffe from a barony to a viscountcy and made him Chairman
of the Mission to the United States. His brother, Lord Rothermere, did not become a
Viscount until 1919, but entered the Government in 1917 as Air Minister, while Sir Max
Aitken, the owner of the *Daily Express*, was immediately rewarded by being created Lord
Beaverbrook, and in 1918 was appointed Chancellor of the Duchy of Lancaster and
Minister of Information.

ably likened to 'a powerful, graceful cat walking delicately and unsoiled across a rather muddy street'.[24]

Margot vented her fury in a wild letter to the traitor's sister-in-law, Betty Balfour, pouring scorn on the new Foreign Secretary's supposed 'patriotism': 'I know chivalry is not his strong point, but this no one would have believed.' What really incensed her was that one of the bones of contention between Asquith and Lloyd George was the former Prime Minister's insistence that Balfour sit on the War Council, whereas she had 'heard Lloyd George say, not once, but 50 times – "Balfour is gaga and will have to retire into private life"'. Characteristically, she quickly apologized once she realized the offence she had caused:

> Darling Betty,
> I hurt you over my spiteful remarks about Arthur – as you know I shall always love Arthur and deeply regret having said this, and hope you have not repeated it to anyone . . . I am not malignant and in spite of having said it I am not angry with Arthur or any of them I think. They made a fatal blunder, but it may be all for the good.[25]

What lay behind Margot's final aside is hard to imagine: perhaps she already hoped that once her husband had recovered his strength, he would return triumphantly to clear up the mess made by the new Government.

Although Asquith remained physically below par for some months, he quickly regained his equanimity, helped by the flood of admiring letters from friends, political colleagues and opponents. Margot's old 'Soul' friend Harry Cust wrote of 'a great sense of loss, but a greater sense of pride', calling himself part of 'a choir "temporarily invisible but immense"'; Katharine's brother, Edward Horner, who had not seen him 'since beloved Raymond's death which I felt too bitterly to be able to think of much besides my own loss', movingly informed the ousted Prime Minister that he had been brought up to think him the most splendid person alive.[26]

The Asquiths' attention was momentarily wrested away from politics when the newspapers reported that Elizabeth was 'engaged' to Hugh Gibson, a young American diplomat. Asquith wrote to Sylvia on 27 December from Easton Grey, where the family spent Christmas: 'I am afraid it has now been so much circulated that it will have to be formally and publicly contradicted. Neither Margot nor I

could consent to anything of the kind . . . The whole thing is a nuis-
ance particularly coming just at this moment. It is less than a month
since she was announced [by the anti-Asquith Press] to be engaged
to [the German Admiral] von Tirpitz's son!'

The Asquiths felt that their daughter, at only nineteen, was too
young to marry and might well live to regret her choice. Apart from
the fact that he was not English, Gibson was poor, and no doubt
they hoped that Elizabeth would eventually fall in love with a more
'suitable' Englishman. However, Elizabeth had inherited too much
of her parents' forceful personalities to be easily talked out of her
romance, and the following week her father went to see Gibson at
his rooms ('to avoid observation and gossip') to persuade him to
drop his suit:

> I told him frankly that I thought Elizabeth in any case too young to
> engage herself at present and that he would understand that, if she came
> to marry, I should much prefer that it should be to a countryman of her
> own . . . He was very sensible and understanding, and has I think a really
> fine character. At any rate he took all I said in good part and was quite
> acquiescent. It is a nuisance, not the less so, that he is an excellent and in
> some ways very nearly a remarkable man.[27]

Gibson agreed not to write to Elizabeth for a year to test the
strength of her feelings. Neither Asquith nor Margot seem to have
been the least suspicious that the diplomat's easy agreement to break
off relations with their daughter might indicate that he was less keen
on her than she on him. Soon afterwards, he was recalled to the
United States, and although Elizabeth continued to write to him, he
failed to respond to her letters even after the expiration of the year to
which he had agreed not to write to her. Elizabeth, meanwhile, did
not waver in her love for him, deluding herself that her feelings were
reciprocated.

Cynthia, who barely noticed Freyberg when Oc introduced him back
in May, was one of the first people to visit the now acclaimed war
hero at the Park Lane Hospital, where he became a patient shortly
after the Asquiths' departure from Downing Street. Afterwards, she
described the wounded man in her diary as a 'splendid animal'. The
interest was mutual and, as soon as he left hospital four weeks later,

Freyberg invited her to lunch at the Carlton Grill with the rich social-ite, Irene Lawley, to whom he had been introduced by the Asquiths during his previous leave, and Eddie Marsh. Cynthia was particularly impressed when, despite still being unable to move one arm, her host 'succeeded where others failed in winding up Irene's car for us'.[28] Over the next few weeks, Cynthia had several long 'dentists' with Freyberg, intrigued by his combination of 'lack of humour, chafing ambition, and a kind of admirable ruthlessness'. He gave her 'the impression of a potentially really great soldier – in the Napoleonic sense rather than the V.C. hero', but at the same time she was touched by his admission that 'he hated pain and would rather die than go through his recent sufferings again'.[29]

Cynthia's irregular flitting between her husband in Brighton and her various 'cuckoo nests' in London and the country, was inevitably remarked on by Beb's fellow officers, and more particularly by their wives. Cynthia herself, though, was merely 'amused' when she heard 'the gossip was the London Society woman who only paid flying visits to her husband'.[30] Her excuse for the infrequency of her visits was her husband's continued insistence on staying at the expensive Royal York Hotel during her stays. Nonetheless, apart from squab-bling over money, they seem to have remained fond of each other. The morning after one tiff, Beb ordered a fly to take her up to the Sussex Downs to see him practising with his guns: 'It was gloriously beautiful up there and I enjoyed it. Beb looked very soldierly and professional. I didn't get back till 12.30 and felt wonderfully ozoned. Beb came back to lunch. We are so comfortable here. It does make such a difference having hot coffee for breakfast and a warm lounge [in the Royal York Hotel]. I wish we could stay, but we oughtn't to, alas!'[31]

Back in November, Cynthia had written in her diary of her 'terror about Beb going out' to France; yet when at the end of February he was at last posted to the Front and simultaneously she became ill, she was strangely reluctant to admit that her affliction was caused by worry about him: 'I don't know what has come over me these days, but I have got a complete mental or nervous collapse, akin to a kind of madness. Such ghastly depression – life seems a sheer nightmare, every prospect a horror, every retrospect a pain. Pangs of the past and fears of the future, with terrible lassitude.'

At the last minute she decided to abandon the idea of going to see off her husband's troopship at Southampton docks, excusing herself that she did not feel physically up to it. She did at least see him off at Waterloo Station on 26 February, buttressed by her mother and her cousins Mary Herbert and Evelyn de Vesci, but could not face waiting for the train to depart. Afterwards, she 'felt rather better. Gone to the Front is better than going.'[32]

Cynthia was surprised rather than offended when a few weeks later Margot 'practically reproached me with my calmness while Beb was at the Front'. She was not even shocked by D. H. Lawrence's mischievous assurance, presumably sparked by her perceived ambivalence about her husband's fate, that 'Beb wouldn't be killed if I didn't want him to be'.[33] Three days earlier, reporting 'a thrilling talk' with Mary Herbert, Cynthia was:

> Astonished to hear my marriage was much canvassed, and by many thought unhappy and detached. How astonishing are impressions given and taken – and I thought I was proverbially 'uxorious', and was almost anxious to soften that impression! It bears out the theory that you cannot have any friendships with men without people drawing the inference that you are detached from your husband. Obviously, from what Mary said, I have been considered in love with Basil . . . No one would believe that Basil had made no sort of declaration until a few months ago – but then I know I am particularly difficult to make love to, and of course outsiders don't know this . . .
>
> She said the Asquiths' opinion was that I neglected Beb, didn't try and make the most of him by sufficient 'taking in hand', and that I thoroughly lowered his spirits and vitality. It is too comic, only it makes one angry. As a matter of fact, it is always in his family that I suffer from feeling Beb underrated.[34]

A few days after Oc returned to France in December 1916, Shute vetoed his appointment to command the Hood, selecting instead Lieutenant Colonel Creagh-Osborne, a regular army officer, on the pretext that the latter had more experience of trench warfare, although Oc later discovered that it was he who was the more battle-hardened of the two. The real reason for his sudden demotion was that, despite the Hood's decisive part in the battle of Beaucourt, the general remained stubbornly determined to impose a strict 'army' regime on the most eccentric of the Naval battalions under his command. When Oc, true to form, challenged the decision, the general rubbed salt into the wound by telling him, in a cattish reference to his earlier forced withdrawal from the front line, that he would not tolerate having a man in charge of a battalion who was liable to be posted to the staff on the eve of an attack. Oc's pleas to be allowed at least to return to being a company commander were ignored and, as a further humiliation, he was sent on a course for staff officers of the rank of captain, even though he had been a lieutenant commander (the equivalent of a major) for eighteen months and had temporarily commanded a battalion.[35]

Creagh-Osborne was wounded and evacuated soon after taking command, to be replaced by another regular army officer. Oc heard that the mood in the Hood was pessimistic, as it passed one of the coldest winters on record holding the area they had helped to capture around Beaucourt. Severe frost made the ground too hard to dig proper trenches and for the most part they had to rely on shell holes for protection against enemy artillery and snipers. Everyone in the battalion was longing for Freyberg's return.

On 2 February Oc was inspecting the site of the fighting at Beaucourt when he met a Royal Naval Division officer who mentioned that the next day the Hood was taking part in an attack on the ridge overlooking nearby Grandcourt. Oc was determined to be in on 'the stunt' and bamboozled his superiors into allowing him to act as an 'observer' for the artillery.[36] The plan was for the Hawke and Hood battalions, with the Nelson in support, to launch a night attack on the German trenches. The Hood's task was particularly complicated since, in the words of Douglas Jerrold, the Divisional historian, 'their objective consisted not only of a well-defined sector of the enemy trenches [on the ridge], but an ill-defined group of posts in the valley. The capture of these necessitated a half-right turn, an obvious source of confusion in a night advance, by the platoons on the right.'

Soon after the assault began at 11 p.m. confusion did indeed result, with the Hood and two Hawke platoons ending up well to the right of their objective.[37] The enemy gunners soon found their range and one of the first casualties was Lieutenant Colonel Munro, the Hood's new commanding officer, who was seriously wounded. The situation appeared desperate as German infantry now counterattacked the disorientated Naval troops. Then 'out of nowhere' Oc appeared and, without any official authority, simply took charge. Thomas Macmillan, a clerk serving at 189th Brigade headquarters, noted the consternation when they heard what had occurred:

No one was more surprised than [the Brigade Major] Barnett when he learned that Asquith was in the thick of it. Turning sharply to me he asked, 'Where the hell did he spring from?' I had the sense not to attempt a reply, for I was as perplexed as the Major. The favoured ones in London, who did not reckon my life as precious as that of Arthur Melland Asquith, were far out when they thought by transferring him to the corps they might sleep at nights without dreading his being killed.[38]

By eight o'clock the following morning the Hood under Oc's command had not only repelled the German counter-attack but had captured most of its original objectives. However, German strong-holds on their left were still holding out, preventing a link-up with the Hawke, so once Oc was satisfied that his men were ready to repel another counter-attack, he returned to brigade headquarters to seek reinforcements. After spending the rest of the day carrying out a detailed reconnaissance of the positions still in enemy hands, at 8 p.m. he picked up the reinforcements: 'B' company of the Drake Battalion, whose company commander, Lieutenant Hugh Kingsmill Lunn, later recalled the impression he made:

> An active imperious figure, strongly contrasted with the tired troops who had been working hard with little rest during the last 24 hours, sprang up on the road . . . Our progress over the torn ground was slow. The men kept falling in and out of shellholes, and Asquith's impatience increased. He seemed to feel as a champion sprinter would who should find himself, on turning out to lower the world's record for the hundred yards, unac-countably compelled to do the course leading a tortoise on a string.[39]

When Oc and the Drakes reached the enemy trenches, the Germans were still defiantly holding out in spite of being pounded all day by the British gunners. Oc led off the attack under rifle fire, and although he was shot in the left arm in the early stages of the action, 'he carried on', according to Macmillan, 'until victory was assured'. It was only then that he calmly informed Lunn that he 'was wounded and must return', leaving him to deal with the remaining defenders.* Macmillan later spotted Oc hobbling unaided into brigade headquar-ters 'looking as white as a winding sheet from loss of blood . . . to give a lucid and most helpful report to the brigade before being evacuated

---

*After Oc left, Lunn lost touch with his men; however, other Naval units cleared out the remaining enemy positions and linked up with the Hawke and Hood Battalions.

to hospital'. Afterwards he was sent to the military hospital in Boulogne, where his wound was classified as 'severe'.[40]

Jerrold, commenting on Oc's role in the battle, wrote: 'To his energy and enthusiasm the success of the 189th Brigade's operations on this occasion was largely due,' calling him 'irresistibly convincing – a born leader who was allowed to lead – the rarest event in war'.[41] Brigadier Philips, putting aside their past disagreements, recommended him for a DSO and, when the decoration was awarded, was generous in his praise: 'Hearty congratulations on getting the DSO, which you thoroughly deserved.'[42]

The one man left with egg on his face was Shute. Oc's remarkable feat of almost single-handedly rescuing the Hood from a shambles brought about by the man Shute had put in command ended the Army's efforts to reshape the Royal Naval Division in its own image. Shute was summarily shifted to another command and replaced by Major General Charles Lawrie, who was to prove much more sympathetic to the Division's unique *esprit de corps*.*

Oc's wound proved less serious than at first feared and a week later he was well enough to be evacuated to the Duchess of Rutland's Hospital in Arlington Street. He characteristically made light of his injury when his father and Margot came to see him. Afterwards Asquith, writing to Sylvia, did not disguise his disappointment that it was not more serious: 'He is up and dressed and carries his arm in a sling. It is only a slight wound, and I fear he will very soon be fit to take himself again to the Front. Meanwhile he is in good quarters, apparently under the sisterhood of Diana Manners.'[43]

A couple of days later Oc was allowed home to Cavendish Square. He was soon reunited with Freyberg and Shaw-Stewart, on leave from Salonika and trying to land a job at the War Office, intending to rejoin the Naval Division, after, so he told Cynthia, 'an interval of London fun'. However, when Patrick's facetious reason for being given a Staff job in London – that he was 'medically unfit' for the Macedonian climate – was rejected, Oc and Freyberg persuaded him over lunch at the Ritz to apply straightaway to rejoin the Hood.[44]

Oc's powers of persuasion proved rather more clumsy when he attempted to renew his suit with Betty Manners. Although she castigated herself for 'selfish bitterness', Betty did give her ever-faithful

---

*Shute's career did not suffer: he was given command of a Corps in 1918 and retired as a full General with a knighthood.

admirer some small ground for hope: 'I know as you tell me I am old and ought to marry and it's quite true and a future as a spinster is all that is struggling and lonely, but my spirit is still fighting and ungoverned by material facts – I shall never stoop. I trust one day my heart and soul will perhaps find a place and a refuge – a strange change will come.'[45] Perhaps the simple truth was that Betty dare not let herself love Oc yet. She could see the misery of so many of her friends all around, young widows with small children to bring up on their own, and, with the apparently endless carnage, little prospect of remarriage.

No war widow was more stricken than Katharine who, six months after Raymond's death, remained inconsolable. She gained some relief from working at a military hospital near Newmarket, from where she wrote to tell Diana how wonderful it was to be numb to anything but physical feeling for eight or nine hours. Katharine's 'numbness', though, was not attributable merely to hard work, for she persuaded a compliant doctor to prescribe her injections of a full half gram of an unspecified narcotic. Not surprisingly, when the 'sweet doctor' was absent, his colleagues refused to oblige with repeat prescriptions. The combination of withdrawal symptoms (which Katharine euphemistically called the after-effect of twilight sleep) and a fever made her hysterical. She movingly described to Diana how she had screamed and ranted and refused to stay in bed. Cynthia came to see her and was marvellously sympathetic, but no one could understand her anguish. Her tears would have 'watered the desert'.[46]

22

'A master of life's rough and tumble'

TOWARDS THE END of February 1917 Beb's division, the 30th, was deployed a few miles south of Arras. He was acting as Forward Observation Officer when he spotted columns of smoke behind enemy lines as the Germans set fire to buildings in preparation for a general retreat. A raid shortly afterwards confirmed that the Germans had abandoned their front line trenches to withdraw to the recently fortified 'Hindenburg Line', defending a much shorter line between Arras and Soissons. Beb's battery of eighteen pounders was sent into No Man's Land to harry the retreating enemy. He later recalled:

> It was dark and drizzling weather, and when we drew near to Arras our advancing troops were lit by dazzling flashes from many batteries of heavy artillery which were lined up by the side of the road and fired over our heads at the retreating Germans. The roar of these heavy howitzers made it almost impossible to hear an order; their flashes lit up the steaming flanks of our horses and the fine lines of rain that fell on the glistening helmets of the drivers; but in spite of the drizzle and the pools of mud, the men were cheerful, there was a sense of adventure in the air, and the pervasive hope of an advance seemed to fill the ranks of our long marching column.
>
> I was ordered to go forward just before dawn as F.O.O. with an infantry battalion which was now entering the old German positions. I had a few hours' sleep in a dugout in the old front line, and the sky was whitening,

but dawn had not yet come, when I went forward with my signaller; it was a slow business finding our way in the dusk through the shell-holes and tangled wire of the old No Man's Land, and when the twilight came it brought slowly to view the bodies of French soldiers lying in tattered uniforms among the rusted stakes. Some of them were little more than skeletons.[1]

As they pushed on into the territory just abandoned by the enemy, everywhere were signs of a desperate scorched earth policy:

Bridges had been blown up and railways destroyed, huge mine-craters gaped in the middle of the roads, orchards had been felled, the fruit trees, severed near the root, lay in rows neatly tilted onto their branches, and even the currant bushes in village gardens had not escaped attention. On this strand of deserted country they had left the print of their nature, the seal of ruthless efficiency, and also, here and there, signs of chivalry. On the slope of a bank behind the reserve trenches I found twelve crosses, some of which supported the weather-worn helmets of French soldiers; a rough board in the centre bore the German inscription to their foes: 'Here lie twelve soldiers of France who have died the *Heldentodt*' [hero's death].[2]

The Germans had suffered some 1.4 million casualties at Verdun and on the Somme and, now outnumbered three to two by the combined Anglo-French forces, were near breaking point. With Russia still undefeated in the East, there was no prospect of reinforcement from that quarter. After the War, Ludendorff himself admitted that after the Battle of the Somme he knew that 'our troops would not be able to withstand such attacks indefinitely, especially if the Enemy gave us no time to rest . . . If the War lasted our defeat seemed inevitable.'[3]

For Beb and the other Allied soldiers around Arras, the scent of victory was in the air. The apparently modest territorial gains made at the Battle of the Somme belied their strategic importance: Haig's armies had succeeded in breaching enemy fortifications expected to withstand any attack. However, instead of renewing the offensive in the New Year, as had already been agreed with Asquith, Haig was obliged by the new Government to support a madcap scheme by the French General Robert Nivelle* to break the German line in just

---

*Nivelle replaced Joffre, who was blamed for the supposed French unpreparedness for the German offensive at Verdun.

forty-eight hours, by concentrating a massive force and overwhelming the enemy in one huge Armageddon.

Lloyd George, who met Nivelle in Paris in January, was captivated by the charming and handsome French general, who had an English mother and spoke her language like an educated Englishman. Without even consulting the War Cabinet, Lloyd George plotted to give Nivelle command of the British forces as well as the French, thus conveniently reducing the dour Haig to what Hankey described as 'a cipher'. However, when the new Prime Minister sprang the demotion on the British Commander-in-Chief in the middle of an Allied Conference on 26 February, both Haig and an apoplectic Robertson, the Chief of the Imperial General Staff, threatened to resign. Lloyd George was only saved from a humiliating climbdown by the skilful intervention of Hankey, who persuaded the generals to accept a compromise formula, by which Haig agreed to put himself under Nivelle for the duration of the battle on the understanding that if the offensive failed – as he was sure it would – he could resume his planned offensive in Flanders.[4]

The role for the British forces in Nivelle's plans was secondary. Haig was ordered not only to extend his own line to free more French troops for the offensive in Champagne, but also to mount a diversionary attack ninety miles to the north around Arras. Preparations for the grand offensive took up the rest of the winter months, giving the Germans, who had been working around the clock to fortify the Hindenburg Line in time for Haig's expected winter offensive, ample time to complete their preparations.

It was not until the beginning of April that Beb's squadron took up their battle positions some four miles south of Arras, opposite the poplar-lined road to Henin across which lay the tangle of rusted barbed wire that marked the front of the Hindenburg Line. No one outside the British High Command suspected that their role in the coming battle was a mere diversion to a French offensive. In any case, General Sir Edmund Allenby, the illustrious commander of the British Third Army – on which the main burden of the attack would fall – intended to hit the enemy as hard as he could with the limited resources available to him. Beb recalled that 'we were ordered to discard all our spare kit and to reduce what was left to the smallest weight that was possible; we were told that Allenby hoped to break the line, and that if it were broken, we and other mobile brigades of light artillery must be ready to go through the gap'.[5]

Nearly 3,000 British guns took part in the preliminary bombardment which lasted for five days. When off duty Beb had little success
in sleeping through the din of an almost continuous stream of shells
passing overhead. There was much muttering among his fellow artillery officers about the length of the barrage, which they believed
would give the Germans too much time in which to bring up their
reserves, not knowing that Haig had overruled Allenby's wish to
restrict it to two days only. The assault began at 5.30 a.m. on 9 April.
Beb's squadron of eighteen pounders opened fire to provide the
'creeping barrage' to cover the infantry as they advanced down the
grassy slope that led to the Hindenburg Line. The noise of their own
guns was almost drowned out by the roar of the heavy artillery
behind them.

> The guns themselves could not be seen; their flashes came through a veil
> of mist and smoke, and they seemed to have a hard gem-like quality, as
> though some giant hand had laid a string of diamonds across the face of
> the country and was shaking their facets in the light. In front our barrage
> was marching steadily forward, a wall of smoke, with its upper fringe
> flashing and sparkling with the glint of bursting shells. Beyond it from the
> Hindenburg Line rose hundreds of golden rockets, the S.O.S. signals to
> the German guns, continuously rising and falling and lifting their brilliant
> shimmering trails high above the smoke. To the eye it was a magnificent
> spectacle, a scene of Aeschylean grandeur; and to the heart, whose friends
> were here engaged, a tragedy deep and strange, whose scale was that of an
> epic, and Fate seemed to brood above it.[6]

The German flares brought an immediate response from their
own artillery. Fortunately, in Beb's words, 'their shooting was not as
good as usual' and most of the shells fell too far forward, and
although shrapnel splinters clanged against their gun shields, none of
the guns in his battery were put out of action. As the day wore on,
news came in that the Canadians had captured part of Vimy Ridge,
while the British had taken the fortified village of Fampoux, four
miles to the west of Arras. However, in Beb's sector the German
machine gunners, safe in ferro-concrete emplacements, withstood
every attempt to dislodge them.

The following day Beb was again the squadron's Forward
Observation Officer. Just before dawn, he and his signaller set off in
the direction of the sunken road where the infantry had taken cover.

The two men could hear the chatter of machine guns all around as they gingerly groped their way through the corpses and buckled steel helmets that lay everywhere. As daylight broke through the sickly yellow mist, shells began to burst close by. Looking around for somewhere to take cover, Beb spotted three wounded and very frightened German soldiers crouching behind a bank trying to shelter from their own gunners:

> Two of them rose to their feet and one held his unwounded arm above his head: 'Do not shoot', he said. 'We come from Schleswig.'* I answered that the British did not shoot wounded men, and at this he seemed greatly relieved. Two of them could walk, but they did not want to leave their comrade who was badly wounded in the leg. I told them where the dressing station was, but it was a long way back, and I thought they would be wiser to stay where they were; in the open there was a strong chance of their being hit by their own machine guns which were now raking the slope.[7]

It took a further twenty minutes for Beb and the signaller to crawl to the relative safety of the sunken country lane where the surviving British infantrymen were lined up against the far bank. The roar of the artillery made it impossible to hear the chatter of the enemy machine gunners (the usual method for observers to locate them), so, taking an infantry officer with him, Beb clambered up the bank and peered cautiously into the smoke-filled landscape beyond, as he tried to pinpoint the source of the bullets whizzing past them. Eventually he managed to identify a concrete enemy machine gun post and spent the rest of the morning trying to target the squadron's guns on this emplacement and the trenches behind it. During the afternoon, they noticed the enemy fire slacken, when

> Suddenly, without any warning, away to our left and then on our own front the Germans rose from their trenches and began to surrender: at first two or three grey figures seemed to emerge from the earth, then tens, and then hundreds, and they came pacing slowly towards us over the thin powdery snow. Some of our walking wounded began to go back over the field; our men in the lane, suddenly released from their tension, rested on their rifles, and an officer near me lit a cigarette.[8]

---

*Schleswig was one of the former Danish provinces annexed by Bismarck in 1864.

By the following day it was apparent that Allenby's 'diversionary' attack had become the greatest British victory so far in the War, pushing the Germans back four miles in forty-eight hours, capturing three miles of the Hindenburg Line, 13,000 prisoners and 200 guns. A few days later, Nivelle's much-vaunted offensive, as Haig had warned Lloyd George, proved an unmitigated disaster. Beb recalled how 'we expected to advance towards the east, but orders came to march southwards'. It was only now that it began to dawn on the British troops that the battle which they had just fought had been a side show.

Beb had time to dash off a quick letter to his father, who reported to Sylvia that his son 'had just been through 8 days of continuous fighting and had not changed his clothes for 4 weeks. Happily was not touched tho'.'[9] But there was to be no respite. The scale of Nivelle's defeat gave Haig no option but to use every available man to continue his offensive through the glutinous mud that now covered the whole Arras area: it was essential that the Germans were given no opportunity to withdraw any of their forces to counter-attack the stricken French armies in Champagne.

While Beb was fighting the Germans, Oc was embroiled in another acrimonious tussle with his superiors when, despite protests from Philips and Freyberg (now back in charge of the Hood), he was ordered to report for Staff training soon after he returned to France. 'I am sick and tired of this conspiracy to make a Staff Officer of me,' he wrote in his diary, bemused at the reasoning behind it now there was not the excuse of putting 'Father off his work'.[10] Echoing Raymond's view of the Staff, he testily complained to Violet about 'long hours in offices, quill driving, telephone chattering, bottlewashing for other people'.[11]

Oc's frustration rose when he heard that the Royal Naval Division was to mount an assault on Gavrelle, a village north-east of Arras, which had been heavily fortified by the Germans, who had occupied it since the early days of the War and so far resisted every attempt to drive them out. The advance of Allenby's forces into the open countryside to the west of the village had left his troops exposed to fire from the German artillery and machine gunners based around Gavrelle, making it now essential to capture it. The assault was scheduled to take place on 23 April, St George's Day and Allenby's fifty-sixth birthday. Three days earlier, in a typical military botch-up, Freyberg was promoted to command a brigade in another division (the 58th Londons). Oc, backed by Philips, urgently applied to take command of the Hood and this time his request was quickly granted. He reached brigade headquarters at 11 p.m., less than thirty hours before the attack was scheduled to begin. Philips was waiting to brief him on the plans. The Drake and Nelson Battalions were to assault the enemy front line trenches on the right (southern) flank, while the 190th Brigade dealt with those to the north. The Hood was to advance twenty minutes later to seize objectives within Gavrelle. If Philips hoped Oc's time on the Staff had made him less headstrong, he was quickly disillusioned as his subordinate forcefully argued that if they waited twenty minutes before going into action they were bound to be targeted by the German artillery, which would anticipate a second wave. However, Philips remained adamant that he could not risk the whole brigade being held up on the wire.

Oc only allowed himself a few hours' sleep in his dug-out before setting out at 7 a.m. to reconnoitre the terrain over which they would advance. Then, after going over the plans with his four company commanders (Lieutenants Asbury, Tamplin, Morrison and Matcham), he sent Lieutenant Commander Ellis, his second in command, to have another go at persuading Philips to let the Hood follow more closely behind the first attack. The brigadier, his irritation mounting, refused to budge in spite of two further attempts to make him change his mind. Oc, however, could be, in the words of his stepmother, 'mulishly obstinate';[12] when, at midnight, he received his fourth refusal, he simply decided to disregard his orders and act on his own initiative, instructing Sub-Lieutenant Hill to go forward with the Nelsons and report back as soon they captured the first line of enemy trenches.

As the first signs of dawn appeared in the sky, Oc took up his position in front of his battalion. Fifteen minutes later, as the British guns opened up, the Nelson and Drake Battalions disappeared into the smoke and dust in the direction of Gavrelle. The German artillery response was almost immediate, and within a few minutes, as Oc had forecast, shells were exploding around them. Without waiting for Hill, he led his men forward. 'His judgement was perfect,' observed Able Seaman Joseph Murray afterwards. 'We were on the line before Jerry knew anything about it. I honestly think that we men of the Hood who survived the battle owe it to Asquith ignoring orders.'[13]

After successfully overrunning the German second line, the Hoods were engaged in fierce house-to-house fighting as they fought their way through the snipers and machine gunners concealed in the ruined buildings and cellars. The road through the centre of Gavrelle soon became congested not just with Hood soldiers but also Nelsons who had lost touch with their own commander and about a hundred men from the Bedfordshire Regiment, which should have been protecting the Hood's flank. However, it was impossible to press on until the British creeping barrage moved forward. 'This pause of 20 minutes is a great mistake,' Oc noted in the Hood Battalion War Diary, 'giving the enemy breathing space just when we have them on the run.'[14] Having sent the Bedfords back to their own regiment, Oc did his best to bring some semblance of order to the Naval troops amidst the falling masonry and crumbling buildings.

Meanwhile, the 190th Brigade had failed to dislodge the Germans from the strategic ridge to the north of Gavrelle (dominated by its famous windmill), from where enemy gunners were shelling the three Naval battalions in the village below them. Immediately below the ridge was the road to Fresnes, dominated by the heavily fortified mayor's house, which covered a strongly manned trench 150 yards to the east. Oc decided that they must capture the *mairie* to have any hope of holding the village against the inevitable counter-attack. Having dispersed his men in ditches and shell holes, behind gravestones in the cemetery and any other available cover in the centre of the village, he took Lieutenant Asbury and two other men to see if they could outflank the enemy trench. Unfortunately, they were spotted creeping along a shallow ditch, and Asbury and one of the men were killed before they could take cover. Oc then turned his attention to the mayor's house itself, returning with another group of men and leading a successful assault on the building, where they found ten German soldiers 'sleeping or shamming sleep in the two cellars'. Oc noted his field notebook: '7.12 a.m. Gavrelle taken'. He later recorded in the Battalion War Diary:

I established snipers in the upper storey [of the *mairie*], from which an excellent view could be obtained of the helmets of the enemy manning the trench due east of the house. These we sniped with good effect. I placed a Lewis gun and snipers in other parts of the house and handed its defence over to Sub-Lieutenant Cooke of the Hood, acting brigade intelligence officer, with orders to harass the enemy as much as possible. Later in the morning he [Cooke] led a Lewis gun team out into the open, to try to get at the enemy occupants of the trench from closer quarters: he and all his team, except Charlton, became casualties. Charlton maintained himself alone for five hours, causing the enemy considerable casualties. Then, his ammunition running out, he withdrew.[15]

It was now clear that the number of German troops in the area had been seriously underestimated, making the position of the Naval troops in Gavrelle, in the understated words of the Divisional historian, 'precarious'.[16] Returning to the centre of the village, Oc busied himself rallying the rest of the Hood and other stray Naval soldiers, who were crowding behind any building left standing to shelter from the shell and machine gunfire, and organizing them to withstand a counter-attack. Meanwhile, a messenger arrived from Philips – completely out of touch with the situation – ordering them to advance. Oc sent the man back with the message: 'Enemy gradually mustering 800–1000 yards East of Village . . . Troops very tired and sluggish . . . Send water, rations and ammunition.' He then set out once more to reconnoitre the enemy positions. When he returned at about midday, he was greeted with the dreadful news that two more of his company commanders had been hit on the road running past the cemetery. He rushed to the spot and found Tamplin was already dead, but he was in time to cradle Morrison in his arms as he lay dying.

Throughout the afternoon, with only one company commander and one other officer left, Oc struggled to prevent the Germans concentrating enough troops to mount a counter-attack. They were under constant fire not only from the enemy artillery and snipers still hidden among the ruins but also from the British gunners, who apparently had not been informed that their own troops had advanced to the northern edge of the village. As the casualties mounted, McCracken, the battalion doctor, and a single orderly left the dressing station behind the lines and entered the village to treat the wounded; on the way they pressed into service a German doctor and fourteen Red Cross orderlies who were led behind the lines as prisoners-of-war, and took them back their former dressing station in a cellar in the middle of the village, where, as Oc later told his father, 'they treated between 100 and 150 of our wounded, many of whom would otherwise have been blown to pieces where they lay'.[17]

At 4.30 p.m. Oc was dismayed to receive another order from the brigadier to name his time for a barrage to cover an advance. His response shows that behind his calm façade he regarded the situation as desperate: 'Men are dog-tired and apathetic. Bedfords' position on our left is weak: they are out-sniped and there seems to be very few of them. I have only two officers left so far as I know . . . Germans have been gathering all day for a big attack . . . all movement subject to severe sniping. I have been unable to trace the arrival of any rations or water. This is badly wanted.'

Oc then sent instructions to his adjutant Hilton, who was manning the old German front line behind him, to try to hold out if he himself was overrun. 'Position is rotten,' he confessed, 'we shall do our best, but I feel very tired.'[18] When the counter-attack came, somehow Oc managed to galvanize his exhausted and outnumbered men into beating the enemy back. The ferocity of the Hood's response deceived the Germans about the strength of their position and they failed to press home their advantage with renewed attacks. Reinforcements finally arrived at 10 p.m., and in the early hours of the following day, still under heavy shell fire, Oc led the weary but victorious survivors of his battered battalion back behind the lines. It was his thirty-fourth birthday.

The following day the Royal Marines rounded off the operation by capturing the ridge to the north of Gavrelle. At the 189th Brigade headquarters, Macmillan noted in his diary:

> The rejoicings over our victory were confined to Army, Corps and Divisional Headquarters, for the men who had accomplished the job were so overcome by fatigue and so depressed at the loss of old comrades that they could not enthuse . . . What shall I say of Commander Asquith? Viewed from any angle he was the outstanding personality in the fight, the one man who, more than any other, carried our arms to victory, and yet he was recommended only for a bar to his DSO. No Victoria Crosses came our way![19]

One of the survivors of the battle, Able Seaman Bryan, summed up the feelings of his comrades about their commanding officer in a letter home: 'We have an excelent [sic] commander in Mr Asquiths son, he is as cool and calm under great shell fire and amid the whizzing of the snipers bullets as though he was walking down the Strand. The boys think the world of him.'

Oc did his best to ensure that the bravery of the men under his command was recognized, securing a DSO for McCracken, but Able Seaman 'Jacky' Charlton, whom he recommended for the Victoria Cross for his intrepid single-handed defence of the *Mairie*, was only awarded the Distinguished Conduct Medal. Oc did, however, ensure that the citizens of Gavrelle, when they returned to rebuild their village, would know the names of the young British soldiers who had died to liberate it. He commissioned a local carpenter to make a large wooden cross and inscribe it with the names of 'The officers and Men of the Hood Battalion killed in the capture of Gavrelle, April 1917'.[20] It can be seen to this day in the parish church.

Oc's other priority was to write to the families of the dead. The Edinburgh-based parents of Lieutenant Morrison were pathetically grateful for his efforts to comfort their mortally wounded son. The young officer's father later asked Oc for a photograph of himself, and in thanking him wrote:

> I value it as that of one under whom my son served during practically all the time he was in the Army, one for whom, as he told me in letters and also when on his only leave, he entertained the highest respect and in whom he had unbounded confidence, of whom he wrote [after the battle of Grandcourt Ridge]: 'he'll likely get a D.S.O., but no honour he will get will be equal to what he deserves', and the one who touched him as a brother and in whose arms he passed away.
>
>   You cannot understand how it touched his mother's heart and mine when we heard of your kindness to our boy, it made us feel that he died in the arms of a friend.[21]

As for Gavrelle, 'captured and held with such determination', it soon had (in the words of Jerrold) 'no more importance than that of any other outpost of a position dictated to us by an unbeaten enemy'.[22]

*

Once Margot's fury over her husband's ejection from power had subsided, she sank into a deep depression, again plagued by feelings of personal and financial insecurity, together with renewed resentment over Violet's continued hold on Asquith's affections. 'My life is over except for Puff, Elizabeth and Henry,' she lamented to Viola Parsons (formerly Tree), in a letter mark 'Bury'. 'I shall return to

Cavendish Square in reduced circumstances and have to have Violet, Cys and Bongie to live with me again . . . Violet who has never cared for me and advises her father <u>always</u> in 1000 ways against me.'[23] Even the birth on 22 April of Violet's first child, a daughter christened (Helen Laura) Cressida, did little to cheer up Margot, as she worked herself up over the baby's sickliness, blaming her nurse for overfeeding her.

In this renewed state of melancholia, Margot felt abandoned even by Oc who, she complained to Freyberg, 'has never written or wired me one line. [He] used to be a very fond of me, but now he doesn't care much. No Asquith has real fire.' Freyberg would have known that the obvious retort was that she had virtually ignored her stepson throughout most of the Gallipoli campaign. But the New Zealander, slowly recovering from wounds sustained at Beaucourt and still deeply affected by the death of his friend Kelly, was grateful for Margot's maternal affection as she scooped him up into her extended family. He tried to reassure her by telling her how much Kelly had appreciated her kindness, but even this induced a bout of self-pity: 'I had no idea he even liked me until you told me!! I never think people care for me. I wish I was like most females who always think everyone cares for them twice as much as they do!'[24]

Margot did at least derive some satisfaction from the travails of the Lloyd George administration. 'Father and I have had and are having real fun over this Ridiculous Government!' she wrote to Oc – soon back in her good books – in June 1917. 'Fat flies [i.e. anglers' bait] thrown daily over both our heads for him to go in and help Lloyd George', who she fondly believed would not 'stay in beyond August, if as long'.[25] The Prime Minister, floundering in the wake of Nivelle's disastrous offensive, was desperate to enlist the support of his predecessor. On 28 May, Reading had arrived at the Wharf as an emissary from 10 Downing Street offering the Foreign Office or the Exchequer as bait to try to tempt Asquith back into the Government. The former Prime Minister, however, was having none of it, bluntly telling the Lord Chief Justice that

> Under no conditions would I serve in a Government of which Lloyd George was the head. I had learned by long and close association to mistrust him profoundly. I knew him to be incapable of loyalty and lasting gratitude. I had always acknowledged, and did still, to the full his many

brilliant and useful faculties, but he needed to have someone over him. In my judgement he had incurable defects, both of intellect and character, which totally unfitted him to be at the head.[26]

The only senior Liberals to succumb to the Prime Minister's blandishments were Montagu, who in June 1917 accepted the new post of Minister for Reconstruction, and Churchill, who, much to the disgust of the Tories in the Cabinet, was brought back as Minister of Munitions in July. Montagu's defection was greeted with mild disdain by Asquith: 'he has swallowed the ginger-bread ungilded' was his acid comment to Sylvia when he heard that his former acolyte was not to be in the Cabinet.[27]

Predictably Margot reacted much more strongly to the 'treachery' of her friend and protégé. She would have been even more incensed had she known that Montagu had been making obsequious overtures to Lloyd George for months. She prided herself on being a good judge of character, but she seriously misjudged Montagu, believing him to be lacking in ambition, whereas he was one of the most ambitious men she knew: had she understood the chronic insecurity that lay behind it, she might have been more forgiving. As it was, the news of his appointment provoked a rare bout of anti-Semitism, naturally spiced by his marriage to her former hated rival: 'he and Venetia are Jews and base', she wrote to Oc.[28]* The full extent of her bitterness (even if she exaggerated her husband's) was revealed in a letter to Viola:

> Henry said to me that he hoped neither <u>you</u> nor anyone else would <u>ever</u> mention Montagu's name to him! . . . Professing under a cloak of patriotism to serve your self-interest instead of serving your Chief [Asquith] is the kind of hardy and morbid egotism that Henry <u>loathes</u>. Henry and I feel we've been taken in up to the eyes – we thought Montagu had almost passionate soppy love for us both! He <u>lived</u> with us and we were his home – Xmas, New Year, Easter etc. . . . When Henry at times doubted his judgement and deplored his self-centredness, I always said it would pass. <u>I</u> never stood by anyone with more affection and persistence when

---

*An amusing sidelight on Venetia's 'Jewishness' was provided by Duff Cooper, who reported to Cynthia Margot's remark 'Of course, she's a Jew. Both Lord Sheffield and Lord Carlisle are Jews.' Duff asked which was her father, and Margot said, 'Neither'. (*Lady Cynthia Asquith Diaries*, p. 283). In fact, Venetia is believed to have been the daughter of the 9th Earl of Carlisle, with whom her mother had an affair.

he was abused than I have done with Montagu. I vomited and was sleep-less 2 nights.[29]

After the Battle of Arras the British forces were engaged in the process of 'gorging the snake from the head downwards', painstak-ingly fighting their way south along the Hindenburg Line: 'this serpent with its bones of concrete, its million stings and its vast skirt of rusted wire was not a morsel easy to digest', as Beb described it, recalling the dreadful conditions that he and his comrades had to endure: 'We slept in the open in heavy squalls of sleet and rain, and we often woke up in the morning lying in pools of slush; behind our battle positions the narrow country roads in this devastated area were congested with the advance of our army . . . transport arrange-ments broke down, and for many days we were without any bread and lived on iron rations'.[30]

For a time, Beb's observation post was a concrete German pill box within the Hindenburg Line itself. The stench was appalling from the unburied corpses that lay all round in a scene of barely imagin-able carnage. Worse than any privations was the continual death of men who had become friends as well as comrades, with always the unspoken thought that it might have been oneself. Once, a few minutes after Beb had been relieved by his 'delightful friend', Lieutenant Cairns, the observation post he had just left was blown apart by a direct hit, instantly killing a man of 'great courage and radiant goodness of heart'.[31]

Oc was never more than a few miles away throughout this period, yet the brothers might have been on different planets. 'No news of Beb, tell Cynthia to write,' Oc wrote to Violet on 22 May, describing 'my first glimpse of <u>Spring</u>', riding over with McCracken to 'a famous ruined town' (Ypres) to dine with Johnny Dodge, now serving with the Royal Sussex Regiment: 'I resent missing it. The only signs in this destroyed area are the patchy pushings of rank grass among the shell holes – an immune stubble on the pock-marked face of the earth – and green foliage on maimed trees along the paved main road.' The Royal Naval Division, having been in the front line 'for eight days of foul weather' before the attack on Gavrelle, had expected a period of recuperation but, to Oc's disgust, within days of the battle they were back on fatigue duties, 'bivouacing in the destroyed area and march-ing and digging most nights 7 p.m. till 4 a.m'.[32]

Oc was soon engaged in a fresh bout of bickering with Philips. It was widely known that Oc had deliberately disobeyed the brigadier's express orders in the opening moments of the assault on Gavrelle, and that he had subsequently held on to the village for a whole day with precious little assistance from brigade headquarters. The fact that Oc was only recommended for a DSO, rather than the VC that most of his men believed he deserved, was regarded by many as spite. Oc's direct line to senior generals – he had been invited to dinner by his Corps commander to give a first-hand account of the battle – only added to Philips' simmering envy. The brigadier foolishly tried to assert his authority with a bureaucratic demand for a list of enemy material captured at Gavrelle. A clearly riled Oc insolently replied: 'The half of Gavrelle village!' He was then ordered to report for a dressing down. The ever attentive Macmillan noted: 'As the Brigade office did not offer sufficient privacy he was taken outside for his telling-off. I dropped my work and observed both men closely. The [Brigadier] General was laying down the law as he paced backwards and forwards, while Asquith followed at his heels looking pale but unrepentant. How the matter ended I cannot say, but neither seemed at all pleased at parting.'[33]

The one crumb of comfort was the return of Patrick Shaw-Stewart, who was posted back to the Hood in early May as a company commander. Oc was delighted to welcome 'poor Patsy fresh from the fleshpots of Mayfair' to share his quarters, which he described in a letter to Diana, as 'a corrugated iron lean-to, all cracks and draughts, no floor and a rather fitful brazier . . . You can imagine what a joy and source of laughter and fun his company has been to me.' Shaw-Stewart, for his part, informed her that his new commanding officer 'is exceedingly sweet and doesn't b—r me about more than is needful to set a good example'.[34]

The arrival of Shaw-Stewart only aggravated Oc's troublesome relationship with Philips. There may have been an element of snobbery in Oc's cavalier treatment of his brigadier, judging by a remark to Violet that 'it would be a comfort to have a sprinkling of officers from Winchester and Eton and other decent public schools, where we have at present no "clientele".'[35] In Philips' case, any feelings of social inferiority towards his confident and well-connected subordinate were bound to be exacerbated by the idea – imagined or otherwise – that Oc and his Etonian friend were mocking him behind his back.

In early June, the Hoods took over the defence of the Windmill ridge north of Gavrelle and Philips ordered new trenches to be dug. Oc instructed Shaw-Stewart to supervise the task. The following day the brigadier received a report that 'no work appears to have been done since the [Hood] Battalion went into the line', and eagerly seized the opportunity to slap down his awkward subordinates, sending Oc a written reprimand that he was 'extremely dissatisfied with the amount of work done' and 'considers this unsatisfactory position is entirely due to lack of proper supervision by the Battalion and Company Commander concerned'. He refused to let the Hood be relieved until the work was completed and copied his note to the commander of the Drake, which had been due to take over.[36]

This near-public rebuke was a red rag to a bull. Oc defiantly complained that he had not been consulted about the original order to dig the trench, nor given the opportunity to explain why, with all the Hood's other duties, his men had not been able to complete the work. He threatened to take the matter up with the divisional commander, Major General Lawrie. Faced with this brazen challenge to his authority, Philips backed down, allowing the Hood to be relieved from its front line duties and to complete the work on the new trenches afterwards. He even tried to adopt a conciliatory tone, condescendingly telling Oc that if he completed the work 'it will be a real feather in your cap' and that he 'was particularly anxious to do away with the impression that the Hood Battalion are not good workers'. Having just been awarded his second DSO, Oc hardly needed a 'feather in his cap' for trench digging, and refused to be placated, demanding an assurance that his battalion was not regarded as slack 'either at Brigade or Divisional Headquarters'.[37]

When a few days later Oc asked for two days' leave to see Churchill, who was visiting Divisional headquarters, Philips grasped the opportunity to back off completely, instructing Macmillan 'to hand back the correspondence entrusted to me, as the matter was now considered closed'.[38] It was game and set to Oc. But as long as Philips remained in command of 189th Brigade and Oc of the Hood Battalion, the trial of strength between the two men was set to continue.

When Cynthia lunched with the Asquiths at 20 Cavendish Square on 12 June she recorded that 'the dear Old Boy [Asquith] was delighted with Oc's great success as colonel of the Hood Battalion – he had just been awarded a clasp to his D.S.O. and his father handed the King's letter of congratulation all round the table with proud sniffs'.[39]

Oc received his father's letter of congratulation just before he set out with McCracken on four days' local leave – a reward for their DSOs. The two men spent most of the time on trains, but in between managed to squeeze in a couple of nights in Paris and a day's sea bathing in Deauville, again staying at the Hôtel·Normandie. Here Oc answered his father's letter, modestly asserting that the award 'came as a complete surprise to me: so few of our officers survived the action'. Characteristically, he gave no hint of his difficulties with his brigadier; indeed the only mention of his military duties in a long chatty letter was a reference to Charles Lawrie – their new Divisional general – whom 'we all like' and who had given him 'a very delight-ful and well favoured chestnut mare', and a single sentence that: 'since our April fighting, we have done one spell in the Front Line trenches – mud and water six inches above the knee – and all the rest of the time we have been digging and fatigues from the gun line forward in that same desolate part of the world'. Otherwise he adopted his customary cheerful banter, recounting how he had renewed his acquaintance with Madame Casaubon (his and Violet's landlady in Paris in 1905), 'whose wig is as golden as it was when she bought it ten years ago to celebrate her golden wedding', had tea with his father's old flame, Mouche,* at Lady Colebrooke's flat, done some shopping and 'dined at the Café de Paris, and after dinner lay on the grass and listened to music outside the Ambassadeurs'. He relates his amusement when the train passed a canal and some sol-diers on board, spotting 'a barge manned by the Inland Water Transport', bawled out of the window: 'Do you get many cases of shell shock down here?' The only clue to the strain he was under was a wistful admission that 'I could do with a week here [in Deauville], but have to start the long journey back at 6 a.m.'[40]

The Royal Naval Division was based around Gavrelle for the rest of the summer, manning the front line or undertaking the dangerous, backbreaking work of digging and repairing trenches, usually at night to avoid detection by the enemy. Cynthia noted that Oc was 'looking very war worn' when she met him on 27 July as he arrived home for

*Married since 1904 to Colonel Everard Baring, third son of the financier Lord Revelstoke.

ten days' leave.[41] His break only added to his anxieties when once again he pressed Betty Manners to marry him. 'You were very nice and I wish I could say more and the war would end and I would know my own mind,' was the only hope she could give him in a letter written after he returned to the Front.

The extent of Oc's irritability is apparent from his field notebook which is full of complaints about bureaucratic interference by Staff officers or minor lapses by his company commanders. Macmillan, who spoke briefly to Oc when he visited Brigade headquarters, noted 'a look of concern which touched me to the core'. The clerk was convinced that there was a clique on the Staff who had it in for him:

> Too often the success in life of a man is due to the fact that he is the son of his father. This could not be said of Commander Asquith.* Here was one who was a master of life's rough and tumble and one who seemed fated to bear more crosses than his own.
>
> Commander Asquith, as he appeared to me, could not by nature do anything underhand, and although I was unable to point a finger at any man or men who were exploiting their brief authority over him, inwardly I now felt convinced that he had enemies behind our lines who gave him more concern than those who wore the dull grey and sought to close with him in battle. Yet, despite the fact of his father's eminence, he seemed to scorn the idea of seeking help from that quarter against those people who were getting him from behind. Perhaps he felt that his father's cross was already enough for an ageing man to bear.[42]

Whatever hostility the Asquith boys might have suffered because they were sons of their father was more than matched by goodwill in other quarters. In spite of the barrage of hostile propaganda directed against the former Prime Minister and his wife, the family name still stood for something, as Alexander Lindsay, the future Master of Balliol, later recalled in a letter to Asquith:

> I remember in the War that my general, who was quite unimpressed by the fact that I was a fellow of Balliol, first began to take notice of me when we met Beb in an ammunition dump. He asked me how I knew him and

---

*The Royal Naval Division still retained naval ranks for non-regular Army officers, so Oc, as Colonel of the Hood, was a Commander, the naval equivalent of Lieutenant Colonel.

when I explained I had been a contemporary with Beb and had tutored another of your sons, said first 'But I thought they were very clever fellows' and, when I assured him that they were, said 'You must be the devil of a swell!' The reflected glory of the Asquiths stood me in good stead.[43]

In the summer of 1917 Beb was transferred to another battery of eighteen pounders, whose gun crews had suffered casualties. He got on well with his new commanding officer, Major MacFarlane, 'a regular soldier of exceptional qualities and a most charming companion'; however, there was little opportunity for fraternization as from 22 July their guns were engaged in the preliminary bombardments leading up to the start of a new offensive, now known by the name of the Flanders village where, four and a half months later, it was to splutter to a halt: Passchendaele.

Haig had originally planned to launch the offensive at the beginning of the year when the ground would have been hardened by winter frosts, the German defences less well prepared and the Allies numerically superior to the enemy. But he was forced to put it off when Lloyd George backed the calamitous Nivelle offensive. Now the French armies were riven by mutinies and in no position to offer support, while the Germans were being steadily reinforced by units redeployed from their Eastern Front, where the Russian Revolution was gathering pace. There was hope from across the Atlantic with the United States finally entering the War on the Allied side, but, with the Royal Navy yet to master the menace of German submarines, it would be another nine months before American troops arrived in Europe in significant numbers.

Haig was not even able to choose the direction of his advance. He was directed to concentrate north of Ypres to threaten the German submarine bases on the Channel. This meant advancing over marshland criss-crossed by flooded streams, overflowing ditches and dykes during what was to emerge as one of the wettest Augusts on record. Beb, who was to see the results, quoted with approval the comment of Marshal Foch that '*Boche* is bad and *boue* [mud] is bad; but *Boche* and *boue* together —!'[44]

The German Army, in such poor shape at the beginning of the year, was now ready for anything that the British could throw at them, countering the preparatory artillery barrages shell for shell. Before the infantry assault even began, four of the six guns in Beb's battery were destroyed, killing one of his three fellow subalterns and severely wounding another. When a neighbouring battery suffered a direct hit on its ammunition store, all that remained of its guns and their crews were 'four gaping chasms in the ground'.

Both sides made regular use of gas shells during their bombardments, so off-duty gunners had to sleep with their gas masks close to their faces. Beb recalled how 'we developed a curious alertness in awaking from the deepest slumber at the sound of that low sinister whistle'.[45] His battery was among those targeted when the Germans first used mustard gas. Fortunately, thanks to their respirators and the gas curtain protecting their dug-outs he and most of his comrades escaped with only minor doses of this sinister new concoction. When some of the men 'developed painful blains [boils] and blisters on their hands and on the tenderest parts of their bodies', the cause was not some devilish new form of germ warfare, as first suspected, but the after-effect of washing in puddles contaminated by mustard gas.

During this period, the most dreaded task was bringing up fresh ammunition every night, with the junior officers taking it in turns to guide the horses along the wooden duckboards that were the only route through miles of desolate, shell strewn and crater-filled landscape. These tracks were easily photographed by enemy airmen for their artillery to bombard with gas and explosives. Beb recollected:

The time came when gas masks were fitted on our horses and mules: we were doubtful at first whether they would consent to wear this new form of head-gear, but some of them thrust their noses into the masks with an eager whinny in the hope that they were filled with oats. The task of leading them forward over that long hazardous track on a night of inky blackness, unaided by any torch, was one of the most difficult duties that fell to an officer. There were certain well-known danger points, one of which was near the ruins of Zillebeke; but the bursts of fire often came at unusual places and irregular intervals, and owing to shell-holes on either side it was impossible to manoeuvre the column away from the track. These journeys were grim reminders of the game of 'Oranges and Lemons' which most of us had played in our childhood. On many nights the baulks of timber that made the track were blown up in front of the advancing column; dead horses lay on either side of it, and the way was often obstructed by groups of animals which had just been killed lying with stiffened legs in the centre of the path. In many parts of this dismal journey the stench was appalling.

Inevitably many horses were killed on these journeys through Hades. On one occasion, as Beb was arriving back at his battery, 'a shell exploded near us and my own horse gave a faint shiver and lowered his head: to my great sorrow he was mortally wounded in the neck and I shot him with my revolver so as to put him out of his pain'.[46] Characteristically, he does not dwell on his own narrow escape.

When the British infantry went 'over the bags', Beb's division was deployed close to the centre of the assault, due west of Ypres and just south of the Menin road. In spite of heavy rain, the British captured Hooge and the strategically important 'Stirling Castle' ridge. However, as the downpour continued day after day, the offensive became, literally, bogged down.

Beb's first stint as Forward Observation Officer came on the third day of the battle. He and his signaller climbed through the notorious 'Sanctuary Wood', by then 'a wood in nothing but name': every tree long since pounded to sawdust and the soil 'poisoned with gas'. They passed shattered pill boxes and the mud-spattered remains of German and British soldiers, to reach the crest of 'Stirling Castle' ridge, where 'we were greeted by heavy fire from German field guns'. Beb's luck held and the explosions were muffled by the mud. They took shelter behind the skeletons of two disabled British tanks before dropping into a trench that led to 'Clapham Junction', the former German stronghold on the highest point of the ridge. Beb was to spend much of the next two weeks at this God-forsaken spot, almost miraculously avoiding being hit by snipers, shellfire or, on one occasion, an aeroplane's machine gunner, as he gazed out over the waterlogged, crater-filled landscape and tried to direct his battery's guns: a small pawn in a deadly and seemingly endless struggle of attack and counter-attack, barrage and counter-barrage conducted over the mudscape below him.

Then, quite suddenly Beb was granted ten days' leave in England, exchanging this hellish world of death and suffering for a brief glimpse of another planet of beautiful, gossiping women, old men arguing over politics, tea and tennis parties, bridge, charades and well-meaning but uncomprehending friends and family.

23

'There is no doubt that Oc is a born soldier'

———◆———

WHEN BASIL BLACKWOOD came home on leave in May 1917 he saw a great deal of Cynthia. Although she gives no clue in her diary as to whether they finally became lovers, on several occasions he stayed on late into the night at the flat she had recently taken in Portman Mansions (near Baker Street) and 'must have murdered my reputation with the hall porter'. For all her thrill about being the subject of gossip, she disliked the idea of being unfaithful to Beb, fretting in her diary: 'Have let myself drift into a very false position. Feel I am cheating and don't know what to do.'[1] Basil returned to the Front on 7 June and, as with Beb, Cynthia could not face seeing him off. They wrote to each other almost daily, Basil illustrating his letters with humorous cartoons, which were a happy complement to the poems sent by Beb. Four weeks later Basil was reported 'missing' after a raid on enemy lines; Cynthia felt 'battered and smashed', confessing that 'Basil and Beb are the only two men who have really got inside my life'. As had happened with her brother, Ego, she clung to the hope that he had been taken prisoner and somehow been missed.

In many ways day-to-day life for Cynthia had changed little since the War began. Although there were shortages of fresh meat, sugar and chocolate, social life went on much as before. She put in a few hours a week at Winchcombe hospital, near Stanway, or at military hospitals in London, mostly doing cleaning work; the rest of the time was spent dining with her male admirers, gossiping with women friends, posing for portraits by McEvoy or Augustus John or, encouraged by her father-in-law, pursuing her dream of becoming an actress in the silent cinema, taking the 'stage' name 'Sylvia Strayte'. Michael remained a constant delight, but John (now under a new 'brain specialist') was still 'an awful shadow over my life'.[2]

Air-raids, which could have brought home the reality of War, were neither frequent enough nor sufficiently devastating to frighten most people not directly affected. Margot heard from her servants, who travelled by Underground, that 'herds of women and children collect there when the warning is given of "Take cover" (by police on bicycles) and shiver and shake and cry',[3] but as far as the Asquiths' own circle was concerned, the raids provided the vicarious thrill of a sensational murder in peacetime. Thus, one morning in July, Asquith was sitting down to write to Sylvia

> when I heard the sound of guns, and looking out of the window saw the sky dotted with a whole fleet of aeroplanes, among which white puffs showed that the shrapnel of the anti-aircraft guns was bursting. They seemed to be almost over us, on the Oxford Circus side, and one quite expected to see the dropping bombs. Apparently some of the machines were our own and in pursuit: for the whole lot wheeled round in the direction of the river and in a few minutes were lost to sight. It was quite exciting while it lasted, but I saw no signs of panic. Most of the inhabitants (including a lot of khaki wounded) turned out into the Square and watched and criticized. Some of the more sanguine (of whom Margot was one) fancied they descried a Zeppelin.[4]

Cynthia proudly recorded how Michael sat up in his pram during one raid and said 'I do like the sound of guns.'* On another occasion she complained about the inconsiderate timing of the spectacle: 'Woken at five by guns – another air-raid at last! I like them with my dinner, not with my dreams, felt sleepy and bored.' When Margot took her family (including, for once, her unmusical husband) to see a performance of *The Marriage of Figaro* on 24 September 1917, the sound of anti-aircraft guns was heard while Sir Thomas Beecham was conducting the Overture and 'about seven people got up and left, but otherwise <u>no one turned a hair</u> . . . Puff hardly looked up from the score'. The one person who was frightened, so Margot

---

*Michael changed his ideas when he grew up and was a conscientious objector during the Second World War.

heard from her former Downing Street staff, was the Prime Minister who, believing himself to be a target, displayed such an 'appearance of terror that two typists fainted at the mere sight of him, thinking some appalling disaster must have taken place'.[5] Her informant was not exaggerating: Sir Harold Nicolson, then a young diplomat at the Foreign Office, saw Lloyd George 'trembling and ashen at the sound of an air raid siren', and according to another official, he 'scuttled into the basement of the Foreign Office when there were raids and sang Welsh hymns to keep up his nerve, beads of perspiration pouring from his face'.[6]

Cynthia was staying with Mary Herbert at Pixton in Somerset when on 18 August she received Beb's telegram announcing his imminent arrival. The next morning:

> At about 5.30 a call of 'Cynthia' interrupted my dreams. I sprang up, wide awake, and found Beb who somehow had got a motor at Taunton and had broken into the house. We talked till nearly seven and then he fell into a heavy sleep. He seems all right – not a bit deaf anyhow – but says his 'guts' are ruined, and that he has had a sort of dysentery all the time. Very full of his experiences. I haven't seen him in a good light, but I really think he is all right.

She left him to sleep on through the morning. He had his lunch in bed and then they walked to a nearby weir with John. After tea she sat with him in the summer house:

> He talked a lot of the war, very interestingly and picturesquely. He has had a ghastly time, both for danger and discomfort – continually in such smells that he had to puff a pipe ceaselessly or be sick, and never coming out of the line for a proper rest. He is undoubtedly *exalté* and exhilarated by some aspects of the fighting, but on the whole is very, very war-weary and I'm afraid, loathes the idea of returning. But he is in good spirits and I see no shadow of a return of his former illness, I think this proves it to have been the effect of one particular explosion and not strain and tension. He has had far more of the latter this time.

A couple of days later Cynthia noted: 'Poor darling! He is already beginning to watch the hands of the clock. Ten days seem a terribly short respite after so long a hell.' They were cheered by a telegram from Margot at The Wharf: "'WHAT DAY DO YOU COME HERE? PLEASE BRING SIX GALLONS OF PETROL WHICH YOU ARE ENTITLED TO'". A good use to put your soldier son to! Beb has never heard of this perquisite. I wonder if it exists for unmotored subalterns.'[7]

Their stay at the Wharf passed off well. Margot had just bought the Mill House next door as a guest annex, having, according to Violet, 'forced Lady Boot (wife of the cash chemist)' to provide the funds.[8] The Asquiths were still basking in their pleasure at Cys's – this time 'approved' – engagement to Anne Pollock, the daughter of Sir Adrian Pollock, a successful solicitor and a prominent figure in the City of London. Anne was, according to her prospective father-in-law, 'a thoroughly nice girl, and attractive to boot'.[9] A few months later Margot noted how: 'The advent of Anne Pollock has already made a marked difference in Cys . . . He is still delicate and devitalised, but this will improve . . . He goes to bed early – by 12 – and doesn't sit up with Elizabeth and a pipe. He is more like the darling boy he always was and never gossips, which he and Violet were apt to do.'[10]

Meanwhile, Cys's father was luxuriating in a new addition to his 'harem' in the shape of Hilda Harrison, who was living in a farmhouse at Easton Grey with her baby daughter while her husband, another artillery officer, was at the Front. The Asquiths first met Mrs Harrison when she was roped in by Lucy to make up a fourth at bridge.

Cynthia was delighted to be complimented by Margot on her 'Septimus yellow' dress, while Beb, according to his father, 'was in excellent form and gave very interesting accounts of the latest development of barrage and counter barrage'.[11] Cynthia was particularly pleased that her husband 'talked very well about his experiences at luncheon – and what is odder – Margot listened very well. I have never known her so nice and so unpainful as on this occasion.'[12]

As Beb's leave came to an end he was 'dreadfully depressed at returning to Hell'. Stormy weather in the Channel gave him a day's reprieve and they rashly went to see a captured German propaganda film at the 'War Cinema' in Piccadilly: 'the sinister spiked helmets made me feel that, even yet, the Germans must win', noted Cynthia pessimistically afterwards.[13]

Ten days later, Freddie Blackwood received a telegram from the Crown Princess of Sweden (representing the Red Cross), confirming that his brother was indeed dead.[14] This final extinction of hope left 'a bewildering blank' in Cynthia's life: 'It gets worse and worse. I did know how <u>fond</u> I was of Basil, but I don't think I quite realized how much an inspiration and occupation he was,' she wrote in her diary.[15]

A few weeks later there was some relief when Freyberg, even more badly wounded than before, arrived at Bryanston Square Hospital. Cynthia found him looking 'very white and subdued', an exploding shell having left him 'riddled like St. Sebastian' with 'a hole the size of his fist in his thigh'.[16] She visited him regularly, fascinated how in spite of all his injuries and the loss of so many friends he was as keen as ever on soldiering: 'I love his love of it,' she recorded. When his leg turned septic and amputation seemed likely, he looked so miserable that she willingly complied when 'he asked me to put my hand on his forehead'. Fortunately, the New Zealander's iron constitution pulled him through.

Cynthia naïvely failed to anticipate how Freyberg would interpret her ministrations. As soon as he was released from hospital at the end of November he made a beeline for her flat, where she found him after returning from a lunch party. She described the outcome in her journal:

> Whether what followed was premeditated or not I don't know – there was a leading up to it in conversation, during which perhaps I could have nipped things in the bud. I don't know how it happened, but suddenly there was an explosion and I found myself involved in the most tremendous melodramatic scene – like something in the *Sicilian Lovers*. Again I felt that strange, detached, spectator feeling and my old dumbness was as bad as ever. I blame myself bitterly for my passivity – inexplicable to me – I can only infer it to his habit of command. I found him terribly difficult to cope with, though his suit only inspired contemptible Narcissus feelings in myself. I do like him very, very much, but would never imagine myself in love with him. I should never have allowed this declaration and I don't know what to do.[17]

Cynthia gave Freyberg a tactful enough brush-off for him to take her out to dinner at the Trocadero the following week. 'He interested me enormously,' she wrote afterwards in a long eulogy. 'I believe him to be a genius . . . I adore his consuming ambition . . . and I like his grimness varied by startling gentleness.' Her vanity was flattered when he told 'he "would do his damnedest" to forget me': it was a new experience to have an 'admirer who hates the yoke and I respect him for it . . . I don't think he should be degraded into the role of "sentimental friend"'.[18]

When Edward Horner was killed shortly after returning to active service, Cynthia was shocked to realize how deadened she had become to the pain of losing yet another close friend, although she naturally felt deep sympathy for his family:

> Oh God, the unutterable cruelty of it! Katharine's one anchor in this world, and he has been so wonderful to her since Raymond's death – and poor, poor Frances! . . . He seems almost the last link with my youth. What a perfect companion he used to be in those years of girlhood which are now like a sort of luminous mist in my memory – he, Raymond, Katharine and Ego all so interwoven. Soon there will be nobody left with whom one can even talk of the beloved figures of one's youth. I felt stupefied with the thought of this new load of misery crushing down on the already broken – but so curiously dried up and sterilised myself. Have I no more tears to shed?[19]

On 15 September 1917 Asquith paid a visit to the Front to be briefed by Haig about the progress of the offensive. Oc was given leave to join his father and Bongie for lunch with General Sir Henry Horne, commander of the First Army, after which they toured Vimy Ridge and watched a duel between the German artillery and the British batteries below them. 'Father looked well and was in excellent spirits,' Oc wrote to Margot afterwards, wryly observing that 'his Gas-Box respirator drill leaves a good deal to be desired'. Asquith, for his part, while finding his son 'very well and in capital form', complained about 'a most infernal and complicated apparatus which has been developed as a safeguard against gas'.[20]

Soon afterwards the Royal Naval Division was moved to what Oc euphemistically described as 'a livelier part of the line',[21] close to St Julien about four miles north-east of Ypres and almost the central point of the offensive, to be used for fatigue duties including the backbreaking and dangerous task of building and repairing the duckboard tracks through the mud. Oc became increasingly concerned about his men's lack of training since March, and after getting nowhere with verbal protests he complained in writing to Philips in a note dated 9 October, pointing out that two-fifths of his men 'have never practised following a barrage'. The brigadier prissily replied:

I feel bound to tell you that the Corps and Divisional Commanders and I myself are quite aware of the condition of this Brigade as regards training and that it is not our business to criticize the orders of our superiors, in fact it is a breach of discipline to which I shall not lend myself by making representations on the subject. I have already told you that you are much too apt to criticize the decisions and orders of your superiors. By constantly doing this, you only weaken any possible case you may as C.O. feel justified in submitting to higher authority. I have been called on to make a special report on all my C.O.s and you must not be surprised if I embody some of the above remarks in my report, which will be sent to you to initial.

As I told you the other day, the work on the roads is most important, and I should be sorry to think that there is a danger of the work suffering by the fact that you seem to think someone else should be doing it. The few men I saw on the road outside St. Julien this morning were not working well, in fact they were sitting or standing about with their hands in their pockets, smoking. I looked for an Officer of the Battalion, but could not find anyone supervising the work. Please impress on all ranks the vital importance of this work, upon which the whole advance depends.

This letter does not require an answer.

Naturally enough, Oc thought it did, insisting that he was not offering criticism but 'counsel' and requesting that a copy of his letter be attached to the brigadier's critical report. He pointedly concluded: 'I am unable to inquire into the alleged slackness of the few men you mention unless I know their Platoon and the time at which they were smoking and doing no work. I have not yet found any signs of slackness, or want of supervision among the officers, of whom one has been killed and two wounded on this work during the last three days.'[22]

On 20 October Oc learnt that the Division was to go into action six days later to cover the left flank of the Canadian Corps (which had just fought its way on to Passchendaele ridge) as it advanced towards the mound of rubble that had once been Passchendaele village. The Hood was to escape Philips and be attached to 188th Brigade as 'the counter attack battalion'. According to Jerrold:

The Division was never confronted with a task which, on the lines laid down to them, was more impossible of fulfilment. Flanders mud had become proverbial, and even under ordinary conditions exposed the troops in the front system to exceptional hardships. Front line and communication trenches were non-existent. The forward system consisted of posts isolated from each other by a sea of mud, and the support line of another line of posts, the elements of a trench, or more probably, of a ruined farmhouse and outbuildings where a company or so could be concentrated. These forward positions were scattered in depth over a wide area, and each was dependent on itself for protection. The enemy posts lay often between our own, and every ration and water party had to be prepared to fight its way forward . . . All supplies and reinforcements had to be brought up on duck-board tracks, which with every advance stretched further and further forward. Off these tracks progress was impossible, yet reliance placed on them was an evil necessity; they marked to the enemy, as to ourselves, our line of supply.[23]

Macmillan graphically described a visit to the front line at the time:

We had to proceed cautiously over the greasy duck-board track, on each side of which the day's casualties lay half-buried in the mud. Occasionally we halted in order to negotiate some awkward bend on the track: to have lost a footing might have meant slow and certain death from drowning in a waterlogged shell-hole.

The clayey soil had been pulped by the enemy's artillery, while the continuous rain had transformed every shell-hole into a muddy pool. Succeeding salvoes had enlarged the shell-holes, and in one of the largest of them I discovered all that remained of a battery of our field artillery. Men and horses, half-submerged, eyed us with a glassy stare, and the brown water ran red with their blood.[24]

It was through this noxious swamp that the Royal Naval Division had to advance. Oc, still conscious of his men's lack of training, formally protested to Brigadier Prentice, commanding the 188th Brigade, that 'this Battalion is not at present trained for offensive action, and has not had time to properly study the ground', before dutifully leading his men into position on the night of 24–25 October.[25] At least his new brigadier proved more flexible than Philips about adapting his orders, and he readily agreed to Oc's suggestion to deploy the Hood closer to the attacking battalions than originally planned.

It was raining heavily when the Anson, Howe and the 1st and 2nd Royal Marines began their advance at 5.40 a.m. on 26 October, and there was no let up in the downpour for the rest of the day. The bombardment of the enemy positions had, according to Jerrold, 'turned the ground over which our troops had to advance, into a mass of shell-holes, flooded to a depth of several feet'.[26] The men of the Hood looked on helplessly as their comrades floundered in the slime while shells splattered amongst them and they were cut down by a hail of machine gun fire from pill boxes around the flooded Paddebeek stream that marked the German front line.

As the gravity of the situation became clear, Oc sent three of his companies forward in readiness for a German counter-attack. Then reports came in from the Canadians that their left flank had lost touch with the British right. Varlet Farm, a strongpoint on the Royal Naval Division's right flank, was said to be still in enemy hands, with a large German force concentrating in the area. Oc set out at about midday to find out what was happening, taking with him Lieutenant Garnham, his artillery FOO, and a single rifleman. Picking their way along the driest available route and running the gauntlet of enemy gunners and snipers, the three men found the pill-box at Varlet Farm was after all in British hands. Characteristically neglecting to mention his own part in the reconnaissance, Oc reported in the Hood Battalion 'War Diary': 'A duel was in progress between the garrison of this pill-box and the two enemy groups to the north-east and north-west. The pill-box, knee deep in water, was being held by Sub Lieutenant Stevenson of Anson Battalion and just 11 survivors of his platoon with one Lewis gun. They were putting up a good fight and keeping at bay a large number of the enemy.'

Several of the surviving Ansons were wounded, as were four German prisoners. Having promised to ensure they were relieved, Oc then proceeded to re-establish contact with the Canadians. According to Jerrold, 'this reconnaissance was a decisive incident in the day's fighting, for it enabled our artillery to safeguard the line won, and prevented any incursions on the flank of the Canadians, who were thus able to make an appreciable advance'. Macmillan heard how 'in the teeth of heavy artillery and machine gun fire, he [Oc] passed from end to end of the line we were holding and superintended the consolidation of our gains'.[27]

Oc returned to the Hood in time to hold off a German counter-attack at 5 p.m., after which the battalion relieved the remnants of the Anson and Howe, still clinging on to their slender territorial gains. When a report came in that the Germans had recaptured

Varlet Farm, which would make the Hood's position untenable, Oc again set forth, this time on his own, through the mud to find Stevenson and seven men still holding out, having never been relieved in spite of his earlier efforts. The Ansons were all wounded, exhausted and almost out of ammunition, so Oc returned to his own battalion and led up three platoons to secure the area and allow the garrison to be evacuated.

By the time the Hood was relieved by the Nelson the following night (27–28 October), the battalion had lost only thirty-five men killed and 114 wounded during the course of the battle, compared to an average of over 500 casualties in each of the attacking battalions.[28] The extraordinarily low casualty toll was largely attributable to Oc's efforts to minimize the risks to almost everyone but himself. McCracken once again displayed amazing courage to save the lives of hundreds of wounded men lying out in the open. Braving enemy fire from Passchendaele Ridge, he walked out carrying a walking stick fluttering a Red Cross flag and eventually got the Germans to cease firing and allow him to bring on his orderlies. Stretcher parties from both sides then worked through the night to evacuate the casualties.

Over the next two days the Canadians advanced further along the drier ground of Passchendaele Ridge, making it essential for the Royal Naval Division, covering their flank below, to capture the remaining enemy fortified positions strung either side of the Paddebeek. On 30 October, line after line of 190th Brigade, made up of non-Naval battalions, struggled forward knee-deep in mud, only to be gunned down by fire from the German pill-boxes. Oc, having witnessed the fruitless bloodshed, suggested a solution to Divisional headquarters that was as simple as it was brilliant, foreshadowing the 'commando' raids that were to become such an important part of twentieth-century warfare. He realized that while in daylight enemy pill-boxes could support each other to mete out appalling punishment to infantry trying to attack them, at night the tables could be turned, with isolated pill-boxes becoming death traps if surprised by 'well trained, fresh, and lightly equipped troops with good knowledge of the ground'.[29]

Lawrie was quick to grasp the potential of a proposal that, at the very least, would avoid further heavy casualties, and he instructed 189th Brigade to carry out the operation. Philips, having sealed his own fate by his critical report on Oc, was peremptorily relieved of his command and temporarily replaced by an affable Indian Army officer, Brigadier Coleridge.

The first prerequisite of Oc's plan was accurate intelligence about each individual enemy strongpoint, so after dark on 1 November he and Sterndale Bennett, the commander of the Drake, conducted a thorough survey of the German front line. The remarkable results of this reconnaissance, at every moment of which the two officers were risking their lives, can be seen in a mud-encrusted map among Oc's papers where each enemy position is ringed in red or blue with a pencilled estimate of the strength of its garrison. According to Oc's military biographer, Christopher Page, who has studied the terrain closely, one of the places surveyed, Tournant Farm, was 'over one thousand yards from the most forward of the recently captured British positions'.[30]

When the new tactics were tried out the following night they proved successful beyond all expectation: Sub-Lieutenant Brealey and eleven men from the Nelson Battalion captured, without a single casualty, concrete defences which two days earlier had held up two battalions; at the same time, a company from the Hawke cleared the enemy out of a key strongpoint on the divisional left. Over the next two days all the remaining German positions in the area were seized. Tragically, Sterndale Bennett was one of the few men killed. The operations paved the way for the final advance by the Canadians, who planted their flag in the ruins of Passchendaele village on 5 November. Of Oc's tactics, 'which saved, without doubt, hundreds of lives', Jerrold has commented that 'too little has been said in published accounts of the battle'.[31] As Asquith remarked to Sylvia, 'there is no doubt that Oc is a born soldier'.[32]

After the battle Macmillan was present when six Hood officers turned up at Brigade headquarters 'to testify to the outstanding gallantry of Commander Asquith and to plead that he be awarded the Victoria Cross'. After listening to what they had to say, Coleridge dictated a citation crediting the success of the operations to Oc's 'magnificent bravery, leadership and utter disregard of his own safety'. When, in Macmillan's words, 'Asquith was again ploughed', the whole brigade shared his indignation. The clerk blamed 'the caprice of soulless Brass Hats and exalted grafters' for 'one of the gravest injustices ever perpetrated on a citizen soldier of the King', believing that 'if his father had still been Prime Minister, the haughty backswoodsmen who barred the way would have been falling over themselves to do him honour'. In fact, it was Oc himself who was responsible: having recommended McCracken for the VC, he was told that only one name could go forward and insisted that it must be the surgeon's. In the end, both men received Bars to their DSOs.[33]

Oc may not have received his just deserts for either his bravery or his tactical brilliance, but when Coleridge took over 188th Brigade after the battle, he was promoted to brigadier general and given command of 189th Brigade. But first he was granted four weeks' much-deserved home leave, which was to prove momentous for his future. While he was in England, Betty Manners told him that she now reciprocated the love he had felt for her for the best part of eleven years. 'I know people think I have treated him abominably,' she told Freyberg (who was recovering in London from his latest wounds), 'but I couldn't help it – I didn't love him before.' Freyberg himself seems to have been instrumental in her apparently sudden change of heart, going out of his way to praise Oc's many qualities to her.

Betty was later to explain to her daughters that the reason why she had taken so long to make up her mind before agreeing to marry their father was because she felt he deserved someone who loved him more intensely. It may well be that she herself, like so many women at the time, was more prepared to compromise on her choice as the carnage on the Western Front continued to shrink the pool of prospective mates. She may also have believed, mistakenly, that now Oc was a brigadier, he was in less danger of being killed. In any case, she freely confessed to Freyberg that she was 'very, very fond' of Oc. As had happened between Margot and Asquith, Betty's love for her husband was to grow ever stronger once she was married.[34]

Unfortunately, before the couple could become officially engaged, or even celebrate properly, Oc's remaining leave was abruptly cut short and he was recalled to the Front. 'I felt stunned when you went off so hastily,' Betty wrote to him afterwards, 'now I don't dare to hope and think, the war brings fresh vistas of danger and loss. I wish I could shut my eyes and wake up, to find you safe in three months and everything over.'[35] Oc himself was none too pleased: 'a bibulous ancestry, the Sudan, and three weeks at Cavendish Square have quite unfitted me for the rigours of a winter campaign', he wrote to his father from his bitterly cold tent.[36]

The reason for the recall was a sudden deterioration in the situation on the Western Front. The combination of the Bolshevik

October Revolution in Russia and the decisive defeat of the Italian
army by the Austrians at Caporetto dramatically shifted the balance
of power in favour of Germany and her allies. As German reinforcements poured west, the British Army was now chronically under
strength. A big German counter-attack in the Cambrai region left
General Sir Hubert Gough's Fifth Army clinging on to a salient
around Flesquières, centred on the strategically important 'Welsh
Ridge'; and it was here that the Royal Naval Division was rushed in
mid-December, as Oc took command of 189th Brigade, with Shaw-
Stewart, who had had the fortune to be on leave in England during
the Paddebeek fighting, replacing him as commander of the Hood.

On 20 December Oc turned up at his former battalion's headquarters to inspect their trenches. Shaw-Stewart, writing to Diana later
that day, described what happened:

> I, having been round at night and round at dawn, like a zealous C.O., and
> was trying to sleep it off (about 11 a.m.), but offered to spring out of bed
> and go round with him – he waved me back and went off alone with his
> runner. An hour later the runner clattered down my dugout pale and wild-
> eye and cried that Oc had been wounded. So he had – he had been stand-
> ing about in my support line, relying on a thin mist, and had been shot by
> a sniper through the bone just above the ankle: a very nasty compound
> fracture, which will take him a very long time (no misfortune to a less
> ardent spirit than his), even if it doesn't go septic, which will be a horror.
> I went with him to the ADS [Dressing Station]. It hurt him like hell, poor
> boy, and the morphia took ages to work and the frost made the stretcher
> bearers slip and the ambulance jolt over the frozen ruts. It is a cruel thing,
> and a great bore for me who counted a deal on general conveniences and
> amenities accruing from him as Brigadier, while I was commanding the
> Battalion – or indeed any time. The incident rather diminished my keen-
> ness for a 'Blighty One', the process seemed so extremely agonizing.[37]

Asquith wrote to Sylvia that he had 'a letter full of appreciation',
from Lawrie: 'He was quite near when he was shot. It was due to a
sudden lifting of the curtain of mist which enabled a German sniper
to take three shots at him with a rifle: happily the third after he had
fallen to the ground, missed and only kicked up the sand . . . It was
bad luck, as he had got his Brigade, and is now called General. But it
has its compensations.'[38]

A grateful Oc told Diana how Shaw-Stewart had met his stretcher
'and was full of "*petit soins*" for me, gave me cigarettes and helped

the stretcher bearers in places where it was difficult going. He and our Doctor [McCracken] bore me company to the Dressing Station two miles away and saw me into an ambulance car.'[39] The following day Oc endured a thirteen-hour train journey to Lady Murray's Hospital in the picturesque little Normandy port of Le Tréport, from where he wrote to his father: 'Except when they are dressing my foot, I have more discomfort from the small of my back and stomach than I do from it – this from being forced to be always in the same position . . . The alternatives before one would appear to be one's own stiff ankle, or a nicely articulated ankle and foot bought in a shop.'[40]

A week later, despite 'some uncomfortable days and nights', he was hopeful that he 'should retain my own leg and foot with stiff ankles'. However, he was upset that yet again his father had failed to be in touch, protesting: 'It's time I had a letter – so far one from Clouder [the butler] is all that has reached me from the family.'[41] This time he was being unfair, for two days earlier Asquith complained to Sylvia about 'breakdown of telegraphs and telephones and we have no report of his progress since just before Xmas Day'.[42]

On 30 December the Germans mounted a determined attack on Welsh Ridge. As reports of the battle began to filter into Le Tréport Hospital, Oc heard a rumour that the Hood Battalion commander had been killed, but when there was no official confirmation he hoped there had been a mistake. A letter the next day from McCracken soon disillusioned him: Shaw-Stewart had indeed been killed. As Oc would have expected, this most reluctant of soldiers died as courageously as his mentor, Raymond, blown to pieces by an incoming shell as, although already wounded, he made a final inspection of the battalion's defences. The surgeon proudly went on to describe how the Hood had stubbornly beaten off four German assaults: 'our fellows simply knocked hell out of them'.[43]

Oc confessed to his father that Shaw-Stewart's death was 'a very bitter blow to me and the Battalion. I had become much attached to Patrick this last summer and autumn. His good company and unfailing good spirits and sense of humour were invaluable . . . I suppose [the Roman Catholic priest] Ronald Knox is now the only survivor of the first class Eton brains of that generation.'[44] Cynthia spoke for their whole circle when she wrote in her diary: 'Poor Patrick – everybody settled he would not be killed. No one ever looked forward to his life more or coveted a glorious death less.'[45] His death marked the departure of the last of Raymond's disciples for the Valhalla that they all so despised.

Oc's hopes of keeping his leg proved to be misplaced: as Shaw-Stewart had foreseen, his ankle turned septic, leaving the Army surgeons no option but to amputate his lower leg. He was eventually shipped back to England on 23 February. Five days later, as a special mark of his affection for the whole Asquith family, the King visited him at his bedside in the King Edward VII Hospital and personally invested him with his DSO and two Bars.[46]

24

Beb's 'Battle in the Mist'*

———————————◆———————————

SHORTLY AFTER BEB returned from leave his division was moved south of the Passchendaele battles to the Messines ridge, where its role was essentially defensive. Although they were spared the horrific casualties of those engaged in the offensive, the 'safety' of their position was, of course, relative as the gunners engaged in regular duels with their German counterparts, which often resulted in casualties. In November they were sent back to the Menin road, where they found that after three months of fighting the British line had moved some 2,000 yards forward. Beb later described the landscape:

> Our new observation post was a German pill box with two storeys, whose grey squat tower rose as a prominent target above the foul swamp of the crater field to the east of Inverness Copse. The slimy ridges between the craters had in many places been pounded away by months of bombardment; they were filled with ponds of torpid and filthy water, tinged by the chemicals of shells that had burst there with strange turgid clouds of blue and green and yellow; in some places the surface of the stagnant ooze was crimsoned with blood and floating near the banks of the pools were some horrible relics of the battle . . .
>
> Though the last big attack was made on 10th of November, there was no sudden dying of the storm: for several weeks the guns and machine guns of both sides were extremely alert and active and I rarely went to the

---

*From the title of Chapter XVIII of Herbert Asquith's *Moments of Memory*.

observation post without seeing fresh casualties lying by the side of the narrow duck-board track that led there. The Germans made very accurate shooting at the duck-boards, and where they had been blown to pieces, it was no simple task making a way over the slimy arretes of the crater field. It would be difficult to exaggerate the hardships of the infantry near our observation post, who sometimes had to lie out all night under heavy fire without any cover except the lips of the poisonous shell-holes. The horse lines, some miles behind us, were bombed at night, often for many hours on end and there were many casualties among the horses: in one battery over fifty horses were hit in a single night.[1]

Shortly before Christmas 1917 Beb saw a man in an unfamiliar uniform gingerly picking his way along the narrow duck-board track that led to their guns: 'he was an American officer of high rank and great courtesy, and he had only lately come to France; he had never before seen the conditions under which we were fighting, and as he approached our dugout he looked round at the crater field, which had so long been our familiar home, with an expression of almost comic bewilderment which he made no effort to hide.'[2]

After Christmas Beb was given three weeks' home leave. Once again, just before he was due to depart, his observation post was destroyed during someone else's shift, killing yet another 'gay and gallant friend', this time Lieutenant Oxley. That evening, as he and his battery commander walked silently back along the cratered Menin road from the ruined look-out, he thought of 'other friends who had fallen there three years before, how short a way we had come since then, and [at] what a cost the journey had been made'.[3]

Cynthia and the boys spent their Christmas holidays at Stanway with her mother, Letty (Ego's widow), and her sisters, Mary (Strickland) and Bibs. The contrast between the pastoral tranquillity of the Gloucestershire countryside and the devastated Flanders landscape he had just left brought an even more 'violent need for adjustment' than usual for Beb.[4] Cynthia was in a gloomy mood: her childhood home brought constant reminders of her two dead brothers, and she was beset by worries about John's deteriorating mental health. Even a Christmas gift from Freyberg of 'a gorgeous enamel fountain pen' failed to lift her spirits.[5]

For Beb, an end to his ordeal – unless it was a German victory – seemed as remote as ever. The frustrated politician in him felt a keen sense of betrayal by the Lloyd George Government, unwilling either to make peace or to prosecute the War with the energy needed to win it. He could have no idea of the official statistics of men being conscripted, but he knew that the British armies in France desperately needed more men if they were to stave off defeat, let alone win the War. Like most soldiers, he felt none of the hatred of the Germans stoked up amongst the civilian population by the London Press. To him, 'our gallant enemies' were fellow victims of a war which the politicians of both sides were too cowardly to end.[6] Cynthia agreed: 'Would it be easier if one hated the Germans?' she wrote in her journal after Basil's disappearance. 'I feel them – poor devils – to be our wretched allies fighting against some third thing.'[7] Nonetheless she was shocked by the force of her normally laconic husband's anger as he poured out his feelings during a long walk they took together on New Year's Eve:

> It was one of the most lovely-looking days I have ever seen. Beb is in very good form – in good, lean looks and very keen and eager – seething with indignation against the Government and the 'hate campaign' of the civilians. He is ashamed of the way England brutally snubs every peace feeler, and reiterates that, either we should negotiate or else fight with all our might, which he says would mean <u>doubling</u> our army in the field. He speaks with rage of the way we are not nearly up to strength at the Front and says it is to a large extent a paper army. In existing circumstances a military victory is quite out of the question until America can really take the field, which will not be for years – and he thinks all the lives now being sacrificed are being wasted, it's like going about with a huge bleeding wound and doing nothing to bind it up. Thank God Beb isn't in the House of Commons! I should never have the moral courage to face the reception given to the kind of speech he would make.[8]

Cynthia was relieved that Beb liked Freyberg when they met him for lunch at the Berkeley Hotel on 5 January 1918: 'Beb was, as I feared, a little shy at first,' she recorded, 'but he soon got happily on to shop and he was charmed with Freyberg.' The two soldiers 'wailed in unison over the incompetency and senility of most of the Army generals'.[9] Even when Mary Herbert joined them for dinner a couple of days later, Cynthia had little chance for a private talk with Freyberg as he and Beb discussed Grand Strategy.

> There was a great struggle to procure port, as it was after 9.30 when the order was given, but Beb acted with commendable firmness and finally

prevailed. Mary and I talked – Beb and Freyberg sat on and on, but finally I roused them and got Beb to walk Mary home, thus leaving Freyberg to a *dentist*. I had thought him looking wonderfully well, and was very sorry to hear that he was constantly fainting – had even done so just before dinner – and was dreadfully depressed. He had tears in his eyes the whole time, lamented Patrick [Shaw-Stewart] and said he envied him and had no wish to survive. He complained of his real loneliness. I was very much touched, but felt very powerless to help him.[10]

Beb and Cynthia's weekend at the Wharf, crammed as usual with Margot's guests, was not a success. There was little chance of rest or repose or, above all, sympathy in the crowded and boisterous atmosphere, and when Beb complained of 'claustrophobia', Cynthia took him out for a walk in the rain.

We agreed the atmosphere was strangely jarring on war nerves. I do think his father is amazing. He is devoted to his sons and it seems odd that, after Beb has been out for five months – liable to be killed at any moment – he should not address one word of enquiry to him, as to what he has been doing and where he has been. I suppose it is part of his habit of optimism – that he likes to blink facts and avoid being confronted by anything unpleasant, just as he avoids what he calls an 'unpleasant novel'. Beb rather feels it, as it is always soothing – at least generally it is – to talk about one's experiences. I think the Wharf atmosphere really hurts him.[11]

Asquith did, in the end, make time for a private chat with his son at 11 p.m. on 17 January, a couple of days before he was due to return to the Front, giving him £50, a sum he could ill afford. That afternoon the former Prime Minister had attended a Secret Session of the House of Commons, where MPs heard the grim news that the Germans were reported to have moved forty divisions to the Western Front following their recent armistice with the Russian Communist Government. Beb the soldier was resigned to the likelihood that he was going to die, as his elder brother and so many of his friends had died (and indeed as the heroes of two semi-autobiographical novels* were to die), in a war that Beb the would-be politician desperately wanted brought to a negotiated end.

---

*Young Orland (1927) and *Roon* (1929).

Beb knew that Lloyd George had recently lunched with his father at Cavendish Square, the first occasion on which the two men had met since December 1916.[12] If Asquith confided in his son what had been said, Beb kept it to himself. Lloyd George, his political position weakening as the prospect of defeat loomed closer, wanted his predecessor's advice on a speech he was about to make to the Parliamentary Labour Party about the possibility of peace talks. Asquith told Margot afterwards that his successor's manner was 'deferential to servility . . . I never saw him more reasonable or half so sensible'.[13] Lloyd George compliantly accepted all his suggestions about the speech and listened carefully to his advice that if he was to suggest peace terms, he must do so at once, before Germany concluded its treaty with Russia. He even joined in condemning the roasting meted out by the newspapers to Lansdowne, the former Tory Foreign Secretary, who had had the temerity to write to *The Times* suggesting negotiations with Germany.* In the event, a hostile Press reaction to Lansdowne's letter sent the Prime Minister scuttling for cover.

The predicament facing Haig was bleak: in September 1917 he had reluctantly agreed to take over nearly thirty extra miles of front line from the exhausted French Army, and by the start of 1918 he had only fifty-nine severely under-strength British and Dominion divisions to keep at bay eighty-one German divisions, still being reinforced by hardened veterans of the Russian campaign. His pleas for reinforcements fell on deaf ears as Lloyd George, determined to avoid the casualties of another Passchendaele, adamantly refused to release over half a million troops stationed in England or the hundreds of thousands stationed around the Mediterranean, choosing to believe instead the siren voices assuring him that Germany had not the stomach for another big offensive.

Lloyd George would dearly have loved to be rid of both Haig and Robertson, but lacking either the resolution or the political strength to sack them, he resorted to encouraging his friends in the Press to denigrate them. Gough, the commander of the Fifth Army (in which both Oc and Beb served), voiced the anger felt by most senior generals towards the Prime Minister's newspaper allies when on 25 January

---

*It was on the grave of Lansdowne's younger son, Major Lord Charles Nairne, that Margot and Major Gordon had fixed the cross entrusted to them by the dead officer's father during their visit to the Western Front in December 1914.

1918 he wrote to Oc to express sympathy about the amputation of
his leg: 'All will be well if the vile campaign now being conducted
by Northcliffe and his Press does not undermine the confidence and
the discipline of the Army.'[14] In the end Haig, backed by his senior
commanders, proved too strong to budge; however, Robertson was
eventually hounded into resignation, to be replaced by one of the
Prime Minister's few allies in the upper reaches of the Army, the
Asquith-hating veteran of the 'Monday Night Cabal', General Sir
Henry Wilson.

A few days after Beb returned to his battery:

> Haig came to review our division which was drawn up in line in a valley,
> the guns and their teams in close order on the right, the infantry on the
> left, making rather a grim array, as they looked to their front beneath the
> brims of their steel helmets. On the crest of a small hill Haig suddenly
> rode into view on his charger and halted for a short time on the sky-line
> to acknowledge our salute: he might have almost been mistaken for a
> figure of bronze, as he sat motionless on his horse, outlined against a grey
> wintry cloud, looking down on this division that had fought in so many of
> his battles, and was now far beneath its proper strength.[15]

Haig based his defensive strategy on a series of heavily fortified
redoubts rather than the usual trench system which he no longer had
the manpower to garrison. The plan was to hold up the enemy long
enough to allow the reserves to be brought into play. The flaw in the
scheme (and it was an unavoidable one) was that the Government's
refusal to provide any extra troops meant British armies had few
reserves and must rely on what Wilson sarcastically called 'Pétain's
charity' to plug the gap with French units, forecasting that it would
be 'very cold charity' by the French Commander-in-Chief.[16]

Haig gambled on the Germans attacking the northern sector of
his line and concentrated his meagre reserves here. However, on 21
March Ludendorff launched two-thirds of sixty-two divisions ear-
marked for his offensive against the British southern flank and in
particular against the fourteen divisions of Gough's Fifth Army – of
which Beb's 30th Division was part. The division had recently taken
over forty-two miles of trenches west of the German held town of St
Quentin. Beb's battery was concealed on the edge of Holnon Wood,

five miles due west of St Quentin, to support the defenders of the nearby redoubt on 'Manchester Hill', held by the Manchester Regiment.

The first sign of German intentions was the appearance of small blue balloons over No Man's Land, 'apparently to test the direction of the wind', and at night 'the dim rumbling of traffic' in the otherwise deserted streets of St Quentin. On 20 March they heard that a German prisoner had revealed that a big offensive was to begin the following day. Beb was sent to warn Lieutenant Harris, the duty Forward Observation Officer on Manchester Hill. Raids on enemy lines later that day brought in eight prisoners 'each belonging to a different division being taken on 2000 yards only of our Northern Sector'. This, Beb later told Oc, 'seemed to clinch the probability of attack into a certainty'.[17] The gunners checked that their gas gloves were near at hand and applied demisting liquid to their goggles, while Beb and his captain built a pyre from the remains of a cherry orchard cut down by the Germans and burnt their copies of the divisional defence scheme.

All the while, on the German side, some 6,000 guns assembled to support the offensive maintained an almost eerie silence. In his letter to Oc, Beb described how:

From 2.30 a.m. to 4.30 a.m. our brigade of eighteen pounders kept up bursts of fire on the German assembly areas and they must have suffered pretty heavily during these hours. At 4.30 their artillery opened with the most terrific crashing of heavy shells intermingled with phosgene and mustard gas . . . the noise was so great that a megaphone was quite useless and it was extremely difficult to get a whistle heard, communications were very difficult. Both our forward telephone lines were cut by shells in the first 5 minutes. I had my [horse] teams close behind in the wood in case it should be necessary to move out against tanks: we kept up communication with the teams by mounted orderly – one of our bombardiers (Vickers): he was killed halfway between the horses and the battery and his horse, which was wounded, stayed with him: a driver (Lynch) took his place and was also killed on his way up.[18]

Writing about the battle in his Memoirs, published nineteen years later, Beb wrote:

The scene that followed is difficult to describe, impossible to forget: it was more a convulsion of nature than the work of man. Among the first sounds was the whistling of gas shells, which I heard as I went from gun to gun, checking the angles of fire, and sucking at the tube of my respirator. It was still pitch-dark above, and the only lights below were the flashes from our own guns or the red flaming cores of exploding shells. The flames from the muzzles were stabbing out into a dense whitish mist which was now mingled with the gas from the German shells and the dark drifting clouds from their explosions. For the fraction of a second a gun and the men who were firing it, gloved, masked, and helmeted, would start into view, lit by a sudden flash, and would then vanish again into blackness.

Fortunately, the German gunners had not ranged their guns (to ensure surprise) and most of their shells fell short, causing casualties among the gun crews and horses, but failing to destroy the guns themselves. Daybreak revealed a thick fog blanketing the whole area. Beb recalled how shortly afterwards Major MacFarlane appeared through the mist and a hail of enemy shells in a mule-cart, bringing with him several wagons of ammunition: 'His arrival had a very cheering effect on the men who were greatly amused by the equipage in which he was riding, and the demure appearance of his mule, which was perfectly groomed, and showed no sign of disturbance at the shattered trees or the thunder of the bombardment.'

The major called a conference of his officers in the dugout, Beb and his captain, both of whom had received doses of gas, joining in 'with our reddened eyes blinking and streaming with water'.[19] The telephone lines to Harris, the FOO on Manchester Hill, had been cut and the fog made signals by flag impossible, so they had no means of knowing whether the German infantry assault had begun until Harris staggered through the exploding shells later that morning to report that the Manchesters had been under attack since 9.40 a.m., but although massively outnumbered, were holding out.* As the gun crews, bathed in sweat and blinking back the gas seeping through their masks, desperately strove to support their comrades manning the redoubt, the fog meant that the machine gunners protecting their flanks from being overrun could only see a few

---

*Beb does not name the FOO, but written in pencil beside his account in the author's second-hand copy of his *Moments of Memory* are the initials 'CKH'. When the author checked the name of the original owner at the front, he found it had belonged to C.K. Harris himself, whose relations must have sold the book after his death, unaware of its significance.

hundred yards ahead. Beb, with Asquithian nonchalance, informed his brother:

> I was sent forward by the Battery Commander to the Round Hill [between Holnon Wood and Manchester Hill] to try and find out the position and look out for tanks. The mist was very thick, the German artillery fire had stopped, and in its place there was a very heavy machine gunfire from both sides. I wandered about for some time, but couldn't find any sign of a German tank. After reporting this I went forward again with a signaller to signal back targets, in case the mist lifted.

Beb later heard how Colonel Elstrob, commanding the Manchesters, 'telephoned by a buried cable at 3.20 p.m. that all the officers there had been hit but that he intended to hold out to the end'.* By now the fog was lifting and a few minutes later 'a large number of grey misty figures, easily recognised as Germans by the shape of their helmets, stood halted on the skyline of Manchester Hill'.[20] After instructing his signaller to convey the news to the battery,

> I went back to an anti-tank gun at the foot of Round Hill to lay it on the Boche – I found a fellow I know in charge (Pearce) and he laid the gun, an eighteen pounder, on open sights and gave them gunfire at a rapid rate. They were advancing by platoons down the North side of the Railway between Manchester Hill and Holnon Wood and also on Savy on our right rear: i.e. we were being outflanked on the right. They saw my signaller and myself signalling from Round Hill and opened on us with a machine gun.

By the time Beb and his signaller got back to Holnon Wood their guns had been withdrawn to Etreillers. Although the wood was still being shelled, Beb, his signaller and MacFarlane (who had waited behind for them) stayed put to direct fire 'onto a long line of Germans who were attacking Savy on our right flank . . . the barrage of our brigade held them up until nightfall'.

The following day Beb returned to the guns when Hardie relieved him as FOO. Their battery was fortunate to lose only an anti-tank gun in the battle, whereas some of their neighbours had been devastated: one team lost all of its officers and most of its guns. German

---

*Elstrob was awarded a posthumous VC.

aeroplanes flew over to pinpoint their position for their artillery, usually spraying them with machine gun fire in the process; when one was shot down, Beb remarked on how it 'swerved downward like a wounded pheasant into a field half a mile behind us'. MacFarlane remained as cool as ever: when a shell buried itself close to where he and Beb were standing and failed to explode 'for a moment the Major contemplated the dark steaming tunnel within a few yards of his feet, and then he continued the conversation at the exact point where he had broken it off'.[21]

During the afternoon German *Sturmtruppen*, their helmets glinting in the sunlight that occasionally punctured the smoke of battle, began to break through the British forward defences. As Hardie, who had relieved Harris as FOO, came limping back 'much begrimed', leading his wounded horse, the battery's officers made a desperate appeal to their men to open 'rapid fire' to cover the retreating infantrymen. Beb recalled how although the gun crews had been on duty for thirty-six hours, their eyes 'inflamed by the gas and by the fumes from the breeches, and their faces were lined with fatigue . . . their response to our appeal was magnificent'. It was at this moment that a messenger from headquarters galloped through the fumes with orders to pull back to Ham:

> Until this point we had thought that we were fighting a delaying action to allow reinforcements time to arrive; we should not have been surprised by an order to retire for half a mile, but as the crow flies, Ham was about seven miles to our rear, and a ten mile march by road. Such an order as this was entirely beyond our experience; we read it with amazement, and it dawned on us at last that the reinforcements we had imagined were creatures of our own fancy.[22]

Gough's only chance to prevent the Germans encircling and destroying his hopelessly outnumbered Fifth Army was to keep his forces on the move. With consummate skill over the next few days, the general would pull his men back a few miles, make a stand, and then retreat again, all the time trying to keep his forces intact, while he waited for reinforcements.

The retreat to Ham was harrowing. All along the road lay groaning, wounded soldiers, but the gunners were forbidden to hoist them on to their gun limbers: nothing must delay the progress of the guns. By the time they reached the town it was already under fire from

German long-range guns aiming for the bridges over the Somme canal as they tried to cut off the retreating British. Everywhere Beb could see signs of the haste in which the civilian population had fled: 'dresses and hats still adorned the windows of the draper, and at the butcher's pieces of meat were still hanging, rather obtrusively by their hooks'. A man ran out into the street with a large box of eggs which he pressed on them to prevent it falling into enemy hands.

It was 1 a.m. before the gunners finished feeding and watering their horses and gulped down a meal of eggs and bully beef, their first meal in two days of fighting. Shortly after 4 a.m., after barely a couple of hours' sleep in a hut beside the main road, Beb was woken by an agitated orderly and told the enemy was about to enter the town and the guns must go into action at once. He later recalled: 'The Germans marched on us in column through Ham: we fired all our ammunition at about 60 rounds a minute up the street and over the bridge into this column and must have caused a good many casualties, as it was very short range.' The charges hurriedly laid by the sappers proved inadequate to destroy the bridges and, in the afternoon, under cover of the fog, the gunners were pulled back to the next village, Esméry Hallon, to make their next stand.

> About 7.30 a.m. the Germans again began to advance covered by great numbers of machine guns and mortars, the tapping and chattering of separate guns being completely lost in the general volume of lashing sound which came out of the mist in front of us. The surviving guns of our brigade were aligned behind a low crest, and opened rapid fire, putting down a barrage in front of our thin line of infantry. Some of our shells were set at fuse 'O', so as to burst near the muzzle in case the Germans tried to rush the guns. After continuing in action for two or three hours we again got orders to retire.

Although 'the morale of the men was excellent', they were by now desperately tired. They regularly encountered infantrymen asleep besides the road even though shells were falling nearby. Beb recollected that 'it was almost impossible to wake them, and when at last we succeeded, I felt no confidence that they would be able to keep their eyes open for more than a few minutes'.[23] He and Hardie kept themselves awake by riding up and down the gun limbers checking their men were not nodding off. Behind the column was a sorry line of wounded horses, those too weak to keep up had to be shot.

At Faverolles, en route for the village of Plessiers, they crossed a road 'blocked with civilians many of whom were in a state of extreme panic: haycarts, dog-carts, wheelbarrows, perambulators, anything that had wheels beneath it, were being loaded under the direction of aged men and women with feather mattresses, chairs, parasols, chickens, goats, pigs and every variety of domestic belonging'.[24] Seeking somewhere to bed down for the night, Beb and some fellow officers found a deserted farmhouse whose occupants had left in the middle of dinner. After ravenously polishing off the food left on the table, Beb went up to the main bedroom where he found an empty jewel case belonging to his 'unknown hostess' lying open on the dressing table and dresses laid out ready to be packed, but left behind in the panic to get away. Scarcely had he laid down on her bed before he was woken with the news that the Germans were closing on the village.

The men were now so exhausted that 'some of the drivers had to be helped to mount their horses . . . four men, instead of two, were needed in order to shift the trail of a gun'. They did their best to counter the far more numerous German gunners, hidden in nearby woods, until an orderly rode in with the news that Plessiers had fallen, and they were about to be encircled. While the rest of the brigade hurriedly limbered up their guns and made a detour north to cross the River Avre at Moreuil, Beb and Howarth, his 'horseholder', rode in the opposite direction across what was now No Man's Land to head off six ammunition wagons due to cross the river at La Neuville. Bob, Beb's horse, 'had had a good feed, and now he seemed to know that something was expected of him'. As the two men galloped though the village 'bullets whizzed over us or struck with a clap on the walls of the houses; but there was no one to be seen, no inhabitants, no soldiers of either side'. When they reached the bridge over the Avre, sappers on the far side were laying charges, and they just managed to clatter across before they blew it up, finding to their 'great relief, that our wagons were still safe on the western bank'.[25]

Over the next few days the four divisions in Beb's corps were reduced to single battalions, but men who had lost touch with their own commanders put themselves under the nearest available officer. Beb later described to Oc how he watched 'infantrymen taking cover behind banks or grubbing themselves holes about 10 inches to 2 feet deep', but still they fought on.

It was soon clear that the British would get little help from Pétain: Gough later complained that 'he sent me reserves armed with only twenty rounds apiece. They blazed away and then beat it back to Verdun or somewhere where Pétain was sitting on his bottom.' In desperation Haig offered to do what until now he had always resisted, put himself and his troops under a French general: his one condition was that it must be Foch, whom he trusted. When, on 3 April, Lloyd George joined the negotiations at Beauvais in time to initial the agreement appointing Foch 'Generalissimo', Haig noted contemptuously that 'the Prime Minister looked as if he had been thoroughly frightened and he seemed still in a funk . . . he appears to me to be a thorough impostor'.[26]

Foch's intervention, even before his formal appointment as 'generalissimo', quickly brought French reservists to fight shoulder to shoulder with the remnants of Gough's army as they mustered behind the River Avre in defence of Amiens. Beb recalled how 'during this battle we made friends with some French dragoons and exchanged our bully beef for theirs'. Each side's meat was equally revolting, but 'the main point was its difference'. However, when it came to swapping 'tough gritty biscuits' for 'good French loaves . . . here again, with a courtesy difficult to exaggerate, the cavalry professed that they were pleased'.

On 31 March Beb and MacFarlane were attached to the French infantry as Forward Observation Officers as the Germans made a final attempt to break through the Allied lines:

Out of a film of mist about 600 yards in front of us came the long grey line of the German infantry, ghostly at first and difficult to discern, but soon becoming clear and solid against the grass as they advanced up the gradual slope of the fields. The impression they gave was very different from that of the storm troops who had attacked at St Quentin; their line now seemed to move more slowly, with the labour of weary men, suffering from want of sleep and food, and the deep physical fatigue of long endurance.

At the moment when they came through the mist, the French opened a heavy fire with their machine guns, and the Major gave out a range and an angle of fire to our signaller who was squatting over his 'buzzer' in the shallow pit of the shell-hole; there was a pause of a few seconds, and then the shells from the surviving guns of our brigade came over our heads and the smoke of the shrapnel curled and glinted in front of the advancing line. They still came, very slowly, for a few hundred yards, and then they suddenly lay down on the grass and began to dig themselves in until the dusk closed over them and hid them from sight.[27]

The Germans had been fought to a standstill. On 5 April Ludendorff accepted that he was not going to break through to Amiens and switched his attention to the British First Army south of Ypres, as he threatened Dunkirk and the vital Allied railway centre of Hazebrouck. Here there was no hinterland into which to retreat and it was now that Haig issued his most celebrated despatch of the War: 'Every position must be held to the last man: there must be no retirement. With our backs to the wall, and believing in the justice of our cause, each one of us must fight on to the end.'

For Beb, there was to be no respite. On 7 April his brigade's remaining guns were loaded on to trains to go into action alongside French gunners near Bailleul. There were four more weeks of bitter fighting before the German advance was finally brought to a halt in early May just outside Ypres. Writing to Oc, Beb reported how, although his brigade had suffered badly in their final engagement on 8 May, he was 'personally rather lucky, as I got off with a small splinter in the arm'.[28] Beb was indeed 'lucky' – if the word can be applied to anyone who went through what he did – having survived relatively unscathed (physically at least) forty days of fighting which produced some quarter of a million British casualties. Even Lloyd George now realized that it was not just offensives that were bloody. Over the next few months, Haig received over a half a million fresh troops, reinforcements that, had they arrived earlier, would have averted a near catastrophe.

Gough, instead of being acclaimed a national hero, became a convenient scapegoat for the Prime Minister's own responsibility for the disaster. He was publicly reviled for allowing his army to 'collapse' and, at the age of forty-eight, was made to retire in disgrace. A disgusted Haig offered to resign himself, but Wilson (the CIGS) persuaded Lloyd George to keep him on since 'he would not get anyone to fight a defensive battle better'.[29] In any case, they would need a much bigger scapegoat than Gough if Germany won the War.*

---

*Eighteen years later Gough received an apology from Lloyd George who, sending him the draft of the relevant passage in his *War Memoirs*, wrote 'I need hardly say that the facts which have come to my knowledge since the War have completely changed my mind as to the responsibility for this defeat. You were completely let down and no general could have won the battle under the conditions which you were placed.' Exactly who let Gough down was not specified. The following year (1937), in a letter read out to a reunion of Fifth Army veterans, the former Prime Minister admitted: 'The refusal of the Fifth Army to run away even when it was broken was the direct cause of the failure of the great German offensive in 1918.' (See Donald McCormick, *The Mask of Merlin*, p. 147)

25

'A gentleman and not a politician'

IT HAD BEEN a 'miserable, gloomy afternoon – pouring with rain', when Cynthia saw Beb off at the station on his way back to the Front on 20 January 1918. She 'felt something more like a presentiment at parting with him than on any previous occasion'.[1] Under the circumstances it was the least she could feel; nonetheless, she soon slipped back into 'cuckooing' and socializing. The latest man in her life was the thirty-nine-year-old Prince Antoine Bibesco, a rich Romanian nobleman serving at his country's embassy in London, who was introduced to her by Elizabeth, whom he was also pursuing. Cynthia, at least, seems to have resisted his best efforts to seduce her, recording that he called her '"an impossible proposition" (meaning for the purpose of erotic attack)'; she noted caustically that 'like most men he talks as though the alternatives were between 'se donnering' [i.e. giving oneself] to <u>him</u> and a nunnery'.[2]

When Ludendorff launched his offensive on 21 March, Cynthia knew that Beb, stationed near St Quentin, must be in the thick of the Fifth Army's desperate rearguard action. But it was not until 4 April, a fortnight after the battle had begun, that she received her first news of him, a field postcard dated 24 March saying he was 'all right'. Feeling 'oppressed' by panic-stricken newspaper reports of British retreat after retreat, she confessed in her journal: 'I have never been so haunted by the War . . . I have never been so frightened about him before.' On 17 April, she finally received a letter from Beb, written eleven days earlier 'saying all his guns were practically knocked out, but none belonging to his battery had fallen into the hands of the Germans'.[3] Two days later Oc sent on his brother's 'excellent letter' congratulating him on his official engagement to Betty Manners (the announcement had been delayed when Oc was wounded), and going on to describe in detail the fighting, before ending: 'What would you like for a wedding present?'[4]

Oc spent the weeks before his wedding in the Mill House, which Margot had now added to The Wharf, looked after by Violet and Bongie. 'I am dismayed at so much happiness coming to me,' Oc replied to Ettie's letter of congratulation. 'No one could ever be good enough for her [Betty] . . . Yet somehow I feel confident about the future.' Asquith reported to Sylvia that his son was 'pretty agile now on his crutches, but his leg still needs dressing and it will be a longish time before he will be able to attempt an artificial limb'.[5] The wedding was celebrated on 30 April in the Manners' tiny parish church at Avon Tyrrell. It was the Asquith family's second that year, Cys having married Anne Pollock on 12 February at St Margaret's, Westminster. However, it was Oc's marriage which had special poignancy after what his father described as 'a wooing of almost patriarchal length, marked by steely persistence on our side and a rather elusive congress on the other'.[6] On the eve of the wedding, Cynthia was amused when 'Ettie told a delicious story of Hoppy [the bride's father, Lord Manners]. He had gone in a state of utmost concern to Con [Betty's mother] and told her that, when inspecting Betty's trousseau, he had said, "Surely, darling, these night gowns are rather thin?" To which she [Betty] had replied, "Oh yes, but it will be all right because I shall wear my combinations under them." What was to be done?'

All seems to have been well, though, as the couple went on successfully to produce four daughters. Cynthia described the wedding ceremony itself as

a poem – really lovely and most touching – much the nicest I have ever seen and it made one think all London weddings indecent. The little chapel was most beautifully decorated – the arch of may was a dream. One felt that no one was there who wasn't really interested. The bridegroom was a brilliantly topical figure, and he stood so well on his one leg, without even a stick, though it made one tired to watch him. The bride looked astonishingly above her average – really delicious – and the sun emerged just in time to gild her hair as they walked out under the arch of New Zealanders'* swords whilst children strewed gorse petals at her feet.

... We went back to the most wonderful pre-war meal and I ate till I was blue – there were actually solid things like ham! Betty and Oc sat beside each other at the wedding breakfast, she still wonderfully pretty, and she cut the cake with his sword. As they motored away to Cranborne,† the New Zealanders mustered and did a Harikro – wuh? [presumably a Maori *Haaka*] – some wild cry which curdles one's blood.[7]

Because of the German offensive, Freyberg had to turn down Oc's request to be his Best Man (he had recently written 'a very dear letter' to Cynthia 'exulting in the battle'[8]). Instead the honour fell to the fifteen-year-old Puffin whose speech, according to his father, was 'a *succès fou*!'.[9] Among the wedding presents was a handsome silver punch bowl inscribed: 'From the old Officers of the Hood Battalion R.N.D. to their adored Commander, Brigadier General A. M. Asquith D.S.O.'[10] Asquith gave his son the royalties from the first 5,000 copies sold of *Occasional Addresses*, a collection of his non-political speeches.[11] Churchill, now Minister of Munitions, offered Oc the job of Controller of Trench Warfare at the Ministry of Munitions when the previous incumbent, Tom Bridges – who had also lost a leg the previous year – joined Balfour's mission to the United States.

Oc's wedding was a brief happy interlude in the Asquiths' lives before they were engulfed once again in a bitter political row. Asquith had been under pressure for months from his own Party to drop his broad support for the Government and take advantage of the growing dissatisfaction with Lloyd George, not only among the Army High Command but among Tory Members of Parliament and even the hitherto slavishly supportive Press, and to mount a strong attack on the Prime Minister's handling of the War effort. Growing public dissatisfaction was exacerbated by misconceived attempts to control the price of food which, without organized rationing, only served to increase the shortages: fresh meat was almost unobtainable, hence Cynthia's ecstasy over the ham at Oc's wedding reception.

---

*Convalescing soldiers who formed 'the Guard of Honour'.
†Lord Salisbury lent Oc and Betty the Manor House at Cranborne in Dorset for their honeymoon.

No one was more irritated than Margot by her husband's 'monotonous and irritating fidelity' to his self-imposed wartime political
truce. 'I am beginning to doubt if he is a born fighter. The types of
"born fighters" bore him! Randolph [Churchill], Joe [Chamberlain],
and later Winston, Lloyd George etc are to him like Journalism
against Literature – perhaps he is too great a gentleman,' she complained in January 1918. A few weeks later, she wrote: 'I long for
Henry to take off the gloves and scatter to the winds all the eye-wash,
intrigue and incapacity of the present lot . . . Things are so serious
that I really don't see how we can let them go uncriticized. I think the
Liberal Party would be dead forever if we hold our tongues now! (Of
course, I may be quite wrong.)' Not for the first time, her own
amateur political judgement was more acute than that of her
husband, who was playing a different game, patriotically determined
not to damage the Lloyd George Government with the strident criticism that had undermined his own administration.[12]

Margot, meanwhile, was left to intrigue against the Government
from the sidelines. When the Asquiths were invited to a reception at
the French Embassy on 15 March, she was taken in to dinner by
Clemenceau (Prime Minister again at the age of seventy-six) and was
delighted when, no doubt prompted by her, he told her 'what contempt he felt for Lloyd George'. Not that she thought much of
Clemenceau's own wartime politics, which she caricatured as: 'Kill
the lot!! And never allow the word Peace and Goodwill towards man
to be whispered.' One can glean some idea of their conversation
from her brutal summing up of her old friend's character in her
journal afterwards:

> He is a man of iron nerve, savage physical health, doubtful methods and
> great powers of speech. I have known him since I was a girl and he is fond
> of me. He is not a bit like a gentleman, he is a figure of the Revolution: an
> evil, ugly, humorous bullet-head and face with an observant suspicious
> eye. Perfectly unforgiving, impenitent and 'cassant'. To him Christ's teach-
> ing would always have been pure 'camouflage'! to forgive an enemy! An
> act of suicide only worthy of a coward or an imbecile![13]

If Margot was trying to stir up trouble for Lloyd George with his
French allies, she was even less successful with Foch, with whom she
had a long talk despite noting that he was 'fascinated by Wilson', the
new Chief of the Imperial General Staff, whose hostility to herself

and Asquith she was well aware of. The following day Wilson himself recorded in his diary that 'Foch showed me an amazing letter of flattery from Mrs Asquith whom he had met at M. Cambon's [the French ambassador] last night. Foch said that she tried without success to get Clemenceau to have a private talk with Asquith.'[14]

The shock of Ludendorff's offensive and the prospect of a decisive Allied defeat temporarily pushed talk of revenge out of the public mind. In spite of Lloyd George's efforts to pin the blame on Gough, as the survivors began to describe what had happened to their families it became widely known just how under-strength the British Army had been to withstand a long-expected German offensive. Growing scepticism about the claims of the Government and its allies in Fleet Street that it was all the fault of 'the generals' was soon reflected in the postbags of MPs of all parties. On 9 April Lloyd George, determined to avoid any blame for what still threatened to become a military catastrophe, rashly hit back at his critics by claiming that the British Army was stronger than it had been at the beginning of 1917. Technically he was correct, if one counted the huge number of non-combatants that had been sent to carry out labour work behind the lines. But everyone in the front line knew that there was a chronic lack of fighting troops. The Prime Minister's statement aroused indignation not just among the Army High Command, already angry about the treatment of Gough, but also among troops serving in the front line.

Major General Sir Frederick Maurice, who until recently had been Director of Military Operations and as such responsible for collating military statistics, wrote to the Press, effectively accusing Lloyd George of lying, 'in the hope that Parliament might see fit to order an investigation into his statements'. The same day, 6 May, he wrote to Asquith to explain that 'I had intended to consult you about this letter, but on second thoughts I came to the conclusion that, if I consulted you, it would be tantamount to asking you to take responsibility for the letter, and that I alone must take that responsibility'.[15]

At 6 p.m. that day, Clouder, the Asquiths' butler, informed Margot that Colonel Repington – now military correspondent for the *Morning Post* – had called to see her husband. It was Repington in *The Times* whose story about the 'shells scandal' in May 1915 had contributed to pushing Asquith into coalition with the Conservatives. Repington subsequently fell out with Northcliffe and in February 1918 was prosecuted and silenced by the Government for reporting on the parlous state of the British forces in France. Margot recorded:

> I went into Henry's study and saw Repington's chalky smile and fat face looking very serious . . . 'I'm afraid it must be me and not my husband as he's at the House of Commons.'
>
> Colonel Repington (with a '*beau geste*' remembering I had treated him like a dog whenever we've met): 'I'm afraid I must reserve what I've got to say – Can I come in after dinner?'
>
> Margot: 'Certainly or before – but p'raps if you wait you will see him as I come to think of it he may run in to say Goodbye to our little boy – Anthony goes to Winchester at 7. I congratulate you on your pluck in attacking the Government in the *Morning Post*. You've shown great courage.'
>
> Col. R.: 'Nothing like the courage that is being shown by another man [Maurice] and of which you will know tomorrow. The Government will fall tomorrow, Mrs Asquith.'
>
> Margot: 'I've heard that so often Colonel Repington! I'm afraid I've ceased to believe in <u>everything</u>!!'
>
> Col. R.: 'This time they are <u>done</u>! finished and will not survive . . . Bonar Law and Lloyd George are Liars and your husband must come back to <u>save</u> this country. He is the only man. <u>Everyone</u> knows this! . . . These scoundrels will lose us the War –'
>
> At this moment Henry came in and greeted Repington coolly.
>
> Col. R: 'Sir, I've come to see you on <u>most</u> vital business – Will you see me?'
>
> Henry: 'Certainly not. I'm going to say goodbye to my little boy. I shall be with you in a few minutes.'

When Margot returned from seeing Puffin on to his school train, Asquith told her 'that Repington had told him the whole of our best soldiers were in revolt at the lies Lloyd George and Co were telling the public thro' the House of Commons and that Sir Frederick Maurice, having protested to General Sir Henry Wilson [the CIGS] in vain, had made up his mind to sacrifice himself tho' he was poor and had seven children* . . . Repington, Henry said, was vibrant with indignation. He gave H. all the correct figures – (which <u>we knew</u> thro' Haig and others . . .).'

According to Asquith's friend and biographer, J. A. Spender, 'during the next two days a multitude of soldiers, politicians and

---

*In fact Maurice had a son and four daughters.

anxious parents either came or wrote to Asquith begging him to stand firm and insist that General Maurice's statements should be probed to the bottom'. Robertson, the former CIGS, who lunched with them the following day, was less sanguine than Repington about the chances of a public outcry against Lloyd George who, despite the defection of the *Morning Post*, still enjoyed overwhelming backing in the Press: 'It is not the fashion to stand by soldiers – not in this war!' he said.[16]

Margot herself was by now almost at fever pitch at the prospect of her husband's imminent return to power. Mary Herbert graphically described to Cynthia (who was at Stanway) how Margot 'went up and down Bond Street like the Ancient Mariner clutching at mannequins, commissionaires, friends, taxi-drivers, policemen, and whispering to them the good news of their return to Downing Street'.[17] Her husband responded to the furore, not by mounting the all-out attack on the Government that his supporters and the generals were craving, but by putting down a motion in the House of Commons calling for a Select Committee to enquire into the issue raised by Maurice. A debate was scheduled by the Speaker for 9 May.

Lloyd George, as an inveterate plotter himself, was convinced that Asquith's motion was a smokescreen for a much wider attack and that his predecessor was conspiring with the generals to seize back the reins of power for himself. The Prime Minister knew that his only hope of survival was to refuse any enquiry and insist that the matter must be decided by a vote of confidence in the Government in the House of Commons. Hankey provided him with a detailed report on the number of British troops serving on the Continent which, although it admitted that 'the rifle strength' of the Army had decreased by 100,000 since Asquith left office, justified Lloyd George's claim that the Army was in fact stronger, by citing Kitchener's rhetorical question: 'Do heavy and field guns, aircraft, machine guns, tanks, trench mortars, gas, railways, roads and entrenchments count for nothing in the fighting strength of the Army?'[18] The problem was that the swollen figures which Hankey contrived for the Prime Minister's defence had little to do with equipment, and included not only non-combatant labour corps, made up of elderly and military unfit men, but even Chinese coolies and enemy prisoners-of-war doing fatigue duties where this was permitted under the Geneva Convention.

In a battle of statistics between Asquith and Lloyd George, there could only be one winner: the former – as Joseph Chamberlain had learnt to his cost in 1905 – was unequalled in his mastery of data, whereas for Lloyd George, as he admitted to Hankey, 'facts and figures were not his strong point'. However, while Asquith kept to his statesmanlike stance of calling for a committee to examine 'two or three very simple issues of fact', Lloyd George, in probably the best speech of his Parliamentary career, made brazen use of Hankey's arguments and figures to justify his claim that the Army on the Western Front was stronger than ever, while never conceding the drop in the 'bayonet strength'. Hankey, sitting in the gallery above, recognized the speech as a 'superb parliamentary effort', but observed ruefully in his diary that 'nevertheless I felt all the time that it was not the speech of a man who tells "the truth; the whole truth; and nothing but the truth" . . . This knowledge embarrassed me a little when MPs of all complexions kept coming to the official gallery to ask me what was the "real truth".'[19]

Lloyd George's bravura performance silenced his critics. Hankey observed how 'Runciman, who was to have wound up for the Opposition, looked miserable, and never rose'. In the Ladies' Gallery, 'a pretty girl' sitting next to Margot turned to her and ruefully remarked 'I suppose, Mrs Asquith, my poor father's case will never be heard!'

'Is your father, General Maurice?' asked Margot.

'Yes.'

'No, my dear – the Government will take good care of that!'

However, it was not the Government that most Liberal MPs were blaming for the failure to make Maurice's letter a *cause célèbre*, but their own leader. Lord Buckmaster, who had briefly served as Lord Chancellor after Haldane, was 'biting' when he remarked to Margot afterwards: 'If we had to die why not go down fighting!!' She felt so depressed at this that she 'could hardly sit still'. When the House divided a mere 98 dispirited Liberal MPs followed Asquith into the Division lobbies, where they were joined by six Labour Members and a single Tory. Margot described how after the vote 'the Press were drunk with pleasure and gave themselves over like dancing Dervishes to an orgy-Praise of their great P.M. and abuse of Henry'.[20]

Predictably, the lone Conservative with the courage to support Asquith was Aubrey Herbert, who was already in trouble with his local Party for supporting Lansdowne's call for peace talks with Germany. Now his wife, Mary, reported to Cynthia, 'his whole constituency [is] in arms and people almost cutting him in the street, while I was railed at across the Ritz dining room'.[21] Aubrey was unrepentant, defiantly informing the irate chairman of his local Conservative Association that 'on certain occasions, I choose to behave as a gentleman and not a politician'.[22]

Coincidentally, Violet and Bongie had been due to stay with the Herberts at Pixton shortly afterwards. When Aubrey's mother, the dowager Lady Carnarvon, suggested that in the circumstances it might be sensible if they put off their visit, Violet happily agreed. However, she unfortunately mentioned the request to Margot, who immediately threw petrol on the flames by cabling Aubrey: 'SAY NOTHING, EXPLAIN NOTHING. IMPORTANT LETTER FOLLOWS. ASQUITH'. The local postmistress soon ensured that her telegram was known to half of Somerset. By the time Margot's eleven-page letter arrived, Aubrey was on his way to Albania on a mission for Military Intelligence, so it fell to Mary to have to read her unsolicited and typically tactless advice to her husband:

> I was very sad you could not have Violet and Bongie for fear of your local press (the *West Somerset Gazette*, as you know, belongs to Northcliffe). I should be <u>very</u> plucky and tell your constituents quite plainly that you won't knuckle under to the Press – that Northcliffe owns the *West Somerset Gazette* – that you don't think a man 'is out to win the war' [i.e. Lloyd George] who doesn't back the fighting man on land or in the air. I'd burn my boats in a speech or letter – it must be published and you'll be as famous as Dizzy [Disraeli] and Randolph [Churchill]. It is useless now for you to retreat – it will be <u>suicide</u> . . . you'll fall between two stools . . . You and Mary go about telling them exactly <u>why</u> you voted for Dear Maurice – that you agree with Asquith it's cruel to snipe at soldiers . . . You would have everyone on your side and heaps of letters backing you in all <u>our</u> papers . . . I envy you and would love to be in your position – you'll romp in the General Election.[23]

Mary, who was already bearing the brunt of the anger being whipped up against Aubrey for his 'pro-German' views, was understandably extremely upset by Margot's letter, which she wrongly assumed that Violet had prompted. Violet quickly wrote to disabuse her:

> Darling Mary . . . you know me and you know Margot well enough to realize that I neither inspire nor control her pen – I am <u>always</u> (and in this

case not less than in others) her victim and not her accomplice . . .
Margot's letter sounds <u>outrageous</u> . . . I can hardly believe that even she –
at her maddest – could accuse Aubrey of lack of hospitality or political
courage!! his two most <u>glaring</u> characteristics.

Still less can I believe that you seriously suspect me of lending even a
'spark' to such charges. You know that I <u>adore</u> Aubrey – have had more
pure happiness from his and your hospitality than almost anyone's . . .

I am no more to be held accountable for Margot's actions (still less
words!) than you for Lady Carnarvon's – (you will admit that of the two,
Margot is the more frenetic and impossible to bridle). Let us dismiss them
both as a pair of (fundamentally benevolent) loonies – but do not for
God's sake let them involve <u>us</u> in controversy or friction – that would be
giving them too much power – and let me come to Pixton later for a
peaceful week alone with you![24]

Margot herself replied to Mary's demand that she withdraw her
imputation against Aubrey's courage with another telegram: 'THE
LAST THING I INTENDED DARLING. EVERYONE THINKS
AUBREY A HERO TORY AND LIBERAL ALIKE. LOVE.
WRITING. MARGOT.'[25] She was by now completely out of touch
with public opinion which was much more affected by the newspaper campaign against the 'pro-Germans' than she could ever
believe.

*

By the spring of 1918 much of the British Press was pervaded by an
almost hysterical witch-hunt against enemy aliens and supposed pro-
Germans at the heart of the Establishment, bent on sabotaging the
country's war effort. Among the publications retailing the more poisonous rumours was a rag called the *Vigilante*, founded in 1917 by
Pemberton Billing, a demagogue who had been elected to the House
of Commons as an 'Independent' MP with the backing of
Northcliffe.

In May 1918 the actress Maud Allen brought an action for criminal libel against the magazine over an article entitled 'The Cult of the
Clitoris', which had alleged that her private production of Oscar
Wilde's *Salome* 'ministered to sexual perverts'. The author of
the story was the American-born Harold Spencer, an obsessive
anti-Semite, whom Billing had appointed as his assistant editor the

previous year following his discharge from Army Intelligence for 'delusional insanity'. An earlier article by Spencer had featured a 'black book' kept by the Germans, which contained a heterogeneous list of 47,000 British 'perverts', who apparently included 'privy councillors, youths of the chorus, wives of cabinet ministers, dancing girls, even cabinet ministers themselves'.

The trial of Billing and Spencer rapidly veered far away from Maud Allen's original action, degenerating into farce as the alleged 'black book' took centre stage and wild allegations were bandied about a German-Jewish conspiracy to bring Asquith back to power, prior to surrendering the country to the enemy. The trial judge, Mr Justice Darling, completely lost control of the proceedings after the defendants alleged that his own name was among the 47,000 'perverts' on the German list, after which he was only too keen to let as many other people as possible be named. Billing and Spencer were acquitted by the jury and then emerged triumphantly from the Old Bailey to be wildly cheered by a huge crowd of supporters gathered outside.

Margot called the Billing case 'the worse sign of the degradation that war brings to any country that we have yet had', and dismissed the results as 'purely political, aimed at one man and <u>one</u> man only – Asquith!!'[26] However, neither she nor her husband seem to have appreciated the extent to which the outcome of the case reflected the extent of public credulity over the most preposterous stories about a corrupt ruling class beholden to sinister 'foreign' influences. Margot's successful libel action three years earlier over her supposed 'dainties' for German prisoners-of-war would now have been inconceivable. The Asquiths had direct experience of the anti-alien feeling at its most petty when Cleg Kelly's Hungarian musician friends, Jelly and Adila d'Arányi, came to stay at the Wharf and the Oxfordshire police, in an exercise of officiousness almost certainly directed at the 'pro-German' former Prime Minister himself, summoned the sisters to report to Didcot police station. Asquith demonstrated his disgust at this bureaucratic harassment by accompanying them to the station and ostentatiously waiting outside in his car while they were being questioned. As it happened, the d'Arányis, whose family were strong Hungarian nationalists, had more reason than most to fear a German-dominated Europe. Nonetheless, they were barred from performing in public (even though serving soldiers were happy to listen to them in private), which caused the unmarried Jelly, in particular, real financial hardship: Margot sent her £5 to cover 'expenses' when she invited her to spend Christmas with them.[27]

Margot could not resist stepping into controversy on the aliens question even when it did not directly concern her. Thus, when the wife of Frederick Leverton Harris, the Parliamentary Secretary to the Minister of Blockade, raised a hornet's nest by visiting the prisoner-of-war son of some German friends, Margot vigorously defended what she saw as an act of Christian charity against 'the zeal and zest' with which 'all my rottenest and even some of my nicest friends rushed like swine into the sea' to condemn the visit. She made a point of attending the debate on the issue in the House of Commons on 12 June, recording in detail an acrimonious argument she had with Mrs Lowther, the wife of the Speaker, who was sitting next to her in the gallery. The quarrel ended with Margot sarcastically asking: 'Do you know this saying of Talleyrand's "*La guerre est trop sérieuse pour la laisser aux militaires*"? I see you don't agree – you think it should be left to the Press. Well, I daresay you're right: the Press will certainly beat the German at home if it can't beat him abroad and we may yet live to be consoled by the internment of the Leverton Harris's.'[28]

In the end, Harris was saved by the firmness of his Minister, Lord Robert Cecil, and the Home Secretary, Sir George Cave, who both threatened to resign if Lloyd George gave way to the outcry and sacked him. Margot did at least find sympathy for her disgust at the anti-German outcry from the King, when the Asquiths lunched *en famille* with him and Queen Mary on 30 July; George V indignantly remarked: 'Intern them all indeed!! Then let them take me first! All my blood is German – my relations are German!'[29]

Margot noticed how the sheer nastiness of the politics of the day seemed to have made her husband lose all appetite for his profession. In a mood of resignation, she was beginning to realize that he was not going to resist his inevitable political nemesis. She reflected in her diary how:

I never talk of politics, they seem to bore him. We [i.e. the Asquiths] are not natural fighters – I am! But he is not; he hates it. The Asquiths are great dialecticians, but have not one drop of wild blood in their veins. They are self-sufficing in the best sense of the word and quite without ambitions. Henry's amazing career has come to him uninvited: no one in this world has taken so little trouble about himself. To please me he gave up pronouncing his A's short (and I made the children do the same); to please me he wore nice clothes and liked pretty furniture and beautiful colours and things. Always an amazingly quick worker his industry and physical strength has been and <u>is</u> enormous: he not only has the finest memory I ever knew, but he has cultivated it. He is a great and real scholar and *literateur*. He is much more than all this – he is a <u>wonderful friend</u>, father, husband and lover, but he is not ambitious nor are any of his children.[30]

Fortunately, the Asquiths do not seem to have heard about the most sickening of all the stories being circulated against them, viz. the 'military fact' propounded by Lloyd George's Private Secretary, Sir William Sutherland (aptly described by Hankey as a 'political parasite'[31]), 'that Raymond Asquith was so disliked by his own men that it was one of their own bombs which accounted for his end'.[32] It was a slander that would have upset Raymond's former comrades as much as it would his family.

That summer Margot was once again distracted from politics by another crisis in the love lives of the children when Hugh Gibson returned to Europe to liaise between General Pershing, the Commander-in-Chief of the American Expeditionary Force, and the Allied Governments. It seems that Gibson had not written to Elizabeth since leaving England some eighteen months earlier, even though he had agreed with her parents not to communicate with her for a year only. Nonetheless, Elizabeth persisted in believing in Gibson's faithfulness, had continued to write to him and told all her friends that they were all but betrothed. Any chance that Elizabeth might realize that Gibson probably wanted to drop her was surprisingly discouraged by Margot. He had been unwell when he returned to America, fearing he had incipient tuberculosis, and Margot believed that he did not write to Elizabeth because

he is ill and poor and firmly believes that by ceasing to write she will get tired of him. He does not know my family. We are faithful unto Death . . . I could wish Hugh Gibson would break finally with her, were it not that passionate grief might not throw her into the arms of a lesser man. No one could have a greater character or finer nature than Hugh, but even if he got well (which I doubt) the life of a minor American diplomatist would not be good for Elizabeth.[33]

It is impossible to do more than surmise what was going through Gibson's mind, but soon after he saw Elizabeth again they became engaged. The likelihood is that a combination of misplaced sense of honour and pressure from a very forceful young woman made him feel he had no option. Margot by now seems to have accepted that Elizabeth was set on marrying Hugh and prepared to welcome him into the family. When Gibson was posted to Paris in August, she busied herself with wedding preparations. However, soon afterwards he came and told the Asquiths that he had been coughing blood and had consulted a doctor at American GHQ, who confirmed that he had tuberculosis and had forbidden him to marry.

Whatever the real reason for Gibson's breaking off the engagement – and at the time both Elizabeth and her mother accepted his explanation – Margot made matters worse by sharing in her daughter's grief to an unhelpful degree.* She described herself in her diary as 'shattered and sleepless', while informing Maud Tree that Elizabeth was 'shattered and will never get over it whoever she marries – if ever she lives thro' it which is doubtful', somewhat unrealistically begging: 'For God's sake allow no one to write or talk of Elizabeth or Gibson or I shall throw myself under a train.'[34] As she had predicted, the loss of Gibson soon threw Elizabeth into someone else's arms, although rather than a 'lesser man', it was to be a more senior (and indubitably rich) diplomat, the Romanian Prince Antoine Bibesco. It was not to be a happy marriage for either party.

The Gibson affair sparked another bout of severe depression in Margot, aggravated by ever-present money worries after her brother, Lord (Eddie) Glenconner, once again refused to help her out financially. In spite of regular resolutions to cut down on her dress bill, she was constitutionally incapable of economizing, refusing to give up their huge house in Cavendish Square or cut down on her entertaining. She was mortified when Violet and Bongie suggested that it might help all their finances if they became paying guests at 20 Cavendish Square for a while, an idea that was quickly abandoned after she threatened to go off and live by herself and let Violet keep house for her father. As always throughout her married life, in the end it was Asquith's kindness and understanding that restored Margot to some semblance of happiness. On 12 September, his 66th

---

*Whatever he believed at the time, Gibson did not have tuberculosis and eventually married.

birthday, he gave her a beautifully bound copy of the text of the Romanes lecture he had delivered at Oxford on 8 June, inscribing the flyleaf with words from Psalm XV:

> Lord, who shall dwell in thy Tabernacle?
> or who shall rest upon thy holy will? Even he, that
> leadeth an uncorrupt life: and doeth the thing which is right,
> and speaketh the Truth from his heart . . .
> Whoso doeth these things shall never fall.

The words could have served as a motto for Asquith's own political career. Margot wrote in her diary: 'I have never had a present that I valued like this. It has healed <u>every</u> wound since my first baby died.'[35] This somewhat extravagant reaction was presumably to the inscription and not the lecture itself (which was on Victorian philosophy) and is a good indication of how desperate Margot was for succour.

Lloyd George expected the War to last at least another two years, with no big Allied offensive until the summer of 1919, by which time the Americans would be ready to play a major part in the battle. Haig, however, now had the men he had been demanding since the start of 1917; he was convinced that with Ludendorff's forces worn out by their failed spring offensive, victory was within the grasp of the Allies. On 8 August the Anglo-Canadian-Australian corps making up Rawlinson's fourth Army, backed by over 500 tanks, launched what was to prove the decisive offensive of the War around Amiens. The German official Monograph called the resulting breakthrough 'the greatest defeat which the German Army had suffered since the beginning of the war'. By the beginning of September, Haig was ready to begin preparations to break through the Hindenburg Line. Yet far from enjoying the support of his own Government, on the eve of his attack the British Commander-in-Chief received a telegram from the CIGS, General Wilson, at Lloyd George's prompting, warning him that 'the War Cabinet would become anxious if we received heavy casualties'.[36] Three weeks later, a few days before the assault, Milner – recently appointed War Minister by Lloyd George – complained to Wilson that Haig was being 'ridiculously optimistic'. Fortunately, Haig ignored his Government's pusillanimity and with the full support of Foch went ahead with the attack and, after two days' ferocious fighting, his forces successfully breached the Hindenburg Line. From that moment Allied victory followed victory. Ludendorff was summarily sacked on 26 October and a fort-night later, 9 November, with Germany on the brink of revolution, the Kaiser abdicated. Two days later the Armistice was signed.

Lloyd George went out of his way to give the credit to everyone but Haig: to Foch, who had had to be persuaded to back Haig's plans, and to the Americans, even though Pershing had only grudgingly provided two divisions to take part in the assault on the Hindenburg Line, both of which had to rescued by the Australians from German counter-attacks in their rear. Foch himself was typically generous in his acknowledgement of the achievement of Haig and the forces under his command, writing: 'Never at any time in history has the British Army achieved greater results in attack than in this unbroken offensive . . . The victory was indeed complete, thanks to the excel-lence of the Commanders of the Armies, Corps and Divisions, thanks above all to the unselfishness, to the wise, loyal and energetic policy of their Commander in Chief.'[37]

There was one man among the war-weary soldiers serving on the Western Front who was actually disappointed that the conflict was over. Freyberg wrote to tell Oc how, when he heard at 9.15 a.m. that hostilities must cease by 11 a.m., he took advantage of the last few moments of the War to lead a detachment of the 7th Dragoon Guards under his command in a raid on the German lines. He proudly recounted how he had managed to take 106 prisoners just two minutes before the Armistice took effect. The captured Germans were predictably 'as fed up as they could be' having been taken 'absolutely by surprise'. Freyberg does not say how many Germans were killed in the assault, but two of his own men were wounded and a horse died – all needless casualties. 'It was,' he wrote, 'a perfect ending to a perfect four years.'[38] For all his fondness for the irrepressible New Zealander, Oc found Freyberg's attitude com-pletely incomprehensible. Apart from anything else, both men had lost almost all of their closest friends in the appalling carnage of the past four years.

Back in London, Elizabeth had answered the telephone at 1 a.m. to be told by Russell Cooke, an official at the War Office, that the Armistice had been signed. Margot recorded

Henry, she [Elizabeth] and I discussed it in Henry's bedroom in our night-gowns not knowing the terms and all felt that curious feeling of Fatigue by which even great news is prevented from penetration. All these days my heart has been <u>so</u> heavy at the raging chaos, famine and huge volcanic up-set of all Europe that any news lightening my heart still leaves it heavy. We all kissed each other and went to bed sleepless. Henry came in on Monday morning 11th November, 1918 and said the news was untrue, the Germans had <u>not</u> signed. I felt no surprise, just went on putting on a new striped rose and purple tweed dress-coat and skirt . . . Just as I was toozling up my hair and powdering my nose Mr Cravath*, my tall and beloved American friend, telephoned to me that at 5 a.m. that morning the armistice was signed.

Margot just had time to despatch telegrams of congratulation to the King, Queen Alexandra and Sir John Cowans – 'the one general who has failed no one, who has fed and clothed <u>our</u> troops in every part of the globe and every-one <u>else</u>'s troops' – before she, her husband, Cys and Elizabeth had to go to Golders Green crematorium to attend the funeral of Asquith's elder brother, Willans, who had died a few days earlier. It was Margot's first cremation and she found it 'mechanical, hideous and uninspiring'. By the time they emerged, the news that the War was over had spread like wildfire. Everywhere she noticed 'little flags and big being run up and groups of people waving and laughing at each other'. When the Asquiths reached Cavendish Square, they found that Clouder, their butler, had already decked their house out in flags including two Scottish standards in deference to Margot's Scottish ancestry – 'a perfect queue, Madam, to get them', he told her.

While Asquith took lunch alone as he prepared the speech he would have to make in the House of Commons that afternoon in response to Lloyd George's announcement of the terms of the Armistice, Vivian Philips, his Private Secretary, accompanied Margot to a lunch party at Maud Cunard's. Margot did not enjoy it, recording that she was '<u>so</u> irritated and bored by the triviality and rot talked that I said I would sit in the hall as Henry was picking me up at 2.30 to go to the House of Commons'. Margot was surprised to find that, although the floor of the House of Commons itself was packed, the Visitors' Gallery was uncrowded and she regretted not bringing

---

*Paul Cravath (1861–1940), then a member of the American delegation to the Inter-Allied Council.

along Elizabeth to witness the historic occasion. She made a point of shaking hands with Margaret Lloyd George and her daughter, the sixteen-year-old Megan. Margot then sat in the front row with her hands and elbows on the rail to hear the Prime Minister read the terms of the Armistice, noting

> Both he and Henry got cheered but Lloyd George the most. My heart beat and my eyes filled with tears at the awful pronouncement. I knew all the time that if the Germans had beaten us, their terms would have been harsher – more humiliating – but it made no difference. A wave of overwhelming compassion came over me 'Love thine enemy' did not seem such a difficult commandment. The Great German Fleet – which I always told our governess, Frau, would ruin Germany – to be given up . . . our armies to occupy every town of importance in Germany and the German armies to give up their swords and surrender on every front.[39]

Beb was among the first Allied troops to enter Spa, the small Belgian town sixteen miles south-east of Liège where the Kaiser and Ludendorff had located their final headquarters. After the German spring offensive Beb had succumbed to the influenza epidemic then ravaging Europe. Weakened by illness and his part in the fighting, he had no qualms about now accepting a Staff appointment (at last promoted to captain) dealing with tactical training. Soon after the Armistice he passed through Spa on his way to visit the first British corps to march into Germany; he later recorded his impressions that day:

> German officers were still in the town and German sentries were still on duty outside their quarters. I walked up the street with a brother officer, and it was a curious experience, tinged with embarrassment, meeting these field-grey figures and passing them on the footpath with punctilious exchange of salutes . . . We stopped at the bank to inquire whether we could change a cheque, and the official beamed with delight when he saw the colour of our uniforms: he gave us a radiant welcome, and putting his cash-shovel on one side, he shook us warmly by the hands and even shewed signs of embracing us, an operation which was luckily prevented by the intervention of the counter . . . He talked much of the Germans and the hardship of foreign domination . . .
>
> On the way to the frontier the flags of the Allies had appeared as though by magic; they fluttered in their thousands in the streets of towns

and villages and the road was spanned by many triumphal arches, decorated with enormous wreaths of laurel. At Liège some French troops were marching proudly through the main street on their way to Germany; they marched like conquerors; their weathered faces were darkly exultant and their chests were glittering with medals. The roads on both sides were scattered with the debris of the German retirement, and a large number of abandoned lorries lay foundered in the ditches. Here and there the corpse of a German charger lay prone by the side of the road with stiffened legs.

The border was not marked in any way, but it was immediately clear when they had entered Germany as the flags and bunting disappeared and gave way to faces marked by 'deep and tragic shock'. Beb went on to chronicle how

> One incident in particular seemed typical of the spirit of the nation: a number of German children, many of whom looked thin and underfed, were marching along the road keeping time with a British battalion that had lately crossed the frontier and was now advancing on its way to Cologne. The English were invaders, but they were also soldiers: it was as though the love of an army lay so deep in the bones of these children that it had overcome the feeling of nationality; perhaps they felt also, by true instinct, that the British soldier is a friend of children, a fact which he frequently shewed in these critical days by giving them a share of his rations, of which they often stood very badly in need.[40]

Any spirit of compassion among the British soldiers towards their former enemies found little reflection in the civilian population at home. Even before the Armistice had been signed, Lloyd George was making preparations to call a snap General Election to exploit his widely trumpeted position as 'the man who won the War', knowing that a now vastly expanded electorate – including newly enfranchised women voters – would be only too eager to support his demands that the German people should (and could) be made to pay the whole cost of the War and German nationals be expelled from the British Isles. The call of the Tory-dominated coalition for 'Revenge and Reparation' soon drowned out the message of 'Reconciliation and Reconstruction' espoused by Lloyd George's former Party, now known as the 'Asquith Liberals'.

When Asquith arrived in his East Fife constituency for the last few days of campaigning he was greeted with posters proclaiming:

'Asquith nearly lost you the War. Are you going to let him spoil the Peace?' The jibe would, in fact, have been much more apt if it had been directed against his successor as Prime Minister: as Haig himself ruefully wrote in his diary about now, 'the real truth, which history will show, is that the British Army has won the war in France in spite of Lloyd George'.[41] As for 'spoiling the peace', the hatred stirred up in the wake of the War would ensure that it would last less than a generation. It would take another World War and the foresight and magnanimity of continental, not British, statesmen to bring lasting peace to Western Europe.

Margot, on the pretext of having to look after Lucy – now suffering worse than ever from arthritis – wanted no part in the election campaign, allowing Elizabeth to act as her father's escort. She wrote bitterly in her diary: 'I have a horrible feeling that the results of this coming General Election will humiliate Henry still more and then I shall know that it does not pay to be good, or dignified or truthful.' Afterwards she blamed the Liberals' disastrous showing above all on members of her own sex, seizing their chance to take their revenge on Asquith, who as Prime Minister, had resisted allowing them to vote: 'I can't help laughing at the silly women who <u>all</u> thought the enfranchisement of women would mean noble and great moral measures passed into Law!! So far from High Morality it was "Hang the Kaiser" and instead of "<u>Peace</u>", they shrieked "<u>Pay</u>!".'[42]

Lloyd George, meanwhile, was curiously keen to remain on good personal terms with the Asquiths in spite of his ruthless political crusade against his former leader. On 27 December Asquith was invited to 10 Downing Street for lunch with the American President, Woodrow Wilson. Eight days earlier, the Asquith and Lloyd George families had met at Charing Cross Station to welcome home Haig and his senior Commanders. Margot and Puffin became separated from Asquith and Elizabeth in the mêlée, and their tickets were examined by 'two rude men' who refused to let them on to the platform where the 'swells' were gathered to welcome the homecoming generals, pushing them towards the opposite platform. Margot recorded how when the Prime Minister saw her predicament:

I observed Lloyd George turn to us and come towards me with his keen, handsome face and knock-kneed slightly waddling walk. He bowed as low as a Frenchman to hide his embarrassment: my eyes <u>never</u> left his face, <u>his</u> <u>never met mine</u>.

> Lloyd George: 'It's absurd this! You must come over here to this side' –
> (holding his hand out).
> Margot: (shaking hands) 'Oh No! Those places are too high for us!'
> Lloyd George made a slight protest and looked extraordinarily uncom-
> fortable and red, then took Anthony's arm and led us forward and
> waddled in to join Henry.

Margot found herself next to her old admirer, Milner, on the platform and took the opportunity to remark acidly that his friend
General Wilson was 'untrustworthy and an intriguer', and then
passed the time chatting to Megan, 'a clever little girl dressed like our
coachman dressed his children on Sundays. She has a pretty little
face. I turned up her black hat which was lined with pink and she
looked <u>much</u> better and she smiled at me with her pretty little eyes.'[43]
The announcement of the election results was delayed until 28
December, a fortnight after the close of the polls, to allow the
troops' votes to be counted. That day the Asquiths were guests at a
big reception at the Guildhall where President Wilson was receiving
the Freedom of the City of London. As Margot congratulated the
President afterwards on his '<u>very</u> good speech', she began to hear
whispered around her the names of former Liberal Cabinet ministers
who had lost their seats. Then, as she made her way past men putting
on their coats towards the cheering crowds gathered outside, she
caught a glimpse of Lord Reading (formerly Sir Rufus Isaacs)
looking '<u>snow white</u>'. Lady Cave – the wife of the Home Secretary –
came up to her and took her by the arm: 'You are a brave woman –
don't turn a hair. The thing <u>can't</u> last! It's a disgrace.' Margot still had
no idea just how bad the results actually were or indeed whether her
husband too had lost his seat.

> I looked at Henry out of the corner of my eyelids. He was a little in front
> of me – not a <u>sign</u> of any kind to be seen on his face. A man pushed up
> against me and whispered 'Never you mind! The Elections have been
> fought on gigantic <u>lies</u> – <u>no one could tell the truth</u>! But it will come out
> some day.'
> Margot: 'Who are you?'
> The man: I've written on the *Morning Post* for fifteen years but I'm a <u>hot</u>
> Liberal – I'm an Asquith man – God bless him.'

After enduring a seemingly endless bow from Reading, the
Asquiths slumped back exhausted in their seats as they were driven

home. It was not until they had almost reached Cavendish Square
that Asquith broke the silence: 'I only hope I have not got in – with
all the others out that would be the last straw!' He tried to make a
joke out of how 'McKenna is always wrong – he was so certain he
was in by three figures!!'

When they arrived at 20 Cavendish Square, the recently widowed
Maud Tree, who had been invited to spend the weekend with them
at the Wharf, was waiting for them. A lot of luggage was piled up in
the hall, but there was 'no note or telephone message of any kind'.
While Asquith went into his study, Margot rang the Liberal Party
headquarters in Abingdon Square to find out what had happened in
East Fife and learnt what practically everyone else at the Guildhall
had known before they left, but no one had dared to tell them:
Asquith had lost the seat he had held since 1886. 'Thank God,' she
exclaimed to Maud, as she tried to maintain her brave face.

'Oh! I can't bear it!!' said Maud, bursting into tears as Asquith
reappeared and asked Margot for the figures. Margot took a pencil
and, after speaking into the telephone again, wrote: 'Asquith 6994 –
Sprott [sic] 8996'.

These were the words with which Margot ended the abridged, and
slightly dramatized, quotation from her diary that she concluded the
second volume of her Autobiography. At the time she told Ettie and
her other friends that 'Henry and I, when we heard we were beaten,
burst out laughing!' She recorded in her journal what actually happened:

> I burst into tears and flung myself into Henry's arms, throwing down the
> telephone receiver.
> Henry (holding me close to him): 'Don't cry darling. It's a great relief! I
> assure you I am too glad. I don't mind at all.' But his beautiful brave face
> showed signs of emotion as he pressed my shaking body in his arms and
> patted my head against his breast.[44]

EPILOGUE

'Servant and son of England'

———————◆———————

T HE GENERAL ELECTION of 1918 left the Liberal Party, which had dominated British politics since the fall of Sir Robert Peel in 1846, in ruins. The 'Asquith' Liberals were reduced to 29 seats while the 'coalition' or 'Lloyd George' Liberals, with 136 seats, were now very much the junior partners to the Unionists, who won 338. Left to himself, there is little doubt that Asquith would have retired to enjoy his books and his grandchildren. However, with no obvious successor, he decided to soldier on as Party Leader, appointing Sir Donald Maclean as acting Party Chairman in the House of Commons pending his own re-election. Lloyd George, meanwhile, ignored the pleas of Hankey and others to include Asquith, the most experienced statesman in Europe, in the Paris peace negotiations.

The Asquiths had the distraction of Elizabeth's wedding in April 1919 to her long-standing Romanian admirer, Prince Antoine Bibesco, nineteen years her senior, who had provided a comforting shoulder to cry on after her break-up with Hugh Gibson. Asquith had warned his daughter not to marry on the 'rebound' and Margot would have found 'easier to bear Elizabeth's leaving me if she were marrying an Englishman of the best type'. But both of them liked the urbane and charming Bibesco and appreciated the 'immense sympathy and understanding to her [Elizabeth] over her Hugh Gibson sorrow'.[1] Although the marriage produced Margot's much-loved only grandchild, Priscilla, it was not to be a happy one, and both parties conducted a series of extra-marital affairs.

Asquith did not have to wait long to re-enter the House of Commons, being triumphantly returned at a by-election in the Scottish seat of Paisley in February 1920 on a platform of opposition to the Government's harsh treatment of Irish Nationalists and the humiliation of Germany by the Versailles Treaty. Asquith's victory was in no small measure due to the vigorous campaigning of Violet, who defended her father's record – besmirched by years of vitriolic criticism in the Press – with a vigour, ferocity and wit fully worthy of her brothers, Raymond and Beb, at their Oxford Union best. However, the House of Commons to which Asquith returned was alien territory; instead of massed ranks of loyal supporters behind him and respectful opponents in front, he was faced with cold indifference. Paisley was to prove a false dawn as over the next decade the Liberals were to be pushed aside by the Labour Party as the main rival to a Conservative Party which was to dominate the British political scene for most of the twentieth century.

It was also in 1920 that the Asquiths were obliged to abandon their beloved 20 Cavendish Square, which was now far too expensive for them to maintain, for the more modest 44 Bedford Square, which they bought from their friend Lady Ottoline Morrell. Margot, meanwhile, had been hard at work on her gloriously indiscreet Autobiography, the first volume of which caused a sensation when it was published in October 1920. In spite of critical reviews – most notably in Northcliffe's *The Times*, which devoted a long article and a leader to rubbishing the author's 'vanity and self love' – the book proved a resounding success on both sides of the Atlantic, and launched Margot on a lucrative literary career which allowed her for a while to continue her extravagant pre-war lifestyle. No one was more pleased by her success than her husband, who admired her 'triumphal progress' when she toured America after the publication of the second volume of her autobiography in 1922.[2]

Margot's Memoirs put her firmly in the limelight. In April 1923 her fame brought an extraordinary meeting in Rome's Palazzo Chigi (the Italian Foreign Office) with Benito Mussolini, who had become dictator only a few months earlier. The thirty-nine-year-old Mussolini, in Asquith's words, 'seems to have been on his best behaviour'. Margot was 'surprised to find him so unselfconscious, easy and humorous', although when she lectured him that 'imprisoning and terrorizing people is not a sign of power, it is a confession of failure', she 'could see he was not listening'.[3]

After the Great War, Oc resumed his business career, making good use of all the contacts he had built up over the years in North Africa and South America. He kept in touch with Freyberg, who in 1918 married Pamela McKenna's widowed sister, Barbara,* Cardy Montagu and McCracken (who became a GP in Yorkshire), and all three would attend reunions of the veterans of the Royal Naval Division, which was disbanded after the War. Oc's relations with Freyberg, however, were never again to be as close as when they had served together in the Hood Battalion. He had been deeply shocked both by his friend's pursuit of Cynthia and by his letter describing his attack on the German lines just before the Armistice. He was appalled to discover later that Freyberg had not told the men whom he led into action that a ceasefire was imminent. For all Oc's qualities as a soldier and leader of men, he himself loathed war, and for the rest of his life remained deeply affected by the loss of so many close friends, although he rarely spoke of his experiences.[4] As if to make up for all the lost years before she agreed to marry him, Oc's wife Betty accompanied her husband on his business trips to North Africa and South America as much as she could. When he was in England, she took a series of cottages by the coast, believing the sea air would be beneficial for his health, though he never recovered from his wounds and the strain of the War.

In the last months of the War, Cynthia had become secretary to the playwright, J. M. Barrie. The job soon turned into a lifeline as it became apparent that she would have to be the main family bread-winner: the trauma of Beb's wartime experiences had killed off any ambition and drive that he may have had. He was also much affected by the death in 1923 of his close friend Aubrey Herbert who, having survived the Great War, died from blood poisoning following a bungled dental operation. Meanwhile the collapse of the Liberal Party barred Beb from the political career that had always been his ultimate ambition, and instead of standing for Parliament he sought to become a poet and writer. He eventually secured a job on the editorial staff of the publishers, Hutchinson. The avuncular Barrie rapidly turned into a fairy godfather to Cynthia, involving himself closely with her sons Michael and Simon (born in 1919) as he had once done with the Llewellyn-Davies boys, and helping to pay for their education and family expenses.

---

*Barbara Jekyll's first husband, Francis McLaren, was killed in the Great War.

Although Asquith was eventually reconciled with both Venetia and Montagu, relations with them never regained their former intimacy. The latter went on to have a distinguished political career as Secretary of State for India under Lloyd George from 1917 until 1922, dying two years later from blood poisoning, like Aubrey, at the age of forty-five. Afterwards Venetia wrote to Asquith 'I know it is not necessary for me to tell you how deeply he loved you and what a lasting grief your political separation was. He always used to say that tho' he was still absorbingly interested in his work after he left you, it was no longer any fun.'[5] Both Sylvia and Viola also lost their husbands while they were still young and were left to bring up their children on their own. Asquith enlisted several new members to his 'harem' including the sculptress Kathleen Scott, the widow of the Arctic explorer, and Christabel McLaren (later Lady Aberconway); but his principal female companion in later years, Margot apart, was Hilda Harrison, whose artillery officer husband had been killed in 1917.

Asquith saw as much as he could of his children and grandchildren. Unfortunately, he saw little of Katharine and her children: their relationship was always marred by her not being quite able to forgive her father-in-law never writing to Raymond while he was in the trenches. Nonetheless, Asquith and Cys intervened on her behalf when, following her conversion to Roman Catholicism in 1923, Beb and Oc, as trustees of a family fund set up by their mother, refused to allow the money to go towards Trim's education if he was not sent to Winchester like his father. He eventually went to Ampleforth. Katharine never remarried and devoted the rest of her life to her children, charitable works and looking after the family estate at Mells in Somerset, of which she became the heiress after the death of her brother, Edward, in the Great War. It eventually passed to Trim. Katharine died in 1976, sixty years after her husband's death on the Somme.

Lloyd George was eventually ditched by his Conservative allies in October 1922 and forced to relinquish office as Prime Minister. The following year the Lloyd George and Asquith Liberals, now reduced to the margins of British politics, came together in time for the General Election called by the new Conservative Prime Minister, Stanley Baldwin. Margot grudgingly accepted 'an absolute necessity unless we want Labour to sweep the country'.[6] In spite of her opinion of Lloyd George as a politician, she could not help but be charmed by him and was soon offering him the benefit of her political advice: '<u>Do not see any Press men</u>, they are fools.'[7]

Although the election went well reasonably well for the Liberals, Asquith supported the formation of a minority Labour Government. The new Prime Minister, Ramsay Macdonald, repaid the favour by calling another snap election, which proved disastrous for the newly united Liberals, who lost three-quarters of their Parliamentary seats and were left with only 40 MPs. Asquith's Paisley constituency was among those to fall to Labour. The following year he accepted the title of Earl of Oxford and Asquith from the King – the 'Asquith' added at the insistence of the Harley family, who had previously held the earldom. However, there was a final electoral blow in 1925 when Oxford University rejected him as its Chancellor in favour of the Tory Lord Cave (formerly Sir George). Asquith fell out once again with Lloyd George in 1926 over their differing approaches to the General Strike, and he resigned the Liberal leadership after suffering a slight stroke in June. He had another stroke the following April, but seemed to make a good recovery. In October he was well enough to receive the freedom of the City of York, and in November he paid what was to be his last visit to Venetia at Breccles Hall, the Norfolk home she and Edwin had bought early in their marriage. He wrote to her afterwards that he 'had enjoyed every minute of my little visit and long to come again when the flowers are all out. It was most good of you to take me in, a "sheer hulk" in need of refitting in your sheltered and delightful haven.'[8]

However, Asquith was not to see another spring. In December he caught a severe chill from which he was never to recover. Over the next few weeks he began at times to become confused. Sensing that the end was near, in the early of hours of Christmas Eve he wrote Margot what was to be his last letter to her:

> Till one by one,
> Some with lives came to nothing,
> Some with deeds as well undone, Death steps tacitly, and took them.
> Where men never see the sun.
>
> I shall see thee, once more, O Soul of my Soul,
> And with God the Rest.
>
> Give this to my 3 daughters [*sic*] and to my son Puffin.

The next few weeks were an agony for his family as he veered between lucidity and complete confusion. On 10 February Margot, in a letter to Viola Parsons, described how all the family 'watch and mourn and wait in turn over him, Violet, Elizabeth and the boys. It is not one of us who have dimmed his hope – it is his own self knowledge – He often talks of plans, places and the future to us . . . when he and I are alone as we are for hours and hours in the day . . . he kisses me and tells me things which I can only tell you when we meet . . . this illness will last a long time. For me it is nothing, but to see him is an anguish.'

But even at this moment, she found herself blaming Lloyd George for breaking her husband's spirit: 'I can see him lying there a great fighter with all his armour taken away from him. No one has helped to undermine his resistance as much as his treacherous colleagues led by Lloyd George. "Ah! if it could only have gone otherwise," he said to me "after the General Strike what a difference it would have made to me!"'[9]

Asquith died five days later, on 15 February 1928 with all his family around him, and was buried in Sutton Courtney churchyard, close to the Wharf. A few days after his death, Margot, struggling to answer piles of letters, revealed her grief to Lord Crewe, 'the wisest and most reliable' of all her husband's former colleagues:

> It is true that Henry was calm and serene – he hated dying, and he and I have suffered untold anguish together alone in the day and in the dark. I prayed for him to die and yet now that it is so, I long to be able to sit with him again to hear him ask for me – when I was there – and to kiss and hold his hands. I feel that in losing him I've lost my own self . . . there is no reason now for me . . . I shall face life boldly for Puffin and Elizabeth: but however much I laugh, or talk, or, read, or listen I shall always be alone.[10]

Encouraged by Barrie, Cynthia was by now launched on a flourishing literary career of her own. Beginning with occasional newspaper articles, she moved on to anthologies, novels and memoirs, but her most successful work was an authorized biography published in 1928 of the young Duchess of York, the late Queen Elizabeth, the Queen Mother. Beb, meanwhile, published four novels, all of which sold well. However, the delayed effects of shell shock and an increasing dependence on alcohol eventually put a stop to his literary career. His last book was a well-received volume of Memoirs, *Moments of Memory*, published in 1937.

Money worries continued to dog Margot to the end of her life. She found it almost impossible to live within her means in spite of her substantial literary earnings, and in 1932 she was forced to sell the Wharf. Margot's main consolation during these years was Puffin, who continued to live with her until her death. His early passion for the theatre soon evolved towards the new medium of the cinema and after coming down from Balliol in 1925 with Second in Greats – much to his father's disappointment – he and Elizabeth went to Hollywood to stay with Douglas Fairbanks to study the work of his studio. After directing five silent films, he made his first 'talkie' in 1931. However, his first big success was in 1938 with *Pygmalion* – based on Bernard Shaw's play – starring Leslie Howard as Professor Higgins and Wendy Hiller as Eliza Doolittle, with David Tree, Viola's twenty-three-year-old son, as Eliza's hapless upper-class admirer, Freddie.

Violet's misfortune was to come of age in an era when Liberalism was banished to the political sidelines and, perhaps appropriately for the daughter of such an ardent anti-suffragist, before women were admitted to the centre stage. However, while Bongie pursued a successful business career as a director of an aircraft manufacturing company, Violet returned to the political fray in the 1930s to campaign alongside Winston Churchill against the policy of appeasement of the Nazi regime in Germany.

In 1936 Betty inherited from her aunt, Christine Hamlyn, the manor house and village of Clovelly on the north Devon coast. Oc had known and loved Clovelly since childhood, but he was not to enjoy it long: in the spring of 1939 he was diagnosed as having Hodgkin's disease (lymphoma). He died on 25 August, aged fifty-six, in the Middlesex hospital in London. Violet, who was with her brother to the end, afterwards wrote to a friend: 'watching beloved Oc dying those last three weeks and knowing oneself quite powerless to help or save him pain was unspeakable . . . I think he was one of the most perfectly and unselfconsciously good people I have ever known.' Freyberg, who also saw Oc just before he died, delivered the funeral oration: 'He was,' he said, 'the bravest man I ever knew.'[11] Oc was buried in the churchyard at Clovelly. A few days later Britain was once again at war and Freyberg soon on his way back to France, in command of a division in the British Expeditionary Force.

The advent of the Second World War led Puffin to direct some of the most successful propaganda films of the period, beginning with

Channel Incident about the evacuation of Dunkirk in 1940 and culmin-ating with *The Way to the Stars* in 1945 celebrating the comradeship of British and American airmen. The War, however, separated Margot and Puffin from Elizabeth, who was trapped in Romania with her husband, where they had gone to look after the Bibesco family estate. The Bibescos' daughter, Priscilla, managed a daring escape across the Balkans to Turkey and ultimately rejoined her grand-mother in London. But Elizabeth, like several other members of her family, suffered from chronic alcoholism and by the end of the War her health was ruined. Margot's preparations to welcome her daugh-ter home were interrupted with the tragic news in April 1945 that she had died suddenly. Margot never recovered from the shock and four months later she too was dead, to be buried beside her beloved husband in Sutton Courtney churchyard.

Puffin was deeply affected by the death of his mother, which trig-gered a serious bout of heavy drinking. He failed to make another film for two years. His drink problem (possibly exacerbated, accord-ing to members of the family, by worries over his repressed homo-sexuality) lasted six years, although in this period he was still able to make some of his best films: his first two collaborations with Terence Rattigan, *The Winslow Boy* (1948) and *The Browning Version* (1950), as well as a classic production of Oscar Wilde's *The Importance of Being Ernest* (1951), starring Michael Redgrave, Michael Denison and Edith Evans as Lady Bracknell. In the end he resorted to a drastic cure that involved continuing to consume alcohol while having injections to make him sick. Fortunately it worked, and he was a teetotaller for the rest of his life. His final film, *The Yellow Rolls Royce* (1964), featured a host of big stars including Ingrid Bergman, Alan Delon, Joyce Grenfell, Rex Harrison, Michael Hordern, Jeanne Moreau, Shirley MacLaine and George C. Scott. Puffin managed to combine his busy life as a director with the Presidency of the Association of Cine Technicians (later the ACTT), of which he was one of the founders. Overwork and his unhealthy lifestyle conspired to give him stomach cancer from which he died in 1968. He was buried alongside his parents.

When Barrie died in 1937, Cynthia found that – apart from Great Ormond Street Children's Hospital, to which he bequeathed the roy-alties of *Peter Pan* – she was the main beneficiary of his will. The money enabled her and Beb to buy Sullington Court, an early nine-teenth-century farmhouse on the edge of the South Downs near

Pulborough in Sussex, from the novelist, A. J. Cronin, in 1939. Although Beb's drinking continued to be a problem, he and Cynthia passed seven happy years in Sussex with their two boys and their dogs while another World War raged across the Channel. They moved to Bath in 1946 as Beb's health deteriorated: he died the following year.

In the 1950s Cynthia had her final love affair, with the journalist Colin Brooks. She was by now a well-known radio and television personality, astounding her audience with her minute knowledge of the novels of Jane Austen when in 1957 she won ITV's pioneering television game show 'The $64,000 Question'. She died in 1960.

Cys, after a distinguished career at the Chancery Bar, was appointed to the High Court Bench in 1938 at the comparatively young age of forty-eight. In 1946 he was promoted to the Appeal Court and in 1951 he became a Law Lord. When Sir Winston Churchill returned to power that same year, he offered Cys the Lord Chancellorship – 'an Asquith sat in my first Cabinet and I want one in my last', the venerable statesman is said to have growled. However, Cys's health, never strong, was by now failing and he had to decline the offer. He died in 1954.

After the Second World War, Violet again found herself a voice in the political wilderness, arguing for Britain's wholehearted participation in the European enterprise at a time when most British politicians were bent on disrupting it. Her leading protégé was Jo Grimond – perhaps the last British politician cast from the Asquithian mould – who married her younger daughter, Laura, in 1938 and led the Liberal Party between 1956 and 1967.

By the time Violet died in 1969, the heyday of Liberalism under her father's Government had become a distant memory. In the succeeding years Asquith's reputation came to be overshadowed by that of his more flamboyant successor. In an age when Parliamentary politics was increasingly eclipsed by the television and print media, Lloyd George, whose public relations skills have arguably never been surpassed in any British Prime Minister, was perhaps inevitably regarded as one of the twentieth century's greatest statesmen. However, as the public tires of Government policy decided by 'spin doctors' and their ilk, it may be that the more substantial qualities and lasting achievements of Lloyd George's thoroughly decent predecessor, Henry Asquith, will serve as a more fitting model for the politicians of the twenty first century.

ON A STATESMAN

A mind humane and generous as the day,
High eloquence with happy wit at play,
Zeal without rancour, and a constant love
Of truth and fairness that no storm could move.
So did he hold his course, and so depart,
Servant and son of England, mind and heart.

(Herbert ['Beb'] Asquith), *Poems 1912–1933*

FINIS

Notes

———◆———

CHAPTER I: THE ASQUITHS

1. I am indebted to the late Mrs Michael Asquith, who was of Swedish descent, for this information.
2. Oxford and Asquith, *Memories and Reflections*, Vol. I, p. 2
3. Frank Elias, *Asquith*, p. 12
4. *Memories and Reflections*, Vol. I, p. 3
5. They are commemorated on the same gravestone as their father and grandparents. No dates are given for Edith Margaret. Emily Willans was born on 20 May and died on 12 June 1859.
6. Clyde Binfield, *A Congregational Formation: An Edwardian Prime Minister's Victorian Education.*
7. Asquith, *Moments of Memory*, p. 13
8. Jan Morris, ed., *The Oxford Book of Oxford*, pp. 272–5
9. John Morley, *Recollections*, Vol. I, p. 371
10. John Jones, *Balliol College*, p. 226, quoting speech by Asquith at a dinner to celebrate his becoming Prime Minister
11. Mells papers, Asquith to Lady (Frances) Horner, 2.9.92. Quoted Spender and Asquith, *Life of Lord Oxford and Asquith*, Vol. I, p. 26
12. Elias, pp. 44–5
13. J. P. Alderson, *Mr Asquith*, p. 19
14. *Moments of Memory*, p. 49
15. Spender and Asquith, p. 73, quoting letter to Frances Horner, 11.9.92
16. Spender and Asquith, pp. 41–43
17. Bonham Carter Papers. Helen to Asquith, 4.2.77
18. A copy of the invitation is among Helen's letters to Asquith in the Bonham Carter manuscripts.
19. Spender and Asquith, p. 73
20. Spender and Asquith, p. 44, *Moments of Memory*, pp. 11, 20, Helen to Asquith, 27.4.77
21. *Moments of Memory*, pp. 49–50
22. *Moments of Memory*, p. 73
23. Augustine Birrell, *Things Past Redress*, p. 252

24. *Moments of Memory*, pp. 24, 43
25. Helen to Asquith, 4.5.81
26. *Moments of Memory*, pp. 20–1
27. *Moments of Memory*, p. 12
28. *Moments of Memory*, p. 22
29. *Moments of Memory*, pp. 17–18
30. *Moments of Memory*, pp. 22–3
31. Mells Papers. Asquith to Frances Horner, 17.10.92
32. Violet Asquith writing in *The Times*, 30.7.1956
33. Haldane Papers. Asquith to Haldane, 2.12.85.
34. Mells Papers: letter to Frances Horner, 17.10.92
35. Helen to Asquith, 1.7.86, 2.7.86
36. Spender and Asquith, pp. 50–51
37. *Moments of Memory*, pp. 23–4
38. Mells Papers: letter to Frances Horner, 17.10.92
39. It is possible to date the move from Haldane's first visit, referred to in a letter to his mother dated 1.11.87.
40. *Moments of Memory*, pp. 57–8
41. Helen to Asquith, 28.5 and 29.5.87
42. *Moments of Memory*, p. 59
43. Much of the above is taken from Isla Brownless, *The Lambrook Legacy 1860–1997*. I am also indebted to Mrs Brownless for looking up the individual Asquith boys' school records.
44. Bonham Carter Papers. Helen to Asquith, 28.9.89, 10.10.89
45. *Isis*, 24.1.03, p. 133 ('Isis Idols'). The evidence is unclear whether Oc sold himself for a penny or sixpence. I credit him with the sense to have demanded the larger sum – even in 1890 1d would not have purchased much chocolate.
46. Helen to Asquith, 3.8.90 and 22.4.91
47. *The Autobiography of Margot Asquith*, Vol. I, p. 261
48. Mells Papers, Asquith to Frances Horner, 17.10.92

CHAPTER 2: MISS MARGOT TENNANT
1. *The Autobiography of Margot Asquith*, Vol. I, p. 10
2. Margot Oxford, *More Memories*, p. 3
3. Frances Horner, *Time Remembered*, p. 161
4. Margot Asquith's Diary, Mss. Eng. d. 3206, p. 76, 16.4.08
5. M. Drew, *Diaries and Letters*, p. 268
6. Chandos Papers. John Tennant, 'A Little Memorial of My Beloved Cousin Laura Lyttelton'
7. Nancy Crathorne, *Tennant's Stalk*, p. 164
8. Margot Asquith's Diary, d. 3202, p. 105, 2.10.97
9. E. A. M. Asquith, *Autobiography*, p. 15
10. Margot Asquith Papers. Margot to Posie Gordon-Duff, 30.4.85
11. Margot Asquith's Diary, d. 3202, p. 92
12. Taken from transcript of diary fragment dated November 1888 in Crathorne Papers
13. Margot Asquith's Diary, Mss. Eng. d. 3198, 28.10.83, p. 284f
14. *The Autobiography of Margot Asquith*, Vol. I, p. 23
15. *The Autobiography of Margot Asquith*, Vol. I, p. 69
16. Margot Asquith's Diary, d. 3198, 23.6.78, p. 50
17. Margot Asquith's Diary, d. 3198, 18.3.79, p. 112
18. Margot Asquith's Diary, d. 3198, p. 51
19. Margot Asquith's Diary, d. 3198, pp. 282, 268
20. *More Memories*, pp. 52–3

21. Philip Magnus, *Gladstone*, p. 382
22. Dudley W. R. Bahlman, ed., *The Diary of Sir Edward Hamilton 1885–1906*, p. 108
23. Margot Asquith's Diary, d. 3198, p. 72
24. Daphne Bennett, *Margot*, p. 39
25. Margot Asquith's Diary, d. 3198 (23.6.81), pp. 203–6
26. A. G. C. Liddell, *Notes from the Life of an Ordinary Mortal*, p. 227
27. Crathorne Papers: *Laura* by Mary Drew, c. 1916
28. A. G. C. Liddell, *Notes from the Life of an Ordinary Mortal*, p. 228
29. Margot Asquith's Diary, d. 3198, Jan 1883
30. Margot Asquith's Diary, d. 3198, 1.3.80, p. 153
31. Margot Asquith's Diary, d. 3198, p. 163f
32. Margot Asquith's Diary, d. 3198, 6.2.82, p. 215
33. Margot Asquith's Diary, d. 3198, 6.6.82, p. 223f
34. Edith Lyttelton, *Alfred Lyttelton*, p. 408
35. Laura and Margot both wrote long accounts of Lyttelton's courtship in their journals. Margot's was written in January 1885, d. 3198, pp. 307–22; Laura's entry is dated 12.1.85. (Margot Asquith Papers)
36. Curzon Papers, Mss. Euro FIII/12. Margot to Curzon, 21.5.85.
37. The account of Laura's death is taken from Margot Asquith's *Autobiography*, pp. 40–46
38. A slightly different account of Laura's death is given in Edith Lyttelton, *Alfred Lyttelton*, Vol. I, pp. 145–6
39. Margot's final entry is dated 1.5.86. There are no surviving regular journals (apart from her journey to Egypt and travel diaries) until 1892. The description of the St Paul's service was written 2.4.93, p. 58.
40. Mary Drew (Gladstone) Papers, Add. Ms. 46238, f. 169
41. *The Autobiography of Margot Asquith*, Vol. I, p. 57
42. *The Autobiography of Margot Asquith*, Vol. I, pp. 217–8
43. Margot Asquith's Diary, d. 3198, 6.8.85
44. Anonymous letter to *The Times* of 17.1.29, almost certainly written by Lady Desborough. Quoted in Jane Abdy and Charlotte Gere, *The Souls*, p. 16
45. *More Memories*, pp. 164–5
46. *More Memories*, pp. 165–6
47. Mary Gladstone Papers, Add. Ms. 46238 f. 13. Letter dated 6.11.188?
48. Different variations of this appear in Margot Asquith's *Autobiography*, Vol. I, p. 167
49. A. J. Balfour, *Chapters of Autobiography*, p. 232
50. Margot dates the meeting to 'one evening in 1888' on p. 107 of her *Autobiography*, Vol. II, and to 1887 on p. 113.
51. *The Autobiography of Margot Asquith*, Vol. I, pp. 103–4. Jowett was commenting on Margot's own description of herself. There is a copy of the letter dated 23.10.90 among Jowett's Papers at Balliol College (II A 21/10)
52. *The Autobiography of Margot Asquith*, Vol. I, pp. 115–6
53. Helen to Asquith, 22.4.86, Chandos Papers, 5/24. Asquith to Mrs Alfred ('DD') Lyttelton, 5.7.13

CHAPTER 3: 'YOU HAVE MADE ME A DIFFERENT MAN'
1. Margot Asquith Papers. Asquith to Margot, March–May 1891
2. A. N. Wilson, *Hilaire Belloc*, p. 248
3. Asquith Papers, Ms. 17, f. 209. Cust to Asquith, 9.12.16
4. Frances Horner, *Time Remembered*, p. 167
5. Mells papers. Asquith to Frances Horner, 11.9.92
6. *The Autobiography of Margot Asquith*, Vol. I, p. 284
7. Spender and Asquith, I, p. 98

8. Helen to Asquith, 4–8.8.91
9. Asquith to Margot, 11.9.91
10. Mells Papers. Asquith to Frances Horner, 11.9.92. Quoted in Spender and Asquith I, p. 73
11. Desborough Papers, D/Erv C72, f.6. Asquith to Lady Desborough 6.11.91
12. Asquith to Margot, 1.10.91
13. Asquith to Margot, 2.10.91
14. Asquith to Margot, 6.10.91
15. Asquith to Margot, 7.10.91
16. Birrell Papers. Asquith to Mrs Birrell, 19.9.91
17. Asquith to Margot, 31.10 and 4.11.91
18. Desborough Papers, D/Erv C72, f. 10. Asquith to Ettie Desborough 17.1.92
19. *Moments of Memory*, pp. 65–6
20. Information supplied by Mrs Isla Brownless
21. Mells Papers. T. D. Mansfield to Asquith, 13.7.92
22. Clovelly Papers. Oc's Lambrook report for Easter 1895
23. Mells Papers. Raymond to Asquith, 21.7.94
24. Beb's school letters to his father are in the possession of his son Michael Asquith. Most are undated.
25. Desborough Papers, D/Erv C71. Margot to Ettie (later Lady Desborough), 23.10.91
26. Desborough Papers, D/Erv C72, f. 10. Asquith to Ettie, 17.1.92. *More Memories*, p. 107
27. Asquith to Margot, 10 and 15.10.91
28. Asquith to Margot, 16.10.91. Spender and Asquith I, p. 102
29. Asquith to Margot, 9.12.91
30. Balfour Papers, Add. Mss, 49794 f. 48. November 1891
31. Margot Asquith's unpublished diary, November 1892 and 31.12.92
32. Chandos Papers I, f5. Margot to DD Lyttelton, 3.3.92
33. Margot Asquith's unpublished diary, November 1892
34. Extracts from Margot's letters (5.3.92, 16.8.92, 2.1.93, 19.2.93) to Milner. Milner Papers, Box 1
35. Asquith to Margot, 5.4.92
36. Asquith to Margot, 27.2.92
37. Balfour Papers, Add. Ms. 49794, f. 52, 26.4.92
38. Asquith to Margot, 10.5.92
39. Asquith to Margot, February to May 1892
40. Asquith to Margot, 26.3.92
41. Spender and Asquith I, p. 99. Asquith to Margot, 8.2.92
42. Asquith to Margot, 24.12.91 and 21.5.92
43. Brian Masters, *E. F. Benson*, p. 102. Mark Bonham Carter wrongly says in his Introduction to the abridged *Autobiography of Margot Asquith* (p. xxii) that it was doubtful if he ever met her. A year before *Dodo*'s publication she told Milner that knew and liked the whole Benson family (see Milner papers, Box 1, f. 12. Margot to Milner 8.9.91).
44. Margot Asquith Papers. Margot to Spencer Lyttelton, 26.9.93
45. Brian Masters, *E. F. Benson*, p. 104. Letter by Margot to Betty Lytton quoted in Tilling Society Newsletter, no. 1, p. 13
46. Margot Asquith Papers. Margot to Spencer Lyttelton, 12.10.93
47. Margot Asquith, *More Memories*, p. 129
48. Asquith to Margot, 6.6.92
49. Asquith to Margot, 17.6.92
50. Mells Papers. Asquith to Raymond, 27.10.98. Asquith to Frances Horner 4–12.7.92. The second letter is quoted in full in Spender and Asquith, I, pp. 74–5.

51. Mells Papers. Asquith to Raymond, 27.10.98
52. Asquith to Margot, 15.8.92
53. Asquith to Margot, 17.8.92
54. Curzon Papers. Margot to Curzon, 3.9.93. Chandos Papers. Margot to DD Lyttelton, n.d.
55. Asquith to Margot, 11.9.92
56. *Moments of Memory*, p. 72
57. Asquith to Margot 2.9.92
58. Mells Papers. Asquith to Frances Horner, 11.9.92. The section of the letter devoted to Helen is quoted in full in Spender and Asquith, I, p. 73
59. Mells Papers. Asquith to Frances Horner, 17.10.92
60. Viscountess Milner, *My Picture Gallery*, pp. 112–17
61. Mells Papers. Frances Horner to Asquith, 24.9.92
62. A favourite phrase of his – see Asquith to Margot, 1.1.93
63. Margot Asquith's Diary, Ms. Eng. d. 3199, 8.3.93
64. Margot Asquith's Diary, Ms. Eng. d. 3199, 6.7.93
65. Asquith to Margot, 15.5.93. Spender and Asquith, I, p. 106
66. Spender and Asquith, I, p. 109
67. Gilmour, *Curzon*, p. 102
68. Margot Asquith's Diary, Ms. Eng. d. 3199, 19.10.93
69. Chandos Papers. Margot to DD Lyttelton (n.d., presumably October 1893)
70. Margot Asquith's Diary, d. 3199, 25.10. and 2.11.93
71. Margot Asquith's Diary, d. 3199, 15.12.93
72. Margot Asquith's Diary, d. 3199, 9.1.94. Interestingly the betrothal itself is not recorded
73. Spender and Asquith, I, pp. 109–10
74. Margot Asquith's Diary, d. 3199, 11.1.94

CHAPTER 4: 'AN ABYSS OF DOMESTICITY'
1. *Moments of Memory*, pp. 78–9. Undated letter from Herbert Asquith in possession of Michael Asquith
2. Margot Asquith Papers. Asquith to Margot, 14.2.94
3. Margot Asquith's Diary. Ms. Eng. d. 3199, 19.4.94
4. Dudley Sommer, *Haldane of Cloan*, p. 93
5. Except where otherwise indicated, the account of the wedding and its aftermath is taken from the account in Margot's unpublished diary, d. 3199 written up on 14 May 1894.
6. *Moments of Memory*, pp. 80–5
7. Curzon Papers. Margot to Curzon, 14.5.94
8. Margot Asquith's Diary, d. 3199, 14.5.94
9. Curzon Papers. Margot to Curzon, 14.5.94
10. *The Autobiography of Margot Asquith*, ed. M. Bonham Carter, p. xxv
11. Violet recounted this to her niece Mrs Susan Boothby (Oc's daughter) who told it to the author.
12. Asquith, *Moments of Memory*, pp. 85–6
13. Margot to Viola Tree, 14.8.19. Viola Tree Papers, BM Add. Man. 5989514
14. Margot to Viola Tree, 13.8.16 and 14.8.19. Viola Tree Papers, BM Add. Man. 5989514
15. *Autobiography*, Vol. I, p. 274. John Buchan also claims to have heard this riposte (*These for Remembrance*, p. 78, and *Memory Hold The Door*, p. 64). Whether he heard the story from Margot or she from him, we will never know.
16. Margot Asquith's Diary, d. 3199. 8 and 27.12.94. Balfour Papers, Add. Ms. 49794, f. 63. MA to AJB, 5.9.94
17. Mells Papers, Asquith to Frances Horner, 19.9.94

18. *Moments of Memory*, pp. 88–9. Clovelly Papers. Oc to Asquith, 30.9.94. Margot Asquith Diaries, d. 3213, p. 79 (August 1915). Margot was told the anecdote by Lord Crewe. A different version – involving a buoy – appears in *Spender and Asquith*, I, p. 213
19. Spender and Asquith, I, p. 214
20. Margot Asquith's Diary, 27.12.94
21. Milner Papers, Box I, f. 74. Margot to Milner, 24.12.94
22. Margot Asquith's Diary, d. 3200, 4.1.95
23. Margot Asquith's Diary, 20.1.95
24. Margot Asquith's Diary, d. 3200, p. 20
25. Milner Papers, Box 1, f. 74
26. Oxford and Asquith, *Memories and Reflections*, Vol I, p. 137
27. Margot Asquith's Diary, d. 3200, 24.6.95. Neither was an early riser, and at least Asquith was usually at home until 10.30 a.m.
28. Ellis Papers. Asquith to Tom Ellis, 30.11.95
29. Margot Asquith's Diary, d. 3200, 18.3.95
30. Margot Asquith's Diary, d. 3200, 10.3.95
31. The account is taken from Margot Asquith's unpublished journal, although she did not write it up until 10 August 1895. In her *Autobiography* (Vol. I, p. 286) Margot mistakenly says her labour began on 18 May.
32. Gladstone Papers. Asquith to Mrs Gladstone, 19.5.95
33. Margot Asquith Papers, Ms. c. 6688
34. Margot Asquith's Diary, d. 3200, 10.8.95
35. Margot Asquith's Diary, d. 3200, 16.10.95
36. Margot Asquith's Diary, d. 3200, 21, 22 and 29.10 and 6.11.95
37. Margot Asquith's Diary, d. 3203, 20.12.99
38. Margot Asquith's Diary, 6.8.96
39. Mells Papers. Arthur Asquith to Asquith, 22.9.95, Herbert Asquith to Asquith, n.d
40. Margot Asquith's Diary, d. 3201, 24.12.96
41. Mells Papers. Raymond to Asquith, 7.10.94
42. Mells Papers. Raymond to Margot, 9.12.95, Jolliffe, p. 20.
43. Mells Papers, n.d., Jolliffe, p. 22
44. Mells Papers. Raymond to Asquith, 29.9.95
45. Ensor Papers. Raymond to Robert Ensor, 10.6.95
46. Mells Papers. Raymond to Asquith, 10.6.95 partially quoted in Jolliffe, p. 22
47. Jolliffe, p. 24. Raymond to H. T. Baker 28.2.97
48. Winchester College Archives
49. Mells Papers. Raymond to Asquith, 10.2.95
50. *The Wykehamist*, March 1896
51. Mells Papers. Asquith to Raymond, 15.6.98
52. *The Wykehamist*, 15.11.98, 15 and 7.2.99
53. *The Wykehamist*, 28.11.1900

CHAPTER 5: 'DIVERTED FROM THE STERNER MODE OF LIFE'
1. Bahlman (ed.), *The Diary of Sir Edward Hamilton 1885–1906*, p. 184
2. Margot Asquith's Diary, d. 3202, 1897, pp. 5–13
3. Margot Asquith's Diary, d. 3202, 1897, p. 20
4. Margot Asquith's Diary, d. 3202, p. 23. Written during a holiday in Malvern in April 1897
5. Margot Asquith's Diary, d. 3203, p. 62. 1.11.99
6. Margot to Raymond, 28.11.96 Mells Papers
7. Ensor Papers, Box 8. Raymond to Robert Ensor, 24.9.97
8. John Jolliffe, *Raymond Asquith, Life and Letters*, p. 28

9. Ensor Papers. Box 8. Raymond to Robert Ensor, 24.9.97
10. Jolliffe, p. 18
11. Margot Asquith Papers. Asquith to Margot, 12.12.97
12. Margot Asquith Papers. Asquith to Margot, 17.12.97; 11.8.98
13. Margot Asquith Papers. Asquith to Margot, 11.8.98; 26.10.98
14. Margot Asquith Papers. Asquith to Margot, 25.10.98
15. Margot Asquith Papers. Asquith to Margot, 29.10.98
16. Mells Papers. Asquith to Raymond, 30.11.98
17. Margot Asquith's Diary, 1899, p. 8, and 20 December. Curzon Papers Mss. Euro F111/12 Margot to Curzon, 9.4.99
18. Balfour Papers, Add. Mss. 49794, f. 89. Margot to Balfour, 18.12.98. Haldane to Balfour Add. Mss. 49724, f. 39, 31.12.98 Margot Asquith Papers. Balfour to Margot 22.12.98 Margot Asquith's Diary 1899, d. 3203, p. 9
19. Curzon Papers. Margot to Curzon, 9.4.99
20. Jolliffe, p. 33. Letter dated October 1897. Mells Papers
21. *Moments of Memory*, p. 126
22. Margot Asquith Papers. Asquith to Margot, 29.11.97
23. Jolliffe, pp. 35–6. Raymond to Margot, probably February 1898
24. Jolliffe, p. 36. Raymond to Asquith, 18.2.98
25. Jolliffe, p. 37. Raymond to Asquith, 30.3.98
26. Jolliffe, pp. 46 and 60
27. Jolliffe, p. 42. Raymond to H. T. Baker, 2.8.98
28. H. W. C. Davis, *History of Balliol College*, p. 227
29. Margot Asquith Papers. Asquith to Margot, f. 43, 26.11.99
30. John Buchan, *Memory Hold the Door*, p. 60
31. John Buchan, *Memory Hold the Door*, pp. 59–60
32. John Buchan, *Memory Hold the Door*, p. 57
33. Maurice Baring, *The Puppet Show of Memory*, p. 223
34. Margot Asquith Papers, Asquith to Margot, 29.11.97
35. *Isis*, 22.2.98. *Oxford Magazine*, 26.2.98. This contradicts John Buchan's later opinion that 'there were no signs of careful preparation' in Raymond's speeches. (*Memory Holds The Door*, p. 58)
36. *Isis*, 19.11.98. *Oxford Magazine*, 23.11.98
37. *Oxford Magazine*, 17.5.99. John Buchan, p. 59
38. *Isis*, 27.1.1900
39. *Isis*, 3.3.1900
40. *Isis*, 26.5.1900. *Oxford Magazine*, 30.5.1900
41. Jolliffe, p. 103. Raymond to H. T. Baker, 22.3.03

CHAPTER 6: 'OF PRESIDENTIAL STOCK'

1. Margot Asquith's Diary, d. 3206, 1.11.99
2. Desborough Papers, D/ERV C71. Margot to Lady Desborough, 19.8.1900
3. Desborough Papers, D/ERV, C71, f.76. Margot to Lady Desborough, n.d.
4. Clovelly Papers. Oc to Asquith, 15.8.1900. Raymond's silence was related by Beb to his son, Michael Asquith.
5. Jolliffe, p. 72. Raymond to H.T. Baker, 9.8.1900
6. Margot Asquith Papers. Raymond to Margot, 19.8.1900
7. Jolliffe, pp. 61–2. Raymond to H. T. Baker, 4.10.99
8. Balliol College Archives. Annandale Minute Book, Trinity Term 1902
9. *Isis*, 17.11.1900
10. *Isis*, 23.2.01. *Oxford Magazine*, 27.2.01
11. *Isis*, 4.5.01
12. *Isis*, 23.11.01. *Oxford Magazine*, 27.11.01

13. *Isis*, 22.2.02
14. *Isis*, 24.1.03, pp. 133–4
15. Margot Asquith Papers. Asquith to Margot, 7.4.02
16. Curzon Papers, Ms. Euro F111/18. Margot to Curzon, 12.8.02
17. Margot Asquith Papers. Asquith to Margot, 4.3.01
18. Margot Asquith's Diary, d. 3204, pp. 44–50
19. Jolliffe, p. 88. Raymond to Buchan, 2.3.02
20. *The Autobiography of Margot Asquith*, Vol. II, p. 53. Although Margot claims the passage is a quotation from her diary it is not there in her surviving manuscript. However, as much of her journal was compiled from contemporary notes, it may well be based on one of these.
21. Margot Asquith's Diary, d. 3204, pp. 130–2. 14.11.05
22. Christopher Page, *Command in the Royal Naval Division*, p. 5
23. Cynthia Asquith *Haply I May Remember*, p. 210
24. *Haply I May Remember*, pp. 222–5
25. *Lady Cynthia Asquith Diaries 1915–18*, p. 241
26. Clovelly Papers. Arthur Asquith's Sudan Diary, 14.9.06. Quoted in Page, p. 9
27. *Lantern Slides*, ed. Mark Pottle, p. 1. Margot Asquith's Diary, 17.10.04
28. *Lantern Slides*, p. 4. Diary 18.10.04
29. *Lantern Slides*, p. 5, 23.10.04
30. Margot Asquith Papers. Margot Asquith's Diary, d. 3205, pp. 3–6
31. Lady Angela Forbes, *Memories and Base Details*, pp. 112–3
32. Margot Asquith's Diary, d. 3205, p. 24. April 1905
33. *Lantern Slides*, p. 42, 3.6.05
34. Margot Asquith's Diary, d. 3208, f.81, 12.11.10 and f.152, 24.7.11
35. *Lantern Slides*, p. 42, 3.6.05
36. *Lantern Slides*, p. 39
37. Margot Asquith's Diary, d. 3205, pp. 89–91, 18.6.06
38. *Lantern Slides*, p. 61
39. *Lantern Slides*, p. 50
40. *Lantern Slides*, p. 58
41. *Lantern Slides*, pp. 94–7
42. Jolliffe, pp. 70 and 80. Raymond to H. T. Baker, 9.8.1900 and 1.8.01
43. Jolliffe, pp. 112 and 113. Raymond to Lady Manners, 1.7.04, and Katharine Horner, 23.7.04
44. Jolliffe, pp. 94, 113
45. Jolliffe, p. 135
46. Margot Asquith Papers. Asquith to Margot, 24.1.06
47. Margot Asquith Papers. Diary, d. 3204, p. 248, 13.6.06

CHAPTER 7: 'HOW DARE YOU BECOME PRIME MINISTER WHEN I'M AWAY'
1. Margot Asquith Papers. Asquith to Margot, 3.8.05
2. Macmichael, *Anglo Egyptian Sudan*, p. 84
3. Clovelly Papers. Arthur Asquith's Sudan Diary
4. *Lantern Slides*, pp. 109 and 115. Violet to Hugh Godley, 26.8.06. Violet's Diary, 18.10.06
5. Sudan Diary, 14.9.06. Quoted Page, *Command in the Royal Naval Division*, p. 7
6. Margot Asquith Papers. Diary, d. 3205, p. 102
7. *Lantern Slides*, p. 111. Oc to Violet, 7.10.06
8. Sudan Diary, 15.9.06 and 23.3.07
9. Sudan Diary, 15.9.06. Partially quoted in Page, p. 9
10. Clovelly Papers. Asquith to Oc, 11.9.06
11. Clovelly Papers. Margot to Oc, 11.9.06

12. Sudan Diary, 7.1.07
13. Sudan Diary, 14.9.06. Quoted in Page, p. 10
14. Sudan Diary, 25.9.06
15. Sudan Diary, 4.10.06
16. Clovelly Papers. The letter, dated 19 September, is transcribed into an entry in Oc's diary dated 4.10.06. It is quoted in Page, p. 10, where it is mistakenly attributed to Lady Manners.
17. Sudan Diary, 29.9.06
18. Sudan Diary, 4.10.06
19. Page, *Command in the Royal Naval Division*, p. 11
20. *Lantern Slides*, pp. 110–12. Oc to Violet, 7.10.06
21. Clovelly Papers. Oc to Asquith, 2.11.06
22. Page, p. 11, quoting letter from Oc to Violet, 16.11.06
23. Clovelly Papers. Oc to Asquith, 24.11.06
24. Clovelly Papers. Oc to Asquith, 24.11.06, 1.1.07. Oc to Margot, 8.12.06
25. Clovelly Papers. Oc to Asquith, 24.11.06
26. H. C. Jackson, *Sudan Days and Ways*, p. 80
27. *Lantern Slides*, p. 119. Oc to Violet, 11.12.06
28. *Lantern Slides*, p. 120. Oc to Violet, 11.12.06
29. Clovelly Papers. Oc to Asquith, 9.3.07
30. Clovelly Papers. Oc to Asquith, 16.4.07
31. Clovelly Papers. Oc to Asquith, 1.7.07. Another paper's version quoted in Page, pp. 13–14
32. Clovelly Papers. Oc to Asquith, 9.3 and 16.4.07
33. Sudan Diary, 23.3.07. Quoted in Page, p. 14
34. Clovelly Papers. Sudan Diary, 7.1.07
35. Clovelly Papers. Sudan Diary, 1.5.07
36. Clovelly Papers. Oc to Asquith, 24.11.06
37. Oc to Margot, 8.12.06
38. *Lantern Slides*, p. 121. Violet to Venetia Stanley, 29.12.06. Margot's Diary, d. 3205, pp. 126–34, January 1907
39. *Moments of Memory*, p. 136
40. Margot Asquith's Diary, 220f. Milner's arguments are based on a letter to Margot of 25 April 1907 and stuck into her diary.
41. Margot Asquith Papers. Diary, d. 3205, pp. 145–8
42. Margot Asquith's Diary, p. 142
43. Margot Asquith Papers. The letter is undated.
44. Desborough Papers, D/ERV, c. 71, f.18. Margot to Lady Desborough, 22.6.07
45. *Lantern Slides*, p. 129. Violet's Diary, 17.6.07
46. Margot Asquith Papers. Diary, d. 3205, pp. 142–58. Chandos Papers I, 5 f.1. Margot to DD Lyttelton, 30.6.07
47. Jolliffe, p. 94
48. Margot Asquith Papers. Asquith to Margot, 4.11.05. Margot's Diary, d. 3206, p. 19 (22.8.07) and d. 3205, p. 191
49. Jolliffe, p. 152. Raymond Asquith to Lady Horner, 9.2.07
50. Jolliffe, p. 152. Raymond Asquith to Lady Horner, 9.2.07
51. Clovelly Papers. Lady Manners to Oc, 11.4.07
52. Clovelly Papers. Lady Manners to Oc, 11.4.07
53. Clovelly Papers. Raymond to Oc, 29.4.07
54. Margot Asquith Papers. Asquith to Margot, 9.7.07
55. Jeanne MacKenzie, *Children of the Souls*, pp. 3–4
56. *Lantern Slides*, p. 135. Raymond to Violet, 13.8.07
57. *Children of the Souls*, p. 22

58. Margot Asquith's Diary, d. 3205, pp. 168–80, 1.10.07
59. Margot Asquith's Diary, d. 3205, p. 180. Asquith to Margot, 11.12.07
60. Margot Asquith's Diary, d. 3205, pp. 171–87
61. Hamilton Papers, Add. Mss. 48614. Margot to Sir Edward Hamilton, 20.10.07
62. Margot Asquith's Diary, d. 3206, p. 36, 29.2.08
63. *Lantern Slides*, p. 145
64. *Lantern Slides*, p. 147. Asquith to Violet, 22.3.07
65. Margot Asquith's Diary, d. 3206, pp. 44–5
66. Margot Asquith's Diary, d. 3206, p. 53. *Lantern Slides*, p. 151. Asquith to Violet, 8.4.08
67. *Lantern Slides*, p. 151

CHAPTER 8: 'THE GOVERNESS OF ALL THE WORLD'

1. Margot Asquith Papers. Asquith to Margot, 13.5.92
2. Violet Bonham Carter, *Winston Churchill As I Knew Him*, p. 15
3. *Winston Churchill As I Knew Him*, p. 16
4. *Lantern Slides*, p. 127. Violet to Hugh Godley, 2.4.07
5. Margot Asquith's Diary, d. 3204, p. 75 (21.7.04), p. 218 (28.2.06); 3206 (23.8.07)
6. Margot Asquith's Diary, d. 3206, pp. 53–4, 8.4.08
7. Margot Asquith's Diary, d. 3206, p. 55
8. Margot Asquith's Diary, d. 3206, pp. 54 and 56, 8.4 and 9.4.08
9. Margot Asquith's Diary, d. 3206, p. 55, 9.4.08
10. Lady Angela Forbes, *Memories and Base Details*, p. 75
11. *Churchill Companion*, Vol. II, Part 2, pp. 771–2
12. Margot Asquith's Diary, d. 3206, p. 58
13. Margot Asquith's Diary, d. 3206, p. 60
14. Margot Asquith's Diary, d. 3206, pp. 50–52
15. Margot Asquith's Diary, d. 3206, p. 62, 12.4.08
16. Margot Asquith's Diary, d. 3206, pp. 62–87
17. *Lantern Slides*, p. 147. Margot Asquith's Diary, d. 3205, p. 195
18. Margot Asquith's Diary, d. 3206, p. 94, *The Autobiography of Margot Asquith*, Vol. II, pp. 106–7
19. *Lantern Slides*, pp. 152–3
20. Margot Asquith's Diary, d. 3206, p. 127 (August 1908)
21. Nicholas Mosley, *Julian Grenfell*, p. 130
22. *Lantern Slides*, p. 162 (Violet to Venetia, 14.8.08)
23. *Lantern Slides*, pp. 129, 146. Violet's Diary, 21.5.07. Archie to Ettie Desborough, 21.3.08
24. Mells Papers. Margot to Raymond, April 1912
25. Margot Asquith's Diary, d. 3206, pp. 129–32
26. Desborough Papers. Margot to Lady Desborough, D/ERV, ff.77 and 78 (n.d.)
27. Margot Asquith's Diary, d. 3206, p. 132
28. Margot Asquith Papers. Asquith to Margot, 25.10.08. *Lantern Slides*, p. 170
29. Margot Asquith's Diary, d. 3206, p. 148
30. Margot Asquith's Diary, d. 3206, p. 149
31. Balfour Papers, Edinburgh
32. Margot Asquith's Diary, d. 3204, p. 223 (March 1906)
33. Margot Asquith's Diary, d. 3207, pp. 15 and 35
34. Margot Asquith's Diary, d. 3206, p. 189
35. Margot Asquith's Diary, d. 3206, p. 193
36. Margot Asquith's Diary, d. 3206, pp. 180–82
37. Margot Asquith's Diary, d. 3206, p. 187 (1.4.09)
38. John Grigg, *Lloyd George: The People's Champion*, p. 178
39. Grigg, pp. 203–9

40. Margot Asquith's Diary, d. 3206, pp. 197–9, 15.9.09
41. Grigg, pp. 223–5
42. *Lantern Slides*, p. 181. Hugh Godley to Violet, 12.5.09
43. *Lantern Slides*, p. 183 (footnote 1)
44. Bonham Carter Papers. Oc to Violet, 18.7.09
45. There is an account of the accident in *Lantern Slides*, p. 190. The details of Archie's injuries come from Margot's Diary, d. 3207, p. 89
46. Margot Asquith's Diary, d. 3207, p. 90, d. 3210, p. 85
47. Margot Asquith Papers. Asquith to Margot, 12.12.09
48. Violet's detailed account of Archie's last moments is in *Lantern Slides*, pp. 191–7
49. Margot Asquith's Diary, d. 3207, p. 93
50. Margot Asquith's Diary, d. 3207, p. 95

CHAPTER 9: A FAMILY CRISIS AND A POLITICAL SETBACK
1. *Lantern Slides*, p. 196
2. Margot Asquith's Diary, d. 3207, pp. 97 and 104
3. Margot Asquith's Diary, d. 3207, p. 104
4. Margot Asquith's Diary, d. 3207, p. 105
5. Margot Asquith Papers. Asquith to Margot, 6.1.10
6. Margot Asquith's Diary, d. 3207, p. 114
7. Margot Asquith's Diary, d. 3207, pp. 1–3
8. Margot Asquith's Diary, d. 3208, p. 6
9. Margot Asquith's Diary, d. 3208, p. 7
10. Margot Asquith's Diary, d. 3208, p. 8
11. Margot Asquith's Diary, d. 3207, p. 82
12. Margot Asquith's Diary, d. 3208, pp. 10–12
13. *Lantern Slides*, p. 202. Montagu to Violet, 7.3.10
14. Margot Asquith's Diary, d. 3208, pp. 22 and 33
15. Margot Asquith Papers. Asquith to Margot, 6.3.10
16. Margot Asquith Papers. Asquith to Margot, 6.3 and 15.3.10
17. Desborough Papers, D/ERV, C7 22. Margot to Lady Desborough, 24.3.10
18. Margot Asquith's Diary, d. 3208, p. 39, 31.3.10
19. Margot Asquith's Diary, d. 3208, p. 24. Asquith to Margot, 28.4.10
20. Margot Asquith's Diary, d. 3206, p. 112. *Lantern Slides*, p. 210
21. Kenneth Rose, *King George V*, p. 76
22. Asquith to Margot, 10.2.09
23. *Haply I May Remember*, p. 75
24. Jane Ridley, *The Letters of Arthur Balfour and Lady Elcho*, p. 238
25. The phrases are taken from Herbert Asquith's novel *Young Orland* (pp. 133–4), and are obviously autobiographical.
26. Nicola Beauman, *Cynthia Asquith*, p. 87
27. *Remember and Be Glad*, pp. 21–2, quoted in Ridley, pp. 239–40
28. Ridley, p. 261, letter to Balfour, 23.3.10
29. Beauman, p. 93
30. Ridley, p. 261
31. Beauman, pp. 93–4
32. *Raymond Asquith, Life and Letters*, p. 173
33. *Haply I May Remember*, p. 28
34. Beauman, p. 96
35. Margot Asquith's Diary, d. 3208, p. 37. *Lantern Slides*, p. 203. Violet's Diary, 18.4.10
36. *Lantern Slides*, p. 211. Violet to Montagu, 6.6.10
37. *Lantern Slides*, p. 216
38. *Lantern Slides*, p. 240

39. *Lantern Slides*, p. 243
40. D'Abernon Papers. Add. Ms. 48928. Violet to Sir Edgar Vincent, 11.1.11
41. *Lantern Slides*, p. 244
42. D'Abernon Papers, Add. Ms. 48928. Violet to Sir Edgar Vincent, 11.1.11. *Lantern Slides*, p. 246
43. *Lantern Slides*, pp. 252, 256–7, 264

CHAPTER 10: 'WHAT A FINE FELLOW HE IS TO SERVE UNDER'

1. Grigg, *The People's Champion*, p. 281
2. Lloyd George Papers, NLW 22522E, f.215. Quoted in Grigg, p. 283
3. Margot Asquith Papers. Diary, d. 3208, p. 93. Lloyd George to Margot, 29.11.10 Reproduced by kind permission of the Clerk of the Records at the House of Lords, on behalf of the Beaverbrook Foundation, and the National Library of Wales
4. Margot Asquith Papers. Diary, d. 3208, pp. 93–4
5. Margot Asquith Papers. Diary, d. 3208, pp. 91–4
6. Lloyd George Papers, NLW 22522E, f. 217. Elibank to Lloyd George, 30.11.10
7. Lloyd George Papers, f. 219–21, 30.11.10. Margot to LG (partially quoted in Grigg, pp. 283–4)
8. Margot Asquith Papers. Diary, d. 3208, p. 95
9. Margot Asquith Papers. Diary, d. 3209, p. 137
10. Margot Asquith Papers. Diary, d. 3209, p. 41 (August 1911)
11. Margot Asquith Papers. Diary, d. 3208, p. 144
12. Margot Asquith Papers. Asquith to Margot, 31.10.11
13. *Letters to Venetia Stanley*, p. 471
14. Margot Asquith, *Off the Record*, p. 122
15. *Letters to Venetia Stanley*, p. 1
16. Tree Papers, Add. Mss. 59895, Asquith to Viola Tree, 10.8.16
17. Tree Papers, Add. Mss. 61727. Asquith to Viola Tree, 24.7.11
18. Margot's account of the debate is taken from her journal, d. 3208, pp. 152–62
19. Alexander MacIntosh, *From Gladstone to Lloyd George*, p. 232
20. Tree Papers, Add. Mss. 61727. Asquith to Viola Tree, 25.7.11
21. Desborough Papers, D/ERV C71. Margot to Lady Desborough, 24.7.11
22. Walter Long Papers, Add. Ms. 62404, LN 3, f. 124 (Margot to Balfour dated 29.2.12, shown to Long but apparently never sent)
23. Tree Papers, Add. Mss. 61727. Asquith to Viola, 15.9.11
24. Battersea Papers. Add. Mss. 47963, ff. 187–90. Lady (Constance) Battersea to The Hon. Mrs Yorke, 17.10.11. I am indebted to Charlotte Mosley for giving me this quotation.
25. Margot Asquith's Diary, d. 3208, 13.11.11, p. 172
26. Beauman, p. 103
27. Lloyd George Papers, NLW 22522E, f. 85, 21.8.11
28. Grigg, *The People's Champion*, p. 293
29. Margot Asquith's Diary, d. 3210, p. 168
30. Margot Asquith Papers. Asquith to Margot, 14.12.11
31. Margot Asquith Papers. Asquith to Margot, 14.12.11
32. Asquith to Margot, 12.1.12
33. *Lantern Slides*, p. 296
34. Asquith to Margot, 12.1.12
35. Asquith to Margot, 26.1.12
36. Brock, p. 532
37. Tree Papers, Add. Mss. 59895. Asquith to Viola, 12.1.12
38. *Lantern Slides*, pp. 297–8
39. Asquith to Margot, 3.2.12

40. *Lantern Slides*, p. 297
41. Tree Papers, Add. Mss. 59895. Asquith to Viola, 10.3.12
42. *Lady Cynthia Asquith Diaries 1915–18*, p. 107
43. L. E. Jones, *An Edwardian Youth*, p. 214
44. *Lantern Slides*, p. 207
45. Tree Papers, Add. Ms. 61727. Asquith to Viola, 23.8 and 15.9.11
46. Asquith to Margot, 3.2.12
47. Spender and Asquith, II, p. 19, *Moments of Memory*, p. 159
48. Tree Papers, Add. Mss. 59895. Asquith to Viola, 10.3.12
49. Margot Asquith's Diary, d. 3210, pp. 18f
50. See *Lady Cynthia Asquith Diaries 1915–1918*, p. 100
51. Margot Asquith's Diary, d. 3210, pp. 28, 30
52. Mosley, p. 217
53. See Margot Asquith's Diary, d. 3208, pp. 174–80, for the story of how she acquired the Wharf.
54. Tree Papers, Add. Mss. 62126, f. 37. Margot to Lady Tree (n.d.)
55. Margot Asquith's Diary, d. 3209, p. 145, 171
56. Chandos Papers. Margot to DD Lyttelton (n.d.)
57. Margot Asquith's Diary, d. 3209, p. 129
58. *Lantern Slides*, p. 331
59. Margot's Diary, d. 3209, p. 35 (July 1911)
60. Mells Papers. Margot to Raymond, 2.4, 6.4 and 13.4.12
61. Mells Papers. Asquith to Raymond, 12.4.12
62. Mells Papers. W. S. Robson K.C. to Asquith, 16.8.10
63. *Letters to Venetia Stanley*, pp. 274, 514
64. L. E. Jones, *An Edwardian Youth*, p. 43
65. Balliol War Memorial Book, p. 14
66. Beauman, p. 86
67. Jolliffe, p. 173
68. *Moments of Memory*, p. 265
69. Balliol War Memorial Book, p. 14
70. *Moments of Memory*, p. 265
71. Jolliffe, p. 179
72. Margot Asquith's Diary, d. 3201, p. 215
73. Philip Ziegler, *Diana Cooper*, pp. 25, 33
74. Lady Diana Cooper, *The Rainbow Comes and Goes*, p. 82
75. Margot Asquith's Diary, d. 3210, p. 216
76. *Letters to Venetia Stanley*, p. 52
77. Margot Asquith's Diary, d. 3210, p. 215
78. Cooper Papers, Add. Mss. 70720, f. 40. Raymond to Diana, 4.10.14
79. *Lady Cynthia Asquith Diaries 1915–18*, p. 79

CHAPTER 11: 'NO ONE WAS LEFT WITH A SHRED OF REPUTATION'
1. Margot Asquith's Diary, d. 3210, p. 34
2. Margot Asquith's Diary, d. 3209, pp. 186–8. Diana Cooper, *The Rainbow Comes and Goes*, pp. 104–5
3. Margot Asquith's Diary, d. 3210, p. 191
4. Margot Asquith's Diary, d. 3209, pp. 190–1
5. Margot Asquith's Diary, d. 3210, pp. 59–68
6. Margot Asquith's Diary, d. 3210, p. 28
7. *Letters to Venetia Stanley*, p. 9
8. Minto Papers, Ms. 12460. Lady Minto's Diary, 23.11 and 24.11.12. I have taken some liberties with the order.

9. Lady Minto's Diary, 25.11.12
10. Margot Asquith's Diary, d. 3210, pp. 77–8. Rosebery Papers, Knollys to Rosebery, 25.11.12
11. *Lantern Slides*, p. 350
12. *Lantern Slides*, pp. 354–6, 367
13. Asquith to Margot, 17.1.13. See *Lantern Slides*, pp. 364, 366
14. Margot Asquith's Diary, d. 3209, p. 225
15. Tree Papers, Add. Mss. 59895. Asquith to Viola, 10.3.12. For Firth-Asquith family backgrounds see Clyde Binfield, *A Congregational Formation: An Edwardian Prime Minister's Victorian Education; Letters to Venetia Stanley*, p. 532.
16. Naomi B. Levine, *Politics Religion and Love*, pp. 194–5
17. *Letters to Venetia Stanley*, p. 2
18. *Letters to Venetia Stanley*, pp. 431 and 467
19. The quotation is from a letter to *The Times*, 14 December 1982, by Alistair Forbes, an old friend of both Venetia and Diana. See Naomi Levine, *Politics, Religion and Love*, pp. 232–5, for an exhaustive discussion of the evidence for and against Asquith and Venetia having been lovers.
20. Artemis Cooper, ed., *A Durable Fire. The Letters of Duff and Diana Cooper*. Levine, p. 233
21. Beauman, p. 195. See *The Shorter Strachey*, ed. Holroyd and Levy, pp. 38–42.
22. For a detailed exposition see Frances Donaldson, *The Marconi Scandal*.
23. Margot Asquith's Diary, d. 3210, p. 126
24. Margot Asquith's Diary, d. 3210, p. 109
25. Margot Asquith's Diary, d. 3210, pp. 127–8
26. Margot Asquith's Diary, d. 3210, pp. 128–9
27. Margot Asquith's Diary, d. 3210, pp. 130–31
28. Reading papers, Mss. Eur.F. 118/63/b, f. 49. Margot to Isaacs, 5.6.13
29. Lloyd George Papers, Series C, 6/10/11. Margot to Lloyd George, 13.6.13
30. Lloyd George Papers. Margot to Lloyd George, 17.6.13
31. Margot Asquith's Diary, d. 3210, p. 133
32. Margot Asquith's Diary, d. 3210, pp. 134–6

CHAPTER 12: 'THERE'S A GERM OF VIOLENCE IN THE AIR'
1. Margot Asquith's Diary, d. 3210, p. 115
2. *Lantern Slides*, p. 437, D'Abernon Papers, Add. Mss. 48928. Violet to Edgar Vincent, 25.9.13
3. Margot Asquith's Diary, d. 3210, p. 123
4. Margot Asquith Papers, d. 3273, 24.10.13
5. Asquith to Margot, 28.12.13
6. Lloyd George Papers. Margot to Lloyd George, 17.11.13. SC, 6/10/1
7. Margot Asquith's Diary, d. 3210, pp. 138–40 and 154
8. Margot Asquith's Diary, d. 3210, p. 153
9. *Letters to Venetia Stanley*, p. 59
10. Margot Asquith Papers, d. 3273, pp. 18–19. Montagu to Margot, 8.3.14
11. Levine, p. 236. Mrs Levine transcribed 'Violet' rather than 'Viola', but I have assumed that whatever Margot wrote in her fraught state, she must have meant Viola. One of the 'two other women' would probably have been Pamela McKenna.
12. Beauman, pp. 105, 111
13. Beauman, p. 106
14. Cynthia Asquith, *Remember and Be Glad*, p. 133
15. *The Letters of D. H. Lawrence*, Vol. II, p. 109. Quoted in Beauman, p. 111
16. *Moments of Memory*, pp. 182–3
17. *Young Orland*, p. 220

18. Margot Asquith's Diary, d. 3209, p. 189
19. Somerset Record Office. Aubrey Herbert's Diary, 29.4.14
20. Aubrey Herbert's Diary, 30.4.14. Quoted in Margaret Fitzherbert, *The Man Who Was Greenmantle*, p. 105
21. Aubrey Herbert's Diary, 4.5 and 5.5.14
22. Asquith to Margot, 28.5.14
23. Margot Asquith's Diary, d. 3210, pp. 230–37
24. Margot Asquith's Diary, d. 3210, pp. 240–1
25. Margot Asquith's Diary, d. 3210, pp. 217–8 (10.7.14)
26. Philip Ziegler, *Diana Cooper*, p. 44

CHAPTER 13: THE ASQUITHS GO TO WAR
1. Margot Asquith's Diary, d. 3210, p. 245
2. *Letters to Venetia Stanley*, pp. 138–9
3. *Letters to Venetia Stanley*, p. 146
4. Margot Asquith's Diary, d. 3210, p. 253
5. *Letters to Venetia Stanley*, pp. 150, 148
6. Margot Asquith's Diary, d. 3211, p. 265
7. M. MacDonagh, *In London During the Great War*, p. 21
8. Margot Asquith's Diary, d. 3211, p. 30
9. Asquith to Margot, 12.8.14
10. *Champion Redoubtable. The Diaries and Letters of Violet Bonham Carter 1914–1945*, pp. 6–7. *The Letters of Arthur Balfour and Lady Elcho 1885–1917*, p. 311
11. Page, p. 24
12. *Champion Redoubtable*, p. 205
13. Herbert Asquith, *The Volunteer and Other Poems*, p. 18
14. *Letters to Venetia Stanley*, p. 228
15. Jolliffe, pp. 190–92
16. Lady Diana Cooper Papers, Add. Mss. 70706, ff. 33 and 36
17. Lady Diana Cooper Papers, Add. Mss. 70706, f. 36. Margaret Fitzherbert, *The Man Who Was Greenmantle*, p. 140
18. *Moments of Memory*, p. 205. Aubrey Herbert, *Mons, Anzac and Kut*, pp. 47–55
19. Asquith to Margot, 16.9.14
20. Page, p. 26
21. Page, pp. 25–6
22. Nigel Jones, *Rupert Brooke*, p. 383
23. Page, p. 29
24. Reproduced in *Moments of Memory*, p. 209
25. *Letters to Venetia Stanley*, p. 275
26. Quoted from cutting on p. 14 of Margot Asquith's Diary, d. 3211
27. The quotations from Cynthia's diary of the expedition are taken from a typescript version sent to Mary Herbert and now in Somerset County Record Office (DD HER 57). See also Beauman, pp. 121–4.
28. *Champion Redoubtable*, p. 11
29. *Champion Redoubtable*, p. 10
30. Margot Asquith's Diary, d. 3211, pp. 19–21, 92. Lloyd George Papers, Series C, 6/10/11. Margot to Lloyd George, 4.11.14
31. Margot Asquith's Diary, d. 3211, p. 93
32. Margot Asquith's Diary, d. 3211, p.101
33. Margot Asquith's Diary, d. 3211, pp. 104–7
34. Margot Asquith's Diary, d. 3211, pp. 110–2
35. Margot Asquith's Diary, d. 3211, pp. 112–8

36. Margot Asquith's Diary, d. 3211, pp. 93–125
37. *Moments of Memory*, pp. 252–3
38. *Letters to Venetia Stanley*, p. 371
39. *Champion Redoubtable*, pp. 25, 26
40. Margot Asquith's Diary, d. 3211, p. 189
41. Margot Asquith's Diary, d. 3211, p. 191
42. Margot Asquith's Diary, d. 3211, p. 191
43. *Champion Redoubtable*, p. 26
44. Margot Asquith's Diary, d. 3211, p. 192
45. *Champion Redoubtable*, p. 27
46. *Champion Redoubtable*, p. 28. Margot Asquith's Diary, d. 3211, p. 194
47. Margot Asquith's Diary, d. 3211, p. 195
48. *Champion Redoubtable*, p. 29
49. *Champion Redoubtable*, p. 30
50. Violet Bonham Carter, *Winston Churchill As I Knew Him*, p. 365

CHAPTER 14: 'TO MAKE A POET'S GRAVE'
1. Herbert Asquith, *Poems 1912–1933*, p. 5
2. Nigel Jones, *Rupert Brooke*, p. 41
3. *Champion Redoubtable*, pp. 26,31,33
4. Margot Asquith Papers, c. 6714, f. 28. Oc to Asquith, 9.3.15; Oc to Margot, 24.3.15
5. Margot Asquith Papers, c. 6714, f. 31. Oc to Asquith, 26.3.15
6. Margot Asquith Papers, c. 6714, Oc to Asquith, 26.3 and 27.3.15
7. Margot Asquith's Diary, d. 3211, p. 226
8. Clovelly Papers. Margot to Oc, 12.4.15
9. Clovelly Papers. Oc to Asquith, 1.4.15. Fitzherbert, *The Man Who Was Greenmantle*, p. 151
10. *Champion Redoubtable*, p. 37. Clovelly Papers. Oc to Violet, 13.4.15
11. Clovelly Papers. Puffin to Oc, 12.4.15
12. Clovelly Papers. Oc to Violet, 13.4.15
13. Clovelly Papers. Oc to Violet, 21.4.15
14. Joseph Murray, *Gallipoli As I Saw It*, p. 61
15. Clovelly Papers. Oc to Violet, 21.4.15
16. Kelly's Diary, 22.4.15
17. Kelly's Diary, 23.4.15
18. *Letters to Venetia Stanley*, p. 571, n. 2
19. *Letters to Venetia Stanley*, p. 569. Aubrey Herbert Papers, DD/HER 57. Violet to Aubrey, 9.10.15
20. Clovelly Papers, 19.5.15
21. Margot Asquith Papers, d. 3289, f. 19. Oc to Margot, 13.10.15
22. Kelly's Diary, 30.4.15. Also see Leonard Sellers, *The Hood Battalion*, pp. 82–3.
23. Kelly's Diary, 1.5.15
24. Margot Asquith Papers, d. 3289, f. 7. Oc to Margot, 15.5.15
25. Margot Asquith Papers, d. 3289, f. 7. Oc to Margot, 15.5.15
26. Ronald Knox, *Patrick Shaw-Stewart*, p. 122
27. Asquith to Sylvia Henley, 9.6.15
28. Martin Gilbert, *Winston S. Churchill Companion*, Vol. II, p. 848. Margot Asquith's Diary, d. 3211, p. 251
29. Clovelly Papers. Margot to Oc, 7.5.15
30. *Champion Redoubtable*, p. 47
31. Margot Asquith's Diary, d. 3211, p. 253
32. Margot Asquith Papers, d. 3289, f. 7. Oc to Margot, 15.5.15

33. Clovelly Papers. Margot to Oc, 13.5.15
34. Adelaide Lubbock, *People in Glass Houses*, p. 82
35. Margot Asquith's Diary, d. 3211, p. 166
36. *Letters to Venetia Stanley*, p. 417. Asquith to Venetia, 7.2.15
37. *Champion Redoubtable*, p. 55
38. *Letters to Venetia Stanley*, pp. 428, 437
39. *Letters to Venetia Stanley*, pp. 452, 394
40. *Letters to Venetia Stanley*, p. 491
41. *Letters to Venetia Stanley*, p. 427
42. *Letters to Venetia Stanley*, p. 446
43. *Letters to Venetia Stanley*, p. 457
44. *Letters to Venetia Stanley*, p. 401
45. Levine, p. 257
46. *Letters to Venetia Stanley*, pp. 445, 530
47. Margot Asquith's Diary, d. 3211, p. 235
48. Asquith to Margot, 13.4.15. Quoted in *Letters to Venetia Stanley*, p. 548
49. *Letters to Venetia Stanley*, p. 547
50. *Letters to Venetia Stanley*, p. 553
51. *Letters to Venetia Stanley*, p. 585
52. *Letters to Venetia Stanley*, p. 589
53. *Letters to Venetia Stanley*, p. 593
54. Asquith to Sylvia Henley, 12.5.15
55. Margot Asquith's Diary, d. 3211, pp. 267–8

CHAPTER 15: 'A TERRIBLE GAMBLE'
 1. Margot Asquith's Diary, d. 3211, p. 269
 2. Margot Asquith's Diary, d. 3212, pp. 12–13
 3. *Champion Redoubtable*, p. 52
 4. Margot Asquith's Diary, d. 3212, pp. 17–18
 5. Asquith to Sylvia Henley, 17.5.15
 6. Margot Asquith's Diary, d. 3212, p. 28
 7. Clovelly Papers. Margot to Oc, 19.5.15
 8. Margot Asquith's Diary, d. 3212, pp. 25–29, 51
 9. Margot Asquith's Diary, d. 3211, p. 143
10. Margot Asquith's Diary, d. 3212, p. 91
11. Margot Asquith Papers, d. 3206, 24.5.15; Diary, d. 3212, p. 59; d. 3271, Haldane to Margot, 24.5.15
12. Mary Soames, *Clementine Churchill*, p. 192
13. Margot Asquith's Diary, d. 3212, p. 49
14. Churchill Papers. 1/118/6–8. Clemmie to Winston, 30.11.15
15. Margot Asquith's Diary, d. 3212, pp. 111–16
16. Asquith to Sylvia Henley, 9.6.15
17. Clovelly Papers. Margot to Oc, 12.4.15
18. Margot Asquith's Diary, d. 3212, pp. 119–23
19. See Margot Asquith's Diary, d. 3212, p. 109.
20. Asquith to Sylvia Henley, 5.6.15
21. Margot Asquith's Diary, d. 3212, p. 31
22. *Letters to Venetia Stanley*, p. 557 (Venetia to Montagu, 20.4.15)
23. Asquith to Sylvia Henley, 27.5, 8.6 and 11.6.15
24. Asquith to Sylvia Henley, 20.6.15
25. *Lady Cynthia Asquith Diaries 1915–18*, p. 34
26. Asquith to Sylvia Henley, 14.6.15
27. Asquith to Sylvia Henley, 30.5.15. Quoted in *Letters to Venetia Stanley*, p. 600

28. Clovelly Papers. Bongie to Oc, 19.7.15
29. Page, p. 51
30. *Champion Redoubtable*, p. 50
31. Clovelly Papers. Violet to Oc, 19.7.15
32. Clovelly Papers. Margot to Oc, 15.6.15
33. Jolliffe, p. 202
34. *Champion Redoubtable*, p. 51
35. *Lady Cynthia Asquith Diaries 1915–1918*, p. 49
36. Herbert Papers, DD\HER 57. Violet to Aubrey, 9.10.15. Quoted in *The Man Who Was Greenmantle*, p. 156
37. *Lady Cynthia Asquith Diaries 1915–1918*, pp. 27, 49
38. Margot Asquith's Diary, d. 3212, pp. 45, 150
39. Clovelly Papers. Margot to Oc, 18.7.15
40. *Champion Redoubtable*, p. 65
41. Compton Mackenzie, *Gallipoli Memories*, p. 123
42. *Champion Redoubtable*, pp. 65–6
43. Margot Asquith Papers, d. 3289, f. 7. Oc to Margot, 15.5.15
44. Joseph Macleod, *The Sisters d'Arányi*, p. 109
45. *Champion Redoubtable*, p. 69
46. Asquith to Sylvia Henley, 21.5 and 27.5.15
47. Margot Asquith's Diary, d. 3212, p. 49

CHAPTER 16: 'FEELING AS IF HE WOULD CRACK UP'
1. *Lady Cynthia Asquith Diaries* 1915–18, pp. 9–10
2. Joliffe, pp. 198, 200
3. Diana Cooper Papers, Add. Mss. 70706, f. 74
4. Diana Cooper Papers, f. 97, f. 40 (4.10.14), f. 138 (8.7.15)
5. Diana Cooper Papers, f. 40 (4.10.14)
6. Diana Cooper Papers, f. 80
7. Jolliffe, p. 201 (11.6.15)
8. *Moments of Memory*, pp. 218–9
9. *Moments of Memory*, p. 227
10. *Lady Cynthia Asquith Diaries 1915–18*, pp. 33, 38
11. Asquith to Sylvia Henley, 31.5.15
12. *Moments of Memory*, p. 230
13. Asquith to Sylvia Henley, 1.6.15
14. Clovelly Papers. Margot to Oc, 2.5.15
15. *Lady Cynthia Asquith Diaries 1915–18*, pp. 43, 46, 49, 50
16. *Moments of Memory*, p. 244
17. *Lady Cynthia Asquith Diaries 1915–18*, p. 44. *The Man Who Was Greenmantle*, p. 155
18. *Moments of Memory*, p. 245. *Lady Cynthia Asquith Diaries 1915–18*, pp. 44, 55
19. Clovelly Papers. Margot to Oc, 18.7.15
20. *Moments of Memory*, p. 234
21. *Moments of Memory*, pp. 245–6
22. *Champion Redoubtable*, p. 75
23. *Lady Cynthia Asquith Diaries 1915–18*, p. 74
24. Beauman, p. 152
25. *The Letters of D. H. Lawrence*, Vol. II, p. 359
26. Tree Papers, Add. Mss. 59895. Raymond to Viola, 11.3.07
27. Herbert Asquith, *Roon*, p. 239
28. *Lady Cynthia Asquith Diaries 1915–18*, pp. 76, 77, 34
29. Margot Asquith's Diary, d. 3213, p. 85
30. Clovelly Papers. Margot to Oc, 15.6, 18.7.15

31. Balfour Papers (Edinburgh), 311 f. 150. Margot to Balfour
32. Margot Asquith's Diary, d. 3213, pp. 73–4. Roskill, p. 228
33. *Lady Cynthia Asquith Diaries 1915–18*, p. 69
34. *Lady Cynthia Asquith Diaries 1915–18*, p. 86
35. Jolliffe, p. 230
36. *Lady Cynthia Asquith Diaries 1915–18*, p. 94

CHAPTER 17: 'TO KNOW MORE DEAD THAN LIVING PEOPLE'
 1. Balliol War Memorial Book, p. 14
 2. Jeanne MacKenzie, *Children of the Souls*, p. 216
 3. *Champion Redoubtable*, p. 81
 4. Diana Cooper Papers, f. 201, f. 203. Jolliffe, p. 204
 5. Jolliffe, pp. 205, 206, 210
 6. Diana Cooper Papers. Raymond to Diana, 27.10.15. Jolliffe, pp. 205, 206, 208
 7. *Lady Cynthia Asquith Diaries 1915–18*, pp. 90–91
 8. *The Man Who Was Greenmantle*, p. 157
 9. *Lady Cynthia Asquith Diaries 1915–18*, pp. 112, 96
10. *Lady Cynthia Asquith Diaries 1915–18*, p. 97
11. *Lady Cynthia Asquith Diaries 1915–18*, pp. 99–101
12. Jolliffe, 219
13. Jolliffe, p. 216. Diana Cooper Papers, Add. Mss. 70706, f. 164 (n.d.)
14. Diana Cooper Papers. Raymond to Diana, 27.10.15. Jolliffe, pp. 213, 214
15. Diana Cooper Papers, f. 201, f. 211 (31.10.15)
16. Diana Cooper Papers f. 243 (10.12.15)
17. Jolliffe, pp. 215, 216
18. Jolliffe, p. 223
19. Jolliffe, p. 230
20. Diana Cooper Papers, f. 248
21. Diana Cooper Papers, f. 249. Quoted in *Children of the Souls*, p. 217
22. Jolliffe, p. 227
23. Jolliffe, pp. 230–31
24. *Speaking for Themselves*, p. 116
25. Jolliffe, p. 220
26. Diana Cooper Papers, Add. Mss. 70706, f. 248
27. Margot Asquith's Diary, d. 3205, p. 198
28. Margot Asquith's Diary, d. 3215 (1916), pp. 110–13; d. 3207 (1909), p. 196. Desborough Papers, D/ERV C7, f. 76. Margot to Ettie Desborough (n.d.), 1900
29. *Lady Cynthia Asquith Diaries 1915–18*, p. xviii
30. Margot Asquith's Diary, d. 3214, 29.12.15
31. Asquith to Sylvia Henley, 24.12.15
32. Clovelly Papers. Oc to Violet, 1.7 and 6.7.15
33. Margot Asquith Papers, d. 3289, f. 10. Oc to Margot, 8.8.15; Clovelly Papers. Oc to Violet, 3.7 and 6.7.15
34. Clovelly Papers. Oc to Violet, 6.7.15
35. Clovelly Papers. Oc to Violet, 6.7.15. Violet to Oc, 19.7.15. Cynthia to Oc, 13.9.15
36. Clovelly Papers. Oc to Violet, 22.8. and 6.7.15
37. Knox, p. 130
38. Jerrold, pp. 145–6
39 Oc to Violet, 24.7.15. Quoted in *Champion Redoubtable*, p. 71
40. Page, p. 53
41. Lord Ribblesdale, *Charles Lister*, p. 211
42. Oc to Violet, 24.7.15. Quoted in *Champion Redoubtable*, p. 72
43. Jerrold, p. 148

44. Asquith Papers, Box 14, ff. 170–73
45. Clovelly Papers. Margot to Oc, 24.9.15
46. Margot Asquith Papers, d. 3289, f. 19. Oc to Margot, 13.10.15
47. Page, p. 55
48. Page, p. 59
49. Margot Asquith Papers, d. 3289, f. 10. Clovelly Papers. Oc to Violet, 3.7.15
50. *Champion Redoubtable*, p. 76
51. *Baron Freyberg VC*, p. 196. The quotation is from the tribute Freyberg gave at Oc's funeral in 1939.
52. Stephen Roskill, *Hankey*, p. 195
53. Margot Asquith Papers, d. 33289, f. 12. Oc to Asquith, 24.9.15
54. Clovelly Papers. Oc to Violet, 31.8.15
55. Asquith Papers, Box 14 f. 12. Oc to Asquith, 24.9.15
56. Roskill, p. 229
57. Roskill, p. 228
58. Margot Asquith Papers, d. 3289, f. 19. Oc to Margot, 13.10.15
59. Page, p. 59
60. Margot Asquith Papers, d. 3289, f. 19. Oc to Margot, 13.10.15
61. Kelly's Diary, 22.11.15. Quoted in Page, p. 61
62. *Champion Redoubtable*, p. 76
63. Page, pp. 62–3
64. Clovelly Papers. Oc to Bongie, 14.12.15
65. Kelly's Diary, 5.1.16
66. Asquith Papers, Box 14, f. 39. Oc to Asquith, 14.1.16
67. Margot Asquith Papers, d. 3289, f. 23. Oc to Margot, 29.12.15
68. Margot Asquith Papers, d. 3318, f. 39. Oc to Asquith, 14.1.16
69. Balfour Papers, Add. Mss. 49794, f. 152. Margot to Balfour, 8.2.16

CHAPTER 18: 'THE AWFUL ANXIETIES OF DOWNING STREET'
 1. See *A Diary by Frances Stevenson*, p. 94.
 2. Margot Asquith's Diary, d. 3212, f. 57. See also *Letters to Venetia Stanley*, p. 586
 3. Margot Asquith's Diary, d. 3213, p. 41
 4. Margot Asquith's Diary, d. 3213, p. 153
 5. Margot Asquith's Diary, d. 3213, p. 175
 6. See Asquith to Sylvia Henley, 28.4.16.
 7. Margot Asquith's Diary, d. 3213, p. 184
 8. Margot Asquith's Diary, d. 3213, p. 95
 9. Spender and Asquith, I, p. 210
 10. Margot Asquith's Diary, d. 3213, p. 174
 11. Margot Asquith's Diary, d. 3211, p. 217. Lloyd George Papers, Series C 6/10/11. Letter dated 24.3.15
 12. Roskill, p. 228. Margot to Hankey, 15.10.15
 13. Margot Asquith's Diary, d. 3213, pp. 185–9
 14. Margot Asquith's Diary, d. 3213, p. 206
 15. Margot Asquith's Diary, d. 3214, p. 59
 16. *Lady Cynthia Asquith Diaries*, p. 117
 17. Margot Asquith's Diary, d. 3214, p. 119
 18. *Champion Redoubtable*, p. 86
 19. Margot Asquith's Diary, d. 3214, p. 163
 20. Margot Asquith's Diary, d. 3214, p. 227
 21. Margot Asquith Papers, d. 3289, f. 98, f. 110. Cys to Margot, 11.1.16
 22. Margot Asquith's Diary, d. 3214, pp. 22–3
 23. *Raymond Asquith Life and Letters*, p. 232

24. *Raymond Asquith Life and Letters*, p. 236
25. *Raymond Asquith Life and Letters*, pp. 232–42
26. *Raymond Asquith Life and Letters*, p. 244
27. *Lady Cynthia Asquith Diaries*, p. 119
28. *The Letters of Arthur Balfour and Lady Elcho*, p. 233
29. Margot Asquith's Diary, d. 3214, p. 147
30. *Lady Cynthia Asquith Diaries*, pp. 123, 124, 243
31 *Collected Letters of D.H. Lawrence*, p. 486. The letter is dated 25.11.16 after Cynthia had sent Lawrence a copy of Beb's poems in response to a belated request by Lawrence to see them.
32. Herbert Asquith, *Poems 1912–1933*, p. 75
33. *The Letters of Arthur Balfour and Lady Elcho*, p. 329
34. *Lady Cynthia Asquith Diaries*, p. 124
35. *Lady Cynthia Asquith Diaries*, pp. 107–8
36. *Lady Cynthia Asquith Diaries*, pp. 129, 161
37. *Lady Cynthia Asquith Diaries*, p. 133
38. Margot Asquith's Diary, d. 3214, pp. 274–5
39. Kelly's Diary, 7.3.16
40. Kelly's Diary, 10.3.16
41. *Lady Cynthia Asquith Diaries*, p. 162
42. Kelly's Diary, 5.5.16
43. Margot Asquith's Diary, d. 3214, p. 324
44. Margot Asquith's Diary, d. 3214, p. 429
45. Asquith to Sylvia Henley, 13.5.15
46. Margot Asquith's Diary, d. 3214, p. 9
47. Balfour Papers, Add. Mss. 49794, f. 146
48. Asquith to Sylvia Henley, 16.6.15
49. *Lady Cynthia Asquith Diaries*, p. 146 (26.3.16)
50. *Lady Cynthia Asquith Diaries*, p. 211 (2.9.16)
51. The *Spectator*, September, 1933
52. Margot to Mrs Alfred Lyttelton (28.9 and 30.9.33). Chandos Papers, 15/.
53. Margot Asquith's Diary, d. 3214, p. 387
54. Margot Asquith's Diary, d. 3214, p. 353 (10.4.16)
55. Margot Asquith's Diary, d. 3214, p. 409 (4.5.16)
56. *The Riddell Diaries*, ed. J. M. McEwen, p. 156

CHAPTER 19: THE BRINK OF DOOM
 1. Jolliffe, pp. 251–2, 257, 259
 2. Jolliffe, pp. 253, 275
 3. Diana Cooper Papers, Add. 70720, f. 125. Raymond to Shaw-Stewart, 29.5.16
 4. Diana Cooper Papers, Add. 70707, f. 58. Raymond to Diana, 23.5.16
 5. Diana Cooper Papers, Add. 70720, f. 125. Raymond to Shaw-Stewart, 29.5.16
 6. Jolliffe, pp. 264, 266
 7. Jolliffe, p. 264
 8. Jolliffe, p. 268
 9. Jolliffe, p. 270
10. Margot Asquith's Diary, d. 3214, p. 449
11. Jolliffe, pp. 269–70
12. Margot Asquith's Diary, d. 3214, p. 477
13. Margot Asquith's Diary, d. 3214, p. 473
14. Margot Asquith's Diary, d. 3214, pp. 477–9
15. Margot Asquith's Diary, d. 3214, p. 481
16. Margot Asquith's Diary, d. 3214, p. 485

17. *Lady Cynthia Asquith Diaries*, pp. 149, 145
18. *Lady Cynthia Asquith Diaries*, p. 149
19. *Lady Cynthia Asquith Diaries*, p. 189
20. *Lady Cynthia Asquith Diaries*, p. 165; Nicola Beaumont, *Cynthia Asquith*, pp. 139, 141
21. *Lady Cynthia Asquith Diaries*, p. 184
22. Jolliffe, p. 273
23. Kelly's Diary, 21.5.16
24. Kelly's Diary, 25.5.16. Quoted in Page, p. 75
25. Page, p. 77
26. Jolliffe, p. 273
27. Margot Asquith's Diary, d. 3215, p. 28 (transcribing Raymond to Margot, 5.7.16). Jolliffe, p. 272 (Raymond to Katharine, 2.7.16. Diana Cooper Papers, Add. Mss. 70707, f. 70 (Raymond to Diana, 10.7.16)
28. Jolliffe, pp. 274, 277
29. Transcribed into Margot Asquith's Diary, d. 3215, p. 23. Letter dated 5.7.16
30. Jolliffe, pp. 271, 273
31. Jolliffe, p. 280
32. Jolliffe, p. 281
33. Kelly's Diary, 13.7.16. Quoted in Page, p. 79
34. Kelly's Diary, 3.8.16
35. Page, p. 82
36. Page, p. 84
37. Margot Asquith's Diary, d. 3214, p. 498
38. Joseph Macleod, *The Sisters d'Arányi*, p. 110
39. Clovelly Papers. Oc to Violet, 21.8 and 4.9.16

CHAPTER 20: NEMESIS ON THE SOMME
1. Diana Cooper Papers, Add. Mss. 70707, f. 96. Raymond to Diana, 13.8.16
2. Jolliffe, p. 274. Raymond to Katharine, 10.7.16
3. Margot Asquith's Diary, d. 3215, p. 26
4. Jolliffe, p. 287
5. Jolliffe, pp. 290–91
6. Jolliffe, p. 293
7. Asquith to Margot, 7.9.16
8. Jolliffe, p. 294
9. Diana Cooper Papers, Add. Mss. 70707, f. 135. Raymond to Diana, 11.9.16
10. Letter to unknown recipient dated 11.10.16. Margot Asquith Papers, Ms. 3319
11. Jolliffe, pp. 292, 295
12. Diana Cooper Papers, Add. Mss. 70707, f. 142. Raymond to Diana, 14.9.16
13. *Nash's Magazine*, August 1928
14. Jolliffe, p. 296
15. Asquith to Sylvia Henley, 23.9.16. *The Autobiography of Margot Asquith*, Vol. I, p. 278
16. Margot Asquith's Diary, d. 3215, p. 62
17. Margot Asquith's Diary, d. 3215, pp. 63–9
18. Asquith to Sylvia Henley, 20.9.16
19. Margot Asquith's Diary, d. 3215, p. 99
20. Viola Parsons Papers. Add. Mss. 59895. Asquith to Viola, 20.9.16
21. Margot Asquith's Diary, d. 3215, p. 90
22. Asquith to Sylvia Henley, 20.9.16
23. Margot Asquith's Diary, d. 3215, p. 91
24. Margot Asquith's Diary, d. 3215, pp. 110–15
25. Desborough Papers, D/ERv C72/2325. Letter dated 25.10.16
26. Kelly's Diary,16.9.16. Quoted in Page, p. 86.

27. Terraine, p. 197
28. Page, p. 87
29. Page, p. 88
30. Oc to Violet, 24.10.16. Quoted in *Champion Redoubtable*, p. 96
31. Asquith to Sylvia Henley, 24.10.16
32. Page, p. 97
33. Page, p. 98
34. Page, p. 99
35. *Champion Redoubtable*, p. 94
36. *Champion Redoubtable*, p. 96
37. Page, p. 98
38. *Lady Cynthia Asquith Diaries*, pp. 236, 239, 222
39. *Lady Cynthia Asquith Diaries*, p. 223 (4.10.16)
40. *Lady Cynthia Asquith Diaries*, p. 237
41. *Lady Cynthia Asquith Diaries*, pp. 240–41 (2–4.12.16)
42. *Lady Cynthia Asquith Diaries*, p. 241

CHAPTER 21: 'AN AERIAL TORNADO FROM WHICH I CANNOT ESCAPE'

1. *Lady Cynthia Asquith Diaries*, p. 234
2. Freyberg Papers. Margot to Freyberg, 20.11.16
3. *The Riddell Diaries*, p. 174
4. Margot Asquith's Diary, d. 3215, p. 123
5. Stephen Roskill, *Hankey*, Vol. 1, p. 323
6. Margot Asquith's Diary, d. 3215, p. 135 (15.12.16)
7. McKenna Family Papers. Asquith to Pamela McKenna, 27.11.16
8. A. M. Gollin, *Proconsul in Politics*, p. 363
9. Margot Asquith's Diary, d. 3215, pp. 139–41
10. Margot Asquith's Diary, d. 3215, pp. 141–2
11. Asquith to Sylvia Henley, 16.12.16
12. Margot Asquith's Diary, d. 3215, pp. 142–4
13. *Lady Cynthia Asquith Diaries*, pp. 242–3
14. Balfour Papers, Edinburgh. Frances to Betty Balfour, 10.12.16
15. Churchill in *Nash's Magazine*, August 1928
16. Roskill, Vol. 1, p. 329
17. Asquith Papers, Box 17, 198. Margot to Asquith, 7.12.16
18. Margot Asquith's Diary, d. 3215, p. 156
19. *Lantern Slides*, pp. 98–9
20. *Champion Redoubtable*, p. 98
21. Asquith to Sylvia Henley, 15.12.16
22. Margot Asquith's Diary, d. 3215, p. 122 (15.12.16)
23. Margot Asquith's Diary, d. 3215, p. 127
24. Winston Churchill, *Great Contemporaries*, p. 231
25. Whittinghame Papers, Edinburgh. Margot to Balfour, 12.12.16
26. Asquith Papers, Box 17 ff., pp. 209, 239
27. Asquith to Sylvia Henley, 27.12.16 and 5.1.17
28. *Lady Cynthia Asquith Diaries*, pp. 246, 257
29. *Lady Cynthia Asquith Diaries*, p. 262
30. *Lady Cynthia Asquith Diaries*, p. 270
31. *Lady Cynthia Asquith Diaries*, p. 254
32. *Lady Cynthia Asquith Diaries*, pp. 136, 22–3
33. *Lady Cynthia Asquith Diaries*, pp. 283, 294
34. *Lady Cynthia Asquith Diaries*, p. 290
35. Page, p. 99

36. Page, p. 103
37. Jerrold, p. 213
38. Sellers, p. 213
39. Sellers, p. 216
40. Sellers, p. 217. Page, p. 106
41. Jerrold, p. 214. *Georgian Adventure*, p. 202
42. Page, p. 106
43. Asquith to Sylvia Henley, 12.2.17
44. *Lady Cynthia Asquith Diaries*, p. 266. Knox, p. 130
45. Page, p. 107
46. Diana Cooper Papers, Add. Mss. 70704, ff. 45 and 54 (March 1917)

CHAPTER 22: 'A MASTER'S LIFE OF ROUGH AND TUMBLE'
 1. *Moments of Memory*, pp. 280–81
 2. *Moments of Memory*, p. 282
 3. Terraine, *Douglas Haig*, p. 230
 4. See *inter alia*, Roskill, *Hankey*, Vol. I, pp. 362–3; Terraine, pp. 254–76.
 5. *Moments of Memory*, p. 284
 6. *Moments of Memory*, p. 286
 7. *Moments of Memory*, p. 288
 8. *Moments of Memory*, p. 289
 9. Asquith to Sylvia Henley, 18.4.16
10. Page, pp. 108–9
11. Oc to Violet, 19.4.17
12. Margot Asquith's Diary, d. 3216, p. 99
13. Sellers, p. 235. From a recording in the Imperial War Museum
14. Sellers, p. 235
15. Sellers, pp. 237–8
16. Jerrold, p. 232
17. Clovelly Papers. Oc to Asquith, 19.6.17
18. Page, p. 121
19. Page, p. 124
20. Page, p. 127
21. Clovelly Papers. James Morrison to Oc, 3.11.18
22. Jerrold, p. 242
23. Viola Parsons Papers, Add. Mss. 59895, f. 126 (n.d.)
24. Freyberg Papers. Margot to Freyberg, 27.12.16, 15.1.17
25. Clovelly Papers. Margot to Oc, 18.6.17
26. Hyde, H. Montgomery, *Lord Reading*, p. 195
27. Asquith to Sylvia Henley, 30.6 and 11.7.17
28. Clovelly Papers. Margot to Oc, 18.6.17
29. Viola Parsons Papers, Add. Mss. 59895. Margot to Viola, 24.7.17
30. *Moments of Memory*, pp. 290–91
31. *Moments of Memory*, pp. 292–3
32. Bonham Carter Papers. Oc to Violet, 22.5.17. Clovelly Papers, Oc to Asquith, 24.4.17
33. Page, p. 125
34. Lady Diana Cooper Papers, Add. Mss. 70704 f. 16. Oc to Diana, 6.1.18; 70714, f. 24. Shaw-Stewart to Diana, 12.5.17
35. Clovelly Papers. Oc to Violet, 22.5.17
36. Page, p. 128
37. Page, pp. 129–30
38. Page, p. 130

39. *Lady Cynthia Asquith Diaries*, p. 311
40. Clovelly Papers, Oc to Asquith, 19.6.17
41. *Lady Cynthia Asquith Diaries*, p. 322
42. Page, pp. 140–41
43. Asquith Papers, Box 35, f. 48. 26.1.25
44. *Moments of Memory*, p. 294
45. *Moments of Memory*, p. 302
46. *Moments of Memory*, p. 300

CHAPTER 23: 'THERE IS NO DOUBT THAT OC IS A BORN SOLDIER'
1. *Lady Cynthia Asquith Diaries*, pp. 308, 310
2. *Lady Cynthia Asquith Diaries*, p. 386
3. Margot Asquith's Diary, d. 3216, p. 6
4. Asquith to Sylvia Henley, 7.7.17
5. *Lady Cynthia Asquith Diaries*, pp. 361, 377, 357. Margot Asquith's Diary, d. 3216, p. 21
6. Donald McCormick, *The Mask of Merlin*
7. *Lady Cynthia Asquith Diaries*, p. 328
8. *Lady Cynthia Asquith Diaries*, p. 334
9. Asquith to Sylvia Henley, 13.8.17
10. Margot Asquith's Diary, d. 3216, p. 86
11. Asquith to Sylvia Henley, 28.8.17
12. *Lady Cynthia Asquith Diaries*, p. 330
13. *Lady Cynthia Asquith Diaries*, p. 331 (29.8.17)
14. *Lady Cynthia Asquith Diaries*, pp. 323, 318, 337
15. *Lady Cynthia Asquith Diaries*, p. 340
16. *Lady Cynthia Asquith Diaries*, p. 350
17. *Lady Cynthia Asquith Diaries*, p. 373
18. *Lady Cynthia Asquith Diaries*, pp. 376–7
19. *Lady Cynthia Asquith Diaries*, p. 370
20. Margot Asquith Papers, Ms. Eng., d. 3289, f. 27, 12.10.17. Asquith to Margot, 15.9 and 17.9.17
21. Margot Asquith Papers, d. 3289, f. 27, 12.10.17
22. Page, pp. 151–2
23. Jerrold, p. 250
24. Sellers, p. 251
25. Page, p. 154
26. Jerrold, p. 253
27. Page, pp. 156–7. Jerrold, p. 256
28. See Page, p. 158, Jerrold, p. 257.
29. Page, p. 162
30. Page, p. 160. See also trench map opposite p. 162
31. Jerrold, p. 263
32. Asquith to Sylvia Henley, 9.6.17
33. Page, pp. 160–61
34. *Lady Cynthia Asquith Diaries*, p. 380 (15.12.17). Conversation between the author and Mrs Susan Boothby
35. Page, p. 168
36. Clovelly Papers. Oc to Asquith, 11.12.17
37. Diana Cooper Papers, Add. Mss. 70704, f. 64. Shaw-Stewart to Diana Manners, 20.12.17
38. Asquith to Sylvia Henley, 28.12.17
39. Diana Cooper Papers, Add. Mss. 70704, f. 1. Oc to Diana Manners, 6.1.18
40. Clovelly Papers. Oc to Asquith, 22.12.17

41. Clovelly Papers. Oc to Asquith, 30.12.17
42. Asquith to Sylvia Henley, 28.12.17
43. Clovelly Papers. McCracken to Oc, 31.12.17. Quoted in Page, p. 171. Jerrold, p. 271
44. Clovelly Papers. Oc to Asquith, 10.1.18
45. *Lady Cynthia Asquith Diaries*, p. 389
46. Page, p. 173

CHAPTER 24: BEB'S 'BATTLE IN THE MIST'

1. *Moments of Memory*, p. 307
2. *Moments of Memory*, p. 306
3. *Moments of Memory*, p. 309
4. *Moments of Memory*, p. 310, where Beb confused this leave with his previous one when he had met Cynthia at Pixton in Devon
5. *Lady Cynthia Asquith Diaries*, p. 384
6. *Moments of Memory*, p. 307
7. *Lady Cynthia Asquith Diaries*, p. 318
8. *Lady Cynthia Asquith Diaries*, pp. 385–6
9. *Lady Cynthia Asquith Diaries*, p. 390
10. *Lady Cynthia Asquith Diaries*, p. 392
11. *Lady Cynthia Asquith Diaries*, p. 391
12. *Lady Cynthia Asquith Diaries*, p. 389
13. Margot Asquith's Diary, d. 3216, p. 72
14. Page, p. 172
15. *Moments of Memory*, p. 311
16. Terraine, *Douglas Haig*, p. 414
17. *Moments of Memory*, p. 315
18. Clovelly Papers. Beb to Oc, 10.4.18
19. *Moments of Memory*, p. 319
20. *Moments of Memory*, p. 321
21. Clovelly Papers. Beb to Oc 10.4.18. *Moments of Memory*, pp. 324–5
22. *Moments of Memory*, p. 326
23. *Moments of Memory*, p. 331
24. *Moments of Memory*, p. 335
25. *Moments of Memory*, pp. 337–9
26. McCormick, p. 145
27. *Moments of Memory*, p. 341
28. Clovelly Papers. Beb to Oc, 10.5.18
29. Terraine, *Douglas Haig*, p. 427

CHAPTER 25: 'A GENTLEMAN NOT A POLICITIAN'

1. *Lady Cynthia Asquith Diaries*, p. 402
2. *Lady Cynthia Asquith Diaries*, pp. 451–2
3. *Lady Cynthia Asquith Diaries*, pp. 423–4, 429–30
4. Clovelly Papers. Beb to Oc, 10.4.18
5. Desborough Papers, D/ERVC 64/1. Oc to Ettie Desborough, 25.3.18; Asquith to Sylvia Henley, 7.4.18
6. Aberconway Papers, Add. Mss. 52550. Asquith to Christabel McLaren, 29.3.18
7. *Lady Cynthia Asquith Diaries*, p. 432
8. *Lady Cynthia Asquith Diaries*, p. 424
9. Aberconway Papers, Add. Mss. 52550. Asquith to Christabel McLaren, 1.5.18
10. Page, p. 175
11. Margot Asquith's Diary, d. 3216, p. 138
12. Margot Asquith's Diary, d. 3216, pp. 79–80, 94

13. Margot Asquith's Diary, d. 3216, pp. 122, 177 and 123
14. Wilson's Diary, 16.3.16
15. Asquith Papers, Box 18, f. 32. Quoted in full Spender and Asquith, Vol. II, p. 303
16. Margot Asquith's Diary, d. 3216, pp. 145–51. Spender and Asquith, Vol. II, p. 304
17. *Lady Cynthia Asquith Diaries*, p. 438
18. Roskill, *Hankey*, I, pp. 541–2
19. Roskill, *Hankey*, I, p. 544
20. Margot Asquith's Diary, d. 3216, pp. 155–6
21. *Lady Cynthia Asquith Diaries*, p. 438
22. Fitzherbert, p. 200
23. Aubrey Herbert Papers (Somerset Records) Margot to Aubrey, 20.5.18
24. Aubrey Herbert Papers (Somerset Records) Violet to Mary Herbert, 25.5.18
25. Fitzherbert, p. 202
26. Margot Asquith's Diary, d. 3216, p. 159
27. See Joseph Macleod, *The Sisters d'Aranyi*
28. Margot Asquith's Diary, d. 3216, pp. 174–8
29. Margot Asquith's Diary, d. 3216, p. 185
30. Margot Asquith's Diary, d. 3216, p. 189
31. Roskill, *Hankey*, I, p. 329
32. Lloyd George Papers. Sutherland to Frances Stevenson (n.d.), F 93/2/3
33. Margot Asquith's Diary, d. 3216, p. 87
34. Maud Tree Papers, Add. Mss. 62126, f. 71 (n.d.)
35. Margot Asquith's Diary, d. 3216, p. 213
36. Terraine, *Douglas Haig*, pp. 458–63
37. Terraine, *The Western Front 1914–1918*, p. 181
38. Clovelly Papers. Freyberg to Oc, 13.11.18
39. Margot Asquith's Diary, d. 3216, pp. 248–53
40. *Moments of Memory*, pp. 349–52
41. McCormick, p. 153
42. Margot Asquith's Diary, d. 3217, pp. 25, 72
43. Margot Asquith's Diary, d. 3217, p. 40
44. Margot Asquith's Diary, d. 3217, pp. 58–70. *Autobiography*, Vol. II, pp. 296–9

EPILOGUE: 'SERVANT AND SON OF ENGLAND'
1. Margot Asquith's Diary, d. 3217, p. 77
2. Margot Asquith Papers. Asquith to Margot, 14.2.22
3. Margot Asquith Papers. Asquith to Margot, 1.4.23; Margot Asquith, *Places and Persons*, pp. 250–51
4. Conversations between the author and Oc's daughter, Mrs Susan Boothby
5. Asquith Papers, Box 18, f. 101. Venetia Montagu to Asquith, 18.11.24
6. Aberconway Papers, Add. Mss. 52550. Margot to Lady Aberconway, f. 104 (n.d., but 1922 from context), f. 107, 23.2.23
7. Churchill Papers, 2/158/121. Margot to Churchill, 5.8.28; Lloyd George Papers, G/16/1. Margot to Lloyd George, 23.12.23
8. *Letters to Venetia Stanley*, p. 608
9. Tree Papers, Add. Mss. 62126. Margot to Viola Parsons, 10.2.28
10. Crewe Papers, C40. Margot to Lord Crewe, 19.2.28
11. Page, pp. 184–5, quoting letter from Violet to Desmond MacCarthy and article by Freyberg in the *Daily Telegraph* of 29.5.61

Selected Bibliography

MANUSCRIPT COLLECTIONS

D'Abernon Papers, British Library
Asquith Papers (H. H. and Margot), Bodleian Library, Oxford
Balfour Papers, British Library
Balliol College Archives, Balliol College, Oxford
Bonar Law Papers, House of Lords Record Office
Campbell-Bannerman Papers
Chandos (Lyttelton) Papers, Churchill College, Cambridge
Churchill Papers, Churchill College, Cambridge
Clovelly Papers, Papers of Arthur ('Oc') Asquith, private collection of Mrs Mary
  Rous
Cooper (Lady Diana, *née* Manners) Papers, British Library
Crathorne Papers, private collection of Tennant family manuscripts in the possession of
  Lord Crathorne
Crewe Papers, Cambridge University Library
Croft House, Morley title deeds (Property of Major and Mrs N. Stevenson)
Curzon Papers, India Office Library
Desborough Papers, Hertfordshire County Record Office
Ellis (Thomas) Papers, National Library of Wales, Aberystwyth
Gladstone Papers (W. E. G., Catherine G., Herbert G. and Mary Drew), British Library
Hamilton (Edward) Papers, British Library
Haldane Papers, National Library of Scotland
Hankey Papers, Churchill College, Cambridge
Harcourt Papers, Bodleian Library
Henley Letters (to Asquith), Bodleian Library
Herbert Papers, Somerset County Records Office and in private possession of Mrs
  Bridget Grant
Jowett Papers, Balliol College, Oxford
Kitchener Papers, Public Records Office, Kew
Lloyd George Papers, House of Lords Record Office and National Library of Wales
Long Papers, British Library

Mells Papers, private Asquith and Horner family Papers, in the possession of the Earl of
    Oxford and Asquith
Midleton Papers, British Library
Milner Papers, Bodleian Librry
Minto Papers, National Library of Scotland
Montagu Papers,Trinity College, Cambridge
Morley Papers, India Office Library
Oxford Union Society Archives, Oxford
Reading Papers, India Office Library
Robinson (Geoffrey Dawson) Papers, Bodleian Library
Rosebery Papers, National Library of Scotland
Spender Papers, British Library
Tree Papers (Maud Tree and Viola Parsons, *née* Tree), British Library
Whittingehame Papers, National Register of Archives (Scotland), Edinburgh
Winchester College Archives

PRINTED SOURCES

The following books have been among the most useful out of the hundreds I have consulted during the seven years spent researching and writing this book. (The literature on
the Great War and the politics of late Victorian and early twentieth-century Britain, in
particular, is self-evidently voluminous.) Unless otherwise specified, London is the place
of publication.

Abdy, Jane, and Gere, Charlotte, *The Souls* (1984), Sidgwick & Jackson
Adams, R. J. Q. and Poirier, Philip P., *The Conscription Controversy in Great Britain, 1900–1918*
    (1987), Basingstoke, Macmillan
Alderson, J. P., *Mr Asquith* (1905), Methuen
Asquith, Lady Cynthia, *Haply I May Remember* (1950), James Barrie
——*Remember and Be Glad* (1952), James Barrie
——*Diaries 1915–18* (1968), Century
Asquith, Herbert, *Moments of Memory* (1937), Hutchinson & Co.
——*Poems 1912–1933* (1934), Sidgwick & Jackson
Asquith, E. Margot, *The Autobiography of Margot Asquith*, 2 vols. (1920 and 1922),
    Thornton Butterworth
——*Places and Persons* (1925), Thornton Butterworth
——*Octavia* (1928), Cassell & Co.
——*More Memories* (1933), Cassell & Co. .
——*More or Less about Myself* (1934), Dutton
——*Off the Record* (1943), Frederick Muller
Bahlman, Dudley (ed.), *The Diary of Sir Edward Hamilton 1885–1906* (1993), Hull, Universtiy
    of Hull Press
Balfour, A. J., *Chapters of Autobiography* (1930), Cassell & Co.
Balfour, Lady Frances, *Ne Obliviscaris* (1930), Hodder & Stoughton
Balliol College War Memorial Book (1924), Glasgow, University Press for Balliol College
Baring, Maurice, *The Puppet Show of Memory* (1922), William Heinemann
Beauman, Nicola, *Cynthia Asquith* (1987), Hamish Hamilton
Beaverbrook, Lord, *Politicians and the War 1914–1916* (1960 edition), Oldbourne Book Co.
Bennett, Daphne, *Margot* (1984), Gollancz
Benson, E. F., *As We Were* (1932), Longmans
Berridge, Virginia, *Opium and the people: opiate use and drug control policy in nineteenth century and
    early twentieth century England* (1999), Free Association
Binfield, Clyde, *A Congregational Formation: An Edwardian Prime Minister's Victorian*

Education. The Congregational Lecture (1996), Congregational Memorial Hall Trust

Birrell, Augustine, *Things Past Redress* (1937), Faber & Faber

Blow, Simon, *Broken Blood* (1987), Faber

Blunt, Wilfred Scawen, *My Diaries: Being a Personal Narrative of Events 1888–1914* (1919), Martin Secker

Bonham Carter, Violet, 'The Souls', *The Listener*, 30 October 1947

Bonham Carter, Lady Violet, *Winston Churchill As I Knew Him* (1965), Eyre & Spottiswode

Brett, Maurice, V. (ed.), *Journal and Letters of Reginald, Viscount Esher*, 2 vols, (1934), Nicholson & Watson

Brock, Michael and Eleanor (eds.), *H. H. Asquith Letters to Venetia Stanley* (1982), Oxford, Oxford University Press

Brock, Michael G., and Curthoys, Mark C., *The History of the University of Oxford*. Vol. VII: *Nineteenth-Century Oxford* (2000), Oxford, University of Oxford

Brownless, Isla, *The Lambrook Legacy 1860–1997* (1998), Aldwick, Evergreen Graphics

Buchan, John, *Memory Hold The Door* (1940), Hodder & Stoughton

——*Those for Remembrance* (privately published 1919, republished in 1987)

Carless, H. W. A., *History of Balliol College*, revised by R. H. C. Davis and Richard Hunt and supplemented by Harold Hartley (1963), Oxford, Basil Blackwell

Cassar, George, *Kitchener, Architect of Victory* (1977), Kimber

——*Asquith as War Leader* (1994), Hambledon Press

Chamberlain, Austen, *Down the Years* (1935), Cassell & Co.

Charmley, John, *Churchill: The End of Glory* (1993), Hodder

Charteris, Brigadier General John, *At GHQ* (1931), Cassell & Co.

Churchill, Randolph S., *Winston S. Churchill, Vol. I 1874–1900* (1966), Heinemann

——*Winston S. Churchill, Vol. II 1900–1914* (1967), Heinemann

Churchill, Winston, *Great Contemporaries* (1937), Thornton Butterworth

Clifford, Rollo, *The Royal Gloucestershire Hussars* (1991), Stroud, Alan Sutton

Cooper, Artemis, *A Durable Fire: Letters of Duff and Diana Cooper 1913–1950* (1983), Collins

Cooper, Diana, *The Rainbow Comes and Goes* (1958), Rupert Hart-Davis

Cooper, Duff, *Old Men Forget* (1953), Rupert Hart-Davis

Crathorne, Nancy, *Tennant's Stalk* (1973), Macmillan

Dangerfield, George, *The Strange Death of Liberal England* (1936), Constable & Co.

David, Edward (ed.), *Inside Asquith's Cabinet: The Diaries of Charles Hobhouse* (1977), John Murray

Dean, Joseph, *Hatred, Ridicule and Contempt* (1953), Constable & Co.

Desborough, Lady, *Pages From a Family Journal, 1888–1915* (1916), privately printed

Donaldson, Frances, *The Marconi Scandal* (1962), Rupert Hart-Davis

Douglas-Smith, A.E., *The City of London School* (1937), Oxford, Basil Blackwell

Egremont, Max, *Balfour* (1980), Collins

Elias, Frank, *The Right Hon. H. H. Asquith M.P.* (1909), James Clarke & Co.

Ensor, R. C. K., *England 1870–1914* (1936), Oxford, Clarendon Press

Faber, Geoffrey, *Jowett* (1957), Faber & Faber

Farnell, L. R., *An Oxonian Looks Back* (1934), Martin Hopkinson

Fisher, John Arbuthnot, Baron, *Memories* (1919), Hodder & Stoughton

Fitzherbert, Margaret, *The Man Who Was Greenmantle: A Biography of Aubrey Herbert* (1983), John Murray

Fitzroy, Sir Almeric, *Memoirs*, 2 vols. (1925), Hutchinson & Co.

Forbes, Lady Angela, *Memories and Base Details* (1922), Hutchinson & Co.

Freyberg, Paul, *Bernard Freyberg VC, Soldier of Two Nations* (1991), Hodder & Stoughton

Gathorne-Hardy, R. (ed.), *The Memoirs of Lady Ottoline Morrell, 1873–1915* (1963), Faber & Faber

Gilbert, Martin, *Winston S. Churchill, Vol. II 1914–16* (1971), Heinemann
——*Winston S. Churchill, Vol. IV 1916–22* (1975), Heinemann
——*Winston S. Churchill, Companion Vol. II* (1977), Heinemann
Gilmour, David, *Curzon* (1994), John Murray
Gladstone, Mary (Mrs Drew) *Some Harwarden Letters* (1917), Nisbet & Co.
——*Her Diaries and Letters*, edited by Lucy Masterman (1930), Methuen & Co.
Glenconner, Pamela, *Edward Wyndham Tennant* (1919), John Lane
Gollin, A. M., *Proconsul in Politics: A Study of Lord Milner* (1964), Anthony Blond
Grey of Fallodon, Viscount, *Twenty-Five Years 1892–1916*, 2 vols (1925), Hodder & Stoughton
Grigg, John, *The Young Lloyd George* (1973), Methuen
——*Lloyd George: The People's Champion 1902–1911* (1978), Eyre Methuen
——*Lloyd George: From Peace to War: 1912–1916* (1985), Methuen
Haldane, Richard Burdon, *An Autobiography* (1929), Hodder & Stoughton
Hankey, Maurice, *The Supreme Command 1914–1918* (1961), George Allen & Unwin
Harrison, Brian (ed.), *The History of the University of Oxford, Vol. VIII: Twentieth-Century Oxford* (1994), Oxford, Clarendon Press
Hassall, Christopher, *Edward Marsh, Patron of the Arts* (1959), Longmans
——*Rupert Brooke* (1964), Faber & Faber
Hazlehurst, Cameron, *Politicians at War* (1971), Jonathan Cape
Herbert, Aubrey, *Mons, Anzac and Kut* (1919), Edward Arnold
Hickey, Michael, *Gallipoli* (1995), John Murray
The History of The Times, Vol. IV (1952), The Times
Hollis, Christopher, *The Oxford Union* (1965), Evans Brothers
Holroyd, Michael, and Levy, Paul (eds.), *The Shorter Strachey* (1980), Oxford, Oxford University Press
Horner, Frances, *Time Remembered* (1933), William Heinemann
Hutchinson, Horace (ed.), *The Private Diaries of Sir Algernon West* (1922), John Murray
Hyde, H. Montgomery, *Carson* (1953), William Heinemann
——*Lord Reading* (1967), Heinemann
Inwood, Stephen, *The Role of the Press in English Politics during the First World War* (unpublished. D. Phil. thesis, Oxford University, 1971)
Jackson, H. C., *Sudan Days and Ways* (1954), Macmillan & Co.
Jenkins, Roy, *Mr Balfour's Poodle. An Account of the Struggle between the House of Lords and the Government of Mr Asquith* (1954), William Heinemann
——*Asquith* (1964, rev. 1986), Collins
——*Churchill* (2001), Macmillan
Jerrold, Douglas, *The Royal Naval Division* (1923), Hutchinson & Co.
——*Georgian Adventure* (1938), 'Right' Book Club
Jolliffe, John, *Raymond Asquith, Life and Letters* (1980), Collins
Jones, John, *Balliol College: A History* (1988), Oxford, Oxford University Press
Jones, L. E., *An Edwardian Youth* (1956), Macmillan & Co.
Jones, Nigel, *Rupert Brooke* (1999), Richard Cohen
Judd, Denis, *Lord Reading: Rufus Isaacs, First Marquess of Reading, Lord Chief Justice and Viceroy of India, 1860–1935* (1982), Weidenfeld & Nicolson
Keegan, John, *The First World War* (1998), Hutchinson
Keynes, Geoffrey (ed.), *Rupert Brooke: Collected Letters* (1968), Faber & Faber
Knox, Ronald, *Patrick Shaw-Stewart* (1920), Collins
Koss, Stephen E., *Lord Haldane, Scapegoat for Liberalism* (1969), New York, Columbia University Press
——*Asquith* (1976), Allen Lane
——*The Rise and Fall of the Political Press in Britain*, Vol. II (1984), Hamilton
Lambert, Angela, *Unquiet Souls* (1984), Macmillan

Lawrence, D. H., *The Collected Letters of D. H. Lawrence*, Vol. II (1981), Cambridge, Cambridge University Press

Levine, Naomi B., *Politics, Religion and Love* (1991), New York, New York University Press

Liddell, A. G. C., *Notes from the Life of an Ordinary Mortal* (1911), John Murray

Liddell Hart, B. H., *History of the First World War* (1970), Cassell

Lister, Beatrice, *Emma Lady Ribblesdale: Letters and Diaries* (1930), privately printed

Lloyd George, David , *War Memoirs*, 2 vols. (1938), Oldhams Press

Longford, Elizabeth, *Victoria RI* (1964), Weidenfeld & Nicolson

——*A Pilgrimage of Passion: The Life of Wilfred Scawen Blunt* (1979), Weidenfeld & Nicolson

Lownie, Andrew, *John Buchan* (1995), Constable

Lubbock, Adelaide, *People in Glass Houses* (1977), Hamish Hamilton

Lyttelton, Edith, *Alfred Lyttelton* (1917), Longmans & Co.

MacCarthy, Desmond (ed.), *H.H.A.: Letters of the Earl of Oxford and Asquith to a Friend, 1915–1922* (1933), Geoffrey Bles

McCormick, Donald, *The Mask of Merlin: A Critical Study of David Lloyd George* (1963), Macdonald

MacDonagh, Michael, *In London During the Great War* (1935), Eyre & Spottiswode

Macdonald, Lyn, *Somme* (1983), Michael Joseph

McEwen, John M. (ed.), *The Riddell Diaries 1908–1923* (1986), Athlone

Mackay, Ruddock, *Balfour: Intellectual Statesman* (1985), Oxford, Oxford University Press

McKenna, Stephen, *Reginald McKenna, 1863–1943* (1948), Eyre & Spottiswode

Mackenzie, Jeanne, *Children of the Souls* (1986), Chatto & Windus

Mackintosh, Alexander, *From Gladstone to Lloyd George* (1921), Hodder & Stoughton

——*Echoes of Big Ben: A Journalist's Parliamentary Diary 1881–1940* (1945), Jarrolds

McLellan, Robert, *The Isle of Arran* (1985), Newton Abbot, David & Charles

Macleod, Joseph, *The Sisters d'Arányi* (1969), Allen & Unwin

Macmichael, Sir Harold, *Anglo Egyptian Sudan* (1934), Faber & Faber

Magnus, Philip, *Gladstone* (1954), John Murray

Marsh, Edward, *A Number of People* (1939), William Heinemann

Masters, Brian, *Great Hostesses* (1982), Constable

——*E. F. Benson* (1991), Chatto & Windus

Matthew, H. C. G., *The Liberal Imperialists* (1973), Oxford University Press

——(ed.), *The Gladstone Diaries: Vol. 13 1892–1896* (1994), Oxford, Clarendon Press

——*Gladstone 1875–1898* (1995), Oxford, Oxford University Press

Maurice, Sir Frederick, *Intrigues of the War* (1922), Loxley Bros

Maurice, Nancy, *The Maurice Case: From the Papers of Major General Sir Frederick Maurice* (1972), Leo Cooper

Midleton, Earl of, *Records and Reactions, 1856–1939* (1939), John Murray

Milner, Viscountess, *My Picture Gallery* (1951), John Murray

Minney, R. J., *Puffin Asquith* (1973), Leslie Frewin

Moore, Henry, T. (ed.), *The Collected Letters of D. H. Lawrence* (1962), Heinemann

Morgan, Kenneth O., *Lloyd George Family Letters* (1973), Oxford University Press

Morley, John, *Recollections* (1917), Macmillan

Morris, Jan (ed.), *The Oxford Book of Oxford* (1978), Oxford University Press

Mosley, Nicholas, *Julian Grenfell: His Life and the Times of his Death 1885–1915* (1976), Weidenfeld & Nicolson

Mosley, Sir Oswald, *My Life* (1968), Nelson

Murray, Bruce, *The People's Budget* (1980), Oxford, Clarendon Press

Murray, Joseph, *Gallipoli As I Saw It* (1965), William Kimber

——*Call to Arms: from Gallipoli to the Western Front* (1980), William Kimber

Newman, Major E. W. Polson, *Great Britain in Egypt* (1928), Cassel & Co.

Nicolson, Harold, *King George V* (1952), Constable

Nicolson, Nigel (ed.), *Harold Nicolson: Diaries and Letters 1939–45* (1967), Collins
Oxford and Asquith, Earl of, *Fifty Years in Parliament*, 2 vols. (1926), Cassell & Co.
——*Speeches* (1927), Hutchinson & Co.
——*Memories and Reflections, 1852–1927*, 2 vols. (1928), Cassell & Co.
Page, Christopher, *Command in the Royal Naval Division: A Military Biography of Brigadier General A. M. Asquith DSO* (1999), Staplehurst, Spellmount
Pottle, Mark (ed.), *Lantern Slides: The Diaries and Letters of Violet Bonham Carter 1904–1914* (1996), Weidenfeld & Nicolson
——*Champion Redoubtable: The Diaries and Letters of Violet Bonham Carter 1914–1945* (1998), Weidenfeld & Nicolson
Pound, R., and Harmsworth, G., *Northcliffe* (1959), Cassell
Repington, Charles A. C., *The First World War 1914–1918: Personal Experiences*, 2 vols. (1920), Constable
Rhodes James, Robert, *Rosebery* (1963), Weidenfeld & Nicolson
Ribblesdale, Lord, *Charles Lister: Letters and Recollections* (1917), Unwin
——*Impressions and Memories* (1927), Cassell & Co.
Ridley, Jane, and Percy, Clayre, *The Letters of Arthur Balfour and Lady Elcho 1885–1917* (1992), Hamish Hamilton
Rose, Kenneth, *Superior Person: a Portrait of Curzon and his Circle* (1969), Weidenfeld & Nicolson
——*King George V* (1983), Weidenfeld & Nicolson
Roskill, Stephen, *Hankey: Man of Secrets*, 3 vols. (1970–4), Collins
Sabben-Clare, James, *Winchester College* (1981), P. Cave Publishers
Sellers, Leonard, *The Hood Battalion* (1995), Leo Cooper
Shaw-Stewart, Basil, *Patrick Shaw-Stewart: A Memorial Volume* (privately printed, 1940)
Simon, Viscount, *Retrospect* (1952), Hutchinson
Soames, Mary, *Clementine Churchill* (1979), Cassell
——(ed.), *Speaking for Themselves: The Personal Letters of Winston and Clementine Churchill* (1998), Doubleday
Sommer, Dudley, *Haldane of Cloan* (1960), Allen & Unwin
Spender, J. A., and Asquith, Cyril, *The Life of Herbert Henry Asquith, Lord Oxford and Asquith*, 2 vols. (1932), Hutchinson & Co.
St. Aubyn, Giles, *Edward VII: Prince and King* (1979), Collins
Stevenson, Frances, *Lloyd George: A Diary*, ed. A. J. P. Taylor (1971), Hutchinson & Co.
Taylor, A. J. P., *English History 1914–1945* (1975), Oxford, Oxford University Press
Terraine, John, *Douglas Haig* (1963), Hutchinson
——*The Western Front 1914–1918* (1964), Hutchinson
Trevelyan, G. M., *Grey of Fallodon* (1937), Longmans & Co.
Walter, David, *The Oxford Union* (1984), Macdonald & Co.
Ward, W. R., *Victorian Oxford* (1965), Frank Cass & Co.
Warwick, Frances, Countess of, *Life's Ebb and Flow* (1929), Hutchinson & Co.
Wemyss, Countess of, *A Family Record* (1932), Plaistow, Curwen Press
West, Sir Algernon, *Recollections 1832–1886*, Vol. 2 (1899), Smith, Elder & Co.
Wilson, A. N., *Hilaire Belloc* (1984), Hamish Hamilton
Wilson, John, *A Life of Sir Henry Campbell-Bannerman* (1973), Constable
Wilson, Trevor (ed.), *The Political Diaries of C. P. Scott, 1911–1928* (1970), Collins
——*The Myriad Faces of War: Britain and the Great War 1914–1918* (1986), Cambridge, Polity
Wood, G., *The Story of Morley* (1916), Sir I. Pitman & Sons
Woodward, David R., *Lloyd George and the Generals* (1983), Newark, New Jersey, Delaware University Press
Young, Kenneth, *Arthur James Balfour: The Happy Life of the Politician, Prime Minister, Statesman and Philosopher, 1848–1930* (1963), G. Bell & Sons
Ziegler, Philip, *Diana Cooper* (1981), Hamish Hamilton

Index

Ranks and titles are generally the highest mentioned in the text.